Growth and Development	Pathology	Change	Illustrative Case
Erogenous zones; oral, anal, phallic stages of development; Oedipus complex	Infantile sexuality; fixation and regression; conflict; symptoms	Transference; conflict resolution; "Where id was, ego shall be"	Little Hans
Congruence and self-actualization versus incongruence and defensiveness	Defensive maintenance of self; incongruence	Therapeutic atmosphere: congruence, unconditional positive regard, empathic understanding	Mrs. Oak
Contributions of heredity and environment to traits	Extreme scores on trait dimensions (e.g., neuroticism)	(No formal model)	69-year old man
Imitation; schedules of reinforcement and successive approximations	Maladaptive learned response patterns	Extinction; discrimination learning; counterconditioning; positive reinforcement; imitation; systematic desensitization; behavior modification	Peter; Reinterpretation of Little Hans
Increased complexity and definition to construct system	Disordered functioning of the construct system	Psychological reconstruction of life; invitational mood; fixed-role therapy.	Ronald Barrett
Social learning through observation and direct experience; development of self-efficacy judgments and standards for self-regulation	Learned response patterns; excessive self-standards; problems in self-efficacy	Modeling; guided participation; increased self-efficacy	Reinterpretation of bombardier case
Development of cognitive competencies, self-schemas, expectancies, attributions	Unrealistic or maladaptive beliefs; errors in information processing	Cognitive therapy—changes in irrational beliefs, dysfunctional thoughts, and maladaptive attributions	Jim

PERSONALITY

THEORY AND RESEARCH

Seventh Edition

Lawrence A. Pervin

Rutgers University

Oliver P. John

University of California, Berkeley

John Wiley & Sons, Inc.

New York   Chichester   Brisbane   Toronto   Singapore

Acquisitions Editor	Christopher Rogers
Marketing Manager	Rebecca Herschler
Production Manager	Pamela Kennedy-Oborski
Production Editor	Deborah Herbert
Copy Editor	Swordsmith Productions
Design Supervisor	Karin Kincheloe
Designer	Laura Ierardi
Manufacturing Manager	Mark Cirillo
Photo Researcher	Hilary Newman
Illustration	Eugene Aiello
Cover Photo	Polaroid photography by Jim Finlayson

This book was set in 10/12 point Aster by LCI Design and
printed and bound by R. R. Donnelly & Sons. the cover
was printed by Lehigh Press.

Recognizing the importance of preserving what has been written, it is a
policy of John Wiley & Sons, Inc. to have books of enduring value published
in the United States printed on acid-free paper, and we exert our best
efforts to that end.

Library of Congress Cataloging-in-Publication Data
Pervin, Lawrence A.
    Personality : theory and research / Lawrence A. Pervin. — 7th ed.
      p. cm.
    Includes bibliographical references and index.
    ISBN 0-471-12804-X (alk. paper)
    1. Personality. I. Title.
BF698.P375 1996
155.2—dc20
                                        96-7678
                                        CIP

Printed in the United States of America

10 9 8 7 6 5 4 3

PREFACE

1995 marked the twenty-fifth anniversary of *Personality: Theory and Research*. This seventh edition marks a new era for the text. Along with the usual updating of all chapters, this edition includes new instructional features designed to make the material even more accessible and personally meaningful to the student. Each chapter begins with an anecdote or personal experience that captures, in vivid language, a core assumption or theme of the chapter. A series of "questions to be addressed" then orients the student to the general issues discussed in the chapter. Moreover, new boxes throughout the book illustrate how the concepts covered in the text can be applied to issues we face in our daily lives.

Perhaps the most exciting change for this new edition is that it involves a collaborative effort by the two of us, Lawrence A. Pervin and Oliver P. John. We first met in 1982 at a European conference in the Netherlands. There we argued about the relative merits of motivational and trait approaches to personality. We've continued to argue ever since, most recently in the pages of *Psychological Inquiry*. At first glance, then, some readers might wonder how two such different individuals could work together this closely. After all, this collaboration had to bridge not only two very different generations of personality researchers, but other differences as well—one of us grew up in Brooklyn, New York, and the other in Bielefeld, Germany; one is associated with a systems-psychodynamic orientation and the other with a cognitive orientation to personality traits; one has spent his professional career on the East Coast and the other on the West Coast. In fact, these differences were not a hindrance but rather turned out to be stimulating, complementary, and synergistic, leading to a broader and more even coverage of personality psychology than either of us could have achieved alone. What has made this collaboration possible and rewarding is a shared fascination with the endless variety of personality differences, a shared respect for the scientific enterprise, and a shared commitment to education.

Personality, in individuals and in the field of psychology that studies it, is always in a state of evolution. This seventh edition of *Personality: Theory and Research* continues to capture this dynamic aspect of people and the field, and to present it effectively to students. The current edition emphasizes four major goals:

1. *Presentation of the major theoretical approaches to personality.* Our intent is to give in-depth coverage to the major theoretical approaches or perspectives rather than to cover many theories in a more superficial manner. At the same time, to a certain extent the grand theory approach of the past (e.g., Freud, Rogers) has been replaced by more diverse *theoretical approaches* (e.g., trait, cognitive information processing) in the present. In focusing, where appropriate, either on grand theories or on theoretical approaches, the text is faithful to past theoretical traditions that remain important as well as to more recent developments.

2. *Integration of theory with research.* Our intent here is to demonstrate the linkage between personality theory and personality research; that is, to show how developments in one of these areas can, and should, be part and parcel of developments in the other.

3. *Integration of case material with theory.* By necessity, theory and research deal with abstractions and generalizations, rather than with specific and unique individuals. To bridge the gap between the general and the individual, we provide a case illustration of each theory and its assessment instruments. Moreover, we follow one individual case throughout the book to show how the various theories relate to the same person. Thus, the student can ask: Are the pictures of a person gained through the lens of each theory completely different from each other, or do they represent complementary perspectives on the same person?

4. *Objective, evenhanded treatment of each theoretical approach.* Our effort has been to understand each theory on its own terms and then to evaluate it in relation to standard criteria. Thus, discussion of each major theory is followed by an analysis of the strengths and limitations of that approach. Rather than persuade the student of the value of one theory over all others, we attempt to present an accurate statement of each one, and to entice the students to come to their own conclusions.

This new edition of *Personality: Theory and Research* offered an opportunity to capture new theoretical developments and new approaches to the study of personality while retaining the important contributions made by earlier approaches. Preparing the revision was a personal learning experience. We had to review the major developments in the field in order to select those to be presented in the new edition, and we tried to find new ways to present the material to enrich the student's learning experience.

The seventh edition retains coverage of the theories included in the preceding edition of the text. It also presents developments on the cutting edge. These developments lie in two particular areas. First, a consensus appears to be emerging among trait researchers concerning the fundamental dimensions of personality traits. Important developments also are occurring in research on inherited aspects of personality traits and the possible biological and evolutionary bases of these traits. These new developments are discussed in Chapters 1, 7, and 8. Second, important developments are occurring in the closely related social-cognitive and information-processing approaches to personality. These approaches have always been strong in their focus on systematic research, but recently the scope of research has broadened to include important aspects of human emotion and motivation. These developments are discussed in Chapters 12 to 14.

We hope that in reading this edition of *Personality: Theory and Research*, students will gain an appreciation of three overarching themes: (1) the mystery of human personality and the efforts of psychologists to unravel this mystery; (2) the contributions that both clinical case studies and empirical research can offer; and (3) the value of alternative theoretical approaches to the field. We also hope that students will both discover a particular theory of personality that makes personal sense to them and gain respect for the insights offered by alternative approaches.

INSTRUCTOR'S RESOURCE GUIDE

The instructor's resource guide for *Personality: Theory and Research* is a full teaching resource for the instructor. It includes (1) suggested lecture topics and resource materials; (2) instructional aids; (3) questions for thought and discussion; and (4) multiple-choice and true-false test items.

Suggested lecture topics in each chapter either expand on the material presented in the text or introduce new material directly related to the text. In following this format, the lectures remain integrated with the text without duplicating it. In most cases, the suggestions include a brief description of content that might be included in the lecture and a number of references (a bibliography is included at the end of the manual) that can be reviewed for discussion of the issue under consideration.

The instructional aids include films, tapes, and demonstrations that can be presented in conjunction with the texts and lectures. For the films and tapes there is a brief description of the content, a listing of the distributor, and in most cases, price information. Distributors' addresses are given at the end of the manual.

The questions for thought and discussion include items designed to challenge the student to make use of what has been learned, as well as to think critically about the new knowledge's implications. The questions require the student to build on and go beyond the information presented. They may also serve as a basis for lecture material, as a foundation for large or small group discussions, or as essay test questions.

Finally, the test items provide a testing resource to check on the progress being made by students. The number of items is greatly expanded and improved, and the items are available to instructors on disk in both IBM and Macintosh versions.

ACKNOWLEDG-MENTS

In our efforts to present a comprehensive, scholarly, and interesting textbook, we have been assisted by many people. Students in our classes have been a constant source of stimulation and useful feedback. We are particularly grateful to Jennifer Pals who made many important contributions to the updating and editing of this edition, and to Kate Shea for her thoughtful comments and suggestions. For their helpful reviews and suggestions for revision, we gratefully acknowledge the following professors:

Daniel Cervone, University of Illinois

Barry Fritz, Quinnipiac College

Joseph Germana, Virginia Polytechnic Institute

Kirby Gilliland, University of Oklahoma

James J. Johnson, Illinois State University

Christopher A. Langston, Purdue University

Thomas J. Schoeneman, Lewis & Clark College

Finally, we are especially grateful for the efforts of the staff at Wiley who contributed their skills and talents to the seventh edition, in particular editors Karen Dubno and Chris Rogers.

Lawrence A. Pervin
Rutgers, the State University

and

Oliver P. John
University of California, Berkeley

CONTENTS

CHAPTER 2

CHAPTER 3

CHAPTER 4

A PSYCHODYNAMIC THEORY: APPLICATIONS AND EVALUATION OF FREUD'S THEORY **111**

CHAPTER 5

A PHENOMENOLOGICAL THEORY: CARL ROGERS'S PERSON-CENTERED THEORY OF PERSONALITY   **165**

CHAPTER 6

A PHENOMENOLOGICAL THEORY: APPLICATIONS AND EVALUATION OF ROGERS'S THEORY   195

CHAPTER 7

TRAIT APPROACHES TO PERSONALITY: ALLPORT, EYSENCK, AND CATTELL   225

CHAPTER 8

TRAIT APPROACHES: THE FIVE-FACTOR MODEL; APPLICATIONS AND EVALUATION OF TRAIT APPROACHES TO PERSONALITY   255

CHAPTER 9

LEARNING APPROACHES TO PERSONALITY   297

CHAPTER 10

CHAPTER 14

A COGNITIVE, INFORMATION-PROCESSING APPROACH TO PERSONALITY   453

CHAPTER 15

1

PERSONALITY THEORY: FROM EVERYDAY OBSERVATIONS TO SYSTEMATIC THEORIES

Chapter Focus

Do you have a friend you know so well that you feel as if you could predict how she would react in any situation? Through your experiences with your friend, you have become familiar with the particular unique patterns and consistencies in the way she thinks, feels, and behaves. Not only do you understand what makes her "tick," you know what makes her different from your other friends. In short, you are an expert on what we would call your friend's personality.

The work conducted by all of us in our daily lives is not fundamentally different from that conducted by the scientist who studies personality. The task for each is to develop a model of human functioning, a method for differentiating people, and a set of rules for predicting behavior. This model, and the rules of prediction that follow from it, form the essence of the personality psychologist's theory as much as it forms the essence of our theories in our everyday lives. The difference is that personality psychologists make their models more explicit, define their terms more clearly, and conduct systematic research to evaluate the accuracy of their predictions. This chapter focuses on what a theory is, what a theory of personality should include, and how to evaluate the quality of a theory. Although in our everyday lives we may accept fuzzy theories and may be capable of distorting events to conform to our beliefs, as personality psychologists we must be clear about our concepts and objective about our findings.

QUESTIONS TO BE ADDRESSED IN THIS CHAPTER

1. It sometimes is said that we are all personality psychologists and each of us has a theory of personality. If this is true, then in which ways do the theories of scientific personality psychologists differ from those of ordinary people in their daily functioning?

2. Are there basic areas of human functioning that we would expect a theory of personality to cover? Put differently, which questions concerning human functioning puzzle us and for which questions do we want a theory of personality to provide answers?

3. Are there broad issues on which theories of personality differ (e.g., the fundamental nature of humans, the importance of genes and experience, the importance of the unconscious)?

WHY THE STUDY OF PERSONALITY?

Why do students choose to take a course in personality? Why do some individuals decide to become personality psychologists? Our sense is that they seek answers to the questions "why are people the way they are? Why am I the way I am?" We are all fascinated with people; we frequently ask how and why people are so different from one another and why they behave the way they do. Why do some struggle with feelings when others do not? Why do some appear to be able to do well in areas in which others, seemingly of equal ability, fail? A course in personality offers some promise of answers to these questions. This text may not answer all the many questions of interest to students of personality, but it does provide a number of answers, as well as a way of thinking about people and of studying the questions of interest.

Personality is the part of the field of psychology that most considers people in their entirety as individuals and as complex beings. The reader of this text will find alternative answers that past and current personality psychologists have provided for why we are the way we are. And, the reader will find discussion of how personality psychologists go about studying their subject matter—that is, the research methods we use to study the ways in which people differ and the causes of these differences. The questions asked by personality psychologists probably are not very different from those asked by the student interested in human behavior. However, often those questions are framed differently, in ways that lend themselves to systematic study. And the research methods used by personality psychologists are likely to be much more systematic and free of error or bias than those most of us use in our daily observations of human behavior.

To summarize, the scientific study of personality continues to address the question of why we are the way we are. In trying to answer this question we cannot help but be aware of the complexity of human behavior. People are alike in many ways yet different in many other ways. Out of this maze of complexity and, at times, seeming chaos, we seek to find order and meaningful relationships. To us, this is what the field of personality is about, why one takes a course in personality and why some of us go on to become personality psychologists.

DEFINING PERSONALITY

The field of personality is concerned with *individual differences.* Although they recognize that all people are similar in some ways, psychologists interested in personality are particularly concerned with the ways people differ from one another. Why do some achieve and others not? Why do some perceive things in one way and others in a different way? Why do some suffer from considerable stress and others not?

Personality theorists also are concerned with the total person, trying to understand how the different aspects of an individual's functioning are all intricately related to each other. For example, personality research is not the study of perception, but rather of how individuals differ in their perceptions and how these differences relate to those individuals' total functioning. The study of personality focuses not only on psychological processes, but also on the relationships among these processes. Understanding how these processes interact to form an integrated whole often involves more than understanding each of them separately. People function as organized wholes, and it is in the light of such organization that we must understand them.

Given this emphasis on individual differences and the total person, how are we to define personality? To the general public, personality may represent a value judgment: if you like someone, it is because he or she has a "good" personality or "lots of personality." To the scientist and student of personality, however, the term **personality** is used to define a field of study. A scientific definition of personality tells us what areas are to be studied and suggests how we might best study them.

For the present, let us use the following working definition of personality: *Personality represents those characteristics of the person that account for consistent patterns of feeling, thinking, and behaving.* This is a very broad definition that allows us to focus on many different aspects of the person. At the same time, it suggests that we attend to consistent patterns of behavior and to qualities inside the person that account for these regularities—as opposed, for example, to looking at qualities in the environment that account for such regularities. The regularities of interest to us include the thoughts, feelings, and overt (observable) behaviors of people. Of particular interest to us is how these thoughts, feelings, and overt behaviors relate to one another to form the unique, distinctive individual.

Although one definition of personality has been suggested here, other definitions are possible. Such definitions are not right or wrong; rather, they may be more or less useful in directing us to important areas of understanding. Thus, a definition of personality is useful to the extent that it helps advance the field as a science.

To summarize, the scientific exploration of personality involves systematic efforts to discover and explain regularities in the thoughts, feelings, and overt behaviors of people as they lead their daily lives. As scientists we develop theories to help us observe and explain these regularities. It is to the nature of theory that we now turn.

PERSONALITY THEORY AS AN ANSWER TO THE QUESTIONS OF WHAT, HOW, AND WHY

A theory of personality suggests ways of bringing together and systematizing a wide variety of findings. It also may suggest which directions in research are potentially most useful. Stated simply, theories help to pull together what we know and suggest how we may discover what is yet unknown.

What do we seek to explain with a theory of personality? If we study individuals intensively, we want to know *what* they are like, *how* they became that way, and *why* they behave as they do. Thus, we want a theory to answer the questions of *what*, *how*, and *why*. The "what" refers to the characteristics of the person and how they are organized in relation to one another. Is the person honest, persistent, and high in need for achievement? The "how" refers to the determinants of a person's personality. To what extent and in what ways did genetic and environmental forces interact to produce this result? The "why" refers to the reasons for the individual's behavior. Answers refer to the motivational aspects of the individual—why he or she moves at all, and why in a specific direction. If an individual seeks to make a lot of money, why was this particular path chosen? If a child does well in school, is it to please parents, to use talents, to bolster self-esteem, or to compete with peers? Is a mother overprotective because she happens to be affectionate, because she seeks to give her children what she missed as a child, or because she seeks to avoid any expression of the resentment and hostility she feels toward the child? Is a person depressed as a result of humiliation, because of the loss of a loved one, or because of a feeling of guilt? A theory should help us understand to what extent depression is characteristic of a person, how this personality characteristic developed, why depression is experienced in specific circumstances, and why the person behaves in a certain manner when depressed. If two people tend to be depressed, why does one go out and buy things whereas the other withdraws into a shell?

Let us consider questions such as these in more systematic detail. Here we will consider five areas that a complete theory of personality should cover: (1) *Structure*—the basic units or building blocks of personality. (2) *Process*—the dynamic aspects of personality, including motives. (3) *Growth and Development*—how we develop into the unique person each of us is. (4) *Psychopathology*—the nature and causes of disordered personality functioning. (5) *Change*—how people change and why they sometimes resist change or are unable to change.

STRUCTURE

Theories can be compared in terms of the concepts they use to determine the what, how, and why of personality. The concept of **structure** refers to the more stable and enduring aspects of personality. They represent the building blocks of personality theory. In this sense they are comparable to parts of the body, or to concepts such as atoms and molecules in physics. Such structural concepts as *response, habit, trait,* and *type* have been popular in efforts to conceptualize what people are like.

The concept of *trait* refers to the consistency of individual response to a variety of situations, and approximates the kind of concept the layman uses to describe people. One way to think about traits is to consider how you would describe yourself or a good friend. For example, you might use adjectives such as "intelligent," "outgoing," "honest," "funny," or "serious." You are using these terms in a way very similar to that used by many personality theorists.

The concept of *type* refers to the clustering of many different traits. Compared to the trait concept, that of type implies a greater degree of

THE FAR SIDE   By GARY LARSON

Drawing by Gary Larson;
© 1990 FarWorks, Inc./
Dist. by Universal Press
Syndicate.

The four basic personality types

regularity and generality to behavior. Although people can have many traits to varying degrees, they are generally described as belonging to a specific type. For example, individuals have been described as being introverts or extroverts, and in terms of whether they move toward, away from, or against others (Horney, 1945).

It is possible to use concepts other than trait or type to describe personality structure. Theories of personality differ in the kinds of units or structural concepts they use; they also differ in the way they conceptualize the organization of these units. Some theories involve a *complex* structural system in which many components are linked to one another in a variety of ways. Other theories involve a *simple* structural system in which a few components have few connections to one another. The human brain is a far more complex structure than the brain of a fish because the human brain has more parts, which can be distinguished from one another, and more linkages or connections among these parts.

Theories of personality also differ in the extent to which they view the structural units as organized in a hierarchy—that is, where some structural units are seen as higher in order, and therefore as controlling the function of other units. The human nervous system is more complex than those of other species, not only because it has more different parts and more linkages among them but also because some parts, like the brain, regulate the functioning of other parts in the system. An analogy can be found in business structures. Some business organizations are more complex than others. Complex business organizations have many units, with many linkages among them, and a ranking of people who have responsibility for making decisions. Simple business organizations have few units, few linkages among the units, and few levels in the chain of command—a mom-and-pop store, say, as opposed to General Motors. Similarly, personality theories differ in the numbers and kinds of structural units they emphasize and in the extent to which they emphasize complexity or organization within the system.

PROCESS

Just as theories can be compared in their structures, they can be compared in the dynamic *motivational concepts* they use to account for behavior. These concepts refer to the **process** aspects of human behavior.

Three major categories of motivational concepts have been employed by personality psychologists: pleasure or hedonic motives, growth or self-actualization motives, and cognitive motives (Pervin, 1996). Pleasure-hedonic motivational concepts emphasize the pursuit of pleasure and the avoidance of pain. There are two major variants of such theories of motivation: **tension reduction models** and **incentive models**. One major personality theorist refers to these as "push" or "pitchfork theories" and "pull" or "carrot theories" (Kelly, 1958a). According to tension reduction "pitchfork" models of motivation, physiological needs create tensions that the individual seeks to reduce by satisfying those needs. For example, hunger or thirst creates tension that can be relieved by eating or drinking. The term *drive* typically has been used to refer to internal states of tension that activate and direct people toward tension reduction. In contrast with such tension reduction models, in "pull" or "carrot" models the emphasis is on end-points, goals, or incentives that the person seeks to achieve. For example, the person may seek to achieve money, fame, social acceptance, or power. Although here it is the goal that is stressed rather than an internal state of tension, it should be clear that nevertheless the pursuit of pleasure is being emphasized, in this case the pleasure associated with achievement of the goal. It is for this reason that incentive theories of motivation as well as tension reduction theories are considered to be hedonic or pleasure-oriented theories of motivation.

In contrast with such pleasure-oriented theories, other motivational theories emphasize the efforts of the organism to achieve growth and self-fulfillment. According to this view, individuals seek to grow and realize their potential even at the cost of increased tension. Finally, in cognitive theories of motivation, the emphasis is on the person's efforts to understand and predict events in the world. Rather than seeking pleasure or self-fulfillment, according to such theories the person has a need for consistency or a need to know. For example, the person may seek to maintain a consistent picture of the self and to have others behave in a predictable way. In this case, consistency and predictability are emphasized even at the price of pain or discomfort. Thus, it is suggested that people at times may prefer an unpleasant event to a pleasant one if the former makes the world seem more stable and predictable (Swann, 1992).

The most widely accepted model in early theories of motivation was that of tension reduction. Research on animals and humans, however, demonstrates that organisms often seek tension. Monkeys, for example, work to solve puzzles independent of any reward; in fact, rewards may interfere with their performance. The exploratory and play behaviors of members of many species are well known. Observations such as these led R.W. White (1959) to conceptualize a process in human functioning that he called *competence motivation.* According to this view, people are motivated to deal competently or effectively with the environment. Indeed, as individuals mature, more of their behavior appears to be involved with developing skills for the sake of mastery or for dealing effectively with the environment, and less of their behavior appears to be exclusively in the service of tension reduction.

Different motivational theories have been popular at various times in the history of the field. Until the 1950s, drive theories of motivation were quite popular. With the decline of interest in drive and the tension reduction theories of motivation in the 1950s, there began to be interest in

Motivation: *Personality theories emphasize different kinds of motivation (e.g., tension-reduction, self-actualization, power, etc.)*

growth and self-fulfillment models. With the cognitive revolution in the 1960s, there developed considerable interest in cognitive motives for consistency and predictability. And today, there is increased interest in goal theories that emphasize a view of the person as actively pursuing anticipated end-points.

Must one choose among the various theories of motivation—tension reduction, self-fulfillment, cognitive, goal? Is one necessarily correct and the others wrong? As we shall see in later chapters in this book, individual personality theorists have tended to emphasize one model of motivation or another. However, it may be that people are capable of various kinds of motivation, sometimes seeking pleasure in the form of tension reduction or achievement of a goal, sometimes seeking self-fulfillment, and sometimes seeking cognitive consistency and predictability. Differences may exist among individuals in the extent to which they are motivated by one or another of these motives. In other words, such individual differences may themselves be an important part of personality. Although such a view is possible, perhaps even desirable, personality theorists have tended to use one model or another to account for the process aspects of human behavior.

GROWTH AND DEVELOPMENT

One of the most profound challenges facing personality psychologists is to account for the development of individual differences and the development of the unique individual that each of us is. Typically the determinants of personality have been divided into genetic determinants and environmental determinants. Unfortunately, this division of determinants also often has led to pitched battles over which of them is more important for personality—the *nature-nurture controversy*, nature referring to the contribution of genes and nurture referring to the importance of the environment. At various points in time, one or another emphasis has been predominant, the pendulum shifting from an emphasis on nature (genes) to one on nurture (environment), and then back to one on nature. In recent years there has been an increased emphasis on the importance of genes, but even some proponents of this point of view suggest that the pendulum may be swinging too far in the direction of nature (Plomin, 1994; Plomin, Chipuer, & Loehlin, 1990).

Once more, is it necessary to choose? Clearly both genetic and environmental determinants are important in the formation of personality. Before considering relations between these determinants, let us consider the importance of each separately.

Genetic Determinants

Genetic factors play a major role in determining personality, particularly in relation to what is unique in the individual (Plomin et al., 1990). Although many psychologists historically have stressed the importance

Genetic Influences on Personality Development: *Personality development reflects the interaction of environmental and genetic forces. The triplets pictured here had been separated in infancy and discovered one another as young men. They found that they not only looked alike, but smiled and talked in the same way.*

of environmental and genetic factors in shaping personality as a whole, recent theorists have recognized that the importance of these factors may vary from one personality characteristic to another. Genetic factors are generally more important in such characteristics as intelligence and temperament, and less important in regard to values, ideals, and beliefs.

One good example of an individual difference due to temperament is activity level and fearfulness (Kagan, 1994). Some infants are more active and less fearful than others. Such differences can last into adulthood, with some individuals always wanting to be on the go and others generally preferring to read a book or take a nap, some individuals being relatively fearless and others generally fearful or cautious. The fact that these differences appear early, are long-lasting, and seem to be relatively independent of one's learning history, suggests that these differences are due to genetic or inherited characteristics. It is often said that parents are "environmentalists" with the birth of their first child, but after viewing the striking differences in their children beginning at birth, become "hereditarians" with the birth of additional children.

Genetic determinants also have come to be emphasized by personality psychologists who emphasize our evolutionary heritage (Buss, 1991, 1995). According to such psychologists, many patterns of behavior date back to our evolutionary heritage and relate to genes shared with members of other species. Although in most cases we tend to think of how genes make us different from one another, it also is important to keep in mind how much of our genetic constitution is shared with one another and with members of other species. Thus, at the most basic level most of us have two eyes, two ears, a nose, and so forth. But beyond this, evolutionary personality psychologists also suggest that we share social patterns of relating to one another. For example, characteristics considered to be desirable in a male or female mate, male-female differences in parenting involvement, altruism, and basic emotions experienced have all been considered to reflect our evolutionary heritage in the form of information contained in genes. Psychologists who emphasize basic emotions (e.g., anger, sadness, joy, disgust, fear) suggest that these emotions are innate, with the relevant information coded into our genes (Ekman, 1992, 1993; Izard, 1991). Thus children as well as adults, and chimpanzees as well as humans, experience such emotions, the reason being the shared evolutionary heritage and the shared genetic structure. This is not to say that experience does not play a role in which emotions an individual is more or less likely to encounter, or in when particular emotions are experienced and how they are expressed, but rather that these developments occur in relation to an underlying genetic structure. In sum, genes play a role in making us alike as humans as well as different as individuals.

Environmental Determinants

Environmental determinants include influences that make many of us similar to one another as well as experiences that make us unique.

Culture   Significant among the environmental determinants of personality are experiences individuals have as a result of membership in a particular *culture*. Each culture has its own institutionalized and sanctioned patterns of learned behaviors, rituals, and beliefs. This means that most members of a culture will have certain personality characteristics in common. Thus, often we are unaware of cultural influences until we come into contact with members of a different culture who view the world differently and perhaps challenge our own accepted view of the world. As much as we may take such influences for granted, their impact is enormous, influencing virtually every aspect of our existence—how we define our needs and our means of satisfying them; our experiences of different emotions and how we express what we are feeling; our relationships with others and with ourselves; what we think is funny or sad; how we cope with life and death; and what we view as healthy or sick (Kitayama & Markus, 1994; Markus & Kitayama, 1991; Triandis, 1989).

Social Class   Although certain patterns of behavior develop as a result of membership in a culture, others develop as a result of membership in a social class. Few aspects of an individual's personality can be understood without reference to the group to which that person belongs. One's social group—whether lower class or upper class, working class or professional—is of particular importance. Social class factors help determine the status of individuals, the roles they perform, the duties they are bound by, and the privileges they enjoy. These factors influence how individuals see themselves and how they perceive members of other social classes, as well as how they earn and spend money. Like cultural factors, social class factors influence the ways people define situations and how they respond to them.

Family   Beyond the similarities determined by environmental factors such as membership in the same culture or social class, environmental factors lead to considerable variation in the personality functioning of members of a single culture or class. One of the most important environmental factors is the influence of the family. Parents may be warm and loving or hostile and rejecting, overprotective and possessive or aware of their children's need for freedom and autonomy. Each pattern of parental behavior affects the personality development of the child. Parents influence their children's behavior in at least three important ways:

1. Through their own behavior, they present situations that elicit certain behavior in children (e.g., frustration leads to aggression).
2. They serve as role models for identification.
3. They selectively reward behaviors.

Recently, researchers have begun to focus on the question: Why are children from the same family so different? The answer lies not only in constitutional differences but also in the different experiences siblings have as members of the same family and in different experiences they

Determinants of Personality: *Genetic differences and different life experiences, both within and outside the family, contribute to personality differences among siblings.*

CURRENT ISSUES

THE LIMITS OF FAMILY INFLUENCE?

For a long time, personality and developmental psychologists have assumed that the family is of paramount importance in shaping personality. More specifically, the assumption has been made that children from the same family share common personality characteristics as a result of shared environmental influences—that is, as a result of being members of the same family. As noted in the text, behavioral geneticists—individuals who study the relation between genetic similarity and personality characteristics, and who thereby seek to determine genetic influences on personality—have come to suggest that siblings growing up in the same family do not share the same environment. Rather, the family environment is distinctive for each sibling.

Beyond this, some behavioral geneticists suggest that the family environment has limited systematic influence on personality altogether! The suggestion is that genes play a larger role in personality development than do family experiences, both in terms of direct genetic influences and in ways that genetic differences lead individuals to respond differently to the same environment. For example, temperamentally aggressive children may select different environments, elicit different responses from others, and

respond differently to the same environmental events than temperamentally passive children. Thus, although environmental experiences may be somewhat important, it is suggested that to a large extent these experiences occur outside the family environment and, again, are influenced by genetic factors.

These views have not gone unchallenged by psychologists who emphasize the importance of family experiences in shaping similarities as well as differences among siblings. In one particularly noteworthy recent study, attitudes toward romantic love relationships were found to be largely influenced by a common family environment and hardly influenced at all by genetic factors. According to the authors of the study, "common family environment plays a sizable role in determining love styles, a finding compatible with theories stressing the importance of family interactions in personality development" (Waller & Shaver, 1994, p. 268). Perhaps the best statement that could be made at the present is that we still have a great deal to learn about how genes and environments interact to shape various personality characteristics.

SOURCES: Harris, 1995; Hoffman, 1991; Rowe, 1994; Scarr, 1992; Waller & Shaver, 1994.

have outside the family (Dunn & Plomin, 1990; Plomin et al., 1990; Plomin & Daniels, 1987). To the surprise of many people, the different experiences of siblings (the nonshared environment) may be even more important for personality development than experiences shared as members of the same family.

Peers   If the shared family environment is not as important as many think, which environmental experiences are important? Perhaps they are the family experiences that are unique for each child. Recently another alternative has been suggested. According to this view, it is the peer environment that accounts for the environmental effects on personality development: "experiences in childhood and adolescent peer groups, not experiences at home, account for environmental influences on personality development. The answer to the question 'Why are children from the same family so different from one another?' (Plomin & Daniels, 1987) is, because they have different experiences outside the home and because their experiences inside the home do not make them more alike" (Harris, 1995, p. 481).

What is suggested here is that children learn many things in the home but these influences are specific to the home environment, and often fade in the face of peer group influences. Thus, the peer group serves to socialize the individual into acceptance of new rules of behavior and provides for experiences that will have lasting influences on personality development. According to this view, parental bonds are important for early development, but it is peer involvement that is important for later, more lasting personality development.

Relations Between Genetic and Environmental Determinants

As noted, psychologists have historically debated the relative importance of genes and environment. At the same time, probably all psychologists would agree that this is a senseless debate, since genes and environments are always interacting with one another—that is, there are never genes without an environment and never an environment without genes. Thus, the question for psychologists becomes one of understanding the process of personality development as a result of the ongoing interactions between genes and environments. For example, consider the concept of *reaction range* (Gottesman, 1963). This concept suggests that heredity fixes a number of possible outcomes but environment ultimately determines the specific outcome. That is, heredity may set a range within which the further development of a characteristic is determined by the environment. For example, heredity may define the limits of talent in music or sports but environment will determine the specific degree and form of development of each talent.

Although useful, the concept of reaction range fails to portray the active process of ongoing interaction between nature and nurture. Once born into the world, infants not only are exposed to different environments but, based on inherited constitutional differences, they evoke different responses from the environment. For example, the hyperactive child evokes different responses from parents than does the tranquil child, the physically appealing child different responses than the physically unappealing child, the girl different responses than the boy. With further development, the person seeks out different environments based in part on constitutional differences and in part based on past experiences of pleasure or pain in specific environments. Thus, rather than a simple cause-effect relationship, we have an ongoing interaction, or reciprocal process, between heredity and environment.

To summarize, personality is determined by many interacting factors, including genetic, cultural, social class, and familial forces. Heredity sets limits on the range of development of characteristics; within this range, characteristics are determined by environmental forces. Heredity provides us talents that a culture may or may not reward and cultivate. It is possible to see the interaction of these many genetic and environmental forces in any significant aspect of personality. A personality theory must account for the development of structures and patterns of behavior. A theory of personality should explain what is developed, how, and why.

Psychopathology and Behavior Change

In attempting to account for these varied aspects of human behavior, a complete theory of personality must include analyses of why some people are capable of coping with the stresses of daily life and generally experience satisfaction, whereas others develop psychopathological responses (abnormal behavior due to psychological causes). Further, such a theory should suggest psychotherapies or means by which pathological forms of behavior can be modified. Although not all personality theorists are therapists, a complete theory of personality should suggest how and why people change or resist change.

SUMMARY

This section has explored five areas that a complete theory of personality must take into account and by which theories of personality can be compared: structure, process, development, psychopathology, and change. These areas represent abstractions or ways of carving up the field. Such conceptual abstractions are found in other sciences as well as psychology. They define the areas to be covered by a theory of personality—what we have labeled the what, how, and why of personality.

Throughout the relatively brief history of personality theory, a number of issues have confronted theorists repeatedly (Pervin, 1990). The ways in which they treat these issues do much to define the major characteristics of each theoretical position. Thus, in reviewing various personality theories we must consider how much attention each theorist gives to these issues and how that theorist resolves each issue.

IMPORTANT ISSUES IN PERSONALITY THEORY

PHILOSOPHICAL VIEW OF THE PERSON

What is the basic nature of people? A philosophical view concerning human nature tends to underlie current personality theories. For example, one theory views the person as an organism that reasons, chooses, and decides (rational view), whereas another views the person as an organism that is driven, compelled, irrational (animal view); one theory views the person as automatically responding to outside stimuli (machine view), whereas another views the person as processing information like a computer (computer view).

Proponents of different points of view have had different life experiences, and have been influenced by different historical traditions. Thus, beyond scientific evidence and fact, theories of personality are influenced by personal factors, by the spirit of the time, and by philosophical assumptions characteristic of members of a given culture (Pervin, 1978b). Although based on observed data, theories selectively emphasize certain kinds of data and go beyond what is known, and therefore can be influenced by personal and cultural factors. To some extent, in developing psychological theories we talk about ourselves. In itself this is not a problem. Only when personal experiences become more important than other kinds of experience and ignore research evidence do personal determinants of a theory become a problem.

INTERNAL AND EXTERNAL DETERMINANTS OF BEHAVIOR

Is human behavior determined by processes inside the person or by external events? The issue here concerns the relationship between internal and external determinants. All theories of personality recognize that factors inside the organism and events in the surrounding environment are important in determining behavior. However, the theories differ in the level of importance given to internal and external determinants (Pervin & Lewis, 1978). Consider, for example, the difference between Freud's view that we are controlled by unknown internal forces and Skinner's suggestion that "a person does not act upon the world, the world acts upon him" (1971, p. 211). Whereas the Freudian views the person as active and responsible for behavior, the Skinnerian views the person as a passive victim of events in the environment. The Freudian view suggests that we focus our attention on what is going on inside the person; the Skinnerian view suggests that such efforts are foolhardy and that we would be wise to concentrate on environmental variables.

Although the Freudian and Skinnerian views represent extremes that many psychologists avoid, most psychologists nevertheless weight their theories in the direction of internal or external factors. Periodically there is a shift in emphasis from internal to external factors or vice versa, with an occasional call for investigation of the relationship between the two. For example, in the 1940s one psychologist spoke out against the prevalent tendency to overestimate the importance of internal (person) relative to external (environmental) factors in personality (Ichheiser, 1943). In the 1970s another psychologist asked, "Where is the person in personality research?" (Carlson, 1971). More recently, debate concerning the role of internal and external forces in governing behavior has been high-lighted in the *person–situation controversy*. In his 1968 book *Personality and Assessment*, social learning theorist Walter Mischel criticized tradi-tional personality theories for their emphasis on stable and enduring internal structures, which leads to the perception of people's behavior as fairly unchanging over time and across situations. Instead of emphasiz-ing broad personality characteristics that function independently of external factors, Mischel suggested that changes in environmental or external conditions modify how people behave. Such changes result in relatively situation-specific behavior: Each environmental situation acts independently to affect individual behavior.

Since the publication of Mischel's book, considerable attention has been paid to the internal–external (or person–situation) controversy. First there was debate about whether persons or situations control behavior, then about whether persons or situations are more important, and, finally, acceptance of the view that both are important and interact with one another (Endler & Magnusson, 1976; Magnusson & Endler, 1977). Almost all researchers today suggest an emphasis on person–situ-ation interaction, even though fundamental disagreements remain. Even when persons, situations, and interactions are all accepted as important, there are theoretical differences about *what* in the person interacts *how* and with *what* in the situation. Thus, the internal–external debate remains lively and is an issue to keep in mind when considering various theoretical points of view (Pervin, 1985).

CONSISTENCY ACROSS SITUATIONS AND OVER TIME

How consistent is personality from situation to situation? For example, to what extent are you "the same person" when with friends as with parents? At a party as in a classroom discussion? In terms of consistency over time, how similar is your personality now to what it was when you were a child? And, how similar will it be twenty years from now? Once more we find that personality theorists take different positions on this issue. The issue of consistency across situations is related to the person–situation controversy just discussed. Whereas some theorists suggest that people are consistent across situations, others suggest that people are very vari-able, virtually being different people in one context than in another. Although clearly people differ in this regard, some being more consistent and others more variable, we can ask whether generally people seem con-sistent or variable in their behavior across situations. More generally, we can ask how a theory accounts for the consistency and variability that does exist in each person's behavior over a range of situations.

Turning to consistency over time, some personality theorists empha-size the continuity of personality over time. From this perspective, the child is "father to the man" and by the time a person reaches the age of twenty-five or so their personality is virtually "set like plaster" (Costa &

McCrae, 1994a). Other personality theorists emphasize the lack of continuity between childhood and adulthood. From this perspective, it is no surprise that it is so hard to predict what will become of a child, and no great surprise when an adult takes a path representing a marked departure from childhood patterns. Indeed, some psychologists suggest that there is very limited predictability from childhood to adulthood, particularly given all of the chance occurrences that play a role in human development (Lewis, 1995).

The question of personality consistency is a complex one and answers depend in part upon the aspect of personality being considered. We would expect people to change more on some characteristics than others, to change more readily on less central personality characteristics and less readily on more central characteristics. Also, the issue partly revolves around one's definition of consistency, that is, does consistency require that the person behave in an identical way or that their behavior reflect the same personality pattern? An aggressive child, for example, may remain aggressive as an adult but channel the aggression in a very different way. Is there consistency in this case? A person may look different on two different occasions, or in two different situations, but the underlying personality may be the same, just as the underlying structure of water, ice, and steam are the same despite the very different appearances. In sum, personality theorists differ in their views concerning the extent to which people are consistent across situations and over time.

THE UNITY OF BEHAVIOR AND THE CONCEPT OF SELF

How are we to account for the integrated nature of much of our functioning, that is, the fact that generally our behavior shows pattern and organization rather than randomness or chaos? Most psychologists agree that human behavior results not only from the operation of specific parts, but also from the relationships among these parts. To a certain extent this is true for a mechanical system such as an automobile; it is even truer for a living system such as the human body. Rather than being made up of isolated responses, human behavior generally expresses *pattern, organization,* and *integration.* Like a smoothly running car, the parts operate in harmony with one another. They all seem to function together to achieve their common goals, instead of each part functioning independently to achieve different goals that may conflict with one another. Indeed, when behavior appears disorganized and unintegrated, we suspect that something is drastically wrong with the person. How, then, are we to formulate this pattern and organization? What is it that gives an integrative quality to behavior? The concept of the self has often been used in this regard. Although many personality theorists give major attention to this concept, others choose to disregard it entirely.

Traditionally, the concept of the self has been emphasized for three reasons. First, our awareness of ourselves represents an important aspect

The Concept of Self: *Personality psychologists are interested in how the concept of self develops and helps to organize experience.*

of our phenomenological or subjective experience. Second, considerable research suggests that how we feel about ourselves influences our behavior in many situations. Third, as noted, the concept of the self is used to express the organized, integrated aspects of human personality functioning. In asking whether the concept of the self is necessary, the noted theorist Gordon Allport (1958) suggested that many psychologists have tried in vain to account for the integration, organization, and unity of the human person without making use of the concept of the self.

Without a concept of self, the theorist is left with the task of developing an alternative concept to express the integrated aspects of human functioning. On the other hand, reliance on the concept of the self leaves the theorist with the task of defining self in a way that makes it possible to be studied systematically, rather than leaving it vaguely defined as some strange inner being. Thus, how to account for the organized aspects of personality, and the utility of the concept of the self in this regard, remains a major issue of concern for personality psychologists.

VARYING STATES OF AWARENESS AND THE CONCEPT OF THE UNCONSCIOUS

To what extent are we aware of much of our internal mental life and the causes of behavior? A fifth issue of continuing concern to most personality theorists is how to conceptualize the role of varying states of consciousness in individual functioning (Kihlstrom, 1990; Pervin, 1996). Most psychologists agree that the potential for different states of consciousness exists. The effects of drugs, along with interest in Eastern religions and techniques of meditation, have served to heighten the concern of personality theorists with the whole range of altered states of consciousness. Most theorists also accept the view that we are not always attentive to or aware of factors that influence our behavior. However, many are uncomfortable with Freud's theory of the unconscious; they feel that it is used to account for too much, and that it does not lend itself to empirical investigation.

But how are we to account for such diverse phenomena as slips of the tongue, dreams, and our ability under some circumstances to remember events of the past that once appeared to have been forgotten? Are these related or separate phenomena? Must they be understood in terms of the working of an unconscious, or are alternative explanations possible? As we shall see, the issue here is important in relation to personality measurement as well as personality theory. To what extent can we rely on people to give accurate reports about themselves? Are they aware of some things but unaware of others? In relation to the concept of the self, are people aware of all their feelings about themselves, or are some of these feelings unconscious? If we cannot recognize some important feelings about ourselves, what are the implications of this fact for attempts to measure perceptions of the self?

RELATIONSHIPS AMONG COGNITION, AFFECT, AND OVERT BEHAVIOR

To what extent are our thoughts, feelings, and overt behavior related to one another? Is one more causal than another, that is, do feelings change our thoughts or do thoughts change our feelings? Or, are both possible?

Personality includes cognitions (thought processes), affects (emotions, feelings), and overt behavior. Not all psychologists agree that these are all worthy of investigation, and even where such agreement exists, there are major differences concerning relationships among them. As we shall see later in the text, radical behaviorism led to a focus on overt behavior and the rejection of investigation of internal processes such as thoughts and feelings. Then, starting in the 1950s, a cognitive revolution took place in psychology that led to domination of the field by cognitive theories. For some time the area of affect was ignored, although in recent years there have been strong signs of a developing interest in affect, both in its own right and in its implications for thought and action.

Personality psychologists differ in the relative weight or attention they give to each of these areas of functioning. This is of particular interest since it concerns what is investigated, how research is conducted, and how we assess personality. That is, different methods of personality investigation and assessment are involved in the study of human thoughts, feelings, and behaviors. Personality psychologists also differ in their views of the causal relations among thoughts, feelings, and behaviors. For example, whereas some personality theorists give primacy to affects, other theorists give primacy to the role of cognition in affect and behavior.

It is interesting to consider the relevance of these phenomena in light of one's own personality. For example, how much of your personality is expressed in overt behavior? Could we know all there is to know about you from observing your overt behavior? From knowing your thoughts? From knowing your feelings? Or does personality involve all three and—most significantly—relationships among what you are thinking, what you are feeling, and how you behave? Is change in one more central to change in the others? Which is easiest to change—thoughts, feelings, or behaviors?

THE INFLUENCE OF THE PAST, PRESENT, AND FUTURE ON BEHAVIOR

To what extent are we "prisoners of our past" as opposed, for example, to always being shaped by our view of the future? The final issue to be noted here concerns the importance of the past, present, and future in governing behavior. Theorists agree that behavior can be influenced only by factors operating in the present. In this sense, only the present is important in understanding behavior. But the present can be influenced by experiences in the remote past or in the recent past. Similarly, what one is thinking about in the present can be influenced by thoughts about the immediate future or the distant future. People vary in the extent to which they worry about the past and the future. And personality theorists differ in their concern with the past and the future as determinants of behavior in the present. At one extreme lies psychoanalytic theory, which attaches importance to early learning experiences. At the other extreme lies cognitive theory, which emphasizes the individual's plans for the

The Effects of Early Experience: *Psychologists generally agree that early experiences can be important for personality development, but they disagree on whether these experiences lead to the development of relatively fixed personality characteristics.*

future. However, the issue is not whether events that happened in the past can have lasting effects or whether anticipations about the future can have effects in the present (theorists undoubtedly agree that both are possible and occur), but how to conceptualize the role of past experiences and future anticipations and connect their influence to what is occurring in the present.

SUMMARY

In attempting to account for the what, how, and why of human functioning, personality theorists are confronted with many issues. Seven issues of particular importance have been mentioned here: (1) the philosophical view of the person; (2) the relation between internal (personal) and external (situational) influences in determining behavior; (3) the consistency of personality across situations and over time; (4) the concept of the self and how to account for the organized aspects of personality functioning; (5) the role of varying states of awareness and the concept of the unconscious; (6) the relationships among cognition, affect, and behavior; and (7) the role of the past, present, and future in governing behavior. Of course, many other issues concern personality theorists and account for differences among them, but the purpose here has been to point to the main ones. The importance of these and other issues will become increasingly clear as we consider the positions of the various theorists in the chapters that follow.

EVALUATION OF THEORIES

In a sense, we are all personality theorists and personality psychologists, that is, we all develop ways of organizing information about people, make predictions about how individuals will behave, make further observations, and revise our views accordingly (G. A. Kelly, 1955). What differentiates the work of professional personality theorists from people in their daily behavior is that professional theorists make their theories more explicit and are more systematic in testing them. Whereas in our daily lives we usually leave our theories implicit, rarely taking the time to spell them out or give them some formal organization, as personality psychologists we make our theories explicit, stating clearly the basic units and processes we see as regulating human behavior.

To pursue this analogy further, how can we compare the evaluation of our theories in our daily lives with that of the evaluation of theories in the scientific work of personality psychologists? In our daily lives presumably we seek to find pattern, regularity, predictability in events. Were we not able to find order and predictability the world would appear chaotic. How would we function? The more we can account for and anticipate events, the better off we are. In addition, since often we are required to make quick decisions, we seek a system for interpreting events and making predictions that is as simple and easy to use as possible. Finally, given that we all are fallible and at best imperfect scientists, we must be open to recognizing mistakes in our views and capable of making corrections in them. Although often we may be hesitant to do so, periodically we must put our ideas to the test and find out just how much stock we can put in them. And although often we are capable of great self-deception in reading the evidence, and may be quite reluctant to believe the data, generally we are at least somewhat open to the need for revision of our views or implicit theories.

These basic principles that most of us follow in our daily lives have parallels in the principles followed by personality psychologists as scientists although, once more, there are differences. As noted, the rules of science require that theories be made explicit rather than left implicit. In addition, whereas we may be unsystematic in the collection of information in our daily lives, the rules of science require that we be systematic in our data collection and that other scientists be able to obtain identical findings to those we reportedly have observed. In terms of evaluation of theories, the criteria used by personality psychologists parallel those we follow in our daily lives and follow from the functions of theory—the organization of existing information and the prediction of new findings. The criteria for evaluation of theories of personality are *comprehensiveness*, *parsimony* or *simplicity*, and *research relevance* (Hall & Lindzey, 1957). As is true for the implicit theories used by us in our daily lives, the explicit theories of personality psychologists can be evaluated in terms of how much data they can account for in a simple, parsimonious way and in terms of how useful they are in helping us to anticipate and explain events. Earlier it was suggested that the function of a theory is to organize what is known and to point toward discovery of what is as yet unknown. The first two criteria, comprehensiveness and parsimony, relate to the organizing function of theory; the third criterion, research relevance, to the guiding function.

COMPREHENSIVENESS

A good theory is comprehensive in that it encompasses and accounts for a wide variety of data. Such a theory is directed to each of the realms of behavior discussed previously. It is important to ask how many different kinds of phenomena the theory can account for. However, we must not be merely quantitative. No theory can account for everything, so one must also ask whether the phenomena accounted for by one theory are as important or central to human behavior as the phenomena encompassed by another. It is important to recognize that comprehensiveness includes both the number and the significance of the facts accounted for by the theory.

While considering how comprehensive a theory is, we also want to consider how specifically it deals with the events to which it relates. In other words, we not only want a theory to cover many different phenomena in a general way but to be very exact in its coverage. Not only should a good theory of personality allow us to make predictions about lots of events but it should also allow us to be very specific in our predictions. The concepts of **bandwidth** and **fidelity** encompass the criteria under consideration. The concept of bandwidth relates to the range of phenomena covered by a theory, what might be called its range of convenience, that of fidelity to the phenomena to which it is particularly applicable, what can be called its focus of convenience. An analogy may be drawn here to a comparison of radios. A truly excellent radio picks up a wide variety of stations (bandwidth) and receives the signals of each with great clarity (fidelity). Similarly, an excellent theory of personality accounts for a large range of phenomena with great clarity and specificity. However, often we are forced to make a tradeoff between bandwidth and fidelity. One radio brings in more signals but with lesser clarity; another radio has great clarity but brings in only a limited number of stations. Similarly, personality theories often are stronger in one characteristic than the other, covering a broader range of phenomena at a lesser degree of specificity or a narrower range of phenomena at a greater degree of specificity. Thus, although recognizing that both comprehensiveness and specificity—bandwidth and fidelity—are desirable, we must at times be prepared to consider tradeoffs between the two.

PARSIMONY

Along with being comprehensive, a theory should be simple and parsimonious. It should account for varied phenomena in an economical, internally consistent way. A theory that makes use of a different concept for every aspect of behavior or of concepts that contradict one another is a poor one. These goals of simplicity and comprehensiveness, in turn, raise the question of the appropriate level of organization and abstraction of a personality theory. As theories become more comprehensive and parsimonious, they tend to become more abstract. Therefore it is important that, in becoming abstract, theories retain concepts that relate clearly to the behavior studied. In other words, fuzzy or unclear concepts should not be the price paid for a theory becoming more parsimonious.

RESEARCH RELEVANCE

Finally, a theory is not true or false, but useful or not useful. A good theory has research relevance in that it leads to many new hypotheses, which can then be confirmed through systematic research. It has what Hall and Lindzey call *empirical translation*: It specifies variables and concepts in such a way that there is agreement about their meaning and about their potential for measurement. Empirical translation means that the concepts in a theory are clear, explicit, and lead to the expansion of knowledge; they must have predictive power. In other words, a theory must contain testable hypotheses about relationships among phenomena. A theory that is not open to the *negative test*—one that potentially cannot be shown to be inaccurate—is a poor theory; it would lead to argument and debate, but not to scientific progress. Whatever the final fate of a theory, if it has led to new insights and research techniques, it has made a valuable contribution to science.

SUMMARY

The criteria of comprehensiveness, parsimony, and research relevance provide the basis for a comparative evaluation of theories of personality. In comparing theories, however, we can ask two questions: Do they address themselves to the same phenomena? Are they at the same stage of development? Two theories that deal with different kinds of behavior may each be evaluated in relation to these three criteria. Nevertheless, we need not choose between the two theories; each can be allowed to lead to new insights, with the hope that at some point both can be integrated into a single more comprehensive theory. Finally, a new and immature theory may be unable to account for many phenomena but may lead to a few important observations and show promise of becoming more comprehensive with time. Such a theory may be unable to explain phenomena considered to be understood by another established theory, but may represent a breakthrough in significant areas formerly left untouched. It is like having a new idea, one that needs to be tested further but which seems to explain phenomena formerly puzzling or unaccounted for.

The field of personality is filled with issues that divide scientists along sharply defined lines and lead to alternative, competing schools of thought. It is important to recognize that such theoretical differences exist and that they may not be speedily resolved by debate or experimental proof. The social sciences are still in an early developmental stage. Therefore, we should not be surprised to find competing views that make a common claim to understanding but emphasize different observations and modes of research.

THEORY AND THE STUDY OF PERSONALITY

What, then, is the role of theory in the study of personality? The entire plan of this book suggests that theory is important to our goals of understanding and explaining human behavior. We can be critical of personality theory, as many rightfully have been, and we can even turn away from theory and devote ourselves to detailed research problems, as many psychologists are doing. But in the final analysis, theory is necessary, and a good theory of personality will be developed.

The position taken in this book is that we are always guided by theory in our efforts to study and understand people. The question is to what extent we spell out and test our theories. The task of personality psychologists is to make their theories explicit and open to scientific examination. Ideally, a theory of personality should involve laws that help us understand how each person is different as well as how all people are the same. In the pursuit of such laws, we must develop theories that permit coherent organization of what is known and leave room for us to move on to insights into the unknown.

MAJOR CONCEPTS

Personality. Those characteristics of the person that account for consistent patterns of behavior.

Structure. In personality theory, the concept that refers to the more enduring and stable aspects of personality.

Process. In personality theory, the concept that refers to the motivational aspects of personality.

Bandwidth. A concept referring to the range of phenomena covered by a theory.

Fidelity. A concept referring to the specificity or clarity with which a theory relates to phenomena.

REVIEW

1. We all act as personality psychologists in our efforts to observe, explain, and predict human behavior.

2. Personality theories address the questions of what (structure), why (process), and how (growth and development) concerning human functioning. They also address questions concerning the nature of psychopathology and personality change.

3. A number of issues have confronted personality theorists throughout the relatively brief history of the field. Responses to these issues play a major role in defining the essential characteristics of the theory developed by each theorist.

4. Compared to the average person, scientific personality psychologists make more systematic observations, make their theories more explicit, and provide for more rigorous testing of specific predictions.

5. In evaluating theories, we are interested in the criteria of comprehensiveness, parsimony, and research relevance.

6. Theories organize what is known and suggest answers to questions about what is not yet known. Although the role of theory in the study of personality has been debated, it is suggested that theory is important to our goals of understanding and explaining human behavior.

2

THE SCIENTIFIC STUDY
OF PEOPLE

Chapter Focus

Three students in a course on personality work together on a research project on the effects of achievement motivation on academic performance. At their first meeting, they realize that they have drastically differing opinions about how to proceed. Alex is convinced that the best approach is to follow one student over the course of the semester, carefully recording all relevant information (grades, changes in motivation, feelings about courses, etc.) to obtain a complete and in-depth picture. Sarah, however, thinks little of Alex's idea because his conclusions would apply only to that one person. Her approach would be to develop a set of general questions and collect written responses from as many students as possible. Yet, Michael thinks that the best way to understand things is to do experiments. His approach would be to make some people feel motivated and some people unmotivated and then measure how well they perform on a test.

Case studies, questionnaire research, and *laboratory experiments* are the three major methodological approaches used in personality research. This chapter first considers four types of information or data personality researchers collect about people. Then we consider the three major approaches to research, and illustrate their relative strengths and limitations by exploring research on stress, helplessness, and control. Theories of personality tend to differ in their preferred approaches to research and methods for assessing individuals. That is, there is a link between our theories and how we go about studying people. Finally, attention is given to the personal and social forces that influence research, from defining a problem for study to the development of public social policy.

QUESTIONS TO BE ADDRESSED IN THIS CHAPTER

1. What kind of information is it important to obtain to conduct studies of people?

2. What do we mean when we say that our observations must be reliable and valid?

3. How should we go about studying people? Should we conduct research in the laboratory or in the natural environment? Through the use of self-reports or reports of others? Through studying many subjects or a single individual?

4. To what extent does it make a difference if we study a person using one or another type of data? One or another approach to research? One or another theoretical perspective? In other words, to what extent will the person "look the same" when studied from different vantage points or perspectives?

In Chapter 1 we suggested that all people are personality psychologists. What makes the theories of scientific personality psychologists different is that their theories are more explicit and more open to systematic examination than those of ordinary people. Similarly, we are all researchers on personality in that we notice differences among people and observe consistent patterns of behavior within individuals. However, the "research" of the ordinary person still differs from that of the personality scientist. As scientists we make our ideas explicit, and we are systematic in our observations. We follow established procedures to ensure that our observations are as accurate as possible and can be duplicated by others. And, as scientists, we follow established procedures to determine whether our observations are reliable and stable, rather than occurring by chance or error. In making our research public through publications, we offer others the opportunity to replicate our findings, check our data, and reexamine our conclusions. Rarely in our daily lives do we do this in any kind of systematic way.

Research involves the systematic study of relationships among events. Generally, theory directs our attention to specific problems for investigation, and research tells us how well our theory is doing and how it might be developed further. Thus, theory and research are closely linked to one another. Theory without research is mere speculation, and unending research without theory is meaningless fact-gathering.

What are the data of interest to personality psychologists? What kind of information is it important to obtain if one is to conduct systematic studies of people? Personality psychologists have defined four categories of information, or data, that are used in research (Block, 1993). These are **life record data (L-data)**, **observer data (O-data)**, **test data (T-data)**, and **self-report data (S-data)**. The four kinds of data can be recalled through the acronym LOTS, as when personality psychologists gather lots of data about people.

THE DATA OF PERSONALITY PSYCHOLOGY

L-data consist of information concerning the person that can be obtained from their life history or life record. For example, if one is interested in the relation between intelligence and school performance, one can make use of records of school grades obtained from school records. Or, if interested in the relation between personality and criminality, one can make use of court records of arrests and convictions as a criterion for criminality. O-data consist of information provided by knowledgeable observers such as parents, friends, or teachers. Generally such data are provided in the form of ratings on personality characteristics. Thus, for example, friends might be asked to rate an individual on personality characteristics such as friendliness, extraversion, or conscientiousness. In some research observers are trained to observe individuals in their daily lives and to make personality ratings based on their observations.

For example, camp counselors can be trained to observe the behavior of campers. Personality-relevant data can then be obtained in the form of observations of specific behaviors (e.g., verbal aggression, physical aggression, compliance) or in the form of ratings on more general personality characteristics (e.g., self-confidence, emotional health, social skills) (Shoda, Mischel, & Wright, 1994; Sroufe, Carlson, & Shulman, 1993). As is clear from these examples, O-data can consist of observations of very specific pieces of behavior or of more general ratings based on observations of behavior. In addition, data on any individual can be obtained from one observer or from multiple observers (e.g., one friend or many friends, one teacher or many teachers). In the latter case, one can check for agreement or reliability among observers.

T-data consist of information obtained from experimental procedures or standardized tests. For example, ability to tolerate delay of gratification might be measured by determining how long a child will work at a task to obtain a larger reward rather than a smaller reward that is immediately available (Mischel, 1990). Performance on a standardized test such as an intelligence test would also be illustrative of T-data. Finally, S-data consist of information provided by the subject himself or herself. Typically such data are in the form of responses to questionnaires. In these cases the person is taking the role of observer and making ratings relevant to the self (e.g., "I am a conscientious person"). Personality questionnaires can be relevant to single personality characteristics (e.g., Optimism) or can attempt to cover the entire domain of personality.

Having considered the four categories of data, we now can ask about the extent to which measures obtained from the different types of data agree with one another. If a person rates herself as high on conscientiousness, will others (e.g., friends, teachers) rate her similarly? If an individual scores high on a questionnaire measure of depression, will ratings given by a professional interviewer lead to a similar score? If an individual rates himself as high on extraversion, will he score high on that trait in a laboratory-designed situation to measure that trait (e.g., participation in a group discussion)? We know that scores obtained from questionnaires often are discrepant from scores obtained from laboratory procedures. Questionnaires tend to involve broad judgments over a great variety of situations (e.g., "I generally am pretty even-tempered") whereas experimental procedures measure personality characteristics in a very specific context. Thus, T-data and S-data tend to be different.

But what of the relation between self-report ratings and ratings by others—S-data and O-data? Here personality psychologists come to differing conclusions. While some personality psychologists suggest that self-ratings on traits are largely supported by trait ratings provided by friends and spouses, others question this conclusion and suggest that self-ratings and ratings provided by others can lead to different conclusions (Coyne, 1994; John & Robins, 1994a; Kenny et al., 1994; McCrae & Costa, 1990; Pervin, 1996). Especially when the attribute being rated is highly evaluative (e.g., stupid, warmhearted), self-perception biases enter the rating process, thus lowering agreement between self and observer ratings (John & Robins, 1993, 1994a). Moreover, some personality characteristics are more observable and easier to judge than others (e.g., sociability vs. neuroticism), leading to greater agreement between self and observer ratings as well as to greater agreement among ratings obtained from different observers of the same person (Funder, 1989, 1993, 1995; John & Robins, 1993). In addition, some individuals appear to be easier to read or more "judgable" (Colvin, 1993). Whereas some "open" personalities are easy to read and can be judged with accuracy and agreement by friends, other individuals are closed books for whom people give widely differing personality ratings. In other words, "judgability" may itself be a personality characteristic. In sum, we cannot say with certainty that personality scores obtained from different data sources will always show high agreement with one another.

If personality measures can differ from one another, can we say that one measure is better, more accurate, more valid than another? Once more, we have a complex question to which it is difficult to give a simple, conclusive answer. Each form of data has its advantages and disadvantages, and some personality psychologists prefer one type of data whereas others prefer a different type of data. For example, some psychologists reject many forms of S-data and argue that people not only consciously lie but often distort things for unconscious reasons. On the other hand, other psychologists suggest that if you want to know something about a person, the best thing to do is to ask them (Allport, 1961; G. A. Kelly, 1955). Whereas some psychologists suggest that the best measure of an individual's personality is ratings by others who know the person, others suggest that often different people rate the same person in quite different ways (Hofstee, 1994; John & Robins, 1994a; Kenny et al., 1994). Whereas some psychologists feel that the "true coin" of personality as a science is objective measures of behavior under defined experimental conditions, others question the relevance of such data to the behavior of an individual in the natural environment. In sum, personality psychologists differ in their evaluations of the merits of the various kinds of data.

Despite these differences, probably almost all personality psychologists would be open to the potential utility of each of the four kinds of data for different purposes. For example, if one is interested in the world of subjective experience—how the person experiences the self and others—then obviously it is necessary to use self-report measures. On the other hand, if one is interested in actual performance on tasks, then obviously it is better to use objective test data. Ideally, perhaps, it would be best in our research to obtain various types of data on the same subjects. One thereby could attempt a more comprehensive picture of the person and attempt to understand why particular measures did or did not show agreement with one another. Indeed, in this text we will have the opportunity to consider relations among various types of data for one person. Our sense is that this is a worthy endeavor that is practiced all too rarely in the field. The reason for this is that studies that involve the intensive study of individuals and make use of varied forms of data are extremely time-consuming. In addition, they rarely provide for the testing of specific hypotheses or straight-forward answers to theoretical questions. Instead, they tend to be more exploratory in nature, although potentially of great value in that regard. Finally, as noted, they violate the general tendency for personality psychologists to have a preference for one or another kind of data.

In relation to trying to understand people, we can ask the following: If you wanted to know about someone's personality, what kind of information would you seek to obtain about them? Would you want to ask them questions about themselves (S-data)? Keep track of your own observations and those of others (O-data)? Check specific records (L-data)? Subject them to objective experimental procedures or tests (T-data)? Rarely do we in our daily lives have the option of obtaining such varied information about a person, so we make do with one or another kind of information, typically what people tell us about themselves and the observations we and others make about them. But, even here often we are confronted with discrepancies among the sources of information—what the people tell us about themselves doesn't square with what we observe about them or what others tell us about them. What, then, are we to do? How are we to make sense out of the differing representations of the same person? Is one or another source of data to be most trusted or can we otherwise account for the differences?

From consideration of such questions, hopefully it can be seen just how complex is the task of personality psychologists. We have become very good at developing personality measures and have become very sophisticated concerning research methods. As we shall see in the following section, we have developed criteria for evaluating the scientific merit of differing measures. Clearly it is not all a matter of personal preference. Yet, we remain confronted with the problem that personality measures obtained from different sources of data may not agree with one another and that there is no overall answer to the question of which is the best, most accurate, most valid measure or source of data. If we are to appreciate people in their complexity, and appreciate the complexity of personality research, then we must be prepared to face challenging questions and accept less than conclusive answers.

GOALS OF RESEARCH: RELIABILITY, VALIDITY, ETHICAL BEHAVIOR

All research efforts share certain common goals. In research, we are seeking systematic observations that can be replicated and that relate to the concept of interest to us; that is, in research we seek reliable and valid observations.

RELIABILITY

The concept of **reliability** refers to the extent to which our observations are stable, dependable, and can be replicated. There are many different kinds of reliability, and many different factors may contribute to a lack of reliability. However, an essential factor in all scientific research is that other investigators must be able to reproduce or replicate the observations reported by one investigator. We must have stable, consistent observations to even begin to make theoretical interpretations.

What are some of the factors that might contribute to unreliable observations? On the subject side, if subject performance is greatly influenced in unsystematic ways by transient factors such as attitude or mood, then unreliable observations are likely. For example, if a person is taking the same personality test on two different days, and responses on one day are altered by a chance event that day, scores on the two days will differ. This resulting lack of agreement, or lack of reliability, is a problem if the test is assumed to measure stable personality characteristics that are relatively uninfluenced by temporary states or moods. On the experimenter side, variations in instructions to subjects, as well as in measuring or interpreting responses, can lead to a lack of reliability. For example, carelessness in scoring a test or ambiguous rules for interpreting scores can lead to a lack of agreement, or lack of reliability, among testers.

VALIDITY

In addition to reliable observations, our data must be valid. The concept of **validity** refers to the extent to which our observations indeed reflect the phenomena or variables of interest to us. What use are reliable observations if they do not relate to what we think they do? Suppose, for example, that we have a reliable test for the personality traits of neuroticism or extraversion, but there is no evidence that the test measures what it purports to measure. Of what use is such a measure? Suppose that we take certain behaviors to be expressive of neuroticism, but they reflect other phenomena. Of what use is such a measure? Problems such as this may seem trivial in some areas. For example, we know that a scale is both a reliable and a valid measure of weight, and we know that a ruler is both a reliable and a valid measure of height. But how do we know that certain behaviors are expressive of extraversion or that answers to certain questionnaire items are indicative of neuroticism?

Unfortunately, in personality research it is not unusual for different tests or measures of the same concept to disagree with one another. Which, then is the true or valid measure? If there are two different measures of temperature, how can we know which one is true or valid? The answer is the measure that gives us the most reliable and theoretically useful results. If there are two different measures of a personality concept, how do we know which one is true or valid? Here, too, we would consider the reliability, meaningfulness, and usefulness of the observations. In sum, validity concerns the extent to which we can be sure that we are measuring the phenomena or variables of interest to us. As we shall see, different kinds of personality research present different challenges in regard to satisfying the criteria of reliability and validity.

THE ETHICS OF RESEARCH AND PUBLIC POLICY

As a human enterprise, research involves ethical issues in terms of how we conduct research and report our results. Over the past decades a number of studies have brought into sharp focus some of the issues involved. For example, in one research effort that won a prize from the American Association for the Advancement of Science, subjects were told to teach other subjects ("learners") a list of paired associate words and to punish them with an electric shock when an error was made (Milgram, 1965). The issue investigated was obedience to authority. Although actual shock was not used, the subjects believed that it was being used and often administered high levels despite pleas from the learners that it was painful. In another research effort in which a prison environment was simulated, subjects adopted the roles of guards and prisoners (Zimbardo, 1973). Subject "guards" were found to be verbally and physically aggressive to subject "prisoners," who allowed themselves to be treated in a dehumanized way.

Such programs are dramatic in terms of the issues they raise, but the underlying question concerning ethical principles of research is fundamental. Do experimenters have the right to require participation? To deceive subjects? What are the ethical responsibilities of researchers to subjects and to psychology as a science? The former has been an issue of concern to the American Psychological Association, which has adopted a list of relevant ethical principles (*Ethical Principles of Psychologists*, 1981). The essence of these principles is that "the psychologist carries out the investigation with respect and concern for the dignity and welfare of the people who participate." This includes evaluating the ethical acceptability of the research, determining whether subjects in the study will be at risk in any way, and establishing a clear and fair agreement with research participants concerning the obligations and responsibilities of each. Although the use of concealment or deception is recognized as necessary in some cases, strict guidelines are presented. It is the investigator's responsibility to protect participants from physical and mental discomfort, harm, and danger.

The ethical responsibility of psychologists includes the interpretation and presentation of results as well as the conduct of the research. Of late there has been serious concern in science generally with "the spreading stain of fraud" (*APA Monitor*, 1982). Some concern with this issue began with charges that Sir Cyril Burt, a once prominent British psychologist, intentionally misrepresented data in his research on the inheritance of intelligence. In other fields of science there have been reports of investigators intentionally manipulating data to enhance their chances of publication, grant funding, promotion, and public recognition. The issue of fraud is one that scientists do not like to recognize or talk about because it goes against the essence of the scientific enterprise. Although fraudulent data and falsified conclusions are rare, psychologists are beginning to face up to their existence and to take constructive steps to solve the problem.

Much more subtle than fraud, and undoubtedly of much broader significance, is the issue of the effects of personal and social bias on the ways in which issues are developed and the kinds of data that are accepted as evidence in support for a given enterprise (Pervin, 1978b). In considering sex differences, for example, to what extent are research projects developed in a way that is free from bias? To what extent is evidence for or against the existence of sex differences equally likely to be accepted? To what extent do our own social and political values influence not only what is studied but how it is studied and the kinds of conclusions we are prepared to reach (Bramel & Friend, 1981)? As noted, although scientists make every effort to be objective and remove all possible sources of error and bias from their research, this remains a human enterprise with the potential for personal, social, cultural, and political influence.

Finally, we may note the role of research in personnel decisions and the formulation of public policy. Though still in an early stage of development as a science, psychology does relate to fundamental human concerns, and psychologists often are called on to administer tests relevant to employment or admissions decisions and to suggest the relevance of research for public policy. Personality tests often are used as part of employment, promotion, or admission to graduate programs; research findings have influenced government policy in regard to immigration policy, early enrichment programs such as Head Start, and television violence. This being the case, psychologists have a responsibility to be careful in the presentation of their findings and to inform others of the limits of their findings in regard to personnel and policy decisions.

Although all personality researchers hold the goals of reliability, validity, and theory development in common, they differ in strategy concerning the best routes to these goals. In some cases, the differences in research strategies are minor, limited to the choice of one experimental procedure or test over another. In other cases, however, the differences are major and express a more fundamental difference in approach. Research in personality has tended to follow one of three directions, and we now turn to a description of these approaches. For comparative purposes, we will consider research from each approach relevant to the topic of stress and helplessness. This will enable us to see how data gathered from different research procedures can be consistent and can lead to a greater understanding of the phenomena of interest. The topic of stress and helplessness is selected because of its intrinsic interest, as well as its current importance in personality research.

THREE GENERAL APPROACHES TO RESEARCH

CASE STUDIES AND CLINICAL RESEARCH

Clinical research involves the intensive study of individuals. The material gathered by the psychoanalyst Sigmund Freud illustrates this approach. Case studies and the in-depth observations made by clinicians working with patients have played an important role in the development of some major theories of personality. As the theories were evolving, and once they were developed, additional efforts were made to formulate hypotheses that could be tested more systematically, through either the use of personality tests and questionnaires, or through experimental means. However, the initial focus of these theorists was on their observations of patients, and these clinical observations by them and their followers continued to play a major role in the further elaboration of the theories.

How has clinical research been used in relation to stress and helplessness? The concept of anxiety, related to that of stress, has received considerable clinical attention. The noted psychoanalyst Rollo May, in an early review of the literature, concluded that "the special characteristics of anxiety are the feelings of uncertainty and helplessness in the face of danger" (1950, p. 191). Uncertainty (or lack of cognitive structure) and a sense of helplessness (or lack of control) are mentioned repeatedly in the clinical literature. The former often is expressed in the "fear of the unknown" and is seen as related to a sense of powerlessness or helplessness: An unknown danger creates a situation where activity cannot be

Tactics of Research: *Case studies represent one approach to personality research.*

directed toward any one goal, with a resultant feeling of mental paralysis and helplessness (Kris, 1944). Among the many valuable clinical investigations of responses to stress have been the studies by Grinker and Spiegel (1945) of the reactions of World War II airmen to battle stress.

Reactions to Battle Stress

After World War II, two psychoanalysts (Grinker & Spiegel, 1945) reported on their experiences in interviewing and treating individuals engaged in air battle. Their book, *Men Under Stress*, is a fascinating account of the stress that is common to all combatants and the varied reactions that occur among different individuals. After describing the kinds of dangers to which the airmen are exposed and their use of group morale to deal with the constant threats facing them, the authors raise the question: Of what is the airman afraid? Their description of the relationship between helplessness and anxiety is as follows:

> Although the fear of the aircraft and of human inefficiency are a constant source of stress, the greatest fear is attached to enemy activity. The enemy has only two forms of defense against our combat aircraft: fighter planes and flak [antiaircraft guns]. The enemy's fighter aircraft are efficient and highly respected by our combat crew members. But they are not as great a source of anxiety as flak. Enemy planes are objects that can be fought against. They can be shot down or outmaneuvered. Flak is impersonal, inexorable, and as used by the Germans, deadly accurate. It is nothing that can be dealt with—a greasy black smudge in the sky until the burst is close.
>
> SOURCE: Grinker and Spiegel, 1945, p. 34

Grinker and Spiegel similarly describe the response of ground forces to enemy air and mortar attack. What is so stressful is that "there is nothing in the environment which can be used to anticipate the approach of danger...any stimuli may actually mean the beginning of an attack. Inhibition of anxiety becomes increasingly difficult" (1945, p. 52). According to these psychoanalysts, the initial reaction to such stress is heightened tension and alertness. The person becomes mentally and physically prepared for trouble so as to counteract the threat and avoid loss of control. A variety of means can be used to deal with the threat, but in the final analysis, "mastery, or its opposite, helplessness, is the key to the ultimate emotional reaction" (p. 129). Confidence is lessened by near misses, physical fatigue, and the loss of friends. Efforts to see the self as invulnerable (incapable of being harmed) become increasingly difficult: "Out of the ensuing helplessness is born the intense anxiety" (p. 129). Some strive to hold on to ideas of personal invulnerability ("It can't happen to me"), whereas others hold on to a faith in magical or supernatural powers ("God is my copilot").

Clinical Research: *During World War II psychiatrists and psychologists treated and studied combat men under stress, such as flying personnel subjected to enemy flak.*

Whatever the nature of the efforts, they can be viewed as attempts to deal with the threatened loss of control or experience of helplessness. With prolonged stress, the development of almost any type of neurotic and psychosomatic (psychologically induced illness) reaction is possible. These reactions are grouped under the term *operational fatigue* and generally include a mixture of anxiety, depression, and psychosomatic reaction. The depression that is so common in such cases is associated with a sense of failure ("I've let my buddies down") and wounded pride. In sum, the main component of the anxiety is the sense of helplessness in the presence of a perceived danger. Prolonged stress of this sort leads to a psychological and physical breakdown expressed in a variety of neurotic reactions that are often accompanied by fatalism and depression.

These observations of Grinker and Spiegel are interesting, not only in relation to stress and helplessness, but in relation to our understanding of depression as well. Note that they tie depression to prolonged stress, to a sense of failure, and to wounded pride. Bibring (1953) emphasizes similar factors in his clinical analysis of patient reports of depression. For example, he describes a patient who became depressed whenever his fear of remaining weak was aroused, another patient who became depressed when confronted with a power beyond her reach, and people who became psychologically depressed during the economic depression of the 1930s and the political crises prior to World War II. The common themes running throughout cases of depression, Bibring suggests, are helplessness, a feeling of doom, and a blow to the person's self-esteem.

LABORATORY STUDIES AND EXPERIMENTAL RESEARCH

Experimental research involves efforts to gain control over the variables of interest and establish if–then causal relationships. In experimental approach, for example, the researcher might create conditions of high, moderate, and low anxiety and observe the effects of such varying degrees of anxiety on thought processes or interpersonal behavior. The goal is to be able to make specific statements about causation; that is, by changing one variable, one can produce changes in another variable. The laboratory provides the setting for such research.

Clinical research and experimental research contrast markedly with one another in many ways. Whereas clinicians make observations as close to life as possible, allow events to unfold, and study only a few individuals, experimental research in the laboratory involves tight control over the variables and the study of many subjects. To appreciate the experimental approach, let us consider a research program directed to an understanding of the effects of stress and helplessness. The focus here is on the use of experimental procedures in the laboratory setting, though we shall see that these efforts have expanded into the use of other research procedures as well.

Tactics of Research: *The experimenter here is testing the development of cognition in children.*

Learned Helplessness

As an illustration of the laboratory approach to research, let us consider the important work of Seligman and the concept of **learned helplessness**. In the course of some early work on fear conditioning and learning, Seligman and his coworkers observed that dogs that had experienced uncontrollable shocks in one situation transferred their sense of helplessness to another situation where shock was avoidable. In the first situation, dogs were put in a situation where no response they made could affect the onset, offset, duration, or intensity of the shocks. When placed in a second, different situation where jumping over a barrier could lead to escape from shock, most of the dogs seemed to give up and accept the shock passively. They had learned in the first condition that they were helpless to influence the shocks and transferred this learning to the second condition. Note that this was true for most of the dogs (about two-thirds), but not for all—an important difference among individuals that will be returned to later.

The behavior of the dogs that had learned they were helpless was particularly striking in contrast with that of dogs that received no shock or shock under different conditions. Given the situation where escape and avoidance were possible, the latter dogs ran frantically until they accidentally stumbled on the response that led to escape. Thereafter they progressively learned to move to that response more quickly until finally, they were able to avoid the shock altogether. In contrast to such "healthy" dogs, the dogs with learned helplessness similarly first ran frantically, but then they stopped, laid down, and whined. With succeeding trials the dogs gave up more and more quickly and accepted the shock more passively—the classic learned helplessness response. The depth of their despair became so great that it became extremely difficult to change the nature of their expectations. The experimenters tried to make it easier for the dogs to escape and tried to get them to come to safety by attracting them with food—to no avail. By and large, the dogs just lay there.

Even outside that situation, the behavior of the helpless dogs was different from that of the nonhelpless dogs: "When an experimenter goes to the home cage and attempts to remove a nonhelpless dog, it does not comply eagerly; it barks, runs to the back of the cage, and resists handling. In contrast, helpless dogs seem to wilt; they passively sink to the bottom of the cage, occasionally even rolling over and adopting a submissive posture; they do not resist" (Seligman, 1975, p. 25).

Further research demonstrated that the same phenomena found in dogs could be produced in humans (Hiroto, 1974). In this research one group of college students heard a loud noise that they could terminate by pushing a button, a second group heard the same noise but could not stop it, and a third (control) group did not hear a noise. All three groups were then put in another situation where in order to escape the noise they had to move their hand from one side of the box to the other once

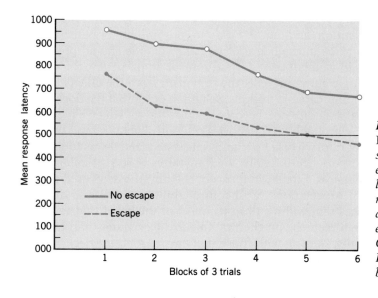

Figure 2.1 Learned Helplessness in Humans. *As in the animal research, subjects who were first in the no-escape treatment condition took longer to respond and failed to escape more often in the test situation than did subjects who were first in the escape condition. (Hiroto, 1974.)* Copyright 1974 by the American Psychological Association. Reprinted by permission.

a light signal had gone on. The members of the first and third groups quickly learned to escape the noise by moving their hands, but the members of the learned helplessness group failed to escape the noise; most sat passively and accepted the painful noise. The measure of the learned helplessness effect was response latency, or how long it took the subjects to move their hand once the light signal went on. In sum, manipulation of the escape versus no-escape conditions in the first phase of the experiment produced clear evidence of differences in learned helplessness in the second phase of the experiment (Figure 2.1).

Additional research demonstrated that such learned helplessness could generalize beyond the initial task to a broad range of behaviors (Hiroto & Seligman, 1975). Studies have demonstrated that learned helplessness can occur through observing helpless models (Brown & Inouye, 1978; DeVellis, DeVellis, & McCauley, 1978). Individuals will give up more easily if they see themselves as similar to a helpless model than if they observe a successful model or if they perceive themselves as more competent than the observed model.

Seligman's explanation of the learned helplessness phenomenon was that the animal or person learns that outcomes are not affected by its behavior. The expectation that outcomes are independent of the organism's response then has motivational, cognitive, and emotional implications: (1) Uncontrollable events undermine the organism's motivation to initiate other responses that might result in control. (2) As a result of uncontrollability of previous events, the organism has difficulty learning that its response can have an effect on other events. (3) Repeated experiences with uncontrollable events eventually lead to an emotional state similar to that identified in humans as depression.

This is the theory of helplessness, a theory that also leads to suggestions concerning prevention and cure. First, to prevent an organism from expecting events to be independent of its behavior, one should provide it with experiences in which it can exercise control. In particular, the experience of controlling trauma protects the organism from the effects caused by experiences of unescapable trauma. Seligman notes that the dogs in the original research that did not become helpless even when exposed to inescapable shock probably had histories of controllable trauma prior to coming to the laboratory. This hypothesis was tested, and it was found that dogs with little experience in controlling anything were particularly susceptible to helplessness. Finally, in terms of therapy, the depressed person who suffers from expectations of uncontrollability needs to be directed toward experiences that will result in recovery of the belief that responding produces reinforcement. In therapy this involves games and tasks of increasing difficulty, starting with those that ensure success (Beck, 1991).

The learned helplessness model and associated research are indeed impressive. The negative effects of experience with uncontrollable events have been produced in cats, fish, and rats, as well as in dogs and humans.

Learned Helplessness: *Childhood experiences associated with the feeling of control and competence can help to prevent the development of earned helplessness.*

However, further research with humans has suggested that factors in addition to experience with uncontrollability appear to be important in determining the consequent effects. At least with humans the effects of experience with uncontrollable events appear to depend on how the person interprets what has occurred. Observation of varying effects, depending on modifications in the experimental design or on individual differences in people, has led to a reformulated model of learned helplessness. Although we have not yet covered all the experimental research on learned helplessness, much of the research following from the reformulated model has used correlational rather than experimental procedures. We shall review some of this research in the next section. At this point, however, we may take stock of some of the defining characteristics of experimental research as seen in the efforts of Seligman. In this research program we have seen the careful manipulation and control of the relevant variables and, by and large, a focus on systematic influences that are independent of individual differences.

PERSONALITY QUESTIONNAIRES AND CORRELATIONAL RESEARCH

Personality tests and questionnaires are used where the intensive study of individuals is not possible or desirable, and where it is not possible to conduct laboratory experiments. Beyond this, the advantage of personality questionnaires is that a great deal of information can be gathered on many subjects at one time. Although no one individual is studied as intensively as with the case study approach, the investigator can study many different personality characteristics in relation to many different subjects. Although the investigator cannot demonstrate control over the variables of interest, as in the experimental method, there is the opportunity to study variables that are not easily produced in the laboratory.

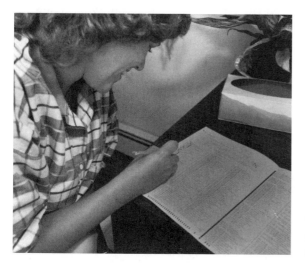

Tactics of Research: *Personality questionnaires are used to obtain a great deal of information about many subjects.*

The use of personality tests and questionnaires has tended to be associated with an interest in differences among individuals. For example, personality psychologists have an interest in individual differences in anxiety, friendliness, or dominance. In addition, there has been a tendency by those psychologists to study whether individuals who differ in one personality characteristic also differ in another characteristic. For example, are individuals who are more anxious also less creative? More inhibited in their interpersonal behavior? Research of this kind is known as **correlational research**. In correlational research the investigator seeks to establish a relationship between two or more variables that do not lend themselves readily to experimental manipulation and control. An association or correlation is established, rather than a cause–effect relationship. For example, we might be able to say that anxiety is associated with an increase in rigidity rather than that anxiety caused an increase in rigidity. Because of the emphasis on individual differences and the study of many variables at one time, questionnaires and correlational research have been very popular among personality psychologists.

Internal–External Locus of Control

An interesting comparison of the experimental and correlational perspectives may be made by returning briefly to the experimental research on learned helplessness in humans (Figure 2.1). Remember that it was demonstrated that human subjects who were first in the no-escape treatment condition took longer to respond to a signal light and more often failed to escape in the test situation than did subjects who were first in the escape condition. The interpretation was that in the no-escape condition the subjects learned that outcomes were not affected by their behavior. Would subjects who already differed in their beliefs concerning their ability to influence outcomes also differ in their performance in the second situation? In other words, could one find in people differences that occurred naturally and also reproduced the effects of the experimental manipulations? We can now consider another feature of Hiroto's research on learned helplessness in humans. Hiroto considered the effects of not only no-escape and escape treatment conditions on later performance, but also differences in the personality characteristic known as **locus of control**.

The concept of locus of control is part of Rotter's (1966, 1982) social learning theory of personality and represents a generalized expectancy concerning the determinants of rewards and punishments in one's life. At one extreme are people who believe in their ability to control life's events, that is, internal locus of control. At the other extreme are people who believe that life's events, such as rewards and punishments, are the result of external factors such as chance, luck, or fate; that is, external locus of control. The **Internal–External (I–E) Scale** has been developed to measure individual differences in perception of the extent to which rewards and punishments are generally under internal or external control. Representative items are presented in Figure 2.2.

1a. Many of the unhappy things in people's lives are due partly to bad luck.
1b. People's misfortunes result from the mistakes they make.
2a. One of the major reasons we have wars is that people don't take enough interest in politics.
2b. There will always be wars, no matter how hard people try to prevent them.
3a. Sometimes I can't understand how teachers arrive at the grades they give.
3b. There is a direct connection between how hard I study and the grades I get.
4a. The average citizen can have an influence in government decisions.
4b. This world is run by the few people in power and there isn't much the little guy can do about it.

Figure 2.2 *Illustrative items from Rotter's Internal–External Locus of Control Scale.*

Since the beliefs of external locus of control people closely resembled the beliefs that are part of learned helplessness, Hiroto suspected that people differing in the personality characteristic of locus of control would perform differently in the test situation. Dividing subjects up into extreme groups of internal and external locus of control on the basis of responses to the I–E Scale, Hiroto exposed members of each group to the no-escape and escape conditions and then looked at their performance in the second or test situation. As expected, he found that external locus of control subjects, regardless of their pretreatment, were slower to escape or to avoid than were the internal locus of control subjects (Figure 2.3).

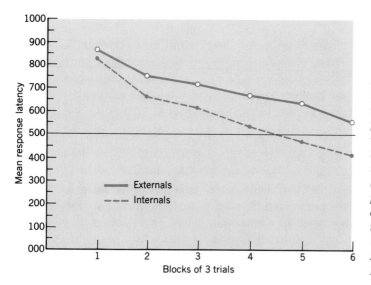

Figure 2.3 Locus of Control and Performance. *The personality variable of externality appears to function like the pretreatment variable of inescapability. In view of the parallel effects created by inescapability and externality, it is likely that the same underlying process exists in each—that is, the expectancy that responding and reinforcement are independent. (Hiroto, 1974. Copyright 1974 by the American Psychological Association. Reprinted by permission.)*

In other words, the personality variable of externality appeared to function like the pretreatment variable of inescapability. An association was found between an already existent personality difference and performance in a test situation.

Causal Attributions: Explanatory Style

To illustrate further the correlational approach to personality research, as well as the combined use of questionnaires with experimental procedures, let us continue with the story of research on learned helplessness. Earlier we noted that the original formulation of learned helplessness could not account for the varied consequences of uncontrollability often found in human subjects. How people interpret the events and the basis for their helplessness seemed to be important. This led to a reformulated model of learned helplessness (Abramson, Seligman, & Teasdale, 1978; Abramson, Garber, & Seligman, 1980). According to this reformulation, when people find themselves helpless, they ask why they are helpless. People answer the question *why* in terms of *causal attributions*. Three dimensions of **causal attribution** are suggested as important. First, people may attribute the cause of their helplessness to themselves or to the nature of the situation. In the former case, the cause of helplessness is seen as being internal or personal. In the latter case, it is seen as being external or universal. Second, people may attribute helplessness to factors specific to the situation they are in, or to more general conditions in the world around them or in themselves. Third, people may perceive the conditions of their situation to be stable and relatively permanent, or unstable and perhaps temporary.

In sum, three dimensions of causal attribution are suggested in the reformulated model of learned helplessness: *internal–external, specific–global, and stable–unstable*. The attribution made by a person is seen as determining a broad range of important consequences. For example, the attribution of lack of control to internal factors is seen as leading to a greater loss of self-esteem than an attribution to external factors. A student who perceives continuous failure to be due to his or her own lack of intelligence or incompetence will experience a much greater loss of self-esteem than the student who perceives continuous failure to be due to poor teaching. If a person attributes lack of control to global factors, there will be greater generalization of the learned helplessness response to other situations than if a more situation-specific attribution is made. And if the person attributes lack of control to stable factors, such as lack of ability or difficulty of the curriculum, there will be greater permanence of the effects over time than if helplessness is attributed to unstable factors such as how the person felt that day or how lucky or unlucky one was. Which attribution is made in response to helplessness, then, will influence whether expectations of future helplessness are chronic or acute, broad or narrow, and whether or not self-esteem is lowered. Particularly important is the suggestion that internal, global, and stable attributions have important implications for the development of depression.

Attributional Style Questionnaire (ASQ)   An experimental approach to the reformulated model of learned helplessness involves the manipulation of causal attributions and observation of the resultant motivational and emotional effects. Thus, for example, subjects could be exposed to conditions that would lead them to make internal or external attributions for failure, and differences in consequent effects on self-esteem would be predicted. Although there is some support for the attributional reformulation from experimental research, most such studies have had methodological problems in producing the desired attributions or helplessness effects. To facilitate research in this area, the **Attributional Style Questionnaire (ASQ)** was developed to measure individual differences in the use of the three specified attributional dimensions (Peterson, 1991). In this questionnaire subjects are asked to give a cause for each of 12 hypothetical events and then to rate the cause on scales relevant to the internal–external, stable–unstable, and specific–global dimensions. An illustrative question appears in Figure 2.4. Six of the hypothetical events are good (e.g., "You become very rich") and six are bad (e.g., "You go out on a date and it goes badly"). In addition, some events are interpersonal,

---

You have been looking unsuccessfully for a job for some time.

1. Write down the *one* major cause. _____

2. Is the cause of your unsuccessful job search due to something about you, or to something about other people or circumstances? (circle one number)

   Totally due to other
   people or circumstances   1 2 3 4 5 6 7   Totally due to me

3. In the future, when looking for a job, will this cause again be present? (circle one number)

   Will never
   again be present   1 2 3 4 5 6 7   Will always be present

4. Is the cause something that influences just looking for a job, or does it also influence other areas of your life? (circle one number)

   Influences just this   Influences all
   particular situtation   1 2 3 4 5 6 7   situations in my life

5. How important would this situation be if it happened to you? (circle one number)

   Not at all important   1 2 3 4 5 6 7   Extremely important

Figure 2.4   *Illustrative Item—The Attributional Style Questionnaire (ASQ).* *(Peterson et al., 1982, p. 292.)*

whereas others have to do with achievement. The assumptions are that people have characteristic attributional tendencies or styles and that these can be measured with a questionnaire.

According to the reformulated learned helplessness model, attributing uncontrollable bad events to internal, stable, and global factors leads to depression. This would suggest that people scoring high on these dimensions on the ASQ should show more depression than people scoring low. Indeed, the authors of the ASQ report an association or correlation between a style in which internal, stable, and global attributions are made for bad events and depressive symptoms in college students, adults, and patients. Scores on the ASQ have been found to be associated with the development of depressive symptoms following poor performance by college students on a midterm examination. Finally, in a study using a similar questionnaire, it was found that depression was associated with blame directed at one's character, but not at one's behavior (Peterson, Schwartz, & Seligman, 1981). Bad events attributed to character ("I'm that kind of person") were viewed as less controllable than events attributed to behavior ("I did something"). In addition, characterological blame was associated with more stable and global attributions than was behavior blame. However, self-blame or characterological blame could not be determined to be a cause of depression. That is, characterological self-blame was found to be associated with, but not a cause of, later depressive symptoms.

The final point made in relation to the above study is important both for the reformulated learned helplessness model of depression and for an appreciation of the limits of correlational research. This research suggests an association between internal, global, and stable attributions for bad events and depression, but the research does not demonstrate that such cognitive attributions cause depression. Could they be a part of depression and caused by the same factors that lead to the depression? Indeed, a major study of people before and after they became depressed found that depression-related cognitions did not predict future depression and appeared to be more of a concomitant of depression than a cause of it. Prior to becoming depressed, the future depressives did not attribute failure to internal causes or perceive themselves as having little control over events in their lives (Lewinsohn, Steinmetz, Larson, & Franklin, 1981).

Explanatory Style   It has been about 10 years since the development of the concept of attributional style, now called *explanatory style*, and the means for measuring it. An impressive body of research, primarily correlational, has been established. A recent review of the literature concerning the meaning and measurement of explanatory style suggests the following (Peterson, 1991; Peterson, Maier, & Seligman, 1993):

1. There is considerable evidence of the widespread impact of learned helplessness in both humans and animals.

2. There is considerable evidence that people have characteristic explanatory styles that are stable over extended periods of time, perhaps over the life span of an individual.

3. Explanatory style has implications for motivation, emotion, and behavior. Most specifically, a pessimistic explanatory style (internal, stable, global explanations for negative events) is associated with less motivation, poorer performance, and more negative emotion than an optimistic explanatory style. In the words of the famous baseball player Yogi Berra: "Ninety percent of the game is fifty percent mental."

4. The symptoms of learned helplessness match those of depression. Depressed individuals, both adults and children, make internal, stable, and global explanations for bad events as well as external, unstable, and specific explanations for good events. Although a pessimistic explanatory style has been found to be *associated* with depression, it has not been demonstrated to be the *cause* of depression (Robins & Hayes, 1995)

5. Cognitive therapy can improve explanatory style and lead to significant relief from depression (DeRubeis & Hollon, 1995).

6. Learned helplessness and pessimistic explanatory style are associated with poor health. A pessimistic explanatory style in early adulthood is a risk factor for poor health in middle and late adulthood.

This impressive body of findings leads Seligman and his coworkers to a very optimistic picture of what can be accomplished in the future: "We know how to remake society in a way that will benefit the individual and the group...At our most utopian, we envision the creation of Optimism Institutes, centers in which basic research on personal control is conducted and then applied to schools, work settings, and society itself" (Peterson, Maier, & Seligman, 1993, pp. 309–310).

Although we have this impressive body of research, we should recognize that not all the findings have been supportive and a number of important problems have been raised. Among them are the following, many of them suggestive of some of the potential limitations of correlational research and the use of questionnaires (*Psychological Inquiry*, 1991, vol. 2, no. 1):

1. Responses to the ASQ may not match actual causal attributions.

2. People may have explanations for specific events rather than more generalized explanatory styles.

3. The specific importance of the components of explanatory style (internal–external, stable–unstable, global–specific) remains to be determined, as does the importance of attributions for positive events.

EXPLANATORY STYLE, JOB SUCCESS, AND HEALTH

Seligman's research on explanatory style has expanded beyond depression to the realms of job performance, athletic success, and health, leading to headlines in the mass media of "Research Affirms Power of Positive Thinking" and "Stop Blaming Yourself."

Do life insurance sales agents with an optimistic explanatory style remain on the job longer and sell more life insurance than those with a pessimistic style? Since sales agents repeatedly encounter failure, rejection, and indifference from prospective clients, Seligman reasoned that "optimists" would weather the challenge better than "pessimists." (Optimists have internal, stable, and global explanations for positive events and external, unstable, and specific explanations for negative events. The opposite holds true for pessimists.) Evidently, the answer to the above ques-

tion is a clear *yes*. According to Seligman, "I think we've got a test for who can face a stressful, challenging job and who can't. My guess is that this test could save the insurance company millions of dollars a year in training alone since it costs about $30,000 each to train new people and half of them quit."

In terms of athletic success, teams and athletes with optimistic explanatory styles have been found to perform better than their competitors with pessimistic explanatory styles, especially under pressure. And, in terms of health, there is evidence that thinking "good" is associated with feeling "well," perhaps because the good immunological system of optimists provides greater resistance to disease than the disease-fighting system of pesssimists.

SOURCE: Peterson, 1995; Rettew & Reivich, 1995; Schulman, 1995; Seligman, 1991.

Optimisim and Job Success:
An optimistic explanatory style is associated with success in sales.

4. It remains unclear whether explanatory style precedes and causes depression as opposed to being a contributing factor, an accompanying ingredient of depression, or even a result of depression.

5. Pessimism scores derived from the ASQ (internal, stable, and global explanatory styles for negative events) do not show high agreement with pessimism scores derived from other personality questionnaires.

Particularly noteworthy are three potential problems with this approach to research: (1) A questionnaire may be used to derive a single, composite score, whereas there may be a number of different components to the questionnaire, each deserving of a separate score. (2) Scores derived from one measure of a personality variable may not agree with scores derived from another measure of what is assumed to be the same personality variable. (3) It is difficult to establish causal relations.

Having considered the goals of all personality research, we are in a position to evaluate the three major research strategies. We shall see that as a consequence of proceeding along different lines, each strategy may be characterized as having both strengths and limitations.

EVALUATING ALTERNATIVE RESEARCH APPROACHES

CASE STUDIES AND CLINICAL RESEARCH: STRENGTHS AND LIMITATIONS

Clinical research has strengths and limitations, depending on what is being investigated and how the research is conducted. Generally in clinical research, one examines the behavior of interest directly and does not have to extrapolate from a somewhat artificial setting to the real world. Clinical research may also be the only feasible means for the study of some phenomena (e.g., wartime stress). And, through the use of case studies, one can observe the full complexity of personality processes and individual–environment relationships. We have already suggested that part of what is distinctive about the field of personality is its emphasis on the organization of structures and processes within the person. In-depth clinical research and case studies provide an opportunity for the study of such organization. At the same time, such research may involve subjective impressions on the part of researchers, resulting in different observations by each investigator. Insofar as researchers make observations on a subjective basis, they accumulate data that decline considerably in reliability and validity.

In-depth study of a few individuals has two main features that stand in contrast with research on groups (Pervin, 1983). First, relationships established for a group as a whole may not reflect the way any individual behaves or the way some subgroups of individuals behave. The average learning curve, for example, may not reflect the way any one individual learns. Second, by considering only group data, one may miss some valuable insights into processes going on in particular individuals. Some time ago, Henry Murray argued for the utility of individual as well as group studies as follows: "In lay words, the subjects who gave the majority response may have done so for different reasons. Furthermore, a statistical answer leaves unexplained the uncommon (exhibited-by-the-minority) response. One can only ignore it as an unhappy exception to the rule. Averages obliterate the `individual characters of individual organisms' and so fail to reveal the complex interaction of forces which determine each concrete event" (1938, p. viii).

The Use of Verbal Reports

Clinical research in personality need not involve the use of verbal reports by subjects, though clearly it often does. In making use of verbal reports, we are confronted with special problems associated with such data. Treating what people say as accurate reflections of what has actually occurred or is actually going on has come under attack from two very different groups. First, psychoanalysts and dynamically oriented psychologists (Chapters 3 and 4) argue that people often distort things for unconscious reasons: "Children perceive inaccurately, are very little conscious of their inner states and retain fallacious recollections of occurrences. Many adults are hardly better" (Murray, 1938, p. 15). Second, many experimental psychologists argue that people do not have access to their internal processes and respond to interviewer questions in terms of some inferences they make about what must have been going on rather than accurately reporting what actually occurred (Nisbett & Wilson, 1977; Wilson, Hull, & Johnson, 1981). For example, despite experimenter evidence that subjects make decisions in accord with certain experimental manipulations, the subjects themselves may report having behaved in a particular way for very different reasons. Or, to take another example, when consumers are asked about why they purchased a product in a supermarket they may give a reason that is very different from what can experimentally be demonstrated to have been the case. In a sense, people give subjective *reasons* for behaving as they do, but may not give the actual *causes*. In sum, the argument is that whether for defensive reasons or because of "normal" problems people have in keeping track of their internal processes, verbal self-reports are questionable sources of reliable and valid data (Wilson, 1994).

Other psychologists argue that verbal reports should be accepted for what they are—data (Ericsson & Simon, 1993). The argument is made that there is no intrinsic reason to treat verbal reports as any less useful data than an overt motor response such as pressing a lever. Indeed, it is possible to analyze the verbal responses of people in as objective, systematic, and quantitative fashion as their other behavioral responses. If verbal responses are not automatically discounted, then the question becomes: Which kinds of verbal responses are most useful and trustworthy?

Here the argument is made that subjects can only report about things they are attending to or have attended to. If the experimenter asks the subject to remember or explain things that were never attended to in the first place, the subject will either make an inference or state a hypothesis about what occurred (White, 1980). Thus, if you later ask persons why they purchased one product over another in the supermarket when they were not attending to this decision at the time, they will give you an inference or a hypothesis rather than an account of what occurred.

Those who argue in favor of the use of verbal reports suggest that when they are elicited with care and the circumstances involved are appreciated, they can be a useful source of information. Although the term *introspection* (i.e., verbal descriptions of process going on inside a person) was discredited long ago by experimental psychologists, there is now increased interest in the potential utility of such data. In accepting the potential utility of verbal reports, we may expand the universe of potential data for rich and meaningful observation. At the same time, we must keep in mind the goals and requirements of reliability and validity. Thus, we must insist on evidence that the same observations and interpretations can be made by other investigators and that the data do reflect the concepts they are presumed to measure. In appreciating the merits and vast potential of verbal reports, we must also be aware of the potential for misutilization and naive interpretation. In sum, verbal reports as data should receive the same scrutiny as other research observations.

LABORATORY, EXPERIMENTAL RESEARCH: STRENGTHS AND LIMITATIONS

In many ways, experimental laboratory research represents the scientific ideal. Ask people for their description of a scientist, and they are likely to conjure up the image of a person in a white smock in a laboratory, clipboard in hand, noting meter readings of machines or making minor adjustments to a piece of apparatus. The strength of the experimental approach to research is the potential for careful manipulation of the variables of interest, the gathering of objective data free from biased or subjective interpretation, and the establishment of cause–effect relationships. In the experiment that is properly designed and carried out, every step is carefully planned to limit effects to the variables of interest. Few variables are studied, so that the problem of disentangling complex relationships does not exist. Systematic relationships between changes in some variables and consequences for other variables are established so that the experimenter can say: "If X, then Y." Full details of the experimental procedure are reported so that the results can be replicated by investigators in other laboratories.

Psychologists who are critical of laboratory research suggest that too often such research is artificial and limited in relevance to other contexts. The suggestion is that what works in the laboratory may not work elsewhere. Furthermore, although relationships between isolated variables may be established, such relationships may not hold when the complexity of actual human behavior is considered. Also, since laboratory research tends to involve relatively brief exposures to stimuli, such research may miss important processes that occur over time. These criticisms are in addition, of course, to the potential limitation due to the fact that not all phenomena can be produced in the laboratory.

As a human enterprise, experimental research with humans lends itself to influences that are part of everyday interpersonal behavior. The investigation of such influences might be called the *social psychology of research*. Let us consider two important illustrations. First, there may be factors influencing the behavior of human subjects that are not part of the experimental design. Among such factors may be cues implicit in the experimental setting that suggest to the subject that the experimenter has a certain hypothesis and, "in the interest of science," the subject behaves in a way that will confirm it. Such effects are known as **demand characteristics** and suggest that the psychological experiment is a form of social interaction in which subjects give purpose and meaning to things (Orne, 1962; Weber & Cook, 1972). The purpose and meaning given to the research may vary from subject to subject in ways that are not part of the experimental design and thereby serve to reduce both reliability and validity.

Complementing these sources of error or bias in the subject are unintended sources of influence or error in the experimenter. Without realizing it, experimenters may either make errors in recording and analyzing data or emit cues to the subjects and thus influence their behavior in a particular way. Such unintended **experimenter expectancy effects** may lead subjects to behave in accordance with the hypothesis (Rosenthal, 1994; Rosenthal & Rubin, 1978). For example, consider the classic case of Clever Hans (Pfungst, 1911). Hans was a horse that by tapping his foot could add, subtract, multiply, and divide. A mathematical problem would be presented to the horse and, incredibly, he was able to come up with the answer. In attempting to discover the secret of Hans' talents, a variety of situational factors were manipulated. If Hans could not see the questioner or if the questioner did not know the answer, Hans was unable to provide the correct answer. On the other hand, if the questioner knew the answer and was visible, Hans could tap out the answer with his foot. Apparently the questioner unknowingly signaled Hans when to start and stop tapping his hoof: The tapping would start when the questioner inclined his head forward, increase in speed when the questioner bent forward more, and stop when the questioner straightened up. As can be seen, experimenter expectancy effects can be quite subtle and neither the researcher nor subject may be aware of their existence.

It should be noted that demand characteristics and expectancy effects can occur as sources of error in all three forms of research. However, they have been considered and studied most often in relation to experimental research. In addition, as noted, experimental research often is seen as most closely approximating the scientific ideal. Therefore, such sources of error are all the more noteworthy in relation to this form of research.

Many of the criticisms of experimental research have been attacked by experimental psychologists. In defending laboratory experiments, the following statements are made: (1) Such research is the proper basis for testing causal hypotheses. The generality of the established relationship is then a subject for further investigation. (2) Some phenomena would never be discovered outside of the laboratory. (3) Some phenomena can be studied in the laboratory that would be difficult to study elsewhere (e.g., subjects are given permission to be aggressive in contrast with the often quite strong restraints in natural social settings). (4) There is little empirical support for the contention that subjects typically try to confirm the experimenter's hypothesis or for the significance of experimental artifacts more generally. Indeed, many subjects are more negativistic than conforming (Berkowitz & Donnerstein, 1982).

CORRELATIONAL RESEARCH AND QUESTIONNAIRES: STRENGTHS AND LIMITATIONS

As previously noted, many of the strengths and limitations of the correlational approach are the opposite of those of experimental research. On the one hand, there may be the opportunity to study a broader range of variables; on the other, there is less control over the variables. Consider the use of personality questionnaires in correlational research. First, many psychologists would question whether we can accept the subjects' responses to questionnaires as accurate statements of what the subjects feel and do. Second, responses to self-report questionnaires are susceptible to particular biases. Research suggests that subjects often respond to qualities in the questionnaire items other than content, or that they have a consistent tendency to respond in one or another way to a test—a **response style**.

Two illustrative response style problems can be considered. The first has been called **acquiescence** and involves the tendency to agree or disagree with items regardless of their content. For example, subjects may have a preference for responses such as "Like" and "Agree" (yea-sayers) or for responses such as "Dislike" and "Disagree" (nay-sayers). The second illustrative potential for bias in response to questionnaires involves the **social desirability** of the items. Instead of responding to the intended psychological meaning of a test item, a subject may respond to it as suggesting a socially acceptable or a socially desirable personality characteristic.

Another criticism of questionnaire research has to do with its reliance on self-report data and thereby the potential for the problems earlier noted in relation to verbal reports. A recent research report highlights the particular issue of distortion of responses for unconscious reasons, and emphasizes the potential value of clinical judgment as well (Shedler,

Mayman, & Manis, 1993). In this research, conducted by psychologists with a psychoanalytic orientation who were skeptical of accepting self-report data at face value, individuals who "looked good" on mental health questionnaire scales were evaluated by a psychodynamically oriented clinician. On the basis of his clinical judgments, two subgroups were distinguished: One defined as being genuinely psychologically healthy in agreement with the questionnaire scales and a second defined as consisting of individuals who were psychologically distressed but who maintained an *illusion* of mental health through defensive denial of their difficulties. Individuals in the two groups were found to differ significantly in their responses to stress. Subjects in the illusory mental health group were found to show much higher levels of coronary reactivity to stress than subjects in the genuinely healthy group. Indeed, the former subjects were found to show even greater levels of coronary reactivity to stress than subjects who reported their distress on the mental health questionnaire scales. The differences in reactivity to stress between the genuinely healthy subjects and the "illusory" healthy subjects were considered not only to be statistically significant but medically significant as well. Thus, it was concluded that "for some people, mental health scales appear to be legitimate measures of mental health. For other people, these scales appear to measure defensive denial. There seems to be no way to know from the test score alone what is being measured in any given respondent" (Shedler, Mayman, & Manis, 1993, p.1128).

Those who defend the use of questionnaires suggest that such problems and sources of bias can be eliminated through careful test construction and interpretation. For example, testgivers suggest that questionnaire responses need not be considered as true or accurate reflections of the subject's feelings and behaviors, but only that the resulting scores relate to phenomena of interest. Also, they suggest that by careful item writing, one can remove the potential effects of biases such as acquiescence and social desirability. Finally, they suggest that test items or scales can be included to measure whether subjects are faking or trying to present themselves in a particularly favorable or socially desirable way.

Although such safeguards may be possible, few of them appear in many personality questionnaires. Furthermore, even when a personality test has reasonable evidence of reliability and validity, its results may disagree with those from another test presumed to measure the same concept. In sum, although personality questionnaires are attractive because they are easy to use and can get at many aspects of personality that would otherwise be difficult to study, the problems in establishing their reliability and validity are often substantial.

SUMMARY OF STRENGTHS AND LIMITATIONS

In assessing these alternative approaches to research we must recognize that we are considering potential, rather than necessary, strengths and

Table 2.1   Summary of Potential Strengths and Limitations of Alternative Research Methods

Potential Strengths	*Potential Limitations*
CASE STUDIES AND CLINICAL RESEARCH	
1. Avoid the artificiality of laboratory.	1. Lead to unsystematic observation.
2. Study the full complexity of person–environment relationships.	2. Encourage subjective interpretation of data
3. Lead to in-depth study of individuals.	3. Entangled relationships among variables.
LABORATORY STUDIES AND EXPERIMENTAL RESEARCH	
1. Manipulates specific variables.	1. Excludes phenomena that cannot be studied in the laboratory.
2. Records data objectively.	2. Creates an artificial setting that limits the generality of findings.
3. Establishes cause–effect relationships.	3. Fosters demand characteristics and experimenter expectancy effects
QUESTIONNAIRES AND CORRELATION RESEARCH	
1. Study a wide range of variables.	1. Establish relationships that are associational rather than causal.
2. Study relationships among many variables.	2. Problems of reliability and validity of self-report questionnaires.

limitations (Table 2.1). What it comes down to is that each research effort must be evaluated on its own merits and for its own potential in advancing understanding rather than on some preconceived basis. Alternative research procedures can be used in conjunction with one another in any research enterprise. In addition, data from alternative research procedures can be integrated in the pursuit of a more comprehensive theory.

In the first chapter we considered the nature of personality theory, the effort to systematize what is known and point research in directions toward discovery of what is as yet unknown. In this chapter we began with consideration of the kinds of data obtained by personality psychologists in their research. We then turned to consideration of three traditions of personality research—clinical research, experimental research, and correlational research. Although following divergent paths, the three traditions share the goals of reliability and validity, that is, the goals of obtaining replicable findings that expand knowledge and can be set within a theoretical context. Until now we have considered theory and research separately. However, what is being emphasized here is that theory and research have important implications for one another. Theory suggests avenues for exploration and research provides means for testing

PERSONALITY THEORY AND PERSONALITY RESEARCH

hypotheses derived from theories. Theory that is not tied to research consists of mere speculation and research unrelated to theory consists of mere fact-gathering. Theory and research are interdependent, deriving much of their significance from one another.

Having emphasized the interdependent nature of theory and research, we also want to suggest that they tend to be related in another way. Earlier in the chapter it was suggested that personality researchers have preferences for one or another kind of data. In addition, researchers have preferences and biases concerning how research should be conducted. The father of American behaviorism, John B. Watson, emphasized the use of animals in research in part because of his discomfort in working with humans. On the other hand, undoubtedly the opposite is true for other researchers. Historically, personality researchers have tended to fall on one or the other side of three issues associated with the three approaches to research: (1) "making things happen" in research (experimental) versus "studying what has occurred" (correlational); (2) all persons (experimental) versus the single individual (clinical); and (3) one aspect or few aspects of the person versus the total individual. In other words, there are preferences or biases toward clinical, experimental, and correlational research. Despite the objectivity of science, research is a human enterprise and such preferences are part of research as a human enterprise. All researchers attempt to be as objective as possible in the conduct of their research and generally they give "objective" reasons for following a particular approach to research. That is, the particular strengths of the research approach followed are emphasized relative to the strengths and limitations of alternative approaches. Beyond this, however, a personal element enters in. Just as psychologists feel more comfortable with one or another kind of data, they feel more comfortable with one or another approach to research.

Further, it can be suggested that different theories of personality are linked with different research strategies and thereby with different kinds of data. In other words, the links among theory, data, and research are such that the observations associated with one theory of personality often are different from those associated with another theory. And, the phenomena of interest to one theory of personality are not as easily studied by the research procedures useful in the study of phenomena emphasized by another theory of personality. One personality theory leads us to obtain one kind of data and follow one approach to research whereas another theory leads us to collect different kinds of data and follow another approach to research. It is not that one or another is better but rather that they are different, and these differences must be appreciated in considering each approach to theory and research. Since the remaining chapters in this text are organized around the major theoretical approaches to personality, it is important to keep such linkages and differences in mind in comparing one theory with another.

As we have seen, personality research involves the effort to measure individuals on a personality characteristic assumed to be of theoretical importance. The term *assessment* generally is used to refer to efforts to measure personality aspects of individuals in order to make an applied or practical decision: Will this person be a good candidate for this job? Will this person profit from one or another kind of treatment? Is this person a good candidate for this training program? In addition, the term assessment often is used to refer to the effort to arrive at a comprehensive understanding of individuals by obtaining a wide variety of information about them. In this sense, assessment of a person involves administering a variety of personality tests or measures in the pursuit of a comprehensive understanding of their personality. As noted, such an effort also provides for a comparison of results from different sources of information. This book assumes that each technique of assessment gives a glimpse of human behavior, and that no one test gives, or can hope to give, a picture of the total personality of an individual. People are complex, and our efforts to assess personality must reflect this complexity. In the chapters that follow, we will consider a number of theories of personality and approaches to personality assessment. In addition, we will consider the assessment of an individual, Jim, from the standpoint of each theory and approach to assessment. Through this approach we will be able to see the relation between theory and assessment, and also to consider the extent to which different approaches result in similar pictures of the person.

Before we describe Jim, some details concerning the assessment project will be presented. Jim was a college student when, in the late 1960s, he volunteered to serve as a subject for a project involving the intensive study of college students. He participated in the project mainly because of his interest in psychology, but also because he hoped to gain a better understanding of himself. At the time, a variety of tests were administered to him. These tests represented a sampling of the tests then available. Obviously, theories of personality and associated tests that had not been developed at the time could not be administered. However, Jim agreed to report on his life experiences and to take some additional tests 5, 20, and 25 years later. At those times, an effort was made to administer tests developed in association with emerging theories of personality.

Thus, we do not have the opportunity to consider all the tests at the same point in time. However, we are able to consider the personality of an individual over an extended period of time, and

PERSONALITY ASSESSMENT AND THE CASE OF JIM

thereby examine how the theories—and the tests—relate to what occurred earlier in life and what followed later. Let us begin with a brief sketch derived from Jim's autobiography and follow him throughout the text as we consider the various approaches to personality.

Autobiographical Sketch

In his autobiography Jim reported that he was born in New York City after the end of World War II and received considerable attention and affection as a child. His father is a college graduate who owns an automobile sales business; his mother is a housewife who also does volunteer reading for the blind. Jim described himself as having a good relationship with his father and described his mother as having "great feelings for other people— she is a totally 'loving' woman." He is the oldest of four children, with a sister four years younger and two brothers, one five years younger and one seven years younger. The main themes in his autobiography concern his inability to become involved with women in a satisfying way, his need for success and his relative failure since high school, and his uncertainty about whether to go on to graduate school in business administration or in clinical psychology. Overall he felt that people had a high estimate of him because they used superficial criteria, but that inwardly he was troubled.

We have here the bare outline of a person. Hopefully, the details will be filled in as he is considered from the standpoint of different personality theories. Hopefully, by the end of the book, a complete picture of Jim will emerge.

MAJOR CONCEPTS

L-data. Life record data or information concerning the person that can be obtained from their life history or life record.

O-data. Observer data or information provided by knowledgeable observers such as parents, friends, or teachers.

T-data. Test data or information obtained from experimental procedures or standardized tests.

S-data. Self-report data or information provided by the subject.

Reliability. The extent to which observations are stable, dependable, and can be replicated.

Validity. The extent to which our observations reflect the phenomena or variables of interest to us.

Clinical research. An approach to research involving the intensive study of individuals in terms of observation of naturally occurring behavior or verbal reports of what occurred in the natural setting.

Experimental research. An approach to research in which the experimenter manipulates the variable and is interested in general laws, in contrast with the correlational approach to research. Interest is in establishing cause–effect relationships among a few variables.

Learned helplessness. Seligman's concept for inappropriate passivity and diminished effort resulting from repeated experiences with uncontrollable events.

Correlational research. An approach to research in which existing individual differences are measured and related to one another, in contrast with the experimental approach to research.

Locus of control. Rotter's concept expressing a generalized expectancy or belief concerning the determinants of rewards and punishments.

Internal–External (I–E) Scale. The personality scale developed by Rotter to measure the extent to which the person has developed a belief that he or she can control life's events (i.e., internal locus of control) as opposed to the belief that life's events are the result of external factors such as chance, luck, or fate (i.e., external locus of control).

Causal attribution. In the revised theory of learned helplessness and depression, attributions made on three dimensions: internal (personal)–external (universal), specific–global, and stable–unstable.

Attributional Style Questionnaire (ASQ). A questionnaire designed to measure attributions concerning learned helplessness along three dimensions: internal (personal)—external (universal), specific–global, and stable–unstable.

Demand characteristics. Cues that are implicit (hidden) in the experimental setting and influence the subject's behavior.

Experimenter expectancy effects. Unintended experimenter effects involving behaviors that lead subjects to respond in accordance with the experimenter's hypothesis.

Response style. The tendency of some subjects to respond to test items in a consistent, patterned way that has to do with the form of the questions and/or answers rather than with their content.

REVIEW

1. Research involves the systematic study of relationships among phenomena or events. Four types of data are obtained in personality research: L-data, O-data, T-data, and S-data (LOTS). Three approaches to personality research are clinical research, laboratory experimentation, and correlational research using questionnaires.

2. All research shares the goals of reliability and validity—of obtaining observations that can be replicated and for which there is evidence of a relation to the concepts of interest. As a human enterprise, research involves ethical questions concerning the treatment of subjects and the reporting of data.

3. Clinical research involves the intensive study of individuals and is illustrated by the study of reactions to battle stress.

4. Experimental research involves the manipulation of specific variables and the ability to state if–then, causal relationships. This approach to research is illustrated by the study of the effects of learned helplessness.

5. In correlational research the investigator gives up control over the variables of interest and tries to associate or correlate already existing phenomena with one another. Questionnaires are particularly important in correlational research, as illustrated by research with the I–E Scale and the ASQ.

6. According to the reformulated model of learned helplessness, people make causal attributions for events along dimensions such as internal–external, global–specific, and stable–unstable. Specific attributional or explanatory styles are suggested to be associated with specific consequences (e.g., internal, global, stable attributions or explanations for negative events associated with depression).

7. The three approaches to research result in similar observations concerning the relation between lack of control or helplessness and stress. The expectation that outcomes are independent of responses (external locus of control, learned helplessness) has significant motivational, cognitive, and emotional implications.

8. Each of the three approaches to research can be viewed as having its own set of potential strengths and limitations (Table 2.1). Thus, each research strategy has the potential to produce particular insights and pitfalls.

9. Theories of personality differ in their preferences for types of data and approaches to research. In other words, there tend to be linkages among theory, type of data, and method of research. It is important to keep such linkages in mind as the major theories of personality are considered in the chapters that follow. A single case studied from the standpoint of each theoretical perspective also will be presented for illustrative and comparative purposes.

3

A PSYCHODYNAMIC THEORY: FREUD'S PSYCHOANALYTIC THEORY OF PERSONALITY

Chapter Focus

The number one player on the tennis team is getting ready to play for the state title. She has never met her opponent before, so she decides to introduce herself before the match. She strolls out onto the court where her opponent is warming up and says, "Hi, I'm Amy. Glad to *beat* you." You can imagine how embarrassed Amy was! Flustered, she corrected her innocent mistake and walked over to her side of the court to warm up. "Wow," Amy thought, "where did *that* come from?"

Was Amy's verbal slip so innocent? Freud wouldn't have thought so. In his view, Amy's silly mistake was actually a very revealing display of *unconscious* aggressive drives. Freud's *psychoanalytic* theory is illustrative of a *psychodynamic* and *clinical* approach to personality. Behavior is interpreted as a result of the dynamic interplay among motives, drives, needs and conflicts. The research consists mainly of clinical investigations as shown in an emphasis on the individual, in the attention given to individual differences, and in attempts to assess and understand the total individual.

QUESTIONS TO BE ADDRESSED IN THIS CHAPTER

1. To what extent did historical and personal events shape Freud's theory?

2. What scientific evidence is there for the existence of unconscious influences on our lives?

3. Anxiety often is a very painful emotion. What are the means people use to protect themselves from too much anxiety?

4. Can people repress memories of childhood trauma and then recover these memories as adults?

5. How important is early experience for later personality development?

Psychoanalysis has reflected changing values in our society and has played a role in changing these values. The psychoanalytic theory of Freud is reviewed because of its prominence in the culture of our society and its importance as a model of a psychodynamic theory of personality. As noted by Norman O. Brown: "It is a shattering experience for anyone seriously committed to the Western tradition of morality and rationality to take a steadfast, unflinching look at what Freud has to say. It is humiliating to be compelled to admit the grossly seamy side of so many grand ideals...To experience Freud is to partake a second time of the forbidden fruit" (1959, p. xi). Freud astutely observed that there had been three hurts to human self-love and self-image—Copernicus's discovery that the earth is not the center of the universe, Darwin's discovery that we do not exist independently of other members of the animal kingdom, and the discovery of the degree to which we are influenced by unknown, unconscious, and at times uncontrollable forces.

Psychoanalytic theory was derived from intensive work with individuals and, in turn, was applied to individuals. Psychoanalysis exemplifies a *psychodynamic* theory in that it gives a prominent role to the interplay among forces in human behavior. In psychoanalytic theory, behavior is a result of struggles and compromises among motives, drives, needs, and conflicts. Behavior can express a motive directly or in a subtle, disguised way. The same behavior can satisfy different motives in different people or a variety of motives in one person. For example, eating can satisfy a hunger need but it also can symbolically satisfy a need for love; being a doctor can satisfy a need to help others, as well as serve as a way of overcoming anxieties about illness and bodily harm. Finally, behavior occurs at different levels of awareness, with individuals being more or less aware of the forces behind their various behaviors.

In sum, in this chapter we will consider a theory that emphasizes behavior as the result of an interplay among forces. In addition, it is a theory grand in scope, one that emphasizes phenomena as simple as the slip of the tongue and as complex as the development of culture.

Sigmund Freud was born in Austria in 1856. He was the first child of his parents, although his father, 20 years older than his mother, had two sons by a previous marriage. His birth was followed by the birth and early death of one sibling and the birth of six more siblings. Described as having been his mother's favorite, Freud himself stated that "a man who has been the indisputable favorite of his mother keeps for life the feeling of a conqueror, that confidence of success that often induces real success" (Freud, 1900, p. 26). As a boy he dreamed of becoming a great general or minister of state but, being Jewish, he was concerned about anti-Semitism in these fields. This led him to consider medicine as a profession. As a medical student (1873–1881), he came under the influence of noted physiologist Ernst Brucke. Brucke viewed humans in terms of a dynamic physiological system in which they are controlled by the physical principles of the conservation of energy. This view of physiological functioning was the foundation for Freud's dynamic view of psychological functioning (Sulloway, 1979).

After obtaining his medical degree, Freud did research and practiced in the field of neurology. Some of his early research involved a comparison of adult and fetal brains. He concluded that the earliest structures persist and are never buried, a view that was paralleled later by his views concerning the development of personality. Professionally, the first years

SIGMUND FREUD (1856–1939): A VIEW OF THE THEORIST

Sigmund Freud

after medical school were filled with theory and research, but then, for financial reasons, Freud turned toward practice. Personally, Freud experienced periodic depressions and attacks of anxiety, occasionally using cocaine to calm the agitation and dispel the depression. During these years he married and had three daughters and three sons.

In 1886 Freud spent a year with French psychiatrist Jean Charcot, who was having some success in treating neurotic patients with hypnosis. Although not satisfied with the effects of hypnosis, Freud was stimulated by the thinking of Charcot. Ernest Jones, Freud's biographer, comments on Freud's development at that time. "All this work would have established Freud as a first class neurologist, a hard worker, a close thinker, but—with the exception perhaps of the book on aphasia—there was little to foretell the existence of genius" (1953, p. 220).

In 1897, the year following his father's death, Freud began his self-analysis. He continued to be plagued by periods of depression, and though intellectual pursuits helped to distract him from his pain, he looked for answers in his unconscious: "My recovery can only come through work in the unconscious; I cannot manage with conscious efforts alone." For the rest of his life he continued self-analysis, devoting the last half-hour of his workday to it. In the 1890s, he tried a variety of therapeutic techniques with his patients. First he used hypnotic suggestion as practiced by Charcot; then he tried a concentration technique in which he pressed his hand upon the patient's head and urged the recall of memories. During these years he also worked with the Viennese physician Joseph Breuer, learned from him the technique of **catharsis** (a release and freeing of emotion through talking about one's problems), and collaborated with him on the book *Studies in Hysteria*. At this point, already in his forties, Freud had developed little, if any, of what was later to become known as psychoanalysis. Furthermore, his judgments of himself and of his work parallel the comment made by his biographer, Jones: "I have restricted capacities or talents. None at all for the natural sciences; nothing for mathematics; nothing for anything quantitative. But what I have, of a very restricted nature, is probably very intense."

The momentum in Freud's work and thinking most clearly dates back to his self-analysis and to the beginnings, in 1896, of his use of the **free association** method with his patients. This method of allowing all thoughts to come forth without inhibition or falsification of any kind resulted, in 1900, in what many still consider to be Freud's most significant work, *The Interpretation of Dreams*. In this book, Freud began to develop his theory of the mind and, although only 600 copies were sold in the first eight years after publication, he began to develop a following. In 1902, a Psychoanalytic Society was formed, and was joined by a number of people who went on to become outstanding psychoanalysts. Freud's writing and development of theory progressed, but with increased public attention came increased public abuse. In 1904, Freud wrote on the *Psychopathology of Everyday Life*, and in 1905 he published *Three Essays on the Theory of Sexuality*. The latter presented Freud's views on infantile sexuality and its relation to perversions and neuroses. This resulted in ridicule of Freud, who was seen as an evil and wicked man with an obscene mind. Medical institutions were boycotted for tolerating Freud's view; an early follower, Ernest Jones, was forced to resign his neurological appointment for inquiring into the sexual life of his patients.

To jump ahead of our story for a moment, it is interesting to note that Freud's books were long scorned in Russia as antithetical to Communist ideology and, even with the recent liberalization, a person seeking to publish his essays on sex was told that "our young people don't need books about Freud" (*The New York Times*, May 2, 1989, A1).

In 1909 Freud was invited by G. Stanley Hall to give a series of lectures at Clark University in Worcester, Massachusetts. During this period, Freud was developing his theories of development and infantile fantasies, his theory of the principles of mental functioning, and his views concerning the psychoanalytic process. He had by now achieved sufficient fame and acceptance to have a waiting list of patients.

But Freud had problems, too. By 1919 he had lost all his savings in World War I. In 1920, a daughter, age 26, died. Perhaps most significant was Freud's fear for the lives of two sons who were in the war. Out of this historical context Freud, age 64, in 1920 developed his theory of the **death instinct**—a wish to die, which is in opposition to the life instinct, or wish for survival.

Just as the war appeared to influence his thinking, so apparently did the growth of anti-Semitism during the 1930s. In 1932, for example, the Nazis in Berlin made a bonfire of his books. Shortly thereafter, Freud published his book *Moses and Monotheism*, in which he suggested that Moses was an Egyptian noble who joined the Jews and gave them a religion. Freud attributed anti-Semitism to resentment against the strict moral code of the Jews and, in this book, appeared to say that it was not a Jew but an Egyptian who bears the onus.

Freud died on September 23, 1939, at the age of 83. Almost to the very end, he was doing analysis daily and continuing his writing. The last 20 years of his life represent a remarkable period of personal courage and productivity. Earlier, it had taken a great deal of courage to go on with his work in spite of attacks from the public and his medical colleagues. During this later period, it took great courage to go on in spite of the loss of many of his disciples and the brutality of the Nazis. During these later years, Freud continued to work despite extreme physical discomfort and pain, including 33 operations for cancer of the jaw. Although not wealthy, he turned down lucrative offers that he felt would jeopardize the stature of his work. In 1920, he refused an offer from *Cosmopolitan* magazine to write on topics such as "The Husband's Place in the Home," replying: "Had I taken into account the considerations that influence your edition from the beginning of my career, I am sure I should not have become known at all, either in America or Europe." In 1924 he turned down an offer of $100,000 by Samuel Goldwyn to collaborate in making films of famous love stories.

Most of what we now recognize as the major elements in Freud's theory were developed during these last 20 years. As a man he was glorified by some as being compassionate, courageous, and a genius. Others, noting his many battles and breaks with colleagues, see him as rigid, authoritarian, and intolerant of the opinions of others (Fromm, 1959). Whatever the interpretation of Freud's personality, most, if not all, would agree that he pursued his studies with great courage. Finally, most students of Freud and of psychoanalysis would agree that factors in Freud's personal life and related historical factors (e.g., the Victorian era, World War I, and anti-Semitism) played a part in the final formulation of his theory and in the development of the psychoanalytic movement.

FREUD'S VIEW OF THE PERSON AND SOCIETY

Implicit in psychoanalysis are a view of the person and a view of society, and perhaps even a total philosophy of life. Although Freud struggled to develop a theory free of biases from his personal life and the historical period of which he was a part, psychoanalytic theory reflects the themes that were current in late nineteenth- and early twentieth-century Europe. Freud's theory was based on observations, but these were primarily observations of middle- and upper-class patients of the Victorian era.

At the heart of the psychoanalytic view of the person is that the human is an **energy system**. Postulated is a system in which energy flows, gets sidetracked, or becomes dammed up. There is a limited amount of energy, and if it is used in one way, there is much less of it to be used in another way. The energy that is used for cultural purposes is no longer available for sexual purposes, and vice versa. If the energy is blocked from one channel of expression, it finds another, generally along the path of least resistance. The goal of all behavior is *pleasure*, that is, the reduction of tension or the release of energy.

Why the assumption of an energy model concerning human behavior? The assumption is traceable to the excitement scientists were then experiencing in the field of energy dynamics. For example, according to the nineteenth-century physicist Helmholtz's principle of the conservation of energy, matter and energy can be transformed but not destroyed. Not only physicists but also members of other disciplines were studying the laws of energy changes in a system. As already noted, while in medical school Freud came under the influence of the physiologist Brucke. Brucke viewed humans as moved by forces according to the principle of the conservation of energy, a view apparently translated by Freud into the psychological realm of behavior. The age of energy and dynamics provided scientists with a new conception of humans, "the view that man is an energy system and that he obeys the same physical laws which regulate the soap bubble and the movement of the planets" (Hall, 1954, pp. 12–13).

Beyond the view of the person as being an energy system, there is the view that humans are driven by sexual and aggressive instincts or drives. Freud's view of the importance of aggression in human behavior was based on observations, but his interpretation of these observations had the definite quality of a philosophical view. For example, in *Civilization and Its Discontents* (1930), Freud commented: "The bit of truth behind all this—one so eagerly denied—is that men are not gentle, friendly creatures wishing for love, who simply defend themselves if they are attacked, but that a powerful measure of desire for aggression has to be reckoned as a part of their instinctual endowment" (p. 85). Freud went on to comment that the instinct of aggression lies "at the bottom of all relations of affection and love between human beings—possibly with the single exception of that of a mother to her male child" (p. 89). We have already noted that Freud published his theory of aggression and the death instinct in 1920, after the extended and bloody period of World War I.

Along with the aggressive drive, Freud placed great emphasis on the sexual drive, and on the conflict between expression of these drives and society. The emphasis on sexual inhibition in particular appears to relate to the Victorian period of which Freud and his patients were a part. For Freud, the person in pursuit of pleasure is in conflict with society and civilization. People function according to the **pleasure principle**, seeking "unbridled gratification" of all desires. Yet, such a mode of operation runs counter to the demands of society and the external world. The energy that would otherwise be released in the pursuit of pleasure and gratification must now be inhibited and channeled to conform to the aims of society. Freud believed that scientific activities and artistic endeavors—in fact the whole range of cultural productivity—were expressions of sexual and aggressive energy that were prevented from expression in a more direct way.

Another possible outgrowth of this conflict between the individual and society is misery and neurosis. In fact, according to Freud, the price of progress in civilization is misery, the forfeiting of happiness, and a heightened sense of guilt.

We can see, then, that beyond the formal conceptualization of a theory of personality, there is a view of the person implicit in psychoanalysis. According to this view, humans—like other animals—are driven by instincts or drives and operate in the pursuit of pleasure. People operate as energy systems, building, storing, and releasing, in one form or another, basically the same energy. All behavior is determined, much of it by forces outside of awareness. In the end, psychoanalysis sides with the instincts and seeks a reduction in the extent to which the instincts are frustrated.

CURRENT QUESTIONS

WHAT PRICE THE SUPPRESSION OF EXCITING THOUGHTS?

Freud suggested that the price of progress in civilization is increased inhibition of the pleasure principle and a heightened sense of guilt. Does civilization require such an inhibition? What are the costs to the individual of efforts to suppress wishes and inhibit "unbridled gratification" of desires?

Recent research by Daniel Wegner and his associates suggests that the suppression of exciting thoughts may be involved in the production of negative emotional responses and the development of psychological symptoms such as phobias (irrational fears) and obsessions (preoccupation with uncontrollable thoughts). In this research, subjects were told not to think about sex. Trying not to think about sex produced emotional arousal, just as it did in subjects given permission to think about sex. Although arousal decreased after a few minutes in both groups, what followed differed for subjects in the two groups. In the first group, the effort to suppress exciting thoughts led to the intrusion of these thoughts into consciousness and the reintroduction of surges of emotion. This was not found when subjects were given the opportunity to think about sex.

The researchers suggest that the suppression of exciting thoughts can promote excitement; that is, the very act of suppression may make these thoughts even more stimulating than when we purposefully dwell on them. In sum, such efforts at suppression may not serve us well either emotionally or psychologically.

SOURCE: Wegner, 1992; 1994; Wegner et al., 1990.

We know that Freud was trained in medical research and appreciated the relationship between theory and research. He felt a need for sharp definitions of concepts, but he also accepted the possibility that vague conceptions and speculative theory might be necessary during the early stages of science.

FREUD'S VIEW OF SCIENCE, THEORY, AND RESEARCH

Although he developed an elaborate theory of personality, Freud's major contribution was in the nature of the observations he made. Freud's observations were based on the analysis of patients and, by and large, he had little use for efforts to verify psychoanalytic principles in the laboratory. When a psychologist wrote to tell Freud of his experimental studies of one psychoanalytic concept, Freud wrote back that psychoanalytic concepts were based on a wealth of reliable observations and thus did not need independent experimental verification. He was satisfied with using the intensive clinical study of the individual patient as his major research method.

This research method allows the accumulation of considerable data about an individual. Probably no other method in psychology even approximates the wealth of material gathered about a single person by the psychoanalyst. On the other hand, as Freud himself pointed out, analysts are unlike other scientists in that they do not use experiments as part of their research. Although Freud viewed psychoanalysis as part of the science of psychology, most of the early research was conducted by medical professionals in a therapeutic setting. Only within the last 20 to 30 years have psychologists tried to apply the traditional scientific techniques of the discipline to the concepts of psychoanalysis. As we consider psychoanalytic concepts, we shall continue to see this struggle between the complex, uncontrolled observations of the clinical setting and the systematic, controlled study of phenomena in the laboratory. Indeed, of late there has been considerable criticism of the uncontrolled nature of Freud's observations and the way he reported them: "Instead of training scientists, Freud ended up training practioners in a relatively fixed system of ideas" (Sulloway, 1991, p. 275).

We now turn to consideration of the details of psychoanalytic theory, keeping in mind its emphasis on clinical investigations and a view of human functioning as the result of an interplay among forces.

PSYCHOANALYSIS: A THEORY OF PERSONALITY

STRUCTURE

What are the structural units used by psychoanalytic theory to account for human behavior? In the early development of the theory the concept of levels of consciousness served as a focal point in psychoanalytic thinking. In fact, Freud claimed that "Psychoanalysis aims at and achieves nothing more than the discovery of the unconscious in mental life" (1924, p. 397).

THE CONCEPT OF THE UNCONSCIOUS

It is hard to overestimate the importance of the concept of the unconscious to psychoanalytic theory. It also is hard to overestimate the moral dilemmas that have resulted from taking the concept seriously and the difficulties scientists have experienced in conducting relevant research. The concept of the unconscious suggests that there are aspects of our functioning of which we are not fully aware. Beyond this, within psychoanalytic theory the concept of the unconscious suggests that much of our behavior, perhaps the majority of it, is determined by unconscious forces, and that much of our psychic energy is devoted either to finding acceptable expression of unconscious ideas or to keeping them unconscious. It is the extent of unconscious influences and the motivated aspects of such influences that is noteworthy in relation to the psychoanalytic concept of the unconscious.

Levels of Consciousness

According to psychoanalytic theory, psychic life can be described in terms of the degree to which we are aware of phenomena: the **conscious** relates to phenomena we are aware of at any given moment, the **preconscious** to phenomena we can be aware of if we attend to them, and the **unconscious** to phenomena that we are unaware of and *cannot* become aware of except under special circumstances.

Although Freud was not the first to pay attention to the importance of the unconscious, he was the first to explore in detail the qualities of unconscious life and attribute major importance to them in our daily lives. Through the analysis of dreams, slips of the tongue, neuroses, psychoses, works of art, and rituals, Freud attempted to understand the properties of the unconscious. What he found was a quality of psychic life in which nothing was impossible. The unconscious is alogical (opposites can stand for the same thing), disregards time (events of different periods may coexist), and disregards space (size and distance relationships are neglected so that large things fit into small things and distant places are brought together). One is reminded of William James's reference to the world of the newly born infant as a "big blooming buzzing confusion."

It is in the dream that the workings of the unconscious become most apparent. Here we are exposed to the world of symbols, where many ideas may be telescoped into a single word, where a part of any object may stand for many things. It is through the process of symbolization that a penis can be represented by a snake or nose, a woman by a church, chapel, or boat, and an engulfing mother by an octopus. It is through this process that we are allowed to think of writing as a sexual act—the pen is the male organ and the paper is the woman who receives the ink (the semen) that flows out in the quick up-and-down movements of the pen (Groddeck, 1923). In *The Book of the It*, Groddeck, gives many fascinating examples of the workings of the unconscious and offers the following as an example of the functioning of the unconscious in his own life.

> I cannot recall her [my nurse's] appearance. I know nothing more than her name, Bertha, the shining one. But I have a clear recollection of the day she went away. As a parting present she gave me a copper three-pfennig piece. A Dreier.... Since that day I have been pursued by the number three. Words like trinity, triangle, triple alliance, convey something disreputable to me, and not merely the words but the ideas attached to them, yes, and the whole complex of ideas built up around them by the capricious brain of a child. For this reason, the Holy Ghost, as the Third Person of the Trinity, was already suspect to me in early childhood; trigonometry was a plague in my school days....Yes, three is a sort of fatal number for me.
>
> SOURCE: Groddeck, 1923, p. 9

The Motivated Unconscious At its roots, psychoanalytic theory is a motivational theory of human behavior. As noted above, psychoanalytic theory suggests that much of our behavior is motivated by unconscious influences. As will be discussed in greater detail later in the chapter, the suggestion is that some thoughts, feelings, and motives exist in the uncon-

While some slips of the tongue may represent merely a confusion among choice of words, others seem to illustrate Freud's suggestion that slips express hidden wishes. (Illustration by Patrick McDonnell, 1987 Psychology Today Magazine, Sussex Publishers, Inc.)

FAILURE, UNHAPPINESS, AND
UNCONSCIOUS MOTIVATION

In his study of "Those Wrecked by Success," Freud described individuals who, because of feelings of guilt, fell ill once they had achieved some long-cherished wish. More recently, psychoanalyst Roy Schafer has described the unconscious meanings that success, failure, happiness, and unhappiness can have for people. He suggests that repetitive failure and chronic unhappiness typically are self-inflicted rather than expressions of inescapable events. For example, in one case a male underachieved to ward off the envy of others, and in another case a young man pursued failure to protect the self-esteem of his unsuccessful father: "Thus, for this young man, failure was also a success of a kind, while being a success was also a failure." In a third case, a woman was extremely self-sacrificing to retain the love of others. Although the "pursuit of failure" and the "idealization of unhappiness" are seen as being found in members of both sexes, Schafer suggests that the former is more prevalent in men and the latter in women. This is not to say, however, that all cases of failure or unhappiness are motivated by the result of unconscious conflicts.

SOURCE: Schafer, 1984.

"He's mad as hell. He has this need to fail and he keeps getting promoted."

Drawing by Stan Hunt; © 1980 The New Yorker Magazine.

scious for motivated reasons. That is, to allow them into awareness would cause us pain and discomfort. For example, to recall painful memories of the past, to recognize feelings of envy or hostility, or to recognize wishes to have sex with a forbidden person or to harm a loved person may create serious discomfort for the person. Thus, in accordance with our pursuit of pleasure and the avoidance of pain, we seek to keep such thoughts, feelings, and motives out of our awareness.

In addition to thoughts, feelings, and memories being kept unconscious for motivated reasons, psychoanalysts suggest that what is in the unconscious can express itself in our daily behavior through slips of the tongue, misperceptions, accidents, and "out of character" or seemingly irrational behavior. In other words, our underlying, "true" feelings and motives can express themselves despite our efforts to bury them in the unconscious. It is not just that there are parts of ourselves that we are unaware of but that these parts influence our daily behavior, often in ways that are perplexing to us and others. For many analysts psychoanalysis is nothing less than the exploration of such unconscious influences.

Relevant Psychoanalytic Research   The unconscious is never observed directly. What evidence, then, is there to support the concept of the unconscious? Let us review the range of evidence that might be considered supportive of the concept of the unconscious, beginning with Freud's clinical observations. Freud realized the importance of the unconscious after observing hypnotic phenomena. As is well known, people under hypnosis can recall things they previously could not. Furthermore, they perform things under posthypnotic suggestion without consciously "knowing" that they are behaving in accordance with that suggestion; that is, they fully believe that what they are doing is voluntary and independent of any suggestion by another person. When Freud discarded the technique of hypnosis and continued with his therapeutic work, he found that often patients became aware of memories and wishes previously buried. Frequently, such discoveries were associated with painful emotion. It is indeed a powerful clinical observation to see a patient suddenly experience tremendous anxiety, sob hysterically, or break into a rage as he or she recalls a forgotten event or gets in touch with a forbidden feeling. Thus, it was clinical observations such as these that suggested to Freud that the unconscious includes memories and wishes that not only are not currently part of our consciousness but are "deliberately buried" in our unconscious.

What of experimental evidence? In the 1960s and 1970s experimental research focused on unconscious perception or what was called **perception without awareness**. Can the person "know" something without knowing that he or she knows it? For example, can the person hear or perceive stimuli, and be influenced by these perceptions, without being aware of these perceptions? Currently this is known as *subliminal perception*, or the registration of stimuli at a level below that required for awareness. For example, in some early relevant research one group of subjects was shown a picture with a duck image shaped by the branches of a tree. Another group was shown a similar picture but without the duck image. For both groups the picture was presented at a rapid speed so that it was barely visible. This was done using a tachistoscope, an apparatus that allows the experimenter to show stimuli to subjects at very fast speeds, so that they cannot be perceived. The subjects then were asked to close their eyes, imagine a nature scene, draw the scene, and label the parts. Would the two groups differ, that is, would subjects in the group "seeing" the picture with the duck image draw different pictures than subjects in the other group? And, if so, would such a difference be associated with differential recall as to what was perceived? What was found was that more of the subjects viewing the "duck" picture had significantly more duck-related images (e.g., "duck," "water," "birds," "feathers") in their drawings than did subjects in the other group. However, these subjects did not report seeing the duck during the experiment and the majority even had trouble finding it when they were asked to look for it. In other words, the stimuli that were not consciously perceived still influenced the imagery and thoughts of the subjects (Eagle, Wolitzky, & Klein, 1966).

The mere fact that people can perceive and be influenced by stimuli of which they are unaware does not suggest that psychodynamic or motivational forces are involved. Is there evidence that such is or can be the case? Two relevant lines of research can be noted. The first, called **perceptual defense**, involves a process by which the individual defends against the anxiety that accompanies actual recognition of a threatening stimulus. In a relevant early experiment, subjects were shown two types of words in a tachistoscope: neutral words such as *apple, dance,* and *child* and emotionally toned words such as *rape, whore,* and *penis.* The words were shown first at very fast speeds and then at progressively slower speeds. A record was made of the point at which the subjects were able to identify each of the words and their sweat-gland activity (a measure of tension) in response to each word. These records indicated that subjects took longer to recognize the emotionally toned words than the neutral words and showed signs of emotional response to the emotionally toned words before they were verbally identified (McGinnies, 1949). Despite criticism of such research (e.g., did subjects identify the emotionally toned words earlier but were reluctant to verbalize them to the experimenter?), there appears to be considerable evidence that people can, outside of awareness, selectively respond to and reject specific emotional stimuli (Erdelyi, 1984).

More recently, research has focused on what has been called **subliminal psychodynamic activation** (Silverman, 1976; 1982; Weinberger, 1992). In this research, there is an effort to stimulate unconscious wishes without making them conscious. In general, the experimental procedure involves using a tachistoscope to show subjects material related to wishes that are expected to be either threatening or anxiety alleviating to them and then observing whether the expected effects do occur. In the case of threatening wishes, the material being presented subliminally (below the threshold for conscious recognition) is expected to stir up unconscious conflict and thus increase psychological disturbance. In the case of an anxiety-alleviating wish, the material being presented subliminally is expected to diminish unconscious conflict and thus decrease psychological disturbance. For example, the content "I Am Losing Mommy" might be upsetting to some subjects, whereas the content "Mommy and I Are One" might be reassuring.

In a series of studies, Silverman and his colleagues have demonstrated that such subliminal psychodynamic activation effects can be produced. In one study this method was used to present conflict-intensifying material ("Loving Daddy Is Wrong") and conflict-reducing material ("Loving Daddy Is OK") to female undergraduates. For subjects prone to conflict over sexual urges, the conflict-intensifying material, presented outside of awareness, was found to disrupt memory for passages presented after the subliminal activation of the conflict. This was not true for the conflict-reducing material or for subjects not prone to conflict over sexual urges (Geisler, 1986). What is key here is that the content that is upsetting or relieving to various groups of subjects is predicted beforehand on the basis of psychoanalytic theory and that the effects occur only when the stimuli are perceived subliminally or unconsciously.

Another interesting use of the subliminal psychodynamic activation model involves the study of eating disorders. In the first study in this area, normal college women and women with signs of eating disorders were compared in terms of how many crackers they would eat following subliminal presentation of three messages: Mama Is Leaving Me, Mama Is Loaning It, Mona Is Loaning It (Patton, 1992). Based on psychoanalytic theory, the hypothesis tested was that subjects with an eating disorder struggle with feelings of loss and abandonment in relation to nurturance and therefore would seek substitute gratification in the form of eating the crackers once the conflict was activated subliminally through the message "Mama Is Leaving Me." Indeed, the eating disorder subjects who received the abandonment stimulus (Mama Is Leaving Me) below threshold showed significantly more cracker eating than subjects without an eating disorder or subjects with an eating disorder exposed to the abandonment stimulus above threshold. This study was replicated with the additional use of pictorial stimuli—a picture of a sobbing baby and a woman walking away along with the "Mommy Is Leaving Me" message and a picture of a woman walking along with the neutral stimulus, in this case "Mommy Is Walking." Once more significantly more crackers were eaten by the eating disorder women subliminally exposed to the abandonment phrase and picture than by eating disorder women exposed to these stimuli above threshold or by women without an eating disorder exposed to the stimuli above or below threshold (Gerard, Kupper, &

THE POWER OF SUBLIMINAL MESSAGES

Ever since subliminal perception was discovered, questions have been raised about the extent to which such messages can influence what we think, feel, and do. Could advertisers use "hidden persuaders" to make people buy things they might not otherwise buy? Can therapeutic tapes with hidden messages telling you to relax actually have a calming effect? A confidence-building effect if they say positive things about you? And what of the parents who claim in a lawsuit that the suicides of their sons were influenced by the message "Do it!" hidden in the music of the rock group Judas Priest?

Psychologists generally agree that subliminal perception exists, but they differ about how powerful and widespread the effect is. There is no evidence of its power in advertising, nor any evidence of the therapeutic value of subliminal tapes; the parents lost their case against Judas Priest. However, some psychologists argue that specific subliminal messages, tailored to the unconscious of the individual, can affect what the person thinks, feels, and does.

Subliminal Perception: *The evidence did not support a claim that a hidden message in the music of Judas Priest influenced behavior.*

Nguyen, 1993). Once more it was suggested that only when the stimuli were presented subliminally were they able to activate unconscious wishes and conflicts.

Some view the research on perceptual defense and subliminal psychodynamic activation as conclusive experimental evidence of the importance of psychodynamic, motivational factors in determining what is "deposited into" and "kept in" the unconscious (Weinberger, 1992). However, the experiments have frequently been criticized on methodological grounds, and at times some of the effects have been difficult to replicate or reproduce in other laboratories (Balay & Shevrin, 1988, 1989; Holender, 1986).

Current Status of the Concept of the Unconscious The concept of a motivated unconscious continues to lie at the heart of psychoanalytic theory. How is the concept viewed more generally by psychologists in the field? At this point almost all psychologists, whether psychoanalytic or otherwise, would agree that unconscious processes are important in influencing what we attend to and how we feel. For example, consider the view of Jacoby, an important investigator in the area of unconscious perception who is *not* a follower of psychoanalytic theory: "Our conclusion, perhaps discomforting for the layperson, is that unconscious influences are ubiquitous. It is clear that people sometimes consciously plan and act. More often than not, however, behavior is influenced by unconscious processes; that is, we act and then, if questioned, make our excuses" (Jacoby, Toth, Lindsay, & Debner, 1992, p.82). At the same time, there are differing points of view concerning principles of unconscious functioning, the contents of the unconscious, and motivated aspects of the unconscious.

Two contrasting points of view can be considered here, that emphasizing the psychoanalytic unconscious and that emphasizing what has been called the *cognitive unconscious* (Kihlstrom, 1990; Pervin, 1996). As we have seen, the psychoanalytic view of the unconscious emphasizes the irrational, illogical nature of unconscious functioning. In addition, the contents of the unconscious are presumed by analysts mainly to involve sexual and aggressive thoughts, feelings, and motives. Finally, analysts emphasize that what is in the unconscious is there for motivated reasons and these contents exert a motivational influence on daily behavior. In contrast to this, according to the cognitive view of the unconscious there is no fundamental difference in quality between unconscious and conscious processes. According to this view, unconscious processes can be as intelligent, logical, and rational as conscious processes. Second, the cognitive view of the unconscious emphasizes the variety of contents that may be unconscious, with no special significance associated with sexual and aggressive contents. Finally, related to this, the cognitive view of the unconscious does not emphasize motivational factors. According to the cognitive view, cognitions are unconscious because they can not be processed at the conscious level, because they

Table 3.1   Comparison of Two Views of the Unconscious: Psychoanalytic and Cognitive

Psychoanalytic View	Cognitive View
1. Emphasis on illogical, irrational unconscious processes.	1. Absence of fundamental difference between conscious and unconscious processes.
2. Content emphasis on motives and wishes.	2. Content emphasis on thoughts.
3. Emphasis on motivated aspects of unconscious functioning.	3. Focus on nonmotivated aspects of unconscious functioning.

never reached consciousness, or because they have become overly routinized and automatic. For example, tying one's shoe is so automatic that we no longer are aware of just how we do it. We act similarly with typing and where letters are on the keyboard. Many of our cultural beliefs were learned in such subtle ways that we can not even spell them out as beliefs. As noted in Chapter 1, we are not even aware of them until we meet members of a different culture. However, such unconscious contents are not kept there for motivated reasons. Nor do they necessarily exert a motivational influence on our behavior.

Many of these contrasting views are captured in the following statement by Kihlstrom, a leading proponent of the cognitive view of the unconscious:

> The psychological unconscious documented by latter-day psychology is quite different from what Sigmund Freud and his psychoanalytic colleagues had in mind in Vienna. Their unconscious was hot and wet; it seethed with lust and anger; it was hallucinatory, primitive, and irrational. The unconscious of contemporary psychology is kinder and gentler than that and more readily bound and rational, even if it is not entirely cold and dry.
>
> SOURCE: Kihlstrom, Barnhardt, & Tataryn, 1992, p. 788

Although efforts are being made to integrate the psychoanalytic and cognitive views of the unconscious (Epstein, 1994), generally these differing points of view remain. In sum, although the importance of unconscious phenomena is recognized, and the investigation of such phenomena has become a major area of research, the uniquely psychoanalytic view of the unconscious remains questionable for many, perhaps most, nonpsychoanalytic investigators.

ID, EGO, AND SUPEREGO

In 1923 Freud developed a more formal structural model for psychoanalysis, defined by the concepts of id, ego, and superego, which refer to different aspects of people's functioning. According to the theory, the **id** represents the source of all drive energy. The energy for a person's functioning originally resides in the life and death, or sexual and aggressive instincts, which are part of the id. In its functioning, the id seeks the release of excitation, tension, and energy. It operates according to the pleasure principle—the pursuit of pleasure and the avoidance of pain. In operating this way the id seeks immediate, total release. It has qualities of a spoiled child: it wants what it wants when it wants it. The id cannot tolerate frustration and is free of inhibitions. It shows no regard for reality and can seek satisfaction through action or through imagining that it has gotten what it wants; the fantasy of gratification is as good as the actual gratification. It is without reason, logic, values, morals, or ethics. In sum, the id is demanding, impulsive, blind, irrational, asocial, selfish, and finally, pleasure-loving.

In marked contrast to the id is the **superego**, which represents the moral branch of our functioning, containing the ideals we strive for and the punishments (guilt) we expect when we have violated our ethical code. This structure functions to control behavior in accordance with the rules of society, offering rewards (pride, self-love) for "good" behavior and punishments (guilt, feelings of inferiority, accidents) for "bad" behavior. The superego may function on a very primitive level, being relatively incapable of reality testing—that is, of modifying its action depending on circumstances. In such cases, the person is unable to distinguish between thought and action, feeling guilty for thinking something even if it did not lead to action. Furthermore, the individual is bound by black–white, all–none judgments and by the pursuit of perfection. Excessive use of words such as *good, bad, judgment*, and *trial* express a strict superego. But the superego can also be understanding and flexible. For example, people may be able to forgive themselves or someone else if it is clear that something was an accident or done under severe stress. In the course of development, children learn to make such important distinctions and to see things not only in all-or-none, right-or-wrong, black-or-white terms.

The third structure conceptualized in the theory is that of the **ego**. Whereas the id seeks pleasure and the superego seeks perfection, the ego seeks reality. The ego's function is to express and satisfy the desires of the id in accordance with reality and the demands of the superego. Whereas the id operates according to the pleasure principle, the ego operates according to the **reality principle**: gratification of the instincts is delayed until the time when the most pleasure can be obtained with the least pain or negative consequences. According to the reality principle, the energy of the id may be blocked, diverted, or released gradually, all in accordance with the demands of reality and the conscience. Such an operation does not contradict the pleasure principle, but rather represents a temporary suspension of it. It functions, in George Bernard Shaw's words, so as "to be able to choose the line of greatest advantage instead of yielding in the direction of least resistance." The ego is able to separate wish from fantasy, can tolerate tension and compromise, and changes over time. Accordingly, it expresses the development of perceptual and cognitive skills, the ability to perceive more and think in more complex terms. For example, the person can begin to think in terms of the future and what is best in the long run. All these qualities are in contrast with the unrealistic, unchanging, demanding qualities of the id.

In comparison with his investigations into the unconscious and the workings of the id, Freud did relatively little work on the functioning of the ego. He pictured the ego as a weak structure, a poor creature that served three harsh masters—the id, reality, and the superego. The "poor" ego has a hard time serving these masters and must reconcile the claims and demands of each. Of particular significance is the relation of the ego to the tyranny of the id.

> One might compare the relation of the ego to the id with that between a rider and his horse. The horse provides the locomotive energy, and the rider has the prerogative of determining the goal and of guiding the movements of his powerful mount towards it. But all too often in the relations between the ego and the id we find a picture of the less ideal situation in which the rider is obliged to guide his horse in the direction in which it itself wants to go.
>
> SOURCE: Freud, 1933, p. 108

In sum, Freud's ego is logical, rational, tolerant of tension, the "executive" of personality, but it is a poor rider on the swift horse of the id and is subject to control by three masters.

Just before his death Freud began to devote more attention to the importance of the ego in personality. This subject was then developed by his daughter, Anna Freud, and a number of analysts whose work has been categorized under the heading of *ego psychology*. Whereas in the earlier view the ego was viewed as existing without energy of its own and obliged to guide the id where it wanted to go, the later view emphasized the importance of the ego in conflict resolution and in adaptation. This view left room for the possibility that the individual may experience pleasure through the conflict-free functioning of the ego, and not only through the release of the energies of the id. According to ego psychology, the ego has a source of energy of its own and takes pleasure in mastery of the environment. This concept is related to R. W. White's (1959) concept of *competence motivation*. In its description of personality, this view stressed the ways in which individuals actively engage their environment and their modes of thinking and perceiving. Although these modes still could be considered as functioning to serve the id and to reduce conflict, they were now viewed as having adaptive functions and importance independent of these other functions.

Personality psychologists have attempted to study individual differences in ego functioning. For example, measures have been developed

"Double Scotches for me and my super-ego, and a glass of water for my id, which is driving."

Psychoanalytic Theory: *Freud emphasized the concepts of id, ego, and superego as structures of personality. (Drawing by Handelsman; © 1972 The New Yorker Magazine, Inc.)*

for concepts such as *ego strength* (Barron, 1953), *ego development* (Loevinger, 1976, 1985, 1993), and *ego resiliency and control* (Block, 1993; Block & Block, 1980; Funder & Block, 1989). Although details of the concepts differ, as well as the means for measuring them, they share an emphasis on qualities such as the ability to tolerate delay of gratification, the ability to tolerate frustration and cope with stress, a firm sense of self, the ability to relate to others in terms of mutuality and intimacy, an internalized set of values, and relatively conflict-free functioning.

The concepts of conscious, unconscious, id, ego, and superego are highly abstract and are not always defined with great precision. Furthermore, there is some lack of clarity because the meaning of some concepts changed as the theory developed, but the exact nature of the change in meaning was never spelled out (Madison, 1961). Finally, it should be clear that these are conceptualizations of phenomena. Even though the language is picturesque and concrete, we must avoid regard-

HOW TO MEASURE EGO FUNCTIONING: LOEVINGER'S SENTENCE COMPLETION TEST

Freud did not put much faith in the ability of the ego to carry out its "executive" function of handling the id, the superego, and reality. Jane Loevinger thought differently. Her theory of *ego development* (1976) focuses on the vast individual differences in the functioning of the ego. Ego functioning refers to the particular way in which individuals interpret experience and act on the world: how they process information, control impulses, and relate to others.

Based on psychoanalytic theory as well as other areas of psychology, Loevinger postulates a sequence of stages of ego functioning. The sequence of stages captures a developmental progression toward what Loevinger considers more and more *mature levels* of ego functioning. Individuals at the lowest stages of ego development think in simplistic, stereotyped ways, are impulsive and self-protective, and are preoccupied with immediate, basic concerns. Individuals in the middle stages of ego development see the world in terms of good and bad, value conformity to rules and loyalty to friends and family, and are preoccupied with social acceptability. Individuals at the highest stages are complex thinkers, try to integrate intimacy and independence in their relationships, and have accepted the complexity and ambiguity of life. People can remain at any stage in the sequence, so that individuals differ dramatically in ego development in any given age group.

How can we measure such a broad and all-encompassing construct? Loevinger developed a Sentence Completion Test (SCT; Loevinger & Wessler, 1970) that con-sists of 36 sentence stems (e.g., "A woman should always…") which subjects complete in any way they want. In Loevinger's own words, "The SCT, being a free-response test, requires the respondent to display his or her own frame of reference. That gives a glimpse of personality structure that objective tests cannot match" (1993, p. 12). Here are two example sentence stems and responses given by individuals low, medium, and high on ego development (ED).

Ego development	(1) A woman should always…	(2) When I am criticized…
Low:	…get what she wants.	…I get mad and hit somebody.
Medium:	…try to look pretty.	…I feel deeply hurt and as if the other person doesn't like me.
High:	…choose roles that she believes reflect her true feelings of self.	…I like it because I can learn from others and see in myself what others see in me.

These response to the two sentence stems exemplify the developmental progression Loevinger describes as ego development. At the low end, we see a rather simple interpretation of experience (e.g., impulsive gratification of immediate needs), whereas individuals at the high end show a much more complex and integrated frame of reference. The sentence completions, all drawn from adults, also illustrate the enormous range of individual differences in ego functioning. While Freud paid relatively little attention to the ego, Loevinger's extensive theory and research highlight the importance of the ego in personality functioning.

ing concepts as real things. There is no energy plant inside us with a little person controlling its power. We do not "have" an id, ego, and superego, but according to the theory there are qualities of human behavior that are usefully conceptualized in these structural terms. The structures achieve greater definition in relation to the processes implied in them, and it is to these processes that we now turn.

PROCESS

Life and Death Instincts

We have discussed Freud's view of the person as an energy system obeying the same laws as other energy systems. Energy may be altered and transformed, but essentially it is all the same energy. Within this overall framework, the processes (dynamics) involved in psychoanalytic theory relate to the ways in which energy is expressed, blocked, or transformed. According to the theory, the source of all psychic energy lies in states of excitation within the body that seek expression and tension reduction. These states are called *instincts*, or *drives*, and represent constant, inescapable forces. In the earlier view, there were ego instincts, relating to tendencies toward self-preservation, and **sexual instincts**, relating to tendencies toward preservation of the species. In the later view, there was the **life instinct**, including both the earlier ego and sexual instincts, and the **death instinct**, involving the aim of the organism to die or return to an inorganic state. The energy of the life instinct was called **libido.** No name has come to be commonly associated with the energy of the death instinct. In fact, the death instinct remains one of the most controversial and least-accepted parts of the theory, with most analysts instead referring to the **aggressive instincts**. Both sexual and aggressive instincts are viewed as being part of the id.

In psychoanalytic theory, the instincts are characterized as aiming at the immediate reduction of tension, at achieving satisfaction and pleasure. In contrast to lower animals, humans are capable of gratifying an instinct in many and varied ways. This provides for uniqueness in personality. Furthermore, in humans the instincts can be delayed and modified before they are released.

The Dynamics of Functioning

In the dynamics of functioning, what can happen to one's instincts? They can, at least temporarily, be blocked from expression, expressed in a modified way, or expressed without modification. For example, affection may be a modified expression of the sexual instinct, and sarcasm a modified expression of the aggressive instinct. It is also possible for the object of gratification of the instinct to be changed or *displaced* from the original object to another object. Thus, the love of one's mother may be displaced to the wife, children, or dog. Each instinct may be transformed or modified, and the instincts can combine with one another. Football, for example, can gratify both sexual and aggressive instincts; in surgery there can be the fusion of love and destruction. It should already be clear how psychoanalytic theory is able to account for so much behavior on the basis of only two instincts. It is the fluid, mobile, changing qualities of the instincts and their many alternative kinds of gratification that allow such variability in behavior. In essence, the same instinct can be gratified in a number of ways and the same behavior can have different causes in different people.

Virtually every process in psychoanalytic theory can be described in terms of the expenditure of energy in an object or in terms of a force inhibiting the expenditure of energy, that is, inhibiting gratification of an instinct. Because it involves an expenditure of energy, people who direct much of their efforts toward inhibition end up feeling tired and bored. The interplay between expression and inhibition of instincts forms the foundation of the dynamic aspects of psychoanalytic theory. The key to this is the concept of **anxiety**. In psychoanalytic theory, anxiety is a painful emotional experience representing a threat or danger to the person. In a state of "free-floating" anxiety, individuals are unable to relate their state of tension to an external object; in contrast, in a state of fear, the source of tension is known. Freud had two theories of anxiety. In the first theory, anxiety was viewed as a result of undischarged sexual impulses—dammed-up libido. In the later theory, anxiety represented a painful emotion that acted as a signal of impending danger to the ego. Here, anxiety, an ego function, alerts the ego to danger so that it can act.

The psychoanalytic theory of anxiety states that at some point the person experiences a trauma, an incident of harm or injury. Anxiety represents a repetition of the earlier traumatic experience, but in miniature form. Anxiety in the present, then, is related to an earlier danger. For example, the child may be severely punished for some sexual or aggressive act. Later in life, the person may experience anxiety in association with the inclination to perform the same sexual or aggressive act. The earlier punishment (trauma) may or may not be remembered. In structural terms, what is suggested is that anxiety develops out of a conflict between the push of the id instincts and the threat of punishment by the superego. That is, it is as if the id says "I want it," the superego says "How terrible," and the ego says "I'm afraid."

Anxiety and the Mechanisms of Defense

Anxiety is such a painful state that we are incapable of tolerating it for very long. How are we to deal with such a state? Why are we not anxious more of the time? The answer is that individuals develop **defense mechanisms** against anxiety. Unconsciously, we develop ways to distort reality and exclude feelings from awareness so that we do not feel anxious. What are some of the ways in which this can be done? One of the most primitive defense mechanisms is **projection**. In projection, what is internal and unacceptable is projected out and seen as external. Rather than recognize hostility in the self, an individual sees others as being hostile. For example, suppose that you feel anxious or guilty about your dislike and hostility toward a friend who has taken advantage of you. You might project your own hostility onto this person and view many of his more innocuous actions as hostile toward you; at the same time, you might deny any hostile feelings on your part. Most of us behave this way from time to time. However, where such a pattern develops and becomes extreme, individuals may project all of their unacceptable feelings onto others, who are viewed as evil, while seeing themselves as virtuous or good.

Efforts to produce projection experimentally have been problematic (Holmes, 1981). In a semiexperimental study, Halpern (1977) tested the psychoanalytic hypothesis that defensive subjects would respond to threat by projecting feared characteristics onto disliked others. First, a measure of sexual defensiveness was obtained by scoring the number of times the subject agreed with questionnaire items such as "I never have sexual fantasies" and "I never have dreams with sexual content." Subjects were thereby divided into a high-defensive group and a low-defensive group. Members of each group were then exposed to one of two conditions. In one group, subjects were exposed to pornographic photographs. In the other group, subjects received no sexual stimuli. Following this, all subjects were asked to rate the most unfavorable person seen in the photographs, as well as themselves, on a list of traits.

How might projection appear, and where? The trait "lustful" was selected as key with the expectation that high-defensive subjects would project this trait onto the unfavorable person when they had been stimulated by the nude photographs. Presumably such stimuli would be threatening to the high sexual defense group and provide the conditions for projection. Indeed, sexually defensive subjects who viewed the nude photographs rated the unfavorable person highest on lustfulness, whereas the nondefensive subjects who viewed the nude photographs gave this person the lowest lustful ratings. In both conditions, the high-defensive subjects rated themselves lower on the trait lustful than did the low-defensive subjects. The study shows that certain conditions were required for projection to occur. In addition, the study recognized that according to psychoanalytic theory, people will project only those traits or motives they are seeking to defend against and will associate these characteristics with an unfavorable person; that is, *projection as a defense is used only in relation to specific characteristics, under particular conditions, and in relation to specific others*. Unfortunately, many research studies are not so careful in their definition and exploration of this mechanism of defense.

A second defense mechanism is **denial**. Here there may be either denial of reality, as in the girl who denies she lacks a penis or in the boy who in fantasy denies the lack of power, or denial of impulse, as when an irate person protests "I do not feel angry." The saying that someone "doth protest too much" gives specific reference to this defense. Denial of reality is commonly seen where people attempt to avoid recognizing the extent of a threat. The expression "Oh, no!" upon hearing of the death of a close friend represents the reflex action of denial. Children have been known to deny the death of a loved animal and long afterward to behave as if it were still alive. When Edwin Meese, former Attorney General in the Reagan administration, was asked how much he owed in legal bills, he replied, "I really don't know. It scares me to look at it, so I haven't looked at it." Initially, such avoidance may be conscious, but later it becomes automatic and unconscious, so that the person is not even aware of "not looking."

Denial of reality is also seen when people say or assume that "It can't happen to me" in spite of clear evidence of impending doom. This defense was seen in Jews who were victims of the Nazis. Steiner (1966), in his book on the Nazi concentration camp Treblinka, describes how the population acted as if death did not exist, in spite of clear evidence to the contrary. He notes that the extermination of a whole people was so unimaginable that the people could not accept it. They preferred to accept lies rather than to bear the terrible trauma of the truth.

Another illustration of denial of reality, one closer to home, has to do with how people cope with unpredictable disasters such as earthquakes. For some time, a major earthquake has been predicted for southern California. In 1983 the University of California at Los Angeles commissioned a panel to study the vulnerability of campus buildings to such an event. The results of the panel's findings were widely distributed in a report to the university community. A study of individuals who were aware of the report and the danger found that respondents in the very poor structures were significantly more likely to deny the seriousness of the situation and to doubt the experts' predictions than were respondents in the better structures. In addition, both groups showed ignorance of basic earthquake safety information and had taken no measures to prepare for an earthquake. It was concluded, "The results of this study suggest that individuals at risk for a catastrophic event whose occurrence is highly likely, but whose timing is unknown, may cope with that threat by ignoring or denying the seriousness of the situation....That respondents were typically aware of the threat and that residents of very poor seismic structures showed more questioning and denial than individuals in good seismic structures suggest that these perceptions are efforts to cope with the event, rather than a result of simple ignorance or misinformation" (Lehman & Taylor, 1987, pp. 551, 553).

Is denial necessarily a bad thing? Should we always avoid self-deception? Psychoanalysts generally assume that although the mechanisms of defense can be useful in reducing anxiety, they also are maladaptive in turning the person away from reality. Recall that in Chapter 2 there was

Denial and Addiction: *One of the most frequently cited characteristics of alcoholics and drug addicts is denial. Former Brooklyn Dodger pitcher Johnny Podres describes how he'd come home drunk, his mother would say he was an alcoholic, and he'd say "Not me." Another former Dodger pitcher, Don Newcombe, also a reformed alcoholic, describes how he and his drinking buddies would all deny their problem: "That's part of the syndrome—the denial syndrome." And in seeking to understand why N.Y. Mets pitcher Dwight Gooden would agree to be tested for cocaine use when he was using cocaine, one expert suggested that "massive denial is the hallmark of cocaine addiction. There is some denial in all addictions, but it is probably greatest in cocaine abuse." (*The New York Times, *July 30, 1983 and April 4, 1987.)*

discussion of defensive subjects with an illusion of mental health who showed signs of greater stress than either healthy subjects or nondefensive psychologically unhealthy subjects (Shedler, Mayman, & Manis, 1993). Thus, psychoanalysts view "reality orientation" as fundamental to emotional health and they doubt that distortions about oneself and others can have value for adaptive functions (Colvin & Block, 1994; Robins & John, 1996).

Yet, some psychologists suggest that positive illusions and self-deceptions, often based on denial or similar distortions of reality, can be constructive and adaptive. For example, it is suggested that positive illusions about one's self, about one's ability to control events, and about the future can be good, perhaps essential, for mental health (Taylor &

DENIAL: HEALTHY OR SICK? ADAPTIVE OR MALADAPTIVE?

Should we avoid self-deception? Is knowing all there is to know a sign of health? Psychoanalysts generally assume that although the mechanisms of defense are useful in reducing anxiety, they also are maladaptive in turning a person away from reality. For example, consider the potentially damaging effects of denial. A person who denies threatening signs may not be in a position to respond adaptively. Thus, women who discover a lump in thier breast and delay going to a doctor because of denial of the possible seriousness of the lump may seriously reduce the chances of surgical success. Or men who deny the symptoms of a heart attack and continue to exercise or climb stairs may turn out to have made a fatal mistake.

However, there is evidence that denial and self-deception can also be constructive and adaptive. For example, take the person who has had a severe, incapacitating illness such as polio or cancer. Denial and self-deception can provide temporary relief from the emotional trauma and help the person to avoid being overwhelmed by anxiety, depression, or anger. Defensive processes can then facilitate optimism, and thereby allow constructive participation in rehabilitative efforts. In this case, denial as a coping process can be adaptive. It can be good for your health!

What sense can one make out of this conflicting evidence? It has been suggested that denial generally is maladaptive where it interferes with action that might otherwise improve the person's condition. However, denial generally is adaptive where action is impossible or irrelevant and where excessive emotion may interfere with recuperative efforts. Should the doctor tell all to the patient? Evidently this depends not only on the above factors, but also on the patient's personality. Some people seek out information and function best when they are fully informed. Other people avoid information and function best when they know only what is essential. In other words, denial may or may not be adaptive, depending on the circumstances, and information may or may not be helpful, depending on the person's coping style.

SOURCE: Lazarus, 1983; Miller & Mangan, 1983; Robins & John, 1996; Taylor, 1989.

Denial: *How much information is useful to the patient?*

Brown, 1988, 1994). The answer to these differing views appears to depend on the extent of distortion, how pervasive it is, and the circumstances under which it occurs. For example, it may be helpful to have positive illusions about oneself as long as they are not too extreme. And, denial and self-deception may provide temporary relief from emotional trauma and help the person avoid becoming overwhelmed by anxiety or depression. Denial may be adaptive where action is impossible, as when a person is in a situation that cannot be altered (e.g., a fatal illness). On the other hand, denial certainly is maladaptive when it prevents one from taking constructive action, as when denial prevents one from taking signs of illness seriously and obtaining proper treatment.

Another way to deal with anxiety and threat is to isolate events in memory or to isolate emotion from the content of a memory or impulse. In **isolation**, the impulse, thought, or act is not denied access to consciousness, but it is denied the normal accompanying emotion. For example, a woman may experience the thought or fantasy of strangling her child without any associated feelings of anger. The result of using the mechanism of isolation is *intellectualization*, an emphasis on thought over emotion and feeling, and the development of logic-tight compartments. In such cases, the feelings that do exist may be split, as in the case where a male separates women into two categories, one with whom there is love but no sex and the other with whom there is sex but no love (madonna–whore complex).

People who use the mechanism of isolation also often use the mechanism of **undoing**. Here the individual magically undoes one act or wish with another. "It is a kind of negative magic in which the individual's second act abrogates or nullifies the first, in such a manner that it is as though neither had taken place, whereas in reality both have done so" (A. Freud, 1936, p. 33). This mechanism is seen in compulsions in which the person has an irresistible impulse to perform some act (e.g., the person undoes a suicide or homicide fantasy by compulsively turning off the gas jets at home), in religious rituals, and in children's sayings such as "Don't step on the crack or you will break your mother's back."

In **reaction formation**, the individual defends against expression of an unacceptable impulse by only recognizing and expressing its opposite. This defense is evident in socially desirable behavior that is rigid, exaggerated, and inappropriate. The person who uses reaction formation cannot admit to other feelings, such as overprotective mothers who cannot allow any conscious hostility toward their children. Reaction formation is most clearly observable when the defense breaks down, as when the model boy shoots his parents or when the man who "wouldn't hurt a fly" goes on a killing rampage. Of similar interest here are the occasional reports of judges who commit crimes.

A mechanism often familiar to students is **rationalization**. Here an action is perceived, but the underlying motive is not. Behavior is reinterpreted so that it appears reasonable and acceptable. Particularly inter-

esting is that with rationalization the individual can express the dangerous impulse, seemingly without disapproval by the superego. Some of
the greatest atrocities of humankind have been committed in the name
of love. Through the defense of rationalization, we can be hostile while
professing love, immoral in the pursuit of morality.

Finally, we come to the major primary defense mechanism, **repression**. In repression, a thought, idea, or wish is dismissed from consciousness. It is as if we say "What we don't know or remember can't hurt
us." Repression is viewed as playing a part in all the other defense mechanisms and, like these other defenses, requires a constant expenditure of
energy to keep that which is dangerous outside of consciousness. There
has been more experimental research on repression than on any other
defense mechanism and perhaps more than on any other single concept
in psychoanalytic theory. An early study in this area was that by
Rosenzweig (1941), who found that when a group of Harvard undergraduates were personally involved with the experiment, they recalled a
larger proportion of tasks that they had been able to complete than tasks
they had been unable to complete. When the students did not feel threatened, they remembered more of the uncompleted tasks.

More recently, women high in sex guilt and women low in sex guilt
were exposed to an erotic videotape and asked to report their level of sexual arousal. At the same time, their level of physiological response was
recorded. Women high in sex guilt were found to report less arousal than
those low in sex guilt but to show greater physiological arousal.
Presumably the guilt associated with sexual arousal led to repression or
blocking of awareness of the physiological arousal (Morokoff, 1985).

In another fascinating study of repression, subjects were asked to
think back to their childhood and recall any experience or situation that
came to mind. They also were asked to recall childhood experiences associated with each of five emotions (happiness, sadness, anger, fear, and
wonder) and to indicate the earliest experience recalled for each emotion. Subjects were divided into repressors and nonrepressors (high anxious and low anxious nonrepressors) on the basis of their response to
questionnaires. Did the subjects differ in recall, as would be suggested by
the psychoanalytic theory of repression? It was found that repressors
recalled fewer negative emotions and were significantly older at the time
of the earliest negative memory recalled (Figure 3.1). The authors concluded: "The pattern of findings is consistent with the hypothesis that
repression involves an inaccessibility to negative emotional memories
and indicates further that repression is associated in some way with the
suppression or inhibition of emotional experiences in general. The concept of repression as a process involving limited access to negative affective memories appears to be valid" (Davis & Schwartz, 1987, p. 155).

Further research along these lines supports the view that some individuals may be characterized as having a repressive style (Weinberger,
1990). Such individuals report little tendency to experience negative

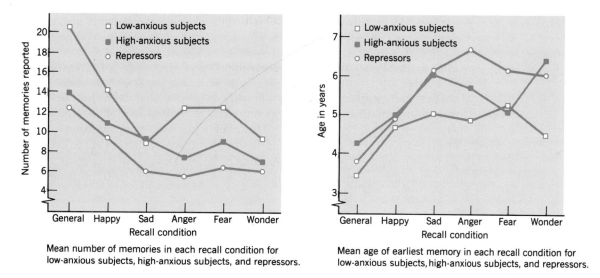

Mean number of memories in each recall condition for low-anxious subjects, high-anxious subjects, and repressors.

Mean age of earliest memory in each recall condition for low-anxious subjects, high-anxious subjects, and repressors.

Figure 3.1 *Repression and Affective Memories. (Davis & Schwartz, 1987) (Copyright © 1987 by the American Psychological Association. Reprinted by permission.)*

affect and have relatively stereotyped emotional responses. They have rather consistent self-images, report little inclination to change, and resist information that might produce such change. Although they are relatively calm, such calmness appears to be bought at a price. Thus, for example, they appear to be physiologically more reactive to stress than are nonrepressors and more prone to develop a variety of illnesses (Weinberger & Davidson, 1994). Reporting on related research, Schwartz indicated that the cheerfulness of repressors masks high blood pressure and high pulse rates, putting them at risk for illnesses such as heart disease and cancer (*APA Monitor*, July 1990, p. 14). This view fits with other evidence suggesting that a lack of emotional expressiveness is associated with increased risk of illness (Cox & MacKay, 1982; Levy, 1991; Temoshok, 1985, 1991).

In considering the status of the concept of repression, we return to issues considered in relation to the concept of the unconscious, which is not surprising since the two are linked so closely. In a plea not to sweep repression under the rug, Erdelyi and Goldberg (1979) have given an enlightening discussion of the problems in defining the concept and in demonstrating related phenomena in the laboratory. Their consideration begins with a quote from Dostoyevsky's *Notes from the Underground*:

Every man has reminiscences which he would not tell to everyone but only to his friends. He has other matters in his mind which he would not reveal even to his friend, but only to himself, and that in secret. But there are other things which a man is afraid to tell even to himself, and every decent man has a number of such things stored away in his mind.

They suggest that there is considerable research evidence that events or memories apparently hopelessly forgotten can be recovered. What is harder to demonstrate in the laboratory is the defensive function of repression, that is, the effort to keep ideas repressed from consciousness to minimize psychological pain. However, rather than arguing that a lack of experimental evidence should lead us to discard the concept, Erdelyi and Goldberg focus on the limitations of laboratory efforts to produce the complex phenomena. In a telling discussion of the results of clinical and

---

CURRENT QUESTIONS

RECOVERED MEMORIES OR FALSE MEMORIES?

Psychoanalysts suggest that through the defense of repression people bury memories of traumatic experiences of childhood in the unconscious. They also suggest that under some conditions, such as psychotherapy, individuals can recall their forgotten experiences. On the other hand, others question the accuracy of adult recall of childhood experiences. The issue has reached headline proportions as individuals report recalling experiences of childhood sexual abuse and initiate lawsuits against individuals now recalled to be the perpetrators of the abuse. Although some professionals are convinced of the authenticity of these memories of sexual abuse, and suggest that a disservice is done to the person when we do not treat them as real, others question their authenticity and refer to them as part of a "false memory syndrome." While some view the recovery of these memories as beneficial to those who previously repressed the trauma of abuse, others suggest that the "memories" are induced by the probing questions of therapists

convinced that such abuse has taken place.

An article in a professional psychological journal asks: "What scientific basis is there for the authenticity of memories of sexual abuse that were 'repressed' but then 'remembered' with the help of a therapist? How are scientists, jurists, and distressed individuals themselves to distinguish true memories from false ones?" Unfortunately, the answers to these questions are not clear-cut. On the one hand, we know that people can forget events that subsequently are remembered. On the other hand, we also know that people can "recall" events that never occurred. However, psychologists are divided on the status of the evidence concerning whether people can recover previously "repressed" memories. In addition, if such memories can be recovered, currently we have no means for distinguishing between "recovered memories" and "false memories."

SOURCES: American Psychological Society *Observer*, July 1992, p. 6; Loftus, 1993; *New York Times*, April 8, 1994, p. A1; Williams, 1994.

laboratory data, they suggest that "the two approaches have had palpably different yields. Such differences, we believe, reflect inherent differences in the two approaches, not some peculiar inconstancy of the phenomenon itself. The genius of the clinical approach is its ability to reveal truly complex cognitive processes.... From the clinical standpoint, the evidence for repression is overwhelming and obvious. The weakness of the clinical approach, on the other hand, is its looseness of method...the strength of the laboratory-experimental approach, unlike the clinical, is its methodological vigor; its overriding weakness is its inability to deal with truly complex processes" (Erdelyi & Goldberg, 1979, pp. 383–384).

In sum, whereas practicing psychoanalysts find the evidence in support of the concept of repression compelling, experimental researchers suggest that there is no controlled laboratory evidence supporting the concept of repression and perhaps it is time to give up the quest for such evidence (Holmes, 1990).

Before ending this discussion of the defenses, it is important to note one further device that is used to express an impulse free of anxiety. This mechanism, of considerable social importance, is **sublimation**. In sublimation, the original object of gratification is replaced by a higher cultural goal, one further removed from direct expression of the instinct. Whereas the other defense mechanisms meet the instincts head on and,

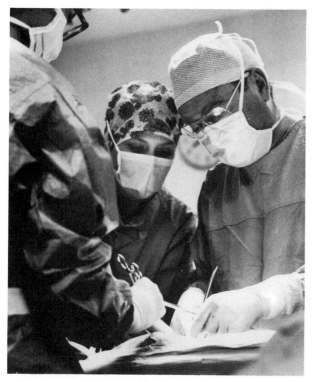

Sublimation: *In performing surgery, aggressive impulses can be turned toward useful, constructive ends.*

by and large, prevent discharge, in sublimation the instinct is turned into a new and useful channel. In contrast to the other defense mechanisms, here the ego does not have to maintain a constant energy output to prevent discharge. Freud interpreted DaVinci's *Madonna* as a sublimation of his longing for his mother. Becoming a surgeon, butcher, or boxer can represent sublimations, to a greater or lesser degree, of aggressive impulses. Being a psychiatrist can represent a sublimation of "peeping tom" tendencies. In all, as noted, Freud felt that the essence of civilization is contained in a person's ability to sublimate sexual and aggressive energies.

GROWTH AND DEVELOPMENT

The psychoanalytic theory of development takes into consideration all aspects of the development of character (personality). There are two major aspects to the theory of development. The first is that the individual progresses through stages of development. The second emphasizes the importance of early events for all later behavior. An extreme psychoanalytic position would go so far as to say that the most significant aspects of later personality have been formed by the end of the first five years of life.

The Development of Thinking Processes

The psychoanalytic theory of the development of thinking processes focuses on the change from **primary process** thinking to **secondary process** thinking. Primary process thinking is the language of the unconscious in which reality and fantasy are indistinguishable. Aspects of primary process thinking are seen in dreams. Here events occur in more than one place at the same time, characteristics of different people and objects are combined, events shift rapidly back and forth in time, and what in waking life is impossible occurs with ease. Secondary process thinking is the language of consciousness and reality testing. Parallel to this is the development of the ego and superego. With the development of the ego, the individual becomes more differentiated, as a self, from the rest of the world and there is a decrease in self-preoccupation.

Recently Epstein (1994) has made a related distinction in types of thinking, that between *experiential thinking* and *rational thinking*. These are viewed as two fundamentally different ways of knowing, one associated with feelings and experience and the other with intellect. Experiential thinking, analogous to primary process thinking, is viewed as earlier in evolutionary development and characterized by being holistic, concrete, and heavily influenced by emotion. Often it is used in interpersonal situations to be empathic or intuitive. Rational thinking, analogous to secondary process thinking, is viewed as later in evolutionary development and characterized by being more abstract, analytical, and following the rules of logic and evidence. For example, rational thinking would be used in solving mathematical problems. The potential conflict between the two systems of thought can be seen in an experiment in which subjects were asked to choose between drawing a winning red jelly bean from a bowl that contained one out of ten red jelly beans, and a bowl that contained eight out of one hundred red jelly beans (Denes-Raj & Epstein, 1994). Having been told the proportion of red jelly beans in the two bowls, subjects *knew* that the rational thing to do was to select the bowl with the higher proportion—one out of ten. Yet, despite this, many subjects *felt* that their chances were better with the bowl that contained more red jelly beans, despite the poorer odds. This conflict between what they *felt* and what they *knew* expressed the conflict between the experiential and rational thought systems. According to Epstein (1994), the two systems are parallel and can act in conjunction with one another as well as in conflict with one another. This is likely the case in most creative activities. Also, there are individual differences in the extent to which each system is developed and available for use in specific enterprises.

The Development of the Instincts

The most significant part of the psychoanalytic theory of development concerns the development of the instincts. The source of the instincts is states of bodily tension, which tend to focus on certain regions of the body, called **erogenous zones**. According to the theory, there is a biologically determined development of, and change in, the major erogenous zones of the body. At any one time the major source of excitation and energy tends to focus on a particular zone, with the location of that zone changing during the early developmental years. The first erogenous zone is the mouth, the second the anus, and the third the genitals. The mental and emotional growth of the child are dependent on the social interactions, anxieties, and gratifications that occur in relation to these zones.

Stages of Development   The first major area of excitation, sensitivity, and energy is the mouth. It is the locus of excitation that leads to the name **oral stage**. Early oral gratification occurs in feeding, thumb sucking, and other mouth movements characteristic of infants. In adult life, traces of orality are seen in chewing gum, eating, smoking, and kissing. In the early oral stage the child is passive and receptive. In the late oral stage, with the development of teeth, there can be a fusion of sexual and aggressive pleasures. In children, such a fusion of instinctual gratification is seen in the eating of animal crackers. In later life, we see traces of orality in various spheres. For example, academic pursuits can have oral associations within the unconscious—one is given "food for thought," asked to "incorporate" material in reading, and told to "regurgitate" what has been learned on exams.

In the second stage of development, the **anal stage** (ages two and three), there is excitation in the anus and in the movement of feces through the anal passageway. The expulsion of the feces is believed to bring relief from tension and pleasure in the stimulation of the mucous membranes in that region. The pleasure related to this erogenous zone involves the organism in conflict. There is conflict between elimination and retention, between the pleasure in release and the pleasure in retention, and between the wish for pleasure in evacuation and the demands of the external world for delay. This latter conflict represents the first crucial conflict between the individual and society. Here the environment requires the child to violate the pleasure principle or be punished. The child may retaliate against such demands by intentional soiling (diarrhea); associate having bowel movements with losing something important, which leads to depression; or associate having bowel movements with giving a prize or gift to others, which may be associated with feelings of power and control.

In the **phallic stage** (ages four and five), excitation and tension come to focus in the genitals. The biological differentiation between the sexes leads to psychological differentiation. The male child develops erections, and the new excitations in this area lead to increased interest in the genitals and the realization that the female lacks the penis. This leads to the fear that he may lose his penis—**castration anxiety**. The father becomes a rival for the affections of the mother, as suggested in the song "I Want a Girl Just Like the Girl That Married Dear Old Dad." The boy's hostility toward the father is projected onto the father, with the consequent fear of retaliation. This leads to what is known as the **Oedipus complex**. According to the Oedipus complex, every boy is fated to kill his father in fantasy and marry his mother. The complex can be heightened by actual seductiveness on the part of the mother. Castration anxiety can be heightened by actual threats from the father to cut off the penis. These threats occur in a surprising number of cases.

For an interesting illustration of an effort to test the concept of the Oedipus complex, we can return to the subliminal psychodynamic activation studies of the unconscious. As previously described, in this research stimuli are presented to subjects subliminally in a tachistoscope. When certain stimuli register subliminally, they presumably activate unconscious conflicts and either intensify or alleviate these conflicts, depending on the nature of the conflict and the stimulus presented. The point of the current experiment was to manipulate the degree of oedipal conflict in males and to observe the effects of their performance in a competitive situation (Silverman, Ross, Adler & Lustig, 1978). The stimuli chosen to intensify or alleviate oedipal conflict were "Beating Dad Is Wrong" and "Beating Dad Is OK." In addition, a number of other stimuli were presented, including the neutral stimulus "People Are Walking." These stimuli were presented tachistoscopically to male college students after they engaged in a dart-throwing competition. The subjects were tested again for dart-throwing performance following subliminal exposure to each of the stimuli. As expected, the two oedipal

Table 3.2 Oedipal Conflict and Competitive Performance

Dart Score	``Beating Dad Is Wrong"	``Beating Dad Is OK"	``People Are Walking"
TACHISTOSCOPIC PRESENTATION OF THREE STIMULI			
Mean, Prestimulus	443.7	444.3	439.0
Mean, Poststimulus	349.0	533.3	442.3
Difference	-94.7	+90.0	+3.3

Partial results adapted from Silverman et al., 1978, p. 346. Copyright by the American Psychological Association. Reprinted by permission.

stimuli had clear-cut effects in different directions. The "Beating Dad Is OK" stimulus was followed by significantly higher scores than those following the neutral stimulus, whereas the "Beating Dad Is Wrong" stimulus was followed by significantly lower scores than those following the neutral stimulus (Table 3.2).

What is interesting about this research is that whereas the theoretical formulation was derived from clinical material with patients, the experimental testing involved normal college males. The assumption of the experimenters was that "since most persons are vulnerable to some degree of neurotic behavior and since, according to psychoanalytic understanding, oedipal conflict often plays a central pathogenic role, we anticipated that the clinically based relationship might apply to a `normal' college population" (p. 342). Two additional points are worthy of note since there have been difficulties in replicating this type of research. First, the results were not obtained when the stimuli were presented above threshold. The psychodynamic activation effects appear to operate at the unconscious rather than at the conscious level. Second, the authors emphasize that the experimental stimuli must relate to the motivational state of the subjects and the response measured must be sensitive to changes in this motivational state. Thus, in the experiment above, subjects were first "primed" with picture and story material containing oedipal content and then the task was presented as one involving competition.

The developmental processes during this stage are somewhat different for the female. She realizes the lack of a penis and blames the mother, the original love object. In developing **penis envy**, the female child chooses the father as the love object and imagines that the lost organ will be restored by having a child by the father.[1] Whereas the Oedipus complex is abandoned in the boy because of castration anxiety, in the female it is started because of penis envy. As with the male, conflict during this

---

[1] Psychoanalytic theory has been criticized by feminists on a variety of grounds. Perhaps more than any other concept, the concept of penis envy is seen as expressing a chauvinistic, hostile view toward women. This issue will be addressed in Chapter 4 in the Critical Evaluation section.

period is in some cases accentuated by seductiveness on the part of the father toward the female child. And, as with the male, the female child resolves the conflict by keeping the father as a love object but gaining him through identification with the mother.

Do children actually display oedipal behaviors or are these all distorted memories of adults, in particular patients in psychoanalytic treatment? A study investigated this question through the use of parents' reports of parent–child interactions, as well as through the analysis of children's responses to stories involving parent–child interaction. It was found that at around age four, children show increased preference for the parent of the opposite sex and an increased antagonism toward the parent of the same sex. These behaviors diminish at around the age of five or six. What is interesting in this study is that although the researchers came from a differing theoretical orientation, they concluded that the reported oedipal behaviors coincided with the psychoanalytic view of oedipal relations between mothers and sons and between fathers and daughters (Watson & Getz, 1990).

As part of the resolution of the Oedipus complex, the child identifies with the parent of the same sex. The child now gains the parent of the opposite sex through **identification** with, rather than defeat of, the parent of the same sex. The development of an identification with the parent of the same sex is a critical issue during the phallic stage and, more generally, is a critical concept in developmental psychology. In identification, individuals take on themselves the qualities of another person and integrate them into their functioning. In identifying with their parents, children assume many of the same values and morals. It is in this sense that the superego has been called the heir to the resolution of the Oedipus complex.

Although Freud gave relatively little attention to developmental factors after the resolution of the Oedipus complex, he did recognize their existence. After the phallic stage, the child enters **latency**. The meaning of the latency stage has never been clear in psychoanalytic theory. An assumption of a decrease in sexual urges and interest during the ages of 6 through 13 might have fit observations of Victorian children, but it does not fit observations of children in other cultures. A more plausible assumption, and one more difficult to test, is that there are no new developments during this stage in terms of the ways in which children gratify their instincts.

The onset of puberty, with the reawakening of the sexual urges and oedipal feelings, marks the beginning of the **genital stage**. The significance of this period for individuals and for their functioning in society is demonstrated in the initiation rites of many cultures and in the Jewish bar mitzvah. Dependency feelings and oedipal strivings that were not fully resolved during the pregenital stages of development now come back to rear their ugly heads. The turmoil of adolescence is partly attributable to these factors.

Oedipus Complex, Competition, and Identification: *For the male child to become competitive, there must not be too much anxiety about rivalry with the father. Jim Burt, of the N.Y. Giants football team, carried his son around the field after winning the 1987 Super Bowl. He describes his son, Jim Jr., age 4 1/2, as "So much like me it's frightening. He's got the same fire in his eyes. And like when we wrestle together on the rug, he always wants to win."*

Erikson's Psychosocial Stages of Development   It is clear that in the psychoanalytic theory of development, major attention is given to the first five years and to the development of the instincts. Ego psychologists have tried, within this framework, to give greater attention to other developments during the early years and to significant developments that take place during the latency and genital stages. Erik Erikson (1902–1994), one of the leading ego psychoanalysts, describes development in psychosocial terms rather than merely in sexual terms (Table 3.3). Thus, the first stage is significant not just because of the localization of pleasure in the mouth, but because in the feeding situation a relationship of trust or mistrust is developed between the infant and the mother. Similarly, the anal stage is significant not only for the change in the nature of the major erogenous zone, but also because toilet training is a significant social situation in which the child may develop a sense of autonomy or succumb to shame and self-doubt. In the phallic stage the child must struggle with the issue of taking pleasure in, as opposed to feeling guilty about, being assertive, competitive, and successful.

For Erikson (1950), the latency and genital stages are periods when the individual develops a sense of industry and success or a sense of inferiority, and perhaps most important of all, a sense of identity or a sense of role diffusion. For him, the crucial task of adolescence is the establishment of a sense of ego identity, an accrued confidence that the way one views oneself has a continuity with one's past and is matched by the

Erik H. Erikson

perceptions of others. In contrast to people who develop a sense of identity, people with role diffusion experience the feeling of not really knowing who they are, of not knowing whether what they think they are matches what others think of them, and of not knowing how they have developed in this way or where they are heading in the future. During late adolescence and the college years, this struggle with a sense of identity may lead to joining a variety of groups and to considerable anguish about the choice of a career. If these issues are not resolved during this time, the individual is, in later life, filled with a sense of despair; life is too short, and it is too late to start all over again.

In his research on the process of identity formation, Marcia (1994) has identified four statuses individuals can have in relation to this process. In *Identity Achievement*, the individual has established a sense of identity following exploration. Such individuals function at a high psychological level, being capable of independent thought, intimacy in interpersonal relations, complex moral reasoning, and resistant to group demands for conformity or group manipulation of their sense of self-esteem. In *Identity Moratorium*, the individual is in the midst of an identity crisis. Such individuals are capable of high levels of psychological functioning, as indicated in complex thought and moral reasoning, and also value intimacy. However, they are still struggling with just who they are and what they are about, and are less prepared than the identity achievers to make commitments. In *Identity Foreclosure*, the individual is committed to an identity without having gone through a process of exploration. Such individuals tend to be rigid, highly responsive to group demands

Table 3.3 Erikson's Eight Psychosocial Stages of Development and Their Implications for Personality

Psychosocial Stage	Age	Positive Outcomes	Negative Outcomes
Basic Trust vs. Mistrust	1	Feelings of inner goodness, trust in oneself and others, optimism	Sense of badness, mistrust of self and others, pessimism
Autonomy vs. Shame and Doubt	2–3	Exercise of will, self-control, able to make choices	Rigid, excessive conscience, doubtful, self-conscious shame
Intitiative vs. Guilt	4–5	Pleasure in accomplishments, activity, direction and purpose	Guilt over goals contemplated and achievements initiated
Industry vs. Inferiority	Latency	Able to be absorbed in productive work, pride in completed product	Sense of inadequacy and inferiority, unable to complete work
Identity vs. Role Diffusion	Adolescence	Confidence of inner sameness and continuity, promise of a career	Ill at ease in roles, no set standards, sense of artificiality
Intimacy vs. Isolation	Early Adulthood	Mutuality, sharing of thoughts, work, feelings	Avoidance of intimacy, superficial relations
Generativity vs. Stagnation	Adulthood	Ability to lose oneself in work and relationships	Loss of interest in work, impoverished relations
Integrity vs. Despair	Later Years	Sense of order and meaning, content with self and one's accomplishments	Fear of death, bitter about life and what one got from it or what did not happen

for conformity and sensitive to manipulation of their self-esteem. They tend to be highly conventional and rejecting of deviation from perceived standards of right and wrong. Finally, in *Identity Diffusion*, the individual lacks any strong sense of identity or commitment. Such individuals are very vulnerable to blows to their self-esteem, often are disorganized in their thinking, and have problems with intimacy. In sum, Marcia suggests that individuals differ in how they go about handling the process of identity formation, with such differences being reflected in their sense of self, thought processes, and interpersonal relations. Although not necessarily establishing fixed patterns for later life, how the process of identity formation is handled is seen as having important implications for later personality development.

Continuing with his description of the later stages of life and the accompanying psychological issues, Erikson suggests that some people develop a sense of intimacy, an acceptance of life's successes and disappointments, and a sense of continuity throughout the life cycle, whereas other people remain isolated from family and friends, appear to survive on a fixed daily routine, and focus on both past disappointments and

Identity vs. Role Diffusion: *In adolescence, a sense of ego identity is developed partly by having one's sense of self confirmed by the perceptions of friends.*

future death. Although the ways in which people do and do not resolve these critical issues of adulthood may have their roots in childhood conflict, Erikson suggests that this is not always the case and that they have a significance of their own (Erikson, 1982). In sum, Erikson's contributions are noteworthy in three ways: (1) he has emphasized the psychosocial as well as the instinctual basis for personality development; (2) he has extended the stages of development to include the entire life cycle and has articulated the major psychological issues to be faced in these later stages; (3) he has recognized that people look to the future as well as to the past, and how they construe their future may be as significant a part of their personality as how they construe their past.

The Importance of Early Experience

Psychoanalytic theory emphasizes the importance of events early in life for later personality development. Others suggest a much greater potential for change across the entire life span. The issue is complex, the prevailing view changes from time to time, and no consensus has ever been reached (Caspi & Bem, 1990).

The complexities of the issue can be illustrated with two studies. The first, conducted by a psychoanalyst (Gaensbauer, 1982), involved the study of affect development in infancy. The infant, Jenny, was first studied systematically when she was almost four months old. Prior to this time, at the age of three months, she had been physically abused by her father. At that time she was brought to the hospital with a broken arm and a skull fracture. She was described by hospital personnel as being a "lovable baby"—happy, cute, sociable, but also as not cuddling when held and as being "jittery" when approached by a male. Following this history of abuse, she was placed in a foster home, where she received adequate physical care but minimal social interaction. This was very much in contrast with her earlier experience with her natural mother, who spent considerable time with her and breast-fed her "at the drop of a hat." The first systematic observation occurred almost a month after placement in the foster home. At this time her behavior was judged to be completely consistent with a diagnosis of depression—lethargic, apathetic, disinterested, collapsed posture. A systematic analysis of her facial expressions indicated five discrete affects, each meaningfully related to her unique history. Sadness was noted when she was with her natural mother. Fearfulness and anger were noted when she was approached by a male stranger but not when approached by a female stranger. Joy was noted as a transient affect during brief play sequences. Finally, interest–curiosity was noted when she interacted with female strangers.

After she was visited in her foster home, Jenny was placed in a different foster home where she received warm attention. Following two weeks in this environment, she was again brought to the hospital for further evaluation, this time by her second foster mother. This time she generally appeared to be a normally responsive infant. She showed no evidence of distress and even smiled at a male stranger. After an additional month at this foster home, she was brought to the hospital *by her natural mother* for a third evaluation. Generally, she was animated and happy. However, when the mother left the room, she cried intensely. This continued following the mother's return despite repeated attempts to soothe her. Apparently separation from her natural mother continued to lead to a serious distress response. In addition, sadness and anger were frequently noted. At eight months old, Jenny was returned to her natural mother, who left her husband and received counseling. At the age of 20 months, she was described as appearing to be normal and having an excellent relationship with her mother. However, there continued to be the problem of anger and distress associated with separation from her mother.

From these observations, we can conclude that there was evidence of both continuity and discontinuity between Jenny's early emotional experiences and her later emotional reactions. In general, she was doing well and her emotional responses were within the normal range for infants of her age. At the same time, the anger reactions in response to separations and frustration appeared to be a link to the past. The psychoanalyst conducting the study suggested that perhaps isolated traumatic events are less important than the repeated experiences of a less dramatic but more persistent nature. In other words, the early years are important, but more in terms of patterns of interpersonal relationships than in terms of isolated events.

The second study, conducted by a group of developmental psychologists, assessed the relationship between early emotional relationships with the mother and later psychopathology (Lewis, Feiring, McGuffog, & Jaskir, 1984). In this study, the attachment behavior toward their mother of boys and girls one year of age was observed. The observation involved a standardized procedure consisting of a period of play with the mother in an unstructured situation, followed by the departure of the mother and a period when the child was alone in the playroom, and then by the return of the mother and a second free play period. The behavior of the children was scored systematically and assigned to one of three attachment categories: avoidant, secure, or ambivalent. The avoidant and ambivalent categories suggested difficulties in this area. Then at six years of age, the competence of these children was assessed through the completion by the mothers of a Child Behavior Profile. The ratings of the mothers were also checked against teacher ratings. On the basis of the Child Behavior Profile the children were classified into a normal group, an at-risk group, and a clinically disturbed group.

What was the relationship between early attachment behavior and later pathology? Two aspects of the results are particularly noteworthy. First, the relationships were quite different for boys than for girls. For boys, attachment classification at one year of age was significantly related to later pathology. Insecurely attached boys showed more pathology at age six than did securely attached boys. On the other hand, no relationship between attachment and later pathology was observed for girls. Second, the authors noted a difference between trying to predict pathology from the early data (prospective) as opposed to trying to understand later pathology in terms of earlier attachment difficulties (retrospective). If one starts with the boys who at age six were identified as being at risk or clinically disturbed, 80 percent would be found to have been assigned to the avoidant- or ambivalent-attachment category at age one. In other words, a very strong statistical relationship exists. On the other hand, if one took all boys classified as insecurely attached (avoidant or ambivalent) at age one and predicted them to be at risk or clinically disturbed at age six, one would be right in only 40 percent of the cases. The reason for this is that far more of the boys were classified as insecurely attached than were later diagnosed as at risk or disturbed. Thus, the clinician viewing later pathology would have a clear basis for suggesting a strong relationship between pathology and early attachment difficulties. On the other hand, focusing on the data in terms of prediction would suggest a much more tenuous relationship and the importance of other variables. As Freud himself recognized, when we observe later pathology, it is all too easy to understand how it developed. On the other hand, when we look at these phenomena prospectively, we are made aware of the varied paths that development can follow.

As previously noted, the issues relevant to the importance of early experience for later personality development are complex. Perhaps we must seek a more differentiated approach to the question rather than a black-or-white answer. For example, the importance of early experience for later personality development might depend on the characteristic being studied. Perhaps some personality characteristics, once formed, are more resistant to change than are others. The role of early experience might also depend on the intensity of particular experiences, their duration, and the extent to which differing experiences occurred earlier and later. Thus, for example, the effects of maternal deprivation may depend on how serious and long-lasting the deprivation is, as well as on the role of positive experiences both before and following deprivation. Finally, we may note the distinction between what may occur and what must inevitably occur. Psychoanalytic theory can be accurate in portraying the *possible* effects of early experience, particularly as seen in various forms of psychological disturbance where a pattern of relationships is established early and maintained over time, without postulating that such effects are inevitable.

MAJOR CONCEPTS

Catharsis. The release and freeing of emotion through talking about one's problems.

Free association. In psychoanalysis, the patient's reporting to the analyst of every thought that comes to mind.

Energy system. Freud's view of personality as involving the interplay among various forces (e.g., drives, instincts) or sources of energy.

Pleasure principle. According to Freud, psychological functioning based on the pursuit of pleasure and the avoidance of pain.

Conscious. Those thoughts, experiences, and feelings of which we are aware.

Preconscious. Freud's concept for those thoughts, experiences, and feelings of which we are momentarily unaware but can readily bring into awareness.

Unconscious. Those thoughts, experiences, and feelings of which we are unaware. According to Freud, this unawareness is the result of repression.

Perception without awareness. Unconscious perception or perception of a stimulus without conscious awareness of such perception.

Perceptual defense. The process by which an individual defends (unconsciously) against awareness of a threatening stimulus.

Subliminal psychodynamic activation. The research procedure associated with psychoanalytic theory in which stimuli are presented below the perceptual threshold (subliminally) to stimulate unconscious wishes and fears.

Id. Freud's structural concept for the source of the instincts or all of the drive energy in people.

Ego. Freud's structural concept for the part of personality that attempts to satisfy drives (instincts) in accordance with reality and the person's moral values.

Superego. Freud's structural concept for the part of personality that expresses our ideals and moral values.

Reality principle. According to Freud, psychological functioning based on reality in which pleasure is delayed until an optimum time.

Sexual instincts. Freud's concept for those drives directed toward sexual gratification or pleasure.

Life instinct. Freud's concept for drives or sources of energy (libido) directed toward the preservation of life and sexual gratification.

Death instinct. Freud's concept for drives or sources of energy directed toward death or a return to an inorganic state.

Libido. The psychoanalytic term for the energy associated first with the life instincts and later with the sexual instincts.

Aggressive instincts. Freud's concept for those drives directed toward harm, injury, or destruction.

Anxiety. In psychoanalytic theory, a painful emotional experience that signals or alerts the ego to danger.

Defense mechanisms. Freud's concept for those devices used by the person to reduce anxiety. They result in the exclusion from awareness of some thought, wish, or feeling.

Projection. The defense mechanism in which one attributes to (projects onto) others one's own unacceptable instincts of wishes.

Denial. The defense mechanism in which a painful internal or external reality is denied.

Isolation. The defense mechanism in which emotion is isolated from the content of a painful impulse or memory.

Undoing. The defense mechanism in which one magically undoes an act or wish associated with anxiety.

Reaction formation. The defense mechanism in which the opposite of an unacceptable impulse is expressed.

Rationalization. The defense mechanism in which an acceptable reason is given for an unacceptable motive or act.

Repression. The primary defense mechanism in which a thought, idea, or wish is dismissed from consciousness.

Sublimation. The defense mechanism in which the original expression of the instinct is replaced by a higher cultural goal.

Primary process. In psychoanalytic theory, a form of thinking that is not governed by logic or reality testing and that is seen in dreams and other expressions of the unconscious.

Secondary process. In psychoanalytic theory, a form of thinking that is governed by reality and associated with the development of the ego.

Erogenous zones. According to Freud, those parts of the body that are the sources of tension or excitation.

Oral stage. Freud's concept for that period of life during which the major center of bodily excitation or tension is the mouth.

Anal stage. Freud's concept for that period of life during which the major center of bodily excitation or tension is the anus.

Phallic stage. Freud's concept for that period of life during which excitation or tension begins to be centered in the genitals and during which there is an attraction to the parent of the opposite sex.

Castration anxiety. Freud's concept of the boy's fear, experienced during the phallic stage, that the father will cut off the son's penis because of their sexual rivalry for the mother.

Oedipus complex. Freud's concept expressing the boy's sexual attraction to the mother and fear of castration by the father, who is seen as a rival.

Penis envy. In psychoanalytic theory, the female's envy of the male's possession of a penis.

Identification. The acquisition, as characteristics of the self, of personality characteristics perceived to be part of others (e.g., parents).

Latency stage. In psychoanalytic theory, the stage following the phallic stage in which there is a decrease in sexual urges and interest.

Genital stage. In psychoanalytic theory, the stage of development associated with the onset of puberty.

REVIEW

1. Psychoanalytic theory illustrates a psychodynamic, clinical approach to personality. The psychodynamic emphasis is expressed in the interpretation of behavior as a result of the interplay among motives or drives. The clinical approach is expressed in the emphasis on material observed during intensive treatment of individuals.

2. Events in Freud's life played a role in the development of his theory and influenced his approach toward science. Illustrative here are the emphasis on the death instincts in relation to World War I, his emphasis on sex in relation to inhibitions concerning sexuality found in Victorian society, and the energy model then popular in other branches of science.

3. Two sets of structural concepts are key to psychoanalytic theory. The first relates to levels of consciousness—conscious, preconscious, and unconscious. The second relates to different aspects of people's functioning as expressed in the concepts of id, ego, and superego, roughly corresponding to drives (instincts), an orientation toward reality, and morals.

4. Experimental research on the unconscious is illustrated by the study of perception without awareness and subliminal psychodynamic activation. Although there remains dispute concerning the importance of unconscious phenomena, almost all psychologists agree that we can be influenced by stimuli that are outside of conscious awareness.

5. In psychoanalytic theory the person is viewed as an energy system,

and the source of energy lies in the life and death instincts or the sexual and aggressive instincts.

6. Crucial to the dynamics of psychological functioning are the concepts of anxiety and the defense mechanisms. Anxiety is a painful emotion that acts as a signal of impending danger. The defense mechanisms represent ways of distorting reality and excluding feelings from awareness so that we do not feel anxious. Repression, in which a thought or wish is dismissed from consciousness, is particularly important in this regard.

7. According to psychoanalytic theory, the individual progresses through stages of development. The development of the instincts is related to changes in the sensitivity of different parts of the body (erogenous zones) and is expressed in the concepts of oral, anal, and phallic stages. The Oedipus complex, which develops during the phallic stage, is seen as a particularly important psychological development and has been the subject of considerable research.

8. Psychoanalyst Erik Erikson attempted to broaden and extend psychoanalytic theory through an emphasis on the psychosocial stages of development.

9. Psychoanalytic theory emphasizes the importance of early experience, particularly during the first five years of life, for later personality development. Research on the relationship between early experiences and later psychopathology illustrates an effort to study the importance of early experience for later personality development. The importance of early events probably is influenced by the intensity of these events and whether subsequent events further strengthen what has been formed or turn personality development in new directions.

4

A PSYCHODYNAMIC THEORY: APPLICATIONS AND EVALUATION OF FREUD'S THEORY

When you were a kid, did you ever play the cloud game? It had to be a day when there were big white fluffy clouds against the blue background of the sky. You would lie on your back in the grass with a friend and stare at the clouds until you "saw" something. If you tried long and hard enough you could find all kinds of interesting things—animals, dragons, the face of an old man. Quite often, pointing out your discoveries to your friend was impossible. Exactly what you saw could only be seen by you. Why did you see the things you saw? It must have been something about you that you "projected" onto the cloud in the sky.

This is the basic idea behind projective tests such as the Rorschach Inkblot Test and the Thematic Apperception Test (TAT). In this chapter, we focus on these tests because they are techniques of personality assessment associated with psychodynamic theory. Projective tests use ambiguous stimuli to elicit highly individualistic responses which can then be interpreted by the clinician. This chapter also considers Freud's attempts to understand and explain the symptoms presented by his patients and his efforts to develop a systematic method of treatment. After considering more recent developments in psychoanalytic theory, we turn to a critical evaluation and summary.

QUESTIONS TO BE ADDRESSED IN THIS CHAPTER

1. Which personality tests are best suited to assess an individual's personality from a psychoanalytic standpoint?

2. How can we understand the diverse forms of psychopathology from a psychoanalytic perspective?

3. How does psychoanalytic therapy attempt to facilitate psychological growth and improved psychological functioning?

4. Why did various early followers of Freud reject psychoanalysis in favor of an alternative theory?

5. How can we evaluate psychoanalysis as a theory of personality?

CLINICAL APPLICATIONS

Psychoanalysis is a clinical theory of personality, focusing on the intensive study of the person. Central to the theory is an emphasis on unconscious processes and the interplay among motives. A key theme in this book is that a theory of personality does not stand alone, but rather is tied to and reflects ways of observing people. In addition, to the extent that the theory is associated with an approach to psychotherapy or change, the theory and therapy will reflect some common basic assumptions. Let us consider, then, how basic psychoanalytic concepts are reflected in approaches to the assessment of people, as well as in the understanding and treatment of psychopathology.

ASSESSMENT: PROJECTIVE TESTS

Although many different personality tests can be used with psychoanalytic theory, **projective tests** are most closely linked to the theory. Projective tests involve the use of relatively ambiguous stimuli to which the subject is free to respond in a highly individualistic way and is unlikely to be aware of how the response will be interpreted by the examiner. The term *projection* in relation to assessment techniques was first used in 1938 by Henry A. Murray, but the importance of projective tests was first emphasized most clearly by L. K. Frank in 1939. Frank argued against the use of standardized tests, which he felt classified people but told little about them as individuals. He argued for the use of tests that would offer insight into individuals' private worlds of meanings and feelings. Such tests would allow individuals to impose their own structure and organization on stimuli and would thereby express a dynamic conception of personality.

In this section we consider two projective tests, the Rorschach Inkblot Test and the Thematic Apperception Test (TAT). Both are unstructured—meaning that they allow subjects to respond in their own unique ways. Both are also disguised tests, in that generally subjects are not aware of their purpose or of how particular responses will be interpreted. Psychoanalytic theory is related to projective tests as follows:

1. Psychoanalytic theory emphasizes individual differences and the complex organization of personality functioning. Personality is viewed as a process through which the individual organizes and structures external stimuli in the environment. Projective tests allow subjects to respond with complete freedom in terms of both content and organization.

2. Psychoanalytic theory emphasizes the importance of the unconscious and defense mechanisms. In projective tests, the directions and stimuli provide few guidelines for responding, and the purposes of the test and interpretations of responses are hidden from the subject.

3. Psychoanalytic theory emphasizes a holistic understanding of personality in terms of relationships among parts, rather than the interpretation of behavior as expressive of single parts or personality characteristics. Projective tests generally lead to holistic

interpretations based on the patterning and organization of test responses rather than on the interpretation of a single response reflecting a particular characteristic.

Having considered some general relationships between psychoanalytic theory and projective tests, let us consider two of them in some detail.

The Rorschach Inkblot Test

The Rorschach Inkblot Test was developed by Hermann Rorschach, a Swiss psychiatrist. Although inkblots had been used earlier, Rorschach was the first to grasp fully the potential use of subjects' responses for personality assessment. Rorschach put ink on paper and folded the paper so that symmetrical but ill-defined forms were produced. These inkblots were then shown to hospitalized patients. Through a process of trial and error, the inkblots that elicited different responses from different psychiatric groups were kept, while those that did not were discarded. Rorschach experimented with thousands of inkblots and finally settled on 10.

Rorschach was well acquainted with the work of Freud, the concept of the unconscious, and the dynamic view of personality. The development of his test certainly seems to have been influenced by this view. Rorschach felt that the data from the inkblot test would increase understanding of the unconscious and have relevance for psychoanalytic theo-

Hermann Rorschach

ry. He used psychoanalytic theory in his own interpretations of subjects' responses.

The Rorschach test consists of 10 cards containing inkblots. When showing the cards, the experimenter tries to make the subjects relaxed and comfortable while providing them with sufficient information to complete the task. Thus, the test is presented as "just one of many ways used nowadays to try to understand people," and the experimenter volunteers as little information as possible—"It is best not to know much about the procedure until you have gone through it." Subjects are asked to look at each card and tell the examiner what they see—anything that might be represented on the card. Individuals are free to select what they will see, where they will see it, and what determines their perceptions. All responses are recorded on the test record.

In interpreting the Rorschach, one is interested in how the response, or percept, is formed, the reasons for the response, and its content. The basic assumption is that the way individuals form their perceptions is related to the way they generally organize and structure stimuli in their environments. Perceptions that match the structure of the inkblot suggest a good level of psychological functioning that is well oriented toward reality. On the other hand, poorly formed responses that do not fit the

Rorschach Inkblot Test— *The Rorschach interpreter assumes that the subject's personality is projected onto unstructured stimuli such as inkblots. Drawing by Ross; © 1974 The New Yorker Magazine, Inc.*

structure of the inkblot suggest unrealistic fantasies or bizarre behavior. The content of subjects' responses (whether they see mostly animate or inanimate objects, humans or animals, and content expressing affection or hostility) makes a great deal of difference in the interpretation of the subjects' personalities. For example, compare the interpretations we might make of two sets of responses, one where animals are seen repeatedly as fighting and a second where humans are seen as sharing and involved in cooperative efforts.

Beyond this, content may be interpreted symbolically. An explosion may symbolize intense hostility; a pig, gluttonous tendencies; a fox, a tendency toward being crafty and aggressive; spiders, witches, and octopuses, negative images of a dominating mother; gorillas and giants, negative attitudes toward a dominating father; and an ostrich, an attempt to hide from conflicts (Schafer, 1954). Two illustrative stimuli and responses are presented in Figure 4.1.

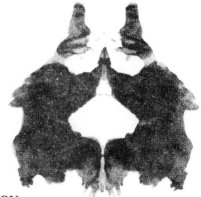

Response: *"Two bears with their paws touching one another playing pattycake or could be they are fighting and the red is the blood from the fighting."*

**ILLUSTRATION
NO. 1**

Response: *"Two cannibals. Supposed to see something in this? African natives bending over a pot. Possibly cooking something—hope they're not man-eaters. I shouldn't make jokes—always liking humor. (Are they male or female?) Could be male or female. More female because of breasts here. But didn't impress me at first glance as being of either sex."*

**ILLUSTRATION
NO. 2**

Figure 4.1 Examples from the Rorschach Inkblot Test. *The inkblot illustrations reproduced here are from the Rorschach location chart. The actual inkblot cards contain color. (Reprinted by permission of Hans Huber, Publishers.)*

It is important to recognize that the Rorschach is not interpreted on the basis of one response alone, but in relation to the total sum of responses. However, each response is used to suggest hypotheses or possible interpretations about the individual's personality. Such hypotheses are checked against interpretations based on other responses, on the total response pattern, and on the subject's behavior while responding to the Rorschach. In relation to the last, the examiner notes all unusual behavior and uses this as a source of data for further interpretation. For example, a subject who constantly asks for guidance may be interpreted as dependent. A subject who seems tense, asks questions in a subtle way, and looks at the back of the cards may be interpreted as suspicious and possibly paranoid.

The Thematic Apperception Test (TAT)

Probably the most widely used projective test is the Thematic Apperception Test (TAT), developed by Henry Murray and Christina Morgan. The TAT consists of cards with scenes on them. Most of the cards depict one or two people in some important life situation, though some cards are more abstract. The subject is asked to make up a story based on the scene on the card, including what is going on, the thoughts and feelings of the participants, what led up to the scene, and the outcome. Since the scenes often are ambiguous, they leave considerable

Henry Murray

Sample Card from the Thematic Apperception Test.

Illustration 1   *This is the picture of a woman who all of her life has been a very suspicious, conniving person. She's looking in the mirror and she sees reflected behind her an image of what she will be as an old woman—still a suspicious, conniving sort of person. She can't stand the thought that that's what her life will eventually lead her to and she smashes the mirror and runs out of the house screaming and goes out of her mind and lives in an institution for the rest of her life.*

Illustration 2   *This woman has always emphasized beauty in her life. As a little girl she was praised for being pretty and as a young woman was able to attract lots of men with her beauty. While secretly feeling anxious and unworthy much of the time, her outer beauty helped to disguise these feelings from the world and, sometimes, from herself. Now that she is getting on in years and her children are leaving home, she is worried about the future. She looks in the mirror and imagines herself as an old hag—the worst possible person she could become, ugly and nasty—and wonders what the future holds for her. It is a difficult and depressing time for her.*

Figure 4.2   *Illustrative TAT Card and Responses to It*

room for individuality in the content of subjects' stories: "The test is based on the well-recognized fact that when a person interprets an ambiguous social situation he is apt to expose his own personality as much as the phenomenon to which he is attending" (Murray, 1938, p. 530).

Some TAT cards are shown to both male and female subjects; others are shown to members of one sex only. An illustrative card and responses given to it by two different individuals are shown in Figure 4.2. The card, given to female subjects, is described by Murray as "The portrait of a young woman. A weird old woman with a shawl over her head is grimacing in the background." Common themes given in response to this card are stories of disappointment with a parent, of parental pressure, and of sad thoughts about the past. In addition, some women appear to see the younger woman as having a vision of her evil self or of herself in old age (Holt, 1978).

The thinking behind the TAT clearly shows its relation to the psychodynamic view. According to Murray (1938), the TAT is used to discover unconscious and inhibited tendencies. The assumption is that subjects are not aware they are talking about themselves and thus their defenses can be bypassed: "If the procedure had merely exposed conscious fantasies and remembered events it would have been useful enough, but it did more than this. It gave the experimenter excellent clues for the divination of unconscious thematic formations!" (p. 534).

TAT responses of subjects can be scored systematically according to a scheme developed by Murray, or on a more impressionistic basis. The test is used both in clinical work and in experimental studies of human motivation. The TAT assumes a close relationship between the expressed fantasy (story about the TAT card) and underlying motivation, as well as a relationship between such fantasy and behavior. Efforts to test these assumptions have met with mixed results. Fantasy can be associated with the expression of motives in behavior and can also substitute for the expression of motives in behavior. Thus, for example, a person with a strong motive to be aggressive with others may express this motive in both fantasy (TAT) and behavior, but the person may also express it in fantasy and block it from expression in overt behavior.

Illustrative Research Use and Evaluation

Projective tests have been used in many types of research, both in relation to psychoanalytic theory and apart from it. A study of comedians, clowns, and actors illustrates the use of projective tests and the psychodynamic approach (Fisher & Fisher, 1981). The study attempted to understand the origins, motivations, and personalities of those who make people laugh as opposed to those who entertain through acting. Professional clowns, comedians, and actors were interviewed and given projective tests such as the Rorschach and TAT.

What can such research contribute to our understanding of comedians and clowns? First, they were found to be funny early in life, particularly in school, despite little support from their parents for their comic endeavors. Second, a number of motivations seemed to contribute to their decision to be comedians. Among the motivations suggested by the data are the following:

1. **Power**. The ability to control an audience and make people laugh.
2. **Preoccupation with good–evil and positive presentation of self**. "We would propose that a major motive of comedians in conjuring up funniness is to prove that they are not bad or repugnant. They are obsessed with defending their basic goodness" (p. 69).

Comedians and Clowns—*Research using psychoanalytic theory and projective techniques suggests that comedians and clowns often are sensitive about a part of their body. Here, in a scene from* Young Frankenstein, *the bulging eyes of the comedian Marty Feldman are highlighted.*

3. **Concealment and Denial**. Humor is used to escape from difficulty and as a screen to hide behind when feeling embarrassed or inferior.

4. **Anarchy**. Comedians belittle accepted norms, leave nothing sacred, and make everything laughable.

Let us consider illustrative Rorschach evidence for two of these motivations. First is the concern with good–bad or virtue–evil. A scoring system was devised to consider how frequently such themes appeared in the Rorschach records. Illustrative responses were those referring directly to good and bad (e.g., bad person, virtuous look), those referring to religious matters (e.g., church, angel, devil, heaven, purgatory), and those referring to persons often linked with good–bad (e.g., police officer, criminal, judge, sinner). The Rorschach records of 35 comedians and clowns were found to have significantly more such good–bad references than did the records of 35 actors who were not comedians. Second is the concern with concealment and denial. Many of the Rorschach responses seemed to express denial that things are as bad or threatening as they seem. For example, consider the following responses: "Faces. Evil looking....The evil not very evil. A put on." "Mephisto...charming character." "Tiger. Lovable tiger." "Monster....He's nice." "Wolfman....He's misunderstood....People are afraid. If you walk up and talk to him, he's a decent thing." "Two devils. Funny devils. Not to be taken seriously." In analyzing the Rorschach records of comics, it was found that they contained significantly more of these "not bad" images than did the records of actors. In addition, the records of comics were found to have significantly more concealment themes (e.g., hiding, mask, disguise, magic, tricks) than did the records of actors.

One final theme noted in this study related to the tendency for comedians and clowns to be sensitive about some part of their body or their sense of self generally. Think, for example, of Jimmy Durante's jokes about his nose. Or consider the film comic Marty Feldman, whose trademark was his bulging eyes. He was quoted as follows in relation to his appearance: "The sum total of the disasters of my life. If I aspired to be Robert Redford, I'd have my eyes straightened and my nose fixed and end up like every other lousy actor, with two lines on Kojak. But this way, I'm a novelty" (*The New York Times*, December 4, 1982). In sum, comedy is seen by comedians as a way of helping themselves deal with some sense of inferiority.

A review of this study allows us to consider briefly the strengths and limitations of such studies and projective tests. The Rorschach, as well as projectives generally, is a marvelous instrument for glimpsing individual fantasy and the complexity of organization of individual perception. However, the difficulties in substantiating theoretical hypotheses or in establishing the reliability and validity of the test itself are enormous. Those who use projective techniques emphasize that only these tests can capture the richness of personality. Ambiguous stimuli elicit individual, idiosyncratic responses. Through these responses, individuals express their personalities. The Rorschach is seen as being the psychologist's microscope or X ray, able to penetrate to the depths of the individual's personality. The data from other tests are seen as trivial and fragmented by comparison. On the other hand, such efforts to give a multidimensional picture of the total personality create problems in empirical investigation. Thus, it is difficult to establish the reliability and validity of the Rorschach, or of other projective tests.

Once more we are involved with the tension between the richness of psychodynamic, clinical data and the scientific requirements of systematic investigation. This tension will remain with us as we now consider the psychoanalytic interpretation of psychopathology and personality change.

PSYCHOPATHOLOGY

Frequently it is difficult to appreciate psychoanalytic theory without first understanding the nature of the often strange and puzzling behaviors that were brought to Freud's attention. Freud spent most of his professional time working with patients with neurotic disorders. In fact, the most critical elements in his theory are based on the observations that came from this work. In the course of these investigations, Freud decided that the psychological processes of his patients were not peculiar to those with neurotic disturbances, but could be found to one degree or another, and in one form or another, in all people. Thus, though originally based on observations with patients, his theory is a general theory of personality functioning rather than only a theory of abnormal behavior.

Personality Types

As noted, Freud thought that the first five years of life were critical in the individual's development. During these years, it is possible for a number of failures to occur in the development of the instincts. Such failures in the development are called **fixations**. If individuals receive so little gratification during a stage of development that they are afraid to go to the next stage, or if they receive so much gratification that there is no motivation to move on, a fixation will occur. If a fixation occurs, the individual will try to obtain the same type of satisfaction that was appropriate for an earlier stage of development during later stages. For example, the individual partially fixated at the oral stage may continue to seek oral gratification in eating, smoking, or drinking. A developmental phenomenon related to that of fixation is **regression**. In regression, the individual seeks to return to an earlier mode of satisfaction, an earlier point of fixation. Regression often occurs under conditions of stress, so that many people overeat, smoke, or drink too much alcohol only during periods of frustration and anxiety.

The Oral Personality   The concepts of the stages of development, fixation, and regression are of tremendous importance to the psychoanalytic theory of development. One of its most fascinating aspects is the way in which personality characteristics are developed in early life and maintained thereafter. For each of the early stages of development, there is a corresponding character type that is developed because of partial fixations at that stage (Table 4.1). The characteristics of the **oral personality**, for example, relate to processes going on during the oral stage of development that the individual maintains in later life. Oral personalities are narcissistic in that they are only interested in themselves and do not have a clear recognition of others as separate entities. Other people are seen only in terms of what they can give (feed). Oral personalities are always asking for something, either in terms of a modest, pleading request or an aggressive demand.

The Anal Personality   The **anal personality** stems from the anal stage of development. In contrast to gratification associated with the mouth and oral activity, which can be expressed in adulthood in a relatively unrepressed form, the gratifications of anal impulses must undergo considerable transformation. In general, the traits of the anal character are related to processes going on at the anal stage of development that have

Table 4.1   Personality Characteristics Associated with Psychoanalytic Personality Types

Personality Type	Personality Characteristics
Oral	Demanding, impatient, envious, covetous, jealous, rageful, depressed (feels empty), mistrustful, pessimistic
Anal	Rigid, striving for power and control, concerned with shoulds and oughts, pleasure and possessions, anxiety over waste and loss of control, concern with whether to submit or rebel
Phallic	*Male:* exhibitionistic, competitive, striving for success, emphasis on being masculine—macho—potent *Female:* naive, seductive, exhibitionistic, flirtatious

not been completely relinquished. The important processes are the bodily processes (accumulation and release of fecal material) and interpersonal relations (the struggle of wills over toilet training). Tying the two together, the anal person sees excretion as symbolic of enormous power. That such a view persists is shown in many everyday expressions such as the reference to the toilet as "the throne." The change from the oral to the anal character is one from "give me" to "do what I tell you," or from "I have to give you" to "I must obey you."

The anal character is known by a triad of traits, called the *anal triad*: orderliness and cleanliness, parsimony and stinginess, and obstinacy. The emphasis on cleanliness is expressed in the saying "Cleanliness is next to godliness." The anal-compulsive personality has a need to keep everything clean and in order, representing a reaction formation against an interest in things that are disorderly and unclean. The second trait of the triad, parsimony–stinginess, relates to the anal-compulsive's interest in holding on to things, an interest dating back to a wish to retain the powerful and important feces. The third trait in the triad, obstinacy, relates to the anal character's infantile defiance against parting with stools, particularly on command by others. Dating back to toilet training and the struggle of wills, anal personalities often seek to be in control of things and have power or dominance over others.

The Phallic Character   Just as the oral and anal character types reflect partial fixations at the first two stages of development, the **phallic character** represents the result of a partial fixation at the stage of the Oedipus complex. Fixation here has different implications for men and women, and particular attention has been given to the results of partial fixation for males. Whereas success for the oral person means "I get," and success for the anal person means "I control," success for the phallic male means "I am a man." The phallic male must deny all possible suggestions that he has been castrated. For him success means that he is "big" in the eyes of others. He must at all times assert his masculinity and potency, an attitude exemplified by Theodore Roosevelt's saying, "Speak softly but carry a big stick." The excessive, exhibitionistic quality to the behavior of these people is expressive of the underlying anxiety concerning castration.

The female counterpart of the male phallic character is known as the *hysterical personality*. As a defense against oedipal wishes, the little girl identifies to an excessive extent with her mother and femininity. She uses seductive and flirtatious behavior to maintain the interest of her father but denies its sexual intent. The pattern of behavior then is carried over into adulthood, where she may attract men with flirtatious behavior but deny sexual intent and generally appear to be somewhat naive. Hysterical women idealize life, their partners, and romantic love, often finding themselves surprised by life's uglier moments.

Conflict and Defense

According to Freud, all psychopathology relates to an effort to gratify instincts that have been fixated at an earlier stage of development. Thus, in psychopathology the individual still seeks sexual and aggressive gratification in infantile forms. However, because of its association with past trauma, expression of this wish may signal danger to the ego and lead to the experience of anxiety. As a result, there is a conflict situation in which the same behaviors are associated with both pleasure and pain. For example, a person may seek to be dependent on others but fear that if this is done he or she will be vulnerable to frustration and loss (pain). Another example is a wish to indulge in sexual behavior that is blocked by feelings of guilt and fear of punishment or injury. A third example is the conflict between a wish to retaliate against powerful others—representing the parents—and a fear that these figures will themselves retaliate with force and destruction. In each case there is a conflict between a wish and anxiety. In such a situation the result is often that the individual can't "say no," can't be assertive, or otherwise feels blocked and unhappy (Table 4.2).

As noted in the preceding discussion, a critical part of the conflict is anxiety. To reduce the painful experience of anxiety, defense mechanisms, as outlined in Chapter 3, are brought into play. Thus, for example, the person may deny his or her aggressive feelings or project them onto others. In either case, the person no longer has to be afraid of the aggressive feelings. In sum, in psychopathology there is a conflict between a drive or wish (instinct) and the ego's sense (anxiety) that danger will ensue if the wish is expressed (discharged). To guard against this and to ward off anxiety, defense mechanisms are used. In structural terms, a neurosis is a result of conflict between the id and the ego. In process terms, an instinct striving for discharge triggers anxiety, leading to a defense mechanism.

In many cases the conflict between the id and ego, between instinct and defense, leads to the development of a **symptom**. A symptom, such

Table 4.2   Psychoanalytic Theory of Psychopathology

Illustrative Conflicts		Behavior Consequences of Defense Mechanisms
WISH	ANXIETY	DEFENSE
I would like to have sex with that person.	Such feelings are bad and will be punished.	Denial of all sexual behavior, obsessive preoccupation with the sexual behavior of others.
I would like to strike out at all those people who make me feel inferior.	If I am hostile they will retaliate and really hurt me.	Denial of wish or fear: "I never feel angry," "I'm never afraid of anyone or anything."
I would like to get close to people and have them feed me or take care of me.	If I do they will smother me or leave me.	Excessive independence and avoidance of getting close to people or fluctuations between approaching people and moving away from them; excessive need to take care of others.

as a tic, psychological paralysis, or compulsion, represents a disguised expression of a repressed impulse. The meaning of the symptom, the nature of the dangerous instinct, and the nature of the defense all remain unconscious. For example, a mother may be painfully obsessed with the fear that something will happen to her child. Underlying the obsession may be rage at her child and anxiety about the harm she may do to the child. The symptom of the obsession expresses both the mother's feelings that she may harm or injure the child and her defense against it in terms of excessive preoccupation with the child's welfare. To take another example, in a hand-washing compulsion—in which a person feels compelled to wash his or her hands continuously—the symptom may express both the wish to be dirty or do "dirty" things and the defense against the wish in terms of excessive cleanliness. In both of these cases the person is unaware of the wish or the defense and is troubled only by the symptom. Many people do not suffer from such specific problems or symptoms, but analysts suggest that all psychological problems can still be understood in these terms.

To summarize the psychoanalytic theory of psychopathology, there is an arrest in the development of the person that is associated with conflicts between wishes and fears. The wishes and fears that were part of a specific time period in childhood are now carried over into adolescence and adulthood. The person attempts to handle the anxiety that is a painful part of this conflict by using defense mechanisms. However, if the conflict becomes too great, the use of defense mechanisms can lead to neurotic symptoms or psychotic withdrawal from reality. Symptoms express the

EMOTIONAL SUPPRESSION AND HEALTH

More than 50 years ago, psychoanalysts suggested a relation between personality dynamics and health, in particular a relation between specific conflicts and specific somatic difficulties. In developing the area of psychosomatic medicine, each disorder was thought to result from a specific emotional constellation. For example, peptic ulcers , described as the "Wall Street stomach," were thought to result from an unconscious craving for love and dependence, which was defended against by an active, productive, agressive lifestyle. Hypertension was thought to be associated with individuals who were gentle in outward manner but boiling with rage inside.

This line of psychology fell into disfavor because the relation between psycho-logical factors and bodily illness seemed more complex than was originally suggested. Although different in form, currently there is a return to interest in some of these early psychoanalytic views. In particular, there is evidence that the continued suppression of emotion can be detrimental to one's health. For example, it may play a negative role in the course of cancer, ulcers, and heart disease. Alternatively, the expression, or nonsuppression, of emotion may represent an active, adaptive style of coping that reduces the risk of illness and bodes well for the course of an illness.

SOURCES: Jensen, 1987; Levy, 1984; Pennebaker, 1985, 1990; Temoshok, 1985, 1991.

I happen to believe a nasty disposition is good for your health.

(Copyright© 1985 American Psychological Association. Reprinted by permission from Psychology Today.*)*

unconscious conflict between the wish or drive and anxiety. In each case of abnormal behavior there is an unconscious conflict between a wish and a fear that dates back to an earlier period in childhood. So as adults there continue to be childlike parts of us that—under stress and some other conditions—may become more active and troublesome.

BEHAVIOR CHANGE

How does behavior change come about? Once a person has established a behavioral pattern, a way of thinking about and responding to situations, through what process does a change in personality take place? The psychoanalytic theory of growth suggests that there is a normal course of human personality development, one that occurs because of an optimum degree of frustration. Where there has been too little or too much frustration at a particular stage of growth, personality does not develop normally and a fixation takes place. When this occurs, the individual repeats patterns of behavior regardless of other changes in situations. Given the development of such a neurotic pattern, how is it possible to break the cycle and move forward?

Insights Into the Unconscious: Free Association and Dream Interpretation

In his early efforts to change behavior, Freud used a method called *cathartic hypnosis*. The view then held was that neurotic symptoms would be relieved by the discharge of blocked emotions. Freud did not like using hypnosis—since not all patients could be hypnotized, the results were often transient, and he did not feel that he was learning much about mental functioning. The second development in technique was that of waking suggestion. Here Freud put his hand on the patient's head and assured the patient that he or she could recall and face repressed past emotional experiences. With the increased interest in the interpretation of dreams, Freud focused on the *free association* method as basic to psychoanalysis. In free association the patient is asked to report to the analyst every thought that comes to mind, to delay reporting nothing, to withhold nothing, to bar nothing from coming to consciousness.

Dreams are the "royal road" to the unconscious. Through the free association method the analyst and patient are able to go beyond the manifest (obvious) content of the dream to the latent content, to the hidden meaning that expresses the unconscious wish. Dreams, like symptoms, are disguises and partial wish fulfillments. In the dream, the person can satisfy a hostile or sexual wish in a disguised and thereby safe way. For example, rather than dreaming of killing someone, one may dream of a battle in which a particular figure is killed. In such a case the wish may remain at least somewhat obvious, but in other cases the wish may be much more disguised. Free association allows the disguise to be uncovered.

At first, Freud thought that making the unconscious conscious was sufficient to effect change and cure. This was in keeping with an early emphasis on repressed memories as the basis for pathology. Freud then realized that more than the recovery of memories was involved. Rather, emotional insight into the wishes and conflicts that had remained hidden was necessary.

The process of therapeutic change in psychoanalysis involves coming to grips with emotions and wishes that were previously unconscious and struggling with these painful experiences in a relatively safe environment. If psychopathology involves fixation at an early stage of development, then in psychoanalysis individuals become free to resume their normal psychological development. If psychopathology involves damming up the instincts and using energy for defensive purposes, then psychoanalysis involves a redistribution of energy so that more energy is available for mature, guiltless, less rigid, and more gratifying activities. If psychopathology involves conflict and defense mechanisms, then psychoanalysis involves reducing conflict and freeing the patient from the limitations of the defensive processes. If psychopathology involves an individual dominated by the unconscious and the tyranny of the id, then psychoanalysis involves making conscious what was unconscious and putting under control of the ego what was formerly under the domination of the id or superego.

The Therapeutic Process: Transference

In sum, then, psychoanalysis is viewed as a learning process in which the individual resumes and completes the growth process that was interrupted when the neurosis began. The principle involved is the reexposure of a patient, under more favorable circumstances, to the emotional situations that could not be handled in the past. Such reexposure is affected by the transference relationship and the development of a transference neurosis. The term **transference** refers to a patient's development of attitudes toward the analyst based on attitudes held by that patient toward earlier parental figures. In the sense that transference relates to distortions of reality based on past experiences, transference occurs in everyone's daily life and in all forms of psychotherapy. For example, there is research evidence that individuals have mental images associated with emotion that are based on early interpersonal relationships. These emotionally laden mental representations influence the ways in which we view and respond to other individuals. Often this occurs in an automatic, unconscious way (Andersen & Baum, 1994; Andersen, Glassman, Chen, & Cole, 1995).

In expressing transference attitudes toward the analyst, patients duplicate in therapy their interactions with people in their lives and their past interactions with significant figures. For example, if patients feel that the analyst's taking notes may lead to exploitation by the analyst, they are expressing attitudes they hold toward people they meet in their daily

Freud's consulting room.

existence and earlier figures in their lives. In free associating, oral characters may be concerned about whether they are "feeding" the analyst and whether the analyst gives them enough in return; anal characters may be concerned about who is controlling the sessions; phallic characters may be concerned about who will win in competitive struggles. Such attitudes, often part of the unconscious daily existence of the patient, come to light in the course of analysis.

Although transference is a part of all relationships and of all forms of therapy, psychoanalysis is distinctive in using it as a dynamic force in behavior change. Many formal qualities of the analytic situation are structured to enhance the development of transference. The patient lying on the couch supports the development of a dependent relationship. The scheduling of frequent meetings (up to five or six times a week) strengthens the emotional importance of the analytic relationship to the patient's daily existence. Finally, the fact that patients become so tied to their analysts, while knowing so little about them as people, means that their responses are almost completely determined by their neurotic conflicts. The analyst remains a mirror or blank screen on which the individual projects wishes and anxieties.

Encouraging transference, or providing the circumstances that allow it to develop, leads to the development of the transference neurosis. It is here that patients play out—full-blown—their old conflicts. Patients now invest the major aspects of their relationship with the analyst with the wishes and anxieties of the past. The goal is no longer to get well, but to gain from the analyst what they had to do without in childhood. Rather than seeking a way out of competitive relationships, they may only seek to castrate the analyst; rather than seek to become less dependent on others, they may seek to have the analyst gratify all their dependency needs. The fact that these attitudes have developed within the analysis allows patients and their analysts to look at and understand the instinctual and defensive components of the original infantile conflict. Because the patient invests considerable emotion in the situation, the increased understanding is emotionally meaningful. Change occurs when insight has been gained, when patients realize, on both an intellectual and an emotional level, the nature of their conflicts and feel free, in terms of their new perceptions of themselves and the world, to gratify their instincts in a mature, conflict-free way.

Whereas guilt and anxiety prevented growth in the past, the analytic situation allows the individual to deal anew with the old conflicts. Why should the response be any different at this time? Basically, change occurs in analysis because of the three therapeutic factors. First, in analysis the conflict is less intense than it was in the original situation. Second, the analyst assumes an attitude that is different from that of the parents. Finally, patients in analysis are older and more mature, that is, they are able to use parts of their ego that have developed to deal with the parts of their functioning that have not developed. These three factors, creating as they do the opportunity for relearning, provide the basis for what Alexander and French (1946) call the "corrective emotional experience." Psychoanalytic theory suggests that through insight into old conflicts, through an understanding of the needs for infantile gratifications and recognition of the potential for mature gratification, and through an understanding of old anxieties and a recognition of their lack of relevance to current realities, patients may progress toward maximum instinctual gratification within the limits set by reality and their own moral convictions.

A Case Example: Little Hans

Although many psychiatrists and psychologists have spent considerable time treating patients, Freud is one of the very few who have reported cases in detail. Most of Freud's cases come from early in his career. Although these case presentations are useful in understanding many aspects of psychoanalytic theory, it is important to remember that they occurred prior to Freud's development of his theory of the sexual and aggressive instincts, prior to the development of the structural model, and prior to the development of the theory of anxiety and defense mechanisms.

Description of the Problem

The case of Little Hans, published in 1909, deals with the analysis of a phobia in a five-year-old boy. It involves the treatment of the boy by his father and does not represent Freud's direct participation in the therapeutic process. The boy was bothered by a fear that a horse would bite him, and therefore refused to leave the house. The boy's father kept detailed notes on his treatment and frequently discussed his progress with Freud. Although the "patient" was not treated by Freud, the case of Little Hans is important because it illustrates the theory of infantile sexuality, the functioning of the Oedipus complex and castration anxiety, the dynamics of symptom formation, and the process of behavior change.

Events Leading Up to Development of the Phobia

Our account of events in the life of Little Hans begins at age three. At this point he had a lively interest in his penis, which he called his "widdler." What was striking about Hans during this period was his pleasure in touching his own penis and his preoccupation with penises or widdlers in others. For example, he wanted to know if his mother had a widdler and was fascinated with the process by which cows are milked. The interest in touching his penis, however, led to threats by his mother. "If you do that, I shall send you to Dr. A. to cut off your widdler. And then what will you widdle with?" Thus, there was a direct castration threat on the part of a parent, in this case the mother. Freud pinpointed this as the beginning of Hans' castration complex.

Hans' interest in widdlers extended to noting the size of the lion's widdler at the zoo and analyzing the differences between animate and inanimate objects—dogs and horses have widdlers, tables and chairs do not. Hans was curious about many things, but Freud related his general thirst for knowledge to sexual curiosity. Hans continued to be interested in whether his mother had a widdler. "I thought you

(mother) were so big you'd have a widdler like a horse." When he was three and a half, a sister was born, who also became a focus for his widdler concerns. "But her widdler's still quite small. When she grows up, it'll get bigger all right." According to Freud, Hans could not admit what he really saw, namely, that there was no widdler there. To do so would mean that he would have to face his own castration anxieties. These anxieties occurred at a time when he was experiencing pleasure in the organ, as witnessed in his comments to his mother while she dried and powdered him after his bath.

HANS: Why don't you put your finger there?

MOTHER: Because that'd be piggish.

HANS: What's that? Piggish? Why? (*laughing*) But it's great fun.

Thus Hans, now more than four years old, was preoccupied with his penis, experienced pleasure in it and concern about the loss of it, and began some seduction of his mother. It was at this point that his nervous disorders became apparent. The father, attributing the difficulties to sexual overexcitation due to his mother's tenderness, wrote Freud that Hans was "afraid that a horse will bite him in the street" and that this fear seemed somehow to be connected with his having been frightened by seeing a large penis. As you remember, he had noticed at a very early age what large penises horses have, and at that time he inferred that, as his mother was so large, she must "have a widdler like a horse." Hans was afraid of going into the street and was depressed in the evenings. He had bad dreams and was frequently taken into his mother's bed. While walking in the street with his nurse, he became extremely frightened and sought to return home to be with his mother. The fear that a horse would bite him became a fear that the horse would come into his room. He had developed a full-blown phobia, an irrational dread or fear of an object. What more can we learn about this phobia? How are we to account for its development? As Freud notes, we must do more than simply call this a small boy's foolish fears.

Interpretation of the Symptom

The father attempted to deal with his son's fear of horses by offering him an interpretation. Hans was told that the fear of horses was nonsense, that the truth was that he (Hans) was fond of his mother and that the fear of horses had to do with an interest in their widdlers. On Freud's suggestion, the father explained to Hans that women do not have widdlers. Apparently this provided some relief, but Hans continued to be bothered by an obsessive wish to look at horses, though he was then frightened by them. At this point, his tonsils were taken out and his phobia worsened. He was afraid that a white horse would bite him. He continued to be interested in widdlers in females. At the zoo, he was afraid of all the large animals and was entertained by the smaller ones. Among the birds, he was afraid of the pelican. In spite of his father's truthful explanation, Hans sought to reassure himself. "And everyone has a widdler. And my widdler will get bigger as I get bigger, because it does grow on me." According to Freud, Hans had been making comparisons among the sizes of widdlers and was dissatisfied with his own. Big animals reminded him of this defect and were disagreeable to him. The father's explanation heightened his castration anxiety, as expressed in the words "it does grow on me," as if it could be cut off. For this rea-

son he resisted the information, and thus it had no therapeutic results. "Could it be that living beings really did exist which did not possess widdlers? If so, it would no longer be so incredible that they could take his own widdler away, and, as it were, make him into a woman."

At around this time, Hans reported the following dream. "In the night there was a big giraffe in the room and a crumpled one; and the big one called out because I took the crumpled one away from it. Then it stopped calling out; and then I sat down on top of the crumpled one." The father's interpretation was that he, the father, was the big giraffe, with the big penis, and the mother was the crumpled giraffe, missing the genital organ. The dream was a reproduction of a morning scene in which the mother took Hans into bed with her. The father warned her against this practice ("The big one called out because I'd taken the crumpled one away from it"), but the mother continued to encourage it. The mother encouraged and reinforced the oedipal wishes. Hans stayed with her and, in the wish fulfillment of the dream, he took possession of her ("Then the big giraffe stopped calling out; and then I sat down on top of the crumpled one").

Freud's strategy in understanding Hans' phobia was to suspend judgment and to give his impartial attention to everything there was to observe. He learned that prior to the development of the phobia, Hans had been alone with his mother at a summer place. There, two significant events occurred. First, he heard the father of one of his friends tell her that a white horse there bit people and that she was not to hold her finger up to its mouth. Second, while pretending to be horses, a friend who rivaled Hans for the affection of the little girls fell down, hit his foot, and bled. In an interview with Hans, Freud learned that Hans was bothered by the blinders on horses and the black band around their mouths. The phobia became extended to include a fear that horses dragging a heavy van would fall down and kick their feet. It was then discovered that the exciting cause of his phobia—the event that capitalized on a psychological readiness for the formation of a phobia—was that Hans had witnessed a horse falling down. While walking outside with his mother one day, Hans had seen a horse pulling a van fall down and begin to kick its feet.

The central feature in this case was the phobia about the horse. What is fascinating in this regard is how often associations concerning a horse came up in relation to the father, the mother, and Hans himself. We have already noticed Hans' interest in his mother's widdler in relation to that of a horse. To his father, he said at one point: "Daddy, don't trot away from me." Could the father, who wore a mustache and eyeglasses, be the horse that Hans was afraid of, the horse that would come into his room at night and bite him? Or could Hans himself be the horse? Hans was known to play horse in his room, to trot about, fall down, kick about with his feet, and neigh. He repeatedly ran up to his father and bit him, just as he feared the horse would do to him. Hans was overfed. Could this relate to his concerns about large, fat horses? Finally, Hans was known to have called himself a young horse and to have a tendency to stamp his feet on the ground when angry, similar to what the horse did when it fell down. To return to the mother, could the heavily laden carts symbolize the pregnant mother and the horse falling down the birth or delivery of a child? Are such associations coincidental or can they play a significant role in our understanding of the phobia?

According to Freud, the major cause of Hans' phobia was his Oedipus conflict.

Hans felt considerable affection for his mother, more than he could handle during the phallic stage of his development. Although he had deep affection for his father he also considered him a rival for his mother's affections. When he and his mother stayed at the summer cottage and his father was away, he was able to get into bed with his mother and keep her for himself. This heightened his attraction for his mother and his hostility toward his father. For Freud, "Hans was really a little Oedipus who wanted to have his father `out of the way,' to get rid of him, so that he might be alone with his handsome mother and sleep with her. This wish had originated during his summer holidays, when the alternating presence and absence of his father had drawn Hans' attention to the condition upon which depended the intimacy with his mother which he longed for." The fall and injury to his friend and rival during one of those holidays was significant in symbolizing the defeat for Hans of his rival.

The Solution to the Oedipal Conflict

When he returned home from the summer holidays, Hans' resentment toward his father increased. He tried to suppress the resentment with exaggerated affection. He arrived at an ingenious solution to the oedipal conflict. He and his mother would be parents to children and the father could be the granddaddy. Thus, as Freud notes, "The little Oedipus had found a happier solution than that prescribed by destiny. Instead of putting his father out of the way, he had granted him the same happiness that he desired himself: he made him a grandfather and let him too marry his own mother." But such a fantasy could not be a satisfactory solution, and Hans was left with considerable hostility toward his father. The exciting cause of the phobia was the horse falling down. At that moment, Hans perceived a wish that his father might similarly fall down and die. The hostility toward his father was projected onto the father and was symbolized in the horse, because he himself nourished jealous and hostile wishes against him. He feared the horse would bite him because of his wish that his father would fall down, and fears that the horse would come into his room occurred at night when he was most tempted by oedipal fantasies. In his own play as a horse and in his biting of his father, he expressed an identification with his father. The phobia expressed the wish and the anxiety and, in a secondary way, accomplished the objective of leaving Hans home to be with his mother.

In sum, both his fear that a horse would bite him and his fear that horses would fall down represented the father who was going to punish Hans for the evil wishes he was harboring against him. Hans was able to get over the phobia and, according to a later report by Freud, he appeared to be functioning well. What factors allowed the change? First, there was the sexual enlightenment by the father. Although Hans was reluctant to accept this and it at first heightened his castration anxiety, it did serve as a useful piece of reality to hold onto. Second, the analysis provided by his father and by Freud was useful in making conscious for Hans what had formerly been unconscious. Finally, the father's interest in and permissive attitude toward Hans' expression of his feelings allowed a resolution of the Oedipus conflict in favor of an identification with the father, diminishing both the wish to rival the father and the castration anxiety, and thereby decreasing the potential for symptom development.

Overall Evaluation

The case of Little Hans has many problems as a piece of scientific investigation. The interviewing was done by the father in an unsystematic way. The father himself was a close adherent of Freud's and therefore was possibly biased somewhat in his observations and interpretations. Freud himself was dependent on secondhand reports. He was aware of the limitations of the data, but he was also impressed with them. Whereas before he had based his theory on the childhood memories of adult patients, now, in the case of Little Hans, he began to observe the sexual life of children.

It is hard to draw conclusions about the theory in terms of this one case. The presentation does not contain all of Freud's observations on Hans. Furthermore, it is but a single case, and it is taken from an early point (1909) in Freud's work. On the other hand, we do get an appreciation of the wealth of information available to the analyst and, moreover, of the problems inherent in evaluating and interpreting such data. We must necessarily get a feeling for Freud's ability to observe and describe phenomena and his efforts to come to terms with the complexity of human behavior. In this one case alone we have descriptions of phenomena relevant to the following: infantile sexuality, fantasies of children, functioning of the unconscious, the process of conflict development and conflict resolution, the process of symptom formation, symbolization, and the dream process. In reading such a case, we cannot fail to be impressed by Freud's courageous efforts to discover the secrets of human functioning and by his willingness to do the job that needed to be done, in spite of limitations in his observations and in full recognition of the complexity of the phenomena he was trying to understand.

Rorschach and TAT: Psychoanalytic Theory

The Rorschach Inkblot Test and the TAT, both projective, were administered to Jim by a professional clinical psychologist. On the Rorschach, Jim gave relatively few responses—22 in all. This is surprising in view of other evidence of his intelligence and creative potential. It may be interesting to follow his responses to the first two cards and to consider the interpretations formulated by the psychologist, who also is a practicing psychoanalyst.

CARD 1

JIM: The first thing that comes to mind is a butterfly.

INTERPRETATION: Initially cautious and acts conventionally in a novel situation.

JIM: This reminds me of a frog. Not a whole frog, like a frog's eyes. Really just reminds me of a frog.

INTERPRETATION: He becomes more circumspect, almost picky, and yet tends to overgeneralize while feeling inadequate about it.

JIM: Could be a bat. More spooky than the butterfly because there is no color. Dark and ominous.

INTERPRETATION: Phobic, worried, depressed, and pessimistic.

CARD 2

JIM: Could be two headless people with their arms touching. Looks like they are wearing heavy dresses. Could be one touching her hand against a mirror. If they're women, their figures are not good. Look heavy.

INTERPRETATION: Alert to people. Concern or confusion about sexual role. Anal-compulsive features. Disparaging of women and hostile to them— headless and figures not good. Narcissism expressed in mirror image.

JIM: This looks like two faces facing each other. Masks, profiles—more masks than faces—not full, more of a façade, like one with a smile and one with a frown.

INTERPRETATION: He presents a façade, can smile or frown, but doesn't feel genuine. Despite façade of poise, feels tense with people. Repeated several times that he was not imaginative. Is he worried about his productivity and importance?

A number of interesting responses occurred on other cards. On the third card Jim perceived women trying to lift weights. Here again was a suggestion of conflict about his sexual role and about a passive—as opposed to an active—orientation. On the following card he commented that "somehow they all have an Alfred Hitchcock look of spooky animals," again suggesting a possible phobic quality to his behavior and a tendency to project dangers into the environment. His occasional references to symmetry and details suggested the use of compulsive defenses and intellectualization while experiencing threat. Disturbed and conflicted references to women come up in a number of places. On Card 7, he perceived two women from mythology who would be good if they were mythological but bad if they were fat. On the next to last card he perceived "some sort of a Count, Count Dracula. Eyes, ears, cape. Ready to grab, suck blood. Ready to go out and strangle some woman." The reference to sucking blood suggested tendencies toward oral sadism, something that also appeared in another percept of vampires that suck blood. Jim followed the percept of Count Dracula with one of pink cotton candy. The tester interpreted this response as suggesting a yearning for nurturance and contact behind the oral sadism; that is, the subject uses oral aggressive tendencies (e.g., sarcasm, verbal attacks) to defend against more passive oral wishes (e.g., to be fed, to be taken care of, and to be dependent).

The examiner concluded that the Rorschach suggested a neurotic structure in which intellectualization, compulsivity, and hysterical operations (irrational fears, preoccupation with his body) are used to defend against anxiety. However, it was suggested that Jim continues to feel anxious and uncomfortable with others, particularly authority figures. The report from the Rorschach concluded: "He is conflicted about his sexual role. While he yearns for nurturance and contact from the motherly female, he feels very guilty about the cravings and his intense hostility toward women. He assumes a passive orientation, a continual role playing and, behind a façade of tact, he continues his rage, sorrow, and ambition."

What kinds of stories did Jim tell on the TAT? Most striking about these stories were the sadness and hostility involved in all interpersonal relationships. In one story a boy is dominated by his mother, in another an insensitive gangster is capable of gross inhumanity, and in a third a husband is upset to learn that his wife is not a virgin. In particular, the relationships between men and women constantly involve one putting down the other. Consider this story.

Looks like two older people. The woman is sincere, sensitive, and dependent on the man. There is something about the man's expression that bespeaks of insensitivity —the way he looks at her, as if he conquered her. There is not the same compassion and security in her presence that she feels in his. In the end, the woman gets very hurt and is left to fend for herself. Normally I would think that they were married but in this case I don't because two older people who are married would be happy with one another.

In this story we have a man being sadistic to a woman. We also see the use of the defensive mechanism of denial in Jim's suggestion that these two people cannot be married since older married people are always happy with one another. In the story that followed the aforementioned one, there is again the theme of hostile mistreatment of a woman. In this story there is a more open expression of the sexual theme, along with evidence of some sexual role confusion.

This picture brings up a gross thought. I think of Candy. The same guy who took advantage of Candy. He's praying over her. Not the last rites, but he has convinced her that he is some powerful person and she's looking for him to bestow his good graces upon her. His knee is on the bed, he's unsuccessful, she's naive. He goes to bed with her for mystical purposes. [Blushes] She goes on being naive and continues to be susceptible to that kind of thing. She has a very, very sweet compassionate look. Could it possibly be that this is supposed to be a guy wearing a tie? I'll stick with the former.

The psychologist interpreting these stories observed that Jim appeared to be immature, naive, and characterized by a gross denial of all that is unpleasant or dirty, the latter for him including both sexuality and marital strife. The report continued: "He is vacillating between expressing sadistic urges and experiencing a sense of victimization. Probably he combines both, often in indirect expressions of hostility while feeling unjustly treated or accused. He is confused about what meaningful relationships two people can have. He is ambivalently idealistic and pessimistic about his own chances for a stable relationship. Since he sees sex as dirty and as a mode for using or being used by his partner, he fears involvement. At the same time he craves attention, needs to be recognized, and is often preoccupied with sexual urges."

Between the Rorschach and the TAT, a number of important themes emerge. One theme involves a general lack of warmth in interpersonal relationships, in particular a disparaging—and at times sadistic—orientation toward women. In relation to women, Jim has a conflict between sexual preoccupation and the feeling that sex is dirty and involves hostility. The second theme involves experiencing tension and anxiety behind a façade of poise. A third theme involves conflict and confusion about his sexual identity. Although there is evidence of intelligence and creative potential, there also is evidence of rigidity and inhibition in relation to the unstructured nature of the projective tests. Compulsive defenses, intellectualization, and denial are only partially successful in helping him deal with his anxieties.

Comments on the Data

What can be said about the data from the projective tests, particularly since these tests relate to psychoanalytic theory? The unstructured quality of these tests led to many personal responses that relate to unique aspects of Jim's personality. Furthermore, the disguised quality of the tests allows us to penetrate the façade of his personality (in psychoanalytic terms, his defenses) to view his underlying needs, motives, or drives. We have a test that allows for considerable uniqueness of response and a theory of personality that is clinical in its emphasis on the individual. We have a test that disguises its true purpose and a theory of personality that is dynamic in its emphasis on behavior as a result of the interplay among forces, drives, conflicts, and layers of personality.

The picture of Jim given in the Rorschach and the TAT is quite different from that presented in the autobiography. In his autobiography Jim indicated that he received unlimited affection from his parents and was quite popular and successful through high school. At the same time, he wrote that people had a high opinion of him because they could use only superficial criteria and that inwardly he was troubled. We thus have support for the interpretation in the Rorschach that he hides his tension and anxiety behind a façade of poise. There also is evidence in his autobiography of a conflicted relationship with women.

> My relationships with women were somewhat better in high school than they are now, but they weren't really satisfying then either. I was operating in a small subculture then, and I was very respected by everyone, so that probably made me more popular than I would have been otherwise. I have never had a really long-term, intimate relationship with a girl and I think those are the only kind that are meaningful. I had a number of superficial relationships, but there was always a barrier set up against my really becoming involved, and that barrier has been reinforced and made stronger over the last four years. Once a girl starts liking me a great deal I start lik-

ing her less—this has obvious implications about my lack of feelings of self-worth. It's a vicious and self-defeating circle: I like a girl only until she starts to like me. Thus in high school I was much sought after, but I managed to remain safely uninvolved.

Jim's Response to the Projective Tests

Jim did not like the Rorschach. He felt that he had to see something and that whatever he perceived would be interpreted as evidence that he was neurotic. He suggested that he didn't feel defensive about his troubles since he was willing to accept having them, but he didn't want them overstated. When he read some of the comments made by the psychologist, he observed that he himself believed that there was a sexual problem and that this would be the major issue if he went into therapy. Jim said that he had fears about ejaculating too quickly, his potency, and his ability to satisfy a female. It is interesting that the fear of losing control, or premature ejaculation, occurs in an individual who uses compulsive defenses and who strives to be in complete control of most situations.

Projective Tests and Psychoanalytic Theory

What can be said about the relationship between the projective data and psychoanalytic theory? Clearly the data from the Rorschach and the TAT are important because of the theoretical interpretations given to the responses, in particular the use of psychoanalytic symbolism. However, aside from this, it is difficult to determine how other theories of personality could make as much use of the data as psychoanalytic theory can. As we shall see, the data from the projectives are qualitatively different from those found in the other tests. It is only on the Rorschach that we obtain content such as "women trying to lift weights," "Count Dracula...ready to grab, suck blood. Ready to go out and strangle some woman," and "pink cotton candy." And only on the TAT are there repeated references to themes of sadness and hostility in interpersonal relationships. It is the content of the responses and the way in which the tests are handled that allow for the psychodynamic interpretations.

Obviously, Jim is not a Count Dracula and there is little overtly to suggest that he is a sadist. But the content of the projectives allows for the interpretation that an important part of his personality functioning involves a defense against sadistic urges. Obviously Jim does not still drink out of a milk bottle, but the references to sucking blood and to cotton candy, together with the rest of his responses, allow for the interpretation that he is partially fixated at the oral stage. In relation to this, it is interesting to observe that Jim has an ulcer, which involves the digestive tract, and that he must drink milk to manage this condition.

Perhaps the point here is that if you let people's imaginations wander, you will be led to the world of the irrational. Freud not only allowed this, but indeed encouraged it. He encouraged his patients to dream, to fantasize, to associate freely. Encouraged to do so, Freud's patients reported feelings and memories that they were previously unaware of. Similarly, in Jim's Rorschach and TAT we have content and themes that seem out of character with the rest of his responses to other personality tests. Having access to these feelings and memories, Freud was able to draw certain relationships between them and the problems that first brought his patients to treatment. Similarly, in Jim's case, we can guess that it is his sexual confusion and latent hostility that make him feel anxious or insecure and prevent him from becoming involved with women. Finding himself making discoveries in the world of the irrational and basing his theory on observations with patients, Freud was led to overemphasize the importance of the unconscious and to overemphasize the pathological in individuals. Similarly, Jim's performance on the projectives gives little indication of the skills, talents, and resources he has used to make some significant achievements.

RELATED POINTS OF VIEW AND RECENT DEVELOPMENTS

The history of psychoanalytic theory includes the development of schools or groups with different, often antagonistic, points of view. Freud changed many aspects of psychoanalytic theory during the course of his professional career. However, he and his followers clashed on many issues. To a certain extent there was what has been described as a religious or political quality (Fromm, 1959) to psychoanalysis, with the traditional followers being considered among the faithful and those who deviated from the fundamental principles being cast out from the movement. This pattern started during Freud's life and continued afterward. A theorist such as Erik Erikson is still highly regarded by most traditional psychoanalysts, whereas the theorists considered below often are not. Frequently it is hard to determine the basis for the response to one or another theorist. However, as a general rule, a theorist must retain a commitment to the following concepts to be considered a part of Freudian psychoanalysis: the sexual and aggressive instincts, the unconscious, and the stages of development. As we shall see, the theorists considered questioned one or another of these concepts and thereby approached the understanding of humans somewhat differently.

TWO EARLY CHALLENGES TO FREUD

Among the many early analysts who broke with Freud and developed their own schools of thought were Alfred Adler and Carl G. Jung. Both were early and important followers of Freud, Adler having been president of the Vienna Psychoanalytic Society and Jung president of the International Psychoanalytic Society. Both split with Freud over what they felt was an excessive emphasis on the sexual instincts. The split with Jung was particularly painful for Freud since Jung was to be his "crown prince" and chosen successor. While other individuals also split with Freud and developed their own schools of thought, Adler and Jung were among the earliest, and remain the best known.

Alfred Adler (1870–1937)

For approximately a decade, Alfred Adler was an active member of the Vienna Psychoanalytic Society. However, in 1911, when he presented his views to the other members of this group, the response was so hostile that he left it to form his own school of *Individual Psychology*. What ideas could have been considered so unacceptable to psychoanalysts? We cannot consider all of Adler's theory, but we can consider some of his early and later views to get a feeling for the important differences between those views and psychoanalysis.

Perhaps most significant in Adler's split from Freud was his greater emphasis on social urges and conscious thoughts than on instinctual sexual urges and unconscious processes. Early in his career Adler became interested in organ inferiorities and how people compensate for them. A person with a weak organ may attempt to compensate for this weakness

Alfred Adler

by making special efforts to strengthen that organ or to develop other organs. For example, someone who stutters as a child may attempt to become a great speaker, or someone with a defect in vision may attempt to develop special listening sensitivities. Whereas initially Adler was interested in bodily organ weaknesses, gradually he became interested in psychological *feelings of inferiority* and *compensatory strivings* to mask or reduce these painful feelings. Thus, whereas Freudians might see Theodore Roosevelt's emphasis on toughness and carrying a "big stick" as a defense against castration anxiety, Adlerians might see him as expressing compensatory strivings against feelings of inferiority associated with boyhood weaknesses. Whereas Freudians might see an extremely aggressive woman as expressing penis envy, Adlerians might see her as expressing a *masculine protest* or rejection of the stereotyped feminine role of weakness and inferiority. According to Adler, how a person attempts to cope with such feelings becomes a part of his or her *style of life*—a distinctive aspect of his or her personality functioning.

These concepts already suggest a much more social rather than biological emphasis. This social emphasis increasingly became an important part of Adler's thinking. At first Adler spoke of a *will to power* as an expression of the person's efforts to cope with feelings of helplessness dating from infancy. This emphasis gradually shifted to an emphasis on *striving for superiority*. In its neurotic form this striving could be

Birth Order: *Alfred Adler emphasized the importance of birth order in personality development. Twenty-one of the first 23 American astronauts were first-born or only sons.*

expressed in wishes for power and control over others; in its healthier form it could be expressed as a "great upward drive" toward unity and perfection. In the healthy person the striving for superiority is expressed in social feeling and cooperation as well as in assertiveness and competition. From the beginning people have a *social interest*, that is, an innate interest in relating to people and an innate potential for cooperation.

Adler's theory is also noteworthy for its emphasis on how people respond to feelings about the self, how people respond to goals that direct their behavior toward the future, and how the order of birth among siblings can influence their psychological development. In relation to the last, many psychologists have noted the tendency for only sons or first-born sons to achieve more than later sons in a family. For example, 21 of the first 23 American astronauts were first-born or only sons. Although many of Adler's ideas have found their way into the general public's thinking and are related to views later expressed by other theorists, Adler's school of individual psychology itself has not had a major impact on personality theory and research.

Carl G. Jung (1875–1961)

Jung split with Freud in 1914—a few years after Adler—and developed his own school of thought called *Analytical Psychology*. Like Adler, he was distressed with what he felt was an excessive emphasis on sexuality. Instead, Jung viewed the libido as a generalized life energy. Although sexuality is a part of this basic energy, the libido also includes other strivings for pleasure and creativity.

Carl Jung

Jung accepted Freud's emphasis on the unconscious but added to it the concept of the *collective unconscious*. According to Jung, people have stored within their collective unconscious the cumulative experiences of past generations. The collective unconscious, as opposed to the personal unconscious, is shared by all humans as a result of their common ancestry. It is a part of our animal heritage, our link with millions of years of past experience: "This psychic life is the mind of our ancient ancestors, the way in which they thought and felt, the way in which they conceived of life and the world, of gods and human beings. The existence of these historical layers is presumably the source of belief in reincarnation and in memories of past lives" (Jung, 1939, p. 24).

An important part of the collective unconscious are universal images or symbols, known as *archetypes*. Archetypes, such as the Mother archetype, are seen in fairy tales, dreams, myths, and some psychotic thoughts. Jung was struck with similar images that keep appearing, in slightly different forms, in far-distant cultures. For example, the Mother archetype might be expressed in a variety of positive or negative forms: as life giver, as all-giving and nurturant, as the witch or threatening punisher ("Don't fool with Mother Nature"), and as the seductive female. Archetypes may be represented in our images of persons, demons, animals, natural forces, or objects. The evidence in all cases for their being a part of our collective unconscious is their universality among members of different cultures from past and current time periods.

Another important aspect of Jung's theory was his emphasis on how people struggle with opposing forces within them. For example, there is the struggle between the face or mask we present to others (*persona*) and the private or personal self. If people emphasize the persona too much, there may be a loss of sense of self and a doubting about who they are. On the other hand, the persona, as expressed in social roles and customs, is a necessary part of living in society. Similarly, there is the struggle between the masculine and feminine parts of ourselves. Every male has a feminine part (*anima*) and every female has a masculine part (*animus*) to their personality. If a man rejects his feminine part he may emphasize mastery and strength to an excessive degree, appearing cold and insensitive to the feelings of others. If a woman rejects her masculine part she may be excessively absorbed in motherhood. Psychologists currently interested in stereotyped sex roles would probably applaud Jung's emphasis on these dual aspects in everyone's personality, although they might question his characterizing some as specifically masculine and others as feminine.

Another contrast in Jung's theory is that between *introversion* and *extraversion*. Everyone relates to the world primarily in one of two directions, though the other direction always remains a part of the person. In the case of introversion, the person's basic orientation is inward, toward the self. The introverted type is hesitant, reflective, and cautious. In the case of extraversion the person's basic orientation is outward, toward the outside world. The extraverted type is socially engaging, active, and adventuresome. For each person there is the task of finding unity in the *self*. For Jung an important task of life is bringing into harmony, or integrating, the preceding and other opposing forces. The integration of the many opposing aspects of our personality into the self is a lifelong struggle: "Personality as a complete realization of the fullness of our being is an unattainable ideal. But unattainability is no counter argument against an ideal, for ideals are only signposts, never goals" (Jung, 1939, p. 287). The struggle described here can become a particularly important aspect of life once people have passed the age of 40 and defined themselves to the outside world in a variety of ways.

As with Adler, we have considered only some of the highlights of Jung's theory. Jung is considered by many to be one of the great creative thinkers of the century, and his theory has influenced the thinking of people in many fields outside of psychology. Although periodically there are signs of the development of a strong interest in Jung within psychology, his views have yet to have a significant impact on the field.

THE CULTURAL AND INTERPERSONAL EMPHASIS

With the later shift in psychodynamic thinking from Europe to the United States, one finds theorists emphasizing social rather than biological forces in behavior. Collectively, these theorists are called *neo-Freudians*, recognizing both their theoretical debt to Freud and their development of new theoretical positions. Some of these theorists, such as Karen Horney, emigrated to the United States prior to World War II. Other theorists, notably Harry Stack Sullivan, were born and trained in this country.

Karen Horney (1885–1952)

Karen Horney was trained as a traditional analyst in Germany and came to the United States in 1932. Shortly thereafter she split with traditional psychoanalytic thought and developed her own theoretical orientation and psychoanalytic training program. In contrast to Adler and Jung, she felt that her views were built on the tremendous contributions of Freud and were not replacements of them. Perhaps the major difference between her and Freud centers on the question of universal biological influences as opposed to cultural influences: "When we realize the great import of cultural conditions on neuroses, the biological and physiological conditions, which are considered by Freud to be their root, recede into the background" (1937, p. viii). She was led to this emphasis by three major considerations. First, Freud's statements concerning women made Horney think about cultural influences: "Their influence on our ideas of what constitutes masculinity or femininity was obvious, and it became just as obvious to me that Freud had arrived at certain conclusions

Karen Horney

because he failed to take them into account" (1945, p. 11). Second, she was associated with another psychoanalyst, Erich Fromm, who increased her awareness of the importance of social and cultural influences. Third, Horney's observations of differences in personality structure between patients seen in Europe and the United States confirmed the importance of cultural influences. Beyond this, these observations led her to conclude that interpersonal relationships are at the core of all healthy and disturbed personality functioning.

Horney's emphasis in neurotic functioning is on how individuals attempt to cope with *basic anxiety*—the feeling a child has of being isolated and helpless in a potentially hostile world. According to her theory of neurosis, in the neurotic person there is conflict among three ways of responding to this basic anxiety. These three patterns, or *neurotic trends*, are known as *moving toward, moving against*, and *moving away*. All three are characterized by rigidity and the lack of fulfillment of individual potential, the essence of any neurosis. In moving toward, a person attempts to deal with anxiety by an excessive interest in being accepted, needed, and approved of. Such a person accepts a dependent role in relation to others and, except for the unlimited desire for affection, becomes unselfish, undemanding, and self-sacrificing. In moving against, a person assumes that everyone is hostile and that life is a struggle against all. All functioning is directed toward denying a need for others and toward appearing tough. In moving away, the third component of the conflict, the person shrinks away from others into neurotic detachment. Such people often look at themselves and others with emotional detachment,

⚹Neurotic Trends: *Karen Horney emphasized the neurotic trends of moving toward, moving away, and moving against (as illustrated in these three photographs) as an attempt to cope with basic anxiety. In more moderate forms, such trends exist in most people.*

as a way of not getting emotionally involved with others. Although each neurotic person shows one or another trend as a special aspect of their personality, the problem is really that there is conflict among the three trends in the effort to deal with basic anxiety.

Before leaving Horney, we should consider her views concerning women. These views date back to her early work within traditional psychoanalytic thought and are reflected in a series of papers collected in *Feminine Psychology* (1973). As has been noted, from the start Horney had trouble accepting Freud's views of women. She felt that the concept of penis envy might be the result of a male bias in psychoanalysts who treat neurotic women in a particular social context: "Unfortunately, little or nothing is known of physically healthy women, or of women under different cultural conditions" (1973, p. 216). She suggested that women are not biologically disposed toward masochistic attitudes of being weak, dependent, submissive, and self-sacrificing. Instead, these attitudes indicated the powerful influence of social forces.

In sum, both in her views of women and in her general theoretical orientation, Horney rejected Freud's biological emphasis in favor of a social, interpersonal approach. Partly as a result of this difference, she held a much more optimistic view concerning people's capacity for change and self-fulfillment.

Harry Stack Sullivan (1892–1949)

Of the theorists considered in this section, Sullivan is the only one born and trained in the United States, the only one who never had direct contact with Freud, and the one who most emphasized the role of social,

Harry Stack Sullivan

interpersonal forces in human development. In fact, his theory has been known as the _Interpersonal Theory of Psychiatry_ (1953), and his followers consider themselves part of the Sullivan school of interpersonal relations.

Sullivan placed great importance on the early relationship between the infant and the mother in the development of anxiety and in the development of a sense of self. Anxiety may be communicated by the mother in her earliest interaction with the infant. Thus, from the start, anxiety is interpersonal in character. The _self_, a critical concept in Sullivan's thinking, similarly is social in origin. The self develops out of feelings experienced while in contact with others and from _reflected appraisals_ or perceptions by a child as to how he or she is valued or appraised by others. Important parts of the self, particularly in relation to the experience of anxiety as opposed to security, are the _good me_ associated with pleasurable experiences, the _bad me_ associated with pain and threats to security, and the _not me_, or the part of the self that is rejected because it is associated with intolerable anxiety.

Sullivan's emphasis on social influences is seen in his views on the development of the person. These views are somewhat similar to Erikson's in their emphasis on interpersonal influences and in their emphasis on important stages beyond the Oedipus complex. Particularly noteworthy is Sullivan's emphasis on the _juvenile era_ and _preadolescence_. During the juvenile stage—roughly the grammar school years—a child's

Peers: _Harry Stack Sullivan emphasized the importance of peers and a close friend of the same sex during preadolescence._

experiences with friends and teachers begin to rival the influence of his or her parents. Social acceptance becomes important, and the child's reputation with others becomes an important source of self-esteem or anxiety. During preadolescence a relationship to a close friend of the same sex becomes particularly important. This relationship of close friendship, of love, forms the basis for the development of a love relationship with a person of the opposite sex during adolescence. Today, many child psychologists suggest that early relationships with peers may equal in importance the early relationships with the mother (Lewis et al., 1975).

As with the other theorists in this section, we have considered only a few of the major concepts of Sullivan's interpersonal theory. Sullivan's work is noteworthy in its social emphasis, in its emphasis on the development of the self, and in the outstanding contributions that he made to the treatment of schizophrenic patients.

RECENT DEVELOPMENTS WITHIN TRADITIONAL PSYCHOANALYTIC THEORY

Within traditional psychoanalytic theory, let us consider the progress associated with clinical investigations and with systematic research. From its inception with Freud and continuing to the present, developments within psychoanalytic theory generally have been based on clinical investigation—that is, on analysis of individual cases. One important development has been the extension of psychoanalytic investigation to age groups and forms of psychopathology rarely treated by Freud and his followers. As noted, Little Hans was treated by his father. Most psychoanalytic material on childhood and adolescence was based on memories reported by adult parents. The situation changed considerably with the efforts of individuals such as Anna Freud and Melanie Klein, who used psychoanalytic concepts in the treatment of children; now much of the psychotherapy of children and adolescents in Great Britain and the United States is based on psychoanalytic theory. The treatment procedure is modified according to the age group being treated (e.g., with children, play therapy is used as a substitute for dream analysis as a route to the unconscious), but the essential theoretical concepts remain the same.

In addition to expanding their clinical efforts to the treatment of children, psychoanalysts increasingly have been concerned with different types of patient problems than those generally faced by Freud. In the words of one analyst, today's patients come from a different social and cultural context than did Freud's, and they bring with them different problems. Rather than presenting with "typical neuroses," they seek help for depression, for feelings of emptiness, and for lives "lacking zest and joy" (Wolf, 1977). Such changes in the major problems coming to the attention of analysts have led to new theoretical advances, not from a dissatisfaction with Freudian theory per se, but from the need to understand and solve different clinical problems.

Object Relations Theory

Clinical concern with problems of self-definition and with an excessively vulnerable sense of self-esteem have led analysts to become increasingly interested in how, during the earliest years, a person develops a sense of self and then attempts to protect its integrity. As a group, the individuals concerned with such questions are known as *object relations theorists* (Greenberg & Mitchell, 1983). The word *object* here refers to people rather than to physical objects. Thus, the interest is in how experiences with important people in the past are represented as parts or aspects of the self and then affect one's relationships with others in the present. Although there are differences among object relations theorists, and although some depart from traditional psychoanalytic theory more than others, generally there is a greater emphasis on people as relationship seeking rather than as focused on the expression of sexual and aggressive instincts. For example, an important relationship with a nurturant grandmother can be represented as a nurturant part of the self. On the other hand, an important relationship with a grandmother perceived to be selfish can lead to a selfish self-representation.

Narcissism and the Narcissistic Personality

In relation to this interest in the disturbances in the sense of self, psychoanalytic attention has focused particularly on the concept of narcissism and the *narcissistic personality*. The two figures most important in this area are Heinz Kohut and Otto Kernberg. In the development of a healthy sense of self and a healthy narcissism, an individual has a clear sense of self, has a satisfactory and reasonably stable level of self-esteem, takes pride in accomplishments, and is aware of and responsive to the needs of others while responding to his or her own needs. In the narcissistic personality, there is a disturbance in an individual's sense of self, a vulnerability to blows to self-esteem, a need for the admiration of others, and a lack of empathy with the feelings and needs of others. While being vulnerable to intense feelings of worthlessness and powerlessness (shame and humiliation), a narcissistic individual has a grandiose sense of self-importance and is preoccupied with fantasies of unlimited success and power. Such individuals tend to have an exaggerated feeling of being *entitled to* things from others, of *deserving* the admiration and love of others, and of being *special* or unique. They are capable of being very giving to others, though generally not on an emotional or empathic level, but also of being very demanding. They at times idealize others around them—as well as themselves—but at other times may completely devalue others. In therapy it is not unusual for the narcissistic individual to idealize the therapist as extremely insightful at one moment, and to berate the same therapist as stupid and incompetent in the next moment.

Henry Murray, who developed the TAT, also developed a questionnaire to measure narcissism (Figure 4.3). More recently a *Narcissistic Personality Inventory (NPI)* (Raskin & Hall, 1979, 1981) has been developed and is

---

Murray's Narcissism Scale (1938, p. 181)

I often think about how I look and what impression I am making upon others.

My feelings are easily hurt by ridicule or by the slighting remarks of others.

I talk a good deal about myself, my experiences, my feelings, and my ideas.

Narcissism Personality Inventory (Raskin & Hall, 1979)

I really like to be the center of attention.

I think I am a special person.

I expect a great deal from other people.

I am envious of other people's good fortune.

I will never be satisfied until I get all that I deserve.

Figure 4.3   *Illustrative Items from Questionnaire Measures of Narcissism.*

beginning to be used in research (Emmons, 1987) (Figure 4.3). In one study, individuals scoring high on the NPI were found to use many more self-references (e.g., I, me, mine) than did those scoring low (Raskin & Shaw, 1987), and in another study a relationship was found between high scores on the NPI and being described by others as exhibitionistic, assertive, controlling, and critical-evaluative (Raskin & Terry, 1987). Individuals scoring high on narcissism have been found to evaluate their performance more positively than it is evaluated by peers or staff, demonstrating a significant self-enhancement bias relative to individuals scoring low on narcissism (John & Robins, 1994a, Robins & John, 1995). Moreover, whereas most people feel uncomfortable and self-conscious when they see themselves in a mirror or on videotape, this was not the case for narcissistic individuals. Just like the mythical Narcissus who admired his own reflection in a pond, narcissistic individuals spent more time looking at themselves in mirrors, preferred to watch themselves rather than another person on videotape, and indeed received an "ego boost" from watching themselves on videotape (Robins & John, 1995). Finally, narcissistic individuals have not only a self-aggrandizing attributional style but also fairly simple self-concepts and a cynical mistrust of others (Rhodewalt & Morf, 1995). These findings are consistent with the picture of the narcissist as a person preoccupied with the maintenance of their exaggerated self-esteem.

Attachment Theory and Adult Personal Relationships

This theory deals with the effect of early experiences on personality development, and their relationship to later personality functioning. Although not specifically a part of psychoanalytic theory or object relations theory, attachment theory has many points in common with both.

   Current attachment theory is largely based on the early theoretical work of the British psychoanalyst John Bowlby and the empirical work of the developmental psychologist Mary Ainsworth (Ainsworth & Bowlby, 1991; Bretherton, 1992; Rothbard & Shaver, 1994). Bowlby was trained as a psychoanalyst and was interested in the effects of early separation from parents on personality development. This was a major problem in England during World War II when many children were sent to the countryside, far from their parents, to be safe from enemy bombing of the cities. In his conceptual work, Bowlby was largely influenced by developments in ethology, a part of the field of biology that focuses on the study of animals in their natural environment, and by developments in general systems theory, a part of the field of biology that focuses on general principles of operation of all biological systems. His clinical observations and reading of the literature led Bowlby to formulate a theory of the development of the **attachment behavioral system (ABS)**. According to this theory, a developing infant goes through a series of phases in the development of an attachment to a major caregiver, generally the mother, and the use of this attachment as a "secure base" for exploration and separations. The ABS is viewed as something programmed within infants, a part of our evolutionary heritage that has adaptive value. It provides for both the maintenance of close contact with the mother and exploration of the environment from that secure base of contact.

As a further part of the development of the ABS, the infant develops **internal working models** or mental representations (images) of itself and its primary caregivers. These working models are associated with emotion. Based on interactional experience during infancy, they provide the basis for the development of expectations about future relationships. In the emphasis on the importance of early emotional relationships for personality development and future relationships, attachment theory is similar to psychoanalytic theory and object relations theory.

In terms of empirical work, a major turning point occurred with the development by Ainsworth of the *Strange Situation procedure*. Basically this procedure involves systematic observation of how infants respond to the departure (separation) and return (reuniting) of the mother or other caregiver. These observations lead to the placement of infants in one of three attachment categories: Secure (about 70 percent of infants), anxious–avoidant (about 20 percent of infants), and anxious–ambivalent (about 10 percent of infants). Briefly, secure infants are sensitive to the departure of the mother but greet her upon being reunited, are readily comforted, and then are able to return to exploration and play. On the other hand, anxious–avoidant infants register little protest over separation from the mother but, upon her return show avoidance in terms of turning, looking, or moving away. Finally, the anxious–ambivalent infants have difficulty separating from the mother and have difficulty reuniting with her upon her return. What is distinctive about their behavior here is the mixture of pleas to be picked up with squirming and insistence that they be let down.

There is much more that could be said about the theory and procedure but first it is important to stop and examine the question of whether individual differences in attachment relate to differences in adult interpersonal relationships—in particular to romantic relationships. In the research to be considered, the psychologists set out to investigate possible relationships between emotional bonds developed in infancy and emotional bonds established as adults in love with another person (Hazan & Shaver, 1987). Specifically, it was hypothesized that early styles of attachment (secure, avoidant, anxious–ambivalent) would relate to adult styles of romantic love—the kind of continuity of emotional and behavioral patterns suggested by psychoanalytic theory.

Subjects in the study were respondents to a newspaper survey or "love quiz." As a measure of attachment style, the newspaper readers described themselves as fitting one of three categories in terms of their relationships with others. These three categories were descriptive of the three attachment styles (Figure 4.4). As a measure of their current style of romantic love, subjects were asked to respond to questions listed under a banner headline in the newspaper: "Tell Us About the Love of Your Life." Responses to the questions concerning the most important love relationship they ever had formed the basis for scores on 12 Love Experience Scales (Figure 4.4). Additional questions were asked concerning each person's view of romantic love over time and recollections of childhood relationships with parents and between parents.

Did the different types of respondents (secure, avoidant, anxious–ambivalent) also differ in the way they experienced their most important love relationships? As the means for the three groups on the Love Scales indicate, this appears to be the case. Secure attachment styles were associated with experiences of happiness, friendship, and trust; avoidant styles with fears of closeness, emotional highs and lows, and jealousy; and anxious–ambivalent styles with obsessive preoccupation with the loved person, a desire for union, extreme sexual attraction, emotional extremes, and jealousy. In addition, the three groups differed in their views or mental models of romantic relationships: secure lovers viewed romantic feelings as being somewhat stable but also waxing and waning, and discounted the kind of head-over-heels romantic love often depicted in novels and movies; avoidant lovers were skeptical of the lasting quality of romantic love and felt that it was rare to find a person one can really fall in love with; anxious–ambivalent lovers felt that it was easy to fall in love but rare to find true love. Finally, secure subjects, in comparison with subjects in the other two groups, reported warmer relationships with both parents, as well as between their two parents.

A further study conducted by the psychologists with college students confirmed the pattern of these relationships and also suggested differences in the ways members of the three groups described themselves: secure subjects described themselves as easy to get to know and liked by most people, whereas anxious–ambivalent subjects described themselves

Adult Attachment Types
Which of the following best describes your feelings

Secure (N = 319, 56%): I find it relatively easy to get close to others and am comfortable depending on them and having them depend on me. I don't often worry about being abandoned or about someone getting too close to me.

Avoidant (N = 145, 25%): I am somewhat uncomfortable being close to others; I find it difficult to trust them completely, difficult to allow myself to depend on them. I am nervous when anyone gets too close, and often love partners want me to be more intimate than I feel comfortable being.

Anxious/Ambivalent (N = 110, 19%): I find that others are reluctant to get as close as I would like. I often worry that my partner doesn't really love me or won't want to stay with me. I want to merge completely with another person, and this desire sometimes scares people away.

Scale Name	Sample Item	Attachment Type Means		
		Avoidant	Anxious/ ambivalent	Secure
Happiness	My relationship with _____ (made/makes) me very happy.	3.19	3.31	3.51
Friendship	I (considered/consider) _____ one of my best friends.	3.18	3.19	3.50
Trust	I (felt/feel) complete trust in _____.	3.11	3.13	3.43
Fear of closeness	I sometimes (felt/feel) complete trust in _____.	2.30	2.15	1.88
Acceptance	I (was/am) well aware of _____'s imperfections but it (did/does) not lessen my love.	2.86	3.03	3.01
Emotional extremes	I (felt/feel) almost as much pain as joy in my relationship with _____.	2.75	3.05	2.36
Jealousy	I (loved/love) _____ so much that I often (felt/feel) jealous.	2.57	2.88	2.17
Obsessive preoccupation	Sometimes my thoughts (were/are) uncontrollably on _____.	3.01	3.29	3.01
Sexual attraction	I (was/am) very physically attracted to _____.	3.27	3.43	3.27
Desire for union	Sometimes I (wished/wish) that _____ and I were a single unit, a "we" without clear boundaries.	2.81	3.25	2.69
Desire for reciprocation	More than anything, I (wanted/want) _____ to return my feelings	3.24	3.55	3.22
Love at first sight	Once I noticed _____, I was hooked.	2.91	3.17	2.97

Figure 4.4 Illustrative items and Means for Three Attachment Types for 12 Love Experience Scales. *(Hazan & Shaver, 1987. Copyright 1987 by the American Psychological Association. Reprinted by permission.)*

as having self-doubts and being misunderstood and underappreciated by others. The avoidant subjects were between these two groups, but closer to the latter in their responses.

In subsequent research, these relationships have been replicated and extended in two ways. First, it has been suggested that attachment style exerts a pervasive influence on people's relationships with others and on their self-esteem (Feeney & Noller, 1990). Second, attachment style appears to be related to orientation toward work: Secure subjects approach their work with confidence, are relatively unburdened by fears of failure, and do not allow work to interfere with personal relationships; anxious–ambivalent subjects are very much influenced by praise and fear of rejection at work and allow love concerns to interfere with work performance; avoidant subjects use work to avoid social interaction and, although they do well financially, are less satisfied with their jobs than secure subjects (Hazan & Shaver, 1990).

It is important to remember that Bowlby suggested that these attachment styles develop as a result of early experiences with the mother-caregiver and involve internal working models of the self and others. Recently an effort has been made to tie the various attachment styles to internal working models of the self and other (Bartholomew & Horowitz, 1991; Griffin & Bartholomew, 1994). Following Bowlby, according to this model attachment patterns can be defined in terms of two dimensions, reflecting the internal working model of the self and the internal working model of others (Figure 4.5). Each dimension involves a positive end and a negative end. Illustrative of the positive self end would be a sense of self-worth and expectations that others will respond positively. Illustrative of the positive other end would be expectations that others will be available and supportive, lending themselves to closeness. As can be seen in Figure 4.5, this model leads to the addition of a fourth attachment style, that of *Dismissing*. Individuals with this attachment pattern are not comfortable with close relationships and prefer not to depend on others, but still retain a positive self-image. Current research suggests some utility to this four-pattern model, relative to the three-pattern model, but it is still an open question as to how many attachment patterns it is best to identify.

The research presented here just scratches the surface of what has become an important area of investigation. Attachment styles have been associated with partner selection and stability of love relationships (Kirkpatrick & Davis, 1994), with the development of adult depression and difficulties in interpersonal relationships (Bartholomew & Horowitz, 1991; Carnelley, Pietromonaco, & Jaffe, 1994; Roberts, Gotlib, & Kassel, 1996), and with how individuals cope with crises (Mikulciner, Florian, & Weller, 1993). In addition, a recent study suggests that attachment style develops out of family experiences shared by siblings, rather than being strongly determined by genetic factors (Waller & Shaver, 1994). Thus, an impressive research record is beginning to develop.

Positive Other

Secure
(Comfortable with
intimacy and autonomy)

Preoccupied
(Preoccupied with
relationships)

Positive Self   **Negative Self**

Dismissing
(Dismissing of intimacy;
counter-dependent)

Fearful
(Fearful of intimacy;
socially avoidant)

Negative Other

Figure 4.5 Bartholomew's Dimensions of Self and Other Internal Working Models and Associated Attachment Patterns SOURCES: *Bartholomew & Horowitz, 1991; Griffin & Bartholomew, 1994. Copyright 1994 by the American Psychological Association. Reprinted by permission.*

At the same time, it is important to keep a number of points in mind. First, despite suggestive evidence of continuity of attachment style, there also is evidence that these styles are not fixed in stone. Second, these studies tend to look at attachment patterns as if each person had just one attachment style. Yet, there is evidence that the same individual can have multiple attachment patterns, perhaps one in relationships with males and another with females, or one for some contexts and another for different contexts (Sperling & Berman, 1994). Finally, it is important to recognize that most of this research involves the use of self-reports and the recall of experiences in childhood. In other words, we need more evidence about the actual behavior of individuals with different adult attachment patterns and research that follows individuals from infancy through adulthood. Some efforts, known as *longitudinal* research, currently are underway (Sroufe, Carlson, & Shulman, 1993). In sum, research to date supports Bowlby's view of the importance of early experience for the development of internal working models that have powerful effects on personal relationships. At the same time, further research is needed to define the experiences in childhood that determine these models, the relative stability of such models, and the limits of their influence in adulthood.

In evaluating psychoanalysis as a theory of personality, we must keep in mind that it is a complex theory with many components, with some concepts being more fundamental to the theory than others. Thus, for exam- **CRITICAL EVALUATION** ple, the concept of the latency stage of development is less fundamental than the emphasis on the importance of early experience in shaping personality development. Also, in considering psychoanalysis as a theory, it is important to keep it distinct from psychoanalysis as a method of therapy. The issue of therapeutic success with psychoanalysis has not been dealt with here because it is not essential to an understanding of the theory or our evaluation of it. The effectiveness of therapy is a very complex matter, still little understood, and it is hard to extrapolate from this area of research to an evaluation of the theory of personality.

MAJOR CONTRIBUTIONS

How good a theory of personality is psychoanalysis? Clearly, Freud made major contributions to psychology. Psychoanalysis has led to the use of new techniques, such as free association and dream interpretation, and has been a significant force in the development and use of special tests in the assessment of personality. In addition, two outstanding contributions are noteworthy. First, psychoanalysis made a major contribution to the discovery and investigation of phenomena. As we go beyond some of the superficialities of human behavior, we are impressed with Freud's observations, which become particularly apparent in clinical work with patients. Whether we choose to interpret these phenomena as characteristic of all human functioning, as Freud did, or merely as idiosyncratic to neurotics, we are forced to take account of these observations as data concerning human behavior.

The first major contribution by Freud, then, was the richness of his observations and the attention he paid to all details of human behavior. The second was the attention he gave to the complexity of human behavior at the same time that he developed an extremely encompassing theory. Psychoanalytic theory emphasizes that seemingly similar behaviors can have very different antecedents and that very similar motives can lead to quite different behavior. Generosity can express genuine affection or an effort to deal with feelings of hostility; the lawyer and the criminal whom he or she defends or prosecutes may, in some cases, be closer to one another psychologically than most of us care to realize. Out of this recognition of complexity comes a theory that accounts for almost all aspects of human behavior. No other theory of personality comes close to psychoanalytic theory in accounting for such a broad range of behavior. Few others give comparable attention to the functioning of the individual as a whole.

LIMITATIONS OF THE THEORY

In making these contributions, Freud stands as a genius and an investigator of tremendous courage. What, then, are the limitations of psychoanalysis as a theory? Two major criticisms are worthy of note. The first involves the scientific status of psychoanalysis, the second the psychoanalytic view of the person.

The Scientific Status of Psychoanalytic Theory

One can raise a variety of questions about the adequacy of psychoanalysis as a theory of personality. These questions can be raised in relation to specific components of the theory as well as in relation to the total enterprise. For example, in terms of the former, consider the problems associated with the energy model found in psychoanalytic theory. We have already noted that this model was based on other scientific models present at the time of Freud's emerging theory. However, such a model now is out of date and research clearly indicates the inadequacy of it. People do not always seek tension reduction; in fact, often stimulation and tension are desired. Thus, the entire model of motivation as based on physiological drives has been found to be wanting in the field. The energy model is perhaps useful as a metaphor for personality functioning but it hardly does justice to the complexity of human functioning.

Of even greater consequence, however, is what are perhaps fundamental scientific flaws in the entire psychoanalytic enterprise. The terms of psychoanalysis are ambiguous. There are many metaphors and analogies that can, but need not, be taken literally. Examples are latency, death instinct, Oedipus complex, and castration anxiety. Does castration anxiety refer to the fear of loss of the penis, or does it refer to the child's fear of injury to his body at a time that his body image is becoming more important to his self-esteem? The language of the theory is so vague that investigators often are hard pressed to agree on precise meanings of the terms. How are we to define libido? Even where the constructs are well defined, often they are *too removed from observable and measurable behavior* to be of much empirical use. Concepts such as id, ego, and superego have considerable descriptive power, but it is often hard to translate them into relevant behavioral observations.

And what of the scientific utility of clinical data? Many critics suggest that psychoanalysts use observations influenced by the theory to support the theory, while glossing over the problem that committed observers (analysts) may bias the response of their subjects and bias their own perceptions of the data. Whereas some suggest that observations drawn from patients in analysis are adequate grounds for testing psychoanalytic concepts (Edelson, 1984), others suggest that clinical data remain suspect and are an inadequate basis for testing the theory (Grunbaum, 1984, 1993). Rather than constituting unbiased observations of experiences and recollections by patients, many critics suggest that Freud often biased his observations through the use of suggestive procedures and by inferring that memories existed at the unconscious level (Crews, 1993; Esterson, 1993; Powell & Boer, 1994). Eysenck, a frequent and passionate critic of psychoanalysis, whose views we will consider later in the book, suggests that "we can no more test Freudian hypotheses on the couch than we can adjudicate between the rival hypotheses of Newton and Einstein by going to sleep under the apple tree" (1953, p. 229).

What we have, then, is a theory that is at times confusing and often difficult to test. This problem is complicated further by the way in which psychoanalysts can account for almost any outcome, even opposite outcomes. If one behavior appears, it is an expression of the instinct; if the opposite appears, it is an expression of a defense; if another form of behavior appears, it is a compromise between the instinct and the defense. The problem with the theory is not that it leaves room for such complexity, but that it fails to state which behavior will occur, given a specific set of circumstances. In not providing such statements, psychoanalytic theory does not leave itself open to disproof or to the negative test.

Finally, there is a problem in the way in which psychoanalysts often defend the theory. Analysts often respond to criticism of the theory by suggesting that the critics are being defensive in not recognizing and accepting the importance of phenomena such as infantile sexuality. Psychoanalysts who advance such arguments in a routine way perpetuate some of the early developments of psychoanalysis as a religious movement rather than as a scientific theory. Kohut, whose influential work on narcissism has been noted, has described the dilemma he faced when he no longer believed in certain traditional aspects of psychoanalysis. Not only did he face difficulties in giving up views formerly dear to him, but he also had to face the condemnation of traditional analysts (Kohut, 1984).

In noting these criticisms of the status of psychoanalysis as a scientific theory, it is important to recognize that Freud was aware of most of these objections. He was not a naive scientist; his position, rather, was that the beginning of scientific activity consists of the description of phenomena, and that at the early stages some imprecision is inevitable. Also, Freud was acutely aware of the difficulties in using psychoanalytic insights for predictive purposes. He noted that the analyst was on safe ground in tracing the development of behavior from its final stage backward, but that if he proceeded in the reverse direction, an inevitable sequence of events no longer seemed to be apparent. His conclusion was that psychoanalysis does a better job of explaining than of predicting. When he developed his theory, Freud did not have the benefit of a discipline in psychology that supported his efforts to develop a scientific theory. Unfortunately, Freud was excessively dependent on a medical, therapeutic environment when he was committed to developing a system with broader relevance.

The Psychoanalytic View of the Person

In addition to these questions raised by scientific critics, psychoanalysis has been criticized by humanists and proponents of the existential point of view in psychology and psychiatry. According to this view, a theory of the person as an energy system oriented toward tension reduction hardly does justice to the creative, self-actualizing efforts of individuals. It is also suggested that psychoanalysis emphasizes the forces within the individual while generally neglecting the forces within the family and the broader society. Relevant here is the criticism that psychoanalytic theory has received from feminists. Although Freud often is misinterpreted, he did see certain traits, such as receptivity, dependence on others, sensitivity, vanity, and submissiveness, as part of the feminine orientation. These characteristics were seen as part of women because of biological influences and because of psychological reactions to their awareness of the lack of a penis—Freud's concept of penis envy. The concept of penis envy symbolizes for many women a "biology is destiny" view on the part of Freud and an inadequate appreciation of cultural factors. Karen Horney, among others, questioned many of Freud's views concerning women and feminine sexuality—and, as noted earlier, proposed instead a view of feminine development that emphasized cultural influences. Interestingly, although psychoanalysis has come under attack by feminists, perhaps more than any other theory, it has almost always had major female figures within its ranks (e.g., Anna Freud, Helene Deutsch, Greta Bibring, Margaret Mahler, Clara Thompson, and Frieda Fromm-Reichman).

SUMMARY EVALUATION

How, then, are we to summarize our evaluation of Freud and psychoanalytic theory (Table 4.3)? As an observer of human behavior and as a person with a creative imagination, Freud was indeed a genius with few, if any, equals. The theory he developed certainly has the virtue of being comprehensive. No other personality theory approximates psychoanaly-

Table 4.3   Summary of Strengths and Limitations of Psychoanalytic Theory

Strengths	Limitations
1. Provides for the discovery and investigation of many interesting phenomena.	1. Fails to define all its concepts clearly and distinctly.
2. Develops techniques for research and therapy (free association), dream interpretation, transference analysis).	2. Makes empirical testing difficult, at times impossible.
3. Recognizes the complexity of human behavior.	3. Endorses the questionable view of the person as an energy system.
4. Encompasses a broad range of phenomena.	4. Tolerates resistance by parts of the profession to empirical research and change in the theory.

FREUD AT A GLANCE		
Structure	**Process**	**Growth and Development**
Id, ego, superego; unconscious, preconscious, conscious	Sexual and aggressive instincts; anxiety and the mechanisms of defense	Erogenous zones; oral, anal, phallic stages of development; Oedipus complex

sis in the range of behavior considered and the interpretations offered. Given such scope, the theory is economical. The structural and process concepts it uses are relatively few. Furthermore, the theory has suggested many areas for investigation and has led to much research. Although relevant to the theory, however, much of this research does not offer an explicit test of a theory-derived hypothesis, and little of it has been used to extend and develop the theory. The major problem with psychoanalytic theory is the way in which the concepts are formulated; that is, ambiguity in the concepts and in the suggested relationships among concepts has made it very difficult to test the theory. The question for psychoanalytic theory is whether it can be developed to provide for specific tests, or whether it will be replaced in the future by another theory that is equally comprehensive and economical but more open to systematic empirical investigation.

MAJOR CONCEPTS

Projective test.   A test that generally involves vague, ambiguous stimuli and allows subjects to reveal their personalities in terms of their distinctive responses (e.g., Rorschach, TAT).

Fixation.   Freud's concept expressing a developmental arrest or stoppage at some point in the person's psychosexual development.

Regression.   Freud's concept expressing a person's return to ways of relating to the world and the self that were part of an earlier stage of development.

Oral personality.   Freud's concept of a personality type that expresses a fixation at the oral stage of development and relates to the world in terms of the wish to be fed or to swallow.

Anal personality.   Freud's concept of a personality type that expresses a fixation at the anal stage of development and relates to the world in terms of the wish for control or power.

Phallic character.   Freud's concept of a personality type that expresses a fixation at the phallic stage of development and strives for success in competition with others.

Symptom.   In psychopathology, the expression of psychological con-

Pathology	Change	Illustrative Case
Infantile sexuality; fixation and regression; conflict; symptoms	Transference; conflict resolution; "Where id was, ego shall be"	Little Hans

flict or disordered psychological functioning. For Freud, a disguised expression of a repressed impulse.

Free association. In psychoanalysis, the patient's reporting to the analyst of every thought that comes to mind.

Transference. In psychoanalysis, the patient's development toward the analyst of attitudes and feelings rooted in past experiences with parental figures.

Attachment behavioral system (ABS). Bowlby's concept emphasizing the early formation of a bond between infant and caregiver, generally the mother.

Internal working model. Bowlby's concept for the mental representations (images), associated with emotion, of the self and others that develop during the early years of development.

1. Projective tests, such as the Rorschach Inkblot Test and Thematic **REVIEW** Apperception Test (TAT), are linked with psychoanalytic theory. Such tests are unstructured and disguised, leaving room for individuals to respond in unique ways and for the interpretation of responses to be hidden from the subject.

2. Projective tests offer an opportunity to study fantasy and the complexity of organization of individual perceptions. However, they also present problems of reliability and validity of interpretation.

3. The psychoanalytic theory of psychopathology emphasizes the importance of fixations, or failures in development, and regression, or the return to earlier modes of satisfaction. The oral, anal, and phallic character types express personality patterns resulting from partial fixations at earlier stages of development.

4. The psychoanalytic theory of psychopathology emphasizes the conflict between instinctual wishes for gratification and the anxiety associated with these wishes. Defense mechanisms represent ways to reduce anxiety but can result in the development of symptoms.

5. Psychoanalysis is a therapeutic process in which the individual

gains insight into and resolves conflicts dating back to childhood. The methods of free association and dream interpretation are used to gain insight into unconscious conflicts. Therapeutic use is also made of the transference situation, in which patients develop attitudes and feelings toward their therapist that relate to experiences with earlier parental figures.

6. The case of Little Hans illustrates how a symptom, such as a phobia, can result from conflicts associated with the Oedipus complex.

7. A number of early analysts broke with Freud and developed their own schools of thought. Alfred Adler emphasized social concepts more than biological concepts, and Carl Jung emphasized a generalized life energy more than a specific sexual energy.

8. Analysts such as Karen Horney and Harry Stack Sullivan emphasize the importance of cultural factors and interpersonal relations, and are part of the group known as neo-Freudians.

9. Recent clinical developments in psychoanalysis have focused on problems in self-definition and self-esteem. Psychoanalysts in this group, known as object relations theorists, emphasize the importance of relationship seeking as opposed to the expression of sexual and aggressive instincts. The concepts of narcissism and the narcissistic personality have gained particular attention. Bowlby's attachment model, and recent related research, illustrate the importance of early experiences for later personal relationships, as well as other aspects of personality functioning.

10. An evaluation of psychoanalysis suggests its tremendous contribution in calling attention to many important phenomena and developing techniques for research and therapy. At the same time, the theory suffers from ambiguous, poorly defined concepts and problems in testing specific hypotheses.

5

A PHENOMENOLOGICAL THEORY: CARL ROGERS'S PERSON-CENTERED THEORY OF PERSONALITY

Chapter Focus

You are really nervous before a first date, and your mother gives you the advice "just be yourself." That does not seem very helpful—after all, you want to impress your date and get him or her to like you! This tension between being yourself and wanting to be liked is a key element of Rogers's theory of personality. His approach is clinical because it makes an effort to understand the total individual. It is phenomenological because it emphasizes the phenomenal world of the individual—how the person perceives and experiences the self and the world. This focus on subjective experience and the self is reflected in Rogers's use of verbal self-reports in assessment and research. Rogerian theory is part of the humanistic movement that emphasizes the fulfillment of the individual's potential for growth.

QUESTIONS TO BE ADDRESSED IN THIS CHAPTER

1. How important a part of personality is a person's self-concept? How can the self-concept be assessed?

2. Freud emphasized the tension-reducing, pleasure-seeking aspects of human motivation. Is it possible to view human motivation in other terms, for example, in terms of seeking growth, self-enhancement, and self-actualization?

3. How important is it for us to have a stable self-concept? How important is it for our internal feelings to match our self-concept? What do we do when feelings are in conflict with our self-beliefs?

4. What are the childhood conditions that produce a positive sense of self-worth?

In the previous chapter we considered Freud's psychoanalytic theory in light of its emphasis on the total individual, the importance of the unconscious, and human behavior as a function of the interplay among various forces—a dynamic model.

In this second chapter on a specific theoretical position, our focus is on the phenomenological theory of Carl Rogers. Originally, the theory was not one of personality, but rather of psychotherapy and the process of change. However, a theory of personality developed out of the theory of therapy. Rogers's position is presented because it typifies an approach to personality that stresses why people can and should be understood in terms of how they view themselves and the world around them—the **phenomenological approach**. Rogers's theory is also presented because it gives attention to the concept of the *self* and experiences related to the self. Finally, it is presented because it illustrates an effort to combine clinical intuition with objective research. In sum, the theory to be considered emphasizes the phenomenal world of the person, the importance of the person's experience of the self, and the combination of clinical work with empirical research.

"I speak as a person, from a context of personal experience and personal learning." This is the way Rogers introduces his chapter "This Is Me" in his 1961 book *On Becoming a Person*. The chapter is a personal, very moving account by Rogers of the development of his professional thinking and personal philosophy. Rogers states what he does and how he feels about it.

CARL R. ROGERS (1902–1987): A VIEW OF THE THEORIST

> This book is about the suffering and the hope, the anxiety and the satisfaction, with which each therapist's counseling room is filled. It is about the uniqueness of the relationship each therapist forms with each client, and equally about the common elements which we discover in all these relationships. This book is about the highly personal experiences of each one of us. It is about a client in my office who sits there by the corner of the desk, struggling to be himself, yet deathly afraid of being himself....It is about me as I try to perceive his experience, and the meaning and the feeling and the taste and the flavor that it has for him....It is about me as I rejoice at the privilege of being a midwife to a new personality— as I stand by with awe at the emergence of a self, a person, as I see a birth process in which I have had an important and facilitating part....The book is, I believe, about life, as life vividly reveals itself in the therapeutic process—with its blind power and its tremendous capacity for destruction, but with its overbalancing thrust toward growth, if the opportunity for growth is provided.
>
> SOURCE: Rogers, 1961a, pp. 4–5

Carl R. Rogers was born on January 8, 1902, in Oak Park, Illinois. He was reared in a strict and uncompromising religious and ethical atmosphere. His parents had the welfare of the children constantly in mind and inculcated in them a worship of hard work. From Rogers's description of his early life, we see two main trends that are reflected in his later work. The first is the concern with moral and ethical matters. The second is the respect for the methods of science. The latter appears to have developed out of exposure to his father's efforts to operate their farm on a scientific basis and Rogers's own reading of books on scientific agriculture.

Rogers started his college education at the University of Wisconsin, majoring in agriculture, but after two years he changed his professional goals and decided to enter the ministry. During a trip to Asia in 1922, he had a chance to observe commitments to other religious doctrines as well as the bitter mutual hatreds of French and German people, who oth-

Carl R. Rogers

erwise seemed to be likable individuals. Experiences like these influenced his decision to go to a liberal theological seminary, the Union Theological Seminary in New York. Although he was concerned about questions regarding the meaning of life for individuals, Rogers had doubts about specific religious doctrines. Therefore, he chose to leave the seminary, to work in the field of child guidance, and to think of himself as a clinical psychologist.

Rogers obtained his graduate training at Teachers College, Columbia University, receiving his Ph.D. in 1931. He described his experience as leading to a "soaking up" of both the dynamic views of Freud and the "rigorous, scientific, coldly objective, statistical" views then prevalent at Teachers College. Again, there were the pulls in different directions, the development of two somewhat divergent trends. In his later life Rogers attempted to bring these trends into harmony. Indeed, these later years represent an effort to integrate the religious with the scientific, the intuitive with the objective, and the clinical with the statistical. Throughout his career, Rogers tried continually to apply the objective methods of science to what is most basically human.

Therapy is the experience in which I can let myself go subjectively. Research is the experience in which I can stand off and try to view this rich subjective experience with objectivity, applying all the elegant methods of science to determine whether I have been deceiving myself. The conviction grows in me that we shall discover laws of personality and behavior which are as significant for human progress or human relationship as the law of gravity or the laws of thermodynamics.

SOURCE: Rogers, 1961a, p. 14

In 1968 Rogers and his more humanistically oriented colleagues formed the Center for the Studies of the Person. The development of the Center expressed a number of shifts in emphasis in the work of Rogers—from work within a formal academic structure to work with a collection of individuals who shared a perspective, from work with disturbed individuals to work with normal individuals, from individual therapy to intensive group workshops, and from conventional empirical research to the phenomenological study of people. From this perspective, Rogers believed that most of psychology is sterile and generally felt alienated from the field. Yet the field continued to value his contributions. He was president of the American Psychological Association in 1946–1947, was one of the first three psychologists to receive the Distinguished Scientific Contribution Award (1956) from the profession, and in 1972 was the recipient of the Distinguished Professional Contribution Award.

With Rogers, the theory, the man, and the life are interwoven. In his chapter on "This Is Me," Rogers lists 14 principles that he learned from thousands of hours of therapy and research. Here are some illustrations:

1. In my relationships with persons I have found that it does not help, in the long run, to act as though I were something that I am not.

2. I have found it of enormous value when I can permit myself to understand another person.

3. Experience is, for me, the highest authority...it is to experience that I must return again and again, to discover a closer approximation to truth as it is in the process of becoming in me.

4. What is most personal and unique in each one of us is probably the very element which would, if it were shared or expressed, speak most deeply to others.

5. It has been my experience that persons have a basically positive direction.

6. Life, at its best, is a flowing, changing process in which nothing is fixed.

SOURCE: Rogers, 1961a, pp. 16–17

For Rogers, the core of our nature is essentially positive. The direction of our movement basically is toward self-actualization. It is Rogers's contention that religion, particularly the Christian religion, has taught us to believe that we are basically sinful. Furthermore, Rogers contends that

ROGERS'S VIEW OF THE PERSON

Freud and his followers have presented us with a picture of the person with an id and an unconscious that would, if permitted expression, manifest itself in incest, murder, and other crimes. According to this view, we are at heart irrational, unsocialized, and destructive of self and others. For Rogers, we may at times function in this way, but at such times we are neurotic and not functioning as fully developed human beings. When we are functioning freely, we are free to experience and to fulfill our basic nature as positive and social animals.

Aware that others may seek to draw parallels between the behaviors of other animals and the behavior of humans, Rogers draws his own parallels. For example, he observes that, although lions are often seen as ravening beasts, actually they have many desirable qualities: they kill only when hungry and not for the sake of destroying, they grow from helplessness and dependence to independence, and they move from being self-centered in infancy to being cooperative and protective in adulthood.

To those who may call him a naive optimist, Rogers is quick to point out that his conclusions are based on more than 25 years of experience in psychotherapy:

> I do not have a Pollyanna view of human nature. I am quite aware that out of defensiveness and inner fear individuals can and do behave in ways which are incredibly cruel, horribly destructive, immature, regressive, antisocial, hurtful. Yet one of the most refreshing and invigorating parts of my experience is to work with such individuals and to discover the strongly positive directional tendencies which exist in them, as in all of us, at the deepest levels.
>
> SOURCE: Rogers, 1961a, p. 27

Here is a profound respect for people, a respect that is reflected in Rogers's theory of personality and his person-centered approach to psychotherapy.

ROGERS'S VIEW OF SCIENCE, THEORY, AND RESEARCH

Although Rogers's theory and specific research tools changed, he remained a phenomenologist. According to his phenomenological position (1951), each individual perceives the world in a unique way. These perceptions make up an individual's **phenomenal field**. The phenomenal field of the individual includes both conscious and unconscious perceptions, including those of which an individual is aware and is not aware. But the most important determinants of behavior, particularly in healthy people, are the ones that are conscious or capable of becoming conscious. Thus, Rogers's approach differs from the psychoanalytic emphasis on the unconscious. Although the phenomenal field is essentially a private world of the individual, we can attempt to perceive the world as it appears to individuals, to see behavior through their eyes and with the psychological meaning it has for them.

Rogers was committed to phenomenology as a basis for the science of the person. According to Rogers, research in psychology must involve a persistent, disciplined effort to understand the phenomena of subjective experience. In following the path of science, these efforts need not start in the laboratory or at the computer. He believed that clinical material, obtained during psychotherapy, offered a valuable source of phenomenological data.

In attempting to understand human behavior, Rogers always started with clinical observations and then used these observations to formulate hypotheses that could be tested in a rigorous way. He viewed therapy as a subjective "letting go" experience, and research as an objective effort with its own kind of elegance; he was as committed to one as a source for hypotheses as he was to the other as a tool for their confirmation.

Throughout his career, Rogers attempted to bridge the gap between the subjective and the objective, just as in his youth he felt a need to bridge the gap between religion and science. Within this context, Rogers was concerned with the development of psychology as a science and with the preservation of people as individuals who are not simply the pawns of science.

Rogers's main focus was on the process of psychotherapy, and his theory of personality is an outgrowth of his theory of therapy. In contrast to the psychoanalytic emphasis on drives, instincts, the unconscious, tension reduction, and early character development, the phenomenological approach emphasizes perceptions, feelings, subjective self-report, self-actualization, and the process of change.

THE PERSONALITY THEORY OF CARL ROGERS

STRUCTURE

The Self

The key structural concept in the Rogerian theory of personality is the **self**. According to Rogers, the individual perceives external objects, and experiences and attaches meanings to them. The total system of perceptions and meanings make up the individual's phenomenal field. Those parts of the phenomenal field seen by the individual as "self," "me," or "I" make up the self. The self-concept represents an organized and consistent pattern of perceptions. Although the self changes, it always retains this patterned, integrated, organized quality.

Two additional points are noteworthy in relation to Rogers's concept of the self. First, the self is not a little person inside of us. The self does not "do" anything. The individual does not have a self that controls

IS THE SENSE OF SELF UNIQUELY HUMAN?

Most dog owners have at some time experimented with placing a mirror in front of their dog. Is there self-recognition? Animal research suggests that species lower than primates do not recognize themselves in mirrors. Chimpanzees are able to do so, provided that they have some exposure to mirrors. Given such experience, chimps will use the mirror to examine and groom themselves (self-directed behavior) rather than ignore the image or react to it as if it is another member of the species (e.g., fish showing aggressive displays toward a mirror image).

Research on the development of self-directed mirror behavior in infants suggests that the development of self-recognition is a continuous process, starting as early as four months of age. At this point infants show some response to relationships between self-movements and

changes in mirror images. And what of recognition of specific features of the self? If an infant looks at itself in the mirror, has rouge placed on its nose, and then looks in the mirror again, will the infant respond to the rouge mark in a way expressive of self-recognition? Such specific feature recognition, in terms of self-directed mirror behavior, appears to begin at about the age of one year.

The recognition of self, whether expressed through self-directed mirror behavior or otherwise, can be related to the development of consciousness and mind. Clearly it is a matter of considerable psychological significance. Not only does it mean that we can be aware of ourselves and have feelings about ourselves, but also that we can have knowledge of and empathy for the feelings of others. It would indeed be ironic if the very processes that allow us to feel worst about ourselves also provided us with the opportunity to feel most empathetic with others.

Mirror mirror on the wall, is that me after all? This appears to be a question that only members of a few species can address. In humans some maturation is required, but self-recognition begins to develop fairly early and remains a significant part of life thereafter.

SOURCE: Lewis & Brooks-Gunn, 1979

Self-Recognition: *Whereas almost all other species are indifferent to their images in a mirror, or react to them as another animal, humans begin to be fascinated with their self-reflection at an early age.*

behavior. Rather, the self represents an organized set of perceptions. Second, the pattern of experiences and perceptions known as the self is, in general, available to awareness—that is, it can be made conscious. Although individuals do have experiences of which they are unaware, the self-concept is primarily conscious. Rogers believes that such a definition of the self is accurate and a necessary one for research. A definition of the self that included unconscious material, according to Rogers, could not be studied objectively.

A related structural concept is the **ideal self**. The ideal self is the self-concept that individual would most like to possess. It includes the perceptions and meanings that potentially are relevant to the self and that are valued highly by the individual.

Measures of the Self-Concept

Rogers maintained that he did not begin his work with the concept of the self. In fact, in his first work he thought that self was a vague, scientifically meaningless term. However, as he listened to clients expressing their problems and attitudes, he found that they tended to talk in terms of the self. Although impressed with the self-statements of clients, Rogers felt that he needed an objective definition of the concept, a way to measure it, and a research tool.

The Q-Sort Technique   Rogers began his research by recording therapy interview sessions and then categorizing all words that referred to the self. After the early research with recorded interviews, he used the **Q-sort** developed by Stephenson (1953). The Q-sort technique has been used frequently to measure the self-concept. In this approach the experimenter gives the subject a group of cards, each containing a statement concerning some personality characteristic. One card might say "Makes friends easily," another might say "Has trouble expressing anger," and so on for each of the cards. Subjects are asked to read these statements (generally about 100) and then sort the cards according to which statements they feel are most descriptive of them and which are least descriptive. The subjects are asked to arrange the cards into a certain distribution, of which one end represents "Most characteristic of me" and the other "Least characteristic of me." Subjects are told how many piles of cards are to be used and how many cards are to go into each pile. For example, with 100 cards the subject might be asked to sort the cards into 11 piles as follows: 2–4–8–11–16–18–16–11–8–4–2. The distribution is a normal one and expresses the subjects' comparative estimates of how descriptive each characteristic is.

Thus, the Q-sort involves a task in which the subject sorts a number of statements, in this case about the self, into categories ranging from most characteristic to least characteristic. In addition, the identical terms can be sorted into the same number of categories in terms of the ideal self— from "most like my ideal self" to "least like my ideal self." This provides

CURRENT QUESTIONS

SELF-IDEAL CONGRUENCE: SEX DIFFERENCES OVER TIME?

Rogers's notion of the ideal self, and the Q-sort method he espoused, still influence contemporary research on the self-concept. One example is the work by Block and Robins (1993) who examined change in self-esteem from adolescence into young adulthood. Has your self-esteem changed from your early teens to your early twenties? According to Block and Robins, the answer to this question may depend on your sex: on average, self-esteem increases for males and decreases for females over these formative years of life.

Level of self-esteem was defined as the degree of similarity between the perceived self and the ideal self. Both of these constructs were measured by an adjective Q-sort, which includes such self-descriptive items as "competitive," "affectionate," "responsible," and "creative." Subjects whose perceived self was highly similar to their ideal self were high in self-esteem. In contrast, subjects whose perceived self was highly dissimilar to their ideal self were low in self-esteem.

Between the ages of 14 and 23 males became more self-confident and females became less self-confident. Whereas at age 14 they were similar in self-esteem, by age 23 males were much higher. Apparently, males and females differ in how they experience the adolescent years and how they negotiate the transition into adulthood. For men, the news is good: this phase of life is associated with coming closer to one's ideal. Unfortunately, the opposite is true for women: they move further away from their ideal as they enter adulthood.

What are the personality attributes that characterize men and women with high self-esteem? Block and Robins used extensive interview data collected at age 23 and found that the high self-esteem women valued close relationships with others. High self-esteem men, in contrast, were more emotionally distant and controlled in their relationships with others. These sex differences in relationships reflect the very different expectations society holds for what it means to be a man or a woman. Not surprisingly, those young adults whose personalities fit these cultural expectations well are more likely to feel good about themselves and have a self-concept that is close to their ideal self.

Left unanswered by this study is a phenomenological question that would have been of interest to Rogers: What is the *content* of the ideal self? Do males and females differ in their perceptions of what constitutes the ideal? The ideal self seems particularly susceptible to external influence—what we perceive as valued in society. The content of the ideal self tells us something about the attributes a person values and thus uses to derive self-esteem. An interesting question for future research is how the content of the ideal self influences psychological adjustment. Does the person's ideal self capture characteristics of a self-actualized human being or society's definition of what constitutes the ideal man or woman?

for a quantitative measure of the difference or discrepancy between self and ideal self. As we shall see (in Chapter 6), such concepts and measures are important in relation to psychopathology and therapeutic change. The Q-sort leads to data that represent a systematic expression of subjects' perceptions of parts of their phenomenal fields. However, it does not represent a completely phenomenological report, since subjects must use statements provided by the experimenter, instead of their own, and must sort the statements into prescribed piles, representing a normal distribution, rather than according to a distribution that makes the most sense to them.

Adjective Checklist and Semantic Differential Other efforts to obtain subjective reports about the self have made use of the *adjective checklist*, in which subjects check adjectives that they feel are applicable to them, and the *semantic differential* (Osgood, Suci, & Tannenbaum, 1957). Developed as a measure of attitudes and the meanings of concepts, rather than as a specific test of personality, the semantic differential has potential as a useful technique for personality assessment. In filling out the semantic differential, the individual rates a concept on a number of seven-point scales defined by polar adjectives such as *good–bad, strong–weak,* or *active–passive.* Thus, a subject would rate a concept such as "My Self" or "My Ideal Self" on each of the polar adjective scales. A rating on any one scale would indicate whether the subject felt that one of the adjectives was very descriptive of the concept or somewhat descriptive, or whether neither adjective was applicable to the concept. The ratings are made in terms of the meaning of the concept for the individual.

Like the Q-sort, the semantic differential is a structured technique in that the subject must rate certain concepts and use the polar adjective scales provided by the experimenter. This structure provides for the gathering of data suitable for statistical analysis but, also like the Q-sort, it does not preclude flexibility as to the concepts and scales to be used. There is no single standardized semantic differential. A variety of scales can be used in relation to concepts such as father, mother, and doctor to determine the meanings of phenomena for the individual. For example, consider rating the concepts "My Self" and "My College" on scales such as liberal–conservative, scholarly–fun-loving, and formal–informal. To what extent do you see yourself and your college as similar? How does this relate to your satisfaction as a student at this college? In some research very similar to this, it was found that the more students viewed themselves as dissimilar to their college environment, the more dissatisfied they were and the more likely they were to drop out (Pervin, 1967a, 1967b).

An illustration of the way in which the semantic differential can be used to assess personality is in a case of multiple personality. In the 1950s two psychiatrists, Corbett Thigpen and Harvey Cleckley, made famous the case of "the three faces of Eve." This was the case of a woman who possessed three personalities, each of which predominated for a period of time, with frequent shifts back and forth. The three personalities were called Eve White, Eve Black, and Jane. As part of a research endeavor, the psychiatrists were able to have each of the three personalities rate a variety of concepts on the semantic differential. The ratings were then analyzed both quantitatively and qualitatively by two psychologists (C. Osgood and Z. Luria) who did not know the subject. Their analysis included both descriptive comments and interpretations of the personalities that went beyond the objective data. For example, Eve White was described as being in contact with social reality but under great emotional stress, Eve Black as out of contact with social reality but quite self-assured, and Jane as superficially very healthy but quite restricted and undiversified. A more detailed, although still incomplete description of the three personalities based on the semantic differential ratings is pre-

---

CURRENT QUESTIONS

ONE SELF OR MANY SELVES?

Rogers emphasized the self-concept as expressing the organizing pattern of perceptions associated with the self. The self represented a patterned whole that could be measured by instruments such as the Q-sort and the semantic differential. However, today many psychologists suggest that the individual may have many selves—some good and some bad, some actualized in the present and some potential selves for the future.

Consider, for example, the following two individuals. Ivan Boesky was a Wall Street superstar who made a fortune and then brought shame to himself and scandal to the industry because of his illegal activities. While on Wall Street he showed a ferocious desire to accumulate wealth, while at the same time contributing to charities, colleges, or public institutions—apparently without much fanfare or wish for special treatment. In 1984 he said of himself: "I'm a person composed of a bunch of sides. There is self-interest, but there is also a second side of me, that affects a hundred things I do. Public service. Philanthropy."

Hector "Macho" Camacho was a boxing champion who had two sides to himself that were "as different as Clark Kent is from Superman." Hector was a rather subdued person, with his own share of doubts and fears. Macho Man liked to drive deluxe autos at fast speeds, posed for *Playgirl* magazine, told others he was handsome and one awesome fighter. In his own words: "Hector is not as bad as Macho Man. Macho Man is the performer, the boxer. Hector is the humble nice guy who lends money out on the street of Spanish Harlem."

Can one speak of a self-concept or must psychologists be concerned with relations among multiple selves?

SOURCES: *The New York Times*, June 13, 1986, and December 22, 1986.

Eve White	Perceives the world in an essentially normal fashion, is well socialized, but has an unsatisfactory attitude toward herself. The chief evidence of disturbance in the personality is the fact that ME (the self-concept) is considered a little bad, a little passive, and definitely weak.
Eve Black	Eve Black has achieved a violent kind of adjustment in which she perceives herself as literally perfect, but, to accomplish this break, her way of perceiving the world becomes completely disoriented from the norm. If Eve Black perceives herself as good, then she also has to accept HATRED and FRAUD as positive values.
Jane	Jane displays the most "healthy" meaning pattern, in which she accepts the usual evaluations of concepts by her society yet still maintains a satisfactory evaluation of herself. The self concept, ME, while not strong (but not weak, either) is nearer the good and active directions of the semantic space.

Figure 5.1   Brief Personality Descriptions, Based on Semantic Differential Ratings, in a Case of Multiple Personality. *(Osgood & Luria, 1954.)*

sented in Figure 5.1. The analysis on the basis of these ratings turned out to fit quite well with the descriptions offered by the two psychiatrists (Osgood & Luria, 1954).

The Q-sort, adjective checklist, and semantic differential all approach the Rogerian ideal of phenomenological self-report; they provide data that are statistically reliable and theoretically relevant. It can be argued that people have many self-concepts rather than a single self-concept, that these tests do not get at unconscious factors, and that the tests are subject to defensive distortion. Rogers felt, however, that these tests provide useful measures for the concepts of self and ideal self.

PROCESS

Self-Actualization

Freud viewed the essential components of personality as relatively fixed and stable, and he developed an elaborate theory of the structure of personality. Rogers's view of personality emphasized change, and he used few concepts of structure in his theory. Freud considered the person as an energy system. Thus, he developed a theory of dynamics to account for how this energy is discharged, transformed, or dammed up. Rogers thought of people as forward moving. Therefore, he tended to deemphasize the tension-reducing aspects of behavior in favor of an emphasis on **self-actualization**. Whereas Freud placed great emphasis on drives, for Rogers there was no motivation in the sense of drives per se. Instead, people's basic tendency is toward self-actualization: "The organism has

Self-actualization: *Rogers emphasizes the basic
tendency of the organism toward self-actualization.*

one basic tendency and striving—to actualize, maintain, and enhance the
experiencing organism" (Rogers, 1951, p. 487).

Rogers chose to postulate a single motivation to life and to stay close
to that idea rather than to be tied to abstract conceptualizations of many
motives. In a poetic passage, he described life as an active process, comparing it to the trunk of a tree on the shore of the ocean as it remains
erect, tough, and resilient, maintaining and enhancing itself in the
growth process: "Here in this palm-like seaweed was the tenacity of life,
the forward thrust of life, the ability to push into an incredibly hostile
environment and not only to hold its own, but to adapt, develop, become
itself" (Rogers, 1963, p. 2).

The concept of actualization involves the tendency of an organism to
grow from a simple entity to a complex one, to move from dependence
toward independence, from fixity and rigidity to a process of change and
freedom of expression. The concept includes the tendency of each person
to reduce needs or tension, but it emphasizes the pleasures and satisfac-
tions that are derived from activities that enhance the organism.

It is always necessary that others approve of what I do. (F)

I am bothered by fears of being inadequate. (F)

I do not feel ashamed of any of my emotions. (T)

I believe that people are essentially good and can be trusted. (T)

Figure 5.2   Illustrative Items from an Index of Self-Actualization. *(Jones and Crandall, 1986.)*

Although Rogers was generally concerned with measures for his concepts, he never did develop a measure of the self-actualizing motive. Over the years a number of scales have been developed to measure self-actualization. The most recent such effort involves a 15–item scale that measures the ability to act independently, self-acceptance or self-esteem, acceptance of one's emotional life, and trust in interpersonal relations (Figure 5.2). Scores on this questionnaire measure of self-actualization have been found to be related to other questionnaire measures of self-esteem and health, as well as to independent ratings of individuals as self-actualizing persons (Jones & Crandall, 1986).

Self-Consistency and Congruence

The concept of an organism moving toward actualization has not been the subject of empirical investigation. Much more critical to the process aspects of the theory and to research has been Rogers's emphasis on **self-consistency** and **congruence** between self and experience. According to Rogers, the organism functions to maintain consistency (an absence of conflict) among self-perceptions and congruence between perceptions of the self and experiences: "Most of the ways of behaving which are adopted by the organism are those which are consistent with the concept of the self" (Rogers, 1951, p. 507).

The concept of self-consistency was developed by Lecky (1945). According to Lecky, the organism does not seek to gain pleasure and to avoid pain but, instead, seeks to maintain its own self-structure. The individual develops a value system, the center of which is the individual's valuation of the self. Individuals organize their values and functions to preserve the self-system. Individuals behave in ways that are consistent with their self-concept, even if this behavior is otherwise unrewarding to them. Thus, if you define yourself as a poor speller, you will try to behave in a manner consistent with this self-perception.

In addition to self-consistency, Rogers emphasized the importance of congruence between the self and experience. This suggests that people will try to bring together, or make congruent, what they feel with how they view themselves. For example, to view oneself as a kind person and feel

CONSISTENT OR VARIABLE VIEW OF THE SELF: WHICH IS BETTER?

In everyday life, people play many different social roles. We are children, friends, lovers, students, workers, sometimes all of these within the same day. For each significant role that we play in life, we develop an image of ourselves within that role. How do you see yourself across the social roles that are important in your life? The following exercise is designed to let you explore this question for yourself.

Think about yourself in the roles of student, friend, and son or daughter. Then describe how you see yourself in that role by rating yourself on the five descriptive statements listed below using the following scale:

DISAGREE			AGREE	
Strongly	A little	Neither/nor	A little	Strongly
1	2	3	4	5

How I see myself in each role:

	Son or Daughter	Friend	Student	Maximum discrepancy
Is assertive.	____	____	____	____
Tries to be helpful.	____	____	____	____
Is punctual.	____	____	____	____
Worries a lot.	____	____	____	____
Is clever, sharp-witted.	____	____	____	____

Once you have made your ratings, you are able to explore how consistent or variable your self-concept is across these roles. For each of the five statements, subtract the lowest from the highest of the three role ratings. Consider the first statement "Is assertive" as an example. If you rated yourself a 5 in the Son/Daughter role, a 3 in the Friend role, and a 1 in the student role, then your maximum discrepancy score would be 5 minus 1 = 4. You might want to ask yourself what such a discrepancy means and how it may have developed. You can also calculate all five discrepancy scores and then add them together to create a total self-concept variability score. Your score should fall within the range of 0 to 20, with 0 representing a highly consistent view of self across these roles and 20 representing a highly variable self view. How variable is your self-concept in general?

As Donahue, Robins, Roberts, and John (1993) showed in two studies, some individuals see themselves as essentially the same person across their various social roles, whereas others see themselves quite differently. For example, one woman saw herself as fun-loving and easygoing across all her roles. In contrast, another woman saw herself as fun-loving and easygoing with her friends but as quite serious with her parents. Which of these two individuals is likely to be better adjusted—the first who has a more consistent self-concept across her roles or the second who has a more variable self-concept?

What would Rogers predict? Recall that Rogers theorized that the psychologically adjusted individual has a coherent and integrated self. Thus, Rogers's theory predicts that very high variability in the self-concept can be bad for mental health because it is indicative of fragmentation and a lack of an integrated "core" self. An alternative prediction is that variability is good because it provides specialized role identities that enable the individual to respond flexibly and adaptively to various role requirements (e.g., Gergen, 1971).

The results reported by Donahue and her colleagues clearly favored Rogers's position. Individuals with highly variable role identities were more likely to be anxious, depressed, and low in self-esteem. Their relationships with parents had been unusually difficult while growing up, and in early adulthood they were less satisfied with how they were doing in their relationships and in their careers. Not surprisingly, they also changed jobs and relationship partners more frequently than did individuals who had more unified self-concepts across their roles.

These findings suggest that various forms of psychological problems and instability are related to inconsistencies in the self-concept across roles. In other words, the inconsistent self is fragmented, rather than specialized. When thinking about your own level of self-concept variability, however, do not assume that a high score is necessarily indicative of psychological problems. What is most important is that you feel comfortable with your particular style of negotiating your own self-image within your various social roles. If you don't feel comfortable, then you may want to consider ways in which you might strive for a more unified self-image across the social roles you act out in your daily life. A recent book by Harary and Donahue (1994) provides many useful exercises and detailed information about these issues.

SOURCES: Donahue, Robins, Roberts, & John, 1993; Harary & Donahue, 1994.

warm and empathic toward others would represent such congruence. On the other hand, to view oneself as a kind person and experience feelings of cruelty toward others would represent a state of incongruence.

States of Incongruence and Defensive Processes   Do individuals ever experience inconsistencies in the self or a lack of congruence between self and experience? If so, how do they function to maintain consistency and congruence? According to Rogers, we experience a state of **incongruence** when there is a discrepancy between the perceived self and actual experience. For example, if you view yourself as a person without hate and you experience hate, you are in a state of incongruence. The state of incongruence is one of tension and internal confusion. When it exists and the individual is unaware of it, he or she is potentially vulnerable to anxiety. Anxiety is the result of a discrepancy between experience and the perception of the self. Again, the person whose self-concept is that he or she never hates anyone will experience anxiety whenever hateful feelings are experienced to any degree at all.

For the most part, we are aware of our experiences and allow them into consciousness. However, we also may perceive an experience as

Incongruence: *A discrepancy between the perceived self and actual experience is experienced as a state of incongruence. (Drawing by H. Martin; © 1971 The New Yorker Magazine, Inc.)*

"Hi, there, the me nobody knows!"

threatening, as being in conflict with the self-concept, and may not allow it to become conscious. Through a process called **subception**, we can be aware of an experience that is discrepant with the self-concept before it reaches consciousness. The response to the threat presented by recognition of experiences that are in conflict with the self is that of *defense*. Thus, we react defensively and attempt to deny awareness to experiences that are dimly perceived to be incongruent with the self-structure.

Two defensive processes are **distortion** of the meaning of experience and **denial** of the existence of the experience. Denial serves to preserve the self-structure from threat by denying it conscious expression. Distortion, a more common phenomenon, allows the experience into awareness but in a form that makes it consistent with the self: "Thus, if the concept of self includes the characteristic `I am a poor student,' the experience of receiving a high grade can be easily distorted to make it congruent with the self by perceiving in it such meanings as, `That professor is a fool'; `It was just luck' " (Rogers, 1956, p. 205). What is striking about this last example is the emphasis it places on self-consistency. What is otherwise likely to be a positive experience, receiving a high grade, now becomes a source of anxiety and a stimulus for defensive processes to be set in operation. In other words, it is the relation of the experience to the self-concept that is key.

Research on Self-Consistency and Congruence   An early study in this area was performed by Chodorkoff (1954) who found that subjects were slower to perceive words that were personally threatening than they were to perceive neutral words. This tendency was particularly characteristic of defensive, poorly adjusted individuals. Poorly adjusted individuals, in particular, attempt to deny awareness to threatening stimuli.

Additional research by Cartwright (1956) involved the study of self-consistency as a factor affecting immediate recall. Following Rogers's theory, Cartwright hypothesized that individuals would show better recall for stimuli that are consistent with the self than for stimuli that are inconsistent. He hypothesized further that this tendency would be greater for maladjusted subjects than for adjusted subjects. In general, subjects were able to recall adjectives they felt were descriptive of themselves better than they were able to recall adjectives they felt were most unlike themselves. Also, there was considerable distortion in recall for the latter, inconsistent adjectives. For example, a subject who viewed himself as hopeful misrecalled the word "hopeless" as being "hopeful," and a subject who viewed himself as friendly misrecalled the word "hostile" as being "hospitable." As predicted, poorly adjusted subjects (those applying for therapy and those for whom psychotherapy had been judged to be unsuccessful) showed a greater difference in recall than did adjusted subjects (those who did not plan on treatment and those for whom psychotherapy had been judged to be successful). This difference in recall scores was due particularly to the poorer recall of the maladjusted subjects for inconsistent stimuli.

In a related study, an effort was made to determine the ability of subjects to recall adjectives used by others to describe them (Suinn, Osborne, & Winfree, 1962). Accuracy of recall was best for adjectives used by others that were consistent with the self-concept of subjects and was poorest for adjectives used by others that were inconsistent with the self-concept. In sum, the accuracy of recall of self-related stimuli appears to be a function of the degree to which the stimuli are consistent with the self-concept.

The studies just discussed relate to perception and recall. What of overt behavior? Aronson and Mettee (1968) found results that were consistent with Rogers's view that individuals behave in ways that are congruent with their self-concepts. In a study of dishonest behavior, they reasoned that if people are tempted to cheat, they will be more likely to do so if their self-esteem is low than if it is high; that is, whereas cheating is not inconsistent with generally low self-esteem, it is inconsistent with generally high self-esteem. The data gathered indeed suggested that whether or not an individual cheats is influenced by the nature of the self-concept. People who have a high opinion of themselves are likely to behave in ways they can respect, whereas people with a low opinion of themselves are likely to behave in ways that are consistent with that self-image.

More recent research supports the view that the self-concept influences behavior in varied ways (Markus, 1983). What is particularly noteworthy here is the suggestion that people often behave in ways that will lead others to confirm the perception they have of themselves—a self-fulfilling prophecy (Darley & Fazio, 1980; Swann, 1992). For example, people who believe they are likable may behave in ways that lead others to like them, whereas others who believe themselves to be unlikable may behave in ways that lead others to dislike them (Curtis & Miller, 1986). For better or for worse, your self-concept may be maintained by behaviors of others that were influenced in the first place by your own self-concept!

The Need for Positive Regard

We have, then, a number of studies supporting the view that the individual attempts to behave in accordance with the self-concept and that experiences inconsistent with the self-concept are often ignored or denied. In Rogers's earlier writing, no mention was made of the reasons for the development of a rift between experience and self and, therefore, the need for defense. In 1959 Rogers presented the concept of the **need for positive regard**. The need for positive regard includes attitudes such as

Positive Regard: *Healthy personality development is fostered through the communication of unconditional positive regard to the child.*

warmth, liking, respect, sympathy, and acceptance and is seen in the infant's need for love and affection. If the parents give the child *unconditional positive regard*, if the child feels "prized" by the parents, there will be no need to deny experiences. However, if the parents make positive regard conditional, the child will be forced to disregard its own experiencing process whenever it conflicts with the self-concept. For example, if a child feels that he or she will only receive love (positive regard) for always being loving, he or she will deny all feeling of hate and struggle to preserve a picture of the self as loving. In this case the feeling of hate not only is incongruent with the self-concept but also threatens a child with the loss of positive regard. Thus the imposition of *conditions of worth* on a child leads to the denial of experiences, the rift between organism and self. The origins of inaccuracies in the self-concept, the origins of conflict between an individual's experience and the self-concept, lie in that individual's attempt to retain love.

To summarize, Rogers did not feel a need to use the concepts of motives and drives to account for the activity and goal-directedness of the organism. For him, the person is basically active and self-actualizing. As part of the self-actualizing process, we seek to maintain a congruence between self and experience. However, because of past experiences with conditional positive regard, we may deny or distort experiences that threaten the self-system.

GROWTH AND DEVELOPMENT

Rogers did not really have a theory of growth and development and did not do research in the area in terms of long-term studies or studies of parent–child interaction. Basically, Rogers believed that growth forces exist in all individuals. The natural growth process of the organism involves greater complexity, expansion, increasing autonomy, greater socialization—in sum, self-actualization. The self becomes a separate part of the phenomenal field and grows increasingly complex. As the self emerges, an individual develops a need for positive regard. If the need for positive regard by others becomes more important than being in touch with one's own feelings, individuals will screen various experiences out of awareness and will be left in a state of incongruence.

Self-Actualization and Healthy Psychological Development

Essentially, then, the major developmental concern for Rogers is whether the child is free to grow within a state of congruence, to be self-actualizing, or whether the child will become defensive and operate out of a state of incongruence. Healthy development of the self takes place in a climate in which the child can experience fully, can accept itself, and can be accepted by its parents, even if they disapprove of particular types of behavior. This point is emphasized by most child psychiatrists and psychologists. It is the difference between a parent saying to a child, "I don't like what you are doing" and saying, "I don't like you." In saying "I don't like what you are doing," the parent is accepting the child while not approving of the behavior. This contrasts with situations in which a parent tells a child, verbally or in more subtle ways, that his or her behavior is bad and that he or she is bad. The child then feels that recognition of certain feelings would be inconsistent with the picture of itself as loved or lovable, leading to denial and distortion of these feelings.

Research on Parent–Child Relationships

A variety of studies suggest that acceptant, democratic parental attitudes facilitate the most growth. Whereas children of parents with these attitudes show accelerated intellectual development, originality, emotional security, and control, the children of rejecting, authoritarian parents are unstable, rebellious, aggressive, and quarrelsome (Baldwin, 1949). What is most critical is children's perceptions of their parents' appraisals. If they feel that these appraisals are positive, they will find pleasure in their bodies and in their selves. If they feel that these appraisals are negative, they will develop insecurity and negative appraisals of their bodies (Jourard & Remy, 1955). Apparently, the kinds of appraisals that parents make of their children largely reflect the parents' own degree of self-acceptance. Mothers who are self-accepting also tend to accept their children (Medinnus & Curtis, 1963).

An extensive study of the origins of **self-esteem** gives further support to the importance of the dimensions suggested by Rogers. Coopersmith (1967) conducted a study of self-esteem, which he defined as the evaluation an individual makes and customarily maintains with regard to the self. Self-esteem, then, is a personal judgment of worthiness. It is a general personality characteristic, not a momentary attitude or an attitude specific to individual situations. Self-esteem was measured by a 50–item Self Esteem Inventory, with most of the items coming from scales previously used by Rogers. Children filled out the inventory and their scores were used to define groups with high, medium, and low self-esteem. Compared to children low in self-esteem, those high in self-esteem were found to be more assertive, independent, and creative. The high self-esteem subjects were also less likely to accept social definitions of reality unless they were in accord with their own observations, were more flexible and imaginative, and were capable of finding more original solutions to problems. In other words, the subjective estimates of self-esteem had a variety of behaviors attached to them.

What of the origins of self-esteem? Coopersmith obtained data on the children's perceptions of their parents, ratings from staff members who interviewed the mothers, and responses from the mothers to a questionnaire relating to child-rearing attitudes and practices. The results indicated that external indicators of prestige such as wealth, degree of education, and job title did not have as overwhelmingly significant an effect on self-esteem as is often assumed. Instead, the conditions in the home and the immediate interpersonal environment had the major effect on judgments of self-worth. Apparently children are influenced in their self-judgments through a process of *reflected appraisal* in which they take the opinions of them expressed by others who are important to them and then use these opinions in their own self-judgments.

What kinds of parental attitudes and behaviors appeared to be important in the formation of self-esteem? Three areas of parent–child interaction seemed to be particularly important. The first area concerned the *degree of acceptance*, interest, affection, and warmth expressed toward the child. The data revealed that the mothers of children with high self-esteem were more loving and had closer relationships with their children than did the mothers of children with low self-esteem. The interest on the part of the mother appeared to be interpreted by children as an indication of their significance, that they were worthy of the concern, attention, and time of those who were important.

The second critical area of parent–child interaction related to *permissiveness and punishment*. The data revealed that the parents of children with high self-esteem made clear demands that were firmly enforced. Reward generally was the preferred mode of affecting behavior. In contrast to this pattern, the parents of children with low self-esteem gave little guidance and were harsh and disrespectful in their treatment. These parents did not establish and enforce guidelines for their children, were apt to use punishment rather than reward, and tended to stress force and loss of love.

Finally, differences were found in parent–child interactions in relation to democratic practices. Parents of children with high self-esteem established an extensive set of rules and were zealous in enforcing them, but treatment within the defined limits was noncoercive and recognized the rights and opinions of the child. Parents of children low in self-esteem set few and poorly defined limits, and were autocratic, dictatorial, rejecting, and uncompromising in their methods of control. Coopersmith summarized his findings as follows: "The most general statement about the origins of self-esteem can be given in terms of three conditions: total or nearly total acceptance of the children by their parents, clearly defined and enforced limits, and the respect and latitude for individual actions that exist within the defined limits" (1967, p. 236). Coopersmith further suggested that it is the perception of the parents by the child, and not necessarily the specific actions they express, that is important. Further, the total climate in the family influences the child's perception of the parents and their motives.

A recent study further supports the relevance of such child-rearing conditions for the development of creative potential. According to Rogers, children raised by parents who provide conditions of psychological safety and psychological freedom are more likely to develop creative

CURRENT QUESTIONS

INTRINSIC MOTIVATION: GET PAID MORE AND BE LESS INTERESTED IN YOUR WORK?

Would you expect children reinforced for drawing to be more or less interested in drawing than children not reinforced? Would you expect college students rewarded for playing with a puzzle to be more or less interested in continuing to play with puzzles than students not rewarded? In perhaps surprising findings that are consistent with Rogers's emphasis on self-actualization, and in conflict with reinforcement theory, in both of these cases intrinsic interest in and motivation to perform the activity were lessened by rewards for performance!

Apparently rewards and other forms of control can interfere with the development of intrinsic motivation or involvement in an activity because of interest in it rather than because of rewards associated with performance. Circumstances that provide for feelings of challenge, competence, and self-determination appear to provide for the development of intrinsic motivation. Thus, parenting styles that are autonomy-oriented rather than control-oriented foster the development of intrinsic motivation.

People oriented toward intrinsic motivation have been found to prefer challenging tasks, to respond with effort and persistence after failure, to be creative and expressive, and to be high in self-esteem. Athletes, employees, and students have all been found to perform better under conditions encouraging intrinsic motivation as opposed to conditions emphasizing extrinsic rewards or external control.

Of course, this doesn't mean that getting paid more will result in enjoying one's work less, although it does suggest that money isn't everything.

SOURCES: Deci & Ryan, 1985, 1991; Kasser & Ryan, 1996; Koestner & McClelland, 1990; Lepper, Greene, & Nisbett, 1973.

potential than children raised by parents who do not provide these conditions. Conditions of psychological safety are provided by parental expressions of unconditional positive regard for the child and empathic understanding, and conditions of psychological freedom are expressed in permission to engage in unrestrained expression of ideas. In a test of this view, child-rearing practices and parent–child interaction patterns were measured for children between the ages of three and five (Figure 5.3). Independent measures of creative potential in the children were obtained prior to their admission to school and in adolescence. In support of Rogers's theory, measures of childhood (preschool) environmental conditions of psychological safety and freedom were significantly associated with creative potential—both in preschool and in adolescence (Harrington, Block, & Block, 1987).

Creativity-fostering Environment

Parents respect the child's opinions and encourage expression of them.

Parents and child have warm, intimate time together.

Children are allowed to spend time with other children or families who have different ideas or values.

Parents are encouraging and supportive of the child.

Parents encourage the child to proceed independently.

The Creative Personality

Tends to be proud of accomplishments.

Is resourceful in initiating activities.

Becomes strongly involved in activities.

Has a wide range of interests.

Is comfortable with uncertainties and complexities.

Perseveres in the face of adversity.

Figure 5.3 Illustrative Characteristics of Creativity-fostering Environments and the Creative Personality. *(Adapted from Harrington, Block, & Block, 1987.)*

Children's Views of the Goodness and Badness of the Self

We come here to research that was not conducted within the Rogerian framework but, since it involves the self-concepts of children, may be viewed within that context. The research started with evidence that children, as well as adults, hold implicit theories about human attributes and that these theories have implications for how they feel and behave. This is a view discussed in Chapter 1. In a series of studies, Dweck and her colleagues investigated the implications of children having one or the other of two kinds of beliefs, the two sets of beliefs differing in how malleable or fixed the relevant trait is believed to be (Dweck, 1991; Dweck, Chiu, & Hong, 1995). According to one set of beliefs, known as an **entity theory**, a particular characteristic or trait is viewed as fixed. According to the other set of beliefs, known as an **incremental theory**, a particular characteristic or trait is believed to be malleable or open to change. For example, an entity view of intelligence suggests that intelligence is a fixed trait. On the other hand, an incremental view of intelligence suggests that intelligence is a malleable trait that can be increased. Differences in views concerning the nature of a trait such as intelligence have implications for goals that are set and responses to failure. For example, children with an entity view of intelligence tend to set *performance goals* and often give up in response to failure, feeling that their performance is a reflection on them and their ability. On the other hand, children with an incremental view of intelligence tend to set *learning goals* and try harder in the face of failure, focusing on increasing their competence.

Apparently children can have comparable theories and goals concerning the self, and it is here that we can see the direct relevance to Rogers. According to Dweck, children make judgments on a good–bad dimension. Included here are judgments concerning the goodness and badness of the self. Children with an entity theory of the self tend to make global judgments of the goodness of the self, compared to children with an incremental theory of the self. In addition, children with an entity theory of the self interpret criticism as reflecting on themselves, whereas children with an incremental theory of the self interpret criticism as a piece of information of which they can make constructive use. Understandably, criticism is a much greater blow to the former children than to the latter. Whereas an entity view of the goodness of the self may be reassuring, an entity view of the badness of the self leaves children vulnerable to continuous blows to their self-esteem. Each failure or criticism experience becomes an indicator of their fundamental badness in relation to which nothing can be done. In contrast, an incremental view of the goodness of the self allows one to experience criticism as specific to the situation and as an opportunity to become a better person. In sum, as in the situation with regard to intelligence, an entity view of goodness–badness is associated with a helpless reaction to failure, whereas a belief in the malleability of goodness–badness is associated with effort and mastery in the face of failure.

Fostering Creative Potential: *Psychological conditions of safety and freedom help develop the creative potential of children.*

Although Dweck and her colleagues have not as yet investigated the parental patterns that lead to the development of one or the other set of beliefs, one can guess that the patterns previously discussed have relevance here as well. And, although Dweck suggests that most beliefs are *specific* to the particular trait or characteristic involved, so that, for example, children may have a fixed, entity view of intelligence but a malleable, incremental view of social skills, she also suggests that children have *general* beliefs concerning the goodness–badness of the self and the fixedness–malleability of the self. It is for this reason that her research may be viewed within the context of the Rogerian emphasis on the development of the self and of feelings of self-worth.

CONCLUSION

Rogers's views on parents' characteristics and practices that influence the child's development of self-esteem have influenced the thinking of researchers and childcare experts. Although they do not always refer to Rogers, in many cases their emphasis on respect for children and protection of children's self-esteem speaks to the influence of Rogers and other members of the human potential movement. His emphasis on the conditions that promote or block self-actualization receives further attention in the next chapter, where we consider the clinical applications of the theory.

MAJOR CONCEPTS

Phenomenology. An approach within psychology that focuses on how the person perceives and experiences the self and the world.

Self-concept. The perceptions and meaning associated with the self, me, or I.

Phenomenal field. The individual's way of perceiving and experiencing his or her world.

Ideal self. The self-concept the individual would most like to possess. A key concept in Rogers's theory.

Q-sort. An assessment device in which the subject sorts statements into categories following a normal distribution. Used by Rogers as a measure of statements regarding the self and the ideal self.

Self-actualization. The fundamental tendency of the organism to actualize, maintain, and enhance itself. A concept emphasized by Rogers and other members of the human potential movement.

Self-consistency. Rogers's concept expressing an absence of conflict among perceptions of the self.

Congruence. Rogers's concept expressing an absence of conflict between the perceived self and experience. Also one of three conditions suggested as essential for growth and therapeutic progress.

Incongruence. Rogers's concept of the existence of a discrepancy or conflict between the perceived self and experience.

Subception. A process emphasized by Rogers in which a stimulus is experienced without being brought into awareness.

Distortion. According to Rogers, a defensive process in which experience is changed so as to be brought into awareness in a form that is consistent with the self.

Denial. A defense mechanism, emphasized by both Freud and Rogers, in which threatening feelings are not allowed into awareness.

Positive regard, need for. Rogers's concept expressing the need for warmth, liking, respect, and acceptance from others.

Self-esteem. The person's evaluative regard for the self or personal judgment of worthiness.

Entity theory. Dweck's concept for beliefs that a personality characteristic is fixed, nonmalleable.

Incremental Theory. Dweck's concept for beliefs that a personality characteristic is malleable or possible to change.

REVIEW

1. The phenomenological approach emphasizes an understanding of how people experience themselves and the world around them. The person-centered theory of Carl Rogers is illustrative of this approach.

2. Throughout his life Rogers attempted to integrate the intuitive with the objective, combining a sensitivity to the nuances of experience with an appreciation for the rigors of science.

3. Rogers emphasized the positive, self-actualizing qualities of the person. In his research he emphasized a disciplined effort to understand subjective experience or the phenomenal field of the person.

4. The key structural concept for Rogers was the self—the organization of perceptions and experiences associated with the "self," "me," or "I." Also important is the concept of the ideal self, or the self-concept the person would most like to possess. The Q-sort is one method used to study these concepts and the relation between them.

5. Rogers deemphasized the tension-reducing aspects of behavior and, instead, emphasized self-actualization as the central human motive. Self-actualization involves continuous openness to experience and the ability to integrate experiences into an expanded, more differentiated sense of self.

6. Rogers also suggested that people function to perceive self-consistency and to maintain congruence between perceptions of the self and experience. However, experiences perceived as threatening to the self-concept may, through defensive processes such as distortion and denial, be prevented from reaching consciousness. A variety of studies support the view that people will behave in ways to maintain and confirm the perception they have of themselves.

7. People have a need for positive regard. Under conditions of unconditional positive regard, children and adults are able to grow within a

state of congruence and be self-actualizing. On the other hand, where positive regard is conditional, people may screen experiences out of awareness and limit their potential for self-actualization.

8. Children are influenced in their self-judgments through the process of reflected appraisal. Parents of children with high self-esteem are warm and accepting but also are clear and consistent in their enforcement of demands and standards.

9. Children develop beliefs concerning the malleability of psychological characteristics, contrasted in terms of an entity theory or an incremental theory. Of particular significance in this regard is the evaluation they make concerning the goodness–badness of the self.

6

A PHENOMENOLOGICAL THEORY: APPLICATIONS AND EVALUATION OF ROGERS'S THEORY

Do you have one particular friend you talk to when you are feeling sad, upset, or angry? During difficult times, it might seem this friend is the only person in the world who can make you feel better. What does he or she have that is so special? Perhaps your friend is good at helping you relax and making you feel safe and comfortable about expressing your feelings.

This was Rogers's goal in therapy. His client-centered therapy was the foundation from which he developed his theory of personality. In his work with clients, he discovered how individuals are led to deny and distort their experiences; he then focused on ways to create conditions that would provide the basis for growth and change. Also considered in this chapter are other significant figures in the human potential movement (Kurt Goldstein, Abraham H. Maslow), existentialism, and an overall evaluation of Rogers's theory of personality.

QUESTIONS TO BE ADDRESSED IN THIS CHAPTER

1. What are the implications of a lack of congruence between self and experience for psychological adjustment?

2. Which kinds of changes in personality functioning constitute improvement in psychological health? What are the critical ingredients determining whether people are able to undergo such positive psychological change?

3. How different does a person look when assessed with self-report measures as compared with projective tests?

4. Why is the Rogerian view of the person considered a corrective force against the Freudian and behaviorist views?

CLINICAL APPLICATIONS

In this chapter we will consider Rogers's views on psychotherapy and personality change. These views are an important part of the theory; in fact, the major part of Rogers's professional life involved these clinical applications. The person-centered approach developed first in counseling and psychotherapy, where it was known as **client-centered therapy**, "meaning that a person seeking help was not treated as a dependent patient but rather as a responsible client" (Rogers, 1977, p. 5). Rather than focusing on an illness model of abnormal behavior and a medical model of a doctor treating a patient, Rogers emphasized the individual's drive toward health, the conditions that may interfere with such growth, and the therapeutic conditions that help to remove obstacles to self-actualization.

PSYCHOPATHOLOGY

Self-Experience Discrepancy

The essential elements of Rogers's view of psychopathology were given in the last chapter. For Rogers, the healthy person can assimilate experiences into the self-structure. In the healthy person, there is a congruence between self and experience, an openness to experience, a lack of defensiveness. In contrast, the neurotic person's self-concept has become structured in ways that do not fit organismic experience. The psychologically maladjusted individual must deny to awareness significant sensory and emotional experiences. Experiences that are incongruent with the self-structure are subceived as threatening and are either denied or distorted. This condition is known as **self-experience discrepancy**. The result is a rigid, defensive maintenance of the self against experiences that threaten the wholeness of the self and frustrate the need for positive self-regard.

Although Rogers did not differentiate among forms of pathology, he did differentiate among types of defensive behaviors. For example, in **rationalization** a person distorts behavior in such a way as to make it consistent with the self. If you view yourself as a person who does not make mistakes, you are likely to attribute a mistake to some other factor. Another example of defensive behavior is *fantasy*. A man who defensively believes himself to be an adequate person may fantasize that he is a prince and that all women adore him, and he may deny any experiences that are inconsistent with this image. A third example of defense behavior is *projection*. Here an individual expresses a need, but in such a form that the need is denied to awareness and the behavior is viewed as consistent with the self. People whose self-concept involves no "bad" sexual thoughts may feel that others are making them have these thoughts.

The descriptions of these defensive behaviors are quite similar to the ones given by Freud. For Rogers, however, the important aspect of these behaviors is their handling of an incongruence between self and experience by denial in awareness or distortion of perception: "It should be noted that perceptions are excluded because they are contradictory, not because they are derogatory" (Rogers, 1951, p. 506). Furthermore, the classification of the defenses is not as critical to Rogerian theory as it is to Freudian theory.

According to Rogers, then, psychological pathology implies that the relation between self-concept and actual experience is disturbed. However, most of the relevant research has examined the relations between self and ideal self. In this research, the discrepancy between self and ideal–self ratings is often used as a measure of adjustment—the smaller the discrepancy between self and ideal self, the more well-adjusted. Many studies have been conducted in support of the view that health and self-esteem are associated with the relation between the self and

CURRENT QUESTIONS

IDEAL SELF AND FEARED SELF—MOTIVATING FACETS OF THE SELF?

The day before a big test you find yourself visualizing what it would feel like to get an *A*. Then you imagine what it would be like to get an *F*. Both possibilities can feel very real. The *A* may seem so ideal, and the *F* so frightening, that you decide to study an extra hour.

What are your ideal and feared selves? Some recent research has emphasized the Ideal self and the Feared self and compared them with the current self as the individual perceives it (e.g., Harary & Donahue, 1994). Here is an exercise that you may find useful for thinking about your ideals and fears in relation to your current self-concept.

First think about how you see yourself in general and rate your *current self-concept* as you perceive it right now using the five descriptive statements listed below. Next, consider your *ideal self*—the way you wish your personality would be—and rate it using the same five statements. Finally, consider your *feared self*—the way you are afraid your personality might become—and rate it accordingly. For all three types of ratings, use the following scale and enter your ratings in the appropriate column:

Once you have completed your ratings, you can compute two discrepancy scores, one for the discrepancy between *current and ideal* self and another between *current and feared* self. For example, consider a person who is quite a partier (a current self rating of 5 on "outgoing") but feels that ideally she should be more reserved and spend more time on schoolwork (an ideal self rating of 3); the resulting current-ideal discrepancy (-2) indicates that she needs to cut back on social activities to get closer to the ideal self. Another person might feel he has overcome his shyness (a current self rating of 3 on "outgoing") but fears that he might drift back into his lonely old self (a feared self-rating of 1). The resulting current-feared discrepancy (+2) is positive and indicates that for now he is successfully avoiding this feared self.

DISAGREE			AGREE	
Strongly	A little	Neither/nor	A little	Strongly
1	2	3	4	5

How I see my various selves:

	Current Self	Ideal Self	Feared Self	Current minus Ideal	Current minus Feared
Outgoing, not reserved.	___	___	___	___	___
Forgiving, doesn't hold grudges.	___	___	___	___	___
Is lazy.	___	___	___	___	___
Is tense, easily stressed out.	___	___	___	___	___
Sophisticated in art, music, or literature.	___	___	___	___	___

You might find it interesting to calculate the two discrepancy scores for each of the five rating dimensions and consider where your current self stands in relation to your ideal self and feared selves. Your current self might be further from your ideal self (and closer to your feared self!) on some dimensions than on others. Are these discrepant aspects of your personality ones that you would like to change? The key is to know what you want for yourself (your ideals), what you don't want (your fears), and what motivates you. Some people are inspired by visualizing their ideal self and others are jump-started into action by the image of their feared self. Which one sounds more like you? If you want to change, a good way to start is to visualize the vast array of possibilities in your life.

ideal–self. For example, Higgins, Bond, Klein, and Strauman (1986) found that people with large discrepancies between self and ideal self are more likely to be depressed. Other research suggests that how close one feels to the feared (or undesired) self may be even more critical to adjustment (Ogilvie, 1987). In other words, self-esteem and life satisfaction may depend more on *not* being like one's feared self than on being like one's ideal self.

Higgins (1987) has proposed a general theory relating self and affect. This theory is an intriguing contemporary elaboration of Rogers's notion that self-inconsistencies produce emotional difficulties. In addition to Rogers's ideal self, Higgins introduced the notion of the "ought self." Whereas the ideal self concept captures the individual's hopes, ambitions and desires, the ought self concept consists of the individual's beliefs about duties, responsibilities and obligations.

According to Higgins's theory, discrepancies between self and ideal lead to dejection-related emotions. For example, if someone has an ideal self of being an *A* student but receives a *C* in a class, he or she would likely feel disappointed, sad, or even depressed. In contrast, discrepancies between self and ought self should lead to agitation-related emotions. For example, if someone has an ought self of being an *A* student but receives a *C*, he or she would likely feel fearful, threatened, or anxious. Thus, the distinction between ideal self and ought self is important because it helps separate two kinds of self-relevant emotions: those related to dejection (e.g., disappointment, sadness, depression) and those related to agitation (e.g., fear, threat, anxiety).

Higgins argues that ideal and ought selves serve as self-guides to direct and organize social behavior. However, while they sometimes work together, these self-guides may also come into conflict. What we idealize for ourselves and what we feel obligated to do are not always the same. For example, some women feel conflict between their own wish to be successful professionals (an ideal self) and societal expectations that they ought to be mothers (an ought self). It is these kinds of conflicts that Rogers felt clients need to become aware of and work through in order to change in therapy.

CHANGE

Although a theory of personality developed out of Rogers's experiences in therapy, his central focus was on the therapeutic process itself. Rogers's main concern was with the manner in which personality change came about. He committed himself to a continuous subjective and objective involvement with the process of change. It was this process, the process of becoming, that was of greatest concern to him.

Therapeutic Conditions Necessary for Change

In his early work, Rogers placed great emphasis on the therapist's use of the technique of reflection of feeling. In this *nondirective* approach, there was minimal therapist activity and guidance of what the client said. Because some nondirective counselors were perceived as passive and uninterested, Rogers changed his focus to an emphasis on counselors being client-centered. Increasingly in the development of his approach to therapy, there was an emphasis on the counselor as actively interested in understanding the experiences of the client, a shift in emphasis from technique to attitude.

Ultimately, Rogers believed that the critical variable in therapy is the therapeutic climate (Rogers, 1966). If therapists can provide three conditions in their relationships with their clients, in a way that is phenomenologically meaningful to the clients, then therapeutic change will occur. The three conditions hypothesized by Rogers to be critical to therapeutic movement are **congruence** or genuineness, **unconditional positive regard**, and **empathic understanding**. Genuine therapists are themselves. They do not present a façade but rather are open and transparent. Therefore, clients feel that they can be trusted. Congruent or genuine therapists feel free to be what they are, to experience events in the therapeutic encounter as they occur. They can be with their clients on a person-to-person basis and be themselves. In a genuine relationship, therapists are free to share feelings with their clients, even when negative feelings toward the client are involved: "Even with such negative attitudes, which seem so potentially damaging but which all therapists have from time to time, I am suggesting that it is preferable for the therapist to be real than to put on a false posture of interest, concern, and liking that the client is likely to sense as false" (Rogers, 1966, p. 188).

The second condition essential for therapeutic movement is unconditional positive regard. This means that the therapist communicates a deep and genuine caring for the client as a person. The client is prized in a total, unconditional way. The unconditional positive regard provided

DRINKING, SELF-AWARENESS, AND PAINFUL FEELINGS

Why do people abuse alcohol and drugs? Why, after treatment, do so many relapse? In Chapter 3 it was suggested that many alcoholics and drug addicts use the defense mechanism of denial to cope with painful feelings. However, evidence of this relationship was not presented, nor was there analysis of how the self is experienced by substance abusers. This would appear to be important since substance abusers commonly report that they use drugs to handle painful feelings, with alcoholics often reporting that they drink to create a blur that blots out the painful aspects of life.

Though not conducted within the Rogerian framework, some recent research in this area is relevant to Rogers's views. The basic hypothesis of this research is that alcohol reduces self-consciousness and that alcoholics high in self-consciousness drink to reduce their awareness of negative life experiences. Individuals high in self-consciousness of inner experiences are those who would describe themselves

in terms of statements such as the following: I reflect about myself a lot; I'm generally attentive to my inner feelings; I'm alert to changes in my mood.

In laboratory research with social drinkers, it has been found that individuals high in self-consciousness consume more alcohol following failure experiences than do members of three other groups—individuals high in self-consciousness following success experiences and individuals low in self-consciousness regardless of whether they experience success or failure. Further, in a study of alcohol use in adolescents, it was found that increased alcohol use was associated with poor academic experience for students high in self-consciousness but not for those low in self-consciousness.

But what of alcoholics? And what about relapse? The latter would appear to be particularly significant since one-half to three-quarters of all treated alcoholics relapse within six months of the end of treatment. In a study of relapse in alcohol abuse following treatment, results comparable to the above were found; relapse appeared to be a joint function of negative events and high self-consciousness.

In many different populations and kinds of studies, a consistent relationship has been found between drinking, high self-consciousness, and experiences of personal failure. The research suggests that many individuals drink to reduce their level of awareness of painful negative experiences.

SOURCES: Baumeister, 1991; Hull, Young, & Jouriles, 1986; Pervin, 1988.

Defensive Behaviors: *Alcohol can be used to reduce awareness of painful feelings.*

by the therapist provides a nonthreatening context in which clients can explore their inner selves.

Finally, the condition of empathic understanding involves the therapist's ability to perceive experiences and their meaning to the client during the moment-to-moment encounter of psychotherapy. It is not a diagnostic formulation of the client's experiences or a rote reflection of what the client says, but instead a "being with" the client while being oneself. It is active listening and understanding of the feelings and personal meanings as they are experienced by the client.

Essentially, Rogers was talking about factors that are independent of the theoretical orientation of the therapist. In one important study, Fiedler (1950) had judges listen to the recorded interviews of experts and nonexperts of the psychoanalytic, nondirective (Rogerian), and Adlerian schools. The judges then sorted a number of descriptive items according to the extent to which they were characteristic of the interview. Fiedler found that, compared to nonexperts, experts were more successful in creating an ideal therapeutic relationship. Independent of orientation, experts were similar to one another in their ability to understand, to communicate with, and to maintain rapport with the client. In a related study, Heine (1950) investigated the relation between the theoretical orientation of therapists and therapeutic progress as viewed by clients. Clients sorted a number of statements to describe the changes they felt had occurred while in treatment and a number of statements to describe the therapeutic factors that they felt were responsible for the changes. Heine found that, according to their own reports, patients from psychoanalytic, nondirective, and Adlerian schools did not differ in the kinds of changes they reported had occurred. Furthermore, the clients who reported the greatest changes described similar factors as being responsible for these changes. A later study by Halkides (1958) found that the existence of the attitudes of genuineness, positive regard, and empathy in the therapist were related to therapeutic success, supporting Rogers's view that these indeed are the conditions necessary for change.

Outcomes of Client-Centered Therapy

One of Rogers's landmark contributions was his opening up the field of psychotherapy for systematic investigation. During the 1940s and 1950s, a number of studies were done by Rogers and others to determine the changes associated with client-centered therapy. Among the changes observed were a decrease in defensiveness and an increase in openness to experience; development of a more positive and more congruent self; development of more positive feelings toward others; and a shift away from using the values of others to asserting their own evaluations.

In addition to his work with neurotic clients, Rogers undertook a major therapeutic and research effort with schizophrenic patients (Rogers, 1967). In this study, scales were developed to measure the critical therapist variables of a therapeutic climate (empathy, congruence, positive regard) and the process of patient experiencing. Once more, Rogers found evidence that a positive therapeutic climate was associated with positive personality change. Indeed, these conditions seemed even more critical for schizophrenics than for neurotics. However, the therapeutic climate was found to depend on a complex dynamic interaction between patient and therapist, rather than on patient or therapist factors alone. Further, there was evidence that patients of therapists who were generally competent and conscientious, yet were unable to establish positive therapeutic conditions, sometimes got worse.

Summary of Distinguishing Characteristics

Although client-centered therapy has been changing, it has retained from its inception certain distinguishing characteristics (Rogers, 1942, 1977). First, there is the belief in the capacity of the client. Because the basic strivings of the organism are toward growth, actualization, and congruence, the therapist need not control or manipulate the therapeutic process. Second, there is an emphasis on the importance of the therapeutic relationship. What is important is that the therapist attempt to understand the client and to communicate this understanding. In contrast to the psychoanalytic search for hidden meanings and insights into the unconscious, the Rogerian therapist believes that personality is revealed in what clients say about themselves. Diagnoses are not important, since they say little about people's views of themselves and do not help to create the necessary therapeutic relationship. Third, there is the belief that client-centered therapy involves a predictable process. Growth occurs as the therapist establishes a helping relationship and is able to help free the strong drive of the individual to become mature, independent, and productive. Finally, with his research emphasis, Rogers tried to maintain ties among theory, therapy, and research. The client-centered theory of therapy is an if–then theory. The theory states that if certain *conditions* exist, then a *process* will occur that will lead to personality and behavioral change.

A Case Example: Mrs. Oak

As noted, one of Rogers's outstanding contributions to the field of psychotherapy was his leadership in opening it up as an area for investigation. He made available verbatim transcripts of therapy, films of client-centered therapy sessions, and a file of recorded therapy sessions that could be used for research purposes. In his 1954 book on psychotherapy and personality change, Rogers presented an extensive analysis of a single case, the case of Mrs. Oak. As Rogers observed, it is the individual case that makes a total research investigation come to life, that brings diverse facts together in the inter-related way in which they exist in life. The case of Mrs. Oak is presented here to illustrate the Rogerian approach to an understanding of personality.

Description of the Client and Problem

Mrs. Oak was a housewife in her late thir-ties when she came to the University of Chicago Counseling Center for treatment. At that time, she was having great diffi-culty in her relationships with her hus-band and with her adolescent daughter. Mrs. Oak blamed herself for her daugh-ter's psychosomatic illness. Mrs. Oak was described by her therapist as a sensitive person who was eager to be honest with herself and deal with her problems. She had little formal education but was intel-ligent and had read widely. Mrs. Oak was interviewed 40 times over a period of five-and-one-half months, at which point she terminated treatment.

Description of the Therapy

In the early interviews, Mrs. Oak spent much of her time talking about specific problems with her daughter and her hus-band. Gradually, there was a shift from these reality problems to descriptions of feelings:

> And secondly, the realization that last time I was here I experienced a—an emotion I had never felt before—which surprised me and sort of shocked me a bit. And yet I thought, I think it has a sort of a...the only word I can find to describe it, the only verbalization is a kind of cleansing. I—I really felt terribly sorry for something, a kind of grief.
>
> p. 311

At first the therapist thought Mrs. Oak was a shy, almost nondescript person and was neutral toward her. He quickly sensed, however, that she was a sensitive and interesting person. His respect for her grew, and he described himself as experi-encing a sense of respect for—and awe of—her capacity to struggle ahead through turmoil and pain. He did not try to direct or guide her; instead, he found satisfaction in trying to understand her, in trying to appreciate her world, in express-ing the acceptance he felt toward her.

MRS. OAK: And yet the—the fact that I— I really like this, I don't know, call it a poignant feel-ing. I mean...I felt things that I've never felt before. I like that, too. Uh-uh...maybe that's the way to do it. I—I just don't know today.

THERAPIST: M-hm. Don't feel at all sure, but you know that you some-how have a real, a real fond-ness for this poem that is yourself. Whether it's the way to go about this or not, you don't know.

p. 314

Given this supportive therapeutic cli-mate, Mrs. Oak began to become aware of feelings she had previously denied to awareness. In the twenty-fourth inter-view, she became aware of conflicts with her daughter that related to her own ado-lescent development. She felt a sense of shock at becoming aware of her own competitiveness. In a later interview, she became aware of the deep sense of hurt inside of her.

MRS. OAK: And then of course, I've come to...to see and to feel that over this...see, I've covered it up. (*Weeps*) But...and...I've covered it up with so much bitterness, which in turn I had to cover up. (*Weeps*) That's what I want to get rid of! I almost don't care if I hurt.

THERAPIST: (*Gently*) You feel that here at the basis of it, as you experienced it, is a feeling of real tears for yourself. But that you can't show, mustn't show, so that's been covered by bitterness that you don't like, that you'd like to be rid of. You almost feel you'd rather absorb the hurt than to...than to feel bitterness. (*Pause*) And what you seem to be saying quite strongly is, "I do hurt, and I've tried to cover it up."

MRS. OAK: I didn't know it.

THERAPIST: M-hm. Like a new discovery really.

MRS. OAK: (*Speaking at the same time*) I never really did know. But it's...you know, it's almost a physical thing. It's...sort of as though I—I—I were looking within myself at all kinds of...nerve endings and—and bits of—of...things that have been sort of mashed. (*Weeping*)

p. 326

At first, this increased awareness led to a sense of disorganization. Mrs. Oak began to feel more troubled and neurotic, as if she were going to pieces. She said she felt as though she were a piece of structure or a piece of architecture that had parts removed from it. In struggling with these feelings, Mrs. Oak began to recognize the dynamics of anxiety that had operated in her and to discover how, in an attempt to

cope with anxiety, she had deserted her self. She described her previous inability to recognize and "sort of simply embrace" fear. She described her feeling that the problem for her and for many others is that they get away from self.

Intermittently, Mrs. Oak expressed her feelings toward the therapist. At first she felt resentful that the therapist was not being very helpful and would not take responsibility for the sessions. During the course of therapy, she felt very strongly at times that the therapist didn't "add a damn thing." But, also in the course of therapy, she developed a sense of relationship with the therapist and how this relationship compared with the descriptions her friends had given of the relationship in psychoanalysis. She concluded that her relationship with the therapist was different, was something she would never be casual about—was the basis of therapy.

I'm convinced, and again I may sound textbookish, that therapy is only as deep as this combination, this relationship, as the need in the client is as deep as the need, and as deep as the willingness for the relationship to grow on the part of the therapist.

p. 399

Description of the Outcome

Progress did not occur in all areas. By the end of therapy, Mrs. Oak still had sexual conflicts. However, significant gains had been made in a number of areas. She began to feel free to be herself, to listen to herself, and to make independent evaluations. Mrs. Oak began to stop rejecting the feminine role and, more generally, began to accept herself as a worthwhile human being. She decided that she could not continue in her marriage, and she arrived at a mutually agreeable divorce with her husband. Finally, she obtained and held a challenging job. Through the conditions created within the therapeutic environment, Mrs. Oak was able to break down defenses that had been maintaining a marked incongruence between her self and her experience. With this increase in self-awareness, she was able to make positive changes in her life and become a more self-actualized human being.

THE CASE OF JIM

Semantic Differential: Phenomenological Theory

Jim filled out the semantic differential, rating the concepts self, ideal self, father, and mother on 104 scales. Typical scales were authoritarian–democratic, conservative–liberal, affectionate–reserved, warm–cold, and strong–weak. Each of the four concepts was rated on the same scales so that comparisons could be made of the meaning of these concepts for Jim. The test is clearly different from the Rorschach in being undisguised rather than disguised. The semantic differential test does not immediately follow from Rogerian theory. However, we can interpret data from the test in relation to Rogerian theory, since there is a phenomenological quality to the data and since we are assessing the individual's perception of his self and his ideal self.

First, we look at the ways in which Jim perceives his self. Jim perceives himself as intelligent, friendly, sincere, kind, and basically good. The ratings suggest that he sees himself as a wise person who is humane and interested in people. At the same time, other ratings suggest that he does not feel free to be expressive and uninhibited. Thus he rates himself as reserved, introverted, inhibited, tense, moral, and conforming. There is a curious mixture of perceptions: being involved, deep, sensitive, and kind while also being competitive, selfish, and disapproving. There is also the interesting combination of perceiving himself as being good and masculine but simultaneously weak and insecure. One gets the impression of an individual who would like to believe that he is basically good and capable of genuine interpersonal relationships at the same time that he is bothered by serious inhibitions and high standards for himself and others.

This impression comes into sharper focus when we consider the self-ratings in relation to those for the ideal self. In general, Jim did not see an extremely large gap between his self and his ideal self. However, large gaps did occur on a number of important scales. In an arbitrary way, we can define a gap of three or more positions on a 7-point scale as considerable and important. Thus, for example, Jim rated his self as 2 on the weak–strong scale and his ideal self as 7 on the same scale—a difference of five positions. In other words, Jim would like to be much stronger than he feels he is. Assessing his ratings on the other scales in a similar way, we find that Jim would like to be more of each of the following than he currently perceives himself to be: warm, active, equalitarian, flexible, lustful, approving, industrious, relaxed, friendly, and bold. Basically two themes appear. One has to do with *warmth*. Jim is not as warm, relaxed, and friendly as he would like to be. The other theme has to do with *strength*. Jim is not as strong, active, and industrious as he would like to be.

Jim's ratings of his parents give some indication of where he sees them in relation to himself in general and to these qualities in particular. First, if we compare the way Jim perceives his self with his perception of his mother and father, he clearly perceives himself to be much more like his father than his mother. Also, he perceives his father to be closer to his ideal self than his mother, although he perceives himself to be closer to his ideal self than either his mother or his father. However, in the critical areas of warmth and strength, the parents tend to be closer to the ideal self than Jim is. Thus, his mother is perceived to be more warm, approving, relaxed, and friendly than Jim and his father is perceived to be stronger, more industrious, and more active than Jim. The mother is perceived as having an interesting combination of personality characteristics. On the one hand, she is perceived as affectionate, friendly, spontaneous, sensitive, and good. On the other, she is perceived as authoritarian, superficial, selfish, unintelligent, intolerant, and uncreative.

Comments on the Data

With the autobiography and the semantic differential we begin to get another picture of Jim. We learn of his popularity and success through high school and of his good relationship with his father. We find support for the suggestions from the projective tests of anxiety and difficulties with women. Indeed, we learn of Jim's fears of ejaculating too quickly and not being able to satisfy women. However, we also find an individual who believes himself to be basically good and interested in doing humane things. We become aware of an individual who has a view of his self and a view of his ideal self, and of an individual who is frustrated because of the feelings that leave a gap between the two.

Given the opportunity to talk about himself and what he would like to be, Jim talks about his desire to be warmer, more relaxed, and stronger. We feel no need here to disguise our purposes, for we are interested in Jim's perceptions, meanings, and experiences as he reports them. We are interested in what is real for Jim—in how he interprets phenomena within his own frame of reference. We want to know all about Jim, but all about Jim as he perceives himself and the world about him.

When using the data from the semantic differential, we are not tempted to focus on drives, and we do not need to come to grips with the world of the irrational. In Rogers's terms, we see an individual who is struggling to move toward self-actualization, from dependence toward independence, from fixity and rigidity to freedom and spontaneity. We find an individual who has a gap between his intellectual and emotional estimates of himself. As Rogers would put it, we observe an individual who is without self-consistency, who lacks a sense of congruence between self and experience.

RECENT DEVELOPMENTS

ROGERS'S SHIFT IN EMPHASIS: FROM INDIVIDUALS TO GROUPS AND SOCIETY

Over the years, Rogers emphasized consistently the phenomenological approach, the importance of the self, and the change process. Whereas earlier there was a clear effort to combine clinical sensitivity with scientific rigor, later Rogers appeared to move increasingly toward sole reliance on personal, phenomenological types of studies: "To my way of thinking, this personal, phenomenological type of study—especially when one reads all of the responses—is far more valuable than the traditional 'hard-headed' empirical approach. This kind of study, often scorned by psychologists as being 'merely self-reports,' actually gives the deepest insight into what the experience has meant" (Rogers, 1970, p. 133). Rogers felt that the yield of orthodox scientific studies was minute compared to the insights obtained from clinical work.

Another shift for Rogers, at least in emphasis, was from the one-to-one therapy relationship to an interest in groups. In his book *On Encounter Groups* (Rogers, 1970), Rogers stated that changes occur more rapidly and clearly in small, intensive groups. Of particular interest to Rogers was the marital partnership group and alternatives to marriage (Rogers, 1972a). This interest focused on the extent to which there was openness, honesty, sharing, and movement toward awareness of inner feelings in the relationship. Finally, Rogers extended his person-centered approach to administration, minority groups, interracial, intercultural, and international relationships. Rogers expressed a revolutionary spirit in his belief that the person-centered approach could produce a change in the concepts, values, and procedures of our culture: "It is the *evidence* of the *effectiveness* of a person-centered approach that may turn a very small and quiet revolution into a far more significant change in the way humankind perceives the possible. I am much too close to the situation to know whether this will be a minor or a major event, but I believe it represents a radical change" (p. 286).

THE HUMAN POTENTIAL MOVEMENT

It was noted in the previous chapter that the tone and spirit of the Rogerian position are apparent in other theories of personality, particularly in the emphasis on the continuous striving of the organism to realize its inherent potential. Together with similar emphases by others, Rogers's position is part of the **human potential movement** that has been called the "third force" in psychology, offering an alternative to psychoanalysis and to behaviorism. Although there are theoretical differences among them, many humanist theories of personality are joined in the human potential movement. These theories respond to current concerns (e.g., anxiety, boredom, and lack of meaning) with an emphasis on self-actualization, fulfillment of potential, and openness to experience. Two major figures in this tradition are Kurt Goldstein and Abraham H. Maslow.

Kurt Goldstein

Kurt Goldstein came to the United States in 1935, at age 57, after achieving considerable status as a neurologist and psychiatrist in Germany. During World War I he had extensive experience working with brain-injured soldiers, and this work formed the foundation for his later views. He was impressed with the separation of functions that often occurs in brain-injured patients in contrast with the smooth, coordinated brain functioning of normal individuals. What he observed as differences in brain functioning and disturbances due to brain injury he extended to other aspects of personality functioning. Thus, for example, a healthy person is characterized by flexible functioning, whereas a disturbed person is characterized by rigid functioning. A healthy person is characterized by planned and organized functioning, whereas a disturbed person is characterized by mechanical functioning. A healthy person can delay and anticipate the future, whereas a disturbed person is bound by the past and the immediacy of the present. Yet, at the same time, Goldstein was impressed with the tremendous adaptive powers of his brain-injured patients, the same powers he felt were basic to all human functioning.

Like Freud, Goldstein (1939) had an energy view of the organism. However, his views concerning the movement and direction of energy flow differed considerably from that of Freud: "Freud fails to do justice to the positive aspect of life. He fails to recognize that the basic phenomenon of life is an incessant process of coming to terms with the environment; he only sees escape and craving for release. He only knows the lust of release, not the pleasure of tension" (1939, p. 333). Rather than seeking tension reduction, Goldstein feels the main motive for people is self-actualization. All aspects of human functioning are basically expressions of this one motive—to actualize the self. It can be expressed in such simple ways as eating or in such lofty ways as our highest creative pro-

Kurt Goldstein

ductions, but in the final analysis it is this motive that guides our behavior. Each person has inner potentials that are there to be fulfilled in the growth process. It is the recognition of this that ties Goldstein to others in the human potential movement.

Goldstein's work with brain-injured patients was important for workers in that area. In addition, his views on the general nature of human functioning have had a significant influence on humanist thinkers in the field of psychology.

Abraham H. Maslow

Abraham Maslow (1968, 1971) was perhaps the major theorist in the human potential movement. It was he who described this psychology as the third force in American psychology. He criticized the other forces, psychoanalysis and behaviorism, for their pessimistic, negative, and limited conception of humans. Instead, he proposed that people are basically good or neutral rather than evil, that there is in everyone an impulse toward growth or the fulfillment of potentials, and that psychopathology is the result of twisting and frustration of the essential nature of the human organism. Society often causes such twisting and frustration, and there is a problem when we assume that the result of this twisting and frustration is the essential nature of the organism. Rather, we should recognize what could occur were these obstacles to be removed. Here we see one of the reasons for the popularity of the human potential movement among those who feel excessively restricted and inhibited by their environment. Maslow speaks to these concerns and encourages the belief that things can be better if people are free to express themselves and be themselves.

In addition to this overall spirit, Maslow's views have been important in two ways. First, he suggested a view of human motivation that distin-

Abraham H. Maslow

guishes between such biological needs as hunger, sleep, and thirst and such psychological needs as self-esteem, affection, and belonging. One cannot survive as a biological organism without food and water; likewise, one cannot develop fully as a psychological organism without the satisfaction of other needs as well. Thus, these needs can be arranged in a hierarchy from basic physiological needs to important psychological needs (Figure 6.1).

Far too often, Maslow suggests, psychologists have been concerned with biological needs and have developed views of motivation suggesting that people respond only to deficiency and only seek tension reduction. While accepting that such motivation exists, Maslow calls on us to rec-

Physiological	I get an adequate amount of rest.
Safety	I think that the world is a pretty safe place these days.
Belongingness	I feel rootless.
Esteem	I feel dissatisfied with myself much of the time.
Self-Actualization	I have a good idea of what I want to do with my life.

Figure 6.1   Illustrative Questionnaire Items Measuring Maslow's Hierachy of Needs (arranged from low to high in the hierachy). *(Lester et al., 1983.)*

OVERCOMING ADVERSITY, BECOMING SELF-ACTUALIZED: THE LIFE OF MAYA ANGELOU

On January 20, 1993, when President Clinton was inaugurated on the steps of the Capitol, one woman stole the heart of America. This woman was Maya Angelou—author, performer, educator, and activist—who read her poem, "On the Pulse of Morning," and created inspiration, emotion, and compassion unmatched by any of the many speeches delivered at the occasion.

Born 1928 in St. Louis, Missouri, and growing up in the South during the Depression, Angelou overcame the hard-ship and adversity of her youth to lead a remarkably rich and productive life. Though pregnant at age 16, she managed to move on to San Francisco in 1944 where she studied music, dance, and drama while supporting herself and her son, in an era which did not look kindly on single mothers. Of this time she writes, with characteristically boundless energy, spirit, humor, and warmth:

> I was a twenty-one-year-old single
> parent with my son in kinder-
> garten. Two jobs allowed me an
> apartment, food, and child care
> payment. Little money was left over
> for clothes, but I kept us nicely
> dressed in discoveries bought at the
> Salvation Army and other second-
> hand shops. Loving colors, I bought
> for myself beautiful reds and
> oranges, and greens and pinks, and
> teals and turquoise...And quite
> often, I wore them in mixtures
> which brought surprise, to say the
> least, to the eyes of people who
> could not avoid noticing
> me...When my son was six and I
> twenty-two, he told me quite
> solemnly that he had to talk to
> me..."Mother, do you have any
> sweaters that match?" I was puz-
> zled at first...Then I realized that

Self-actualizing Individuals: *Maya Angelou overcame adversity to become a self-actualizing person..*

my attire, which delighted my heart and certainly activated my creativity, was an embarrassment to him...I learned to be a little more discreet to avoid causing him displeasure. As he grew older and more confident, I gradually returned to what friends thought of as my eccentric way of dressing. I was happier when I chose and created my own fashion...Seek the fashion which truly fits and befits you. You will always be in fashion if you are true to yourself and only if you are true to yourself.

SOURCE: Angelou, 1993, pp. 53–57.

In spite of her modest background, Angelou was cast first in an international tour of *Porgy and Bess* and then on Broadway; she went on to compose and direct, took an active leadership role in the civil rights movement, spent time working in Africa, held academic appointments at several universities, and published numerous stories, poems, and articles.

Beginning with her first autobiographical book, *I Know Why the Caged Bird Sings* (1970), she has told of her personal journey: a young Black girl who worked her way out of poverty and abuse and gradually transformed herself into an acclaimed writer, performer, and activist. Her life is exemplary in that she has responded to the demands of reality, resisted pressures for conformity, learned to accept and appreciate herself, and realized her extraordinary talents. In many ways, her life and her writings capture the essence of Maslow's concept of self-actualization:

It is wise to take the time to develop one's own way of being, increasing those things one does well and eliminating the elements in one's character which can hinder and diminish the good personality.

SOURCE: Angelou, 1993, p. 28.

This passage vibrantly expresses the basic tenet of Maslow's theory of personality, and the human potential movement more generally: Humans should always aim to realize their full and unique potential in life. Maya Angelou is one person who certainly has.

SOURCES: Angelou, 1993; McPherson, 1990.

ognize motivation that is not based on deficiency and that often involves an increase in tension—motivation that is expressed when people are being creative and fulfilling their potential.

A second major contribution by Maslow (1954) was his intensive study of healthy, self-fulfilling, self-actualizing individuals. These were figures from the past as well as some who were living at the time. From this research Maslow concluded that actualizing people have the following characteristics: they accept themselves and others for what they are; they can be concerned with themselves but also are free to recognize the needs and desires of others; they are capable of responding to the uniqueness of people and situations rather than responding in mechanical or stereotyped ways; they can form intimate relationships with at least a few special people; they can be spontaneous and creative; and they can resist conformity and assert themselves while responding to the demands of reality. Who are such people? Illustrative figures are Lincoln, Thoreau, Einstein, and Eleanor Roosevelt. Clearly these are very special individuals, and few people have all or even most of these characteristics to any substantial degree. What is suggested, however, is that all of us have the potential to move increasingly in the direction of these qualities.

At times, the views of Maslow and other leaders of the human potential movement sound almost religious and messianic. At the same time, they speak to the concerns of many people and serve as a corrective influence on other views that represent the human organism as passive, fragmented, and completely governed by tension-reducing motives from within or rewards from the environment.

Existentialism

The approach known as **existentialism** is not new to psychology, but one could hardly say that it has an established or a secure place in mainstream academic psychology. Existentialism is an approach that many people are deeply moved by, yet there is no single representative figure, nor is there agreement about its basic theoretical concepts. There are religious existentialists, atheistic existentialists, and antireligion existentialists. There are those who emphasize hope and optimism, as well as those who emphasize despair and nothingness. There are those who emphasize the philosophical roots of existentialism and those who emphasize the phenomena of clinical cases.

Granted all this diversity, what is it that establishes a common ground among those who would define themselves as existentialists? What is it about this approach that captivates some and leads others to reject it? Perhaps the most defining element of existentialism is the concern with *existence*—the person in the human condition. The existentialist is concerned with phenomena that are inherent in the nature of being alive, human, existing. What constitutes the essence of existence varies for different existentialists; however, all agree that certain concerns are fundamental to the very nature of our being and cannot be ignored, dismissed, explained away, or trivialized. Perhaps most of all, for the existentialist, people and experience are to be taken seriously (Pervin, 1960b).

Another major aspect of the existential view is the significance of the individual. The existentialist sees the person as singular, unique, and irreplaceable. For the philosopher Kierkegaard, the only existential problem is to exist as an individual. A number of additional emphases are related to this valuing of the individual. First, there is an emphasis on freedom. In the existentialist view freedom, consciousness, and self-reflection are what distinguish humans from other animals. Second, freedom involves responsibility. Each person is responsible for choices, for action, for being authentic, or for acting in "bad faith." Ultimately, each person is responsible for his or her own existence. Third, there is the existential concern with death, for it is here as nowhere else that the individual is alone and completely irreplaceable. Finally, there is an emphasis on phenomenology and an understanding of the unique experience of each person. Events are looked at in terms of their meaning for the individual rather than in terms of some standardized definition or the confirmation of some hypothesis. Thus, there is an interest in how any intrinsically human phenomenon can be experienced and given meaning—time, space, life, death, the self, or whatever.

We can perhaps better appreciate this approach by considering a few illustrations. For one, we can consider Rogers's (1980) discussion of loneliness. What is it that constitutes the existential experience of loneliness? Rogers suggested a number of contributing factors: the impersonality of our culture, its transient quality and anomie, the fear of a close relationship. However, what most defines loneliness is the effort to share something very personal with someone and to find that it is not received or is rejected: "A person is most lonely when he has dropped something of his outer shell or façade—the face with which he has been meeting the world—and feels sure that no one can understand, accept, or care for the part of his inner self that lies revealed" (quoted in Kirschenbaum, 1979, p. 351). On the other hand, there may also be the feeling of being understood (Van Kaam, 1966). Here the person has the sense that another individual can empathize in an understanding, accepting way. The feeling of being understood is associated with safety and relief from existential loneliness.

Another illustration involves the search for meaning in human existence (Frankl, 1955, 1958). The existential psychiatrist Viktor Frankl struggled to find meaning while in a concentration camp during World War II. He suggests that the will to meaning is the most human phenomenon of all, since other animals never worry about the meaning of their existence. Existential frustration and existential neurosis involve frustration and lack of fulfillment of the will to meaning. Such a "neurosis" does not involve the instincts or biological drives but rather is spiritually rooted in the person's escape from freedom and responsibility. In such cases the person blames destiny, childhood, the environment, or fate for what is. The treatment for such a condition, *logotherapy*, involves helping patients to become what they are capable of being, helping them to realize and accept the challenges of the opportunities that are open to them.

These are brief vignettes of representative existential concerns. Can they help us understand why existentialism is such a powerful force among some and so dismissed by others? For many people, existentialism speaks in a profound, humane way to issues that are of concern to them. On the other hand, other psychologists are critical of existentialism. In particular, there is criticism of an approach that abandons hope of predicting behavior in a lawful way and that has yet to establish its utility as a therapy.

CRITICAL EVALUATION

Except for occasional comments and questions, little has been done in this and the last chapter to assess the strengths and weaknesses of Rogers's theory of personality. It is time, however, to take a more critical look at the theory. Three questions, each related to the other, form the basis for this evaluation: (1) To what extent does Rogers's philosophical view of the person lead to omissions or to minimal consideration of critical causes of behavior? (2) To what extent does Rogers pay a price for defining (for research purposes) the self in terms of conscious perceptions? (3) In the elaboration of his theory in general, and in his views of the nature of anxiety and defense in particular, to what extent does Rogers represent a departure from Freud?

PHENOMENOLOGY

The phenomenological approach has been part of a significant effort by many psychologists to come to terms with human experience as it occurs. This approach seeks to consider life as it is experienced by the person without neglecting that which is most human, without splitting it into unrelated parts, and without reducing it to physiological principles. Two questions may be raised in relation to this approach: What are the limitations of a phenomenological approach to psychology? To what extent does the Rogerian counselor in fact take a phenomenological approach?

Clearly there are potential major limitations to the phenomenological approach in psychology. First, it may exclude from investigation certain critical variables, in particular those that are outside of human consciousness. If we restrict ourselves to that which people report, we may ignore important aspects of human functioning. Second, to build a science of psychology, one must go beyond the phenomenal world to develop concepts that are related to objective measures. The study of the phenomenal self is a legitimate part of psychology as long as it is studied empirically, with a boundless curiosity that is tempered by discipline and not with carefree speculation. Empathy is a legitimate mode of observation, but we must make sure that the observations made are reliable and that they can be checked against data from other modes of observation. Rogers was aware of these challenges to the phenomenological approach. His response was that the phenomenological approach is a valuable, perhaps necessary, one for psychology, but not the only one to be used (Rogers, 1964).

To turn to our second question, to what extent is the theory based on unbiased phenomenological investigation? The question was well put by MacLeod (1964, p. 138) in response to a presentation by Rogers: "On what basis are you so convinced that you have understood your client better than Mr. Freud has understood his patient?" Rogers's response was that the client-centered therapist brings fewer biases and preconceptions to therapy because of a lighter "baggage of preconceptions." The client-centered therapist is more likely to arrive at an understanding of the phenomenal world of an individual than is the Freudian analyst. In an early paper, Rogers (1947) stated that if one read the transcripts of a client-centered therapist, one would find it impossible to form an estimate of the therapist's views about personality dynamics. But we do not know that this is actually the case. Furthermore, that statement was made at a time when the theory was not well developed and therapists were being nondirective. With the development of the theory and the increased emphasis on client-centered but active involvement by the therapist, is this still true? We know that minor behaviors of the interviewer, including expressions such as "m-hm," may exert a profound effect on the verbalizations and behavior of the person being interviewed (Greenspoon, 1962). As one reads the transcripts of the therapy sessions, the comments of the counselor do not appear to be random or inconsequential as far as content is concerned. Counselors appear to be particularly responsive about the self and about feelings, and appear to formulate some of their statements in theory-related terms:

THERAPIST OF MRS.OAK: I'd like to see if I can capture a little of what that means to you. It is as if you've gotten very deeply acquainted with yourself on a kind of a brick-to-brick experiencing basis, and in that sense you have become more self-ish...in the discovering of what is the core of you as separate from all the other aspects, you come across the realization, which is a very deep and pretty thrilling realization, that the core of the self is not only without hate but is really something more resembling a saint, something really very pure, is the word I would use.

SOURCE: Rogers, 1954, p. 239

This point (of influence of the interviewer on the client) is critical, since so much of Rogers's data comes from clinical interviews.

In summary, the phenomenological approach has distinct merits and potential dangers. Rogers recognized that it is not the only approach to psychology and that it must be associated with empirical investigation. However, he did not consider adequately the role of unconscious forces in behavior. Furthermore, we are still unclear about the extent to which the behavior of the client in client-centered therapy is, in fact, free of the biases and preconceptions of the counselor.

THE CONCEPT OF SELF

The concept of self is an important area for psychological investigation, and one to which we shall return in future chapters. A number of questions are relevant to the status of the concept and to its measurement. The concept of self, as developed by Rogers, assumes constancy over time and across situations; that is, the way people view themselves at one point in time and in one situation is related to their views of themselves at other points in time and in other situations. Furthermore, the Rogerian concept of self assumes a total whole instead of a composite of unrelated parts.

Is there evidence to support these assumptions? Research supports the view that the self-concept is fairly stable across situations and over time (Coopersmith, 1967). Donahue, Robins, Roberts, and John's (1993) findings (see the box on Current Questions in Chapter 5, p. 180) support Rogers's views; having a self-concept that is consistent rather than variable across social roles is associated with good psychological adjustment. Similarly, high self-esteem has been related to both the temporal stability and internal consistency of the self-concept (Campbell & Lavallee, 1993). Other studies suggest, however, that individuals may have multifaceted views of self (Markus & Nurius, 1986). Does this multifaceted perspective on the self contradict Rogers's conception of a unified core self? Not necessarily. Rogers's conception emphasized *coherence*, not simplicity; having a self with the multiple components that are integrated with one another is consistent with Rogers's view of the self.

Finally, the basic structure of the self may vary from culture to culture. For example, one of the distinctive differences between Eastern and Western cultures is the degree to which the self is viewed as connected to others (Markus & Cross, 1990). In Eastern cultures, the self-concept consists of connection with others, and individuals are parts that cannot be understood when separated from the greater, collective whole. This cultural understanding of self stands in contrast to the dominant view of the self in Western civilization, which views the self as unique and separate from others. It is an interesting and important to consider whether Rogers's notions of the self, ideal self, self-consistency and self-actualization are applicable outside the Western cultures in which it originated.

In accepting the concept of the self as important for us as personality psychologists, we must be concerned with assessment hazards. One problem with many of the tests used to assess the self is that the items are not relevant to certain populations or miss important aspects of particular individuals. Our concepts of self are so varied that it is hard to develop a standard test that will tap the uniqueness of each individual. A second problem concerns the extent to which subjects are willing to give, or are capable of giving, honest self-reports. There is considerable evidence that self-reports can be influenced by conscious efforts to present oneself in socially desirable ways as well as by unconscious defensive processes (John & Robins, 1994a; Paulhus, 1990). It is assessment problems such as these that have frustrated so many investigators and left so many questions unanswered (Wylie, 1974).

The concept of self has a long history in psychology, receiving major attention during some periods and virtually disappearing from the literature during others (Pervin, 1996). Because of the difficulties in conceptualization and measurement, some psychologists have concluded that the relevant research has led us toward intellectual bankruptcy. Still, despite the many conceptual and methodological problems, the concept of self remains important to the layperson and to the field of psychology. Rogers, more than any other theorist, gave it the attention it deserves in theory, research, and clinical work.

CONFLICT, ANXIETY, AND DEFENSE

Critical attention has been given to Rogers's concepts of congruence, anxiety, and defense, and we have already compared these process concepts with the Freudian model of anxiety and defense. We can recall that, according to the theory, the individual may prevent awareness (through denial or distortion) of experiences that are subceived as threatening to the current structure of the self. Anxiety is the response of the organism to the subception that an experience incongruent with the self-structure may enter awareness, thus forcing a change in the self-concept. The incongruence between self and experience remains as a constant source of tension and threat. The constant need to use defensive processes results in a restriction of awareness and freedom to respond.

We have, then, a model in which the essential ingredients are conflict (incongruence), anxiety, and defense. Both the Freudian and Rogerian theories involve conflict, anxiety, and defense. In both theories the defenses are used to reduce anxiety. However, the sources of anxiety and, therefore, the processes through which anxiety is reduced are different in the two theories. For Freud, the conflict leading to anxiety is generally between the drives and some other part of the personality—the ego, or the superego as mediated by the ego. For Freud, the defenses are used to deal with the threatening nature of the instincts. The result may be formation of symptoms—symptoms representing partial expressions of the instinct and partial drive reduction. Rogers rejects the assumption that the defenses involve forbidden or socially taboo impulses such as those that Freud describes as coming from the id. Instead, he emphasizes perceptual consistency. Experiences that are incongruent or inconsistent with the self-concept are rejected, whatever their social character.

As observed previously, according to Rogers, favorable aspects of the self may be rejected because they are inconsistent or discrepant with the self-concept. Whereas Freud emphasized instincts and drive reduction, Rogers stressed experiences and their perceptual inconsistency with the self-concept. The ultimate goal for Freud was the proper channeling of the drives. The ultimate goal for Rogers was a state of congruence between organism and self. Rogers's description of possible modes of defense was similar to Freud's and was undoubtedly influenced by psychoanalytic theory. Generally, however, Rogers gave much less attention to differences in types of defense and did not try to relate the type of defense used to other personality variables, as is the case in psychoanalytic theory.

The above distinctions seem fairly clear until Rogers attempts to account for the development of a rift between organismic experience and self and introduces the concept of the need for positive regard. According to Rogers, if parents make positive regard conditional, their children will not accept certain values or experiences as their own. In other words, children keep out of awareness experiences that, if they were to accept them, might result in the loss of love. According to Rogers, the basic estrangement in humans is between self and experience, and this estrangement has come about because humans falsify their values for the sake of preserving the positive regard of others (Rogers, 1959, p. 226). This statement complicates Rogers's position, since it suggests that the individual disregards experiences that formerly were associated with pain (loss of love). This view is not unlike that of Freud's concerning trauma and the development of anxiety. In essence, one can again see a conflict model, in which experiences that were associated in the past with pain later become sources of anxiety and defense.

In the theoretical formulations of both Freud and Rogers, the concepts of conflict, anxiety, and defense play a major role in the dynamics of behavior. Both view well-adjusted people as less concerned with these processes and neurotic people as more concerned with them. For Freud, the process aspects of behavior involve the interplay among drives and the efforts of the defenses to reduce anxiety and to achieve drive reduction. For Rogers, the process aspects of behavior involve the efforts of the individual toward actualization and toward self-consistency. Although at times Rogers appears to emphasize the pain associated with the loss of positive regard, his major emphasis appears to be on the maintenance of congruence, which includes disregarding positive characteristics that are inconsistent with a negative self-concept and accepting negative characteristics that are consistent with this self-concept.

PSYCHOPATHOLOGY AND CHANGE

The Rogerian theory of psychopathology relates to a lack of congruence between experience and self, and the self–ideal self measure is not critical to the theory. On the other hand, self–ideal self discrepancies have been used consistently by Rogerians as a measure of adjustment. A variety of studies have found a relationship between the size of the self–ideal self discrepancy and characteristics such as psychopathology, self-depreciation, anxiety, and insecurity. On the other hand, other studies have found a relationship between high self–ideal self congruence and defensiveness. For example, Havener and Izard (1962) found a relationship between high congruence and unrealistically high self-esteem in paranoid schizophrenics. These subjects appeared to be defending against a complete loss of positive self-regard. Thus, it appears that the self–ideal self relationship is far too complex to be an altogether satisfactory measure of adjustment.

SUMMARY EVALUATION

How, then, may Rogers's theory be evaluated? Is it comprehensive, parsimonious, and relevant to research? The theory would appear to be reasonably comprehensive, though many areas of neglect remain. The theory says little about the course of growth and development or about the specific factors that determine one or another pattern. In contrast with Freud, one finds strikingly little mention of sex and aggression or of feelings such as guilt and depression, yet much of our lives seem to be concerned with these feelings.

The theory appears to be economical, particularly in relation to the process of change. Out of all the complexities of psychotherapy, Rogers attempted to define the few necessary and sufficient conditions for positive personality change.

In terms of research relevance, much of the theory expresses a philosophical, perhaps religious, view of the person. Assumptions most related to this view, such as the drive toward actualization, have remained assumptions and have not provided the basis for research. Also, the system is still without a measure of self-experience congruence. However, it is clear that the theory has provided extremely fertile ground for research. Rogers always kept clinical work, theory, and research in close touch with one another. Most of his work reflected a reluctance to sacrifice the rigors of science for the intuitive aspects of clinical work, and all of his work reflected an unwillingness to sacrifice the rich complexities of behavior for the empirical demands of science. As is properly the case, the development of his system was the result of a constant interplay among gross observations, theoretical formulations, and systematic research efforts.

This chapter on Rogers concludes by stating four major contributions (Table 6.1). Going beyond the discipline of psychology, Rogers developed

Table 6.1 Summary of Strengths and Limitations of Rogers's Theory and Phenomenology

Strengths	Limitations
1. Focuses on important aspects of human existence.	1. May exclude certain phenomena (unconscious processes, defenses, etc.) from research and clinical concern.
2. Attempts to recognize the holistic, integrated aspects of personality.	2. Lacks objective measures of behavior beyond self-report.
3. Tries to integrate humanism and empiricism.	3. Ignores the impossibility of being totally phenomenological—that is, making observations that are totally free of bias and preconception.
4. Aims at systematic inquiry into the necessary and sufficient conditions for therapeutic change.	

ROGERS AT A GLANCE

Structure	Process	Growth and Development
Self; ideal self	Self-actualization; congruence of self and experience; incongruence and defensive distortion and denial	Congruence and self-actualization versus incongruence and defensiveness

a point of view and an approach toward counseling that have influenced teachers, members of the clergy, and people in business. Within psychology, Rogers opened up the area of psychotherapy for research. By recording interviews, by making interviews and transcripts available to others, by developing clinically relevant measures of personality, and by demonstrating the potential value of research in the area, Rogers led the way in the legitimization of research on psychotherapy.

Finally, more than any other personality theorist, Rogers focused both theoretical and empirical attention on the nature of the self. The study of the self has always been a part of psychology, but it has, at times, been in danger of being dismissed as "mere philosophy." As MacLeod (1964) notes, you may not find many papers on the self at meetings of experimental psychologists, but clinicians find the problem staring them in the face. More than any other personality theorist, Rogers attempted to be objective about what is otherwise left to the artists:

> Slowly the thinker went on his way and asked himself: What is it that you wanted to learn from teachings and teachers, and although they taught you much, what was it they could not teach you? And he thought: It was the Self, the character and nature of which I wished to learn. I wanted to rid myself of the Self, to conquer it, but I could not conquer it, I could only deceive it, could only fly from it, could only hide from it. Truly, nothing in the world has occupied my thoughts as much as the Self, this riddle, that I live, that I am one and am separate and different from everybody else, that I am Siddartha; and about nothing in the world do I know less than about myself, about Siddartha.
>
> SOURCE: Hesse, 1951, p. 40

MAJOR CONCEPTS   *Client-centered therapy.* Rogers's term for his earlier approach to therapy in which the counselor's attitude is one of interest in the ways in which the client experiences the self and the world.

Pathology	Change	Illustrative Case
Defensive maintenance of self; incongruence	Therapeutic atmosphere: congruence, unconditional positive regard, empathic understanding	Mrs. Oak

Self-experience discrepancy. Rogers's emphasis on the potential for conflict between the concept of self and experience—the basis for psychopathology.

Congruence. Rogers's concept expressing an absence of conflict between the perceived self and experience. Also one of three therapist conditions suggested as essential for growth and therapeutic progress.

Unconditional positive regard. Rogers's term for the acceptance of a person in a total, unconditional way. One of three therapist conditions suggested as essential for growth and therapeutic progress.

Empathic understanding. Rogers's term for the ability to perceive experiences and feelings and their meanings from the standpoint of another person. One of three therapist conditions essential for therapeutic progress.

Human potential movement. A group of psychologists, represented by Rogers and Maslow, who emphasize the actualization or fulfillment of individual potential, including an openness to experience.

Existentialism. An approach to understanding people and conducting therapy, associated with the human potential movement, that emphasizes phenomenology and concerns inherent in existing as a person. Derived from a more general movement in philosophy.

1. For Rogers, the neurotic person is one who is in a state of incongruence between self and experience. Experiences that are incongruent with the self-structure are subceived as threatening and may be either denied or distorted.   **REVIEW**

2. Research in the area of psychopathology has focused on the discrepancy between the self and ideal-self concepts and the extent to which individuals disown or are vague about their feelings.

3. Rogers's focus was on the therapeutic process. The critical variable in therapy was seen as the therapeutic climate. Conditions of congruence (genuineness), unconditional positive regard, and empathic understanding were seen as essential to therapeutic change.

4. The case of Mrs. Oak, an early case published by Rogers, illustrates his publication of recorded therapy sessions for research purposes.

5. Rogers's views are part of the human potential movement, which emphasizes self-actualization and the fulfillment of each individual's potential. Kurt Goldstein, Abraham H. Maslow, and existentialists like Viktor Frankl are also representatives of this movement.

6. Although there are major differences in the theoretical formulations of Freud and Rogers, in both of their formulations the concepts of conflict, anxiety, and defense played a major role in the dynamics of behavior.

7. Rogers made an important contribution in focusing attention on the self as an important area for psychological investigation and in opening up the area of psychotherapy for research. His work focused on important aspects of human experience, emphasized the positive strivings of people, and suggested that basic conditions are necessary for therapeutic change. At the same time, questions can be raised about the phenomenological approach as a method of research and about the lack of adequate measures for concepts such as the self-actualization motive.

7

TRAIT APPROACHES TO PERSONALITY: ALLPORT, EYSENCK, AND CATTELL

Chapter Focus

Chris has just graduated from college and started a job in a new city. He feels lonely and wants to meet some new people. After some hesitation, he decides to place a personals ad. He stares at the piece of blank paper—what should he write? What kinds of personality characteristics would you choose to describe yourself? Here is one possibility: *"Unconventional, sensitive, fun-loving, happy, humorous, kind, slender graduate, 22, seeks similar qualities in sane soulmate."* Somebody who can be described by this list of *traits* may indeed be a desirable date!

Traits are those personality characteristics that are *stable over time* and *across situations*, so it's a good bet that somebody who is sensitive and kind today will also be sensitive and kind a month from now. This chapter is about traits, defined as broad internal dispositions to behave in particular ways. We review three theories and research programs that attempt to identify the basic dimensions of personality traits. Many trait researchers use a particular statistical procedure, *factor analysis*, to determine the basic traits that make up the human personality. The trait approach has been popular in American psychology and is rooted in common-sense or "folk" understandings of personality.

QUESTIONS TO BE ADDRESSED IN THIS CHAPTER

1. How can we characterize the consistent ways in which individuals differ in their feelings, thoughts, and behavior? How many different traits are needed to adequately describe these personality differences?

2. To what extent do individual differences have a genetic, inherited basis?

3. If individuals can be described in terms of their characteristic traits, how are we to explain variability in behavior across time and situations?

In the preceding chapters, we emphasized one major representative of each theoretical point of view. In this chapter on trait theory, we consider the views of a number of theorists. In the earlier chapters it was easy to pinpoint a major figure to represent that school of thought. This is not nearly as easy with trait theory.

THE TRAIT CONCEPT   Let us put aside the question of who is the leading theorist or representative of trait theory and consider instead the essentials of the point of view itself. This approach has been an influential part of personality theory and research. The basic assumption of the trait point of view is that people possess broad predispositions, called **traits**, to respond in particular ways. In other words, people may be described in terms of the likelihood of their *behaving, feeling,* or *thinking* in a particular way—for example, the likelihood of their acting outgoing and friendly, or feeling nervous and worried, or thinking about an artistic project or idea. People having a strong tendency to behave in these ways may be described as being high on these traits, for example, high on the traits of "extraversion" or "nervousness," whereas people with a lesser tendency to behave in these ways would be described as low on these traits. Although various trait theorists differ on how to determine the traits that make up the human personality, they all agree that traits are the fundamental building blocks of the human personality.

Beyond this, trait theorists agree that human behavior and personality can be organized into a hierarchy. An illustration of this hierarchical point of view comes from the work of Eysenck (Figure 7.1). Eysenck suggests that at its simplest level behavior can be considered in terms of specific responses. However, some of these responses are linked together and form more general habits. Again, we generally find that groups of habits tend to occur together to form traits. For example, people who prefer meeting people to reading also generally enjoy themselves at a lively party, suggesting that these two habits can be grouped together under the trait of sociability. To take another example, people who act without thinking first also tend to shout back at others, suggesting that these two habits can be grouped together under the trait of impulsiveness. At an even higher level of organization, various traits may be linked together to form what Eysenck has called secondary, higher-order factors or **superfactors.** How we find such traits and determine the hierarchical

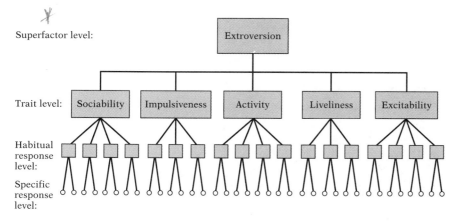

Figure 7.1 Diagrammatic Representation of Hierarchical Organization of Personality. *(Adapted from Eysenck, 1970) Reprinted by permission, Methuen & Co. publishers.*

organization of personality will be discussed shortly. What is important to recognize here is the conceptualization of personality as organized at various levels.

In sum, trait theories suggest that people have broad predispositions to respond in certain ways and that there is a hierarchical organization to personality.

THE TRAIT THEORY OF GORDON W. ALLPORT (1897–1967)

Gordon W. Allport probably will be remembered more for the issues he raised and the principles he emphasized than for a particular theory. Throughout his long and influential career, he emphasized the human, healthy, and organized aspects of behavior. This is in contrast with other views that emphasized the animalistic, neurotic, tension-reducing, and mechanistic aspects of behavior. In this regard, he was critical of aspects of psychoanalysis and was fond of telling the following story. While traveling through Europe at age 22, Allport decided it would be interesting to visit Freud. When he entered Freud's office, he was met with expectant silence as Freud waited to learn of Allport's mission. Finding himself unprepared for silence, Allport decided to start an informal conversation with the description of a four-year-old boy with a dirt phobia, whom he had met on the train. After he completed his description of the boy and his compulsive mother, Freud asked, "And was that little boy you?" Allport describes his response as follows:

> Flabbergasted and feeling a bit guilty, I contrived to change the subject. While Freud's misunderstanding of my motivation was

Gordon W. Allport

amusing, it also started a deep train of thought. I realized that he was accustomed to neurotic defenses and that my manifest motivation (a sort of rude curiosity and youthful ambition) escaped him. For therapeutic progress he would have to cut through my defenses, but it so happened that therapeutic progress was not here an issue. This experience taught me that depth psychology, for all its merits, may plunge too deep, and that psychologists would do well to give full recognition to manifest motives before probing the unconscious.

SOURCE: Allport, 1967, p. 8

A particularly amusing aspect of this episode is that Allport was indeed a person who was very meticulous, punctual, neat, and orderly—possessing many of the characteristics associated by Freud with the compulsive personality. In fact, Freud may not have been as far off in his question as Allport suggested.

Allport's first publication, written with his older brother Floyd, centered on traits as an important aspect of personality theory (Allport & Allport, 1921). Allport believed that traits are the basic units of personality. According to him, traits actually exist and are based in the nervous system. They represent generalized personality dispositions that account for regularities in the functioning of a person across situations and over time. Traits can be defined by three properties—*frequency, intensity*, and *range of situations*. For example, a very submissive person would frequently be very submissive over a wide range of situations.

TRAITS, STATES, AND ACTIVITIES

In a now classic analysis of personality descriptors, Allport and Odbert (1936) differentiated personality traits from other important units of analysis in personality research. Allport and Odbert defined traits as "generalized and personalized determining tendencies—consistent and stable modes of an individual's adjustment to his environment" (1936, p. 26). Traits are thus different from states and activities which describe those aspects of personality that are temporary, brief, and caused by external circumstances. Chaplin, John, and Goldberg (1988) replicated Allport and Odbert's classifications of personality descriptors into three categories: traits, states, and activities. Table 7.1 lists examples of each of the three categories. For example, whereas a person may well be *gentle* throughout his or her lifetime, an *infatuation* (an internal state) typically does not last and even the most enjoyable *carousing* must come to an end.

KINDS OF TRAITS

Allport made a distinction among **cardinal traits**, **central traits**, and **secondary dispositions**. A cardinal trait expresses a disposition that is

Table 7.1   Prototypical Examples of Traits, States, and Activities

Traits	States	Activities
Gentle	Infatuated	Carousing
Domineering	Pleased	Ranting
Trustful	Angry	Snooping
Timid	Invigorated	Leering
Cunning	Aroused	Reveling

SOURCE: Chaplin et al., 1988.

so pervasive and outstanding in a person's life that virtually every act is traceable to its influence. For example, we speak of the Machiavellian person, named after Niccolo Machiavelli's portrayal of the successful Renaissance ruler; of the sadistic person named after the Marquis de Sade; and of the authoritarian personality who sees virtually everything in black–white, stereotyped ways. Generally people have few, if any, such cardinal traits. Central traits (e.g., honesty, kindness, assertiveness) express dispositions that cover a more limited range of situations than is true for cardinal traits. Secondary traits represent dispositions that are the least conspicuous, generalized, and consistent. In other words, people possess traits with varying degrees of significance and generality.

It is important to recognize that Allport did not say that a trait is expressed in all situations independent of the characteristics of the situation. Indeed, Allport recognized the importance of the situation in explaining why a person does not behave the same way all the time. He wrote: "traits are often aroused in one situation and not in another" (Allport, 1937, p. 331). For example, even the most aggressive people can be expected to modify their behavior if the situation calls for nonaggressive behavior, and even the most introverted person may behave in an extraverted fashion in certain situations. A trait expresses what a person *generally* does over many situations, not what will be done in any one situation. According to Allport, both trait and situation concepts are necessary to understand behavior. The trait concept is necessary to explain the consistency of behavior, whereas recognition of the importance of the situation is necessary to explain the variability of behavior.

FUNCTIONAL AUTONOMY

Allport is known for his emphasis not only on traits but also on the concept of **functional autonomy**. This concept suggests that although the motives of an adult may have their roots in the tension-reducing motives of the child, the adult grows out of them and becomes independent of these earlier tension-reducing efforts. What originally began as an effort to reduce hunger or anxiety can become a source of pleasure and motivation in its own right. What began as an activity designed to earn a liv-

Functional Autonomy: *Sometimes a person may select an occupation for one reason, such as job security, and then remain in it for other motives, such as pleasure in the activity itself.*

ing can become pleasurable and an end in itself. Although hard work and the pursuit of excellence can be motivated originally by a desire for approval from parents and other adults, they can become valued ends in themselves—pursued independently of whether they are emphasized by others. Thus, "what was once extrinsic and instrumental becomes intrinsic and impelling. The activity once served a drive or some simple need; it now serves itself, or in a larger sense, serves the self-image (self-ideal) of the person. Childhood is no longer in the saddle; maturity is" (Allport, 1961, p. 229).

IDIOGRAPHIC RESEARCH

Finally, Allport is known for his emphasis on the uniqueness of the individual. Allport emphasized the utility of **idiographic research**, or the in-depth study of individuals, for the purpose of learning more about people generally. One part of such research involves using materials unique to the individual. For example, Allport published 172 letters from a woman that provided the basis for clinical characterization of her personality as well as for quantitative analysis. Another part of idiographic research involves using the same measures for all people but comparing an individual's scores on one scale with his or her scores on other scales, rather than with the scores of other people on each scale. For example, it may be important to know whether a person values being with people more or less than acquiring possessions, a comparison within the individual. This may be more important than knowing whether that individual values being with people more or less than does another person, or values acquiring possessions more or less than another person, both being across persons comparisons. This aspect of the idiographic approach leads to an emphasis on the pattern and organization of traits within a person rather than an emphasis on how a person stands on each trait relative to other people. Finally, Allport's emphasis on the uniqueness of the individual led him to suggest that there are unique traits for each person that cannot be captured by science. Allport's emphasis on the idiographic approach to research was important and is regaining popularity (Pervin, 1983). However, his emphasis on unique traits was interpreted to mean that a science of personality was not possible, and resulted in considerable controversy that did not help to advance the field.

COMMENT ON ALLPORT

In 1924 Allport gave the first course on personality ever taught in the United States and in 1937 published *Personality: A Psychological Interpretation*, which for 25 years was a basic text in the field. His interests ranged broadly across social psychology as well as personality. He raised many critical issues and discussed the trait concept with such balance and wisdom that he can still be read with profit today (e.g., John & Robins, 1993). Thus, for example, Allport (1961) suggested that behavior generally expresses the action of many traits, that conflicting dispositions can exist within the person, and that traits are expressed in part by the person's *selection of* situations as opposed to his or her *response to* situations. Although Allport emphasized the concept of trait and tried to clarify its relation to the situation, he did little research to establish the existence and utility of specific trait concepts. Similarly, although he believed that many traits were hereditary, he did not conduct research to substantiate this. To consider illustrations of such conceptual and research efforts, we must turn to the works of Hans J. Eysenck and Raymond B. Cattell.

THE THREE-FACTOR THEORY OF HANS J. EYSENCK (1916–)

Hans J. Eysenck was born in Germany in 1916 and later fled to England to escape Nazi persecution. His work has been influenced by methodological advances in the statistical technique of factor analysis; by the thinking of European typologists such as Jung and Kretschmer; by the research on heredity of Sir Cyril Burt; by the experimental work on classical conditioning by the Russian physiologist Pavlov; and by the American learning theory of Clark Hull. Although his work has included a sampling of both normal and pathological populations, most of it has been done at the Institute of Psychiatry, Maudsley Hospital, England.

Hans J. Eysenck

TRAIT MEASUREMENT: FACTOR ANALYSIS

Eysenck is strict in his standards for scientific pursuits and places great emphasis on conceptual clarity and measurement. For this reason he has been consistently one of the harshest critics of psychoanalytic theory. Although he supports trait theory, he has emphasized the need to develop adequate measures of traits, the need to develop a theory that can be tested and is open to disproof, and the importance of establishing biological foundations for the existence of each trait. Eysenck emphasizes efforts such as these as being important to avoid a meaningless circularity of explanation, whereby a trait is used to explain behavior that serves as the basis for the concept of the trait in the first place. For example, Jack talks to others because he is high on the trait of sociability, but we know that he is high on this trait because we observe that he spends a lot of time talking to others.

The basis for Eysenck's emphasis on measurement and the development of a classification of traits is the statistical technique of **factor analysis**. In a factor-analytic study, a large number of test items is administered to many subjects. How are their responses to these items related? Individuals who agree with the item "I often go to large and noisy parties," also tend to agree with the item "I enjoy spending time with others" and to disagree with the item "If I can help it, I'd rather stay home than go out at night." Factor analysis is a statistical technique that can identify groups, clusters, or factors of related items. For example, the factor formed by these three items is defined by two gregariousness items on one end and by an item about reclusiveness on the other end, and thus suggests that a dimension akin to sociability is common to these three items. According to trait theory, there are natural structures in personality, and factor analysis allows us to detect them. If things (variables, test responses) covary, that is, if they appear and disappear together, then one can infer that they have some common feature behind them, that they belong to the same aspect of personality functioning. Factor analysis assumes that behaviors that covary across individuals are related. Factor analysis is thus a statistical device for determining which behaviors are related but independent of others, thereby determining the units or natural elements in personality structure.

The resulting trait factors (e.g., sociability) can then be interpreted and named by considering the characteristic that seems common to the items or behaviors found to be interrelated. Through further ("secondary") factor analyses, Eysenck determines the basic dimensions that underlie the trait factors found in the initial round of analysis. These dimensions represent secondary or **superfactors**. Thus, for example, the traits of sociability, impulsiveness, activity, liveliness, and excitability can be grouped together under the superordinate concept of extraversion (Figure 7.1). The term *superfactor* makes clear it defines a dimension with a low end (introversion) and a high end (extraversion), such that people may fall along various points between the two extremes.

BASIC DIMENSIONS OF PERSONALITY

In his earlier research Eysenck found two basic dimensions of personality that he labeled as **introversion–extraversion** and **neuroticism** (emotionally stable–unstable). The relationship of these two basic dimensions of personality to the four major temperamental types distinguished by the Greek physicians Hippocrates and Galen and to a wider range of personality characteristics is presented in Figure 7.2.

Following the initial emphasis on only two dimensions, Eysenck has added a third dimension, which he calls **psychoticism**. People high on this dimension tend to be solitary, insensitive, uncaring about others, and opposed to accepted social custom. Eysenck and Long (1986) note that there is considerable support for the existence of these three dimensions. They have been found in studies of different cultures, and there is evidence of an inherited component to each.

A further appreciation of Eysenck's theoretical system can be gained from a more detailed consideration of one of these three dimensions, that of introversion–extraversion. According to Eysenck, the typical extravert is sociable, likes parties, has many friends, craves excitement, acts on the spur of the moment, and is impulsive. As can be seen, there appear to be two aspects to this dimension, sociability and impulsiveness, that can be separated to a certain extent but that have been found to be related sufficiently to be linked under the same concept of extraversion. In contrast to these characteristics, the introverted person tends to be quiet, introspective, reserved, reflective, distrustful of impulsive

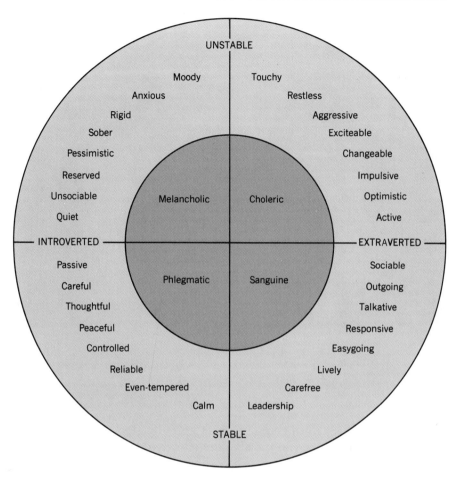

Figure 7.2 The Relationship of Two Dimensions of Personality Derived from Factor Analysis to Four Greek Temperamental Types. *(Eysenck, 1970). Reprinted by permission, Routledge & Kegan Paul Ltd., publishers.*

decisions, and prefers a well-ordered life to one filled with chance and risk.

Questionnaire Measures

Eysenck has developed numerous questionnaires to measure people along the dimension of introversion–extraversion—the Maudsley Personality Inventory, the Eysenck Personality Inventory, and most recently the Eysenck Personality Questionnaire. The typical extravert will answer yes to questions such as: Do other people think of you as very lively? Would you be unhappy if you could not see lots of people most of the time? Do you often long for excitement? In contrast, the typical intro-

Introversion–Extraversion: *Hans Eysenck suggests that a basic dimension of personality involves whether people tend to be unsociable, quiet, and passive (introverts) or sociable, outgoing, and active (extraverts).*

vert will answer yes to these questions: Generally, do you prefer reading to meeting people? Are you mostly quiet when you are with people? Do you stop and think things over before doing anything? Other illustrative items from the Maudsley and Eysenck personality inventories are presented in Figure 7.3. These include items relevant to neuroticism and a lie scale to detect individuals who are faking responses to look good, as well as items relevant to extraversion–introversion. Although the content and direction of scored responses may be obvious in some cases, in other cases this is not true. In addition to such questionnaires, other, more objective measures have been devised. For example, there is some suggestion that the "lemon drop test" may be used to distinguish between introverts and extraverts. In this test a standard amount of lemon juice is placed on the subject's tongue. Introverts and extraverts differ in the amount of saliva produced when this is done.

Research Findings

Are there other significant and theoretically meaningful differences in behavior associated with varying scores on the extraversion—introversion dimension? A review of the dimension presents an impressive array of findings. For example, introverts are more sensitive to pain than are

	Yes	No
1. Do you usually take the initiative in making new friends?	___	___
2. Do ideas run through your head so that you cannot sleep?	___	___
3. Are you inclined to keep in the background on social occasions?	___	___
4. Do you sometimes laugh at a dirty joke?	___	___
5. Are you inclined to be moody?	___	___
6. Do you very much like good food?	___	___
7. When you get annoyed, do you need someone friendly to talk about it?	___	___
8. As a child did you always do as you were told immediately and without grumbling?	___	___
9. Do you usually keep "yourself to yourself" except with very close friends?	___	___
10. Do you often make up your mind too late?	___	___

Note: The above items would be scored in the following way: *Extraversion:* 1 Yes, 3 No, 6 Yes, 9 No; *Neuroticism:* 2 Yes, 5 Yes, 7 Yes, 10 Yes; *Lie Scale:* 4 No, 8 Yes.

Figure 7.3   *Illustrative Items for Extraversion, Neuroticism, and Lie Scale from the Maudsley Personality Inventory and Eysenck Personality Inventory.*

extraverts, they become fatigued more easily than do extraverts, excitement interferes with their performance whereas it enhances performance for extraverts, and they tend to be more careful but less fast than extraverts (Wilson, 1978). The following additional differences have been found:

1. Introverts do better in school than extraverts, particularly in more advanced subjects. Also, students withdrawing from college for academic reasons tend to be extraverts, whereas those who withdraw for psychiatric reasons tend to be introverts.

2. Extraverts prefer vocations involving interactions with other people, whereas introverts tend to prefer more solitary vocations. Extraverts seek diversion from job routine, whereas introverts have less need for novelty.

3. Extraverts enjoy explicit sexual and aggressive humor, whereas introverts prefer more intellectual forms of humor such as puns and subtle jokes.

4. Extraverts are more active sexually, in terms of frequency and different partners, than introverts.

5. Extraverts are more suggestible than introverts.

This last finding is illustrated in a study of a hyperventilating epidemic in England (Moss & McEvedy, 1966). An initial report by some girls of fainting and dizziness was followed by an outbreak of similar complaints, with 85 girls needing to be taken to the hospital by ambulance—"they were going down like ninepins." A comparison of the girls who were affected with those who were not demonstrated that, as expected, the affected girls were higher in both neuroticism and extraversion. In other words, those individuals whose personalities were most predisposed to suggestion proved most susceptible to influence by suggestions of a real epidemic.

Finally, the results of an investigation of study habits among introverts and extraverts may be of particular interest to college students. The research examined whether such personality differences are associated with differing preferences for where to study and how to study, as would be predicted by Eysenck's theory. In accord with Eysenck's theory of individual differences, the following was found: (1) extraverts more often chose to study in library locations that provided external stimulation than did introverts; (2) extraverts took more study breaks than did introverts; (3) extraverts reported a preference for a higher level of noise and for more socializing opportunities while studying than did introverts (Campbell & Hawley, 1982). Extraverts and introverts differ in their physiological responses to the same noise level (introverts show a greater level of response), and each functions best at his or her preferred noise level (Geen, 1984). An important implication of such research is that different environmental designs for libraries and residence units might best fit the needs of introverts and extraverts.

Biological Basis

What is the theoretical underpinning of this dimension? Eysenck suggests that individual variations in introversion–extraversion reflect differences in neurophysiological functioning. Basically introverts are more easily aroused by events and learn social prohibitions more easily than extraverts. As a result, introverts are more restrained and inhibited. There also is some evidence that introverts are more influenced by punishments in learning, whereas extraverts are more influenced by rewards. It is hypothesized that individual differences along this dimension have both hereditary and environmental origins. Indeed, several studies of identical and fraternal twins suggest that heredity plays a major part in accounting for differences between individuals in their scores on this dimension (Loehlin, 1992; Plomin, 1994; Plomin, Chipuer, & Loehlin, 1990). Evidence that the dimension of introversion–extraversion consistently shows up in cross-cultural studies, that individual differences are stable over time, and that genetic factors make a strong contribution to such individual differences all argue for a strong biological basis for the dimensions. Indeed, many studies of various indices of biological functioning (e.g., brain activity, heart rate, hormone level, sweat gland activity) can be cited in support of this conclusion (Eysenck, 1990).

In sum, the introversion–extraversion dimension represents an important organization of individual differences in behavioral functioning that is rooted in inherited differences in biological functioning. These differences can be discovered through the use of factor analysis and measured through the use of questionnaires as well as laboratory procedures.

Let us now turn to the other two dimensions and briefly consider how the theory is extended into other realms. According to Eysenck, people high on neuroticism tend to be emotionally labile and frequently complain of worry and anxiety, as well as of bodily aches (e.g., headaches, stomach difficulties, dizzy spells, etc.). Here, too, an inherited biological difference in nervous system functioning is suggested as the basis for individual differences on this dimension. In this case, the underlying principle is that individuals high on neuroticism respond quickly to stress and show a slower decrease in the stress response once the danger has disappeared than is true for more stable (low neuroticism) individuals. Although less is known about the basis for the psychoticism dimension, here, too, a genetic association is suggested, in particular an association linked with maleness. In general, then, genetic factors play a major role in determining personality and social behavior. Indeed, according to Eysenck, "genetic factors contribute something like two-thirds of the variance in major personality dimensions" (1982, p. 28). More recent research, however, suggests that two-thirds is likely an overestimate and that the figure is closer to 40 percent (Loehlin, 1992; Plomin, 1994).

PSYCHOPATHOLOGY AND BEHAVIOR CHANGE

Eysenck's theory of personality is closely linked to his theory of abnormal psychology and behavior change. The kind of symptoms or psychological difficulties one is likely to develop are related to basic personality characteristics and principles of nervous system functioning. According to Eysenck, a person develops neurotic symptoms because of the joint action of a biological system and because of experiences that contribute to the learning of strong emotional reactions to fear-producing stimuli. Thus, the vast majority of neurotic patients tend to have high neuroticism and low extraversion scores (Eysenck, 1982, p. 25). In contrast, criminals and antisocial persons tend to have high neuroticism, high extraversion, and high psychoticism scores. Such individuals show weak learning of societal norms.

Despite the strong genetic component in the development and maintenance of such disorders, Eysenck claims that one need not be pessimistic concerning the potential for treatment: "The fact that genetic factors play a large part in the initiation and maintenance of neurotic disorders and also of criminal activities, is very unwelcome to many people who believe that such a state of affairs must lead to therapeutic nihilism. If heredity is so important, they say, then clearly behavior modification of any kind must be impossible. This is a completely erroneous interpretation of the facts. What is genetically determined are predispositions for a person to act and behave in a certain manner, when put in certain situations" (1982, p. 29). Accordingly, it is possible for a person to avoid certain potentially traumatic situations, to unlearn certain learned fear responses, or to learn (acquire) certain codes of social conduct. Thus, while emphasizing the importance of genetic factors, Eysenck has been a major proponent of behavior therapy, or the systematic treatment of abnormal behavior according to the principles of learning theory.

We will not extend Eysenck's discussion of behavior therapy here since the basic principles will be covered in the chapter on learning foundations of personality (Chapter 9). However, we may conclude our discussion by noting that Eysenck has been a frequent, outspoken critic of psychoanalytic theory and therapy. In particular, his criticism has emphasized the following points: (1) psychoanalysis is not a scientific theory since it is not falsifiable; (2) neurotic and psychotic disorders constitute separate dimensions rather than points on a continuum of regression; (3) abnormal behavior represents learned maladaptive responses rather than disguised expressions of underlying, unconscious conflicts; (4) all therapy involves the application, intended or otherwise, of learning principles. In particular, therapy with neurotic behaviors involves the unlearning or extinction of learned responses (Eysenck, 1979). According to Eysenck, psychoanalysis is not generally an effective method of treatment and succeeds only to the extent that the principles of behavior therapy are unwittingly or accidentally brought into play by the analyst.

Most recently, Eysenck (1991) has attempted to relate personality traits to the likelihood of developing disorders such as heart disease and cancer, and has described behavioral forms of therapy that increase longevity when such illnesses do occur. These studies are not described here in detail because the results remain controversial and because they are not as directly tied to the theory as would be desired.

COMMENT ON EYSENCK

Befitting a trait theorist, Eysenck's scientific record has been consistent in a number of ways. Noteworthy among the positive aspects of this record are the following: (1) Eysenck has been a prolific contributor to diverse areas. In addition to his continuing focus on individual differences and principles of behavior change, he has contributed to the study of criminology, education, aesthetics, creativity, genetics, psychopathology, and political ideology. His personality tests have been translated into many foreign languages and are used in research around the world. (2) Eysenck has consistently emphasized the value of both correlational and experimental research. Referring to Cronbach's discussion of the two disciplines of scientific psychology (Chapter 2), Eysenck suggests that he has "always looked upon these two disciplines not as in any sense rivals, but as complementary to each other, and indeed each one essential for the success of the other" (1982, p. 4). (3) Eysenck has tied his personality variables to methods of measurement, a theory of nervous system functioning and learning, and an associated theory of psychopathology and behavior change. His theory goes beyond description and can be tested. (4) Historically, Eysenck has been prepared to swim against the tide and argue in favor of unpopular views: "I have usually been against the establishment and in favor of the rebels. Readers who wish to interpret this in terms of some inherited oppositional tendency, some acquired Freudian hatred of father substitutes, or in any other way are of course welcome. I prefer to think that on these issues the majority were wrong, and I was right. But then of course I would think that; only the future will tell" (1982, p. 298).

Given these noteworthy contributions, one might wonder, as did one recent reviewer of Eysenck's work, why Eysenck has not been "universally celebrated by psychologists everywhere" (Loehlin, 1982, p. 623). Prominent among the reasons for this is Eysenck's tendency to dismiss the contributions of others and exaggerate the empirical support for his own point of view (Buss, 1982; Loehlin, 1982). Most psychologists familiar with Eysenck's work feel that it is significant, but that frequently he ignores contradictory findings and overstates the strength of positive results. In relation to this, two additional points can be made. First, alternative models have been proposed that better fit the available data. In one such model, it is suggested that individual differences on the dimensions of impulsivity and anxiety are critical (Gray, 1990). Here there is acceptance of the data emphasized by Eysenck and of the import of tying personality variables to biological functions, but different personality dimensions are emphasized. Second, many psychologists feel that it is impossible to account for individual differences with only two or three dimensions. As we shall see in the next section, the trait theorist Cattell suggests that we consider a larger number of traits and stay at the level of traits, rather than move to the superfactor level of personality description. Finally, there are psychologists who do not share the trait point of view at all, an issue that we will address in some detail in the next chapter.

Raymond B. Cattell was born in 1905 in Devonshire, England. He obtained a B.Sc. degree in chemistry from the University of London in 1924. Cattell then turned to psychology and obtained a Ph.D. degree at the same university in 1929. Before coming to the United States in 1937, Cattell did a number of studies in personality, and acquired clinical experience while directing a child guidance clinic. Since coming to the United States he has held positions at Columbia, Harvard, Clark, and Duke Universities. For 20 years he was Research Professor of Psychology and Director of the Laboratory of Personality Assessment at the University of Illinois. During his professional career, he has written more than 200 articles and 15 books.

THE FACTOR-ANALYTIC TRAIT APPROACH OF RAYMOND B. CATTELL (1905–)

Raymond B. Cattell

Although relatively little is known of the experiences that shaped Cattell's life and work, a number of influences seem apparent. First, Cattell's interest in the use of factor-analytic methods in personality research and his attempt to develop a hierarchical theory of personality organization can be related to his associations with two of the same British psychologists who influenced Eysenck: Spearman and Burt. Second, Cattell's views on motivation were influenced by another British psychologist, William McDougall.

His years spent jointly in personality research and clinical experience were a third influence on Cattell. These years sensitized him to the assets and limitations of clinical and experimental research. Finally, Cattell's earlier experience in chemistry influenced much of his later thinking in psychology. In chemistry, the development of the periodic table by Dmitry Mendeleyev in 1869 led to renewed experimental activity. Just as Mendeleyev developed a classification of the elements in chemistry, much of Cattell's work can be viewed as an attempt to develop a classification of variables for experimental research in personality. Cattell hoped that factor analysis would lead psychology to its own periodic table of the elements.

CATTELL'S VIEW OF SCIENCE

Cattell distinguishes among three methods in the study of personality: **bivariate**, **multivariate**, and **clinical**. The typical *bivariate* experiment, which follows the classical experimental design of the physical sciences, contains two variables, an independent variable that is manipulated by the experimenter and a dependent variable that is measured to observe the effects of the experimental manipulations. In contrast to the bivariate method, the *multivariate* method studies the interrelationships among many variables at once. Furthermore, in the multivariate experiment the investigator does not manipulate the variables. Instead, the experimenter allows life to make the experiments and then uses statistical methods to extract meaningful dimensions and causal connections. The method of factor analysis illustrates the multivariate method. Both the bivariate method and the multivariate method express a concern for scientific rigor. The difference between them is that, in the bivariate method, experimenters limit their attention to a few variables that they can manipulate in some way, whereas in the multivariate methods, experimenters consider many variables as they exist in a natural situation.

Cattell is quite critical of the bivariate method. Many of his criticisms are similar to those discussed in Chapter 2 in relation to laboratory research. First, he argues that attention to the relationship between two variables represents a simplistic and piecemeal approach to personality. Human behavior is complex and expresses the interactions among many variables. Having understood the relationship between two variables, one is left with the problem of understanding how these relate to the many other variables that are important in determining behavior. Second, the fact that bivariate experimenters attempt to manipulate the independent variable means that they must neglect many matters that are of real importance in psychology. Since the more important emotional situations cannot be manipulated and therefore cannot be used in controlled experiments in humans, the bivariate researcher has been forced to attend to trivia, to look for answers in the behavior of rats, or to look for answers in physiology.

In contrast to the bivariate method, the *clinical* method has the advantage that researchers can study important behaviors as they occur and look for lawfulness in the functioning of the total organism. Thus, in scientific aims and in philosophical assumptions, the clinical and multivariate methods are close to one another and separate from the bivariate method. Both the clinician and the multivariate researcher are interested in global events; both are interested in complex patterns of behavior as they occur in life; both allow life itself to be the source of experimental manipulation; and both are interested in understanding the total personality rather than isolated processes or fragmented pieces of knowledge. The difference between the clinician and the multivariate researcher is that whereas the former uses intuition to assess variables and memory to keep track of events, the latter uses systematic research procedures and statistical analyses. Thus, according to Cattell, "the clinician has his heart in the right place, but perhaps we may say that he remains a little fuzzy in the head" (1959c, p. 45).

In the light of these similarities and differences, Cattell concludes that the clinical method is the multivariate method but without the latter's

Table 7.2 Cattell's Description of Bivariate, Clinical, and Multivariate Research Methods

Bivariate	Clinical	Multivariate
Scientific rigor, controlled experiments	Intuition	Scientific rigor, objective and quantitative analysis
Attention to few variables	Consideration of many variables	Consideration of many variables
Neglect of important phenomena	Study of important phenomena	Study of important phenomena
Simplistic, piecemeal	Interest in global events and complex patterns of behavior (total personality)	Interest in global events and complex patterns of behavior (total personality)

concern for scientific rigor. In sum, Cattell thinks the multivariate method combines the desirable qualities of the bivariate and clinical methods (Table 7.2). For Cattell, the most important statistical technique in multi-variate research is **factor analysis**, previously described in the section on Hans Eysenck. The major difference between the two theorists is that Cattell prefers to work with a larger number of factors at the trait level, which have a more narrow definition but tend to correlate with each other. In contrast, Eysenck uses secondary factor analysis to combine traits into a smaller number of superfactors, which cover a broader range of behavior and tend to be uncorrelated. This difference between Eysenck and Cattell in their preferred level in the trait hierarchy is easily apparent in Figure 7.1, and they have continued to differ sharply about this choice.

CATTELL'S THEORY OF PERSONALITY

Kinds of Traits

The basic structural element for Cattell is the trait, which was defined earlier as a predisposition. The concept of trait assumes that behavior follows some pattern and regularity over time and across situations. Among the many possible distinctions between traits, two are of particular importance. The first is that among **ability traits**, **temperament traits**, and **dynamic traits**, and the second is that between **surface traits** and **source traits**.

Ability traits relate to skills and abilities that allow the individual to function effectively. Intelligence is an example of an ability trait. Temperament traits relate to the emotional life of the person and the stylistic quality of behavior. Whether one tends to work quickly or slowly, be generally calm or emotional, or act after deliberation or impulsively, all have to do with qualities of temperament that vary from individual to individual. Dynamic traits relate to the striving, motivational life of the individual, the kinds of goals that are important to the person. Ability, temperament, and dynamic traits are seen as capturing the major stable elements of personality.

The distinction between surface traits and source traits relates to the level at which we observe behavior. Surface traits express behaviors that on a superficial level may appear to go together but in fact do not always move up and down (vary) together and do not necessarily have a common cause. A source trait, on the other hand, expresses an association among behaviors that do vary together to form a unitary, independent dimension of personality. Whereas surface traits can be discovered through subjective methods such as asking people which personality characteristics they think go together, the refined statistical procedures of factor analysis are necessary to discover source traits. These source traits represent the building blocks of personality.

Sources of Data: L-data, Q-data, and OT-data

How do we discover source traits that cover a variety of responses across many situations? Where do we find our building blocks? Cattell distinguishes three sources of data which are similar to the L-O-T-S classification of data sources we discussed in the beginning of Chapter 2: life record data (*L-data*) which include both objective life-event data and ratings by observers and peers, questionnaire data (*Q-data*) which are based on self-reports, and objective-test data (*OT-data*). The first, L-data, relates to behavior in actual, everyday situations such as school performance or interactions with peers. These may be actual counts of behaviors or ratings made on the basis of such observations. The second, Q-data, involves self-report data or responses to questionnaires, such as the Maudsley and Eysenck personality inventories discussed earlier in the chapter. The third, OT-data, involves behavioral miniature situations in which the subject is unaware of the relationship between the response and the personality characteristic being measured. According to Cattell, if multivariate, factor-analytic research is indeed able to determine the basic structures of personality, then the same factors or traits should be obtained from the three kinds of data. This is an important, logical, and challenging commitment.

Originally Cattell began with the factor analyses of L-data and found 15 factors that appeared to account for most of personality. He then set out to determine whether comparable factors could be found in Q-data. Thousands of questionnaire items were written and administered to large numbers of normal people. Factor analyses were run to see which items went together. The main result of this research is a questionnaire known as the *Sixteen Personality Factor (16 P.F.) Questionnaire*. Initially, Cattell made up neologisms, such as "surgency," to name his personality trait factors, hoping to avoid misinterpretations of them. Nonetheless,

Table 7.3   Cattell's 16 Personality Factors Derived from
Questionnaire Data

Reserved	Outgoing
Less intelligent	More intelligent
Stable, Ego Strength	Emotionality/Neuroticism
Humble	Assertive
Sober	Happy-go-lucky
Expedient	Conscientious
Shy	Venturesome
Tough-minded	Tender-minded
Trusting	Suspicious
Practical	Imaginative
Forthright	Shrewd
Placid	Apprehensive
Conservative	Experimenting
Group-dependent	Self-sufficient
Undisciplined	Controlled
Relaxed	Tense

the terms given in Table 7.3 roughly capture the meanings of these trait
factors. As can be seen, they cover a wide variety of aspects of personality, particularly in terms of temperament (e.g., emotionality) and attitudes (e.g., conservative). In general, the factors found with Q-data
appeared to be similar to those found with L-data, but some were unique
to each kind of data. Illustrative L-data ratings and Q-data items for one
trait are presented in Figure 7.4.

Cattell is committed to the use of questionnaires, in particular, factor-
analytically derived questionnaires such as the 16 P.F. On the other hand,
he also has expressed concern about the problems of motivated distortion and self-deception in relation to questionnaire responses. Also, he
feels that the questionnaire is of particularly questionable utility with
mental patients. Because of problems with L-data and Q-data, and
because the original research strategy itself called for investigations with
OT-data, Cattell's efforts have been concerned more recently with personality structure as derived from OT-data. It is the source traits as
expressed in objective tests that are the "real coin" for personality
research.

The results from L-data and Q-data research were important in guiding
the development of miniature test situations; that is, the purpose was to
develop objective tests that would measure the source traits already discovered. Thus, for example, a tendency to be assertive might be expressed
in behaviors such as long exploratory distance on a finger maze test, fast
tempo in arm-shoulder movement, and fast speed of letter comparisons.
More than 500 tests were constructed to cover the hypothesized personality dimensions. These tests were administered to large groups of sub-

---

SOURCE TRAIT EGO STRENGTH VS. EMOTIONALITY/NEUROTICISM (L-DATA AND Q-DATA)

Behavior Ratings by Observer

Ego Strength		*Emotionality/Neuroticism*
Mature	vs.	Unable to tolerate frustration
Steady, persistent	vs.	Changeable
Emotionally calm	vs.	Impulsively emotional
Realistic about problems	vs.	Evasive, avoids necessary decisions
Absence of neurotic fatigue	vs.	Neurotically fatigued (with no real effort)

Questionnaire Responses*

Do you find it difficult to take no for an answer even when what you want to do is obviously impossible?
   (a) yes   (b) *no*

If you had your life to live over again, would you:
   (a) *want it to be essentially the same?*   (b) plan it very differently?

Do you often have really disturbing dreams?
   (a) yes   (b) *no*

Do your moods sometimes make you seem unreasonable even to yourself?
   (a) yes   (b) *no*

Do you feel tired when you've done nothing to justify it?
   (a) *rarely*   (b) often

Can you change old habits, without relapse, when you decide to?
   (a) *yes*   (b) no

*answer in italic type indicates high ego strength.

Figure 7.4 *Correspondence Between Data from Two Different Test Domains: L-data Ratings and Q-data Responses. (Cattell, 1965.)*

jects, and repeated factoring of data from different research situations eventually led to the designation of 21 OT-data source traits.

As mentioned before, the source traits or factors found in L-data and Q-data could, for the most part, be matched to one another. How, then, do the OT-data factors match those derived from L-data and Q-data? Despite the years of research effort, the results were disappointing; although some relations were found across all three data sources, no direct one-to-one mapping of factors was possible.

Summary In this section, we have described four steps in Cattell's research. (1) Cattell set out to define the structure of personality in three areas of observation, called L-data, Q-data, and OT-data. (2) He started his research with L-data and through the factor analysis of ratings came up with 15 source traits. (3) Guided in his research on Q-data by the L-data findings, Cattell developed the 16 P.F. Questionnaire, which con-

"THE RIGHT STUFF": CHARACTERISTICS OF SUCCESSFUL BUSINESS EXECUTIVES

Some time ago Tom Wolfe wrote a book about the first U.S. team of astronauts. An all-male group, these were men who felt that they had the "right stuff"—the manly courage it took to make it as a test pilot and astronaut. Others had the necessary skill, but if they didn't have the right stuff they just didn't make it.

Most demanding occupations have their own kind of right stuff—the personality characteristics or traits that, in addition to skill, make for success. For example, what makes for a top business executive? According to some recent research, the difference between senior executives who make it to chief executive officer and those who do not often is subtle. Members of both groups show considerable talent and have remarkable strengths, as well as a few significant weaknesses. Although no one trait discriminates between the two

groups, those who fall short of their ultimate goal frequently are found to have the following characteristics: they are insensitive to others, untrustworthy, cold—aloof—arrogant, overly ambitious, moody, volatile under pressure, and defensive. In contrast, the successful executives are most characterized by the traits of integrity and understanding others.

Actually, there is a long history of efforts to define the abilities and personal qualities of leaders. At one point, researchers began to give up on the hope of finding general leadership qualities. Leadership was seen as entirely situational in origin, with different skills and personal qualities being required in different situations. However, a recent review of the literature suggests that sounding the death knell of a trait approach to leadership probably was premature. Certain general qualities such as courage, fortitude, and conviction do stand out. In addition, the following traits seem to be generally characteristic of leaders: energetic, decisive, adaptive, assertive, sociable, achieving, and tolerant of stress.

Trait researchers, particularly those in industrial psychology, continue to try to define those personality characteristics that are essential for success in various fields. A variety of personality tests, including the 16 P.F., are then used in many important aspects of personnel selection.

SOURCES: *Psychology Today*, February, 1983; Holland, 1985.

"The Right Stuff": *Success in different occupations requires possessing certain traits. Sally Ride is America's first female astronaut to be a crew member aboard the space shuttle.*

tains 12 traits that match traits found in the L-data research and 4 traits that appear to be unique to questionnaire methods. (4) Using these results to guide his research in the development of objective tests, Cattell found 21 source traits in OT-data that appear to have a complex and low-level relation to the traits found in the other data.

The source traits found in the three types of observation do not complete Cattell's formulation of the structure of personality. However, the traits presented in this section do describe the general nature of the structure of personality as formulated by Cattell. In other words, here we have the foundation for psychology's table of the elements—its classification scheme. But what is the evidence for the existence of these traits? Cattell (1979) cites the following: (1) the results of factor analyses of different kinds of data; (2) similar results across cultures; (3) similar results across age groups; (4) utility in the prediction of behavior in the natural environment; (5) evidence of significant genetic contributions to many traits.

Stability and Variability in Behavior

Although Cattell has been concerned with the consistency of behavior and the structure of personality, he has also focused on process and motivation. As with the earlier traits, his efforts to determine dynamic traits, the motivational sources of behavior, continue to involve an emphasis on factor analysis (Cattell, 1985). His analysis of the courses of action people take in specific situations, and the patterns of behaviors that go together, has led him to conclude that human motivation consists of innate tendencies, called **ergs**, and environmentally determined motives, called **sentiments**. Illustrative ergs are security, sex, and self-assertion. Illustrative sentiments are religious ("I want to worship God."), career ("I want to learn skills required for a job."), and self-sentiment ("I want never to damage my self-respect."). Generally our activities involve the effort to satisfy many motives, and efforts to satisfy sentiments are made in the service of the more basic ergs or biological goals.

Clearly Cattell does not view the person as a static entity or as behaving the same way in all situations. How a person behaves at any one time depends on the traits and motivational variables relevant to the situation. In addition, two other concepts are vital in attempts to account for variability in behavior—states and roles. Cattell's distinction between states and traits is similar to Allport's (see Table 7.1). He uses the concept of **state** to refer to emotional and mood changes that are partly determined by the provocative power of specific situations. Illustrative states are anxiety, depression, fatigue, arousal, and curiosity. Whereas traits describe stable and general action patterns, Cattell emphasizes that the *exact* description of an individual at a given moment requires measurement of both traits and states: "Every practicing psychologist—indeed every intelligent observer of human nature and human history—realizes that the state of a person at a given moment determines his or her behavior as much as do his or her traits" (1979, p. 169). In other words, behavior in a particular situation cannot be predicted from traits alone without regard for whether the person is angry, tired, fearful, and so on.

The second important transient influence relates to the concept of **role**. According to Cattell, certain behaviors are more closely linked to environmental situations than to the general run of personality factors. Thus, customs and mores may modify the influence of personality traits so that "everyone may shout lustily at a football match, less lustily at dinner, and not at all in church" (1979, p. 250). In addition, the concept of role expresses the fact that the same stimulus is perceived in a different way by an individual according to his or her role in the situation. For example, a teacher may respond differently to a child's behavior in the classroom than when no longer in the role of teacher.

In sum, although Cattell believes that personality factors lead to a certain degree of stability in behavior across situations, he also believes that a person's mood (state) and the way he is presenting himself in a given situation (role) will influence his behavior: "How vigorously Smith attacks his meal depends not only on how hungry he happens to be, but also on his temperament and whether he is having dinner with his employer or is eating alone at home" (Nesselroade & Delhees, 1966, p. 583). Cattell's theory suggests that behavior expresses the individual's traits that operate in a situation, the ergs and sentiments associated with attitudes relevant to a situation, and the state and role components that may vary from time to time or situation to situation.

Role: *Cattell suggests that a person's behavior may vary according to their role in different situations.*

In addition to his concern with the structure of personality and with the dynamics of functioning, Cattell has conducted research on the development of personality and psychopathology. The former focuses mainly on the relative contribution of genes and environment to each trait, the latter on trait differences between members of various patient groups. In contrast with Eysenck, who has focused specifically on the application of behavior therapy to abnormal behavior, Cattell has not been associated with any particular form of psychotherapy.

COMMENT ON CATTELL

One cannot help but be impressed with the scope of Cattell's efforts. His research has touched on almost every dimension we have outlined as relevant to personality theory. Cattell has been a major force in the development of new multivariate techniques, as well as techniques for determining the genetic contribution to personality. To further multivariate research, Cattell founded the *Society for Multivariate Experimental Research* (SMEP) in the 1960s. Most factor-analytic personality researchers in the United States became members of this prestigious society. Furthermore, Cattell has endeavored to put his work in a cross-cultural perspective. In the words of one admirer: "Cattell's theory turns out to be a much more impressive achievement than has been generally recognized...It seems fair to say that Cattell's original blueprint for personality study has resulted in an extraordinarily rich theoretical structure that has generated more empirical research than any other theory of personality" (Wiggins, 1984, pp. 177, 190).

At the same time, many personality psychologists ignore the work of Cattell, in part because they question the validity of the tests Cattell used, his heavy reliance on factor analysis, and his theoretical speculation far beyond the data. Also, as was true for Eysenck, Cattell often overstates his data. Unfortunately, in being so committed to his point of view, he is at times unduly accepting of his own efforts and disparaging of the works of others. For example, the gains of clinical and bivariate approaches are minimized and those of the multivariate approach are overstated.

TRAIT THEORY: ALLPORT, EYSENCK, AND CATTELL

In the introduction to this chapter we suggested that there was no one leading trait theorist and decided to focus on trait research as a more general perspective. The basic assumption of this perspective is that individuals differ widely on personality traits, that is, broad dispositions to respond in particular ways.

Allport, Eysenck, and Cattell can be considered representative trait theorists because they all emphasize these individual differences in broad dispositions. At the same time, there are important differences among them in how they approach the study of traits and the place of trait theory in relation to other theories of personality. A major difference in this regard concerns the use of factor analysis to determine the number and nature of personality traits. Allport was critical of the method, whereas Eysenck and Cattell are major proponents of it. At the same time, whereas Eysenck has emphasized only three broad trait dimensions, Cattell has emphasized as many as 20 distinct traits. Allport, of course, went even further than Cattell in suggesting that there are unique traits for each person, opening the door to investigation of an endless number of traits.

In addition to the issues of methodology and number of traits, these three trait theorists differ in their approach to the study of motivation. Whereas Eysenck does not use the concept of motive, both Allport and Cattell left room in their theories for this concept and suggested that research could explore the relation between traits and motives. Finally, whereas both Allport and Eysenck are very critical of psychoanalytic theory, Cattell has been less rejecting.

The point here, then, is that within a common point of view, major differences remain among the three theorists. Notwithstanding these differences, trait theory and research have remained an important part of the personality field for over 50 years. As we will see in the following chapter, a more unified trait point of view is emerging. And, despite periodic attacks on the fundamental assumptions of trait theory, it remains a powerful force in the personality field.

MAJOR CONCEPTS

Trait.   A disposition to behave in a particular way, as expressed in a person's behavior over a range of situations.

Cardinal trait.   Allport's concept for a disposition that is so pervasive and outstanding in a person's life that virtually every act is traceable to its influence.

Central trait.   Allport's concept for a disposition to behave in a particular way in a range of situations.

Secondary disposition.   Allport's concept for a disposition to behave in a particular way that is relevant to few situations.

Functional autonomy.   Allport's concept that a motive may become independent of its origins; in particular, motives in adults may become independent of their earlier basis in tension reduction.

Idiographic approach.   An approach emphasized by Allport in which particular attention is given to the intensive study of individuals and the organization of personality variables in each person.

Factor analysis.   A statistical method for determining those variables or test responses that increase and decrease together. Used in the development of personality tests and of some trait theories (e.g., Cattell, Eysenck).

Superfactor.   A higher-order or secondary factor, representing a higher level of organization of traits than the initial factors derived from factor analysis.

Introversion. In Eysenck's theory, one end of the introversion–extraversion dimension of personality characterized by a disposition to be a quiet, reserved, reflective, and risk avoiding.

Extraversion. In Eysenck's theory, one end of the introversion–extraversion dimension of personality characterized by a disposition to be sociable, friendly, impulsive, and risk taking.

Neuroticism. In Eysenck's theory, a dimension of personality defined by stability and low anxiety at one end and by instability and high anxiety at the other end.

Psychoticism. In Eysenck's theory, a dimension of personality defined by a tendency to be solitary and insensitive at one end and to accept social custom and care about others at the other end.

Bivariate method. Cattell's description of the method of personality study that follows the classical experimental design of manipulating an independent variable and observing the effects on a dependent variable.

Clinical methods. Cattell's description of the method of personality study in which there is an interest in complex patterns of behavior as they occur in life but variables are not assessed in a systematic way.

Multivariate methods. Cattell's description of the method of personality study, favored by him, in which there is study of interrelationships among many variables at once.

Ability, temperament, and dynamic traits. In Cattell's trait theory, these categories of traits capture the major aspects of personality.

Surface trait. In Cattell's theory, behaviors that appear to be linked to one another but do not in fact increase and decrease together.

Source trait. In Cattell's theory, behaviors that vary together to form an independent dimension of personality, which is discovered through the use of factor analysis.

L-data. In Cattell's theory, life-record data relating to behavior in everyday life situations or to ratings of such behavior.

Q-data. In Cattell's theory, personality data obtained from questionnaires.

OT-data. In Cattell's theory, objective test data or information about personality obtained from observing behavior in miniature situations.

Erg. Cattell's concept for innate biological drives that provide the basic motivating power for behavior.

Sentiment. Cattell's concept for environmentally determined patterns of behavior that are expressed in attitudes (i.e., readiness to act in a certain direction) and are linked to underlying ergs (i.e., innate biological drives).

State. Emotional and mood changes (e.g., anxiety, depression, fatigue) that Cattell suggested may influence the behavior of a person at a given time. The assessment of both traits and states is suggested to predict behavior.

Role. Behavior considered to be appropriate for a person's place or status in society. Emphasized by

Cattell as one of a number of variables that limit the influence of personality variables on behavior relative to situational variables.

REVIEW

1. The trait concept represents a broad disposition to behave in a particular way. Traits are viewed as being organized in a hierarchy from specific responses to general styles of psychological functioning.

2. Allport differentiated the importance of traits for a person's personality with the concepts of cardinal traits, central traits, and specific dispositions. Allport also is known for the concept of functional autonomy, suggesting that adult motives may become independent of earlier roots, and for his emphasis on the utility of in-depth study of individuals (idiographic research).

3. Many trait theorists use the statistical technique of factor analysis to develop a classification of traits. Through this technique a group of items or responses (factors) are formed, the items in one group (factor) being closely related to one another and distinct from those in another group (factor).

4. According to Eysenck, the basic dimensions of personality are introversion–extraversion, neuroticism, and psychoticism. Questionnaires have been developed to assess people along these trait dimensions. Research has focused particularly on the introversion–extraversion trait dimension, where differences in activity level and activity preferences have been found. Eysenck suggests that individual differences in traits have a biological and genetic (inherited) basis. However, he also suggests that through behavior therapy important changes in personality functioning can occur.

5. Cattell distinguished among bivariate, multivariate, and clinical approaches to research in personality, favoring the multivariate study of interrelationships among many variables. Cattell also distinguished among ability, temperament, and dynamic traits, as well as between surface and source traits. Source traits represent an association of behaviors discovered through the use of factor analysis and are the building blocks of personality. Although his main research efforts have involved the use of questionnaires (16 P.F. Questionnaire), he has attempted to demonstrate that the same factors show up with the use of ratings and objective tests. Finally, Cattell suggested that behavior in a specific situation reflects motivation variables, such as ergs and sentiments, as well as more temporary influences, such as states and roles.

6. Trait theorists such as Allport, Eysenck, and Cattell share an emphasis on broad dispositions to respond as central to personality. However, their approaches differ in many ways, most importantly concerning the use of factor analysis to discover traits and the number of traits to be used in the description of personality.

8

TRAIT APPROACHES: THE FIVE-FACTOR MODEL; APPLICATIONS AND EVALUATION OF TRAIT APPROACHES TO PERSONALITY

Chapter Focus

You are applying to graduate school and Allport, Eysenck, and Cattell are writing you letters of recommendation. What would their three letters look like? Certainly they would be very different. Eysenck would discuss your behavior and accomplishments in terms of his three broad superfactors, Cattell would consider twenty-some more specific traits, and Allport might weave a richly detailed idiographic portrayal, including many entirely unique trait configurations. While there might be some common themes in the letters, none of the theorists would ever give up his preferred theoretical position. That leads us to the question: How can we ever reach agreement about the basic traits if we cannot break this stalemate?

Suppose we proceed as follows. We ask a thousand people to write personality descriptions of a thousand others. Then we collect together all the trait-descriptive adjectives used in these descriptions. The result would be a list of personality descriptors that is not biased by any theoretical preconceptions, a list that faithfully includes all those attributes that people consider important in their lives. Certainly, there would be considerable redundancy (e.g., *perfect* and *flawless* mean pretty much the same thing), permitting us to reduce the size of the list. If we then factor-analyze personality ratings on these traits, we should end up with the major dimensions of personality trait descriptions. The result may be a compromise that does not please everybody but at least it is arrived at via a fair set of procedures, and its practicality and usefulness will determine whether it is generally accepted in the field.

In this chapter we continue our discussion of trait theory and consider the efforts of trait researchers to reach a consensus using the procedures outlined above. We focus on the emerging consensus on the importance of five basic trait dimensions, and consider the evidence supporting this Five-Factor Model, as well as its application to the individual. The chapter concludes with an overall evaluation of the trait approach to personality.

QUESTIONS TO BE ADDRESSED IN THIS CHAPTER

1. Is it possible for trait researchers to reach a consensus on one model?

2. How many—and which—trait dimensions are necessary for a basic description of personality?

3. Can a trait model derived from factor analysis be connected to the personality terms we use in everyday language? Would we expect such a model to be universal across cultures? To make sense in terms of our evolutionary heritage?

FoxTrot
by Bill Amend

Drawing by Bill Amend; © 1993 Universal Press Syndicate

4. What are the implications of individual differences in traits for career choice, physical health, and psychological well-being?

5. How stable or variable are traits over time and across situations? That is, how much does one's personality change over time and from situation to situation?

In the last chapter we considered the trait approaches of Allport, Eysenck, and Cattell. As indicated, these theorists share the view that traits are the fundamental units of personality, representing broad dispositions to respond in particular ways. At the same time, the three theorists have substantially different views about the use of factor analysis and about the number and nature of the trait dimensions that are needed for an adequate description of personality.

Such differences among trait theorists have raised a fundamental question in the minds of many personality psychologists: If traits are basic units of personality, why can't trait theorists agree on which and how many units are basic? At this time, a consensus is indeed emerging on the **five-factor model** of personality, or what has come to be known as the **Big Five**.

The past decade has witnessed an electrifying burst of interest in the most fundamental problem of the field—the search for a scientifically compelling taxonomy of personality traits. More importantly, the beginning of a consensus is emerging about the general framework of such a taxonomic representation.

SOURCE: Goldberg, 1993, p. 26

TOWARDS A CONSENSUAL MODEL: THE FIVE-FACTOR MODEL OF PERSONALITY TRAITS

> Today we believe it is more fruitful to adopt the working hypothe-
> sis that the five-factor model of personality is essentially correct in
> its representation of the structure of traits...If this hypothesis is
> correct—if we have truly discovered the basic dimensions of per-
> sonality—it marks a turning point for personality psychology.
>
> SOURCE: McCrae & John, 1992, p. 176

Support for the five-factor model comes from three main areas: factor
analyses of large sets of trait terms in language, the relation of trait questionnaires to other questionnaires and ratings, and the analysis of genetic (inherited) contributions to personality (Digman, 1990). We will now
consider each of these areas, as well as some recent suggestions that
place trait theory within an evolutionary perspective.

ANALYSIS OF TRAIT TERMS IN THE NATURAL LANGUAGE AND IN QUESTIONNAIRES

One approach to the discovery of the basic units of personality is to consider terms we use to describe people's personalities. The basic procedure
followed in this research is to have individuals rate themselves or others
on a wide variety of traits carefully sampled from the dictionary (John,
Angleitner, & Ostendorf, 1988). The ratings are then factor-analyzed to see
which traits go together. For example, basing his research on earlier work
by Allport, Cattell, and others, Norman (1963) did a factor-analytic study
of peer ratings and found five basic personality factors. Similar five-factor solutions have been found repeatedly in numerous studies, conducted
by many different researchers in a wide range of data sources, samples,
and assessment instruments (John, 1990). Moreover, all five factors have
been shown to possess considerable reliability and validity and to remain
relatively stable throughout adulthood (McCrae & Costa, 1990; 1994).

Lewis R. Goldberg

In 1981, Goldberg reviewed the work of others, as well as the results of his own research. Impressed with the consistency of the results, he suggested that "it should be possible to argue the case that any model for structuring individual differences will have to encompass—at some level—something like these 'Big Five' dimensions" (p. 159). Thus came into existence the designation of the factors as the **Big Five**. *Big* was meant to refer to the finding that each factor subsumes a large number of more specific traits. The Big Five are almost as broad and abstract in the personality hierarchy as Eysenck's "superfactors." Although slightly different terms have been used for the Big Five factors, we shall use the terms *Neuroticism (N), Extraversion (E), Openness (O), Agreeableness (A),* and *Conscientiousness (C)* (Table 8.1). Note that the first letters of the Big Five dimensions can be reordered to spell out the word **OCEAN** (John, 1990, p. 96)—an easy way to remember all five dimensions.

To illustrate the meaning of the factors, Table 8.1 lists a number of trait adjectives that describe individuals scoring high and low on each

Table 8.1 The Big Five Trait Factors and Illustrative Scales

Characteristics of the High Scorer	*Trait Scales*	*Characteristics of the Low Scorer*
	NEUROTICISM (N)	
Worrying, nervous, emotional, insecure, inadequate, hypochodriacal	Assesses adjustment vs. emotional instability. Identifies individuals prone to psychological distress, unrealistic ideas, excessive cravings or urges, and maladaptive coping responses	Calm, relaxed, unemotional, hardy, secure, self-satisfied
	EXTRAVERSION (E)	
Sociable, active, talkative, person-oriented, optimistic, fun-loving, affectionate	Assesses quantity and intensity of interpersonal interaction; activity level; need for stimulation; and capacity for joy.	Reserved, sober, unexuberant, aloof, task-oriented, retiring, quiet
	OPENNESS (O)	
Curious, broad interests, creative, original, imaginative, untraditional	Assesses proactive seeking and appreciation of experience for its own sake; toleration for and exploration of the unfamiliar.	Conventional, down-to-earth, narrow interests, unartistic, unanalytical
	AGREEABLENESS (A)	
Soft-hearted, good-natured, trusting, helpful, forgiving, gullible, straightforward	Assesses the quality of one's interpersonal orientation along a continuum from compassion to antagonism in thoughts, feelings, and actions.	Cynical, rude, suspicious, uncooperative, vengeful, ruthless, irritable, manipulative
	CONSCIENTIOUSNESS (C)	
Organized, reliable, hardworking, self-disciplined, punctual, scrupulous, neat, ambitious, persevering	Assesses the individual's degree of organization, persistence, and motivation in goal-directed behavior. Contrasts dependable, fastidious people with those who are lackadaisical and sloppy.	Aimless, unreliable, lazy, careless, lax, negligent, weak-willed, hedonistic

SOURCE: Costa & McCrae, 1985, p. 2.

factor. *Neuroticism* contrasts emotional stability with a broad range of negative feelings, including anxiety, sadness, irritability, and nervous tension. *Openness to Experience* describes the breadth, depth, and complexity of an individual's mental and experiential life. *Extraversion* and *Agreeableness* both summarize traits that are interpersonal—that is, they capture what people do with each other and to each other. Finally, *Conscientiousness* primarily describes task- and goal-directed behavior and socially required impulse control.

The factor definitions in Table 8.1 are based on the work by Costa and McCrae (1985; 1992). The definitions suggested by other researchers are quite similar. For example, Goldberg (1992) has suggested a "Transparent Bipolar Inventory" that individuals can use to quickly rate their own standing on the Big Five dimensions. An abbreviated version of this inventory follows below. Please consider the following guidelines as you complete this inventory:

> Try to describe yourself as accurately as possible. Describe yourself as you see yourself at the present time, not as you wish to be in the future. Describe yourself as you are generally or typically, as compared with other persons you know of the same sex and of roughly your same age. For each of the trait scales listed below, circle a number that best describes you on this dimension.

INTROVERSION VERSUS EXTRAVERSION

	Very		Moderately		Neither		Moderately		Very	
silent	1	2	3	4	5	6	7	8	9	talkative
unassertive	1	2	3	4	5	6	7	8	9	assertive
unadventurous	1	2	3	4	5	6	7	8	9	adventurous
unenergetic	1	2	3	4	5	6	7	8	9	energetic
timid	1	2	3	4	5	6	7	8	9	bold

ANTAGONISM VERSUS AGREEABLENESS

unkind	1	2	3	4	5	6	7	8	9	kind
uncooperative	1	2	3	4	5	6	7	8	9	cooperative
selfish	1	2	3	4	5	6	7	8	9	unselfish
distrustful	1	2	3	4	5	6	7	8	9	trustful
stingy	1	2	3	4	5	6	7	8	9	generous

LACK OF DIRECTION VERSUS CONSCIENTIOUSNESS

disorganized	1	2	3	4	5	6	7	8	9	organized
irresponsible	1	2	3	4	5	6	7	8	9	responsible
impractical	1	2	3	4	5	6	7	8	9	practical
careless	1	2	3	4	5	6	7	8	9	thorough
lazy	1	2	3	4	5	6	7	8	9	hardworking

EMOTIONAL STABILITY VERSUS NEUROTICISM

relaxed	1	2	3	4	5	6	7	8	9	tense
at ease	1	2	3	4	5	6	7	8	9	nervous
stable	1	2	3	4	5	6	7	8	9	unstable
contented	1	2	3	4	5	6	7	8	9	discontented
unemotional	1	2	3	4	5	6	7	8	9	emotional

CLOSEDNESS VERSUS OPENNESS TO NEW EXPERIENCE

unimaginative	1	2	3	4	5	6	7	8	9	imaginative
uncreative	1	2	3	4	5	6	7	8	9	creative
uninquisitive	1	2	3	4	5	6	7	8	9	curious
unreflective	1	2	3	4	5	6	7	8	9	reflective
unsophisticated	1	2	3	4	5	6	7	8	9	sophisticated
	Very		Moderately		Neither		Moderately		Very	

How did you score? Keep in mind that this inventory is not a formal test but rather a useful exercise to familiarize yourself with the Big Five dimensions and how they apply to yourself. Nonetheless, if you are interested in your overall Big Five scores, you may want to total up your responses for each factor. Simply add together all the five number you circled for **E** and divide that sum by 5. Then do the same for each of the other factors. On which factor did you have your highest score? On which one did you score lowest? Do the five scores correspond to what you would have expected? Or were there some surprising discrepancies with the way you see yourself in general?

The Fundamental Lexical Hypothesis

The Big Five were designed to capture those personality traits that people consider most important in their lives. Goldberg has spelled out the rationale for this approach in terms of the **fundamental lexical** (language) **hypothesis**:

> The variety of individual differences is nearly boundless, yet most of these differences are insignificant in people's daily interactions with others and have remained largely unnoticed. Sir Francis Galton may have been among the first scientists to recognize explicitly the fundamental lexical hypothesis—namely that the most important individual differences in human transactions will come to be encoded as single terms in some or all of the world's languages.
>
> SOURCE: Goldberg, 1990, p. 1216

Thus, Goldberg suggests that over time humans have found some individual differences particularly important in their interactions and have developed terms for easy reference to them. These trait terms communicate information about individual differences that are important to our own well-being or that of our group or clan. Thus, they are useful because they serve the purpose of prediction and control—they help us predict what others will do and thus control our life outcomes (Chaplin et al., 1988). They help answer questions about how an individual is likely to behave across a wide range of relevant situations.

If there are universal questions concerning individual differences and human interaction, then one might expect the same basic trait dimensions to appear in all languages. Is there evidence that this is the case? Recent reviews of studies in other languages as diverse as German, Japanese, and Chinese, conducted in a variety of cultures, appear to support the fundamental lexical hypothesis (Bond, 1994; Church, Katigbak, & Reyer, 1995; John, 1990). In other words, there is growing evidence that people in diverse cultures, using very different languages, construe personality in accord with the five-factor model.

The Big Five in Personality Questionnaires

By now it probably is clear to the student of personality that the field does not suffer from a shortage of questionnaires. A questionnaire has been developed for almost every concept and in association with almost every theory of personality. In Chapter 7, we discussed the Eysenck Personality Inventory and Cattell's 16 P.F. A variety of other questionnaires have been developed by other trait researchers. For example, we have presented above an abbreviated version of one of Goldberg's (1992)

Paul T. Costa, Jr.

Robert R. McCrae

inventories measuring the Big Five with trait adjectives. In addition to these adjective-based measures, a very elaborate and widely used questionnaire is also available to measure the Big Five.

In three stages of test construction and revision, Costa and McCrae (1992) have developed a questionnaire, the *NEO-Personality Inventory Revised (NEO-PI-R),* to measure the Big Five personality factors. Originally they had focused only on the three factors of Neuroticism, Extraversion, and Openness, thus the title NEO-Personality Inventory. Subsequently they added the factors of agreeableness and conscientiousness to conform to the five-factor model. Moreover, they differentiated each of the Big Five factors (or domains) into six more specific **facets**; facets are the more specific traits or components that make up each of the broad Big Five factors (Table 8.2). For example, in Costa and McCrae's NEO-PI-R, Extraversion is defined by the six facets of *Activity Level, Assertiveness, Excitement Seeking, Positive Emotions, Gregariousness,* and *Warmth.* Each facet is measured by 8 items, so that the most recent NEO-PI-R consists of a total of 240 items (i.e., 5 factors x 6 facets x 8 items). For example, two items from the *Activity* facet scale are "When I do things, I do them vigorously" and "My life is fast-paced" (Costa & McCrae, 1992, p. 70). For each item, subjects indicate the extent to which they agree or disagree, using a five-point rating scale. The resulting scales all have good reliability and show validity across different data sources and with other instruments, such as Goldberg's (1992) adjective inventories. Finally, McCrae and Costa (1990) argue strongly for the use of questionnaires to assess personality and are critical of projective tests and clinical interviews.

Assuming that the NEO-PI is an adequate measure of the five-factor model of personality, to what extent does it correlate with other established measures? The authors accept this as a challenge to the validity of the test, as well as the utility of the five-factor model, and offer considerable evidence suggesting that scores on the NEO-PI-R correlate well with scores on other personality questionnaires (McCrae & Costa, 1987). In particular, this is true for scores from other questionnaires based on factor analysis (see Chapter 7), such as the Eysenck's inventories and Cattell's 16 P.F. (Costa & McCrae, 1992, 1994b). These findings are important because they provide an integration of the older factor-analytic models with the Big Five. For example, Eysenck's superfactors of Extraversion and Neuroticism were found to be virtually identical to the same-named dimensions in the Big Five, and Eysenck's Psychoticism superfactor was found to be a combination of low Agreeableness and low Conscientiousness—people high in Psychoticism, such as criminals, are disagreeable and irresponsible (Costa & McCrae, 1995). Similarly, Cattell's 16 P.F. scales map systematically onto the broader Big Five dimensions (McCrae & Costa, 1990).

Moreover, evidence is presented to support the view that the NEO-PI-R correlates well with personality measures obtained through other means (e.g., Q-sort ratings). In addition, there is evidence that scores on the NEO-PI-R correlate well with scores on questionnaires derived from different theoretical orientations (e.g., Murray's motivational model of personality). The latter is particularly important since it provides the possibility of establishing a link between traits and motives. On the basis of these kinds of studies, McCrae and Costa argue that the five factors, as assessed by the NEO-PI, are both necessary and sufficient for describing the basic dimensions of personality. Indeed, they go beyond this to suggest that "no other system is as complete and yet as parsimonious" (1990, p. 51).

Table 8.2   NEO-PI-R Facet Scales Associated with the Big Five Trait Factors

---

NEUROTICISM: anxiety, angry hostility, depression, self-consciousness, impulsiveness, vulnerability

EXTRAVERSION: warmth, gregariousness, assertiveness, activity, excitement seeking, positive emotions

OPENNESS TO EXPERIENCE: fantasy, aesthetics, feelings, actions, ideas, values

AGREEABLENESS: trust, straightforwardness, altruism, compliance, modesty, tendermindedness

CONSCIENTIOUSNESS: competence, order, dutifulness, achievement, striving, self-discipline, deliberation

---

SOURCE: *The NEO Personality Inventory Manual* (p. 2), by P. T. Costa, Jr. and R. R. McCrae, 1985, Odessa, FL: Psychological Assessment Resources; *NEO-PI-R, Professional Manual* (p. 3), by P. T. Costa and R. R. McCrae, 1992, Odessa, FL: Psychological Assessment Resources.

Another interesting aspect of the NEO-PI-R is that forms are available for both self-report and ratings by others. In several studies, subjects' self-ratings have been compared with ratings by their peers and spouses. McCrae and Costa (1990) report substantial agreement of self-ratings with ratings by peers and with ratings by spouses on all five factors. Agreement between self and spouse is greater than that between self and peer, perhaps because spouses generally know each other better than do friends or because spouses talk a lot about each others' personalities (see Kenny et al., 1995). Two major findings have emerged from this research: (1) following the distinction between S-data and O-data sources we made in Chapter 2, the same five factors are found in both self-reports and observer ratings, and (2) there is agreement among observers concerning the standing of an individual on a trait. These findings are taken as further evidence for the utility of self-report measures and the five-factor model of personality.

GROWTH AND DEVELOPMENT

Changes with Age

In general, trait researchers have focused their work on personality in adulthood, leaving to developmental psychologists the questions of how personality develops from infancy into the Big Five structure we know in adulthood. As we will see later in this chapter, trait researchers suggest that an individual's standing on the Big Five traits remains quite stable after about age 30. Before that age, however, there seems to be considerable growth and change, leading some to conclude that "Like intelligence and height, personality traits appear to have a point of full maturity...personality development is not complete until the end of the decade of the 20s" (Costa & McCrae, 1994a, pp. 139, 142).

A number of studies show that adolescents and young adults in their early twenties are significantly higher in *neuroticism* and *extraversion* and lower in *agreeableness* and *conscientiousness* than older adults (Costa & McCrae, 1994a). These findings make intuitive sense when one compares high school and college students with their parents. On average, teenagers seem to be beset by more anxieties and concerns with acceptance and self-esteem (higher *N*), spend more time on the phone and in social activities with their friends (higher *E*), are more critical and demanding of specific others and society in general (lower *A*), and tend to be less conscientious and responsible than others expect them to be (lower *C*). Not surprisingly, we speak of "angry *young* men," rather than of "angry middle-aged men" or "angry grandfathers." Indeed, the teenage years and early twenties are the times of greatest discontent, turbulence, and revolt. More generally, the findings of changes on the Big Five during the twenties have been interpreted as indicating growth toward greater maturity by age thirty; the assumption of adult roles in career and parenting bring about greater confidence and emotional balance as well as increased socialization and competence.

What about earlier periods of development? Research on the connections between infant temperament, childhood personality, and the Big Five in adulthood has barely begun, but an impressive research effort is under way (Halverson, Kohnstamm, & Martin, 1994). It is safe to suggest that earlier temperamental characteristics, such as *sociability, activity,* and *emotionality* develop and mature into dimensions we know as *Extraversion* and *Neuroticism* in adulthood. However the exact linkages, and the processes by which this development takes place, have not yet been determined. One intriguing finding is that personality structure appears to be more complex and less integrated in childhood than in adulthood. Rather than the usual number of five factors, researchers in the U.S. and the Netherlands have found seven in their studies of children (John, Caspi, Robins, Moffitt, & Stouthamer-Loeber, 1994; van Lieshout & Haselager, 1994). These findings suggest that the organization of personality may change over the course of development, with initially separate dimensions (i.e., the seven of childhood) merging together to form broader, more integrated personality dimentions (i.e., the five of adulthood). Thus, for example, two largely inherited temperament traits such as *sociability* and *activity* may be distinct in childhood but subsequently merge to form the adult *Extraversion* factor.

Traits as Inherited Personality Characteristics

What mechanisms might explain both these age-specific changes in traits and the long-term stability that characterizes personality traits in adulthood? We have already seen that Eysenck and Cattell emphasized the genetic, inherited aspect of traits. Over the past decade, an impressive amount of evidence has been gathered to support the view that many important personality traits have a substantial inherited component (Bouchard et al., 1990; Loehlin, 1992; Plomin, 1994; Tellegen et al., 1988). For example, recently scientists reported discovery of a gene linked to the trait of novelty seeking (Benjamin et al., 1996; Ebstein et al., 1996). Such individuals tend to be extraverted, impulsive, quick-tempered, excitable, and exploratory. Recent estimates of the overall genetic contribution to personality traits converge on roughly 40 percent. In other words, about 40 percent of individual differences in personality traits are due to inheritance. At the same time, the degree of inheritance varies from trait to trait. Thus, the suggestion of some newspapers that "Personality Traits Are Mostly Inherited," or that "People Are Born, Not Made" has some validity, but also represents a gross oversimplification of these complicated issues.

For a long time, some psychologists—as well as people generally—have been reluctant to accept the view that personality has a genetic basis. However, at this point there is a fair amount of data indicating clearly that genetic factors play an important role, in particular for traits relating to temperament. As part of the effort to determine the genetic contribution to personality, psychologists have compared the similarity of personality test scores of identical twins reared together with the similarity of personality test scores of identical twins reared apart. If genes are of primary importance, identical twins reared apart should be as similar to one another as are identical twins reared together. On the other hand, if environment is of primary importance, identical twins reared apart should be much less similar to one another than are identical twins reared together.

The evidence suggests remarkable similarity between identical twins reared apart, often approximating that between identical twins reared together. One recent report suggests: "For almost every behavioral trait so far investigated, from reaction time to religiosity, an important fraction of the variation among people turns out to be associated with genetic variation. This fact need no longer be subject to debate" (Bouchard et al., 1990, p. 227).

An interesting aspect of this research has been the effort to determine which aspects of the environment are important for the development of personality. The natural assumption would be that the family environment plays an important role. This is an assumption shared by many theories of personality, most notably psychoanalytic theory. Yet, psychologists involved with twin research are led to the conclusion that children within a family do not share much of the same environment (Plomin & Daniels, 1987). To the extent that family environmental factors are important in the development of personality, they are experienced differently by children growing up in the same family. Siblings resemble each other in personality, but mostly because of common genes rather than shared experience (Plomin, 1994; Plomin et al., 1990). The data summarized in Figure 8.1 suggest that the unique family environment experienced by each child is far more significant than any common, shared environment experienced by children in the same family. Beyond this, experiences outside the family (school, peers) help to shape differences among children from the same family.

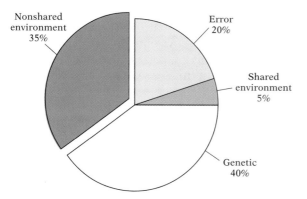

Figure 8.1 Percent of Personality Variance Due to Genetic Factors, Shared Environment Influence, Nonshared Environment Influence, and Measurement Error *(Dunn & Plomin, 1990, p.50) Copyright 1990 by Basic Books, Inc. Reprinted by permission of Basic Books, a division of HarperCollins Publishers, Inc.*

Why Children from the Same Family Are So Different: *Each sibling experiences a different, unique family environment.*

In the above discussion, we have suggested that genes play an important role in shaping personality, and that the environment, in particular the nonshared environment, also plays a major role. A further finding from this research is that there are genetic influences on the environment the parents provide for their children; that is, the personality characteristics of children, which are partly inherited, influence the way parents treat them (Plomin & Bergeman, 1991; Plomin et al., 1990). In other words, genes influence personality not only directly through the biological make-up of the person, but indirectly through the way the person selects, modifies, and creates environments. For example, a calm, cuddly infant elicits a very different parental response than does an irritable, withdrawn infant. Similarly, an aggressive, hyperactive child elicits a vastly different response from parents, peers, and teachers than does a quiet, passive child. Such children also seek out different environments—the aggressive child gravitating to environments offering greater excitement, challenge, and stimulation than the passive child. In this sense, it is true that people make their own environments (Caspi & Bem, 1990).

Having emphasized the role of genes in personality formation, some cautionary notes are in order. The following four points are noteworthy:

1. The conclusion that genetic factors play an important role does not mean that the development of personality is entirely biologically driven, or that nongenetic factors are unimportant.

2. Although genetic factors can influence the family environment encountered by the child, nongenetic factors are mainly responsible for environmental differences among people.

3. The family environment differs for each child due to the child's sex, birth order, or unique events in the family life of each child; nonetheless, family experiences are important even when these experiences are not the same for children growing up in the same family.

4. It is important to realize that strong genetic influences do not imply that a trait is fixed or cannot be influenced by the environment.

What is suggested here is an appreciation for the constant interplay between genes and environment and an avoidance of an either–or position. Perhaps the best way to put this is to quote from those who recently have emphasized the importance of genetics for personality development: "It is good for the field of personality that it has moved away from simple-minded environmentalism. The danger now, however, is that the rush from environmentalism will carom too far—to a view that personality is almost completely biologically determined" (Plomin et al., 1990, p. 225).

AN EVOLUTIONARY PERSPECTIVE

Many trait theorists now view the five-factor model, and traits generally, within an evolutionary perspective. There are two major components to this picture. First, returning to Goldberg's (1990) fundamental lexical hypothesis, there is the view that trait terms have emerged to help people categorize behaviors fundamental to the human condition. Which aspects of interaction would seem to be of particular importance? Goldberg (1981) argued that people ask five fundamental and universal questions when they interact with another person (*X*):

1. Is *X* active and dominant or passive and submissive (Can I bully *X* or will *X* try to bully me)?

2. Is *X* agreeable (warm and pleasant) or disagreeable (cold and distant)?

3. Can I count on *X* (Is *X* responsible and conscientious or undependable and negligent)?

4. Is *X* crazy (unpredictable) or sane (stable)?

5. Is *X* smart or dumb (How easy will it be for me to teach *X*)?

Not surprisingly, these five questions correspond to the Big Five trait factors.

Second, there is the view that humans are biologically similar to the great apes and therefore share certain characteristics with them. According to one view, seven traits are shared by primates and humans: activity level, fearfulness, impulsiveness, sociability, nurturance, aggres-

CURRENT APPLICATIONS

ARE CRIMINALS BORN OR MADE?

The extent to which personality characteristics are inherited is an important questions for psychologists and one with potential social applications. Some people suggest that there is an "aggressive personality" and that criminals are born, not made. Others suggest otherwise.

A fair amount of evidence, based on twin studies and adoption studies, suggests that perhaps heredity accounts for as much as 40 percent of individual differences in the trait of aggressiveness. Further, there is growing evidence of a genetic contribution to criminality. For example, identical twins are twice as likely as fraternal twins to be similar in their criminal activity. Also, a close relationship has been found between antisocial behavior in adopted children and such behavior in their biological parents.

Sarnoff Mednick, one major investigator, concludes: "These studies all suggest that we should take seriously the idea that some biological characteristics that can be genetically transmitted may be involved in causing a person to become involved in criminal activity."

Does this mean that criminal behavior is inevitable in some people? Not necessarily. When a biological parent but not an adoptive parent had a record of conviction, only a minority of the children later had a record of court convictions. Thus, although genetic influences can lead to the development of criminal behavior, improved social conditions can also reduce the likelihood of such a development.

SOURCES: *Psychology Today*, March, 1985; Rushton & Erdle, 1987.

Criminality: *Although there is evidence of a genetic link to antisocial behavior, social conditions also play a role.*

siveness, and dominance (A. H. Buss, 1988). Some of these traits relate to prosocial behavior, others to ways in which we attempt to handle conflict with others or struggle for power.

According to the evolutionary view, important individual differences exist because they have played some role in the processes of evolution by natural selection (D. M. Buss, 1991; 1995). The fundamental question asked is: *How did traits evolve to solve adaptive tasks, since were it not for this reason, why would they exist?* Presumably these individual differences relate to such basic evolutionary tasks as survival and reproductive success. Traits such as extraversion and emotional stability (as opposed to neuroticism) might be particularly important for mate selection (Kenrick et al., 1990), and conscientiousness and agreeableness might be particularly important in relation to group survival. Thus, the trait terms in our daily language reflect individual differences important to the tasks humans have had to face in the long history of their evolutionary development.

The evolutionary perspective within trait theory is relatively recent, and much theoretical and research work needs to be done. At the same time, it is important in that it seeks to anchor personality theory in biological principles common to other species. In the words of one of its proponents: "There is no reason to believe that we are somehow exempt from the organizing forces of evolution by natural selection. Personality theories inconsistent with evolutionary theory stand little chance of being correct" (D. M. Buss, 1991, p. 461). Together with the work on inheritance and that on individual differences in physiological functioning associated with traits, it holds the potential for valuable links with the field of biology.

APPLICATIONS OF THE MODEL

As has been indicated, the five-factor model is viewed by many current trait theorists as the basis for an adequate representation of the structure of personality. In addition, the NEO-PI is viewed as an adequate measure of these traits. This would suggest many potential applications of the model and the personality inventory, including the areas of career choice, diagnosis of personality and psychopathology, and decisions concerning psychological treatment. Developments in these areas are very recent, and it will take time to evaluate them. However, in the meantime, some of the suggested applications can be considered.

Vocational Interests

Psychologists interested in the area of vocational (career) behavior suggest that personality is associated with the kinds of careers people choose and how they function in these occupations. The idea is that people with certain characteristics will select and function better in some occupations than in others. For example, according to the five-factor model, individuals high in extraversion should prefer and do better in social and enterprising occupations relative to individuals high in introversion. To take another example, people high on openness to experience should prefer and do better in artistic and investigative occupations (e.g., journalist, freelance writer) than individuals low on this trait. Since artistic and investigative occupations require curiosity, creativity, and independent thinking, they will be more suitable for individuals high on the openness to experience factor.

Health and Longevity

The idea that personality is related to health dates back at least to the ancient Greeks, who believed there to be a link between disease and temperament. Recent research suggests there may be some truth to this belief. A long-term study points to the importance of conscientiousness in predicting who lives longer (Friedman et al., 1995a, 1995b). In this study, a large sample of children was followed for 70 years by several generations of researchers who kept track of which participants died and the causes of death. Adults who were conscientious as children (according to parent and teacher ratings at age 11) lived significantly longer and were about 30 percent less likely to die in any given year.

Why do conscientious individuals live longer? That is, what are the causal mechanisms that lead to these differences in longevity? First, the researchers ruled out the possibility that environmental variables, such as parental divorce, explain the conscientiousness effects. Second, throughout their lives, conscientious individuals were less likely to die from violent deaths, whereas less conscientious individuals took risks that led to accidents and fights. Third, conscientious people were less likely to smoke and drink heavily. The researchers suggest that conscientiousness is likely to influence a whole pattern of health-relevant behaviors. Thus, in addition to less likelihood of smoking and drinking heavily, they were more likely to do the following: engage in regular exercise, eat a balanced diet, have regular physicals and observe medication regimens, and avoid environmental toxins.

In sum, the effects of being careless or carefree add up throughout one's life and can be quite harmful in the end. More generally, the effects of conscientiousness illustrate that individuals play an important role in making healthy or unhealthy environments for themselves. Friedman et al. (1995a) conclude that "Although common wisdom might argue that a self-indulgent boor may prosper by stepping on others, this does not seem to be the case. Nor do we find a triumph of the lazy, pampered drop-out. In terms of the rush toward death, the encouraging news may be that good guys finish last" (p.76).

Diagnosis of Personality Disorders

The five-factor model and the NEO-PI are seen as measuring the basic emotional, interpersonal, and motivational styles of people. A number of

Big Five researchers have argued recently that many kinds of abnormal behavior are best considered exaggerated versions of normal personality traits (Costa & Widiger, 1994). In other words, many forms of psychopathology are seen as falling on a continuum with normal personality rather than as representing a distinct departure from the normal (Widiger, 1993). For example, the compulsive personality might be seen as someone extremely high on the conscientiousness factor and the antisocial personality as someone extremely low on the agreeableness factor. Although these illustrations focus on scores on individual factors, it is the pattern of scores on the five factors that may be most important.

Treatment

The five-factor model may be useful in providing psychological treatment to individuals. With an understanding of the individual's personality, the therapist may be in a better position to anticipate problems and plan the course of treatment (MacKenzie, 1994; Sanderson & Clarkin, 1994). Another potentially important contribution may be the guidance that can be given in selecting the optimal form of therapy (Costa & Widiger, 1994; Costa & McCrae, 1992; Miller, 1991). The principle here is that just as individuals with different personalities function better or worse in different vocations, so too they may profit more or less from different forms of psychological treatment. For example, individuals high in openness may profit more from therapies that encourage exploration and fantasy than would individuals low on this factor. The latter may prefer and profit better from more directive forms of treatment, including the use of medication. One clinician writing about this notes that he has often heard a patient low on openness say something like, "Some people need to lie on a couch and talk about their mother. My 'therapy' is working out at the gym" (Miller, 1991, p. 426). In contrast, the person high on openness may prefer the exploration of dreams found in psychoanalysis or the emphasis on self-actualization found in the humanistic–existential approach.

Another application of the five-factor model may be in the area of marital counseling. Recall that the NEO-PI has a form in which individuals rate themselves and a form in which they rate someone else. Using these forms with individuals in marital counseling may facilitate understanding of each individual, the relationship between their personalities, and ways in which each has a different perception of the partner than the partner has of the self. In marital counseling, part of the problem commonly is that one individual sees the self very differently from the way he or she is perceived by his or her partner. Often the partners are not aware of such differences and are puzzled about why they have such difficulties communicating. For example, one person may rate herself as high on extraversion and conscientiousness, but her partner rates her low on these factors. The counselor may be able to use such information to give the partners feedback about the differences in their perceptions and then help them to deal more constructively with the differences.

Summary and Comment

In sum, proponents of the Five-Factor Model suggest that as a full portrait of the individual, the model will likely have many valuable applications to the areas of vocational guidance, diagnosis, and treatment. The full implications of the model in this regard, as well as of the NEO-PI as an assessment device, remain to be explored. At the same time, a few points are noteworthy. First, this work is recent, and it is not clear to what extent the five factors will be useful in distinguishing among the many different types of personalities that can succeed in most occupations or among the many different forms of psychopathology of interest to clinicians. Second, the model currently shows more promise as a way of describing various forms of psychopathology than of explaining these disorders (Miller, 1991). Whereas other theories of personality provide explanations for many personality disorders (e.g., the psychoanalytic theory of the stages of development and personality disorders), the five-factor model offers little insight in this regard. Finally, it should be noted that the model offers no therapeutic approach. In contrast with the theories covered so far, each of which is associated with a model for the treatment of individuals with psychological difficulties, the five-factor model is silent in regard to how people can change.

---

*A Case Example: A 69-Year-Old Man**

Case illustrations of trait theory do not appear often in the literature, despite the trait emphasis on individual differences. With the publication of the NEO-PI-R we now have descriptions of individuals from the trait perspective. As described earlier in this chapter, the NEO-PI-R is a questionnaire that consists of 240 items for which the person indicates the extent of agreement on a five-point scale. Scores can be obtained for the five basic factors.

In addition, scores on six more specific *facet scales* are given for each of the five factors. These scales provide for a more fine-grained analysis within each trait category.

This case involves a 69-year-old man who was referred to a behavioral medicine clinic for treatment of chest pains and high blood pressure. He was a self-employed businessman who had undergone bypass surgery two years earlier and was afraid that he might die, leaving his wife and business in a vulnerable state. He stated during the intake interview that he had a lifelong history of anxieties, especially in social situations and unfamiliar surroundings. He is well above average in intelligence.

---

*Sections of this material are reproduced by special permission of the publisher, Psychological Assessment Resources, Inc., Odessa, FL 33556, from the NEO-PI-R Professional Manual, by Paul T. Costa, Jr. and Robert R. McCrae, Copyright 1992 by PAR, Inc.

Shown in Figure 8.2 are the patient's scores on the five factors and the facet scales for each factor. Also shown in Figure 8.2 are scores derived from ratings of him by his wife. That is, both self-report (Form S) and observer (in this case, wife - Form R) ratings are plotted on the same form and can be compared with one another. In general, the self-report and observer (wife) ratings are quite consistent. Both depict him as being introverted, open to experience, and conscientious. The largest discrepancies concern facets of Neuroticism, especially *N4: Self-Consciousness* and *N6: Vulnerability*. His wife clearly underestimated his standing on these facets, and discussions with the couple showed that he had been reluctant to share the extent of his distress with his wife. More open communication of his fears and vulnerabilities became one of the goals of treatment

Global Description of Personality in Terms of the Big Five

The most distinctive feature of this individual's personality is his standing on *Neuroticism*. Individuals scoring in this range are prone to experience a high level of negative emotion and frequent episodes of psychological distress. They are moody, overly sensitive, and dissatisfied with many aspects of their lives. They are generally low in self-esteem and may have unrealistic ideas and expectations. They are worriers who typically feel insecure about themselves and their plans. Friends and neighbors of such individuals might characterize them as nervous, self-conscious, high-strung, and vulnerable in comparison with the average person.

The facet scores for *Neuroticism* suggest that this individual is anxious, generally apprehensive, and prone to worry. He often gets angry at others but has only the usual periods of unhappiness that most men experience. Embarrassment or shyness when dealing with strangers is often a problem for him. He reports being good at controlling his impulses and desires, but he is unable to handle stress well.

This person is very high in *Conscientiousness*. Men who score in this range lead very well-ordered lives, striving to meet their goals in a planned and deliberate manner. They have a high need for achievement. They are neat, punctual, and well-organized and can be counted on to carry through on commitments they make. They take moral, civic, and personal obligations quite seriously and put business before pleasure. They have good self-discipline and have developed a number of competencies. Raters describe such people as careful, reliable, hard-working, and persevering.

Next, consider his level of *Openness to Experience*. Very high scorers like him have a strong interest in experience for its own sake. They seek out novelty and variety and have a marked preference for complexity. They have a heightened awareness of their own feelings and are perceptive in recognizing the emotions of others. They are very responsive to beauty in art and nature. Their attraction to new ideas and alternative value systems may make them especially tolerant of others and may lead them to adopt unconventional attitudes. Peers rate such people as imaginative, daring, independent, and creative.

This person is very low in *Extraversion*. Such people are quite introverted, preferring to do most things alone or with small groups of people. They avoid large, loud parties and do not enjoy meeting new people. They are usually quiet and unassertive in group interactions. They rarely experience strong positive feelings like joy or excitement. Those who know such people would probably describe

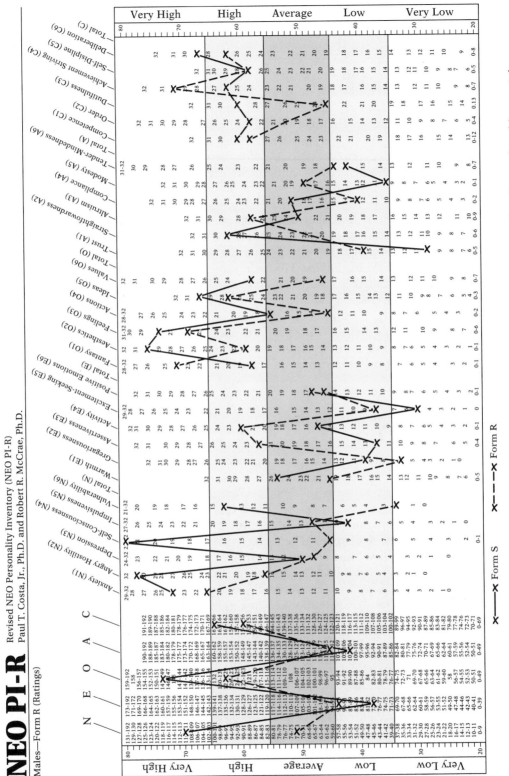

Figure 8.2 Self-ratings and spouse-ratings on the NEO PI-R (Costa & McCrae, 1992, p.27) Adapted and reproduced by special permission from the publisher, Psychological Assessment Resources, Inc., Odessa, FL 33556, from the NEO PI-R, by Paul Costa and Robert McCrae. Copyright 1992 by PAR, Inc. Further reproduction is prohibited without permission of PAR, Inc.

them as reserved, serious, retiring, and loners. The fact that these individuals are introverted does not necessarily mean that they lack social skills—many introverts function very well in social situations, although they might prefer to avoid them. Note also that introversion does not imply introspection; these individuals are likely to be thoughtful and reflective only if they are also high in Openness.

With respect to *Extraversion*, the facet scores indicate that this person is average in his level of interpersonal warmth but rarely enjoys large and noisy crowds or parties. He has trouble asserting himself and prefers to stay in the background in meetings and group discussions. The respondent has a moderate level of personal energy and an average activity level. Excitement, stimulation, and thrills have little appeal to him, but he experiences as much joy and happiness as most men.

Finally, this individual scores in the average range in *Agreeableness*. People who score in this range are about as good-natured as the average person. They can be sympathetic but can also be firm. They are trusting but not gullible, and ready to compete as well as to cooperate with others.

Personality Correlates: Some Possible Implications

In coping with the stresses of everyday life, this individual is likely to react with ineffective responses, such as hostile reactions toward others, self-blame, or escapist fantasies. He is more likely than most adults to use humor and less likely to use faith in responding to threats, losses, and challenges. In addition, he is somewhat less likely to use positive thinking and direct action in dealing with problems.

In terms of *somatic complaints*, this person may be overly sensitive in monitoring and responding to physical problems and illnesses. In medical evalua-

tions, it may be particularly important to seek objective confirmation of his subjective symptom reports where possible.

Considering his *psychological well-being*, it is important to note that his mood and satisfaction with various aspects of his life will vary with the circumstances. However, in the long run this individual is likely to be more sensitive to life's problems than to its rewards, and thus feel relatively unhappy. Because he is open to experience and introspection, his moods can be more intense and varied than those of the average man. Because he is high in *Conscientiousness*, his accomplishments and achievements may give him greater satisfaction with life.

In terms of *cognitive processes*, this individual is likely to be more complex and differentiated in his thoughts, values, and moral judgments than others of his level of intelligence and education. Because he is open to experience, this individual is likely to perform better than average on tests of divergent thinking ability; that is, he can generate fluent, flexible, and original solutions to many problems. He may be considered creative in his work or hobbies.

Finally, this respondent is likely to show high levels of the following needs and motives: achievement, cognitive structure, endurance (persistence), harm avoidance (avoiding danger), order, sentience (enjoyment of sensuous and aesthetic experiences), succorance (support and sympathy), and understanding (intellectual stimulation) and low levels of the following needs: abasement, dominance, and impulsivity.

Treatment Results

Because this patient was very high on Openness to Experience, he was able to benefit from imagery and self-hypnotic techniques designed to enhance relaxation and reduce blood pressure. Because he was high in Conscientiousness, he practiced these new skills regularly at home. As a result, at the end of the tenth session, he had substantially reduced his mean blood pressure and was able to discontinue therapy.

THE CASE OF JIM

The 16 P.F. Questionnaire: Trait, Factor-Analytic Theory

Let us now return to the case of Jim and consider how his personality is depicted by personality trait questionnaires. We begin with the *16 P.F. Questionnaire* developed by Cattell. Jim completed both forms (A and B) of the 16 P.F. The following brief description of Jim's personality was written by a psychologist who assessed the results of the 16 P.F. but was unaware of any of the other data on Jim.

> Jim presents himself as a very bright and outgoing young man although he is insecure, easily upset, and somewhat dependent. Less assertive, conscientious, and venturesome than he may initially appear, Jim is confused and conflicted about who he is and where he is going, tends toward introspection, and is quite anxious. His profile suggests that he may experience periodic mood swings and may also have a history of psychosomatic complaints. Since the 16 P.F. has been administered to college students throughout the country, we can also compare Jim with the average college student. Compared to other students, Jim is more outgoing, intelligent, and affected by feelings—easily upset, hypersensitive, and often depressed and anxious.

Recall that the factor-analytic method allows us to reduce the number of specific traits necessary to describe Jim's personality. Four second-order factors have been derived from Cattell's 16 first-order trait factors: Low Anxiety–High Anxiety, Introversion–Extraversion, Tenderminded Emotionality–Alert Poise, and Subduedness (group-dependent, passive)–Independence. Jim's scores are extreme on two of these factors. First, as expected, Jim is extremely high on anxiety. This suggests that he is dissatisfied with his ability to meet the demands of life and to achieve what he desires. The high level of anxiety also suggests the possibility of physical disturbances and bodily symptoms. Second, Jim is very low on alert poise or, conversely, he is high on tenderminded emotionality. This suggests that rather than being an enterprising and decisive personality, Jim is troubled by emotionality and often becomes discouraged and frustrated. Although sensitive to the subtleties of life, this sensitivity sometimes leads to preoccupation and to too much thought before he takes action. Jim's other two scores indicate that he is neither particularly introverted nor extraverted, and neither excessively dependent nor independent. In summary, his outstanding characteristics are anxiety, sensitivity, and emotionality.

Comments on the Data

Before we leave the 16 P.F., it should be noted that two important features came out in sharper focus on this test than on any of the other assessment devices. The first is the frequency of Jim's mood swings. In reading the results on the 16 P.F., Jim stated that he has frequent and extreme mood swings, ranging from extreme happiness to extreme depression. During the latter periods, he tends to take his feelings out on others and becomes hostile to them in a sarcastic, "biting," or "cutting" way. The second feature of importance concerns psychosomatic complaints. Jim has had considerable difficulty with an ulcer and frequently must drink milk for the condition. Notice that although this is a serious condition that gives him considerable trouble, Jim did not mention it at all in his autobiography.

From the data on the 16 P.F. we can discern many important parts of Jim's personality. The concept of trait, expressing a broad reaction tendency and relatively permanent features of behavior, appears to be useful for the description of his personality. We learn from the 16 P.F. that although Jim is outgoing, he is basically shy and inhibited. Again the characteristics of being anxious, frustrated, and conflicted come through. But one is left wondering whether 16 dimensions are adequate for the description of personality, particularly when they are reduced to four broad dimensions. One also wonders whether a score in the middle of the scale means that the trait is not important for understanding Jim or simply that he is not extreme on that characteristic. The latter appears to be the case. Yet, when one writes up a personality description based on the results of the 16 P.F., the major emphasis tends to fall on scales with extreme scores.

Perhaps most serious, however, is the fact that Cattell has failed to retain the virtues of the clinician in spite of his efforts to do so. The results of the 16 P.F. have the strengths and limitations of being a trait description of personality. The results are descriptive, but they are not interpretive or dynamic. Although Cattell has attempted to deal with the individual as a whole, the results of the 16 P.F. leave one only with a pattern of scores—not a whole individual. Although the theory takes into consideration the dynamic interplay among motives, the results of the 16 P.F. appear unrelated to this portion of the theory. Jim is described as being anxious and frustrated, but anxious about what and frustrated for what reason? Why is Jim outgoing and shy? Why does he find it so hard to be decisive and enterprising? The theory recognizes the importance of conflict in the functioning of the individual, but the results of the 16 P.F. tell us nothing about the nature of Jim's conflicts and how he tries to handle them. The factor traits appear to have some degree of validity, but they also tend to be abstract and leave out the richness of personality found in data from other assessment devices.

The Stability of Personality: Jim 5 and 20 Years Later

The material on Jim presented so far was written at approximately the time of his graduation from college in the late 1960s. Since then, sufficient time has elapsed to consider changes in his life and possible changes in his personality. This is particularly important in relation to trait theory since, as we have seen, considerable stability is suggested.

Five Years Later: Self-report of Life Experiences and Personality Changes

Five years after graduation Jim was contacted and asked (1) to indicate whether there had been significant life experiences for him since graduation and, if so, to describe how they had affected him and (2) to give a brief description of his personality and to describe the ways, if any, in which he had changed since graduation. His response follows.

Life Experiences

"After leaving college, I entered business school. I only got into one graduate school in psychology; it was not particularly prestigious, whereas I got into a number of excellent business schools, and so on that basis I chose to go to business school. I did not really enjoy business school, though it was not terribly noxious either, but it was clear to me that my interest really was in the field of psychology, so I applied to a couple of schools during the academic year but did not get in. I had a job in a New York import–export firm over the summer, and disliked it intensely enough to once more write to graduate schools over the summer. I was accepted at two, and then went into a very difficult decision-making process. My parents explicitly wanted me to return to business school, but I eventually decided to try graduate school. My ability to make that decision in the face of parental opposition was very significant for me; it asserted my strength and independence as nothing else in my life ever had.

"Going through graduate school in the Midwest in clinical psychology was extremely significant for me. I have a keen professional identification as a clinician which is quite central to my self-concept. I have a system of thinking which is well-grounded and very central to the way I deal with my environment. I am entirely pleased with the decision I made, even though I still toy with the idea of returning to business school. Even if I do it, it would be to attain an adjunct degree; it would not change the fact that my primary identification is with psychology. I also fell in love during my first year in graduate school, for the first and only time in my life. The relationship did not work out, which was devastating to me, and I've not gotten completely over it yet. Despite the pain, however, it was a life-infusing experience.

Last year I lived in a communal setting and it was a watershed experience for me. We worked a lot on ourselves and each other during the year, in our formal once-a-week groups and informally at any time, and it was a frequently painful, frequently joyful, and always a growth-producing experience. I am convinced that I would like to live communally as my basic style of life, though I need a very special group of people to do it with and would rather live alone or with one or two other people than with just any group. Our group is thinking about getting together again in a more permanent arrangement, and I may very well decide to live with them again beginning next year. Whether or not this happens, last year's experience was very significant for me, and therapeutic in every respect.

"Toward the end of last year, I began a relationship which has now become primary for me. I am living with a woman, Kathy, who is in a master's program in social work. She has been married twice. It is a sober relationship with problems involved; basically, there are some things about her that I am not comfortable with. I do not feel `in love' at this point, but there are a great many things about her that I like and appreciate, and so I am remaining in the relationship to see what develops, and how I feel about continuing to be with her. I have no plans to get married, nor much immediate interest in doing so. The relationship does not have the passionate feeling that my other significant relationship had, and I am presently trying to work through how much of my feeling at that time was idealization and how much real, and whether my more sober feelings for Kathy indicate that she's not the right woman for me or whether I need to come to grips with the fact that no woman is going to be "perfect" for me. In any event, my relationship with Kathy also feels like a wonderful growth-producing experience, and is the most significant life experience I am currently involved in.

"I think these constitute my significant life experiences since leaving college."

Personality Changes

"I do not think I've changed in very basic ways since leaving college. As a result of going into psychology, I think of myself as somewhat more self-aware these days, which I think is helpful. As I remember your interpretation of the tests I took back then, you saw me as primarily depressive. At this point, however, I think of myself as being primarily obsessive. I think I am prone to depression, but on balance see myself as happier these days— less frequently depressed. I see my obsessiveness as a deeply ingrained characterological pattern, and have been thinking for some time now about going into analysis to work on it (amongst other things, of course). Though I consider my thinking about this serious, I am not yet very close to actually doing it. This is at least in part because I expect to be leaving Michigan at the end of this academic year, and so entering analysis at this point obviously makes no sense. On the other hand, it's a frightening proposition requiring a serious commitment, so there is some resistance to overcome over and above the geographic issue. Nevertheless, I see it as a definite possibility for myself in the next couple of years.

"Let me say a word about my history with psychotherapy as a patient. I have made a number of abortive efforts to become involved, only one of which was even moderately successful. I saw someone at college a handful of times, but as I remember it, it was very superficial in every sense. I did nothing my year at business school. During my first year in graduate school, I saw an analytically oriented psychiatrist for three 'evaluative sessions,' after which he recommended: (1) analysis; (2) group therapy; (3) analytically oriented individual therapy. I was not ready to enter either analysis or a group, and did not want to continue with what he considered a third alternative, so I stopped. My second year in graduate school, I saw an analytically oriented psychiatrist for between six and eight sessions, but became very frustrated with his giving me so little, so that when he recommended increasing the frequency of visits from once to twice a week, I terminated. A big issue for me was how good a therapist he was: I saw him as pretty average, and felt I wanted someone special. This is clearly a form of resistance, I know, though I still feel there was some reality to my impressions of him. During my third year in graduate school, I saw a non-traditional psychiatrist about ten times. He used a mixed bag of techniques: cathartic, gestalt, behavioral, and generally folksy and friendly (very antianalytic). At the end of our relationship, which I thought was somewhat useful at the time, we both felt I'd had enough therapy, and that what I needed were 'therapeutic' life experiences: e.g., a relationship with a woman, some time to play, etc. Since then I have had some important therapeutic life experiences, the most significant of which was living in the house I lived in last year. As a result, I feel less immediate pressure to get help, and think of going into analysis to work through basis characterological issues (like my obsessiveness). In other words, I feel in less acute pain these days.

"As I said previously, I see myself as more similar to, than different from, the way I was five years ago. I think of myself as a witty, aware, interesting and fun-loving person. I continue to be quite moody, so sometimes none of these characteristics is in evidence at all. My sexual relationship with my girlfriend has put to rest my concern about my sexual adequacy (especially about premature ejaculation).

"I still see myself as having an 'authority' issue—i.e., being quite sensitive and vulnerable to the way in which those who have authority over me treat me. However, I see myself as having a number of important professional skills, and as being in the field I want to be in. I still have money issues—i.e., I am concerned about being paid fairly for what I do, I resent psychiatrists making more than me, I am vigilant around making sure I am not 'ripped off,' etc. I still have not fully come to grips with my father having money, and the fact that I will be getting some of that, but on the other hand I'm not terribly concerned about it, and it feels more like an intellectualized concern about the future than an emotional concern in the present. I am extremely compulsive, I very efficiently get done what needs to be done, and experience considerable anxiety when I am not on top of things. My life must be very well ordered for it to be possible for me to relax and enjoy myself. Unfortunately, the compulsiveness spills over into my personal life, so that my room must be orderly, my books stacked appropriately, etc., or else I experience anxiety. Again, this feels like a deeply ingrained pattern which would not be easy to overcome."

Twenty Years Later

Jim is now 40, practicing as a consulting psychologist in a medium-sized city on the West Coast. The most important events over the past years for him have been his marriage, the birth of a child, and the stabilization of a professional identity.

Prior to his marriage he was involved in lengthy relationships with two women. Though they were very different from one another, he found himself critical and discontented with each. He met his current wife about four years ago. He describes her as calm and peaceful, with a good sense of perspective on life. Although she is somewhat like one of the earlier women, he feels that he has changed in a way that makes a lasting relationship more possible: "I have a greater capacity for acceptance of the other and a clearer sense of boundaries between me and others— she is she and I am I. And, she accepts me, foibles and all."

Jim feels that he has made progress in what he calls "getting out of myself," but feels that his narcissism remains an important issue: "I'm selectively perfectionistic with myself, unforgiving of myself. If I lose money I punish myself. As a teenager I lost twenty dollars and went without lunches all summer long. I didn't need the money. My family has plenty of it. But what I did was unforgiveable. Is it perfectionistic or compulsive? I push myself all the time. I must read the newspaper thoroughly seven days a week. I feel imprisoned by it a lot of the time. Can I give up these rituals and self-indulgences with the birth of a child? I must."

Five-Factor Model: Self-ratings and Ratings by Wife on the NEO-PI

The NEO-PI as a measure of the five-factor model of personality was not available at the time of the original testing. Therefore, it seemed like a good idea to have Jim take the test at this time. In addition to the self-ratings, it was possible to obtain ratings of Jim by his wife. This offers an interesting opportunity to examine the degree of self-observer agreement, which the authors of the NEO-PI report to be generally high.

In terms of self-ratings, the most distinctive feature of Jim's personality is his very low standing on agreeableness. The testing report based on his responses indicates that people with his score are antagonistic and tend to be brusque or even rude in dealing with others. In addition, they prefer competition to cooperation and express hostile feelings directly, with little hesitation. They are described by people as relatively stubborn, critical, manipulative, or selfish.

Two other significant features of Jim's responses were his very high ratings on Extraversion and Neuroticism. In terms of the former, the report indicates that such people greatly enjoy the company of others and often are described by others as sociable, fun-loving, and talkative. The more specific subscale scores indicate that he sees himself as forceful and dominant, and prefers to be a group leader rather than a follower. In terms of neuroticism, Jim's score is characteristic of individuals prone to have a high level of negative emotion and frequent episodes of psychological distress. According to his Interpretive Report, such individuals

tend to be moody, overly sensitive, low in self-esteem, dissatisfied, worriers, and described by friends as nervous, self-conscious, and high-strung.

In terms of the two remaining factors, Jim scored high on conscientiousness, indicating a high need for achievement and ability to work in an organized way toward goals, and average on
openness, indicating he values the new and the familiar about
equally. Additional personality correlates suggested in the report
were that he likely uses ineffective coping responses in dealing
with the stresses of everyday life and that he is overly sensitive to
signs of physical problems and illnesses.

How similar a picture of Jim is given by his wife? On three of
the five factors there is very close agreement. Both Jim and his
wife saw him as very high on Extraversion, average on Openness,
and very low on Agreeableness. There was a small difference in
relation to Conscientiousness, with Jim rating himself slightly
higher than his wife rated him. The big difference in ratings
occurred in relation to Neuroticism, where Jim rated himself as
very high and his wife rated him as low. The more specific sub-
scales indicated that Jim saw himself as much more anxious,
hostile, and depressed than his wife rated him to be. In addition,
he viewed himself as somewhat more self-conscious and vulnerable than his wife rated him, although both agreed that he is
average or below average in regard to these traits. Whereas Jim's
self-ratings suggests a person who is anxious and prone to worry,
his wife's ratings suggest an individual who is calm and generally free of worry. In addition, whereas his responses suggest a person with ineffective devices for coping with stress and oversensi-
tivity to physical problems, his wife's ratings portray an individual with effective coping devices and a tendency to discount
physical and medical complaints.

How are we to evaluate such a level of agreement? In some
ways, this is like asking whether a glass is half-filled or half-
empty. The generally high level of agreement supports the suggestion that self-ratings tend to be accurate. On the other hand,
in one area the disagreement is dramatic. Perhaps Jim's wife
generally sees him in a more positive way, perhaps even in a more
accurate way, since Jim can be very self-critical. Another possibility is that, as indicated in the Rorschach report some 20 years
ago, he hides some of these negative emotions behind a façade of
poise and does not share with his wife the negative emotions he
actually feels. Of course, what we do not know is just how these
differences in ratings influence their marriage, that is, whether
the differences in perception represent areas of difficulty
between them or instead are acceptable, perhaps even desirable,
in terms of their marital relationship.

EVALUATION: THE PERSON–SITUATION CONTROVERSY

Over the past two decades trait theory has come in for considerable criticism because of its emphasis on stable and enduring properties of the person. As McCrae and Costa (1994) aptly summarize, the trait position has not been very popular: "If few findings in psychology are more robust than the stability of personality, even fewer are more unpopular. Gerontologists often see stability as an affront to their commitment to continuing adult development; psychotherapists sometimes view it as an alarming challenge to their ability to help patients; humanistic psychologists and transcendental philosophers think it degrades human nature. A popular account in *The Idaho Statesman* ran under the disheartening headline "Your personality—You're Stuck With It" (McCrae & Costa, 1994, p.175). Critics of trait theory argue that behavior is much more variable from situation to situation than trait theorists suggest (Mischel, 1968, 1990; Pervin, 1994b). Furthermore, critics claim that trait theory is not very effective in predicting behavior. Instead of an emphasis on broad predispositions in the *person*, many of these critics emphasize the importance of *situations*, or rewards in the environment, in the control of human behavior. Thus, for some time, debate raged over whether regularities in behavior could be accounted for by aspects of the person, such as traits, or by aspects of the situation—the **person–situation** controversy.

In considering whether people are stable in their personality traits, we may consider two aspects of such stability: longitudinal and cross-situational. The first, longitudinal, asks whether people high on a trait at one point in time are also high on that trait at another point in time. The second, cross-situational, asks whether people high on that trait in some situations are also high on that trait in other situations. Trait theorists suggest that both are true—that is, that people are stable over time and across situations in their trait personality characteristics. Of course, it is this view, particularly the aspect of cross-situational stability, that is attacked by proponents of a more situationist position.

LONGITUDINAL STABILITY

There is good evidence of the longitudinal stability of traits, even over extended periods of time (Block, 1993; Conley, 1985; McCrae & Costa, 1994). One study reports the conclusion that personality changes little after age 30 in most people: "In the course of thirty years, most adults will have undergone radical changes in their life structures. They may have married, divorced, remarried. They have probably moved their residence several times....And yet, most will not have changed appreciably in their standing on any of the five dimensions" (McCrae & Costa, 1990, p. 87). This conclusion may seem surprising given discussion of the "seasons" of people's lives and of periods such as midlife crises (Levinson et al., 1978). Despite the possible importance of many such events, the authors suggest that the basic personality does not change. Further, this picture of stability resulting from self-ratings is confirmed by the reports of others: "Husbands' and wives' views of their spouses' personalities confirm the essential stability of personality" (McCrae & Costa, 1990, p. 95).

Why should there be considerable longitudinal stability to personality? In part this is because of the genetic contribution to traits. In addition, people select and shape their environments so as to reinforce their traits (Caspi & Bem, 1990; Scarr, 1992). An extravert does not just wait for social situations to happen but seeks out others and often encourages them to be extraverted as well. Finally, once perceived in a certain way, others behave toward a person in a way that perpetuates already existing characteristics (Swann, 1992). Thus, although personality can change, there are powerful forces operating to maintain stability over time. Such stability is viewed by trait psychologists as having adaptive value: "Because personality is stable, life is to some extent predictable. People can make vocational and retirement choices with some confidence that their current interests and enthusiasms will not desert them. They can choose friends and mates with whom they are likely to remain compatible...They can learn which co-workers they can depend on, and which they cannot. The personal and social utility of personality stability is enormous" (McCrae & Costa, 1994, p.175).

CROSS-SITUATIONAL STABILITY

The issue of cross-situational consistency is more complex than that of longitudinal consistency. How are we to decide that a person has acted consistently over many situations? It would not make sense for a person to behave the same way in all situations, nor would trait theorists expect this to happen. One would hardly expect evidence of aggressiveness in a religious ceremony or of agreeableness in a football game. The trait position is that one expects evidence of consistency over a range of situations where many different behaviors are considered expressive of the same trait.

Concerning the issue of range of situations, trait psychologists suggest that it is an error to measure behavior in one situation as evidence of a person's standing on a trait. A single situation may not be relevant to the trait in question, and it is possible for an error in measurement to be made. On the other hand, sampling over a wide range of situations ensures that relevant and reliable measures will be obtained (Epstein, 1983). One reason trait psychologists like to use questionnaires is that they provide for the assessment of behavior in a wide range of situations that might be impossible to measure by other means.

In addition, behaviors that appear to be different may in fact be expressive of the same trait. Thus, for example, being talkative, having many friends, and seeking strong stimulation all reflect the trait of extraversion. One would expect this trait to be reflected in different behaviors in different situations. If room is left for such observations and measurements, consistency is often observed (Buss & Craik, 1983; Loevinger & Knoll, 1983).

CURRENT APPLICATIONS

CROSS-SITUATIONAL CONSISTENCY IN PUNCTUALITY: ARE SOME PEOPLE NOTORIOUSLY LATE?

"Five people showed up late to class the other night. This would be no big deal, except that the class they were late for was a class on how not to be late. The class, called 'Never Be Late Again,' is given once a month in a downtown San Francisco hotel by the Learning Annex…Della, a truck driver, said she has been late to work all her life. If she is late one more time, even by a single minute, she stands to lose her job. 'I need help,' she said."

John Carroll,
San Francisco Chronicle,
May 3, 1991, p. e10

Is it true that there is considerable cross-situational consistency in how late people are? Dudycha (1936) was the first psychologist to study punctuality empirically. He recorded children's arrival times to various school and social activities and found a modest degree of consistency. More recently, Mischel and Peake (1982) assessed various behavioral manifestations of conscientiousness, including several measures of subjects' arrival times. Using correlational indices, they concluded that behavioral consistency across situations was low at best.

Ware and John (1995) asked a slightly different question: Does the broad Conscientiousness factor from the Five-Factor Model help us predict individual differences in punctuality? The subjects were Berkeley students in the Masters of Business Administration Program whose arrival times at a managerial assessment program were recorded on several days. Conscientiousness was measured with the NEO-PI self-report scale two weeks prior to the experiment, thus allowing the researchers to divide up the sample beforehand into high and low Conscientiousness groups. Individual differences in lateness were substantial; subjects' arrival times ranged from 30 minutes *early* (a score of -30) to 46 minutes *late* (a score of +46 on lateness).

There were two kinds of situations: one was an easy appointment time (5 p.m. in the afternoon), and the other was a difficult appointment time (8 a.m. in the morning). The findings are illustrated in the figure below. As situationist accounts of behavior would suggest, the average participant was 2 minutes early for the afternoon appointment but 6 minutes late for the early morning one. Now consider the trait effect: the students high in Conscientiousness consistently arrived earlier than the students low in Conscientiousness, by about 5 minutes, and this effect held in both situations. Generally students were consistent in their relative promptness across the situations and their conscientiousness scores predicted lateness to a statistically significant degree (see accompanying figure).

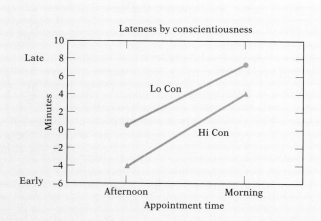

How large is this conscientiousness effect? Five minutes late on *one* day may not seem that much. But consider that 50 percent of the students were classified as relatively low on Conscientiousness and they arrived an average of 5 minutes later for *each* of their appointments. That adds up to an hour late in 12 appointments. At a job, it would translate into almost a half hour of work missed per week, two hours per month, and 24 hours (that is, three whole work days) per year. Thus, what seems like a small effect can quickly snowball. No wonder that Della, the truck driver, is in trouble at her job!

These findings illustrate that both the situation and our personality traits affect how we behave at any given time. There is *some* cross-situational consistency in lateness but the personality trait of Conscientiousness is only one of many influences that determines whether we are late in any one specific situation.

SOURCES: Dudycha, 1936; Mischel & Peake, 1982; Ware & John, 1995.

GEECH®

by Jerry Bittle

Drawing by Jerry Bittle; ©1991 Universal Press Syndicate

Finally, one can consider the ways that one looks for evidence of consistency in personality functioning. The evidence of consistency is better when self-report data and observations in the natural environment are used as opposed to laboratory test data (Block, 1977). Why should this be so? One reason is that laboratory situations restrict the opportunities for individual differences to emerge (Monson et al., 1982). Most students who have been subjects in laboratory experiments will be aware that most laboratory situations leave relatively little room for a wide range of responses. This is consistent with the effort of the experimenter to gain control over the experimental variables and establish cause–effect relations. In addition, unlike the real world, laboratory tests do not provide the opportunity to seek, select, and shape the situation. In the real world, people behave consistently in part because they select and shape the very situations that influence their behavior (Caspi & Bem, 1990; Scarr, 1992).

CONCLUSION

Where does this leave us in terms of the person–situation controversy? Can a conclusion based on the evidence be reached at this time? A fair judgment might suggest that there is evidence of trait consistency, but there appears to be more consistency *within* certain domains of situations (e.g., home, school, work, friends, recreation) than *across* domains. Since in everyday life we observe others over a limited range of situations, we may think there is greater consistency than actually exists. Beyond this, the conclusions drawn about cross-situational consistency tend to vary with the psychologist's point of view. There is evidence both for some cross-situational consistency and for some cross-situational variability. To a certain extent people are the same regardless of context, and to a certain extent they also are different depending on the context. Trait theorists are impressed with the former and use such evidence to support their position, whereas situationist theorists are impressed with the latter and use such evidence to support their position.

OVERALL EVALUATION OF TRAIT APPROACHES

Having reviewed various trait theories and some of the relevant evidence, it is time to evaluate the trait position. Although differences exist among trait theorists, they share an emphasis on individual differences in broad dispositions to behave in particular ways. During the 1970s and 1980s, it seemed as if the trait position might be buried by situationist criticism and the cognitive revolution. Today, trait research is again flourishing, so much so that one critical reviewer suggests that "after decades of doubt and discrimination, traits are back on top" (McAdams, 1992, p. 329).

Although it is true that reports of the death of trait theory were unfounded, it is equally the case that proclamations of discovery of the basic structure of personality seem premature (Block, 1995; Pervin,

1994a). Let us try to provide a more balanced assessment of the strengths and limitations of this important and controversial part of the field. We will begin by considering three important contributions of trait psychologists: the developments of an active research effort, of interesting hypotheses, and of potential ties to the field of biology. Then we will consider three problem areas: problems with the method of factor analysis, problems with the trait concept, and the neglect of important aspects of personality.

STRENGTHS OF THE APPROACHES

Active Research Effort

As a group, trait psychologists have been very active in research. If the person–situation controversy has not been settled, at least there is considerable evidence of stability in personality functioning (Kenrick & Funder, 1988). Recognizing that human behavior is complex and generally determined by many traits, evidence of the predictive utility of traits has been obtained (Ahadi & Diener, 1989; Barrick & Mount, 1991; Brody, 1988; McCrae & John, 1992). As noted earlier, important gains have been made in research on genetic contributions to personality and on physiological aspects of trait characteristics (Eysenck, 1990; Loehlin, 1992; Plomin, 1994; Zuckerman, 1990, 1995). Finally, important research programs are investigating the relation of traits to interpersonal behavior and psychopathology (Costa & Widiger, 1994; Widiger & Trull, 1992; Wiggins et al., 1989; Wiggins & Pincus, 1994). Over a decade ago, in response to situationist criticism, it was suggested that traits were alive and well (Epstein, 1977). If this was true at that time, then they are alive and doing even better now.

Interesting Hypotheses

At this point, a number of interesting hypotheses are emerging from proponents of the trait point of view. Three have already been discussed in this chapter. First, there is the fundamental lexical hypothesis, suggesting that important individual differences will be encoded in language (Goldberg, 1993). Early studies have provided cross-cultural evidence in support of this hypothesis, although the results are less clear-cut when individuals using non-Western languages generate their own personality descriptions (Bond, 1994; Yang & Bond, 1990). Second, there is the interesting hypothesis that environments are important in personality development, but that it is the environment that is *not* shared by members of the same family that is crucial (Plomin, 1994; Plomin et al., 1990). Third, there is the evolutionary-based hypothesis that traits evolved to solve adaptive problems (D. M. Buss, 1995; Tooby & Cosmides, 1990). All three hypotheses are intriguing. Future research associated with them will warrant careful attention.

Potential Ties to Biology

Theoretical and research work in relation to genetics, physiological functioning, and evolutionary theory suggests a link between personality psychology and biology that may hold promise for the future. For example, linkages have been suggested between individual differences in personality traits and differences in brain functioning (Depue, Luciana, Arbisi, Colins, & Leon, 1994). The field of biology has made enormous gains over the past decade. As a minimum, concepts in personality cannot violate what is known about the biological functioning of humans. Beyond this, however, developments in biology may guide some of our research efforts. Tremendous gains are being made in the assessment of biological functioning, and the field of biopsychology is gaining strength. Without losing some of the distinctive focus of the field of personality, it would seem likely that personality research informed by biological findings can make a major contribution to the field.

LIMITATIONS OF THE APPROACHES

These, then, are some of the strengths of the trait position, gains both made and promised for the future. What of the limitations?

Problems with the Method: Factor Analysis

The method of factor analysis is central to trait research, in particular to the development of the five-factor model. Just as Cattell suggested that factor analysis could be used to discover personality's equivalent of chemistry's periodic table of the elements, today's proponents suggest that it has resulted in discovery of the basic dimensions of personality traits—the Big Five (McCrae & John, 1992). At the same time, the method has its critics. Although Allport was committed to trait theory, he was critical of the factor-analytic approaches of Eysenck and Cattell and stated that the factors identified through this procedure "resemble sausage meat that has failed to pass the pure food and health inspection" (1958, p. 251). Others are equally critical, suggesting that the method is comparable to putting people through a centrifuge and expecting the "basic stuff" to come out (Lykken, 1971; Tomkins, 1962).

If factor analysis is as powerful as its proponents suggest, the same factors should be derived from different studies. Although it has been stated that the five-factor model is a basic discovery of personality psychology and that five factors are "just right" (McCrae & John, 1992), some researchers still insist that fewer than five are sufficient (Eysenck, 1993; Zuckerman, 1990) and others suggest that five is not nearly enough (Benet & Waller, 1995; A. H. Buss, 1988; Cattell, 1990; Tellegen, 1993). Despite suggestions of an emerging consensus concerning the Big Five, there is currently a lively and at times heated debate about the status of the Big Five (Block, 1995; Goldberg & Saucier, 1995; Pervin, 1994a;

Eysenck, 1993). A number of critics suggest that the degree of correspondence among the findings from different studies has been less than ideal. In the words of one supporter of trait theory, "the resemblance is more fraternal than identical" (Briggs, 1989, p. 248). In sum, we must question whether factor analysis will provide the basic units of personality.

Problems with the Trait Concept

The trait concept suggests a disposition to respond similarly across a variety of situations. At this point it might seem as if trait theorists agree about what a trait is and what it includes. Yet, as was suggested over 20 years ago, "what is to be included in a definition of traits is not self-evident" (Borgatta, 1968, p. 510). According to some definitions, the existence of a trait implies a consistent pattern of overt, observable behavior (Buss & Craik, 1983; Mischel & Peake, 1982; Pervin, 1994a). However, many trait researchers include many nonobservable behaviors in their definition of traits, such as individual differences in emotions, motives, and attitudes (A. H. Buss, 1989; McCrae & Costa, 1990; McCrae & John, 1992; Watson & Clark, 1992). Indeed, from this standpoint, Henry Murray (Chapter 4) is considered to be a trait theorist!

Trait theorists can define the concept in any way they want, and include within it whatever they choose, but what is included and whether there is agreement on the definition does make a difference. Particularly important is whether the distinction between a trait and a motive is useful (Pervin, 1994a). Murray's (1938) thinking is important here since he specifically contrasted the concept of *need* with that of *trait*. According to Murray, traits are enduring over time and manifested in behavior. In contrast, needs can be either momentary or enduring, and they can be present within the organism without becoming manifest in behavior. Thus, Murray suggested that "according to my prejudice, trait psychology is over-concerned with recurrences, with consistency, with what is clearly manifested (the surface of personality), with what is conscious, ordered, and rational" (1938, p. 715). These are not trivial differences between needs and traits, and they call attention to Murray's skepticism concerning people's ability to report accurately about their thoughts, feelings, and behavior, and his emphasis on a dynamic conceptualization of personality.

Another question concerns the explanatory status of the trait concept. Are traits *descriptions* of behavioral regularities or *explanations* of observed regularities (Briggs, 1989; Tellegen, 1993; Wiggins, 1973; Zuroff, 1986)? In its simplest form, we can ask whether traits are "real" or whether they are "convenient fictions by which we communicate" (Briggs, 1989, p. 251). Remember that Eysenck was very much concerned with this matter, suggesting that without a theory there was the danger of circularity—the use of a trait concept to explain behavior that serves as the basis to infer the trait concept in the first place (Wiggins, 1973). In other words, how much do we add to our understanding of per-

TRAIT APPROACHES AT A GLANCE

Structure	Process	Growth and Development
Traits	Dynamic traits, motives associated with traits	Contributions of heredity and environment to traits

sonality if we infer a person is an extravert because they performed a number of extraverted behaviors and then say that the person behaved that way because he or she is an extravert? More generally, the five-factor model by itself is not an explanatory model of personality (McCrae, 1994; Pervin, 1994a).

What Is Left Out or Neglected?

Does the trait concept and the five-factor model provide us with a comprehensive model of personality? In part, this question follows from the discussion of what is to be included in the trait concept. Even many trait theorists would suggest, however, that there is more to personality than the Big Five—for example, people's self-concepts, their identities, their cognitive styles, and the unconscious (Block, 1995; A. H. Buss, 1988; McAdams, 1992).

Another question is, does the model say anything about the organization of personality? Is a person just a bundle of traits or is an important part of personality the way in which the traits are organized? It is interesting that Allport (1961) placed pattern and organization at the core of personality. Modern trait theorists would appear to agree that "the essence of personality is the organization of experience and behavior" (McCrae & Costa, 1990, p. 118). Yet, trait research is noticeably lacking in this regard and only recently have efforts been made to describe how the Big Five traits combine within individuals to form personality types (Robins, John, Caspi, Moffitt, & Stouthamer-Loehber, 1996; York & John, 1992). And, as noted, for a theory of individual differences there is a surprising paucity of studies of the individual. Thus, in the words of one recent critic: "The five-factor model is essentially a psychology of the

Table 8.3   Summary of Strengths and Limitations of Trait Theory

Strengths	Limitations
1. Active research effort	1. The method: factor analysis
2. Interesting hypotheses	2. What does a trait include?
3. Potential ties to biology	3. What is left out or neglected?

Pathology	Change	Illustrative Case
Extreme scores on trait dimensions (e.g., neuroticism)	(No formal model)	69-year-old man

stranger—a quick and simple portrait of someone" (McAdams, 1992, p. 333). Students can form their own opinion on the matter by considering the case presented in this chapter, as well as by comparing the various personality descriptions of Jim presented in Chapter 15.

Finally, with the exception of Eysenck, trait theory does not have much to say with regard to a theory of personality change. It is one thing to document the stability of personality and to suggest reasons for such stability—genetic (temperament) factors, selection and shaping of situations, and stereotyped or self-confirming responses by others. It is another thing to entirely omit an account of how change comes about. Even with an emphasis on stability, our sense is that relatively few trait theorists think that most personality traits are as fixed and enduring as intelligence. For example, there is considerable personality change on the Big Five in early adulthood at least until age 30. And, even if one questions the efficacy of psychotherapy, a way of accounting for change that occurs sometimes would appear to be a reasonable requirement of a comprehensive theory of personality (Brody, 1988). Some research on these issues is finally appearing; for example, trait researchers have attempted to predict how particular life experiences bring about systematic changes in personality traits (Helson, 1993; Helson & Wink, 1992).

In sum, trait theory is alive and well, but some aches and pains remain. In what form the patient will develop and change remains to be seen.

MAJOR CONCEPTS

Five-factor model. An emerging consensus among trait researchers that there are five basic dimensions or factors to describe all human personality traits.

Big Five. The five broadly defined dimensions included in the Five-Factor Model: neuroticism, extraversion, openness, agreeableness, and conscientiousness

OCEAN. The acronym for the five basic traits: **O**penness, **C**onscientiousness, **E**xtraversion, **A**greeableness, and **N**euroticism.

Fundamental lexical hypothesis. The hypothesis that over time the most important individual differences in human interactions have been encoded as single terms into language.

Facets. Facets are the more specific traits (or components) that make up each of the broad Big Five factors. For example, facets of Extraversion are *Activity Level, Assertiveness, Excitement Seeking, Positive Emotions, Gregariousness*, and *Warmth*.

Person–situation controversy. A controversy between psychologists who emphasize the importance of personal (internal) variables in determining behavior and those who emphasize the importance of situational (external) influences.

REVIEW

1. A consensus among trait theorists is emerging around the Big Five dimensions (O-C-E-A-N) specified by the five-factor model. Support for the model comes from the factor analysis of trait terms in language, the factor analysis of ratings and questionnaire (e.g., NEO-PI) data, and the analysis of genetic (inherited) contributions to personality.

2. The fundamental lexical hypothesis suggests that over time the fundamental individual differences among people have been encoded into language.

3. From an evolutionary perspective, it has been suggested that fundamental personality traits exist because they played an adaptive role in the process of natural selection.

4. Proponents of the five-factor model suggest that it has important potential applications in areas such as vocational guidance, health and longevity, personality diagnosis, and psychological treatment. It was noted that developments in these areas are recent and remain to be evaluated. In addition, the model offers no specific recommendations concerning the process of personality change.

5. Critics of trait theory suggest that human behavior is very variable. Instead of emphasizing broad dispositions within the person, the importance of situational influences should be recognized. This has led to the person–situation controversy. There is evidence for longitudinal stability in personality and for cross-situational consistency where a broad range of situations and behaviors is sampled (aggregation). At the same time, there is evidence for variability in individual behavior, particularly where situations are very different from one another. The task remains to account for patterns of stability and variability in behavior.

6. An overall evaluation of current trait theory suggests strengths in research, the formulation of interesting hypotheses, and the potential for ties to biology in relation to work on genetic contributions to personality and evolutionary developments. At the same time, questions can be raised concerning the method of factor analysis, the clarity of definitions of the trait concept, and the neglect of such important areas of psychological functioning as the organization of personality traits within the individual and a theory of personality change.

9

LEARNING APPROACHES TO PERSONALITY

Chapter Focus

Have you ever dated someone who did something that really annoyed you? A woman was particularly bothered by her boyfriend's constant moaning about how much schoolwork he had to do. She grew tired of constantly providing him with attention and sympathy—after all, she had just as much work! What if she simply ignored her boyfriend every time he complained? When she stopped pampering him, his complaining gradually disappeared; all she had to do was to remove the positive reinforcement which had taught him to complain in the first place.

Without realizing it, this woman was using some of the basic principles of learning theory to change her boyfriend's behavior. This chapter considers approaches to personality that are based on theories of learning. There are many different learning theories, all of which aim to explain how people learn and unlearn specific behaviors. In this chapter, we will focus on three such theories—Pavlov's *classical conditioning*, Skinner's *operant conditioning*, and *stimulus–response* (S–R) theory. These theories all share a commitment to the experimental testing of clearly defined hypotheses. Approaches to assessment and change are then considered, along with an overall critical evaluation of these approaches to personality.

QUESTIONS TO BE ADDRESSED IN THIS CHAPTER

1. How does a focus on laboratory research and cause–effect relationships lead to different observations and different theories than those associated with clinical research and correlational research?

2. To what extent can basic principles of learning, often based on the study of learning in nonhuman animals, provide the basis for a theory of personality?

3. To what extent is our behavior controlled by reinforcers (i.e., rewards and punishments)? Can abnormal behaviors be understood in terms of learning principles?

4. If normal behavior is learned or acquired like all other behavior, can therapeutic change occur as the result of the application of learning principles? To what extent, then, is psychopathology more a problem of faulty learning than of a disease or illness?

In this chapter we will discuss three approaches to learning: Pavlov's classical conditioning, Skinner's operant conditioning, and Hull's stimulus–response learning. They share common features, in particular an emphasis on the importance of learning and a commitment to rigorous methodology. There are, however, many important differences in how they interpret the principles of learning and understand behavior.

During the period between the 1950s and the 1970s, these approaches greatly influenced thinking in the area of personality and clinical psychology. Subsequently their influence was replaced by other, generally more cognitive approaches. However, they are important to understand in terms of the history of developments in the field.

To understand the learning theory approach to personality, one must be prepared to make new assumptions and to consider new strategies for research. The learning theory approach to personality has two basic assumptions from which a number of critical points follow. The first assumption is that nearly all behavior is learned, and the second is that objectivity and rigor in the testing of clearly formulated hypotheses are crucial (Table 9.1).

THE LEARNING VIEW OF THE PERSON AND SCIENCE

Whereas Eysenck and Cattell viewed learning as part of the broader area of personality, the theoretical approaches discussed in this chapter suggest that the study of personality is a branch of the general field of learning. For example, psychopathology is understood in terms of the learning of maladaptive behaviors or the failure to learn adaptive behaviors. Rather than speaking of psychotherapy, followers of the learning–behavioral view speak of *behavior modification* and *behavior therapy*. Specific behaviors are to be modified or changed, rather than underlying conflicts resolved or a personality reorganized. Since most problematic behaviors have been learned, they can be unlearned or otherwise changed through the application of learning-based procedures.

The emphasis on objectivity and rigor, on testable hypotheses and the experimental control of variables, is perhaps even more significant. It has led to an emphasis on the laboratory as the place for studying behavior, to an emphasis on simple rather than complex behavior, and to the use of animals, such as rats and pigeons, as subjects. Further, the emphasis on the careful manipulation of objectively defined variables has led to

Table 9.1 Basic Points of Emphasis of Learning Approaches to Personality

1. Empirical research is the cornerstone of theory and practice.
2. Personality theory and applied practice should be based on principles of learning.
3. Behavior is responsive to reinforcement variables in the environment and is more situation specific than suggested by other personality theories (e.g., trait, psychoanalytic).
4. Rejection of the medical symptom-disease view of psychopathology and emphasis instead on basic principles of learning and behavior change.

an emphasis on forces *external* to the organism as opposed to ones *internal* to it. According to the learning–behavioral approach, one manipulates variables in the environment and observes the consequences of these manipulations in behavior. Whereas psychodynamic theories emphasize causes of behavior that are inside the organism (e.g., instincts, defenses, self-concept), learning theories emphasize causes that are in the external environment. Stimuli in the environment that can be experimentally manipulated, such as food rewards, are emphasized instead of concepts that cannot be manipulated, such as the self, the ego, and the unconscious.

The behavioral emphasis on external, environmental determinants also has been associated with an emphasis on **situational specificity** in behavior. In contrast with the emphasis in psychodynamic and trait theories on characteristics that are expressed in a range of situations, behavior theory suggests that whatever consistency is found in behavior is the result of the similarity of environmental conditions that evoke these behaviors.

Before we consider the three approaches to learning, a word should be said about psychologist John Watson, whose views so much influenced the course of American psychology and developments in parts of the field of personality.

WATSON'S BEHAVIORISM

John B. Watson (1878–1958) was the founder of the approach to psychology known as **behaviorism**. He began his graduate study at the University of Chicago in philosophy and then switched to psychology. During these years he took courses in neurology and physiology and

John B. Watson

began to do a considerable amount of animal research. Some of this research concerned the increased complexity of behavior in the rat and the associated development of the central nervous system. During the year before he received his doctorate, Watson had an emotional breakdown and had sleepless nights for many weeks. He described this period as useful in preparing him to accept a large part of Freud (Watson, 1936, p. 274). The graduate work at Chicago culminated in a dissertation on animal education and was associated with the development of an important attitude regarding the use of human subjects.

> At Chicago, I first began a tentative formulation of my later point of view. I never wanted to use human subjects. I hated to serve as a subject. I didn't like the stuffy, artificial instructions given to subjects. I always was uncomfortable and acted unnaturally. With animals I was at home. I felt that, in studying them, I was keeping close to biology with my feet on the ground. More and more the thought presented itself: Can't I find out by watching their behavior everything that the other students are finding by using O's (human subjects)?
>
> SOURCE: Watson, 1936, p. 276

Watson left Chicago in 1908 to become a professor at Johns Hopkins University, where he served on the faculty until 1919. During his stay there, which was interrupted by a period of service during World War I, Watson developed his views on behaviorism as an approach to psychology. These views, which emphasized the study of observable behavior and which excluded the study of self-observation or introspection, were presented in public lectures in 1912 and were published in 1914 in Watson's book *Behavior*. Watson's call for the use of objective methods and the end of speculation about what goes on inside the person was greeted enthusiastically, and he was elected president of the American Psychological Association for 1915. His views were further developed to include the work of the Russian physiologist Pavlov; those views can be found in his most significant work, *Psychology from the Standpoint of a Behaviorist* (1919).

Watson was divorced in 1919, immediately married his student Rosalie Rayner, and was forced to resign from Hopkins. The circumstances of this departure from Johns Hopkins led him to earn his livelihood in the business world. Although he had already established a considerable reputation as a psychologist, he now was forced to do studies of potential sales markets. He found, however, "that it can be just as thrilling to watch the growth of a sales curve of a new product as to watch the learning curve of animals or men" (Watson, 1936, p. 280). After 1920, Watson did write some popular articles and published his book *Behaviorism* (1924), but his career as a productive theorist and experimenter ended with his departure from Johns Hopkins.

PAVLOV'S THEORY OF CLASSICAL CONDITIONING

Ivan Petrovich Pavlov (1849–1936) was a Russian physiologist who, in the course of his work on the digestive process, developed a procedure for studying behavior and a principle of learning that had a profound effect on the field of psychology. Around the beginning of the twentieth century Pavlov was involved in the study of gastric secretions in dogs. As part of his research, he placed some food powder inside the mouth of a dog and measured the resulting amount of salivation. Coincidentally he noticed that after a number of such trials the dog began to salivate to certain stimuli before the food was placed in its mouth. This salivation occurred in response to cues such as the sight of the food dish or the approach of the person who generally brought the food. In other words, stimuli that previously did not lead to this response (called *neutral stimuli*) could now elicit the salivation response because of their association with the food powder that automatically caused the dog to salivate. To animal owners this may not seem to be a startling observation. However, it led Pavlov to conduct significant research on the process known as **classical conditioning**.

PRINCIPLES OF CLASSICAL CONDITIONING

The essential characteristic of classical conditioning is that a previously neutral stimulus becomes capable of eliciting a response because of its association with a stimulus that automatically produces the same or a similar response. In other words, the dog salivates to the first presentation of the food powder. One need not speak of a conditioning or learn-

Ivan Petrovich Pavlov

Drawing by Norm Rockwell
Reprinted by permission.

ing process at this point. The food can be considered to be an *unconditioned stimulus* (US) and the salivation an *unconditioned response* (UR). This is because the salivation is an automatic, reflex response to the food. A neutral stimulus, such as a bell, will not lead to salivation. However, if on a number of trials the bell is sounded *just before* the presentation of the food powder, the sounding of the bell itself without the subsequent appearance of food may have the potential to elicit the salivation response. In this case, conditioning has occurred since the presentation of the bell alone is followed by salivation. At this point, the bell may be referred to as a *conditioned stimulus* (CS) and the salivation as a *conditioned response* (CR).

In a similar way, it is possible to condition withdrawal responses to previously neutral stimuli. In the early research on conditioned withdrawal, a dog was strapped in a harness and electrodes were attached to his paw. The delivery of an electric shock (US) to the paw led to the withdrawal of the paw (UR), which was a reflex response on the part of the animal. If a bell was repeatedly presented just before the shock, eventually the bell alone (CS) was able to elicit the withdrawal response (CR).

The experimental arrangement designed by Pavlov to study classical conditioning allowed him to investigate a number of important phenomena. For example, would the conditioned response become associated with the specific neutral stimulus alone or would it become associated with other similar stimuli? Pavlov found that the response that had become conditioned to a previously neutral stimulus would also become associated with similar stimuli, a process called **generalization**. In other words, the salivation response to the bell would generalize to other sounds. Similarly, the withdrawal response to the bell would generalize to sounds similar to the bell.

DEATH BY HEROIN OVERDOSE:
A CLASSICAL CONDITIONING EXPLANATION

Dwayne Goettel, 31, keyboardist and programmer for the influential industrial band Skinny Puppy, died from an apparent heroin overdose Aug. 23, 1995, in a bathroom at his parents' house. How could this have happened? As a bandmate told *Rolling Stone Magazine*, Goettel had just returned to his parents' house to kick his habit.

Goettel is one of hundreds of heroin addicts who die each year of a reaction typically known as an "overdose." Yet, how these deaths happen still remains unclear. Why do some long-term heroin users die from a dose that would not be expected to be fatal for them? Research by Sheppard Siegel and his colleagues suggests that some instances of heroin overdose may result from a *failure of tolerance*. How does a heroin addict, who has spent years building up a tolerance to heavy doses of the drug, experience such a failure of tolerance? Pavlov's theory of classical conditioning provides the basis for an answer to this question.

Pavlov proposed that drug administration constitutes a conditioning trial. The unconditioned stimulus (US) is the bodily effect of the drug, and the unconditioned response (UR) is how the body compensates for those effects. Conditioning occurs when the US (the effect of the drug) becomes associated with a conditioned stimulus (CS)—such as environmental cues present when the drug is taken. In other words, as heroin users establish an addiction, they learn to associate the effects of the drug with the environment in which they usually take it. Soon, the environmental cues alone can bring about the compensatory effects even before the drug is taken. Thus, the environmental cues serve as a *signal* to the body that the effects of the drug are about to take place. In preparation, the body reacts to the cues in a manner that helps compensate for the anticipated effects of the drug. This conditioned response (CR) builds tolerance to the drug by lessening the drug's effects.

This Pavlovian model of drug tolerance has an important implication: heroin addicts are at risk for overdose when they take the drug in an environment that has not previously been associated with the drug. If the environmental cues typically associated with the drug are absent, the conditioned response cannot occur, causing a failure of tolerance. The heroin user takes a heavy dose of the drug and the body is left unprepared for its effects.

Is there empirical evidence for this explanation? In an *animal study*, rats received daily injections of increasing dosages of heroin in one of two environments. In the final session of the experiment, all the rats were administered a dose of heroin; for this injection, half of the rats were in the same environment in which they had been administered heroin in the past (*same-environment rats*) and the other half were in an environment in which they had never been administered heroin before (*different-environment rats*).

The different-environment rats were significantly more likely to die from the injection than the same-environment rats. Why? The different-environment rats had lower tolerance to heroin because they were in an environment not previously associated with the drug. Unlike the same-environment rats, they did not have the conditioned response stimulated by cues in the environment to prepare them for the effects of the drug.

The rat experiment supports the model, but does the same phenomenon occur in humans? For obvious reasons, the parallel experiment cannot be conducted on people, so we must rely on what heroin users who have survived an overdose tell us about their experience.

This is exactly what Siegel did to complement the results of the rat experiment. He interviewed former heroin addicts who had been hospitalized for drug overdoses. The majority of the survivors reported that the setting in which the overdose episode occurred was *atypical*. For example, one person reported that he injected the drug in the bathroom of a car wash—for him, an unusual place to take the drug. These reports from human victims show that the Pavlovian model of drug tolerance is relevant and useful in understanding such tragic deaths as that of the musician Dwayne Goettel in his parents' bathroom.

SOURCES: *Rolling Stone Magazine*, Oct. 1995, p. 25; Siegel (1984); Siegel et al. (1982).

What are the limits of such generalization? If repeated trials indicate that only some stimuli are followed by the unconditioned stimulus, the animal recognizes differences among stimuli, a process called **discrimination**. For example, if only certain sounds but not others are followed by shock and reflexive paw withdrawal, the dog will learn to discriminate among sounds. Thus, whereas the process of generalization leads to consistency of response across similar stimuli, the process of discrimination leads to increased specificity of response. Finally, if the originally neutral stimulus is presented repeatedly without being followed at least occasionally by the unconditioned stimulus, there is an undoing or progressive weakening of the conditioning or association, a process known as **extinction**. Whereas the association of the neutral stimulus with the unconditioned stimulus leads to the conditioned response, the repeated presentation of the conditioned stimulus without the unconditioned stimulus leads to extinction. For example, for the dog to continue to salivate to the bell, there must be at least occasional presentations of the food powder with the bell.

Although the illustrations used relate to animals, the principles can be seen to apply to humans as well. For example, consider a child who is bitten or merely treated roughly by a dog. The child's fear of this dog may now be extended to all dogs—the process of generalization. Suppose, however, by getting help, the child begins to discriminate among dogs of various kinds and begins to be afraid only of certain dogs. We can see here the process of discrimination. Over time, the child may have repeated positive experiences with all dogs, leading to the extinction of the fear response altogether. Thus, the classical conditioning model may be potentially very helpful in understanding the development, maintenance, and disappearance of many of our emotional reactions.

PSYCHOPATHOLOGY AND CHANGE

The phenomena of generalization, discrimination, and extinction are important to classical conditioning theory as well as to other theories of learning. In addition to his work on these phenomena, Pavlov did research that was significant in terms of a possible explanation for other phenomena, such as conflict and the development of neuroses. An early demonstration of what came to be known as *experimental neuroses* in animals was completed in Pavlov's laboratory. A dog was conditioned to salivate to the signal of a circle. Differentiation between a circle and an ellipse was then conditioned by not reinforcing the response to the ellipse. When the ellipse was gradually changed in shape to approximate a circle, the dog first developed fine discriminations but then, as it became impossible to discriminate between the circle and the ellipse, its behavior became disorganized. Pavlov described the events as follows:

> After three weeks of work upon this discrimination not only did the discrimination fail to improve, but it became considerably worse, and finally disappeared altogether. The hitherto quiet dog began to squeal in its stand, kept wriggling about, tore off with its teeth the apparatus for mechanical stimulation of the skin, and bit through the tubes connecting the animal's room with the observer, a behavior which never happened before. On being taken into the experimental room the dog now barked violently, which was also contrary to its usual custom; in short, it presented all the symptoms of a condition of acute neurosis.
>
> SOURCE: Pavlov, 1927, p. 291

Conditioned Emotional Reactions

Pavlov's work on the conditioning process clearly defined stimuli and responses and provided an objective method for the study of learning phenomena. It therefore played an influential role in the thinking of later behaviorists such as Watson. For example, shortly after the publication of *Psychology from the Standpoint of a Behaviorist* (1919), Watson reported on the conditioning of emotional reactions in an infant. The research on Albert, an 11–month-old child, has become a classic in psychology. In this research, the experimenters, Watson and Rayner (1920), trained the infant to fear animals and objects that previously were not feared. They found that striking a hammer on a suspended steel bar produced a startle and fear response in the infant. They then found that if the bar was struck immediately behind Albert's head just as he began to reach for a rat, he began to fear the rat, whereas previously he had not shown this response. After doing this a number of times, the experimenters found that the instant the rat alone (without the sound) was shown to Albert, he began to cry. He had developed what is called a **conditioned emotional reaction**.

Albert now feared the rat because of its emotional association with the frightening sound. Furthermore, there was evidence that Albert began to fear other objects that somewhat resembled the rat. Despite some evidence that Albert's emotional reaction was not as strong or as general as expected (Harris, 1979), Watson and Rayner concluded that many fears are conditioned emotional reactions. On this basis they criticized the more complex psychoanalytic interpretations.

> The Freudians twenty years from now, unless their hypotheses change, when they come to analyze Albert's fear of a seal skin coat...will probably tease from him the recital of a dream upon which their analysis will show that Albert at three years of age attempted to play with the pubic hair of the mother and was scolded violently for it....If the analyst has sufficiently prepared Albert to accept such a dream when found as an explanation of his avoiding tendencies, and if the analyst has the authority and personality to put it over, Albert may be fully convinced that the dream was a true revealer of the factors which brought about the fear.
>
> SOURCE: Watson and Rayner, 1920, p. 14

The "Unconditioning" of Fear of a Rabbit

For many psychologists, the classical conditioning of emotional reactions plays a critical role in the development of psychopathology and a potentially important role in behavioral change. Behavior therapy based on the classical conditioning model emphasizes the extinction of problematic responses, such as conditioned fears, or the conditioning of new responses to stimuli that elicit such undesired responses as anxiety.

An early utilization of this approach, one that followed Watson and Rayner's (1920) study of the conditioning of the fear emotional response in Albert, was the effort of Jones (1924) to remove a fear under laboratory conditions. In this study, described as one of the earliest, if not the first, systematic utilization of behavior therapy, Jones attempted to treat the exaggerated fear reaction in a boy, Peter, who then was two years and ten months old. Peter was described as a generally healthy, well-adjusted child with a fear of a white rat that also extended to a rabbit, fur coat, feather, and cotton wool. Jones carefully documented the nature of the child's fear response and the conditions that elicited the greatest fear. She then set out to determine whether she could "uncondition" the fear

WHAT MAKES SOME FOODS A TREAT AND OTHERS DISGUSTING?

Most people love some odors and food tastes and are disgusted by others. Often these responses date back to childhood and seem nearly impossible to change. Can classical conditioning help us to understand them and their power?

Consider some research on food tastes. What makes some foods so unpleasant—even disgusting—that we have emotional reactions to just the thought of them? Eating worms, or drinking milk that has a dead fly or dead cockroach in it are examples. The interesting thing about some of these reactions is that a food that evokes disgust in one culture can be considered a delicacy in another, and disgust might be evoked by a dead fly or cockroach in the milk even if one is told that the insect was sterilized before it was put in the milk. Having seen the dead insect in the milk, one might not even be prepared to drink a different glass of milk; the disgust reaction now having generalized to the milk itself.

According to the researchers of such reactions, a possible explanation lies in the strong emotional reaction that becomes associated with a previously neutral object. In classical conditioning terms, the disgust response becomes associated with, or conditioned to, a previously neutral object such as milk or another food: "We believe that Pavlovian conditioning is alive and well, in the flavor associations of billions of meals eaten each day, in the expression of affects of billions of eaters as they eat away, in the association of foods and offensive objects, and in the association of foods with some of their consequences."

If this is the case, then it sugests that many things that we like, perhaps even feel addicted to, are the result of classical conditioning. This being the case, it may be possible to change our emotional reactions to certain objects through the process of classical conditioning.

SOURCE: *Psychology Today*, July 1985; Rozin & Zellner, 1985. Copyright © 1985 American Psychological Association. Reprinted by permission from *Psychology Today*.

Conditioned food responses: *Many strong and persisting emotional responses to foods, such as a disgust response to worms, are acquired through the process of classical conditioning. (Copyright © 1985 American Psychological Association. Reprinted by permission from* Psychology Today.)

response to one stimulus and whether such unconditioning would then generalize to other stimuli. Jones chose to focus on Peter's fear of the rabbit since this seemed even greater than his fear of the rat. She proceeded by bringing Peter to play at a time when the rabbit was present, as well as three other children who were selected because they were fearless toward the rabbit. Gradually Peter moved from almost complete terror at the sight of the rabbit to a completely positive response. The steps noted along the way to this progress are presented in Figure 9.1.

Peter's progression through these steps was not even or unbroken, and fortunately Jones gives us a careful, explicit accounting of a fascinating chain of events. Peter had progressed through the first nine steps listed in Figure 9.1 when he was taken to the hospital with scarlet fever. After a delay of two months, Peter returned to the laboratory with his fear response at the original level. Jones describes the cause of this relapse as follows:

> This was easily explained by the nurse who brought Peter from the hospital. As they were entering a taxi at the door of the hospital, a large dog, running past, jumped at them. Both Peter and the nurse were very much frightened....This seemed reason enough for this precipitate descent back to the original fear level. Being threatened by a large dog when ill, and in a strange place and being with an adult who also showed fear, was a terrifying situation against which our training could not have fortified him.

1. Rabbit anywhere in the room in a cage causes fear reactions.
2. Rabbit 12 feet away in cage tolerated.
3. Rabbit 4 feet away in cage tolerated.
4. Rabbit 3 feet away in cage tolerated.
5. Rabbit close in cage tolerated.
6. Rabbit free in room tolerated.
7. Rabbit touched when experimenter holds it.
8. Rabbit touched when free in room.
9. Rabbit defied by spitting at it, throwing things at it, imitating it.
10. Rabbit allowed on tray of high chair.
11. Squats in defenseless position beside rabbit.
12. Helps experimenter to carry rabbit to its cage.
13. Holds rabbit on lap.
14. Stays alone in room with rabbit.
15. Allows rabbit in play pen with him.
16. Fondles rabbit affectionately.
17. Lets rabbit nibble his fingers.

Figure 9.1 *Steps in the "Unconditioning" of Peter's Fear of a Rabbit.* (M. C. Jones, 1924)

Thus, at this point Jones began anew with another method of treatment, "direct conditioning." Here Peter was seated in a chair and given food he liked as the experimenter gradually brought the rabbit in a wire cage closer to him: "Through the presence of pleasant stimulus (food) whenever the rabbit was shown, the fear was eliminated gradually in favor of a positive response." In other words, the positive feelings associated with food were counterconditioned to the previously feared rabbit. However, even in the later sessions the influence of other children who were not afraid of the rabbit seemed to be significant. And what of the other fears? Jones notes that after the unconditioning of Peter's fear of the rabbit, he completely lost his fear of the fur coat, feathers, and cotton wool as well. Despite the lack of any knowledge concerning the origins of Peter's fears, the unconditioning procedure was found to work successfully and to generalize to other stimuli as well.

Additional Applications of Classical Conditioning

Another important early procedure was one developed by Mowrer and Mowrer (1928) for the treatment of bedwetting. In general, bedwetting in children occurs because the child does not respond to stimuli from the bladder in time to awaken and urinate in the bathroom. To deal with this condition, Mowrer and Mowrer developed a device based on the classical conditioning model. This consisted of an electrical device in the child's bed. If the child urinated, the device activated a bell that awakened the child. Gradually stimuli from the bladder became associated with the awakening response. Eventually, the response was anticipated so that bedwetting no longer took place.

The classical conditioning procedure also has been used in treating alcoholics. For example, an aversive stimulus such as shock or a nausea-inducing agent is applied immediately after the alcoholic takes a drink. The aversive stimulus acts as an unconditioned stimulus, and the avoidance response is conditioned to the alcohol (Nathan, 1985).

Systematic Desensitization

By far the most influential development in this area has been that of Joseph Wolpe's method of **systematic desensitization**. Interestingly, this method of therapy was developed by a psychiatrist rather than a psychologist, and by someone who originally practiced within a psychoanalytic framework. After a number of years of practice, however, Wolpe read and was impressed by the writings of Pavlov and Hull. He came to believe that a neurosis is a persistent, maladaptive learned response that is almost always associated with anxiety. Therapy, then, involves the inhibition of anxiety through the counterconditioning of a competing response. In other words, therapy involves the conditioning of responses that are antagonistic to or inhibitory of anxiety. A variety of anxiety-inhibiting responses can be used for counterconditioning purposes.

However, the one that has received most attention is deep muscle relaxation. Through the process of systematic desensitization, the patient learns to respond to certain previously anxiety-arousing stimuli with the newly conditioned response of relaxation.

Systematic desensitization involves a number of phases (Wolpe, 1961). First, there is a careful assessment of the therapeutic needs of the patient. After determining that the patient's problems can be treated by systematic desensitization, the therapist trains the patient to relax. A detailed procedure is described for helping the patient to relax first one part of the body and then all parts. Whereas, at first, patients have limited success in freeing themselves from muscle tension, after about six sessions most are able to relax the entire body in seconds. The next phase of treatment involves the construction of an anxiety hierarchy. This is a procedure in which the therapist tries to obtain from the patient a list of stimuli that arouse anxiety. These anxiety-arousing stimuli are grouped into themes such as fear of heights or fear of rejection. Within each group or theme, the anxiety-arousing stimuli are then arranged in order from most disturbing to least disturbing. For example, a theme of claustrophobia (fear of closed spaces) might involve placing the fear of being stuck in an elevator at the top of the list, an anxiety about being on a train in the middle of the list, and anxiety in response to reading of miners trapped underground at the bottom of the list. A theme of death might involve being at a burial as the most anxiety-arousing stimulus, the word *death* as somewhat anxiety-arousing, and driving past a cemetery as only slightly anxiety-arousing. Patients can have many or few themes and many or few items within each anxiety hierarchy.

"Leave us alone! I am a behavior therapist! I am helping my patient overcome a fear of heights!"

Behavior Therapy: *One aspect of behavior therapy involves the extinction of learned fears or phobias. (© copyright Sidney Harris)*

With the construction of the anxiety hierarchies completed, the patient is ready for the desensitization procedure itself. The patient has learned to calm the self by relaxation, and the therapist has established the anxiety hierarchies. Now the therapist encourages the patient to achieve a deep state of relaxation and then to imagine the least anxiety-arousing stimulus in the anxiety hierarchy. If the patient can imagine the stimulus without anxiety, then he or she is encouraged to imagine the next stimulus in the hierarchy while remaining relaxed. Periods of pure relaxation are interspersed with periods of relaxation and imagination of anxiety-arousing stimuli. If the patient feels anxious while imagining a stimulus, he or she is encouraged to relax and return to imagining a less anxiety-arousing stimulus. Ultimately the patient is able to relax while imagining all stimuli in the anxiety hierarchies. Relaxation in relation to the imagined stimuli generalizes to relaxation in relation to these stimuli in everyday life. "It has consistently been found that at every stage a stimulus that evokes no anxiety when imagined in a state of relaxation will also evoke no anxiety when encountered in reality" (Wolpe, 1961, p. 191).

A number of clinical and laboratory studies have indicated that systematic desensitization can be a useful treatment procedure. These successful results led Wolpe and others to question the psychoanalytic view that, as long as the underlying conflicts remain untouched, the patient is prone to develop a new symptom in place of the one removed (symptom substitution) (Lazarus, 1965). According to the behavior therapy point of view, no symptom is caused by unconscious conflicts. There is only a maladaptive learned response, and once this response has been eliminated, there is no reason to believe that another maladaptive response will be substituted for it.

A REINTERPRETATION OF THE CASE OF LITTLE HANS

In this section the application of the learning theory approach will be observed in a case presented by Wolpe and Rachman (1960) that gives us an excellent opportunity to compare the behavioral approach with that of psychoanalysis. In fact, it is not a case in the same sense as other cases that have been presented. Rather, it is a critique and reformulation of Freud's case of Little Hans.

As we learned in Chapter 4, the case of Little Hans is a classic in psychoanalysis. In this case, Freud emphasized the importance of infantile sexuality and oedipal conflicts in the development of a horse phobia, or fear. Wolpe and Rachman are extremely critical of Freud's approach to obtaining data and of his conclusions. They make the following points. (1) Nowhere is there evidence of Hans' wish to make love to his mother. (2) Hans never expressed fear or hatred of his father. (3) Hans consistently denied any relationship between the horse and his father. (4) Phobias can be induced in children by a simple conditioning process and need not be related to a theory of conflicts or anxiety and defense. The view that neuroses have a purpose is highly questionable. (5) There is no evidence that the phobia disappeared as a result of Hans' resolution of his oedipal conflicts. Similarly, there is no evidence that insight occurred or that information was of therapeutic value.

Wolpe and Rachman feel handicapped in their own interpretation of the phobia because the data were gathered within a psychoanalytic framework. They do, however, attempt an explanation. A phobia is regarded as a *conditioned anxiety reaction*. As a child, Hans heard and saw a playmate being warned by her father that she should avoid a white horse lest it bite her: "Don't put your finger to the white horse." This incident sensitized Hans to a fear of horses. Also, there was the time when one of Hans' friends injured himself and bled while playing horses. Finally, Hans was a sensitive child who felt uneasy about seeing horses on the merry-go-round being beaten. These factors set the condition for the later development of the phobia. The phobia itself occurred as a consequence of the fright Hans experienced while watching a horse fall down. Whereas Freud suggested that this incident was an exciting cause that allowed the underlying conflicts to be expressed in terms of a phobia, Wolpe and Rachman suggest that this incident was *the* cause.

Wolpe and Rachman see a similarity here to Watson's conditioning of a fear of rabbits in Albert. Hans was frightened by the event with a horse and then generalized his fear to all things that were similar to or related to horses. The recovery from the phobia did not occur through the process of insight, but probably through a process of either extinction or counterconditioning. As Hans developed, he experienced other emotional responses that inhibited the fear response. Alternatively it is suggested that perhaps the father's constant reference to the horse in a nonthreatening context helped to extinguish the fear response. Whatever the details, it appears that the phobia disappeared gradually, as would be expected by this kind of learning interpretation, instead of dramatically, as might be suggested by a psychoanalytic, insight interpretation. The evidence in support of Freud is not clear, and the data, as opposed to the interpretations, can be accounted for in a more straightforward way through the use of a learning theory interpretation.

FURTHER DEVELOPMENTS

Most of the work on classical conditioning has focused on relatively simple reflex mechanisms that humans share with other animals. However, Pavlov also recognized the importance of speech and thought in what he called the second signal system. The concept of the second signal system provides for an understanding of much more complex organizations of stimuli and responses. The importance of this concept is illustrated by Razran's (1939) research on semantic conditioning. In this research with human subjects, Razran paired the visual presentation of the words *style, urn, freeze,* and *surf* with food reinforcement, leading to the development of a salivary response to the words. He then tested whether the conditioned response would generalize to words that sounded similar (*stile, earn, frieze,* and *serf*) or to words that sounded different but were similar in meaning (*fashion, vase, chill,* and *wave*). What would one expect to find—generalization to sound or to meaning? Razran found a significant difference in terms of the latter, suggesting that conditioning processes can be influenced by meaning or semantics. Pavlov himself did relatively little research on the second signal system, but it has continued to be a major area of investigation in Russian psychology, including developmental studies of changes in the factors controlling conditioning processes.

The concepts of conditioned emotional responses and a second signal system considerably expand the interpretation of the importance of classical conditioning in human behavior. For example, it has been suggested that people acquire motives or goals by associating positive and negative affect with stimuli, including symbols (Pervin, 1983; Staats & Burns, 1982).

For some time interest in classical conditioning declined among personality psychologists. However, recently there has been increased recognition of the potential contributions of concepts and procedures associated with classical conditioning theory. One illustrative area of research is the use of classical conditioning procedures to demonstrate that people can unconsciously develop fears and attitudes toward others (Krosnick, Betz, Jussim, & Lynn, 1992; Ohman & Soares, 1993). For example, a stimulus such as a picture with positive or negative affective value, can be presented subliminally (i.e., below the threshold of awareness) in association with another stimulus, such as another photo. Thus, a person will come to dislike a photo unconsciously associated with negative emotion and come to like a photo unconsciously associated with positive emotion. One can speculate in this regard how many of our attitudes and preferences are classically conditioned on a subliminal or unconscious basis. To attach even greater significance to the process, there now is evidence that, whereas conditioned responses may readily generalize across contexts, the extinction of these responses may be very context-specific (Bouton, 1994). Thus, you may learn a fear or disgust response in one context and have it generalize to many other contexts. However, extinguishing the response in one context does not mean that it will be extinguished in other contexts as well. The person who has acquired a fear of authority figures in one context may find the fear generalizing to other contexts as well. However, in extinguishing the fear in one context the person may be surprised to find that the fear remains in other contexts. This suggests that the extinction of strongly conditioned and widely generalized problematic responses, often the goal in psychotherapy, may be a particularly difficult enterprise.

Another very recent effort in relation to classical conditioning is investigation of the conditioning of health-related responses (Ader & Cohen,

1993). For example, patients undergoing repeated chemotherapy for cancer often develop a classically conditioned nausea and vomiting response, that is, the nausea and vomiting associated with the chemotherapy become conditioned to stimuli associated with the chemotherapy. There then is anticipatory nausea and vomiting, just as Pavlov's dog developed an anticipatory salivation response to the bell that preceded the food stimulus. Another example of research in this area involves exploration of the classical conditioning of the immune system. Here the question is whether unconditioned responses of the body's disease-fighting system can be conditioned to other stimuli. There is some evidence that this is the case, raising the potential for the utilization of classical conditioning procedures to enhance the immune-system functioning of the body. In sum, classical conditioning procedures are being used to investigate important aspects of social behavior and health functioning.

B. F. Skinner (1904–1990) is the most influential supporter of an extreme behaviorist point of view. He is perhaps the best-known American psychologist, and his views about psychology and society have been the source of considerable controversy.

SKINNER'S THEORY OF OPERANT CONDITIONING

A VIEW OF THE THEORIST

> The scientist, like any organism, is the product of a unique history. The practices which he finds most appropriate will depend in part upon his history.
>
> SOURCE: Skinner, 1959, p. 379

In this passage, Skinner takes the point of view that has been argued in each of the theory chapters in this book, that is, that psychologists' orientations and research strategies are, in part, consequences of their own life history and expressions of their own personalities.

B. F. Skinner was born in New York, the son of a lawyer who was described by his son as having been desperately hungry for praise and a mother who had rigid standards of right and wrong. Skinner (1967) described his home during his early years as a warm and stable environment. He reported a love for school and showed an early interest in building things. This interest in building things is particularly interesting in relation to the behavioral emphasis on laboratory equipment in the experimental setting, and because it contrasts with the absence of such an interest in the lives and research of the clinical personality theorists.

At about the time Skinner entered college, his younger brother died. Skinner commented that he was not much moved by his brother's death and that he probably felt guilty for not being moved. Skinner went to Hamilton College and majored in English literature. At that time, his

B. F. Skinner

goal was to become a writer, and at one point he sent three short stories to Robert Frost, from whom he received an encouraging reply. After college, Skinner spent a year trying to write, but concluded that at that point in his life he had nothing to say. He then spent six months living in Greenwich Village in New York City. During this time he read Pavlov's *Conditioned Reflexes* and came across a series of articles by Bertrand Russell on Watson's behaviorism. Russell thought that he had demolished Watson in these articles, but they aroused Skinner's interest in behaviorism.

Although Skinner had not taken any psychology courses in college, he had begun to develop an interest in the field and was accepted for graduate work in psychology at Harvard. He justified his change in goals as follows: "A writer might portray human behavior accurately, but he did not therefore understand it. I was to remain interested in human behavior, but the literary method had failed me; I would turn to the scientific" (Skinner, 1967, p. 395). Psychology appeared to be the relevant science. Besides, Skinner had long been interested in animal behavior (recalling his fascination with the complex behaviors of a troupe of performing pigeons). Furthermore, there would now be many opportunities to make use of his interest in building gadgets.

During his graduate school years at Harvard, Skinner developed his interest in animal behavior and in explaining this behavior without reference to the functioning of the nervous system. After reading Pavlov, he disagreed with Pavlov's contention that, in explaining behavior, one could go "from the salivary reflexes to the important business of the organism in everyday life." However, Skinner believed that Pavlov had given him the key to understanding behavior. "Control your conditions (the environment) and you shall see order!" During these and the following years, Skinner (1959) developed some of his principles of scientific methodology: (1) When you run into something interesting, drop everything else and study it. (2) Some ways of doing research are easier than others. A mechanical apparatus often makes doing research easier. (3) Some people are lucky. (4) A piece of apparatus breaks down. This presents problems, but it can also lead to (5) serendipity—the art of finding one thing while looking for something else.

After Harvard, Skinner moved first to Minnesota, then to Indiana, and then returned to Harvard in 1948. During this time he became, in a sense, a sophisticated animal trainer; he was able to make organisms engage in specific behaviors at specific times. He turned from work with rats to work with pigeons. Finding that the behavior of any single animal did not necessarily reflect the average picture of learning based on many animals, he became interested in the manipulation and control of individual animal behavior. Special theories of learning and circuitous explanations of behavior were not necessary if one could manipulate the environment so as to produce orderly change in the individual case. In the meantime, as Skinner notes, his own behavior was becoming controlled by the positive results being given to him by the animals "under his control" (Figure 9.2).

The basis of Skinner's operant conditioning procedure is the control of behavior through the manipulation of rewards and punishments in the environment, particularly the laboratory environment. However, his conviction concerning the importance of the laws of behavior and his interest in building things led Skinner to take his thinking and research far beyond the laboratory. He built a "baby box" to mechanize the care of a baby, teaching machines that used rewards in the teaching of school subjects, and a procedure whereby pigeons could be used militarily to land a missile on target. He committed himself to the view that a science of human behavior and the technology to be derived from it must be developed in the service of humankind. His novel, *Walden Two*, describes a utopia based on the control of human behavior through positive reinforcement (reward).

Figure 9.2   "Boy, have I got this guy conditioned! Every time I press the bar down he drops a piece of food." *(Skinner, 1956)*

Skinner was considered by many to be the greatest contemporary American psychologist. He received many awards, including the American Psychological Association's award for Distinguished Scientific Contribution (1958) and the National Medal of Science (1968). In 1990, shortly before his death, he became the first recipient of the American Psychological Association's Citation for Outstanding Lifetime Contribution to Psychology.

SKINNER'S THEORY OF PERSONALITY

Before turning to Skinner's theory in relation to personality, it may be useful to contrast its general qualities with those of theories considered in earlier chapters. Each of the theories covered in these chapters emphasized structural concepts. Freud used structural concepts such as id, ego, and superego; Rogers used concepts such as self and ideal self; and Allport, Eysenck, and Cattell used the concept of traits. The concept of structure relates to relatively enduring qualities of organization and is important in accounting for individual differences. But the behavioral approach to personality emphasizes situational specificity and minimizes the importance of broad response predispositions relative to the importance of stimuli in the external environment. Therefore, it is not surprising to find few structural concepts. While deemphasizing structure, the behavioral approach stresses the concepts of process and, in particular, processes that hold true for all individuals. In summary, because the theory is based on assumptions that are different from those of other theories, the formal properties of the theory are different from those already studied.

Structure

The key structural unit for the behavioral approach in general, and Skinner's approach in particular, is the *response*. A response may range from a simple reflex response (e.g., salivation to food, startle to a loud noise) to a complex piece of behavior (e.g., solution to a math problem, subtle forms of aggression). What is critical to the definition of a response is that it represents an external, observable piece of behavior that can be related to environmental events. The learning process essentially involves the association or connection of responses to events in the environment.

In his approach to learning, Skinner distinguishes between responses elicited by known stimuli, such as an eyeblink reflex to a puff of air, and responses that cannot be associated with any stimuli. These responses are emitted by the organism and are called **operants**. Skinner's view is that stimuli in the environment do not force the organism to behave or incite it to act. The initial cause of behavior is in the organism itself. "There is no environmental eliciting stimulus for operant behavior; it simply occurs. In the terminology of operant conditioning, operants are emitted by the organism. The dog walks, runs, and romps; the bird flies; the monkey swings from tree to tree; the human infant babbles vocally. In each case, the behavior occurs without any specific eliciting stimulus...It is in the biological nature of organisms to emit operant behavior" (Reynolds, 1968, p. 8).

Process: Operant Conditioning

Before discussing some of the processes that this theory views as underlying behavior, it is important to consider the concept of the reinforcer. The Skinnerians define a **reinforcer** as an event (stimulus) that follows a response and increases the probability of its occurrence. If a pigeon's pecking at a disk, which is a piece of operant behavior, is followed by a reinforcer such as food, the probability of its pecking at the disk is increased. According to this view, a reinforcer strengthens the behavior it follows, and there is no need to turn to biological explanations to determine why a stimulus reinforces behavior. Stimuli that originally do not serve as reinforcers can come to do so through their association with other reinforcers. Some stimuli, such as money, become **generalized reinforcers** because they provide access to many other kinds of reinforcers.

It is important to observe here that a reinforcer is defined by its effect on behavior, an increase in the probability of a response. Often it is difficult to know precisely what will serve as a reinforcer for behavior, as it may vary from individual to individual or from organism to organism. Finding a reinforcer may turn out to be a trial-and-error operation. One keeps trying stimuli until one finds a stimulus that can reliably increase the probability of a certain response.

The Skinnerian approach focuses on the qualities of responses and their relationships to the rates and intervals at which they are reinforced, or **schedules of reinforcements**. A simple experimental device, the Skinner box, is used to study these relationships. In this kind of box there are few stimuli, and behaviors such as a rat's pressing of a bar or a pigeon's pecking of a key are observed. It is here, according to Skinner, that one can best observe the elementary laws of behavior. These laws are discovered through the control of behavior, in this case the bar-pressing activity of the rat or the key-pecking activity of the pigeon. Behavior is understood when it can be controlled by specific changes in the environment. To understand behavior is to control it. Behavior is controlled through the choice of responses that are reinforced and the rates at which they are reinforced. Schedules of reinforcement can be based on a particular *time interval* or a particular *response interval*. In a time interval schedule, the reinforcement appears after a certain period, say every minute, regardless of the number of responses made by the organism. In a response interval, or a response ratio schedule, reinforcements appear after a certain number of responses (e.g., presses of a bar, pecks of a key) have been made.

Thus, reinforcements need not be given after every response, but can instead be given only sometimes. Furthermore, reinforcements can be given on a regular or *fixed* basis—always after a certain period of time or after a certain number of responses—or they can be given on a *variable* basis—sometimes after a minute and sometimes after two minutes, or sometimes after a few responses and sometimes after many responses. Each schedule of reinforcement tends to stabilize behavior in a different way.

In a sense, operant learning represents a sophisticated formulation of the principles of animal training. Complex behavior is *shaped* through a process of **successive approximation**; that is, complex behaviors are developed by reinforcing pieces of behavior that resemble the final form of behavior one wants to produce.

> Operant conditioning shapes behavior as a sculptor shapes a lump of clay. Although at some point the sculptor seems to have produced an entirely novel object, we can always follow the process back to the original undifferentiated lump, and we can make the successive stages by which we return to this condition as small as we wish. At no point does anything emerge which is very different from what preceded it....An operant is not something which appears full grown in the behavior of the organism. It is the result of a continuous shaping process.
>
> SOURCE: Skinner, 1953, p. 91

The process of shaping or successive approximation is seen most clearly in the work of animal trainers. The difficult tricks performed by circus animals are not learned as complete wholes. Rather, the trainer gradually builds up sequences of learned responses through the reinforcement of particular behaviors that are then linked or chained to one another. What started off as the learning of individual behaviors ends up as the display of a complex series of acts before a circus audience. The animal ultimately is rewarded for its behavior, but the final reward is made dependent, or contingent, on the performance of the series of previously learned behaviors. In a similar way, complex behaviors in humans may be developed through the process of successive approximation.

Although operant conditioning primarily emphasizes the use of positive reinforcers such as food, money, or praise, Skinnerians also emphasize the importance of reinforcers based on the organism's *escape from*, or *avoidance of*, aversive (unpleasant) stimuli. In such cases responses are reinforced by the removal or avoidance of an unpleasant stimulus rather than by the appearance of a pleasant stimulus. In all these cases the effect is to reinforce or increase the strength of the response. Such response–outcome contingencies can be contrasted with the case of *pun-

ishment. In punishment, an aversive stimulus follows a response, decreasing the probability of that response's occurring again. However, the effect of punishment is temporary and it appears to be of little value in eliminating behavior. For this reason, Skinner has emphasized the use of positive reinforcement in shaping behavior.

Growth and Development

The Skinnerian view of growth and development continues to emphasize the importance of schedules of reinforcement in acquiring and performing behavior. As the child develops, responses are learned and remain under the control of reinforcement contingencies in the environment. The emphasis is on specific responses as they are influenced by specific environmental reinforcers. Children become self-reliant through the reinforcement of acts in which they take care of themselves, for instance, in eating and dressing. The child is reinforced immediately after completing those acts, both by material rewards such as food and by social rewards such as praise. In learning to tolerate delay of gratification (reinforcement), the child may first be reinforced after a brief period of delay and then gradually may be reinforced for longer periods of delay. After a while, delay behavior becomes stabilized, and one can say that the child has developed an ability to tolerate delays in gratification.

What of children who imitate the behavior of parents, siblings, and others? Are such behaviors tied to the same principles of reinforcement? Behaviors can be imitated without being directly reinforced (Skinner, 1990). However, this occurs only where imitation has been reinforced many times; through generalization, imitation itself takes on the qualities of a reinforcer. Whereas initially the child is reinforced for imitating specific responses, it is now reinforced to be generally imitative and a generalized imitative response tendency has developed. Thus, from the Skinnerian point of view, new behaviors may be acquired through the process of successive approximations or through the development of a generalized imitative repertoire. In either case, the behaviors are under the control of reinforcement contingencies in the environment.

Psychopathology

The learning theory position on psychopathology may be stated as follows: the basic principles of learning provide a completely adequate interpretation of psychopathology. Explanations in terms of symptoms with underlying causes are not necessary. According to the behavioral point of view, behavioral pathology is not a disease. Instead, it is a response pattern learned according to the same principles of behavior as are all response patterns.

The Skinnerians argue against any concept of the unconscious or a "sick personality." Individuals are not sick, they merely do not respond appropriately to stimuli. Either they fail to learn a response or they learn a maladaptive response. In the former case, there is a **behavioral deficit**. For example, individuals who are socially inadequate may have had faulty reinforcement histories in which social skills were not developed. Having failed to be reinforced for social skills during socialization, as adults they have an inadequate response repertoire with which to respond to social situations.

Reinforcement is important not only for the learning of responses but also for the maintenance of behavior. Thus, one possible result of an absence of reinforcement in the environment is depression. According to this view, depression represents a lessening of behavior or a lowered response rate. The depressed person is not responsive because positive reinforcement has been withdrawn (Ferster, 1973).

When a person learns a **maladaptive response**, the problem is that a response has been learned that is not considered acceptable by society or by others in the person's environment. This may be because the response itself is considered unacceptable (e.g., hostile behavior) or because the response occurs under unacceptable circumstances (e.g., joking at a formal business meeting). Related to this situation is the development of *superstitious behavior* (Skinner, 1948). Superstitious behavior develops because of an accidental relationship between a response and reinforcement. Thus, Skinner found that if he gave pigeons small amounts of food at regular intervals regardless of what they were doing, many birds came to associate the response that was coincidentally rewarded with systematic reinforcement. For example, if a pigeon was coincidentally rewarded while walking around in a counterclockwise direction, this response might become conditioned even though it had no cause–effect relationship with the reinforcement. The continuous performance of the behavior would result in occasional, again coincidental, reinforcement. Thus, the behavior could be maintained over long periods of time.

Superstitious Behavior: *Skinner suggested that superstitious behavior is based on an accidental relationship between a response and reinforcement.*

In sum, people develop faulty behavior repertoires, what others call "sick" behavior or psychopathology, because of the following: they were not reinforced for adaptive behaviors, they were punished for behaviors that later would be considered adaptive, they were reinforced for maladaptive behaviors, or they were reinforced under inappropriate circumstances for what would otherwise be adaptive behavior. In all cases there is an emphasis on observable responses and schedules of reinforcement rather than on concepts such as drive, conflict, unconscious, or self-esteem.

Behavioral Assessment

The emphasis on specific behaviors tied to defined situational characteristics forms the basis for what has come to be known as **behavioral assessment**. Heavily influenced by the thinking of Skinner, the behavioral approach to assessment emphasizes three things: (1) identification of specific behaviors, often called **target behaviors** or **target responses**; (2) identification of specific environmental factors that elicit, cue, or reinforce the target behaviors; and (3) identification of specific environmental factors that can be manipulated to alter the behavior. Thus a behavioral assessment of a child's temper tantrums would include a clear, objective definition of temper tantrum behavior in the child, a complete description of the situation that sets off the tantrum behavior, a complete description of the reactions of parents and others that may be reinforcing the behavior, and an analysis of the potential for eliciting and reinforcing other nontantrum behaviors (Kanfer & Saslow, 1965; O'Leary, 1972). This **functional analysis** of behavior, involving the effort to identify the environmental conditions that control behavior, sees behavior as a function of specific events in the environment. The approach has also been called the **ABC assessment**: one assesses the *A*ntecedent conditions of the behavior, the *B*ehavior itself, and the *C*onsequences of the behavior.

Behavioral assessment generally is closely tied to treatment objectives. For example, consider the task of assisting a mother who came to a clinic because she felt helpless in dealing with her four-year-old son's temper tantrums and general disobedience (Hawkins et al., 1966). The psychologists involved in this case followed a fairly typical behavioral procedure to assessment and treatment. First, the mother and child were observed in the home to determine the nature of the undesirable behaviors, when they occurred, and which reinforcers seemed to maintain them. The following nine behaviors were determined to constitute the major portion of the boy's objectionable behavior: (1) biting his shirt or arm; (2) sticking out his tongue; (3) kicking or biting himself, others, or objects; (4) calling someone or something a derogatory name; (5) removing or threatening to remove his clothing; (6) saying "NO!" loudly and vigorously; (7) threatening to damage objects or persons; (8) throwing objects;

and (9) pushing his sister. Observation of the mother–child interaction suggested that the objectionable behavior was being maintained by attention from the mother. For example, often she tried to distract him by offering him toys or food.

The treatment program began with a behavioral analysis of how frequently the boy expressed one of the objectionable behaviors during one-hour sessions conducted in the home two to three times a week. Two psychologists acted as observers to ensure that there was high reliability or good agreement concerning recording of the objectionable behavior. This first phase, known as a *baseline period*, lasted for 16 sessions. During this time, mother and child interacted in their usual way. Following this careful assessment of the objectionable behavior during the baseline period, the psychologists initiated their intervention or treatment program. Now the mother was instructed to tell her son to stop or to put him in his room by himself without toys each time he emitted an objectionable behavior. In other words, there was a withdrawal of the positive reinforcer for objectionable behavior. At the same time, the mother was instructed to give her son attention and approval when he behaved in a desirable way. In other words, the positive reinforcers were made contingent on desirable behavior. During this time, known as the *first experimental period*, the frequency of objectionable behaviors was again counted. As can be seen in Figure 9.3, there was a marked decline in the frequency of objectionable behavior from 18 to 113 such responses during a one-hour period (preexperimental baseline) to 1 to 8 such responses per session (first experimental period).

Following the first experimental treatment period, the mother was instructed to return to her former behavior to determine whether it was the shift in her reinforcement behavior that was determining the change in her son's behavior. During this *second baseline period*, her son's objectionable behavior ranged between 2 and 24 per session (Figure 9.3). There was an increase in this behavior, though not a return to the former baseline level. However, the mother reported that she had trouble responding in her previous way because she now felt more "sure of herself." Thus, even during this period she gave her son more firm commands, gave in less after denying a request, and gave more affection in response to positive behaviors in her son than was previously the case. Following this there was a return to a full emphasis on the treatment program, resulting in a decline in objectionable behavior (*second experimental period*). The rate of objectionable behavior was found to remain low after a 24-day interval (*follow-up period*), and the mother reported a continuing positive change in the relationship.

ABA Research Design   In sum, in this case it was possible to assess the target responses in the home environment as well as their reinforcers, and then to specify a treatment regimen that resulted in measurable changes in the frequency of these behaviors. As well as illustrating behavioral assessment, this study illustrates an interesting variant of the experi-

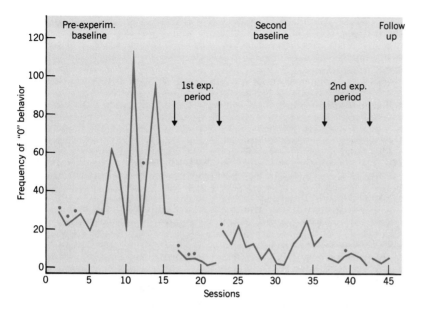

Figure 9.3 Number of 10-second Intervals per 1-hour Session, in Which Objectionable Behavior Occurred. *Dots indicate sessions in which reliability was tested. (Hawkins et al., 1966) Copyright 1966 by Academic Press, Inc. Reprinted by permission.*

mental method—the Skinnerian **ABA research design** or **own-control** design (Krasner, 1971). Basically the ABA, own-control research design involves the experimental manipulation of a specific behavior and the demonstration that changes in behavior can be attributed directly to specific changes in environmental events. One subject is used and serves as his or her own control relating to variations in experimental conditions. In the first or baseline phase (A) of this design, the current rate of occurrence of the behavior of interest is recorded. In the second or reinforcement phase (B), a reinforcer following the behavior of interest is introduced to increase the frequency of that behavior. Once the behavioral response has been established at the desired frequency, the reinforcer may be withdrawn (A phase) to see whether the behavior returns to the original (baseline period) rate. This is called the *nonreinforcement period*. Instead of comparing a subject who is reinforced with one who is not, the subject is treated differently in the various phases—he is his own control. In some research, a fourth phase is also included in which the reinforcer is reintroduced to reestablish the desired behavior (see Figure 9.3). Also, some experiments may begin with the reinforcement phase and then move to nonreinforcement and then reintroduction of reinforcement. This approach is typical when it does not make sense to begin with a baseline period, such as when a new behavior is being taught.

PARENTAL BEHAVIORAL TRAINING FOR CHILD NONCOMPLIANCE

What are parents to do with a noncompliant child, one who refuses to do as asked or told? At one time or another most parents have experienced the sense of frustration and helplessness when their child becomes stubborn, obstinate, defiant. For most parents this is an occasional period of stress, but for others it is a continuing source of concern. Indeed, noncompliance is a major basis for bringing children to psychological clinics for treatment and an important predictor of later psychological problems. Can the behavior therapist be of help?

According to Wierson and Forehand, two psychologists concerned with such problems, noncompliant behavior is learned and reinforced through interactions with others in the environment, in particular parents. Typically parents of noncompliant children positively reinforce such behavior through attention. In addition, negative reinforcement is given in that often parents "give in" to the child in order to stop the protesting, thereby reinforcing the behavior they are attempting to avoid. Here the noncompliance serves to get the child out of the situation that is considered distressing (i.e., the parent "gives in" and removes the command from the child). If applied in an inconsistent, intermittent fashion, such parental behavior creates a strong response in the child (noncompliance) that is resistant to extinction.

Can parents understand these principles and be taught to apply them in ways that will reduce noncompliance? According to Wierson and Forehand, parents can be taught parenting skills that involve better reinforcement and contingency management strategies. In their parent behavioral training program, parents are taught positive ways of changing behavior (e.g., reinforcing desired behaviors with praise and attention) and the use of disciplinary techniques (e.g., ignoring noncompliance, giving firm commands that are enforced). Emphasis is particularly given to the positive reinforcement of behaviors in the child that are incompatible with noncompliance behavior. In addition, nonaversive and nonpainful punishment techniques are taught (e.g., placing the child in a chair in the corner). Verbal instruction to parents is followed by modeling of reinforcement techniques by the therapist, role playing by parent and therapist of the application of the prescribed parental behaviors, and supervised practice sessions in the clinic and home.

The results? According to the psychologists parents often are amazed at just how quickly change can occur in their children's behavior. Relative to nontreatment control cases, children in the parental training program show a significant reduction in noncompliance behavior. Indeed, at post-treatment they are as compliant as children who have not been referred to any clinic. Beyond this, there is evidence of generalization to other inappropriate behaviors in the child and from

the child to siblings not involved in treatment. The effects seem to be maintained
over a period of years, although there is
not evidence of generalization from the
home to school. The conclusion drawn is
that "overall, research demonstrates that
parent behavioral training is an effective

clinical strategy for dealing with child
noncompliance and that it accomplishes
its underlying goal—to disrupt coercive
parent-child interchanges by providing
parents with more effective strategies for
dealing with their children" (p. 149).
SOURCE: Wierson and Forehand, 1994.

Sign and Sample Approaches to Assessment   As can be seen, in behavioral assessment there is emphasis on single variables (specific target behaviors) and
the gathering of reliable, objective data. What is different about behavioral assessment in comparison to some other personality measures is
that the behavior itself is of interest, not some theoretical construct (ego
strength, extraversion) presumed to be expressed in the behavior.
Mischel (1968, 1971) has contrasted these differences in terms of **sign
and sample approaches to assessment**. In the *sign* approach, traits are
inferred from test behavior. Test items are assumed to be adequate to
reflect personality characteristics and interpretations are made of test
behavior relative to assumed underlying traits. There is, in other words,
a high level of inference from test behavior to interpretations concerning
personality characteristics. In the *sample* approach, interest is in the
behavior itself and how it is affected by alterations in environmental conditions. Interest is in overt behavior, and it is assumed that one must
understand the surrounding stimulus conditions to understand the relevant behavior. There is a low level of inference from test behavior to
other similar behaviors in the individual. The sign approach asks about
motives and traits that act together to result in observed behavior; the
sample approach asks about environmental variables that affect behaviors in terms of their frequency, intensity, and duration.

Behavior Change

Use of the principles of operant conditioning to regulate behavior can be
seen in a **token economy** (Ayllon & Azrin, 1965). Under a token economy, the behavioral technician rewards, with tokens, the various patient
behaviors that are considered desirable. The tokens, in turn, can be
exchanged by the patient for desirable products, such as candy and cig-
arettes. Thus, for example, patients could be reinforced for activities
such as serving meals or cleaning floors. In a tightly controlled environment, such as a state hospital for long-term psychiatric patients, it is feasible to make almost anything that a patient wants contingent on the
desired behaviors. There is evidence to support the effectiveness of token
economies in increasing such behaviors as social interaction, self-care,

and job performance in severely disturbed patients and mentally retarded individuals. They also have been used to decrease aggressive behavior in children and to decrease marital discord (Kazdin, 1977).

In sum, the Skinnerian behavioral technician seeks a straightforward application of operant conditioning to the problem of behavior change. Target behaviors are selected and reinforcement is made contingent on performance of the desired responses. We have here, then, a view that emphasizes how the environment acts upon people, as opposed to how people act upon the environment. This view has resulted in the development of a group of social engineers who are committed to acting on the environment. Watson suggested that through control of the environment he could train an infant to become any type of specialist he might select. Skinnerian social engineers take this principle one step further. As seen in the development of token economies, as well as in the development of communes based on Skinnerian principles, there is an interest in the design of environments that will control broad aspects of human behavior.

STIMULUS–RESPONSE THEORY: HULL, DOLLARD, AND MILLER

Stimulus–response (S–R) theory was being developed by people such as Hull and Dollard and Miller while Skinner was developing his operant conditioning view. However, S–R theory probably reached its peak of systematization and influence earlier than did Skinner's approach. For some time the operant and S–R approaches represented competitive points of view, and considerable debate existed over their relative merits.

A VIEW OF THE THEORISTS

Several theorists have made significant contributions to the development of S–R learning theory. Among these, however, three figures are of particular significance. The first, Clark L. Hull, made a major effort to develop a systematic, comprehensive theory of learning. The second two, John Dollard and Neal E. Miller, are particularly well known for their efforts to bring together the remarkable accomplishments of Freud and Hull.

Clark L. Hull (1884–1952)

Clark Hull was born in New York, but early in his life he and his family moved to a farm in Michigan. During his early school years, Hull was very interested in mathematics and described the study of geometry as the most important event of his intellectual life. In college, he began studying math, physics, and chemistry, with the goal of becoming a mining engineer. However, after two years at school, he became ill with polio and was forced to consider a new occupation. His interest in scientific theory and in the design of automatic equipment led him to the study of psychology. After a difficult and incomplete recovery from polio, Hull

Clark L. Hull

returned to college to concentrate in psychology at the University of Michigan.

After a brief stint as a teacher in Kentucky, Hull went on to graduate work in psychology at the University of Wisconsin. He first developed an interest in finding a scientific basis for aptitude testing, and then systematically studied what takes place during hypnosis. While he was at the University of Wisconsin, word was spreading of Watson's views of behaviorism and Hull found himself sympathetic to this new emphasis on objectivity.

In 1929, Hull went to Yale as a professor of psychology. He had just read a translation of Pavlov's *Conditioned Reflexes* and was interested in comparisons between Pavlov's research and the experiments that were being conducted in this country. Also, he was forced to end his research on hypnosis because of other psychologists' attitude of fear toward hypnosis. The following years witnessed a coming together of his interests in math, geometry, theory, apparatus construction, and psychology as a natural science. In 1940 he published his *Mathematico-Deductive Theory of Rote Learning* and in 1943, his *Principles of Behavior*. Of particular importance was Hull's emphasis on a systematic theory of the process of instrumental learning.

Hull's emphasis on a systematic theory of learning, careful experimentation, and the development of habits (S–R associations) as a result of reward laid much of the groundwork for a learning theory approach to social psychology and to the study of personality.

John Dollard (1900–1980) and Neal E. Miller (1909–)

John Dollard was born in Wisconsin and received his undergraduate degree from the University of Wisconsin in 1922. In 1931, he obtained his graduate degree (Ph.D.) in sociology from the University of Chicago. Following this he taught sociology, anthropology, and psychology at Yale University. An unusual aspect of Dollard's professional development—one that significantly influenced his later thinking—was his training in psychoanalysis at the Berlin Psychoanalytic Institute. His interest in psychoanalysis, clinical work, and the social sciences continued throughout his professional career.

Neal E. Miller also was born in Wisconsin. He received his undergraduate degree from the University of Washington and his Ph.D. from Yale University in 1935. During this time he came into contact with Hull and Dollard, and also obtained training in psychoanalysis at the Vienna Institute of Psychoanalysis. He continued to spend the major part of his professional career at Yale until 1966, when he joined the faculty at Rockefeller University. During his time at Yale, Miller made many significant experimental and theoretical contributions to S–R theory, particularly in the area of motivation and learned drives. Subsequently he has become a major figure in the area of biofeedback, or the learning of voluntary control over bodily processes such as heart rate and blood pressure (Miller, 1978, 1983). In 1951 Miller was elected president of the American Psychological Association.

The collaborative work of Dollard and Miller is expressed in three major books. In the first, *Frustration and Aggression* (1939), completed with colleagues at Yale's Institute of Human Relations, there was an attempt to develop a scientific theory of aggressive behavior based on the assumption that aggression is a response to frustration. In the second, *Social Learning*

John Dollard

Neal E. Miller

and Imitation (1941), Miller and Dollard attempted to apply Hull's theory to personality and social psychology. Finally, in the third book, *Personality and Psychotherapy* (1950), Dollard and Miller attempted to integrate the achievements of learning theory, as expressed in the works of Pavlov, Hull, and others, with the achievements of psychoanalysis, as expressed in the works of Freud. In this book they attempted to apply the basic principles of learning to complex personality functioning, neurotic phenomena, and psychotherapy. This attempt was significant in that it directed attention onto the application of learning theory to clinical phenomena. However, in contrast with the approaches of current behavior modificationists and behavior therapists, the use of learning theory did not itself lead to the development of new therapeutic techniques.

THE S–R THEORY OF PERSONALITY

The helpless, naked, human infant is born with primary drives such as hunger, thirst, and reactions to pain and cold. He does not have, however, many of the motives that distinguish the adult as a member of a particular tribe, nation, social class, occupation, or profession. Many extremely important drives, such as the desire for money, the ambition to become an artist or a scholar, and particular fears and guilts are learned during socialization.

SOURCE: Dollard and Miller, 1950, p. 62

Structure

As in Skinner's operant theory, the key structural concept for S–R theory is the response. However, whereas Skinner places little importance on the stimulus that leads to and becomes associated with the response, the S–R view is that stimuli become connected to responses to form S–R bonds. According to Hullian theory, an association between a stimulus and a response is called a **habit**; personality structure is largely composed of learned habits, or S–R bonds.

Another structural concept used by the followers of Hull is that of **drive**. A drive is broadly defined as a stimulus strong enough to activate behavior. Using the Hullian model, it is drives that make the individual respond. A distinction is made between innate, **primary drives** and learned, **secondary drives**. The primary drives, such as pain and hunger, are generally associated with physiological conditions within the organism.

Secondary drives are drives that have been acquired on the basis of their association with the satisfaction of the primary drives. An important acquired drive is anxiety or fear. Based on the primary drive of pain, the secondary drive of anxiety is important because it can be learned quickly and can become strong. Anxiety can lead an organism to a variety of behaviors and is of particular importance in relation to abnormal behavior.

Process

In the Hullian model, there is an emphasis on drives (primary and secondary) that consist of internal stimuli leading to responses. Learning occurs when responses are rewarded in terms of a reduction in drive stimuli. In **instrumental learning** there is an emphasis on the use of learned responses to reduce drive stimuli (e.g., reward, escape from pain, avoidance of pain).

In the typical experiment in instrumental learning, the intensity of a drive and the amount of a reward are manipulated to see the effects on learning. For example, an experimenter might seek to study maze learning in a rat. The experimenter could manipulate the number of hours of food deprivation (hunger drive) in a rat, as well as the amount of food reward for making a correct response in the maze, and determine the effects on maze learning. The instrumental responses (correct turns in the maze) are reinforced through reduction of the hunger drive stimuli.

Another illustration is instrumental escape learning. In this type of experiment (Miller, 1951), a rat is put into a box with two compartments: a white compartment with a grid as a floor, and a black compartment with a solid floor. The compartments are separated by a door. At the beginning of the experiment, the rats are given electric shocks while in the white compartment and are allowed to escape into the black compartment. Thus, a fear response is conditioned to the white compartment. A test is then made as to whether the fear of the white compartment can lead to learning a new response. Now, in order for the rat to escape to the black compartment, it must turn a wheel placed in the white compartment. The turning of the wheel opens the door to the black compartment and allows the rat to escape. After a number of trials, the rat begins to rotate the wheel with considerable speed. The interpretation is that the rat has acquired a fear drive in relation to the white compartment. This drive operates to activate the rat and to set the stage for reinforcement, just as the hunger drive did in the maze experiment. Escape from the white into the black compartment involves learning a new response—turning a wheel. This instrumental learning is based on the escape from the white compartment and the associated reduction in the strength of the fear drive stimuli.

Growth and Development

In general, S–R theory interprets growth and development as consisting of the accumulation of habits, which are then related to one another in a hierarchical arrangement or order of importance. Miller and Dollard's social learning interpretation of development included an emphasis on the role of **imitation**. According to them, the imitative process is based on the positive reinforcement of matching behavior. For example, a boy might hear his father approach and run to greet him, following which he receives some candy. His younger sister might on one occasion run when she sees her older brother run. She too receives candy, resulting in a reward for matching the behavior of the older brother. Subsequently, through the process of generalization, the younger girl might imitate other behaviors of the older brother. In an experimental analysis of such a situation, Miller and Dollard rewarded rats for going in the same direction in a maze as the leader. Whereas the leader was trained to use a cue for finding food, the other rats were not. In other situations, the rats continued to imitate the behavior of the leader rather than use the available cues independently. In sum, rats reinforced for following the behavior of a leader learned the response of imitating, and this learned response generalized from the original situation to other situations.

Other efforts to translate Hullian theory into principles of growth and development have emphasized the importance of rewards in parental childrearing practices. For example, in one research program the pattern of childrearing found to be most likely to result in "high conscience" development in children was one in which the mother is generally warm and loving but also uses the threat of withdrawal of affection as a method of control (Sears et al., 1965). S–R theory emphasizes the learning of personality characteristics (S–R bonds) through patterns of parental reward and punishment, as well as rewards and punishments from other important people in the environment.

Psychopathology

Dollard and Miller (1950) were among the first to relate the principles of learning theory to personality phenomena, in general, and to abnormal behavior, in particular. In this effort they emphasized the concepts of drive, drive conflict, anxiety, and reinforcement through the reduction of anxiety.

According to Dollard and Miller, in the course of development children must learn socially accepted outlets for their drives. Particularly critical learning situations are those involving feeding, toilet training, and sexual and aggressive behavior. As children grow, they may wish to express certain drives but be punished for doing so by their parents. The result of punishment is the development of an acquired fear drive in relation to certain stimuli. As described earlier, Miller demonstrated that the fear response could be conditioned to a previously neutral stimulus (white compartment) and then itself take on properties of a drive stimulus. Similarly, because of the pain associated with punishment, a child may learn to fear many stimuli or situations that otherwise would be experienced in a neutral way. Responses that result in the reduction of the acquired fear drive are then learned. Guilt and avoidance are examples of possible learned responses under such conditions.

Types of Conflict   In the course of development, the same stimulus may come to elicit both an approach response and an avoidance response. At this point, the individual experiences an **approach–avoidance conflict**. Thus a boy may be torn between making sexual advances toward a girl (approach) and the fear of doing so (avoidance). Or an individual might wish to express anger but be afraid to do so because of past punishment for this behavior. Most people can think of many such approach–avoidance conflicts they face in their daily lives.

The approach–avoidance conflict between two drives is the basic ingredient for the development of neurotic behavior. As a result of the conflict and the anxiety involved, the individual develops a symptom. The symptom reduces the anxiety and relieves the pressure of the conflict. For example, Dollard and Miller described the case of a 23-year-old married woman who had developed a number of fears, one of which was that her heart would stop beating if she did not concentrate on counting the beats. The difficulties started with her feeling faint in a store, then developed into a fear of going out alone, and then into a fear of heart trouble. Dollard and Miller interpreted her symptoms as involving a sex–fear conflict. When on the streets alone, the woman was afraid of sexual temptation. She felt that someone might try to seduce her and that she would be vulnerable to the seduction. The increased sex desire accompanying the fantasized seduction touched off anxiety and guilt, leading to the sex–anxiety conflict. Going home and avoiding being alone on the streets were reinforced because they reduced the anxiety and relieved the conflict. The counting of heartbeats was similarly reinforcing because it preoccupied her and did not allow her to think of possible seductions. The counting habit was reinforced by the drop in anxiety.

The case illustrates how Dollard and Miller used the concepts of drive, drive conflict, anxiety, and reinforcement through drive reduction to account for the development of a neurosis. Although the details are sketchy, the case also illustrates how Dollard and Miller attempted to use Hullian theory in a way that was consistent with psychoanalytic theory.

Conflict: *This girl is facing an approach–approach conflict as to which food to choose.*

Although most attention has been given to approach–avoidance conflicts in the development of neuroses, Dollard and Miller also emphasized the importance of approach–approach and avoidance–avoidance conflicts. In an *approach–approach conflict* a person is torn between two desirable alternatives. Should a person date one or another attractive individual, watch this or the other great movie, buy this or that car? In an *avoidance–avoidance conflict* a person is torn between undesirable, unpleasant alternatives. Should a person pay the bill now and be without money or pay a larger bill later, is divorce or living in an unpleasant situation worse, should a child tell his or her parent and risk punishment or stay silent and feel guilty?

As noted, Dollard and Miller attempted to apply principles of S–R learning theory to psychoanalytic concepts. Their book *Personality and Psychotherapy* (1950) contains many brilliant illustrations of how such psychoanalytic concepts as repression, symptom, and transference can be understood in S–R, instrumental learning terms. Other personality psychologists and clinicians used S–R theory but rejected the medical symptom—disease model as well as the translation into psychoanalytic theory. In neither case, however, did new methods of behavior change develop.

This chapter has considered learning, behavioral approaches, in particular those based on principles of classical conditioning, operant conditioning, and S–R learning. To an even greater extent than any of the approaches considered previously, there is a diversity of views and even hostility among alternative camps. Such diversity makes comparison with earlier views difficult. At the same time, the approaches considered

A COMPARISON OF LEARNING APPROACHES WITH EARLIER VIEWS

Table 9.2   Contrasting General Points of Emphasis of Learning Views and Traditional Theories of Personality

Learning Views	Traditional Personality Theory
Processes of learning	Personality structures
Specific behaviors	General characteristics
General laws	Individual differences
Laboratory data	Clinical data & questionnaires
Environmental variables	Internal variables

in this chapter have enough in common for them to be considered together, and contrasted with the views presented earlier.

Perhaps the most significant comparison between the theories presented in this chapter and those considered previously is the emphasis on *processes* of learning rather than on *structures*, such as motives, traits, or the self-concept. In part following from this, learning–behavioral approaches tend to emphasize the importance of specific behaviors rather than general personality characteristics. In addition, there is an interest in general laws of learning rather than in individual differences. Also, in terms of method of research, there is an emphasis on laboratory experiments rather than clinical investigation or the use of questionnaires. Finally, there tends to be a difference in the extent to which the focus is on variables internal to the organism as opposed to those external to it. Compared with the views presented earlier, the theories considered in this chapter emphasize the importance of variables in the environment in the regulation and control of behavior (Table 9.2).

CRITICAL EVALUATION

We have now covered considerable ground, including a variety of theoretical and applied approaches. It is time to take stock of learning, behavioral approaches to personality.

STRENGTHS OF LEARNING APPROACHES

Three major contributions have been made by learning approaches: a commitment to systematic research and theory development; a recognition and exploration of the role of situational and environmental variables in influencing behavior; and a pragmatic approach to treatment leading to important new developments.

Learning psychologists share a commitment to empiricism or systematic research. Whatever the differences in theory, the various approaches are characterized by a respect for scientific methodology and for evidence in support of a new point of view. In contrast with the development of psychoanalysis—and to a certain extent with that of phenomenology and humanistic approaches—learning approaches have been largely tied to academic departments. There the emphasis is on clarity in defining constructs and on replicability in verifying data. Although at times this may limit what is studied and how phenomena are conceptualized, it also sets some useful boundaries on armchair speculation and quasi-religious debate. Thus, to a greater extent than most other approaches considered to this point, the learning approach emphasizes laboratory research that leads to the establishment of causal relationships.

The second contribution and strength of learning approaches is a recognition of the role of environmental and situational variables in behavior. Most learning approaches emphasize the importance of regulating or maintaining conditions in the environment; all emphasize the importance of situational analysis. For some time, traditional personality theory and assessment gave minimal attention to such variables. The importance of the situation or environment was noted by psychoanalytic and trait theorists, but there was no active exploration or conceptual development. In many ways, it has been unfortunate that the emphasis on situational variables and situation-specific aspects of performance became associated with the person–situation controversy. As most personality psychologists now recognize, both person and situation variables enter into behavior, and we must try to understand how they relate to one another. The learning approach has called attention to the variability and flexibility that are characteristic of much human behavior, as well as to the diversity of skills that are relevant to specific tasks.

Related to this has been a pragmatism that has led to the development of important procedures for behavior change. In contrast with many traditional treatment programs, which focused on young, verbal, intelligent, and successful patients, many behavior modification programs started by treating individuals on whom almost everyone else gave up—the chronic schizophrenic, the autistic child, the retarded, the addicted, and so on. Traditional therapy programs were not working and new approaches were required. Behavior therapists filled the void, in particular with the application of Skinnerian principles in behavior modification programs. These programs have raised moral and ethical issues concerning the control of human behavior, but on the whole significant gains have been made in assisting people who otherwise would have been left untouched.

LIMITATIONS OF LEARNING APPROACHES

If the strengths outlined above seem significant, the limitations to be detailed are no less noteworthy. In some cases they speak to the same issues already covered, suggesting that the reality is not always as pretty as the picture presented. For example, with its concern for objectivity and rigor, the learning approach has oversimplified personality and neglected important phenomena.

Table 9.3   Summary of Strengths and Limitations of Learning Approaches

Strengths	Limitations
1. Committed to systematic research and theory development.	1. Oversimplifies personality and neglects important phenomena.
2. Recognizes the role of situational and environmental variables in influencing behavior.	2. Lacks a single, unified theory; gap between theory and practice.
3. Takes a pragmatic approach to treatment which can lead to important new developments.	3. Requires further evidence to support claims of treatment effectiveness.

There are many components to the criticism that learning theorists oversimplify behavior. One component is the claim that the principles of learning used are derived from research on rats and other subhuman animals. Are the same principles involved in human learning? In other words, can rat laws be applied to human behavior? A second component of this criticism is the claim that the behaviors studied by learning theorists are superficial. In their effort to gain experimental control over relevant variables, learning theorists have limited themselves to simple, specific responses and have avoided complex behaviors. We may recall here Cattell's argument that the bivariate method limits investigators to the study of a few variables, and this means that they must ignore behaviors that cannot be produced in the laboratory.

A third and critical component of the criticism regarding oversimplification concerns cognitive behavior. Cognitive behavior involves the way in which the individual receives, organizes, and transmits information. The work of many psychologists demonstrates the importance of understanding cognitive behavior. Yet, for a long time behaviorists avoided considering these phenomena. Perhaps because of a reluctance to look at internal processes or to consider complex processes, learning theorists clung to their attempts to understand all behavior in terms of stimulus–response bonds or in terms of operants and successive approximation.

Critics of the approaches considered in this chapter also emphasize that there is no agreed-on theory of learning and that a large gap exists between theory and practice. Some time ago a supporter of behavior therapy suggested that it is a group of techniques rather than a theory-based scientific procedure: "When you eliminate the polemics and politics and gratuities, however, what remains of the theory to define the field and to tell you what it is about? Not a whole lot" (London, 1972, p. 916). Further, although there is evidence that procedures can be effective, such as with systematic desensitization, there is a question concerning the processes involved—that is, such a procedure may be working for reasons other than those suggested by behavior therapists (Kazdin & Wilson, 1978; Levis & Malloy, 1982).

Finally, let us consider the effectiveness of learning approaches to treatment. There is a need for evidence concerning the effectiveness of most behavioral treatment procedures, particularly where they are used with actual clinical populations and in relation to significant effects that are maintained over time. Initially, there was a burst of enthusiasm for the successes of behavior therapy, as is often the case with a new development. Following this, some sobering questions were raised, including the following: To what extent does behavior therapy generalize successfully from one situation to another and from one response to another? To what extent are the results durable or stable over time? Are the originally published success rates accurate, and are behavioral techniques equally successful with all patients?

Historically, a problem with behavior therapy has been that often the results do not generalize and/or do not remain stable over time. Questions have been raised, for example, as to whether results obtained in the laboratory or clinic are maintained in the natural environment (Bandura, 1972; Kazdin & Bootzin, 1972). In addition, some studies suggest that in many patients gains are eventually lost (Eysenck & Beech, 1971). Finally, techniques found to be useful with mild problems in the laboratory may be far less significant when applied to clients with more serious difficulties.

Although Skinnerian and S–R learning theory dominated much of psychology—including personality and clinical psychology—during the 1940s and 1950s, their influence has greatly diminished since that time (see also Chapter 15). What happened? There are many explanations that can be given but perhaps the dominant factor was what has been called *the cognitive revolution*. Starting approximately in the 1960s, psychologists became increasingly interested in how people think and process information. Whereas the metaphor for S–R learning theory was the telephone switchboard, in which stimulus–response connections were made just as were telephone connections, the metaphor for cognitive theories was the computer, in which information is encoded, stored and retrieved. The computer revolution became the cognitive revolution, the unfolding of which we continue to witness to this day. In the chapters that follow we will consider the personality theories that are a part of this revolution.

MAJOR CONCEPTS

Situational specificity. The emphasis on behavior as varying according to the situation, as opposed to the emphasis by trait theorists on consistency in behavior across situations.

Behaviorism. An approach within psychology, developed by Watson, that restricts investigation to overt, observable behavior.

Classical conditioning. A process, emphasized by Pavlov, in which a previously neutral stimulus becomes capable of eliciting a response because of its association with a stimulus that automatically produces the same or a similar response.

Generalization. In conditioning, the association of a response with stimuli similar to the stimulus to which the response was originally conditioned or attached.

Discrimination. In conditioning, the differential response to stimuli depending on whether they have been associated with pleasure, pain, or neutral events.

Extinction. In conditioning, the progressive weakening of the association between a stimulus and a response; in classical conditioning because the conditioned stimulus is no longer followed by the unconditioned stimulus; and in operant conditioning because the response is no longer followed by reinforcement.

Conditioned emotional reaction. Watson and Rayner's term for the development of an emotional reaction to a previously neutral stimulus, as in Little Albert's fear of rats.

Systematic desensitization. A technique in behavior therapy in which a competing response (relaxation) is conditioned to stimuli that previously aroused anxiety.

Operant conditioning. Skinner's term for the process through which the characteristics of a response are determined by its consequences.

Operants. In Skinner's theory, behaviors that appear (are emitted) without being specifically associated with any prior (eliciting) stimuli and are studied in rela-

tion to the reinforcing events that follow them.

Reinforcer. An event (stimulus) that follows a response and increases the probability of its occurence.

Generalized reinforcer. In Skinner's operant conditioning theory, a reinforcer that provides access to many other reinforcers (e.g., money).

Schedule of reinforcement. In Skinner's operant conditioning theory, the rate and interval of reinforcement of responses (e.g., response ratio schedule and time intervals).

Successive approximation. In Skinner's operant conditioning theory, the development of complex behaviors through the reinforcement of behaviors that increasingly resemble the final form of behavior to be produced.

Behavior deficit. In the Skinnerian view of psychopathology, the failure to learn an adaptive response.

Maladaptive response. In the Skinnerian view of psychopathology, the learning of a response that is maladaptive or not considered acceptable by people in the environment.

Behavioral assessment. The emphasis in assessment on specific behaviors that are tied to defined situational characteristics (e.g., ABC approach).

Target behaviors (target responses). In behavioral assessment, the identification of specific behaviors to be observed and measured in relation to changes in environmental events.

Functional analysis. In behavioral approaches, particularly Skinnerian, the identification of the environmental stimuli that control behavior.

ABC assessment. In behavioral assessment, an emphasis on the identification of antecedent (A) events and the consequences (C) of behavior (B); a functional analysis of behavior involving identification of the environmental conditions that regulate specific behaviors.

ABA (own-control) research. A Skinnerian variant of the experimental method consisting of exposing one subject to three experimental phases: (A) a baseline period, (B) introduction of reinforcers to change the frequency of specific behaviors, and (A) withdrawal of reinforcement and observation of whether the behaviors return to their earlier frequency (baseline period).

Sign approach. Mischel's description of assessment approaches that infer personality from test behavior, in contrast with sample approaches to assessment.

Sample approach. Mischel's description of assessment approaches in which there is an interest in the behavior itself and its relation to environmental conditions, in contrast to sign approaches that infer personality from test behavior.

Token economy. Following Skinner's operant conditioning theory, an environment in which individuals are rewarded with tokens for desirable behaviors.

Habit. In Hull's theory, an association between a stimulus and a response.

Drive, primary. In Hull's theory, an innate internal stimulus that activates behavior (e.g., hunger drive).

Drive, secondary. In Hull's theory, a learned internal stimulus, acquired through association with the satisfaction of primary drives, that activates behavior (e.g., anxiety).

Instrumental learning. In S–R theory, the learning of responses that are instrumental in bringing about a desirable situation.

Imitation. Behavior that is acquired through the observation of others. In S–R theory, the result of the process called *matched-dependent* behavior in which, for example, children match their behavior to that of their parents and are then rewarded.

Approach–avoidance conflict. In S–R theory, the simultaneous presence of opposing drives to move toward an object and away from it.

REVIEW

1. The learning approach to personality emphasizes principles of learning and the experimental testing of clearly defined hypotheses. Associated with this is an emphasis on the situational specificity of behavior, the application of principles of learning to behavior change, and rejection of the medical symptom–disease model of psychopathology.

LEARNING APPROACHES AT A GLANCE

	Structure	Process	Growth and Development
	Response	Classical conditioning; instrumental conditioning; operant conditioning	Imitation; schedules of reinforcement and successive approximations

2. Watson spelled out the rationale for a behaviorist approach to psychology.

3. Pavlov's work on classical conditioning illustrates how a previously neutral stimulus can become capable of eliciting a response because of its association with a stimulus that produces the same or a similar response (e.g., the dog salivates to the bell stimulus associated with the food powder). Generalization, discrimination, and extinction are three important processes studied by Pavlov.

4. The classical conditioning procedure suggests that many abnormal behaviors are the result of conditioning responses to inappropriate stimuli. Watson and Rayner's case of Little Albert illustrates such a conditional emotional reaction. The application of principles of classical conditioning is seen in the classic case of Peter's fear of a white rabbit, in the treatment of bedwetting in children, and in the method of systematic desensitization. In systematic desensitization the relaxation response is counterconditioned to a graded, imagined hierarchy of stimuli that formerly were associated with anxiety.

5. Freud's case of Little Hans has been reinterpreted according to the principles of classical conditioning. The phobia is viewed as a conditioned anxiety reaction precipitated by his viewing a horse fall down, rather than as an expression of underlying conflicts.

6. Skinner, considered by many to be the greatest contemporary American psychologist, developed the principles of operant conditioning. The emphasis here is on responses emitted by the organism (operants) and the schedules of reinforcement that shape behavior. Complex behavior is shaped through successive approximation.

7. The Skinnerian interpretation of psychopathology emphasizes behavioral deficits and the development of maladaptive responses that are maintained by reinforcers in the environment. Behavioral assessment includes an analysis of the Antecedent conditions of the behavior of interest, and Behavior itself, and the Consequences of the

Pathology	Change	Illustrative Case
Maladaptive learned response patterns	Extinction; discrimination learning; counterconditioning; positive reinforcement; imitation; systematic desensitization; behavior modification	Peter; Reinterpretation of Little Hans

behavior—the ABCs of behavioral assessment. A distinction is drawn between sign and sample approaches to assessment. Whereas in sign approaches personality is inferred from test responses, in sample approaches interest is in the behavior itself and how it is affected by environmental conditions.

8. Although there is no single method of behavior therapy or behavior modification, its procedures emphasize principles of learning theory. In behavior modification involving Skinnerian principles of operant conditioning, desired behaviors are shaped through stages of successive approximation. The ABA or own-control design can be used to demonstrate that the reinforcers being manipulated are the causal agents in the change process. The application of these principles to behavior regulation in an institutional setting is seen in a token economy.

9. In the S–R, instrumental learning approach of Hull and of Dollard and Miller, habits are learned through the reinforcement of stimulus–response (S–R) connections. Reinforcement consists of the reduction of drive stimuli—either of primary, innate drives or of secondary, learned drives such as anxiety. In terms of growth and development, the emphasis is on habits acquired through reinforcement and imitation. The S–R interpretation of psychopathology places major emphasis on the roles of approach–avoidance conflicts and anxiety drive stimuli. As with other learning approaches, the basic principles of learning are seen as adequate for an understanding of abnormal behavior.

10. Learning approaches are diverse in their specifics. As a group, however, they can be contrasted with traditional personality theories in terms of their greater emphasis on specific behaviors and general laws of learning.

11. Learning approaches share a commitment to research and generally are open to theoretical developments. Additional strengths are recog-

nition of the importance of environmental variables and a pragmatic approach to treatment that has fostered the development of new procedures for behavior change. At the same time, these approaches tend to oversimplify personality and neglect important phenomena. In addition, there is still no unified theory of learning, and further evidence is required to support claims of treatment effectiveness.

A COGNITIVE THEORY OF PERSONALITY: GEORGE A. KELLY'S PERSONAL CONSTRUCT THEORY OF PERSONALITY

Chapter Focus

You've just finished a novel that you thoroughly enjoyed. Excitedly, you call a friend to recommend the book, telling him about the exquisitely detailed descriptions of the characters and the settings. To your dismay, your friend informs you that he has read the book, and worse, he hated it! How could this be? He explains that he found the plot thin and slow-moving. He and you read the exact same book in two very different ways. The two of you attended to different aspects of the story, *constructing* your own *personal* interpretations along the way.

This is what George Kelly's *personal construct theory* is all about: how each individual uniquely perceives, interprets, and conceptualizes the world. Each person construes the world differently, just as you and your friend read the book differently. In Kelly's clinical, cognitive theory, the person is viewed as a *scientist* who develops a theory (*construct system*) to make sense of the world and predict events. Kelly's most important contribution to personality assessment is the *Rep test*. The Rep test is one procedure to elicit the individual's personal construct system and thereby helps understand the individual's personality.

QUESTIONS TO BE ADDRESSED IN THIS CHAPTER

1. In which ways do people behave like scientists in their psychological functioning?

2. To what extent does personality involve how people construe the world, that is, if you knew how an individual construed or interpreted events, would you know their personality?

3. Can one think of motivated behavior in terms other than Freud's tension-reduction–pursuit of pleasure model or Rogers's self-actualization model?

4. How do people deal with unpredictable situations? Do people seek complete predictability of events, even if it means potential monotony or boredom?

In earlier chapters, two clinical theories of personality were discussed—the psychodynamic theory of Freud and the phenomenological theory of Rogers. Both theories were derived from clinical contacts with patients; both emphasize individual differences; both view individuals as having some consistency across situations and over time; and both view the person as a total system. Freud and Rogers attempted to understand, predict, influence, and conceptualize behavior without fragmenting people into unrelated parts. Although having these common characteristics, the two theories were presented as illustrative of different approaches to theory and research.

In this chapter, we study a third theory that is representative of the clinical approach toward understanding personality. The *personal construct theory* of George Kelly, like the theories of Freud and Rogers, was developed mostly out of contact with clients in therapy. Like the theories of Freud and Rogers, Kelly's personal construct theory emphasizes the whole person. As Kelly observed, the first consideration of personal construct theory is the individual person, rather than any part of the person, any group of persons, or any particular process in a person's behavior. The personal construct clinician cannot fragment the client and reduce the client's problem to a single issue. Instead, the clinician must view the client from a number of perspectives at the same time.

Although sharing these characteristics with other clinical theories, Kelly's theory is vastly different from the theories of Freud and Rogers. Kelly's theory interprets behavior in *cognitive* terms; that is, it emphasizes the ways in which we perceive events, the ways we interpret these events in relation to already existing structures, and the ways that we behave in relation to these interpretations. For Kelly a **construct** is a way of perceiving or interpreting events. For example, good–bad is a construct frequently used by people as they consider events. An individual's personal construct system is made up of the constructs—or ways of interpreting events—and the relationships among these constructs.

How are we to characterize Kelly's theory, particularly in relation to other theories of personality? This is no small problem since others have construed the theory in a variety of ways and Kelly himself refused to attach any labels to it. Kelly's theory has been viewed as phenomenological, since it emphasizes the ways in which individuals construe the world. Because it also emphasizes the person as an active agent in engaging the world, Kelly's theory has been described as existential as well. Because his approach to therapy emphasizes things people can *do* to change the way they *think*, personal construct theory also has been described as behavioral. Because the theory emphasizes the interplay among the elements of a person's construct system, and because, as noted, Kelly viewed the person as an active agent in engaging the world, personal construct theory also has been called a dynamic theory. Although Kelly indeed viewed his theory as dynamic, once more he rejected a particular label for it (Winter, 1992).

In this text we will consider personal construct theory as a cognitive approach to personality. It should be noted that Kelly rejected the term *cognitive* because he felt that it was too restrictive and suggested an artificial division between cognition (thinking) and affect (feeling). Despite this, cognitive remains the most popular classification of Kelly's theory, and for good reason (Neimeyer, 1992; Winter, 1992). Kelly's theory is a constructivist theory—that is, it emphasizes the construction of the world by the individual. This is a cognitive process. In its emphasis on how the individual attributes meaning to events and on the efforts of the person to predict events, personal construct theory clearly emphasizes cognitive processes. Another reason for describing Kelly's theory as cognitive, and the reason for considering it at this point in the text, is that it clearly anticipated later cognitive developments in personality theory. Much of current personality theory, as well as current psychology more generally, has become increasingly cognitive. The chapters that follow in this text will describe in detail many of these developments and Kelly's theory forms a bridge to them. Thus, as one supporter of personal construct theory noted, "Kelly's theory enjoys the irony of becoming increasingly contemporary with age" (Neimeyer, 1992, p.995).

In sum, in this and the following chapter we will consider a theory of personality derived primarily from clinical experience, one that has similarities to some of the theories previously considered yet is distinctive in its cognitive emphasis. As noted, it is a theory whose developer insisted that it not be categorized or labeled in terms already familiar to psychologists. Rather, Kelly suggested that we be prepared to think of his theory in new terms, just as he dared to reconstrue—that is, to reinterpret—the field of psychology. This is an enormously challenging task, one that can involve a mix of excitement and anxiety. But, as we shall see, this is the stuff that Kelly suggested life was made of, so we might as well set ourselves to be ready for the task.

GEORGE A. KELLY (1905–1966): A VIEW OF THE THEORIST

Less has been written about Kelly than about Freud and Rogers, but we do know something of his background, and the nature of the man comes through in his writing. He appears to be the kind of person he encourages others to be—an adventuresome soul who is unafraid to think unorthodox thoughts about people and who dares to explore the world of the unknown. Kelly's philosophical and theoretical positions stem, in part, from the diversity of his experience (Sechrest, 1963). Kelly grew up in Kansas and obtained his undergraduate education there at Friends University and at Park College in Missouri. He pursued graduate studies at the University of Kansas, the University of Minnesota, and the University of Edinburgh, and received his Ph.D. from the State University of Iowa in 1931. He developed a traveling clinic in Kansas, was an aviation psychologist during World War II, and was a professor of psychology at Ohio State University and Brandeis University.

Kelly's early clinical experience was in the public schools of Kansas. While there, he found that teachers referred pupils to his traveling psychological clinic with complaints that appeared to say something about the teachers themselves. Instead of verifying a teacher's complaint, Kelly decided to try to understand it as an expression of the teacher's construction or interpretation of events. For example, if a teacher complained that a student was lazy, Kelly did not look at the pupil to see if

George A. Kelly

the teacher was correct in the diagnosis; rather he tried to understand the behaviors of the child and the way the teacher perceived these behaviors—that is, the teacher's construction of them—that led to the complaint of laziness. This was a significant reformulation of the problem. In practical terms, it led to an analysis of the teachers as well as the pupils, and to a wider range of solutions to the problems. Furthermore, it led Kelly to the view that there is no objective, absolute truth—phenomena are meaningful only in relation to the ways in which they are construed or interpreted by the individual.

George Kelly, then, was a person who refused to accept things as black or white, right or wrong. He was a person who liked to test new experiences; who dismissed truth in any absolute sense, and therefore felt free to reconstrue or reinterpret phenomena; who challenged the concept of objective reality and felt free to play in the world of make-believe; who perceived events as occurring to individuals and, therefore, was interested in the interpretations of these events by individuals; who viewed his own theory as only a tentative formulation and who, consequently, was free to challenge views that others accepted as fact; who experienced the frustration and challenge, the threat and joy, of exploring the unknown.

Theories of personality have implicit assumptions about human nature. Often, they can be uncovered only as we study why a theorist explores one phenomenon instead of another, and as we observe that theorists go beyond the data in ways that are meaningful in relation to their own life

KELLY'S VIEW OF THE PERSON

experiences. In general, Kelly's view of the person is explicit. In fact, he begins his presentation of the psychology of personal constructs with a section on his perspectives of the person. Kelly's assumption about human nature is that every person is a scientist. The scientist attempts to predict and control phenomena. Kelly believes that psychologists, operating as scientists, try to predict and control behavior, but that they do not assume that their subjects operate on a similar basis. Kelly describes this situation as follows:

> It is as though the psychologist were saying to himself, "I, being a psychologist, and therefore a scientist, am performing this experiment in order to improve the prediction and control of certain human phenomena; but my subject, being merely a human organism, is obviously propelled by inexorable drives welling up within him, or else he is in gluttonous pursuit of sustenance and shelter."
>
> SOURCE: Kelly, 1955, p. 5

Scientists have theories, test hypotheses, and weigh experimental evidence. Kelly considered this an appropriate view of people as well. As noted in Chapter 1, all people experience events, perceive similarities and differences among these events, formulate concepts or constructs to order phenomena, and, on the basis of these constructs, seek to anticipate events. In this respect, all people are scientists.

The view of the person as a scientist has a number of further consequences for Kelly. First, it leads to the view that we are essentially oriented toward the future. "It is the future which tantalizes man, not the past. Always he reaches out to the future through the window of the present" (Kelly, 1955, p. 49). Second, it suggests that we have the capacity to "represent" the environment, rather than merely respond to it. Just as scientists can develop alternative theoretical formulations, so can individuals interpret and reinterpret, construe and reconstrue, their environments. Life is a representation, or construction, of reality, and this allows us to make and remake ourselves.

Some people are capable of viewing life in many different ways, whereas others cling rigidly to a set interpretation. However, people can perceive events only within the limits of the categories (constructs) that are available to them. In Kelly's terms, we are free to construe events, but we are bound by our constructions. Thus we come to a new understanding of the issue of free will and determinism. According to Kelly, we are both free *and* determined. "This personal construct system provides him [humankind] with both freedom of decision and limitations of action—freedom, because it permits him to deal with the meaning of events rather than forces him to be helplessly pushed about by them, and limitation, because he can never make choices outside the world of alternatives he has erected for himself" (Kelly, 1958a, p. 58). Having "enslaved" ourselves with these constructions, we are able to win freedom again and again by reconstruing the environment and life. Thus, we are not victims of past history or of present circumstances—unless we choose to construe ourselves in that way.*

KELLY'S VIEW OF SCIENCE, THEORY, AND RESEARCH

Much of Kelly's thinking, including his view of science, is based on the philosophical position of **constructive alternativism**. According to this position, there is no objective reality or absolute truth to discover. Instead, there are efforts to construe events—to interpret phenomena in order to make sense of them. There are always alternative constructions available from which to choose. This is as true for the scientist as it is for people who behave as scientists. In Kelly's view the scientific enterprise is not the discovery of truth, or as Freud might have suggested, the uncovering of things in the mind previously hidden. Rather, the scientific enterprise is the effort to develop construct systems that are useful in anticipating events.

Kelly was concerned about the tendency toward dogma in psychology. He thought psychologists believed that constructs of inner states and traits actually existed rather than understanding them as "things" in a theoretician's head. If someone is described as an introvert, we tend to check to see whether he *is* an introvert, rather than checking the person who is responsible for the statement. Kelly's position against "truth" and dogma is of considerable significance. It allows one to establish the "invitational mood" in which one is free to invite many alternative interpretations of phenomena and to entertain propositions that initially may seem absurd. The invitational mood is a necessary part of the exploration of the world, for the professional scientist as well as for the patient in therapy. It is the mood established by the creative novelist; but where the novelist publishes make-believe and may even be unconcerned with the evidence supporting his or her constructions, the professional scientist tends to minimize the world of make-believe and to focus on evidence.

According to Kelly, it is the freedom to make believe and to establish the invitational mood that allows for the development of hypotheses. A hypothesis should not be asserted as a fact, but instead should allow the scientist to pursue its implications *as if* it were true. Kelly viewed a theory as a tentative expression of what has been observed and of what is expected. A theory has a **range of convenience**, indicating the boundaries of phenomena the theory can cover, and a **focus of convenience**, indicating the points within the boundaries where the theory works best. For example, Freud's theory has a broad range of convenience, providing interpretations for almost all aspects of personality, but its focus of con-

---

*Kelly's references to "man the scientist" and "man the biological organism" may strike students as sexist. It should be remembered that Kelly was writing in the 1950s, prior to efforts to remove sexism from language.

venience was the unconscious and abnormal behavior. Rogers's theory has a narrower range of convenience, and its focus of convenience is more on the concept of the self and the process of change. The focus of convenience for trait theory is the structure of personality and broad generalizations concerning dispositional differences among individuals. Different theories have different ranges and different foci of convenience.

For Kelly, theories were modifiable and ultimately expendable. A theory is modified or discarded when it stops leading to new predictions or leads to incorrect predictions. Among scientists, as well as among people in general, how long one holds onto a theory in the face of contradictory information is partly a matter of taste and style.

Kelly's view of science is not unique, but it is important in terms of its clarity of expression and its points of emphasis (Figure 10.1). It also has a number of important ramifications. First, since there are no "facts," and since different theories have different ranges of convenience, we need not argue about whether one theory is right and another wrong; they are different constructions. Second, Kelly's approach involved criticism of an extreme emphasis on measurement. Kelly felt that such an approach can lead to viewing concepts as things rather than as representations, and to making a psychologist into a technician rather than a scientist. Third, Kelly's view of science leaves room for the clinical as opposed to the experimental method. He considered the clinical method useful because it speaks the language of hypothesis, because it leads to the emergence of new variables, and because it focuses on important questions. Here we have a fourth significant aspect of Kelly's view of science: it should focus on important issues. In Kelly's belief, many psychologists are afraid of doing anything that might not be recognized as science, and they have given up struggling with important aspects of human behavior. He suggested that they stop trying to be scientific and get on with the job of understanding people. Kelly believed that a good

1. There is no objective reality and there are no "facts." Different theories have different constructions of phenomena. These theories also have different ranges of convenience and different foci of convenience.
2. Theories should lead to research. However, an extreme emphasis on measurement can be limiting and lead to viewing concepts as "things" rather than as representations.
3. The clinical method is useful because it leads to new ideas and focuses attention on important questions.
4. A good theory of personality should help us to solve the problems of people and society.
5. Theories are designed to be modified and abandoned.

Figure 10.1   *Some Components of Kelly's View of Science*

scientific theory should encourage the invention of new approaches to the solution of the problems of people and society.

Finally, as noted, Kelly took a firm stand against dogma. It was his contention that many scholars waste time trying to disprove their colleagues' claims to make room for their own explanations. It is a tribute to Kelly's sense of perspective, sense of humor, and lack of defensiveness concerning his own work that he could describe one of his own theoretical papers as involving "half-truths" only, and that he could view his theory as contributing to its own downfall. It is this theory—the theory of personal constructs—that we now discuss.

STRUCTURE

THE PERSONALITY THEORY OF GEORGE A. KELLY

Kelly's key structural concept for the person as a scientist is that of the *construct*. A construct is a way of *construing*, or interpreting, the world. It is a concept that the individual uses to categorize events and to chart a course of behavior. According to Kelly, a person anticipates events by observing patterns and regularities. A person experiences events, interprets them, and places a structure and a meaning on them. In experiencing events, individuals notice that some events share characteristics that distinguish them from other events. Individuals distinguish similarities and contrasts. They observe that some people are tall and some are short, that some are men and some are women, that some things are hard and some are soft. It is this construing of a similarity and a contrast that leads to the formation of a construct. Without constructs, life would be chaotic.

At least three elements are necessary to form a construct: two of the elements must be perceived as similar to each other, and the third element must be perceived as different from these two. The way in which two elements are construed to be similar forms the **similarity pole** of the construct; the way in which they are contrasted with the third element forms the **contrast pole** of the construct. For example, observing two people helping someone and a third hurting someone could lead to the construct kind–cruel, with kind forming the similarity pole and cruel the contrast pole. Kelly stressed the importance of recognizing that a construct is composed of a similarity–contrast comparison. This suggests that we do not understand the nature of a construct when it uses only the similarity pole or the contrast pole. We do not know what the construct *respect* means to a person until we know what events the person includes under this construct and what events are viewed as being opposed to it. Interestingly, whatever constructs one applies to others are potentially applicable to the self. "One cannot call another person a bastard without making bastardy a dimension of his own life also" (Kelly, 1955, p. 133).

A construct is not dimensional in the sense of having many points between the similarity and contrast poles. Subtleties or refinements in construction of events are made through the use of other constructs, such as constructs of quantity and quality. For example, the construct black–white in combination with a quantity construct leads to the four-scale value of black, slightly black, slightly white, and white (Sechrest, 1963).

Types of Constructs

It is fascinating as well as enlightening to think of the constructs people use. Often they are part of the person's everyday language, though the individual might be surprised to learn that these are only constructs and that alternative ways of viewing the world are possible. Think, for example, of the constructs that are part of your own construct system. What are the terms or characteristics you use to describe people? Does each term include an opposite one to form a similarity–contrast pair, or is one end of the construct missing in some cases? Can you think of constructs that people you know use to say something about themselves as individuals? What constructs are shared by members of one social class or culture and not shared by members of a different social class or culture?

It is interesting to consider whether such differences in construct systems are often part of the problem in communications between groups. In fact, consider a specific application of this point: Can you think of constructs that people use and that often result in problems in interpersonal relationships? For example, a frequent problem in marital relationships is when both partners emphasize the core construct guilty–innocent. Typically, each then argues that he or she is the "innocent" party and their partner is "to blame" for the difficulties. Both may initially see the counselor as a judge who will render a verdict rather than as someone who may help them to view things in another light or revise their constructs.

Another example concerns a friend who once said to me: "Isn't there a winner and a loser in every relationship?" That person was obviously unaware that "winner–loser" is a possible, but not a necessary, construct. Another person might have used the construct compromising–uncompromising person or compassionate–uncompassionate person. Such different constructions might lead to very different patterns of relationships. Many marital relationships run into trouble because they are construed in power terms and tests of will rather than in terms of help and empathy. Thus, although seemingly abstract, constructs can be seen as very much influencing basic aspects of our daily lives.

We need not assume from this discussion that constructs are verbal or that they are always verbally available to a person. Although Kelly emphasized the cognitive aspects of human functioning—the ones that Freudians would call the conscious—he did take into consideration phenomena described by Freudians as being unconscious. Kelly did not use the conscious–unconscious construct; however, he did use the verbal–preverbal construct to deal with some of the elements that are

CURRENT
APPLICATIONS

HAVING WORDS FOR WHAT YOU SEE, TASTE, AND SMELL

"Why are we so inarticulate about these things?" said a student in referring to tastes, odors, and touch sensations. What would the implications be if we had a greater vocabulary for experience, that is, if we had more constructs for such phenomena? Can having more taste constructs develop one's sense of taste? More odor constructs one's sense of smell? Is the secret to becoming a food connoisseur the development of one's construct system?

At one time it was thought that language determines how we perceive and organize the world. In light of today's evidence, such a view seems too extreme. We are capable of sensing and recognizing many things for which we have no name or concept. However, having a concept or construct may facilitate experiencing and recalling some phenomena. For example, research on odor identification suggests that having the right words to describe an odor facilitates recognition of the odor: "People can improve their ability to identify odors through practice. More specifically, they can improve it through various cognitive interventions in which words are used to endow odors with perceptual or olfactory identity." A name for a smell helps to transform it from vague to clear. Not just any word will do, since some words seem to capture better the sensory experience than others do. The important fact, however, is that cognition does play an important role in virtually all aspects of sensory experience.

In sum, expanding one's sensory construct system alone may not provide for increased sensitivity to sensory experience but, together with practice, it can go a long way toward doing so. Want to become a food connoisseur? Practice, but also expand your construct system.

SOURCE: *Psychology Today*, July 1981.

Unity of Constructs: *Having a relevant construct may facilitate sensitivity to tastes and odors.*

otherwise interpreted as conscious or unconscious. A **verbal construct** can be expressed in words, whereas a **preverbal construct** is one that is used even though the person has no words to express it. A preverbal construct is learned before the person develops the use of language. Sometimes, one end of a construct is not available for verbalization; it is characterized as being **submerged**. If a person insists that people do only good things, one assumes that the other end of the construct has been submerged since the person must have been aware of contrasting behaviors to have formed the "good" end of the construct. Thus, constructs may not be available for verbalization, and the individual may not be able to report all the elements that are in the construct—but this does not mean that the individual has an unconscious. In spite of the recognized importance of preverbal and submerged constructs, ways of studying them have not been developed and generally this area has been neglected.

The constructs used by a person in interpreting and anticipating events are organized as part of a system. Each construct within the system has a range of convenience and a focus of convenience. A construct's range of convenience comprises all those events for which the user would find application of the construct useful. A construct's focus of convenience comprises the particular events for which application of the construct would be maximally useful. For example, the construct caring–uncaring, which might apply to people in all situations where help is given (range of convenience), would be particularly applicable in situations where special sensitivity and effort are required (focus of convenience). In addition, some constructs are more central to the person's construct system than are others. Thus, there are **core constructs** that are basic to a person's functioning and can be changed only with great consequences for the rest of the construct system, and **peripheral constructs** that are much less basic and can be altered without serious modification of the core structure.

Also, there is a hierarchical arrangement of constructs within a system. A **superordinate construct** includes other constructs within its context, and a **subordinate construct** is one that is included in the context of another (superordinate) construct. For example, the constructs bright–dumb and attractive–unattractive might be subordinate to the superordinate construct good–bad.

It is important to recognize that the constructs within the person's construct system are interrelated to at least some extent. A person's behavior generally expresses the construct system rather than a single construct, and a change in one aspect of the construct system generally leads to changes in other parts of the system. Generally the constructs are organized to minimize incompatibilities and inconsistency. However, some constructs in the system can be in conflict with other constructs, and thus produce strain and difficulties for a person in making choices (Landfield, 1982).

Core Constructs: *Marital difficulties can revolve around the use of core constructs such as guilty–innocent.*

To summarize, according to Kelly's theory of personal constructs, an individual's personality is made up of his or her construct system. A person uses constructs to interpret the world and to anticipate events. The constructs a person uses thus define his or her world.

People differ both in the content of their constructs and in the organization of their construct systems. Individuals differ in the kinds of constructs they use, in the number of constructs available to them, in the complexity of organization of their construct systems, and in how open they are to changes in these construct systems. Two people are similar to the extent that they have similar construct systems. Most important, if you want to understand a person, you must know something about the constructs that person uses, the events subsumed under these constructs, the way in which these constructs tend to function, and the way in which they are organized in relation to one another to form a system.

The Role Construct Repertory (Rep) Test

Knowing other people, then, is knowing how they construe the world. How does one gain this knowledge of a person's constructs? Kelly's answer is direct—ask them to tell you what their constructs are. "If you don't know what is going on in a person's mind, ask him; he may tell you" (1958b, p. 330). Instead of using tests that had been developed by others in relation to different theoretical systems, Kelly developed his own assessment technique—the **Role Construct Repertory Test (Rep test)**. As an assessment technique the Rep test is probably more closely related to a theory of personality than is any other comprehensive personality test. The Rep test was developed out of Kelly's construct theory and was designed to be used as a way of eliciting personal constructs.

Basically the Rep test consists of two procedures—the development of a list of persons based on a *Role Title List* and the development of constructs based on the comparison of triads of persons. In the first procedure, the subject is given a Role Title List or list of roles (figures) believed to be of importance to all people. Illustrative role titles are mother, father, a teacher you liked, or a neighbor you find hard to understand. Generally, 20 to 30 roles are presented and subjects are asked to name a person they have known who fits each role. Following this, the examiner picks three specific figures from the list and asks the subject to indicate the way in which two are alike and are different from the third. The way in which two of the figures are seen as alike is called the *similarity pole* of the construct, and the way in which the third is different is called the *contrast pole* of the construct. For example, a subject might be asked to consider the persons named for Mother, Father, and Liked Teacher. In considering the three, the subject might decide that the people associated with the titles Father and Liked Teacher are similar in being outgoing and different from Mother, who is shy. Thus, the construct outgoing–shy has been formed. The subject is asked to consider other groups of three persons (triads), usually 20 to 30 of them. With each presentation of a triad, the subject generates a construct. The construct given may be the same as a previous one or a new construct. Illustrative constructs given by one person are presented in Table 10.1.

One can see how the Rep test follows from Kelly's theory since it elicits people's constructs—or ways of perceiving the world—based on their consideration of the way in which two things are similar to each other and dif-

Table 10.1   Role Construct Repertory Test: Illustrative Constructs

Similar Figures	Similarity Construct	Dissimilar Figure	Contrasting Construct
Self, Father	Emphasis on happiness	Mother	Emphasis on practicality
Teacher, Happy person	Calm	Sister	Anxious
Male friend, Female friend	Good listener	Past friend	Trouble expressing feelings
Disliked person, Employer	Uses people for own ends	Liked person	Considerate of others
Father, Successful person	Active in the community	Employer	Not active in the community
Disliked person, Employer	Cuts others down	Sister	Respectful of others
Mother, Male friend	Introvert	Past friend	Extravert
Self, Teacher	Self-sufficient	Person helped	Dependent
Self, Female friend	Artistic	Male friend	Uncreative
Employer, Female friend	Sophisticated	Brother	Unsophisticated

A REP TEST FOR CHILDREN: HOW DO THEY CONSTRUE PERSONALITY?

What kinds of constructs do you use to differentiate among people you know? For example, how are your mother and father similar to each other but different from yourself? Has the way you construe the similarities and differences between your parents and yourself changed since you were a child? A recent study by Donahue (1994) suggests that your construct system has changed both in content and in form. Donahue used a simplified version of Kelly's Rep test to elicit the constructs 11–year-olds use to describe personality. The children nominated nine individuals: self, best friend, an opposite-sex peer "who sits near you at school," a disliked peer, mother (or mother figure), father (or father figure), a liked teacher, the ideal self, and a disliked adult. The individuals' names were written on cards, and presented in sets of three. For example, to elicit the first construct, the children had to consider the self, the best friend, and the liked teacher. They then generated a word or phrase to describe how two of the individuals were alike, and an opposite word to describe how the third person was different from the other two. In this way, each child generated nine constructs.

What kinds of constructs did the children use? In terms of *content*, Donahue categorized the constructs according to the "Big Five" dimensions of personality description—extraversion, agreeableness, conscientiousness, emotional stability, and openness to experience (see Chapter 8). Although the children used constructs from all Big Five domains, the vast majority of their constructs dealt with Agreeableness (e.g., "is nice" versus "gets into fights") and Extraversion ("wants to be in charge" versus "likes to play quiet"). In contrast to the personality descriptions of adults, the children used the other three Big Five dimensions much less frequently. Thus, most of their constructs were interpersonal in nature—reflecting the importance of getting along with their peers, parents, and teachers.

In terms of *form*, Donahue coded six distinct ways of structuring or expressing personal constructs: facts ("from Oklahoma"), habits ("eats lots of sweets"), skills ("is the marble champion"), preferences ("likes comic books"), behavioral trends ("always in trouble with the teacher"), and traits ("shy"). As expected, the children used fewer trait descriptors and many more facts than adults. These findings suggest that children's construct systems are more concrete and become more abstract and psychological as they mature into adults.

These findings show that the Rep test allows us to see how personal construct systems are defined across ages in terms of both content and form. Of course, many other interesting comparisons are possible. For example, how do you think the construct systems of women and men differ? What about those of different ethnic groups or cultures? The Rep test allows us to explore both what is unique and what is shared in the way we construe the world around us.

ferent from the third. It is particularly attractive since subjects are completely free to express how they construe the world. At the same time, however, it makes a number of important assumptions. First, it is assumed that the list of roles presented to the subjects is representative of the important figures in their lives. Second, it is assumed that the constructs verbalized by the subject are, indeed, the ones used to construe the world. In turn, this assumes that the subjects can verbalize their constructs and that they feel free to report them in the testing situation. Finally, it is assumed that the words the subjects use in naming their constructs are adequate to give the examiner an understanding of how the subjects have organized their past events and how they anticipate the future.

One of the remarkable features of the Rep test is its tremendous flexibility. By varying the role titles or instructions, one can determine a whole range of constructs and meanings. For example, a modification of the Rep test has been used to determine the constructs consumers use in purchasing cosmetics and perfumes. These constructs are then used by advertisers to develop advertisements that will appeal to consumers (Stewart & Stewart, 1982). In a recent study, a Sex Rep was developed to measure the meanings men and women associate with the concepts masculinity and femininity. Earlier research on sex role stereotypes had found that both men and women perceive personality characteristics associated with the concept of masculinity more positively than they do characteristics associated with the concept of femininity. In contrast with such results, research using the Sex Rep suggested that women could see themselves as feminine and still be high on self-esteem and health. In other words, the cultural image or stereotype of the concepts masculinity and femininity may be quite different from the personal meanings associated with these concepts (Baldwin et al., 1986). At the stereotype level, the personality characteristics associated with the concept of masculinity may be more favorable or desirable for both men and women. At the personal level, however, psychological health may be reflected in men seeing themselves as masculine and women seeing themselves as feminine, with neither being perceived as intrinsically better than the other. The Rep test offers a method for getting at such personal meanings.

Cognitive Complexity–Simplicity

As noted, one can describe people not only in terms of the content of their constructs but also in terms of the structure of the construct system. Both the Rep test and modifications of it have again proved to be useful in this regard. An early effort to look at structural aspects of the construct system was Bieri's (1955) study of cognitive complexity. Bieri designated the degree to which a construct system is broken down (levels in the hierarchy) or differentiated as reflecting the system's **cognitive complexity–simplicity**. A cognitively complex system contains many constructs and provides for considerable differentiation in perception of

CURRENT
APPLICATIONS

COGNITIVE COMPLEXITY, LEADERSHIP, AND INTERNATIONAL CRISES

A series of fascinating studies suggests that cognitive style, in particular the dimension of cognitive complexity–simplicity, may have important implications for leadership and international relations. For example, would one suspect that greater or lesser cognitive complexity would be advantageous for a revolutionary leader? In a study of successful and unsuccessful leaders of four revolutions (American, Russian, Chinese, Cuban), it was found that low cognitive complexity was associated with success during the phase of revolutionary struggle but high complexity was associated with success in the poststruggle consolidation phase. The suggestion made was that a categorical, singleminded approach is desirable during the early phase but that a more flexible and integrated view is necessary during the later phase. Cognitive complexity would also appear to be valuable in exercising leadership in a large corporation. Thus successful corporate leaders are able to develop flexible plans, to include various kinds of information in their decisions, and to make connections between decisions.

How would such a characteristic relate to international relations? Evidence suggests that diplomatic communications prior to international crises are lower in cognitive complexity than are those prior to crises that do not result in war. For example, communications between the United States and the Soviet Union were much less complex prior to the outbreak of the Korean War than prior to the Berlin blockade or the Cuban missile crisis. Also, analysis of samples of Israeli and Arab speeches delivered to the United Nations General Assembly found that complexity was significantly reduced prior to each of the four wars in the Middle East (1948, 1956, 1967, 1973). Can such measures be used to predict and possibly avoid future wars or would deception be too easy?

SOURCES: Suedfeld & Tetlock, 1991; Tetlock, Peterson, & Berry, 1993.

---

phenomena. A cognitively simple system contains few constructs and provides for poor differentiation in perception of phenomena. A cognitively complex person sees people in a differentiated way, as having a variety of qualities, whereas a cognitively simple person sees people in an undifferentiated way, even to the extent of using only one construct (e.g., good–bad) in construing others. Using a modified Rep test, Bieri compared cognitively complex and cognitively simple subjects in relation to their accuracy in predicting the behavior of others and in relation to their ability to discriminate between themselves and others. As predicted, it was found that cognitively complex subjects were more accurate in predicting the behavior of others than were cognitively simple subjects. Furthermore, cognitively complex subjects were more able to recognize differences between themselves and others. Presumably the greater number of constructs available to complex subjects allows for both greater accuracy and greater potential for recognition of differences.

Bieri went on to construe cognitive complexity–simplicity as a dimension of personality, defining it as an information-processing variable: "Cognitive complexity may be defined as the capacity to construe social behavior in a multidimensional way" (Bieri et al., 1966). In one study of the way in which individuals process information, it was found that subjects high in complexity differed from subjects low in complexity in the way that they handled inconsistent information about a person. Subjects high in complexity tended to try to use the inconsistent information in forming an impression, whereas subjects low in complexity tended to form a consistent impression of the person and to reject all information inconsistent with that impression (Mayo & Crockett, 1964). Later research has also indicated that more complex individuals are better able to take the role of others (Adams-Webber, 1979, 1982; Crockett, 1982). In terms of the Big Five dimensions described in Chapter 8, complexity is related most strongly to the fifth factor, openness to new experiences (Tetlock, Peterson, & Berry, 1993).

Thus, the Rep test can be used to determine the content and structure of an individual's construct system, as well as to compare the effects of different construct system structures. The Rep test has the advantages of arising from a theory and of allowing subjects to generate their own constructs, instead of forcing subjects to use dimensions provided by the tester. In sum, Kelly posits that the structure of personality consists of the construct system of the individual. An individual is what he construes himself and others to be, and the Rep test is a device to ascertain the nature of these constructions.

PROCESS

In his process view of human behavior, Kelly radically departed from traditional theories of motivation. As already mentioned, the psychology of personal constructs does not interpret behavior in terms of motivation, drives, and needs. For personal construct theory, the term *motivation* is redundant. This term assumes that a person is inert and needs something to get started. But, if we assume that people are basically active, the controversy as to what prods an inert organism into action becomes a dead issue. "Instead, the organism is delivered fresh into the psychological world alive and struggling" (Kelly, 1955, p. 37). Kelly contrasted other theories of motivation with his own position in the following way:

> Motivational theories can be divided into two types, push theories and pull theories. Under push theories we find such terms as

drive, motive, or even stimulus. Pull theories use such constructs as purpose, value, or need. In terms of a well-known metaphor, these are the pitchfork theories on the one hand and the carrot theories on the other. But our theory is neither of these. Since we prefer to look to the nature of the animal himself, ours is probably best called a jackass theory.

SOURCE: Kelly, 1958a, p. 50

Anticipating Events: Predicting the Future

The concept of motive traditionally has been used to explain why humans are active and why their activity takes a specific direction. Since Kelly did not feel the need for the concept of motive to account for a person's activity, how did he account for the direction of activity? Kelly's position is simply stated in his fundamental postulate: *A person's processes are psychologically channeled by the ways in which he anticipates events.* Kelly offers this postulate as a given and does not question its truth. The postulate implies that we seek prediction, that we anticipate events, that we reach out to the future through the window of the present.

In experiencing events, an individual observes similarities and contrasts, thereby developing constructs. On the basis of these constructs, individuals, like true scientists, anticipate the future. As we see the same events repeated over and over, we modify our constructs so that they will lead to more accurate predictions. Constructs are tested in terms of their predictive efficiency. But what accounts for the direction of behavior? Again, like the scientist, people choose the course of behavior that they believe offers the greatest opportunity for anticipating future events. Scientists try to develop better theories, theories that lead to the efficient prediction of events, and individuals try to develop better construct systems. Thus, according to Kelly, a person chooses the alternative that promises the greatest further development of the construct system.

In making a choice of a particular construct, the individual, in a sense, makes a "bet" by anticipating a particular event or set of events. If there are inconsistencies in the construct system, the bets will not add up; they will cancel each other out. If the system is consistent, a prediction is made that can be tested. If the anticipated event does occur, the prediction has been upheld and the construct validated, at least for the time being. If the anticipated event does not occur, the construct has been invalidated. In the latter case, the individual must develop a new construct or must loosen or expand the old construct to include the prediction of the event that took place.

In essence, then, individuals make predictions and consider further changes in their construct systems on the basis of whether those changes have led to accurate predictions. Notice that individuals do not seek reinforcement or the avoidance of pain; instead, they seek validation and expansion of their construct systems. If a person expects something unpleasant and that event occurs, he or she experiences validation regardless of the fact that it was a negative, unpleasant event. Indeed, a painful event may even be preferred to a neutral or pleasant event if it confirms the predictive system (Pervin, 1964).

One should understand that Kelly is not suggesting that the individual seeks certainty, such as would be found in the repetitive ticking of a clock. The boredom people feel with repeated events and the fatalism that comes as a result of the inevitable are usually avoided wherever possible. Rather, individuals seek to anticipate events and to increase the range of convenience or boundaries of their construct systems. This point leads to a distinction between the views of Kelly and the views of Rogers. According to Kelly, individuals do not seek consistency for consistency's sake or even for self-consistency. Instead, individuals seek to anticipate events, and it is a consistent system that allows them to do this.

Anxiety, Fear, and Threat

Thus far, Kelly's system appears to be reasonably simple and straightforward. The process view becomes more complicated with the introduction of the concepts of anxiety, fear, and threat. Kelly defined **anxiety** in the following way: Anxiety is the recognition that the events with which one is confronted lie outside the range of convenience of one's construct system. One is anxious when one is without constructs, when one has "lost his structural grip on events," when one is "caught with his constructs down." People protect themselves from anxiety in various ways. Confronted by events they cannot construe—that is, that lie outside their range of convenience—individuals may broaden a construct and permit it to apply to a greater variety of events, or they may narrow their constructs and focus on minute details. For example, suppose an individual who has the construct caring person–selfish person and considers herself a caring person then finds herself acting in a selfish way. How can she construe herself and events? She can broaden the construct caring person to include selfish behavior, or—probably more easily in this case—restrict the construct caring person to important people in her life, rather than people generally. In the latter case, the construct applies to a more limited set of people or events.

In contrast to anxiety, one experiences **fear** when a new construct appears to be about to enter the construct system. Of even greater significance is the experience of **threat**. Threat is defined as the awareness of imminent comprehensive change in one's core structure. A person feels threatened when a major shakeup in the construct system is about to occur. One feels threatened by death if it is perceived as imminent and if it involves a drastic change in one's core constructs. Death is not threatening when it does not seem imminent or when it is not construed as being fundamental to the meaning of one's life.

Threat, in particular, has a wide range of ramifications. Whenever people undertake some new activity, they expose themselves to confusion and threat. Individuals experience threat when they realize that their construct system is about to be drastically affected by what has been discovered. "This is the moment of threat. It is the threshold between confusion and certainty, between anxiety and boredom. It is precisely at this moment when we are most tempted to turn back" (Kelly, 1964, p. 141). The response to threat may be to give up the adventure—to regress to old constructs to avoid panic. Threat occurs as we venture into human understanding and when we stand on the brink of a profound change in ourselves.

Threat, the awareness of imminent comprehensive change in one's core structure, can be experienced in relation to many things. Consider, for example, the experience of music majors who are going to perform before a music jury that will determine whether they pass for the semester. To what extent can they be expected to experience threat associated with the possibility of failure? Why should some music majors experience more performance anxiety than others? Following Kelly, two psychologists tested the hypothesis that students would feel threatened by the possibility of failure by a music jury to the extent that such failure implied reorganization of the self-construal component of their construct system. To test this hypothesis, at the beginning of the semester, music majors were administered a Threat Index consisting of 40 core constructs (e.g., competent–incompetent, productive–unproductive, bad–good) in relation to which they first rated the *self* and then the *self if*

Construct Change: *Peace Corps volunteers, such as this one, have had to be prepared to develop new constructs as they have been exposed to new values, attitudes, and behaviors in different cultures.*

performed poorly on the jury. The Threat Index score consisted of the number of core constructs on which the *self* and *self if performed poorly* were rated on opposite poles. Anxiety was measured through the use of a questionnaire at the beginning of the semester and three days before the onset of the music juries. Consistent with personal construct theory, those students who reported that failure on the jury would result in the most comprehensive change in self-construal were also those who reported the greatest increase in anxiety as the date of the jury approached (Tobacyk & Downs, 1986).

Unfortunately, the investigators in this study used the concept of anxiety in a way that was not necessarily consistent with Kelly's views. Even more significant, what was not studied in this case was the experiences of students anticipating the possibility of performing much better before the jury than would be expected on the basis of their self-construal; that is, would comprehensive change as a result of unexpected exceptional performance also be associated with threat? This is important since in Kelly's view it is the awareness of imminent comprehensive change in the construct system that is threatening, not failure per se.

Recently some personal construct psychologists have focused their research attention on attitudes toward death, both in terms of the ways in which death is construed and the amount of threat associated with death (Moore & Neimeyer, 1991; Neimeyer, 1994). In terms of how death is construed, research suggests that people use constructs such as purposeful–purposeless, positive–negative, acceptance–rejection, anticipated–unanticipated, and final–afterlife. In terms of the amount of threat associated with death, research has involved measurement of the discrepancy between the ways in which individuals construe themselves and the ways in which they construe death. In other words, in personal construct theory terms death threat is high when the person is unable to construe death as relevant to the self. As measured by the *Threat Index*, individuals rate themselves and their own death on constructs such as healthy–sick, strong–weak, predictable–random, and useful–useless. An individual's threat score represents the difference between the two sets of ratings. Presumably in the case of a large self–death discrepancy, interpretation of the death construct as relevant to the self would involve comprehensive change in one's construct system. Death threat, as defined in this way, has been found to be lower in hospice patients than general hospital patients, lower in individuals open to feelings as opposed to those who repress feelings, and lower in self-actualizing individuals as opposed to individuals less oriented toward growth and self-actualization.

What makes the concepts of anxiety, fear, and threat so significant is that they suggest a new dimension to Kelly's view of human functioning. The dynamics of functioning can now be seen to involve the interplay between the individual's wish to expand the construct system and the desire to avoid the threat of disruption of that system. Individuals always seek to maintain and enhance their predictive systems. However, in the face of anxiety and threat, individuals may rigidly adhere to a constricted system instead of venturing out into the risky realm of expansion of their construct systems.

Summary of the Process View

To summarize, Kelly assumes an active organism, and he does not posit any motivational forces. For Kelly, people behave as scientists in construing events, in making predictions, and in seeking expansion of the construct system. Sometimes, not unlike the scientist, we are made so anxious by the unknowns and so threatened by the unfamiliar that we seek to hold on to absolute truths and become dogmatic. On the other hand, when we are behaving as good scientists, we are able to adopt the invitational mood and to expose our construct systems to the diversity of events that make up life.

GROWTH AND DEVELOPMENT

Kelly was never explicit about the origins of construct systems. He stated that constructs are derived from observing repeated patterns of events. But he did little to elaborate on the kinds of events that lead to differences like the ones between simple and complex construct systems. Kelly's comments relating to growth and development are limited to an emphasis on the development of preverbal constructs in infancy and the interpretation of culture as involving a process of learned expectations. People belong to the same cultural group in that they share certain ways of construing events and have the same kinds of expectations regarding behavior.

Developmental research associated with personal construct theory generally has emphasized two kinds of change. First, there has been exploration of increases in complexity of the construct system associated with age (Crockett, 1982; Hayden, 1982; Loevinger, 1993). Second, there has been exploration of qualitative changes in the nature of the constructs formed and in the ability of children to be more empathic or aware of the construct systems of others (Adams-Webber, 1982; Donahue, 1994; Morrison & Cometa, 1982; Sigel, 1981). In terms of construct system complexity, there is evidence that as children develop they increase the number of constructs available to them, make finer differentiations, and show more hierarchical organization or integration. In terms of empathy, there is evidence that as children develop they become increasingly aware that many events are not related to the self and increasingly able to appreciate the constructs of others (Sigel, 1981).

Two studies have been reported that are relevant to the question of the determinants of complex cognitive structures. In one study, the subjects' level of cognitive complexity was found to be related to the variety of cultural backgrounds to which they had been exposed in childhood

Development of the Construct System: *Being exposed to many stimuli facilitates development of the construct system. Aware of this, some parents try to develop "superbabies."*

(Sechrest & Jackson, 1961). In another study, parents of cognitively complex children were found to be more likely to grant autonomy and less likely to be authoritarian than were the parents of children low in cognitive complexity (Cross, 1966). Presumably, the opportunity to examine many different events and to have many different experiences is conducive to the development of a complex structure. One would also expect to find that children who experience a longstanding and severe threat from authoritarian parents would develop constricted and inflexible construct systems.

The question of factors determining the content of constructs and the complexity of construct systems is of critical importance. In particular, it is relevant to the field of education, since a part of education appears to be the development of complex, flexible, and adaptive construct systems. Unfortunately, Kelly himself made few statements in this area, and research is only now beginning to elaborate on this part of the theory.

MAJOR CONCEPTS

Construct. In Kelly's theory, a way of perceiving, construing, or interpreting events.

Constructive alternativism. Kelly's view that there is no objective reality or absolute truth, but only alternative ways of construing events.

Range of convenience. In Kelly's personal construct theory, those events or phenomena that are covered by a construct or by the construct system.

Focus of convenience. In Kelly's personal construct theory, those events or phenomena that are best covered by a construct or by the construct system.

Similarity pole. In Kelly's personal construct theory, the similarity pole of a construct is defined by the way in which two elements are perceived to be similar.

Contrast pole. In Kelly's personal construct theory, the contrast pole of a construct is defined by the way in which a third element is perceived as different from two other elements that are used to form a similarity pole.

Verbal construct. In Kelly's personal construct theory, a construct that can be expressed in words.

Preverbal construct. In Kelly's personal construct theory, a construct that is used but cannot be expressed in words.

Submerged construct. In Kelly's personal construct theory, a construct that once could be expressed in words, but now either one or both poles of the construct cannot be verbalized.

Core construct. In Kelly's personal construct theory, a construct that is basic to the person's construct system and cannot be altered without serious consequences for the rest of the system.

Peripheral construct. In Kelly's personal construct theory, a construct that is not basic to the construct system and can be altered without serious consequences for the rest of the system.

Subordinate construct. In Kelly's personal construct theory, a construct that is lower in the construct system and is thereby included in the context of another (superordinate) construct.

Superordinate construct. In Kelly's personal construct theory, a construct that is higher in the construct system and thereby includes other constructs within its context.

Role Construct Repertory Test (Rep test). Kelly's test to determine the constructs used by a person, the relationships among constructs, and how the constructs are applied to specific people.

Cognitive complexity–simplicity. An aspect of a person's cognitive functioning that is defined at one end by the use of many constructs with many relationships to one another (complexity) and at the other end by the use of few constructs with limited relationships to one another (simplicity).

Anxiety. An emotion expressing a sense of impending threat or danger. In Kelly's personal construct theory, anxiety occurs when the person recognizes that his or her construct system does not apply to the events being perceived.

Fear (Kelly). In Kelly's personal construct theory, fear occurs when a new construct is about to enter the person's construct system.

Threat (Kelly). In Kelly's personal construct theory, threat occurs when the person is aware of an imminent, comprehensive change in his or her construct system.

REVIEW

1. The personal construct theory of George Kelly emphasizes the way in which the person construes or interprets events.

2. Kelly viewed the person as a scientist—an observer of events who formulates concepts or constructs to organize phenomena and uses these constructs to predict the future.

3. According to the position of constructive alternativism, there is no absolute truth. Rather, people choose among alternative constructs and always are free to reconstrue events.

4. According to Kelly, a theory has a range of convenience, including what is covered by it, and a focus of convenience, indicating where within that range the theory works best.

5. Kelly viewed personality in terms of the person's construct system—the types of constructs the person formed and how they were organized. Constructs are formed on the basis of observations of similarities among events. Core constructs are basic to the system, whereas peripheral constructs are less important. Superordinate constructs are higher in the hierarchy and include other constructs under them, whereas subordinate constructs are lower in the hierarchy.

6. Kelly developed the Role Construct Repertory Test (Rep test) to assess the content and structure of the person's construct system. The Rep test has been used to study the extent to which the person can be described as cognitively complex or simple, indicating the extent to which the person can view the world in differentiated terms.

7. Kelly did not feel the need for a motive concept. Instead, he assumed that people are active, and postulated that people anticipate events and seek to predict the future. Change in the construct system is dictated by efforts to improve prediction.

8. According to Kelly, the person experiences anxiety when aware that events lie outside the construct system, experiences fear when a new construct is about to emerge, and experiences threat when there is the danger of comprehensive change in the construct system.

9. Some constructs are learned prior to the development of language (preverbal constructs), but the majority of constructs can be expressed in words. A healthy, developing construct system becomes more complex—both more differentiated and more integrative. However, if the person feels threatened to construe life in a different way, the construct system may remain simple, rigid, and fixed.

A COGNITIVE THEORY OF PERSONALITY: APPLICATIONS AND EVALUATION OF KELLY'S THEORY

A good actor spends a lot of time and energy "getting into character." She must think about and understand her character so that she can submerge herself in her character's world and see that world through her character's eyes. Kelly would probably say that the actor must learn how to use the character's *construct system*. In fact, he espoused a therapeutic approach called *fixed-role therapy* which was based on this idea.

In fixed-role therapy, clients are instructed to act as if they were another person—a person whose construct system will combat the dysfunctional aspects of their own. In this chapter we consider the clinical applications of Kelly's personal construct theory. Kelly felt that any significant theory of personality has to suggest ways to help people. He saw the area of psychotherapy not only as a major source of interest and concern, but also as a major "focus of convenience" of personal construct theory.

QUESTIONS TO BE ADDRESSED IN THIS CHAPTER

1. How can one understand disturbed psychological functioning from a cognitive–personal construct perspective?

2. Given Kelly's theory of personality, what kind of approach to therapy might be expected to follow from it?

3. Does Kelly's emphasis on constructs suggest ways of comparing personality theories with one another?

CLINICAL APPLICATIONS

PSYCHOPATHOLOGY

According to Kelly, psychopathology is a disordered response to anxiety. As in the theories of Freud and Rogers, the concepts of anxiety, fear, and threat play a major role in Kelly's theory of psychopathology. However, it must be kept in mind that these concepts, although retained, have been redefined in terms relevant to personal construct theory.

For Kelly, psychopathology is defined in terms of disordered functioning of a **construct system**. Only a poor scientist retains a theory and makes the same predictions despite repeated research failures. Similarly, abnormal behavior involves efforts to retain the content and structure of the construct system despite repeated incorrect predictions or invalidations. At the root of this rigid adherence to a construct system are anxiety, fear, and threat. Kelly stated that one could construe human behavior as being directed away from ultimate anxiety. Psychological disorders are disorders involving anxiety and faulty efforts to reestablish the sense of being able to anticipate events:

> There is a sense in which all disorders of communication are disorders involving anxiety. A "neurotic" person casts about frantically for new ways of construing the events of his world. Sometimes he works on "little" events, sometimes on "big" events, but he is always fighting off anxiety. A "psychotic" person appears to have found some temporary solution for his anxiety. But it is a precarious solution, at best, and must be sustained in the face of evidence which, for most of us, would be invalidating.
>
> SOURCE: Kelly, 1955, pp. 895–896

Problems in the Construct System

What are some of the faulty ways in which people try to hold on to their construct systems? These efforts involve problems in (1) the ways in which constructs are applied to new events, (2) the ways in which constructs are used to make predictions, and (3) the ways in which the overall system is organized. Let us consider an illustration of each. An example of the pathological application of constructs is that of making constructs excessively **permeable** or excessively **impermeable**. An excessively permeable construct allows almost any new content into it, whereas an excessively impermeable construct admits no new elements into it. Excessive permeability can lead to the use of just a few very broad constructs and the lack of recognition of important differences among people and events. Too much becomes lumped together, as in stereotypes. Excessive impermeability can lead to pigeonholing each new experience, as if everything is distinctive, and to rejecting events that cannot be pigeonholed. This pattern of response is found in people who are described as being very compulsive.

An illustration of the pathological use of constructs to make predictions is excessive **tightening** and excessive **loosening**. In excessive tightening, the person makes the same kinds of predictions regardless of the circumstances. In excessive loosening, the person makes excessively varied predictions with the same construct. In neither case can prediction be very accurate since both involve ignoring circumstances that might call for shifts in the construct system—in the first case through always predicting the same and in the second case through random, chaotic predictions. Tightening can be seen in the compulsive person who rigidly expects life to be the same regardless of changes in circumstances, whereas loosening can be seen in the psychotic person whose construct system is so chaotic that it cannot be used to communicate with others: "They [schizophrenic clients] are not caught short of constructs. But what constructs!" (Kelly, 1955, p. 497).

Personal construct researchers have investigated the extent to which schizophrenics construe people in unstable and loose ways. For example, in one study subjects were asked to rank eight photographs on six characteristics: kind, stupid, selfish, sincere, mean, and honest. They were then asked to make the ratings again without relying on their memory for the previous ratings. Two questions were of particular interest. First, to what extent would people see the concepts as being related? An intensity score was derived as a measure of the extent to which the subject's eight rank orderings were related to one another. A low intensity score suggested that the subject was treating these six characteristics as if they had no relation to one another. Second, to what extent would people maintain their rankings from the first series to the second series? Because the photographs remained the same and there had been no intervening experience, this correlation essentially measured the test–retest reliability or consistency of the person's ratings. Here a consistency score was used; a low consistency score indicated that the person applied the concepts in very different ways on the two trials.

A number of patient groups and a normal group of subjects were tested in the above ways. The average intensity scores and consistency scores were then calculated for the members of each group. The hypothesis tested was that thought-disordered schizophrenics would have particularly low intensity and consistency scores, indicative of loose and unstable construing. Indeed, this was found to be the case. Relative both to other patient groups as well as to the normal group, the thought-disordered schizophrenic group showed significantly lower intensity and consistency scores (Bannister & Fransella, 1966). In sum, such patients can be characterized in terms of the types of constructs formed, as well as in terms of how these constructs are employed.

Finally, we come to disordered efforts to maintain the overall organization of the construct system, as illustrated in **constriction** and **dilation**. Constriction involves a narrowing of the construct system to minimize incompatibilities. The range and focus of convenience of the construct system become quite small. Constriction tends to be found in people who are depressed and who limit their interests, narrowing their attention to a smaller and smaller area. In contrast, in dilation the person attempts to broaden the construct system and to reorganize it at a more comprehensive level. Extreme dilation is observed in the behavior of the manic person who jumps from topic to topic and who makes sweeping generalizations with few ideas. It is as if everything can now be included in the construct system of this person.

Note should be made that all of these problems involve aspects of the structure of the construct system rather than the content of the constructs. Relatively little research has been done on problematic construct content, reflecting personal construct theory's emphasis on alternative ways of construing reality (Winter, 1992). Some personal construct theorists suggest, however, that even if alternative constructions are possible, specific construct content can be problematic for the individual. For example, the lack of abstract constructs may make it difficult for the individual to see relationships among events, and the lack of interpersonal constructs or emotion constructs will limit the person's ability to differentiate among interpersonal relationships or emotional experiences.

In sum, fundamental to Kelly's views of psychopathology is the effort to avoid anxiety, the experience that one's construct system is not applicable to events, and to avoid threat, the awareness of imminent comprehensive change in the construct system. To protect against anxiety and threat, an individual employs protective devices, a view not far from the Freudian view of anxiety and defense. Indeed, Kelly suggested that in the face of anxiety, individuals may act in ways that will make their constructs unavailable for verbalization. Thus, for example, in the face of anxiety, individuals may **submerge** one end of a construct or suspend elements that do not fit well into a construct. These are responses to anxiety that seem very similar to the concept of repression.

Suicide and Hostility

These faulty devices to prevent anxiety and avoid the threat of change in the construct system illustrate Kelly's efforts to interpret pathological behavior within the framework of personal construct theory. Another such illustration concerns suicide. According to the psychoanalytic view, every suicide is a potential homicide. Because of anxiety or guilt, the hostility that would otherwise be directed toward some other person becomes directed instead toward the self. Not so, according to the psychology of personal constructs. Kelly (1961) interpreted suicide as an act to validate one's life or as an act of abandonment. In the latter case, suicide occurs because of fatalism or total anxiety—because the course of events is so obvious that there is no point in waiting around for the outcome (fatalism), or because everything is so unpredictable that the only definite thing to do is to abandon the scene altogether. As noted, we often must choose between immediate certainty and wider understanding. In suicide, the choice is for the former and represents ultimate constriction. "For the man of constricted outlook whose world begins to crumble, death may appear to provide the only immediate certainty which he can lay his hands on" (Kelly, 1955, p. 64).

Although Kelly did not emphasize the concept of hostility in relation to suicide, he did recognize its importance in human functioning. Again, however, the concept is redefined in terms relevant to personal construct theory. Kelly made an important distinction between aggression and hostility, one that often is absent in other theories. According to Kelly, **aggression** involves the active expansion of a person's construct system. This expansion does not interfere with the functioning of other people. In contrast, **hostility** occurs when one tries to make others behave in an expected way. For example, it would be hostile for a person to intimidate someone because the former expects the latter to behave in a submissive way. According to this view, the hostile person does not intend to do harm. Rather, injury is an accidental outcome of the effort to protect the construct system by attempting to make people behave in expected ways; the emphasis is on protection of the construct system. The opposite of hostility is curiosity and respect for the freedom of movement of others.

Summary

To summarize Kelly's view of psychopathology, we return to the analogy of the scientist. Scientists attempt to predict events through the use of theories. Scientists develop poor theories when they fear venturing out into the unknown, when they fear testing hypotheses and making bets, when they adhere rigidly to their theory in the face of contradictory evidence, when they can account only for trivia, and when they try to say that they are accounting for things that, in fact, are outside the range of convenience of their theories. When scientists construe in these ways, we say they are bad scientists. When people construe in these ways, we refer to them as sick. When people know how to stay loose and also tighten up, we call them creative and reward them for their efforts. When people stay too loose or too "uptight," we say they are ill and consider hospitalization. It all depends on their constructs—and on how others construe the constructs.

CHANGE

The process of positive change is discussed by Kelly in terms of the development of better construct systems. If sickness represents the continued use of constructs in the face of consistent invalidation, psychotherapy is the process of helping clients to improve their predictions. In psychotherapy, clients are trained to be better scientists. Psychotherapy is a process of reconstruing—of reconstructing the construct system. This means that some constructs need to be replaced and some new ones added; some need to be tightened, others loosened; and some need to be made more permeable, others less permeable. Whatever the details of the process, *psychotherapy is the psychological reconstruction of life.*

Conditions Favoring Change

According to Kelly's theory, three conditions are favorable to the formation of new constructs. *First, and perhaps most important, there must be an atmosphere of experimentation.* This means that, for example, in therapy "one does not 'play for keeps.' Constructs, in the true scientific tradition, are seen as 'being tried on for size' " (Kelly, 1955, p. 163). In psychotherapy, one creates the invitational mood and accepts the language of hypothesis. Psychotherapy is a form of experimentation. In therapy, constructs (hypotheses) are developed, experiments are performed, and hypotheses are revised on the basis of empirical evidence. By being permissive and responsive, by providing the client with the tools of experimentation, and by encouraging the client to make hypotheses, the therapist helps the client to develop as a scientist.

The second key condition for change is the *provision of new elements*. Conditions favorable to change include new elements that are relatively unbound by old constructs. The therapy room is a "protected environment" in which new elements can be recognized and confronted. Therapists themselves represent a new element in relation to which their clients can start to develop new constructs. It is here that the question of *transference* emerges, and the therapist must ask: "In what role is the client now casting me?" Clients may attempt to transfer a construct from their repertory that was applicable in the past and to use it in relation to their therapists. They may construe the therapist as a parent, as an absolver of guilt, as an authority figure, as a prestige figure, or as a stooge. Whatever the content of the transference, the therapist tries to provide fresh, new elements in an atmosphere of make-believe and experimentation.

Along with this, therapists provide the third condition for change; they make *validating data available*. We are told that knowledge of results facilitates learning. We know that, given a supportive atmosphere and the permeable aspects of the construct system, invalidation does lead to change (Bieri, 1953; Poch, 1952). The therapist provides new elements in a situation in which the client will at first attempt to use old constructs. It is the therapist's task to share personal perceptions of and reactions to the client, against which the client can check his or her own hypotheses: "By providing validating data in the form of responses to a wide variety of constructions on the part of the client, some of them quite loose, fanciful, or naughty, the clinician gives the client an opportunity to validate constructs, an opportunity which is not normally available to him" (Kelly, 1955, p. 165).

Fixed-role Therapy

We know that there are individual differences in resistance to change and that rigidity is related to psychopathology (Pervin, 1960a). However, given an atmosphere of experimentation, given new elements, and given validating data, people do change. Conversely, the conditions unfavorable for change include threat, preoccupation with old material, and the lack of a "laboratory" in which to experiment. It is within the context of the former conditions of change that Kelly developed a specific therapeutic technique—**fixed-role therapy**.

Fixed-role therapy assumes that, psychologically, people are what they represent themselves to be and that people are what they do. Fixed-role therapy encourages clients to *represent themselves in new ways*, to *behave in new ways*, to *construe themselves in new ways*, and thereby to *become new people*. The purpose of this entire procedure is to reestablish the spirit of exploration, to establish the construction of life as a creative process. Kelly was wary of the emphasis on "being oneself" as Rogers had suggested (see Chapters 5 and 6); how could one be anything else but oneself? To Kelly, remaining what one is seemed uninteresting and unadventurous. Instead he suggested that people should feel free to make believe, to play, and thereby to become.

In fixed-role therapy, clients are presented with a new personality sketch that they are asked to act out. On the basis of some understanding of the client, a group of psychologists gets together to write a description of a new person. The task for the clients is to behave as if they were that person. The personality sketch written for each client involves the development of a new personality. Many characteristics presented in the sketch are in sharp contrast with the person's actual functioning. In the light of construct theory, Kelly suggested that it might be easier for people to play up what they believe to be the opposite of the way they generally behave than to behave just a little bit differently. Design of the sketch involves setting in motion processes that will have effects throughout the construct system. Fixed-role therapy does not aim at the readjustment of minor parts. Instead, it aims to reconstruct a personality. It offers a new role, a new personality for the client in which new hypotheses can be tested; it offers the client the opportunity to test out new ways of construing events under the full protection of make-believe.

How does the process of fixed-role therapy work? After a personality sketch is drawn up, it is presented to the client. The client decides whether the sketch sounds like someone he would like to know, and whether he would feel comfortable with such a person. This is done to make sure that the new personality will not be excessively threatening to the client. In the next phase of fixed-role therapy, the therapist invites the client to act as if he were that person. For about two weeks, the client is asked to forget who he is and to be this other person. If the new person is called Tom Jones, then the client is told the following: "For two weeks, try to forget who you are or that you ever were. You are Tom Jones. You act like him. You think like him. You talk to your friends the way you think he would talk. You do the things you think he would do. You even have his interests and you enjoy the things he would enjoy." The client may resist, he may feel that this is play-acting and that it is hypocritical, but he is encouraged, in an accepting manner, to try it and see how it works. The client is not told that this is what he should eventually be, but he is asked to assume the new personality. He is asked to give up being himself temporarily so that he can discover himself.

During the following weeks, the client eats, sleeps, and feels the role. Periodically, he meets with the therapist to discuss problems in acting the role. There may be some rehearsing of the personality sketch in the therapy session so that the therapist and client will have a chance to examine the functioning of the new construct system when it is actually in use. The therapist must be prepared to act as if he or she were various persons and to accept the invitational mood. The therapist must at every moment "play in strong support of an actor—the client—who is continually fumbling his lines and contaminating his role" (Kelly, 1955, p. 399).

Fixed-Role Therapy—*In Kelly's fixed-role therapy clients are encouraged to behave and represent themselves in new ways. Drawing by Lippman; Copyright © 1972 The New Yorker Magazine, Inc.*

Fixed-role therapy was not the only therapeutic technique discussed or used by Kelly (Bieri, 1986). However, it is one that is particularly associated with personal construct theory, and it does exemplify some of the principles of the personal construct theory of change. The goal of therapeutic change is the individual's reconstruction of the self. The individual drops some constructs, creates new ones, does some tightening and loosening, and develops a construct system that leads to more accurate predictions. The therapist encourages the client to make believe, to experiment, to spell out alternatives, and to reconstrue the past in the light of new constructs. The process of therapy is complex. Different clients must be treated differently, and the resistance to change must be overcome. However, positive change is possible in a situation where a good director assists in the playing of the human drama or a good teacher assists in the development of a creative scientist.

Illustrative Research

Research in psychotherapy has focused on factors in the construct system and in the therapeutic relationship that affect change. As one might expect, there is evidence that superordinate constructs are harder to change than subordinate constructs, presumably because they threaten much more disruption of the construct system. It also appears that constructs must loosen before change can occur. A critical factor in the loosening process is the recognition of new elements. In this regard, Landfield (1971) found that a certain amount of similarity in therapist–client construct systems is necessary to facilitate communication but, at the same time, a certain amount of structural difference appears to facilitate change. Psychotherapy, then, involves a therapist–client relationship that facilitates the reconstruction of the client's construct system.

Personal construct therapists have attempted to explore the potential utility of Kelly's theory in varied ways and in different settings (Epting, 1984). In some cases, this has involved substantial changes in procedure. In one approach, imagery is used to recall past events, leading to a reconstruction of these events (Morrison & Cometa, 1982). For example, one patient construed her father only in negative terms. However, with the use of imagery techniques, she was able to recall and imagine scenes in which her father had acted in positive ways, leading to the addition of new constructs or the increased permeability of some that already existed. Despite these and related efforts, however, much of Kelly's theory of therapy remains unexplored.

Comparison with Other Approaches

As with the theory as a whole, personal construct therapy has similarities with but is not identical to other therapeutic approaches (Winter, 1992). In relation to psychoanalysis, Kelly respected Freud as a clinician and accepted—at times in a revised form—such psychoanalytic concepts as the unconscious, anxiety and defense, transference, and resistance to change. At the same time, Kelly rejected psychoanalytic theory and the psychoanalytic emphasis on insight as the discovery of truth or reality. For Kelly, therapy was much more a process of construction and reconstruction than one of discovering some reality or unconscious truth.

Kelly's approach to therapy may also be seen as similar to the phenomenological (Rogers) and humanistic-existential emphasis on meaning, experience, self-actualization, and a holistic view of the person. At the same time, Kelly viewed the therapist as a much more active participant in the therapeutic endeavor and, as in his emphasis on role playing, placed much less emphasis on the genuineness of the therapist. Contrasting his approach with that of Rogers, Kelly suggested that "the client comes to the therapist not to watch him be 'sincere' for an hour, but to get help" (Kelly, 1955, p.1153). In comparison with learning-behavioral approaches, Kelly shared an emphasis on experimentation and the testing out of constructs through new ways of behaving. However, he also suggested that "to look only at behaviors is to lose sight of man" (Kelly, 1969, p.137). Personal construct therapists also are critical of what they view as a tendency for behavior therapists to impose their own constructions on clients. Finally, a brief comparison can be made with cog-

Table 11.1   Comparison of Personal Construct Therapy with Other Therapeutic Approaches

Psychotherapeutic Approach	Similarity	Contrast
Psychoanalysis	Unconscious (submerged constructs), anxiety and defense, transference	Constructive alternativism vs. discovery of truth (insight)
Phenomenology Humanistic-Existential	Holistic, focus on meaning and experience, emphasis on growth	"The client comes to the therapist not to watch him be 'sincere' for an hour but to get help" (Kelly, 1955, p.1153).
Learning-Behavioral	Emphasis on experimenting with new ways of behaving and testing out hypotheses (constructs)	"To look only at behaviors is to lose sight of man" (Kelly, 1969, p.137)

(Adapted from Winter, 1992)

nitive therapies, to be considered in later chapters. Although personal construct therapy shares with them an emphasis on problematic cognitions and construct systems, personal construct therapy is more accepting of the importance of emotion and places less emphasis on unrealistic thoughts and cognitions. In sum, personal construct therapists view therapy as involving the reconstruction of the construct system, a process in which therapists are active participants in helping clients behave, feel, and think in different ways while discovering new ways of construing the self and life (Table 11.1).

A Case Example: Ronald Barrett

From the phenomenological point of view, and from that of personal construct theory, the client is always right. Although clinicians may choose to construe events differently, they should never ignore the constructions of their clients. Hence, Kelly was led to say: "If you do not know what is wrong with a person, ask him: He may tell you." A useful approach in understanding clients is to have them write a character sketch of themselves. One client who did this was Ronald Barrett, a university student who came to a counseling service with complaints regarding academic, vocational, and social adjustments.

Self-descriptive Sketch

In his character sketch, Ronald began by indicating that he appears to be quiet and calm, and that he dislikes drawing unfavorable attention to himself. Aside from this quiet behavior in public, however, he reported that he was likely to flare up easily. He showed little overt anger, but he readily became frustrated and worked up about his own errors or those of others.

He thought much of his behavior was an effort to impress others and to show that he was considerate and sincere. He considered morals and ethics as guides to behavior and guilt the result of not being sufficiently kind. Ronald described himself as striving to be logical, accurate, and aware of minor technicalities. Finally, he described himself as relatively inflexible and as attaching too much importance to kissing women.

Kelly's Construction

In his discussion of the sketch, Kelly observed that a conventional approach to Ronald's self-discipline approach would emphasize its compulsive aspects. However, beyond this view, Kelly suggested attempting to see the world through the client's eyes. In his analysis of Ronald's account, Kelly emphasized the need to look at the order in which the material is presented, the way it is organized, the terms (inconsiderate, sincerity, conscientiousness, morals, ethics, guilt, kindhearted) that are used, the themes that are repeated, and the similarities and contrasts that are made. In approaching the material in these ways, Kelly referred to the following:

1. Ronald's vehement assertion that he ought to appear quiet and calm suggests that he is sensitive to the public. The effort to retain a public mask seems critical.

2. The contrast between external calm and the feeling of sitting on a lid of explosive behavior seems significant. He appears to get upset by behaviors in others that he sees in himself and rejects—the loss of intellectual controls.

3. He reports inconsistencies in his behavior and appears to be aware of breakdowns in his construct system.

4. Sincerity is a key construct and is linked with consideration and kindheartedness. By implication, the characteristics of insincerity, inconsideration, and unkindheartedness are also critical in his construing of events. He appears to vacillate between these poles and to find neither totally satisfactory.

5. He appears to use criticism and correction as an intellectual process to avoid flare-ups. His stress on technicalities is a way of leading a righteous life.

6. Ronald appears to think in terms of "nothing but," preemptive constructs, and stereotypes. He is concrete in his formulations of events and is not terribly imaginative.

Fixed-role Therapy

At the time of Ronald's self-description, he had completed several therapy sessions. These, however, were not part of a fixed-role therapy program. Such a program was undertaken, and it began with the writing of a fixed-role sketch by a panel of clinicians. The central theme of the sketch was the effort to seek answers in the subtle feelings of others rather than in dispute with them. The sketch, given the name of Kenneth Norton, emphasized attention to feelings. Here is the sketch of Kenneth Norton that was presented to Ronald Barrett.

Kenneth Norton is the kind of man who, after a few minutes of conversation, somehow makes you feel that he must have known you intimately for a long time. This comes about, not by any particular questions that he asks, but by the understanding way in which he listens. It is as if he had a knack of seeing the world through your eyes. The things which you have come to see as being important he, too, soon seems to sense as similarly important. Thus he catches not only your words but the punctuations of feeling with which they are formed and the little accents of meaning with which they are chosen.

Kenneth Norton's complete absorption in the thoughts of the people with whom he holds conversations appears to leave no place for any feelings of self-consciousness regarding himself. If indeed he has such feelings at all, they obviously run a poor second to his eagerness to see the world through other people's eyes. Nor does this mean that he is ashamed of himself, rather it means that he is too much involved with the fascinating worlds of other people with whom he is surrounded to give more than a passing thought to soul-searching criticisms of himself. Some people might, of course, consider this itself to be a kind of fault. Be that as it may, this is the kind of fellow Kenneth Norton is, and this behavior represents the Norton brand of sincerity.

Girls he finds attractive for many reasons, not the least of which is the exciting opportunity they provide for his understanding the feminine point of view. Unlike some men, he does not "throw the ladies a line" but, so skillful a listener is he, soon he has them throwing him one—and he is thoroughly enjoying it.

With his own parents and in his own home he is somewhat more expressive of his own ideas and feelings. Thus his parents are given an opportunity to share and supplement his new enthusiasms and accomplishments.

SOURCE: Kelly, 1955, pp. 374–375

At first, Ronald had trouble understanding the role he was to play and found that he was not too successful. However, he met a former classmate at a movie and found that the role worked better with her than with anyone else. In fact, after a while she was paying him several compliments and indicated that he had changed (presumably for the better) since he had gone away to college. Some role playing was tried in the therapy sessions. At times, Ronald would lapse back into dominating the conversation. At other times, however, he was able to draw out the therapist, who was now acting the role of various people in Ronald's life. When Ronald performed as Kenneth Norton, the therapist rewarded him with compliments.

Although the early presentations of himself as Kenneth Norton had no spontaneity or warmth, Ronald began to feel more comfortable in the role. He reported to the therapist that he felt less insecure in social situations, that he had fewer quarrels with others, and that he seemed to be more productive in his work. When a difficult situation was described, the therapist asked Ronald how Kenneth Norton would have handled it and then proceeded to engage Ronald in a role-playing rehearsal of the situation. Ronald behaved with greater warmth and spontaneity, and the therapist congratulated him to reinforce the new behavior. In general, the therapist tried to reinforce whatever new behavior Ronald exhibited.

The therapy of Ronald Barrett was necessarily incomplete, since after only a few sessions it was time for him to leave school. Unfortunately, we have no data on the exact kinds of changes that did occur and how long they lasted. For example, it would have been interesting to obtain Ronald's responses to the Rep test before treatment, at the end of treatment, and at a later time. This, of course, is the procedure Rogers used in some of his research. In any case, we do have a picture of how a Kellyian might construe an individual and might seek to engage a client in a creative process of change.

THE CASE OF JIM   Rep Test: Personal Construct Theory

Jim took the group form of Kelly's Rep test separately from the other tests (Figure 11.1). Here we have a test that is structured in terms of the roles given to the subject and the task of formulating a similarity–contrast construct. However, the subject is given total freedom in the content of the construct formed. As noted in Chapter 10, the Rep test is derived logically from Kelly's theory of personal constructs. Two major themes appear in these constructs. The first theme is the *quality of interpersonal relationships*. Basically this involves whether people are warm and giving or cold and narcissistic. This theme is expressed in constructs such as *gives love–is self-oriented, sensitive–insensitive, and communicates with others as people–is uninterested in others*. A second major theme concerns *security* and is expressed in constructs such as *hung up–healthy, unsure–self-confident*, and *satisfied with life–unhappy*. The frequency with which constructs relevant to these two themes appear suggests that Jim has a relatively constricted view of the world—that is, much of Jim's understanding of events is in terms of the warm–cold and secure–insecure dimensions.

How do the constructs given relate to specific people? On the sorts that involved himself, Jim used constructs expressing insecurity. Thus, Jim views himself as being like his sister (so hung up that her psychological health is questionable), in contrast to his brother, who is basically healthy and stable. In two other sorts of constructs, he sees himself as lacking self-confidence and social poise. These ways of construing himself contrast with those involving his father. His father is construed as being introverted and retiring, but also as self-sufficient, openminded, outstanding, and successful.

The constructs used in relation to Jim's mother are interesting and again suggest conflict. On the one hand, his mother is construed to be outgoing, gregarious, and loving; on the other, she is construed to be mundane, predictable, closeminded, and conservative. The closeminded, conservative construct is particularly

CONSTRUCT	CONTRAST
Self-satisfied	Self-doubting
Uninterested in communicating with students as people	Interested in communicating with students as people
Nice	Obnoxious
Sensitive to cues from other people	Insensitive to cues
Outgoing–gregarious	Introverted–retiring
Introspective–hung up	Self-satisfied
Intellectually dynamic	Mundane and predictable
Outstanding, successful	Mediocre
Obnoxious	Very likable
Satisfied with life	Unhappy

CONSTRUCT	CONTRAST
Shy, unsure of self	Self-confident
Worldly, openminded	Parochial, closeminded
Open, simple to understand	Complex, hard to get to know
Capable of giving great love	Somewhat self-oriented
Self-sufficient	Needs other people
Concerned with others	Oblivious to all but his own interests
So hung up that psychological health is questionable	Basically healthy and stable
Willing to hurt people in order to be "objective"	Unwilling to hurt people if he can help it
Closeminded, conservative	Openminded, liberal
Lacking in self-confidence	Self-confident
Sensitive	Insensitive, self-centered
Lacking social poise	Secure and socially poised
Bright, articulate	Average intelligence

Figure 11.1 Rep Test Data—Case of Jim.

interesting since, in that sort, Jim's mother is paired with the person with whom he feels most uncomfortable. Thus the mother and the person with whom he feels most uncomfortable are contrasted with his father, who is construed to be openminded and liberal. The combination of sorts for all persons suggests that Jim's ideal person is someone who is warm, sensitive, secure, intelligent, openminded, and successful. The women in his life—his mother, sister, girlfriend, and previous girlfriend—are construed as having some of these characteristics but also as missing others.

Comments on the Data

The Rep test gives us valuable data about how Jim construes his environment. With it we continue to use the phenomenological approach discussed in relation to Rogers, and again find that Jim's world tends to be perceived in terms of two major constructs: warm interpersonal–cold interpersonal relationships and secure, confident–insecure, unhappy people. Through the Rep test we gain an understanding of why Jim is so limited in his relationships to others and why he has so much difficulty in being creative. His restriction to only two constructs hardly leaves him free to relate to people as individuals and instead forces him to perceive people and problems in stereotyped or conventional ways. A world filled with so little perceived diversity can hardly be exciting, and the constant threat of insensitivity and rejection can be expected to fill Jim with a sense of gloom.

The data from the Rep test, like Kelly's theory, are tantalizing. What is there seems so clear and valuable, but one is left wondering about what is missing. There is a sense of the skeleton for the structure of personality, but one is left with only the bones. Jim's ways of construing himself and his environment are an important part of his personality. Assessing his constructs and his construct system helps us to understand how he interprets events and how he is led to predict the future. But where is the flesh on the bones—the sense of an individual who cannot be what he feels, the person struggling to be warm amid feelings of hostility and struggling to relate to women although confused about his feelings toward them?

RELATED POINTS OF VIEW AND RECENT DEVELOPMENTS

Almost all personality theorists today attempt to conceptualize cognitive variables, regardless of whether they interpret these variables as only part of the organism or as virtually all of the organism. As noted in the introduction, Kelly's theory anticipated many of these developments. In the words of one supporter, "Kelly's theory enjoys the irony of becoming increasingly contemporary with age" (Neimeyer, 1992, p. 995).

Although Kelly's theory attracted considerable attention when it was presented in 1955, it spawned little research in the following decade. Since then, however, many leads suggested by personal construct theory have been explored (Neimeyer & Neimeyer, 1992). A major focus has been the Rep test and the structure of construct systems. Studies of the reliability of the Rep test suggest that the responses of individuals to the role title list and constructs used are reasonably stable over time (Landfield, 1971). Beyond this the Rep test has been used to study a variety of individuals with psychological problems, the construct systems of married couples, and people with varied interpersonal relationships (Duck, 1982). Modifications of the Rep test have been used to study the structural complexity of construct systems, the perception of situations, and, as noted, the use of nonverbal constructs. Indeed, so much research has been conducted on the Rep test that Landfield, a major proponent of personal construct theory, has asked: " 'Would we become experimentally paralyzed within Personal Construct Psychology if we accepted a five-year moratorium in the use of the conventional Rep Grids?' " (quoted in Bonarius, Holland, & Rosenberg, 1981, p. 3).

Almost every aspect of Kelly's theory has received at least some study (Mancuso & Adams-Webber, 1982). The organization of the construct system and changes in this organization associated with development are particularly noteworthy topics (Crockett, 1982). The developmental principles emphasized suggest many similarities in the developmental theories of Kelly and Piaget: (1) an emphasis on progression from a global, undifferentiated system to a differentiated, integrated one; (2) increasing use of abstract structures to handle more information more economically; (3) development in response to efforts to accommodate new elements in the cognitive system; and (4) development of the cognitive system as a system, as opposed to a simple addition of new parts or elements.

Despite the wide variety of research studies and the increasing use of personal construct theory, however, certain problems remain. It is to these problems that we now turn.

We had a chance to consider a theory of personality that dares us to change our way of thinking, to reconstrue the nature of the person and of personality processes. While attempting to construe the theory within its own framework, it is time to assess its strengths and limitations and compare it with the other approaches considered previously.

CRITICAL EVALUATION

STRENGTHS AND LIMITATIONS OF THE THEORY

Kelly's theory can be viewed as primarily cognitive in its emphasis on the ways individuals receive and process information about the world, and in its use of the Rep test as a way of determining a person's concepts. As such, Kelly's personal construct theory certainly tends to take (insofar as one can) a cognitive view of behavior. The structural model, with its emphasis on constructs and the construct system, is a significant contribution to personality theory. The interpretation of behavior in terms of the individual's construing of events is useful in theory and in practice. This interpretation allows one to consider the unique aspects of the behavior of individuals, as well as the lawfulness or regularity of much of this behavior. To the extent that Kelly's emphasis on cognitive structures has influenced current research in cognitive style, the theory has made a significant contribution to research. The Rep test, which has the advantage of being derived from the theory, is an important assessment device. Although it has been criticized by some as being so flexible as to be unmanageable (Vernon, 1963), it is recognized by others as an extremely imaginative technique, quite amenable to quantification (Kleinmuntz, 1967; Mischel, 1968). A remaining unresolved problem for the Rep test, as well as for the theory as a whole, is that it requires the individual to use words even though the theory recognizes that preverbal or submerged constructs exist. Given the clinical significance of such constructs, the lack of means for assessing them remains a serious limitation.

The process view of Kelly has several interesting facets. It clearly represents a departure from the drive-reduction or tension-reduction views of Freud and other theorists. However, the process view leaves open a number of issues. The basis for action of an individual is not really clear. For example, how does the individual know which construct will be the best predictor? How does one know which end of the construct (similarity or contrast) to use? Also, what determines the individual's response to invalidation (Sechrest, 1963)? For example, when is new information forced into old constructs and when are constructs altered to accommodate new information?

In his review of Kelly's theory, Bruner (1956) referred to it as the single greatest contribution of the decade between 1945 and 1955 to the theory of personality functioning. Clearly, much of the theory was new and worthwhile. However, some areas of psychology appear to be more within the range of convenience of the psychology of personal constructs than other areas. For example, until recently the theory has had little to say about growth and development. Kelly's theory offers an interesting analysis of anxiety, but it has almost nothing to say about the important emotion of depression. In fact, for all its worthwhile emphasis on cognition, the theory offers a limited view of the person. Although Kelly denied the charge, the theory is noticeably lacking in emphasis on human feelings and emotions. In his review, Bruner stated that people may not be the pigs that reinforcement theory makes of them, but he wondered also whether people are only the scientists that Kelly suggests. Bruner commented further: "I rather suspect that when some people get angry or inspired or in love, they couldn't care less about their systems as a whole! One gets the impression that the author is, in his personality theory, overreacting against a generation of irrationalism" (Bruner, 1956, p. 356). Despite efforts to come to grips with the area of human emotions (McCoy, 1981), many interpretations within the context of personal construct theory seem strained and, on the whole, human emotions remain an area outside of its range of convenience.

Two additional relevant issues are worthy of consideration. First, although construct systems have been widely studied, there is little evidence that measures of these systems are related to overt behavior

(Crockett, 1982; Duck, 1982). The theory would certainly suggest that this is the case, but evidence is needed. Second, Kelly's theory of motivation remains problematic. As noted, Kelly failed to be specific about the basis for many decisions people make in terms of their construct systems. Beyond this, more traditional views of motivation enter the discussion of personal construct theorists. For example, it is suggested that people do not like boredom or surprise (Mancuso & Adams-Webber, 1982). However, emphases on intermediate degrees of novelty or stimulation have typically been associated with pleasure, reinforcement, or hedonic theories of motivation. An emphasis on emotion or pleasure often enters clinical discussions. For example, Landfield (1982) suggests that a person chooses that end of a construct that is positively valued. Furthermore, in his discussion of a case he suggests that the patient stopped having an affair for emotional rather than purely cognitive reasons: "After all, she did like her husband better than her lover" (p. 203).

A final note in the evaluation of Kelly's theory concerns its current status as a basis for active research. Clearly there has been activity and growing interest. However, two reviews of these efforts question whether much progress is being made or whether development is being held back by reverence, insularity, and orthodoxy (Rosenberg, 1980; Schneider, 1982). As noted by a follower of Kelly, without new ideas no theory of personality can survive (Sechrest, 1977).

It is now over 30 years since the publication of Kelly's theory. A review of personal construct psychology assessed the impact of Kelly's ideas over this time and suggested that, except for a group of enthusiasts, they are relatively neglected (Jankowicz, 1987). This is less true in England, where Kelly's ideas are widely known and are part of the training of most clinicians. However, in this country, although his ideas are respected by many, they have had relatively little impact on the field in general. And, despite psychotherapy being a focus of convenience of personal construct theory, its approach to therapy receives little coverage in clinical courses and is not greatly followed in clinical practice (Winter, 1992).

Why should this be? Two factors appear to be relevant. First, Kelly was a rather reserved and private person. Thus, he did not spread his own word and did not have many graduate student disciples who advanced his view. Second, in attempting a radical departure from traditional views, Kelly set himself and his work apart from that of others: "It was part of Kelly's character that he avoided forging the links of his ideas to those of others" (Bieri, 1986, p. 673). They, in turn, ignored his views to a great extent.

Summary

In sum, personal construct theory has both strengths and limitations (Table 11.2). On the positive side, there is the following: (1) the theory makes a significant contribution by bringing to the forefront of person-

Table 11.2   Summary of Strengths and Limitations of Personal Construct Theory

Strengths	Limitations
1. Places emphasis on cognitive processes as a central aspect of personality.	1. Has not led to research that *extends* the theory.
2. Presents a model of personality that provides for both the lawfulness of general personality functioning and the uniqueness of individual construct systems.	2. Leaves out or makes minimal contributions to our understanding of some significant aspects of personality (growth and development, emotions).
3. Includes a theory-related technique for personality assessment and research (Rep test).	3. Is not as yet connected with more general research and theory in cognitive psychology.

ality the importance of cognition and construct systems; (2) it is an approach to personality that attempts to capture both the uniqueness of the individual and the lawfulness of people generally; (3) it has developed a new, interesting, and theoretically relevant assessment technique, the Rep test. On the negative side, there is the following: (1) the theory shows relative neglect of certain important areas such as emotion and motivation; (2) despite Kelly's view that theories are there to be reformulated and abandoned, no one since 1955 has formulated any significant new theoretical developments in personal construct theory; (3) it has remained outside of mainstream research relating work in cognitive psychology to personality. Many of these approaches give lip service to Kelly's contributions but proceed along independent lines.

COMPARISON WITH OTHER THEORIES

Kelly's theory suggests that at least three elements are necessary to form a construct—a perceived similarity between two elements to form a similarity pole and a perceived difference in the third element to form a contrast pole. Given the major approaches covered to this point, we have sufficient elements (theories) to make some comparisons and form some constructs. We can begin by comparing Kelly with each of the previously considered theories and then conclude with some suggested constructs relevant to theories of personality.

KELLY AND FREUD

Although Kelly was extremely critical of psychoanalytic theory, he appreciated the many important observations and clinical contributions made by Freud. The criticisms of Freud are mainly in three areas—Freud's view of the person, the considerable dogmatism in psychoanalytic thinking, and the weaknesses of psychoanalysis as a scientific theory. Kelly was critical of Freud's view of the person as biological-organism and substituted the view of the person as scientist. Kelly was critical of Freud's metaphors and of his emphasis on unconscious drives and instincts.

Kelly placed great reliance on understanding the individual's construction of events and on the tentativeness with which theories are put forward. Both of these reflect an openminded attitude. Against this background, Kelly was critical of Freud's emphasis on understanding what clients mean by examining what they *do not* say. For Kelly, this approach makes psychoanalysis needlessly dogmatic and closeminded. Furthermore, Kelly viewed the followers of Freud as unnecessarily opposed to change.

The third major criticism of psychoanalysis was its standing as a scientific enterprise. Kelly observed that Freud's observations of the unconscious were difficult to explore scientifically. As far as Kelly was concerned, the psychoanalytic movement had shunned scientific methodology in favor of impressionist observation. Hypotheses were so elastic that they could not be invalidated. They were what Kelly called "rubber hypotheses"; they could be stretched to fit any kind of evidence. For Kelly, this was the most vulnerable point of psychoanalysis.

Although Kelly was critical of psychoanalysis, he also believed that the psychoanalytic system of dynamics permitted the clinician to determine that something was going on inside the client. According to Kelly, Freud made many astute observations, and his adventurousness helped to open up the field of psychotherapy for exploration. What is particularly striking in reading Kelly is the number of times that he seems to be describing phenomena that were also described by Freud, even though he may interpret them in a different way. For example, Kelly placed great emphasis on the closeness of opposites, a view quite evident in Freud's thinking. In fact, in dreams, ideas were frequently represented by their opposites. Both Freud and Kelly were sensitive to the fact that the way people view others may also express views they hold about themselves; both were aware that one is threatened only by something that seems plausible, and that one "protests too much" about things one does not want to acknowledge to be true; both viewed people as at times functioning in relation to principles they are unaware of, although in one case the concept of the unconscious was emphasized, whereas in the other the emphasis was on preverbal constructs; both noted that at times an individual may feel uncomfortable with praise, although in one case the concept of guilt was stressed and in the other the emphasis was on the strangeness of new praise and the complex internal reorganization it could imply; both placed emphasis on the concept of transference in therapy; both felt that patients are resistant to change. Not surprisingly, the theories of Freud and Kelly share a number of observations, since the foci of convenience of the two theories are somewhat similar.

KELLY AND ROGERS

There also are a number of similarities in the works of Kelly and Rogers. Both view the person as more active than reactive; both theories emphasize the phenomenological approach, although Kelly believed that personal construct psychology was not just phenomenology. In both, there is an emphasis on consistency, although for Rogers this is on self-consistency per se, and for Kelly it is so that predictions can add up rather than cancel each other out. Both stress the total system functioning of the organism.

Probably their common emphasis on the phenomenological approach and their common avoidance of a drive model of human functioning lead to the appearance of considerable similarity between Kelly and Rogers. At one point, Kelly asked: "Is the therapist ever more familiar with the client's construct system than the client is himself?" His answer was clear: "We think not" (Kelly, 1955, p. 1020). Despite these similarities, however, there are major differences between the two theories. Kelly placed far less emphasis on the self. Although Kelly agreed with Rogers that the present is what counts most, he refused to take a completely ahistorical approach toward behavior. Kelly was interested in the past because individuals' perceptions of their past give clues to their construct system and because a reconstruing of the past can be important in treatment. In general, Kelly was interested in a whole range of clinical phenomena (e.g., transference, dreams, diagnosis, the importance of preverbal constructs), which brought him closer to Freud than to Rogers in this regard.

Kelly viewed Rogers's position as more of a statement of philosophical convictions about the nature of the person than a true psychological theory. Kelly was critical of the Rogerian principle of growth and contrasted it with personal construct theory. Whereas the former emphasized an unfolding of inner potential, the latter emphasized the continuous development of a changing and ever-expanding construct system. Whereas Rogers emphasized the importance of being and becoming, Kelly emphasized the importance of make-believe and doing. The difference has important ramifications for treatment, a point that was made explicit by Kelly: "The nondirectionist, because of his faith in the emerging being, asks the client to pay attention to himself as he reacts with his everyday world. Somewhere the mature self is waiting to be realized....The personal-construct psychologist is probably more inclined to urge the client to experiment with life and to seek his answers in the succession of events which life unveils than to seek them within himself" (1955, pp. 401–402).

Kelly emphasized the verbal fluency and acting skill of the therapist. He opposed the view that the therapist must be known as a real person and was critical of phenomenologically oriented therapists who became involved in "lovely personal relationships." The differences between Kelly and Rogers as people are important and have been translated into views concerning therapy. Rogers (1956), in his review of Kelly's work, stated that Kelly had found an approach congenial to his personality. However, he was critical of Kelly's apparent interpretation of therapy as an intellectual process. Rogers was influenced by Kelly and used the concepts of construct complexity and construct flexibility in his analysis of changes in therapy. However, Rogers was critical of the excessive activity and control assumed in fixed-role therapy. For Rogers, therapy is much more a process of feeling than of thinking, and it is important for therapists to be congruent; skill in manipulating the situation is less important.

KELLY AND TRAIT THEORY

Of the other theories considered to this point, Kelly's theory differs most fundamentally from trait theory. First, the two are based on different approaches to discovery and research, the clinical approach for personal construct theory and the correlational approach for trait theory. Again, this is not to say that alternative methods are not used within the two theoretical contexts, but rather that they come from different starting points. Associated with this are completely different approaches to assessment, for example, the NEO-PI in the case of trait theory and the Rep test in the case of personal construct theory. Associated with this as well is the emphasis on cognitive processes in Kelly's theory, something which is virtually absent in trait theory.

Perhaps even more significant than these differences is the fundamentally different view of the functioning of the human organism. Whereas the trait emphasis is on what is fixed, stable, and unchanging across situations, Kelly's emphasis was on the person as an active, interpreting, discriminating agent who is always potentially in the act of changing. In terms of the person–situation controversy (Chapter 8), Mischel's emphasis on the person discriminating among, and differentially responding to, situations was influenced by the work of Kelly. Thus, while recognizing predictability in individual behavior, Kelly viewed people as behaving differently in situations according to how each situation was construed or interpreted. People's behavior was limited only by their behavioral skills and their ability to construe situations in alternative ways. Whereas trait theorists view a person's personality as pretty much fixed by the mid-twenties, in part for genetic reasons, Kelly was much more optimistic concerning the potential for change. And, whereas trait theorists view the person in relatively static terms, Kelly viewed his theory as a dynamic theory of personality (Pervin, 1994a).

Finally, we may consider two additional differences between trait theory and personal construct theory. First, there is a difference in the focus of convenience of the two theories. For trait theory, personality structure is the focus of convenience and psychotherapy, or the process of person-

KELLY AT A GLANCE

Structure	Process	Growth and Development
Constructs	Processes channelized by anticipation of events	Increased complexity and definition to construct system

ality change, lies pretty much outside its range of convenience. In contrast, the process of personality change is the focus of convenience of personal construct theory. Second, although trait theorists are interested in individual differences, they seek to place all individuals on common dimensions (e.g., the Big Five). In contrast, although Kelly was interested in general principles that applied to all humans, and in individual differences, he also placed a great deal of emphasis on the unique or idiographic aspects of each individual's construct system. In all likelihood Kelly would have viewed the Big Five as some psychologists' constructs, not to be confused with the basic structure of personality.

KELLY AND LEARNING THEORY

From a personal construct theory perspective, the various learning approaches considered represent overly simplified, mechanistic accounts of human behavior. The personal construct theorist is much more interested in the whole person than in individual responses, more interested in how the person construes events than in what is "actually" going on inside the organism (classical conditioning) or in what the experimenter defines as going on outside the organism (operant conditioning). And, whereas S–R theory emphasized the importance of a drive, tension-reduction, "push" model of motivation, Kelly emphasized a cognitive, increasing expansion of the construct system, "jackass" model of motivation. To a great extent these learning theories were supplanted by developments in the cognitive revolution in psychology, and Kelly's theory can be viewed as a part of that revolution in the field of personality.

CONSTRUCTS RELEVANT TO PERSONALITY THEORY

With the theories covered to date, can one develop a construct system relevant to personality theories? For example, what would happen if the theories considered to date were listed as roles on a Rep test grid, and the student was asked to compare triads of theories to define constructs with similarity and contrast poles? What would be the constructs formulated

Pathology	Change	Illustrative Case
Disordered functioning of the construct system	Psychological reconstruction of life; invitational mood; fixed-role therapy.	Ronald Barrett

as relevant to the theories of personality? How different would they be from student to student, from personality theorist to personality theorist? Here are some to consider, others are left to the individual student's developing personal construct system: *holistic–emphasis on elements, dynamic–static, personality as relatively fixed–personality as relatively changing, unconscious emphasized–unconscious not emphasized, self emphasized–self not emphasized, constructivism–"reality," person as active–person as passive or responsive.*

MAJOR CONCEPTS

Permeable construct. In Kelly's personal construct system, a construct that allows new elements into it.

Impermeable construct. In Kelly's personal construct theory, a construct that does not allow new elements into it.

Tightening. In Kelly's personal construct theory, the use of constructs to make the same predictions regardless of circumstances.

Loosening. In Kelly's personal construct theory, the use of the same construct to make varied predictions.

Constriction. In Kelly's personal construct theory, the narrowing of the construct system so as to minimize incompatibilities.

Dilation. In Kelly's personal construct theory, the broadening of a construct system so that it will be more comprehensive.

Submerged construct. In Kelly's personal construct theory, a construct that once could be expressed in words but now either one or both poles of the construct cannot be verbalized.

Aggression (Kelly). In Kelly's personal construct theory, the active expansion of the person's construct system.

Hostility (Kelly). In Kelly's personal construct theory, making others behave in an expected way to validate one's own construct system.

Fixed-role therapy. Kelly's therapeutic technique that makes use of scripts or roles for people to try out, thereby encouraging people to behave in new ways and to perceive themselves in new ways.

REVIEW

1. For Kelly, psychopathology is a disordered response to anxiety leading to malfunctioning of the construct system.

2. Disordered responses to anxiety can be seen in the way constructs are applied to new events (excessively permeable or impermeable), in the way constructs are used to make predictions (excessive tightening or loosening), and in the organization of the entire construct system (constriction or dilation).

3. According to Kelly, suicide and hostility represent efforts to reduce the threat to the construct system. In suicide one escapes either from certainty (fatalism) or complete uncertainty; in hostility one tries to make others behave in expected ways.

4. For Kelly, psychotherapy is the process of reconstructing the construct system. Conditions favoring positive change are an atmosphere of experimentation, the provision of new elements and constructs, and the availability of new validating data.

5. In fixed-role therapy, clients are encouraged to represent themselves in new ways, behave in new ways, and construe themselves in new ways.

6. The case of Ronald Barrett illustrates Kelly's efforts to apply a personal construct analysis to an individual and to use fixed-role therapy as a technique to produce change in the construct system.

7. Research on personal construct theory has focused mainly on the Rep test.

8. Despite Kelly's refusal to label his theory, it can be described as a cognitive theory of personality in that it emphasizes how people process information about the world and uses the Rep test to assess construct systems.

9. An evaluation of personal construct theory recognizes its strengths in emphasizing cognitive processes, in developing a way of suggesting broad principles while capturing the uniqueness of the individual, and in developing an assessment device and a method of therapy directly related to the theory. At the same time, the theory neglects some important areas, fails to come to grips with some fundamental questions, and has had a limited impact on the research and therapeutic efforts of others.

10. Following the spirit of personal construct theory, it is possible to take three theorists such as Freud, Rogers, and Kelly to develop constructs, involving a similarity pole and a contrast pole, and to compare personality theories in terms of these constructs.

SOCIAL COGNITIVE THEORY: BANDURA AND MISCHEL

Chapter Focus

Do you remember your first day of high school? Perhaps you don't care to! What could be more unnerving than not knowing how to act, especially in an environment where "fitting in" is paramount? Although she was really anxious and unsure of what to expect, one young woman decided to approach the first day of high school as an opportunity to learn. Her plan was to model herself after the most successful seniors in the school. She paid close attention to what they talked about, what they wore, where they went and when they went there. Soon, she was the coolest freshman in the class.

This young woman was very influenced by her new environment, but she was also an active agent in choosing how to respond to that influence. This idea, that behavior is the result of an interaction between the person and the environment, is a key concept in the *social cognitive theory* of personality. This theory is distinctive in its emphasis on the social origins of behavior and the importance of cognition (thought processes) in human functioning. People are viewed as capable of actively directing their own lives and learning complex patterns of behavior in the absence of rewards. While evolving from traditional learning theory, social cognitive theory has taken on new dimensions and today is an important force in the field of personality.

QUESTIONS TO BE ADDRESSED IN THIS CHAPTER

1. How consistent are people in their behavior from situation to situation?
2. How essential is reinforcement for learning?
3. How important are role models for personality development?
4. How important are beliefs concerning one's competence for motivation and performance? Is it useful to speak of a general sense of self-efficacy or self-esteem?

Social cognitive theory has its roots in traditional learning theory (Chapter 9). Originally it was known as *social learning theory* and was presented in previous editions of this text as one of the learning approaches to personality. Over time the theory has evolved; increasingly it has emphasized cognition (thought processes) in human functioning and has become more systematic. Today it is known as *social cognitive theory*, and warrants consideration separate from other learning approaches to personality.

Social cognitive theory emphasizes the *social* origins of behavior and the importance of *cognitive* thought processes in all aspects of human functioning—motivation, emotion, and action. In defining their position, social cognitive theorists have been critical of many aspects of the theories already presented. For example, Bandura (1986) is critical of the psychoanalytic emphasis on internal instincts and unconscious forces that cannot be studied systematically. As noted in Chapter 8, Mischel (1968, 1990; Mischel & Shoda, 1995) has been critical of traditional trait and psychoanalytic theories for their emphasis on internal dispositions that are seen as leading to consistency in behavior across situations. Instead, there is an emphasis on the variability of behavior as the person responds to changes in the environment. According to social cognitive theory, behavior is situation-specific and people have distinctive patterns of behaving in situations (Shoda, Mischel, & Wright, 1994). These distinctive situation-behavior patterns are viewed as more defining of personality than the aggregate, cross-situational differences emphasized by trait theorists. For example, social cognitive theorists suggest that it is more important to know about the kinds of situations in which the person is extraverted and introverted than to know their overall level of extraversion–introversion relative to other individuals. In attempting to go beyond traditional debate in the field concerning the relative importance of internal and external determinants of behavior, social cognitive theorists suggest that there is always a process of interaction between the organism and its environment.

In addition, social cognitive theorists attempt to go beyond the traditional division of the field into behavioral "as opposed to" humanistic views of the person. These psychologists are behavioral in their emphasis on the systematic study of human behavior, but they are humanists in their emphasis on the potential for people to influence their destinies and to develop within their biological limits. Finally, there is a break from traditional reinforcement learning theory in an emphasis on cognitive processes, and in the suggestion that learning occurs in the absence of rewards (Table 12.1).

Within the academic community, social cognitive theory is probably the most popular personality theory, and it is gaining increasing numbers of adherents in the clinical community as well. It is most clearly represented in the works of two psychologists, Albert Bandura and Walter Mischel.

Table 12.1 Distinguishing Features of Social Cognitive theory

1. Emphasis on people as active agents.
2. Emphasis on social origins of behavior.
3. Emphasis on cognitive (thought) processes.
4. Emphasis on behavior as situation-specific.
5. Emphasis on systematic research.
6. Emphasis on the learning of complex patterns of behavior in the absence of rewards.

A VIEW OF THE THEORISTS

ALBERT BANDURA (1925–)

Albert Bandura grew up in northern Alberta, Canada and went to college at the University of British Columbia. After graduation he chose to do graduate work in clinical psychology at the University of Iowa because it was known for the excellence of its research on learning processes. Even then Bandura was interested in the application of learning theory to clinical phenomena. In an interview Bandura indicated that he "had a strong interest in conceptualizing clinical phenomena in ways that would make them amenable to experimental test, with the view that as practitioners we have a responsibility for assessing the efficacy of a procedure, so that people are not subjected to treatments before we know their effects" (quoted in Evans, 1976, p. 243). At Iowa he was influenced by Kenneth Spence, a follower of Clark Hull, and by the general emphasis on careful conceptual analysis and rigorous experimental investigation. During that time he was also influenced by the writings of Neal Miller and John Dollard.

After obtaining his Ph.D. at Iowa in 1952, Bandura went to Stanford and began to work on interactive processes in psychotherapy, as well as on family patterns that lead to aggressiveness in children. The work on familial causes of aggression, with Richard Walters—his first graduate student—led to an emphasis on the central role of modeling influences (learning through observation of others) in personality development. These findings and consequent laboratory investigations of modeling processes resulted in the books *Adolescent Aggression* (1959) and *Social Learning and Personality Development* (1963).

Albert Bandura

Bandura describes himself as conducting a multifaceted research program aimed at clarifying aspects of human capability that should be emphasized in a comprehensive theory of human behavior. His 1986 book *Social Foundations of Thought and Action* represents an effort to develop such a theory. His emphasis on human capabilities is related to an interest in personality development and therapeutic change. His recent work focuses on human motivation and the implications of feelings of personal efficacy (competence) for psychological and physical well-being. In addition, his most recent work focuses on how societal factors, such as social and economic conditions, influence people's beliefs about their ability to influence events (Bandura, 1995).

Bandura has received a number of distinguished scientific achievement awards. In 1974 he was elected president of the American Psychological Association, and in 1980 he received the Association's Distinguished Scientific Contribution Award "for masterful modeling as researcher, teacher, and theoretician."

WALTER MISCHEL (1930–)

Walter Mischel was born in Vienna and lived his first nine years "in easy playing distance of Freud's house." He describes the possible influence of this period as follows:

> When I began to read psychology Freud fascinated me most. As a
> student at City College (in New York, where my family settled
> after the Hitler-caused forced exodus from Europe in 1939), psy-
> choanalysis seemed to provide a comprehensive view of man. But
> my excitement fizzled when I tried to apply ideas as a social work-

Walter Mischel

er with "juvenile delinquents" in New York's Lower East Side: somehow trying to give those youngsters "insight" didn't help either them or me. The concepts did not fit what I saw, and I went looking for more useful ones.

SOURCE: Mischel, 1978, personal communication

The experience with juvenile delinquents is of particular interest for two reasons. First, it probably relates to Mischel's longstanding interest in the psychological mechanisms underlying delay of gratification and self-control. Second, there is a similarity to Bandura in that both did their early clinical work with aggressive youngsters.

Mischel did his graduate work at Ohio State University, where he came under the influence of George Kelly and Julian Rotter. He describes their influence as follows:

> George Kelly and Julian Rotter were my dual mentors and each has enduringly influenced my thinking. I see my own work both with cognition and with social learning as clearly rooted in their contributions, a focus on the person both as construer and actor, interacting with the vicissitudes of the environment, and trying to make life coherent even in the face of all inconsistencies.

SOURCE: Mischel, 1978, personal communication

After completing his graduate work at Ohio State, Mischel spent a number of years at Harvard University and then joined Bandura at Stanford. During this time (1965) he participated in a Peace Corps assessment project that had a profound influence on him. In this project it was found that global trait measures did a poor job of predicting performance; in fact, they did less well than self-report measures. This increased Mischel's skepticism concerning the utility of traditional personality theories, such as trait and psychoanalytic theory, that emphasize stable and broadly generalized personality characteristics (Mischel, 1990). The culmination of this skepticism was the 1968 publication of his book *Personality and Assessment*, mentioned in Chapter 8, which became the focus of the person–situation controversy. Mischel describes his skepticism concerning the utility of broadly generalized personality characteristics such as traits as follows:

> Characterizations of individuals on common trait dimensions (such as "Conscientiousness" or "Sociability") provided useful overall summaries of their average levels of behavior but missed, it seemed to me, the striking discriminativeness often visible within the same person if closely observed over time and across situations. Might the same person who is more caring, giving, and supportive than most people in relation to his family also be less caring and altruistic than most people in other contexts? Might these

variations across situations be meaningful stable patterns that characterize the person enduringly rather than random fluctuations? If so, how could they be understood and what did they reflect? Might they be worth taking into account in personality assessment for the conceptualization of the stability and flexibility of human behavior and qualities? These questions began to gnaw at me and the effort to answer them became a fundamental goal for the rest of my life.

SOURCE: Mischel, as quoted in Pervin, 1996, p. 76

In 1978 Mischel received the Distinguished Scientist Award from the Clinical Psychology Division of the American Psychological Association and in 1983 was cited by the Association for his outstanding contributions to personality theory and assessment. Since 1984 he has been a professor of psychology at Columbia University.

VIEW OF THE PERSON

Both Bandura and Mischel recognize the relationship of a general view of the person to a theory of personality, and both have attempted to be explicit concerning this view. Bandura notes that "views about human nature influence which aspects of psychological functioning are studied most thoroughly and which remain unexamined. Theoretical conceptions similarly determine the paradigms used to collect evidence which, in turn, shape the particular theory" (1977a, p. vi). In other words, there is a back-and-forth or reciprocal relationship between a view of the person, a program of research, and a theory of personality.

Current social cognitive theory emphasizes a view of the person as active and as using cognitive processes to represent events, anticipate the future, choose among courses of action, and communicate with others (Mischel & Shoda, 1995). Alternative views of the person as a passive victim of unconscious impulses and past history or as a passive respondent to environmental events are rejected. Theories of personality that emphasize internal factors to the exclusion of environmental events are rejected because of their disregard for the individual's responsiveness to varying situations (Shoda, Mischel, & Wright, 1994). At the same time, theories that emphasize external factors to the exclusion of internal factors are rejected because of their failure to consider the role of cognitive functioning in behavior.

Rejecting both the view that people are driven by inner forces and the view that they are buffeted by environmental stimuli, social cognitive theory suggests that behavior can be explained in terms of an interaction between the person and the environment, a process Bandura calls **reciprocal determinism**. People are influenced by environmental forces, but they also choose how to behave. The person is both responsive to situations and actively constructs and influences situations. People select situations as well as being shaped by them; they influence the behavior of others as well as being shaped by the behavior of others.

Mischel describes the emerging image of the human being as follows:

> The image is one of the human being as an active, aware problem-solver, capable of profiting from an enormous range of experiences and cognitive capacities, possessing great potential for good or ill, actively constructing his or her psychological world, and influencing the environment but also being influenced by it in lawful ways....It is an image that has moved a long way from the instinctual drive-reduction models, the static global traits, and the automatic stimulus–response bonds of traditional personality theories. It is an image that highlights the shortcomings of all simplistic theories that view behavior as the exclusive result of any narrow set of determinants, whether these are habits, traits, drives, reinforcers, constructs, instincts, or genes and whether they are exclusively inside or outside the person.
>
> SOURCE: Mischel, 1976, p. 253

VIEW OF SCIENCE, THEORY, AND RESEARCH

Both Bandura and Mischel are committed to the use of theory and empirical research. There is a strong concern for concepts that are clear and based on systematic observations. Theories that emphasize motivational forces in the form of needs, drives, and impulses are criticized for being vague, of little utility in predicting or changing behavior.

Whereas extreme behaviorism rejects the study of cognitive processes because of a distrust for introspective data, Bandura and Mischel feel that such inner processes must be studied and that the use of some types of self-report is both legitimate and desirable. They suggest that self-reports that are specific and given under conditions that do not arouse evaluative apprehensions can be valuable aids in understanding cognitive processes.

In sum, social cognitive theory is concerned with both a variety of aspects of human behavior and scientific rigor. There is a concern with both important inner processes and systematic observations. In all likelihood it is this blend of concern with important human events and scientific respectability that most accounts for the theory's current popularity.

SOCIAL COGNITIVE THEORY OF PERSONALITY

The stage has been set for considering the details of the social cognitive theory of personality. In doing so, we must keep in mind the importance of cognitive processes in human motivation, emotion, and action, as well as the social origins of human behavior.

STRUCTURE

The personality structures emphasized by social cognitive theory mainly involve cognitive processes. Three structural concepts are particularly noteworthy: expectancies–beliefs, competencies–skills, and goals.

Expectancies–Beliefs

Social cognitive theory emphasizes the expectancies people have concerning events and the beliefs they have concerning themselves. For example, people have expectancies concerning the behavior of others and rewards or punishments for their own behavior in specific types of situations. They also have beliefs concerning their own abilities to handle the tasks and challenges presented by particular kinds of situations. Clearly these involve cognitive processes such as the categorization of situations (e.g., work situations and fun situations, formal and informal situations, relaxed and threatening situations), anticipation of the future, and self-reflection. What is emphasized here is the situational specificity of a person's expectancies and beliefs; that is, although people may have some generalized expectancies and beliefs, such as the internal locus of control generalized expectancies emphasized by Rotter, what is of greater significance are the expectancies and beliefs developed in relation to specific situations or groups of situations. Were we to not discriminate among situations, we would act the same in all of them. No animal could survive under such circumstances. Discrimination among situations in terms of needs that can be met (e.g., hunger, sex, safety) is essential for survival. In addition, humans, because of their tremendous cognitive capacity, make an incredible variety of discriminations among situations. And, the ways in which individuals view particular situations or group them together are highly idiosyncratic. Thus, one individual views a situation as threatening that another views as exciting, and one individual views two situations as very similar that another views as completely different. Not surprisingly, behavior differs in accordance with these differing perceptions of situations. According to social cognitive theorists, the essence of personality lies in the differing ways in which individuals perceive situations and in the behavior patterns established in accord with these differing perceptions.

Discriminations Among Situations and the Consistency of Personality
As noted, according to social cognitive theory individuals differ in their patterns of behavior across situations. According to the theory, individuals develop *if...then* expectancies: *if* this kind of situation *then* this is what I can expect to happen. As a consequence, they develop stable patterns of situation–behavior relationships. Is there evidence of such individuality in the organization of situations and can individuals be described in terms of stable profiles of situation–behavior relationships? This is the question that Mischel suggests has gnawed at him and the answering of which has consumed much of his research efforts.

Research using self-report data clearly supports the view that people see themselves as feeling and acting differently in different groups of situations (Pervin, 1976). For example, a subject will report that she experiences relaxation and behaves in an extraverted fashion in peer–social situations but is tense and introverted at home. Or, another subject reports that he is angry and domineering at work but feels tender and is nurturant at home. The ways in which individuals group the situations in their lives and the feelings and behaviors they associate with these groups of situations differ, but all report feeling and behaving differently in various groups of situations. These, however, are self-reports. Would objective measures of behavior confirm such observations?

A recent study by Mischel and his associates provides important clues to the answer (Shoda, Mischel, & Wright, 1994). In this research boys and girls were observed in various camp settings during a 6-week period. Illustrative settings were woodworking, cabin meeting, classroom, mealtime, playground, and watching TV. Within these settings, situations were defined in terms of whether the interaction involved a peer or an adult counselor and whether the interaction was positive or negative in nature (e.g., the child was praised vs. punished by a counselor or teased by a peer). For each child observations were made regularly on the basis of the frequency with which each of five types of behavior occurred in each of the defined situations: verbal aggression (teased, provoked, or threatened); physical aggression (hit, pushed, physically harmed); whined or displayed babyish behavior; complied or gave in; talked prosocially. These observations were made on an hourly basis, 5 hours a day, 6 days a week, for 6 weeks—an average of 167 hours of observation per child. In sum, there was an incredible amount of observation of each child in terms of behaviors expressed in a variety of situations over the course of time.

What were the findings? Of course there was evidence of considerable differences in behaviors expressed in different situations. People do behave differently in different types of situations. In general, behavior is different on the playground than in the classroom, in a cabin meeting than in woodworking. And, of course there were individual differences in average expressions of each of the five observed types of behavior. As trait theorists suggest, there are individual differences in average expressions of behavior across situations. However, the more critical question for social cognitive theory is whether individuals can be described in terms of their distinctive patterns of situation-behavior relationships. In other words, do individuals differ in their patterns of behavior even if their overall levels are the same? Can two individuals express the same average level of aggressive behavior, be the same on a trait such as aggressiveness, but differ in the kinds of situations in which they express their aggressiveness? Mischel and his associates indeed found clear evidence that individuals have distinctive, stable profiles of expressing particular behaviors in specific groups of situations. Consider, for example,

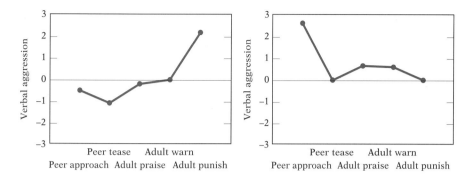

Figure 12.1   *Illustrative intraindividual profiles of verbal aggression across five types of psychological situations. (Adapted from Shoda, Mischel, & Wright, 1994, p.6)*

the verbal aggression profiles of two individuals in relation to five types of psychological situations (Figure 12.1). Clearly the two differ in their profiles of expressing verbal aggression across the various situations. Each behaves reasonably consistently *within* specific groups of situations but differently *between* groups of situations. Averaging behavior across situations would mask such distinctive patterns of situation-behavior relationships.

What can be concluded from this research? Mischel and his associates suggest that individuals have distinctive profiles of situation–behavior relationships, what are called **behavioral signatures**. According to them, in contrast with the trait emphasis on aggregating behavior across situations, "it is this type of intraindividual stability in the pattern and organization of behavior that seems especially central for a psychology of personality ultimately devoted to understanding and capturing the uniqueness of individual functioning" (Shoda, Mischel, & Wright, 1994, p.683).

The Self and Self-Efficacy Beliefs   The social cognitive concept of self refers to processes that are part of the person's psychological functioning. In a sense, the person does not have a structure called "the self," but rather self-processes that are part of the person. In addition, earlier concepts of the self are criticized for being too global. Rather than having a self-concept, social cognitive theory suggests that people have self-conceptions and self-control processes that may vary from time to time and from situation to situation.

A particular aspect of the perception of self has become central to Bandura's thinking: that concerning **self-efficacy** or the perceived ability to cope with specific situations (Bandura, 1995). The concept of self-efficacy relates to judgments people make concerning their ability to act in a specific task or situation. According to Bandura, self-efficacy judgments influence which activities we engage in, how much effort we expend in a situation, how long we persist at a task, and our emotional reactions while anticipating a situation or involved in it. Clearly, we think, feel, and behave differently in situations in which we feel confident of our ability than in situations in which we are insecure or feel incompetent. In sum, self-percepts of efficacy influence thought patterns, motivation, performance, and emotional arousal.

These influences of self-efficacy are spelled out further throughout this chapter. For now, however, it is important to consider how Bandura assesses self-efficacy and how he distinguishes it from what might appear to be related concepts. In terms of assessment, Bandura emphasizes what he calls a **microanalytic research** strategy. According to this strategy, detailed measures of perceived self-efficacy are taken before performance of behaviors in specific situations. Thus, subjects are asked to designate in a specific situation those tasks they can do and their degree of certainty about doing them successfully. This strategy reflects the view that self-efficacy judgments are situation specific and do not represent global dispositions that can be measured by comprehensive personality inventories. As noted before, a global self-concept is criticized because it "does not do justice to the complexity of self-efficacy perceptions, which vary across different activities, different levels of the same activity, and different situational circumstances" (Bandura, 1986, p. 41).

Goals

The concept of **goals** relates to the ability of people to anticipate the future and be self-motivated. It is goals that guide us in establishing priorities and in selecting among situations. It is goals that enable us to go beyond momentary influences and to organize our behavior over extended periods of time. A person's goals are organized in a system, so that some are more central or important than others. However, generally this is not a rigid or fixed system. Rather, a person may select among goals, depending on what seems most important to him or her at the time, what the opportunities in the environment appear to be, and his or her judgments of those goals' self-efficacy relative to the demands of the environment.

Competencies—Skills

Social cognitive theory emphasizes the **competencies** or skills possessed by the individual. Of particular interest are cognitive competencies and skills, that is, the person's ability to solve problems and cope with the problems of life (Cantor, 1990; Mischel, 1990). Rather than emphasizing the traits a person has, social cognitive theory emphasizes the competencies expressed in what a person does. These competencies involve both ways of thinking about life problems and behavioral skills in enacting solutions to them. Of particular importance is the suggestion that people often possess such competencies in specific contexts; that is, a person competent in one context may or may not be competent in another. People competent in the academic realm may or may not be competent in the social or business realm. Thus, there is a shift from context-free traits to an emphasis on how the person functions in relation to specific situations.

PROCESS

According to social cognitive theory, behavior is maintained by **expectancies** or anticipated consequences, rather than just by immediate consequences. Through the cognitive development of expectations concerning the results of various actions, people are able to think about the consequences of behavior before undertaking action and are able to anticipate rewards and punishments far into the future.

Goals, Standards, and Self-regulation

In terms of motivational processes, two concepts are noteworthy. First, there is the suggestion that people have **internal standards** for evaluating their own behavior and that of others. These standards represent goals for us to achieve and bases for expecting reinforcement from others and from ourselves. Second, the process of **self-reinforcement** is particularly important in maintaining behavior over extended periods of time in the absence of external reinforcers. Thus, through such internal self-evaluative responses as praise and guilt, we are able to reward ourselves for meeting standards or punish ourselves for violating them.

In its emphasis on goals, social cognitive theory emphasizes the human capacity for foresight, our ability to anticipate outcomes and make plans accordingly (Bandura, 1990). Thus, according to Bandura, "most human motivation is cognitively generated" (1992, p.18). People vary in the standards they set for themselves. Some individuals set challenging goals, others easy goals; some individuals have very specific goals, others ambiguous goals; some emphasize short-term, proximal goals while others emphasize long-range, distal goals (Cervone & Williams, 1992). In all cases, however, it is the anticipation of satisfaction with desired accomplishments and dissatisfaction with insufficient accomplishments that provides the incentives for our efforts. In sum, performance standards and anticipated consequences explain goal-directed behavior.

In terms of this analysis, two features are noteworthy. First, people are seen as proactive rather than as merely reactive; that is, people set their own standards and goals, rather than merely responding to demands from the environment. Second, through the ability to set one's own standards and the potential for self-reinforcement, considerable **self-regulation** of functioning is possible. Rather than being dependent on external motivators and rewards, we can set our own goals and reward ourselves for accomplishing them. Thus, through the development of cognitive mechanisms such as expectancies, standards, and self-reinforcement we are able to establish goals for the future and gain control over our own destiny (Bandura, 1989a,b).

Self-Efficacy and Performance

As previously noted, Bandura (1995) has increasingly emphasized the importance of self-perceptions of efficacy as cognitive mediators of action. While considering action and once engaged in it, people make judgments concerning their ability to perform various task requirements. These **self-efficacy judgments** influence thought ("This is what I need to do and I can make it." versus "I'll never manage this. What will people think of me?"), emotion (excitement, joy versus anxiety, depression), and action (greater commitment versus inhibition, immobilization). A person sets standards and goals and makes judgments concerning the ability to perform the tasks necessary for goal achievement.

An earlier edition of this text criticized social cognitive theory for its relative lack of concern with human motivation. More recently this has been an important area of concern, and Bandura (1990, 1995) has increasingly emphasized a purposive view of human action. In a relevant piece of research, Bandura and Cervone (1983) studied the effects of goals and performance feedback on motivation. The hypothesis tested was that performance motivation reflects both the presence of goals and the awareness of how one is doing relative to standards: "Simply adopting goals, whether easy or personally challenging ones, without knowing how one is doing seems to have no appreciable motivational effects" (1983, p. 123). The assumption was that greater discrepancies between standards and performances would generally lead to greater self-dissatisfaction and efforts to improve performance. However, a critical ingredient of such efforts is self-efficacy judgments. Thus the research tested the hypothesis that self-efficacy judgments, as well as self-evaluative judgments, mediate between goals and goal-directed effort.

In this research, subjects performed a strenuous activity under one of four conditions: goals with feedback on their performance, goals alone, feedback alone, and absence of goals and feedback. Following this activity, described as part of a project to plan and evaluate exercise programs for postcoronary rehabilitation, subjects rated how self-satisfied or self-dissatisfied they would be with the same level of performance in a following session. In addition, they recorded their perceived self-efficacy for various possible performance levels. Their effortful performance was then again measured. In accord with the hypothesis, the condition combining goals and performance feedback had a strong motivational impact, whereas neither goals alone nor feedback alone had comparable motivational significance (Figure 12.2). Also, subsequent effort was most intense when subjects were both dissatisfied with substandard performance and

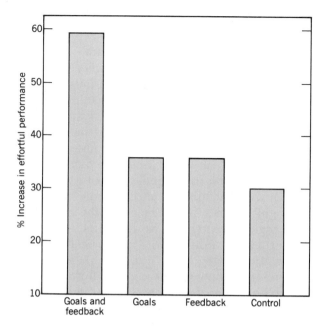

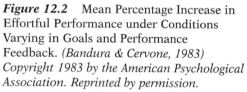

Figure 12.2 Mean Percentage Increase in Effortful Performance under Conditions Varying in Goals and Performance Feedback. *(Bandura & Cervone, 1983) Copyright 1983 by the American Psychological Association. Reprinted by permission.*

high on self-efficacy judgments for good attainment. Neither dissatisfaction alone nor positive self-efficacy judgments alone had a comparable effect. Often effort was reduced where there was both low dissatisfaction with performance and low perceived self-efficacy. The authors concluded that there was clear evidence in support of the theory that goals have motivating power through self-evaluative and self-efficacy judgments.

Performance feedback and self-efficacy judgments have been found to be particularly important in the development of intrinsic interest. Thus, psychologists have been able to enhance the interest of students in learning and their level of performance by helping them to break down tasks into subgoals, helping them to monitor their own performance, and providing them with feedback that increased their sense of self-efficacy (Bandura & Schunk, 1981; Morgan, 1985; Schunk & Cox, 1986). Intrinsic interest thus develops when the person has challenging standards that provide for positive self-evaluation when met, and the sense of self-efficacy in the potential for meeting those standards. It is such intrinsic interest that facilitates effort over extended periods of time in the absence of external rewards. Conversely, it is difficult to sustain motivation where one feels that the external or internal self-evaluative rewards are insufficient, or where one's sense of efficacy is so low that a positive outcome seems impossible. Self-perceived inefficacy can nullify the motivating potential of even the most desirable outcomes. For example, no matter how attractive it might seem to become a movie star, people will not be motivated in that direction unless they feel that they have the necessary skills. In the absence of such a sense of self-efficacy, becoming a movie star remains a fantasy rather than a goal that is pursued in action.

The effects of self-efficacy beliefs on effort and performance can be so great as to wipe out otherwise large differences in ability. For example, in one study males and females engaged in a competitive muscular leg endurance task. Self-efficacy beliefs of the subjects were manipulated by telling some that they were competing against an individual with a knee injury (high self-efficacy) and others that they were competing against a varsity track athlete (low self-efficacy). Not surprisingly, high self-efficacy subjects clearly performed better than low self-efficacy subjects and male subjects generally performed better than female subjects. What was particularly striking, however, was that subjects in the female, high self-efficacy group performed slightly better than subjects in the male, low self-efficacy group on the strength task. In other words, shifts in self-efficacy beliefs wiped out earlier large sex differences in physical strength (Weinberg, Gould, & Jackson, 1979).

Self-efficacy beliefs also influence how people cope with disappointments and stress in the pursuit of life goals. Research generally suggests that human functioning is facilitated by a personal sense of control (Schwarzer, 1992). Self-efficacy beliefs represent one aspect of such a sense of control . A study of women coping with abortion demonstrated the importance of self-efficacy beliefs in coping with stressful life events (Cozzarelli, 1993). In this research women about to obtain an abortion completed questionnaire measures of personality variables such as self-esteem and optimism, as well as a self-efficacy scale measuring expectations concerning successful post-abortion coping. For example, the scale included items asking about whether the women thought they would be able to spend time around children or babies comfortably and whether they would continue to have good sexual relations following abortion. Following abortion and then three weeks later measures of mood and depression were obtained (e.g., the degree to which the women were feeling depressed, regretful, relieved, guilty, sad, good). The results clearly supported the hypothesis that self-efficacy was a key determinant of post-abortion adjustment. The contribution of personality variables such as self-esteem and optimism to post-abortion were related to post-abortion adjustment. However, their effects appeared to occur through their contribution to feelings of self-efficacy.

In sum, self-efficacy beliefs have a broad impact on motivational processes. Most specifically these effects can be described as follows:

Selection   Self-efficacy beliefs influence the goals individuals select (e.g., individuals with high self-efficacy beliefs select more difficult, challenging goals than do low self-efficacy belief individuals).

Effort, Persistence, Performance   Individuals with high self-efficacy beliefs show greater effort and persistence, and perform better relative to individuals with low self-efficacy beliefs.

**CURRENT
APPLICATIONS**

SELF-EFFICACY AND CONDOM USE:
HOW TO CHANGE BEHAVIOR

The AIDS epidemic has complicated sexual relations in the 1990s, particularly for young people. In effect, sex education has become a form of preventative medicine. Awareness is definitely a step in the right direction, and knowing the facts about HIV, AIDS, and risky behavior is certainly important. But is it enough to influence young people's behavior? One recent study suggests not. This research tested whether an intervention program based on *social-cognitive theory* could improve HIV prevention. More specifically, would it help to increase *safe-sex self-efficacy*?

Bandura (1992) had proposed a conceptual model linking social cognitive theory and *perceived self-efficacy* to the control of sexual activities that would put individuals at risk for HIV infection and AIDS. Essentially, Bandura's model promotes the idea that how we perceive our ability to cope with a situation and to control its outcome is the key to influencing actual behavior.

A study by Basen-Engquist (1994) tested Bandura's model with a quasi-experimental field study involving college students. The subjects were divided into 3 groups. One group participated in a safe-sex efficacy workshop, another group heard a didactic lecture on HIV, and the third group was a control who heard a

lecture about an unrelated topic. As expected, an immediate post-test showed that the first and second groups scored higher on safe-sex self-efficacy and were more likely to report the *intention* to use a condom than the control group. The follow-up two months later, however, revealed that the group in the safe-sex efficacy workshop was more likely than both other groups to have increased in *actual* condom use. In other words, it was the manipulation of safe-sex self-efficacy, not mere information about HIV, that produced the change in behavior.

This research demonstrates that HIV prevention efforts must consider the psychology of safe-sex behavior. So much attention has been placed on increasing awareness through education that the question of how information is actually used by young people has been obscured. The discrepancy between *intended* and *actual* condom use in the group who received the HIV lecture suggests that information does not get translated into actual behavior as readily as educators would hope. Social cognitive theory, and perceived self-efficacy in particular, may provide the important psychological link between education and behavior change.

SOURCE: Basen-Engquist (1994)

Emotion   Individuals with high self-efficacy beliefs approach tasks with better moods (i.e., less anxiety and depression) than individuals with low self-efficacy beliefs.

Coping   Individuals with high self-efficacy beliefs are better able to cope with stress and disappointments than are individuals with low self-efficacy beliefs.

Bandura summarizes the evidence concerning the effects of self-efficacy beliefs on motivation and performance as follows: "The emerging evidence indicates that the successful, the innovative, the sociable, the nonanxious, the nondespondent, and the social reformers take an optimistic view of their personal efficacy to exercise influence over events that affect their lives" (1992, p. 24).

Summary of the View of Motivation

To summarize the social cognitive view of motivation, a person develops goals or standards that serve as the basis for action. People consider alternative courses of action and make decisions on the basis of the anticipated outcomes (external and internal) and the perceived self-efficacy for performing the necessary behaviors. Once action has been taken, the outcome is assessed in terms of the external rewards from others and one's own internal self-evaluations. Successful performance may lead to enhanced self-efficacy and either a relaxation of effort or the setting of higher standards for further effort. Unsuccessful performance or failure may lead to giving up or continued striving, depending on the value of the outcome to a person and to his or her sense of self-efficacy in relation to further effort.

Illustrating these concepts in relation to academic work, it is possible to remain motivated in one's studies when one has high standards, positive outcomes, feelings of pride associated with meeting those standards, and the sense that one is capable of meeting them. On the other hand, boredom and low motivation are likely when standards are low and few external or internal rewards are expected for accomplishment, or when one perceives successful performance as impossible.

GROWTH AND DEVELOPMENT

Social cognitive theory emphasizes the development of cognitive competencies, expectancies, goals-standards, self-efficacy beliefs, and self-regulatory functions through observation of others and through direct experience. Observational learning involves the ability to learn complex behaviors by watching others. "Because people can learn from example what to do, at least in approximate form, before performing any behavior, they are spared needless error" (Bandura, 1977b, p.22).

Observational Learning

The theory of **observational learning** suggests that people can learn merely by observing the behaviors of others. The person being observed is called a *model*. There is evidence to suggest that an individual can learn behaviors by observing a model perform these behaviors. Thus, for exam-

Observational Learning: *Aggressive behavior can be learned from the observation of such behavior on television. Etta Hulme, reprinted by permission of NEA, Inc.*

ple, the child may learn language by observing parents and other people speaking, a process called *modeling*. The type of behaviors under consideration are often included under the terms *imitation* and *identification*. However, imitation has the very narrow connotation of response mimicry and, at the other extreme, identification implies an incorporation of entire patterns of behavior. Modeling involves something broader than imitation but less diffuse than identification. In addition, these terms are rejected because they have been associated with stimulus–response reinforcement

Modeling—*Social learning theorists emphasize the importance of observing others in the acquisition of behavior. (Drawing by Opie; © 1978 The New Yorker Magazine, Inc.)*

theories and with psychoanalytic theory. Those theories are considered inadequate in accounting for the observed data.

Acquisition versus Performance   An important part of the theory of modeling is the distinction between **acquisition** and **performance**. A new, complex pattern of behavior can be learned or acquired regardless of reinforcers, but whether or not the behavior is performed will depend on rewards and punishments. Consider, for example, the classic study by Bandura and his associates to illustrate this distinction (Bandura, Ross, & Ross, 1963a). In this study three groups of children observed a model express aggressive behavior toward a plastic Bobo doll. In the first group, the aggressive behavior by the model was not followed by any consequences (No Consequences). In the second group, the model's aggressive behavior was followed by rewards (Reward), and in the third group it was followed by punishment (Punishment). Following observation of the model's aggressive behavior, children from the three groups were presented with two conditions. In the first condition, the children were left alone in a room with many toys, including a Bobo doll. They were then observed through a one-way mirror to see if they would express the aggressive behaviors of the model (No Incentive condition). In the next condition, the children were given attractive incentives for reproducing the model's behavior (Positive Incentive condition).

Two relevant questions can be asked. First, did the children behave aggressively when they were given an incentive to do so as opposed to when they were not? Many more imitative aggressive behaviors were shown in the Incentive condition than in the No Incentive condition (Figure 12.3). In other words, the children had learned (acquired) many aggressive behaviors that were not performed under the No Incentive condition but were performed under the Incentive condition. This result demonstrated the utility of the distinction between acquisition and performance. Second, did the consequences to the model affect the children's display of aggressive behavior? Observation of behavior in the No Incentive condition indicated clear differences; children who observed the model being punished performed far fewer imitative acts than did children in the Model Rewarded and No Consequences groups (Figure 12.3). This difference, however, was wiped out by offering the children attractive incentives for reproducing the model's behavior (Positive Incentive). In sum, the consequences to the model had an effect on the children's performance of the aggressive acts but not on the learning of them.

Vicarious Conditioning   A number of other studies have since demonstrated that the observation of consequences to a model affects performance but not acquisition. The difference between acquisition and performance suggests, however, that in some way the children were being affected by what happened to the model; that is, either on a cognitive basis, on an emotional basis, or both, the children were responding to the conse-

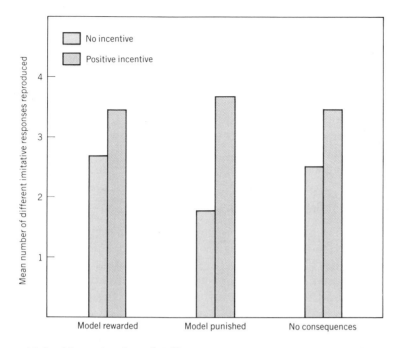

Figure 12.3 Mean Number of Different Imitative Responses Reproduced by Children as a Function of Response Consequences to the Model and Positive Incentives. *(Bandura, 1965) Copyright 1965 by the American Psychological Association. Reprinted by permission.*

quences to the model. The suggestion here is that the children learned certain emotional responses by sympathizing with the model, that is, vicariously by observing the model. Not only can behavior be learned through observation, but emotional reactions such as fear and joy can also be conditioned on a vicarious basis: "It is not uncommon for individuals to develop strong emotional reactions toward places, persons, and things without having had any personal contact with them" (Bandura, 1986, p. 185).

The process of learning emotional reactions through observing others, known as **vicarious conditioning**, has been demonstrated in both humans and animals. Thus, human subjects who observed a model express a conditioned fear response were found to develop a vicariously conditioned emotional response to a previously neutral stimulus (Bandura & Rosenthal, 1966; Berger, 1962). Similarly, in an experiment with animals it was found that an intense and persistent fear of snakes developed in younger monkeys who observed their parents behave fearfully in the presence of real or toy snakes. What was particularly striking about this research is that the period of observation of their parents' emotional reaction was sometimes very brief. Further, once the vicarious conditioning took place, the fear was found to be intense, long-lasting, and present in situations different from those in which the emotional reaction was first observed (Mineka et al., 1984).

Although observational learning can be a powerful process, one should not think that it is automatic or that one is bound to follow in the footsteps of others. Children, for example, have multiple models and can learn from parents, siblings, teachers, peers, and television. In addition, they learn from their own direct experience. Beyond this, as children get older they may actively select which models they will observe and attempt to emulate.

Learning Delay of Gratification Skills

Research has demonstrated the importance of modeling and observational learning in the development of performance standards for success and reward that may then serve as the basis for **delay of gratification**. Children exposed to models who set high standards of performance for self-reward tend to limit their own self-rewards to exceptional performance to a greater degree than do children who have been exposed to models who set lower standards or to no models at all (Bandura & Kupers, 1964). Children will model standards even if they result in self-denial of available rewards (Bandura, Grusec, & Menlove, 1967) and will also impose learned standards on other children (Mischel & Liebert, 1966). Children can be made to tolerate greater delays in receiving gratification if they are exposed to models exhibiting such delay behavior.

The effects of a model on delay behavior in children are well illustrated in research by Bandura and Mischel (1965). Children found to be high and low in delay of gratification were exposed to models of the opposite behavior. In a live-model condition, each child individually observed a testing situation in which an adult model was asked to choose between an immediate reward and a more valued object at a later date. The high-delay children observed a model who selected the immediately available reward and commented on its benefits, whereas the low-delay children observed a model who selected the delayed reward and commented on the virtues of delay. In a symbolic-model condition, children read verbal accounts of these behaviors, the verbal account again being the opposite of the child's pattern of response. Finally, in a no-model condition, children were just appraised of the choices given the adults. Following exposure to one of these three procedures, the children were again given a choice between an immediate reward and a more valuable reward. The results were that the high-delay children in all three conditions significantly altered their delay-of-reward behavior in favor of immediate gratification. The live-model condition produced the greatest effect (Figure 12.4). The low-delay children exposed to a delay model significantly altered their behavior in terms of greater delay, but there was no significant difference between the effects of live and symbolic models. Finally,

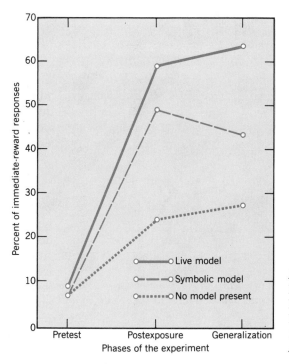

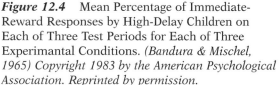

Figure 12.4   Mean Percentage of Immediate-Reward Responses by High-Delay Children on Each of Three Test Periods for Each of Three Experimantal Conditions. *(Bandura & Mischel, 1965) Copyright 1983 by the American Psychological Association. Reprinted by permission.*

for both groups of children, the effects were found to be stable when the tests were readministered four to five weeks later.

As mentioned previously, the performance of observed behaviors clearly is influenced by the observed consequences to the model. For example, children who watch a film in which a child is not punished for playing with toys that were prohibited by the mother are more likely to play with prohibited toys than are children who see no film or see a film in which the child is punished (Walters & Parke, 1964). The old saying "Monkey see, monkey do" is not completely true. It would be more appropriate to say "Monkey sees rewarded or not punished, monkey does." After all, the monkey is no fool.

The ability to delay gratification involves the development of **cognitive and behavioral competencies**. Relevant behaviors are acquired through the observation of others and through direct experience. The ability to delay gratification is determined by the expected outcomes, as influenced by past direct personal experience, observation of consequences to models such as parents and peers, and self-reactions.

Mischel (1990, 1996) has done considerable research on the cognitive mechanisms children use to delay gratification and overcome the temptations of stimuli immediately before them. In addition to the development of rules and internal self-statements ("You are not supposed to do this."), children develop strategies for being able to resist temptation.

Delay of Gratification: *Children must learn to postpone pleasure until the proper time. Here, a child considers how much he will have to save to buy a desired toy.*

One such strategy is distraction or diverting attention away from the tempting object. Another is focusing on the more abstract or "cool" qualities of the desired object, rather than on its concrete or "hot" qualities. For example, one can focus on pictures of food rather than on the actual taste of food: "Thus, what is in the children's heads—not what is physically in front of them—crucially affects their ability to purposefully sustain delay in order to achieve their preferred but delayed goals....If the children imagine the real objects as present they cannot wait long for them. In contrast, if they imagine pictures of the objects, they can wait for long time periods" (Mischel, 1990, p. 123).

Summary of the View of Growth and Development

In addition to the importance of direct experience, social cognitive theory emphasizes the importance of models and observational learning in personality development. Individuals acquire emotional responses and behaviors through observing the behaviors and emotional responses of models (i.e., the processes of observational learning and vicarious conditioning). Whether acquired behaviors are performed similarly depends on directly experienced consequences and the observed consequences to models. Through the experiencing of **direct external consequences** individuals learn to expect rewards and punishments for specific behaviors in specific contexts. Through **vicarious experiencing of consequences** to others individuals acquire emotional reactions and learn expectancies without going through the often painful step of experiencing consequences directly. Thus, through direct experience and observation, through direct experiencing of rewards and punishments and through vicarious conditioning, individuals acquire such important personality characteristics as competencies, expectancies, goals-standards, and self-efficacy beliefs. In addition, through such processes individuals acquire self-regulatory capacities. Thus, through the development of cognitive competencies and standards they are able to anticipate the future and reward or punish themselves for relative progress in meeting chosen goals. The latter **self-produced consequences** are of particular significance in maintaining behavior over extended periods of time in the absence of external reinforcers.

It is important to recognize that social cognitive theory is opposed to views that emphasize fixed stages of development and broad personality types. According to Bandura and Mischel, people develop skills and competencies in particular areas. Rather than developing consciences or healthy egos, they develop competencies and motivational guides for action that are attuned to specific contexts. Such a view emphasizes the ability of people to discriminate among situations and to regulate behavior flexibly according to internal goals and the demands of the situation.

MAJOR CONCEPTS

Reciprocal determinism. The mutual effects of variables on one another (e.g., Bandura's emphasis on person and environmental factors continuously affecting one another).

Behavioral Signatures. Individually distinctive profiles of situation–behavior relationships.

Self-efficacy. In social cognitive theory, the perceived ability to cope with specific situations.

Microanalytic research. Bandura's suggested research strategy concerning the concept of self-efficacy in which specific rather than global self-efficacy judgments are recorded.

Goals. In social cognitive theory, desired future events that motivate the person over extended periods of time and enable the person to go beyond momentary influences.

Competencies. A structural unit in social cognitive theory reflecting the individual's ability to solve problems or perform tasks necessary to achieve goals.

Expectancies. In social cognitive theory, what the individual anticipates or predicts will occur as the result of specific behaviors in specific situations (anticipated consequences).

Internal standards. A concept in social cognitive theory emphasizing how behavior may be regulated and maintained by learned standards for reinforcement (e.g., pride, shame) that are now part of the individual.

Self-reinforcement. In social-cognitive theory, the process by which individuals reward themselves involves self-evaluative responses such as praise and guilt. Such self-reinforcement processes are particularly important in the self-regulation of behavior over extended periods of time.

Self-regulation. Bandura's concept for the process through which persons regulate their own behavior.

Self-efficacy judgments. In social cognitive theory, the person's expectations concerning his or her ability to perform specific behaviors in a situation.

Observational learning. Bandura's concept for the process through which people learn merely by observing the behavior of others, called models.

Modeling. Bandura's concept for the process of reproducing behaviors learned through the observation of others.

Acquisition. The learning of new behaviors, viewed by Bandura as independent of reward and contrasted with performance—which is seen as dependent on reward.

Performance. The production of learned behaviors, viewed by Bandura as dependent on rewards, in contrast with the acquisition of new behaviors, which is seen as independent of reward.

Vicarious conditioning. Bandura's concept for the process through which emotional responses are learned through the observation of emotional responses in others.

Delay of gratification. The postponement of pleasure until the optimum or proper time, a concept particularly emphasized in social cognitive theory in relation to self-regulation.

Cognitive competencies. Abilities to think in a variety of ways, particularly emphasized in social cognitive theory in relation to the ability to delay gratification.

Behavioral competencies. Abilities to behave in particular ways, particularly emphasized in social cognitive theory in relation to performance, as in delay of gratification.

Direct external consequences. In social cognitive theory, the external events that follow behavior and influence future performance, contrasted with vicarious consequences and self-produced consequences.

Vicarious experiencing of consequences. In social cognitive theory, the observed consequences to the behavior of others that influence future performance.

Self-produced consequences. In social cognitive theory, the consequences to behavior that are produced personally (internally) by the individual and that play a vital role in self-regulation and self-control.

REVIEW

1. Social cognitive theory emphasizes learning independent of reinforcement and the importance of cognitive processes. The two main representatives of it are Albert Bandura and Walter Mischel. The emphasis is on the interaction between person and environment, as expressed in the concept of reciprocal determinism.

2. The personality structures emphasized are competencies–skills, goals, and the self. Of particular import are cognitive competencies that enable the person to solve problems in everyday life. Goals guide the individual toward future outcomes. The person is viewed as having self-conceptions and self-control processes. A particularly important aspect of the perception of the self is that of self-efficacy, or the perceived ability to cope with particular situations. These concepts all involve emphasis on functioning in specific situations as opposed to broad dispositions or global, context-free traits. Individuals are viewed as having behavioral signatures or patterns of situation-behavior relationships. Thus, the emphasis is on a microanalytic research strategy.

3. The social cognitive view of motivation emphasizes the importance of standards–goals. Through cognitive processes of foresight and anticipation, individuals strive to reduce discrepancies between current levels of performance and standards or goals of performance levels. Action is undertaken in terms of expected consequences (i.e., rewards and punishments) from external or internal sources. The pursuit of goals is maintained over extended periods of time through the setting of more immediate, proximal goals and through self-reinforcement (e.g., pride). People can take charge of their own destiny through self-regulatory processes involving both the selection of goals and self-reinforcement in the pursuit of them.

4. Self-efficacy judgments, or the perceived ability to perform tasks relevant to a situation, play a key role in motivation through their influence on selection of goals, effort and persistence toward achieving the goal, the emotions with which tasks are approached (i.e., anxiety and depression associated with low self-efficacy), and success in coping with stress and negative events.

5. Social cognitive theory emphasizes the acquisition of skills-competencies, standards, and self-efficacy judgments through the observation of others, through reinforcement by others, and through direct experience. The importance of models in the process of observational learning is emphasized. One aspect of this process involves the learning of emotional reactions through observation of the emotional reactions of models, known as vicarious conditioning. An important distinction is made between acquiring patterns of behavior in the absence of rewards and performing those behaviors, the latter being dependent on expected consequences (i.e., expected rewards and punishments).

6. Research on the development of cognitive and behavioral competencies associated with delay in gratification illustrates the social cognitive principles of growth and development. Standards are learned through the observation of models and through reinforcement. The ability to delay gratification involves the development of cognitive

and behavioral competencies that are acquired through observation of others and through direct experience. Delay behavior, then, is influenced by outcome expectancies, including both responses from others and self-evaluative responses.

7. Throughout social cognitive theory there is an emphasis on the development of cognitive skills and competencies in particular areas. The emphasis is on the ability of the person to discriminate among situations and regulate behavior according to internal goals and external demands. Thus, once more, there is a shift from context-free traits to functioning in specific situations.

13

SOCIAL COGNITIVE THEORY: APPLICATIONS AND EVALUATION

A college senior was trying to work on his medical school applications late one evening, and found himself so paralyzed by anxiety that he had to stop. How could he possibly cope with not getting accepted anywhere? He became so focused on the possibility of total rejection that he was unable to complete his applications by the deadlines. He eventually sent them in, but by being late he significantly worsened his chances of getting into medical school. Thus, his own behavior had increased the likelihood that the unwanted outcome would become a reality.

This young man is displaying cognitions that include some dysfunctional expectancies and equally dysfunctional self-conceptions. Such dysfunctional cognitive processes are the focus of clinical applications of social cognitive theory. This chapter considers the role of dysfunctional cognition in abnormal behavior and discusses procedures for producing change. More specifically, attention is given to the role of self-efficacy beliefs and to procedures that enhance people's beliefs about their ability to cope with specific situations. In conclusion, social cognitive theory is compared with the approaches to personality previously considered in the text.

QUESTIONS TO BE ADDRESSED IN THIS CHAPTER

1. What is the role of disordered self-efficacy beliefs in abnormal psychological functioning?
2. Are there factors common to all therapeutic change?
3. Can psychotherapy rely on cognitive processes alone, or is actual experience a necessary component of therapeutic change?

CLINICAL APPLICATIONS

PSYCHOPATHOLOGY

According to social cognitive theory, maladaptive behavior is the result of dysfunctional learning. Like all learning, maladaptive responses can be learned as a result of direct experience or as the result of exposure to inadequate or "sick" models. Thus, Bandura suggests that the degree to which parents themselves model forms of aberrant behavior is often a significant causal factor in the development of psychopathology. Again, there is no need to look for traumatic incidents in the early history of the individual or for the underlying conflicts. Nor is it necessary to find a history of reinforcement for the initial acquisition of the pathological behavior. On the other hand, once behaviors have been learned through observational learning, it is quite likely that they have been maintained because of direct and vicarious reinforcement. Recall the research on the vicarious conditioning of emotional responses. Monkeys who observed their parents express a fear of snakes developed a conditioned emotional response that was intense, long-lasting, and generalized beyond the context in which it was first learned. Thus, it is suggested that observational learning and vicarious conditioning may account for a great proportion of human fears and phobias.

Dysfunctional Expectancies and Self-conceptions

Although the learning of specific overt behaviors and emotional reactions is important in psychopathology, increasingly social cognitive theory has come to emphasize the role of **dysfunctional expectancies** and **self-conceptions**. People may erroneously expect painful events to follow some events or pain to be associated with specific situations. They then may act so as to avoid certain situations or in a way that creates the very situation they were trying to avoid. An example is the person who fears that closeness will bring pain and then acts in a hostile way, resulting in rejection by others and presumably confirming the expectancy that closeness leads to disappointment and rejection.

Cognitive processes also play a role in psychopathology in terms of dysfunctional self-evaluations, in particular in terms of *perceived low self-efficacy* or *perceived inefficacy*. Remember that perceived self-efficacy is the perception that one can perform the tasks required by a situation or cope with a situation. In perceived inefficacy, one feels that one cannot perform the necessary tasks or cope with the demands of the situation. Thus, according to social cognitive theory, it is perceived inefficacy that plays a central role in anxiety and depression (Bandura, 1988, 1989c, 1992).

Self-efficacy and Anxiety   Let us first consider the role of perceived self-efficacy in anxiety. According to social cognitive theory, people with perceptions of low self-efficacy in relation to potential threats experience high anxiety arousal. It is not the threatening event per se but the perceived inefficacy in coping with it that is fundamental to anxiety. Research indicates that those who believe they cannot manage threatening events experience great distress. They may also develop further dysfunctional cognitions such as a preoccupation with what may happen. In other words, the anxious person may focus attention on the disaster that lies ahead, and on his or her inability to cope with it, rather than focusing on what might be done to cope with the situation. The perception of inability to cope with the situation may then be complicated further by the perceived inability to cope with the anxiety itself—a fear-of-fear response that can lead to panic (Barlow, 1991).

Self-efficacy and Depression   Whereas perceived inefficacy in relation to threatening events leads to anxiety, perceived inefficacy in relation to rewarding outcomes leads to depression; that is, depression represents the response to perceived inability to gain desired rewarding outcomes. Part of the problem with depressives, however, may be their excessively stringent standards. In other words, individuals prone to depression impose upon themselves excessively high goals and standards. When they fall short of these exacting standards, they blame themselves and their lack of ability or competence for what has happened. Excessive self-criticism is, in fact, often a major feature of depression. In sum, although perceived self-inefficacy to fulfill desired goals is fundamental to depression, part of the problem may be the excessive goals themselves. In addition, the low self-efficacy beliefs may contribute to diminished performance, leading to falling even further below standards and additional self-blame (Kavanagh, 1992).

Bandura (1992) raises the interesting point that discrepancies between standards and performance can have varied effects—they can lead to greater effort, to apathy, or to depression. What determines which effect will occur? According to him, discrepancies between performance and standards lead to high motivation when people believe they have the efficacy to accomplish the goal. Beliefs that the goal are beyond one's capabilities because they are unrealistic will lead to abandoning the goal and perhaps to apathy, but not to depression. For example, a person may say "This task is just too hard" and give up—perhaps becoming frustrated and angry, but not depressed. Depression occurs when a person feels inefficacious in relation to a goal but believes the goal to be reasonable; therefore that person feels he or she must continue to strive to meet the standard. Thus the effects of a discrepancy between standards and performance on effort and mood depend on self-efficacy beliefs and whether the standard is perceived to be reasonable, possible to achieve, and important.

Self-efficacy and Health   One of the most active areas of social cognitive research has been on the relation between self-efficacy beliefs and health. The results of this research can be easily summarized: Strong, positive self-efficacy beliefs are good for your health. Conversely, weak and negative self-efficacy beliefs are bad for your health (Schwarzer, 1992). There are two major ways in which self-efficacy beliefs affect health. These ways are the beliefs' effects on health-related behaviors and their effects on physiological functioning (Contrada, Leventhal, & O'Leary, 1990; Miller, Shoda, & Hurley, 1996). Self-efficacy beliefs affect both the likelihood of developing various illnesses and the process of recovery from illness (O'Leary, 1992).

Self-efficacy beliefs have been related to such varied behaviors as cigarette smoking, alcohol use, and condom use with relation to pregnancy and AIDS. For example, perceptions of self-efficacy to practice safer sexual behavior have been related to the probability of adopting safer sexual practices. Modeling, goal-setting, and other techniques have been used to increase self-efficacy beliefs and thereby reduce risky behavior (O'Leary, 1992). Changes in self-efficacy beliefs also have been found to

SELF-EFFICACY AND HEALTH

According to social cognitive theory, perceptions of self-efficacy have important implications for emotional reactions to situations and motivations to undertake various behaviors. Such a concept would appear to have important implications for health in terms of understanding people's emotional and behavioral responses to stressful conditions and health-related programs.

Recent research by Bandura and others suggests that this is indeed the case. A variety of studies indicate that feelings of low self-efficacy are associated with increased stress responses, poorer responses to pain, and low motivation to pursue health-related programs. Conversely, increased feelings of self-efficacy are associated with lower self-reported stress, decreased physiological responses indicative of stress, increased coping, and increased involvement in programs prescribed by health-care workers. In one treatment program, arthritic patients were given treatment to enhance their perceived self-efficacy in

coping with their difficuly. The treatment not only accomplished this but also resulted in reduced pain and joint inflammation, as well as in improved psychosocial functioning. In another treatment program with bulimics—or individuals who binge eat and then vomit to purge themselves of the food—increases in self-efficacy were found to be associated with greater self-control in eating and decreases in vomiting frequency. Finally, in a third program, changes in perceived self-efficacy for walking were found to be associated with increased exercise in an activity program prescribed for patients at risk for heart disease.

Research to date suggests that self-efficacy theory has important implications for such diverse health-related behaviors as smoking cessation, pain experience and management, control of eating and weight, and adherence to preventive health programs.

SOURCES: Bandura, 1995; O'Leary, 1993; O'Leary et al., 1988; Schneider et al., 1987; Schwarzer, 1992.

Programs that increase self-efficacy help arthritic patients overcome their fears of pain and disability.

be of importance in relation to the process of recovery from illness. For example, in recovery from a heart attack it is important to have an appropriate amount of physical activity. That is, sometimes individuals recovering from a heart attack may have unrealistically high self-efficacy beliefs and exercise beyond what is constructive for them. In these cases patients must monitor their self-efficacy beliefs to bring them into more accord with reality and, correspondingly, to bring their exercise into healthier patterns (Ewart, 1992).

Turning to the relation between self-efficacy beliefs and bodily functioning, there is evidence that high self-efficacy beliefs buffer the effects of stress and enhance the functioning of the body's immune (disease-fighting) system. There is evidence that excessive stress can lead to impairment of the immune system, whereas improvement of the ability to ameliorate stress can enhance its functioning (O'Leary, 1990). In an experiment designed to examine the impact of perceived self-efficacy of control over stressors on the immune system, Bandura and his associates found that perceived self-efficacy indeed enhanced immune system functioning (Wiedenfeld et al., 1990).

In this research, subjects with a phobia (excessive fear) of snakes were tested under three conditions: a baseline control phase involving no exposure to the phobic stressor (snake), a perceived self-efficacy acquisition phase during which subjects were assisted in gaining a sense of coping efficacy, and a perceived maximal self-efficacy phase once they had developed a complete sense of coping efficacy. During these phases, a small amount of blood was drawn from the subjects and analyzed for the presence of cells that are known to help regulate the immune system. For example, the level of helper T cells, known to play a role in destroying cancerous cells and viruses, was measured. These analyses indicated that increases in self-efficacy beliefs were associated with increases in enhanced immune system functioning, as evidenced, for example, by the increased level of helper T cells (Figure 13.1). Thus, although the effects of stress can be negative, the growth of perceived efficacy over stressors can have valuable adaptive properties at the level of immune system functioning.

CHANGE

Therapeutic work within the social cognitive framework is relatively recent, though it has become an important area of theory and research. Bandura increasingly has worked to develop methods of therapeutic change and a unifying theory of behavioral change. Although Bandura emphasizes the importance of developing such procedures, he is extremely cautious in his approach. He suggests that therapeutic procedures should be applied clinically only after the basic mechanisms involved are understood and after the effects of the methods have been adequately tested.

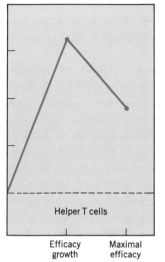

Figure 13.1 Changes in Helper T Cells During Exposure to Phobic Stressor While Acquiring Perceived Coping Self-Efficacy and After Perceived Coping Self-Efficacy Develops to Maximal Level. *(Wiedenfeld et al., 1990) Copyright 1990 by the American Psychological Association. Adapted by permission.*

Modeling and Guided Participation

According to Bandura, the change process involves not only the acquisition of new patterns of thought and behavior, but also their generalization and maintenance. The social cognitive view of therapy consequently emphasizes the importance of changes in the sense of efficacy. The treatment approach most emphasized by social cognitive theory is the acquisition of cognitive and behavioral competencies through **modeling** and **guided participation**. In the former, desired activities are demonstrated by various models who experience positive consequences or at least no adverse consequences. Generally, the complex patterns of behavior to be learned are broken down into subskills and increasingly difficult subtasks so as to ensure optimal progress. In guided participation the individual is assisted in performing the modeled behaviors.

Relevant Research Much of the research on therapeutic modeling and guided participation has been carried out in the laboratory, using severe snake phobias and children's avoidance of dogs as targets of behavior change. In one early study, the modeling technique was compared with systematic desensitization and with a no-treatment control condition (Bandura, Blanchard, & Ritter, 1967). The subjects were individuals who answered a newspaper advertisement offering help to people with a snake phobia. Subjects were tested for how much contact they could tolerate with a snake both before and after they participated in one of the following four conditions: (1) *live modeling with participation*, in which a model demonstrated the desired behavior and then assisted the subject to learn increasingly more difficult responses; (2) *symbolic modeling*, in which subjects observed a film that showed children and adults engaged

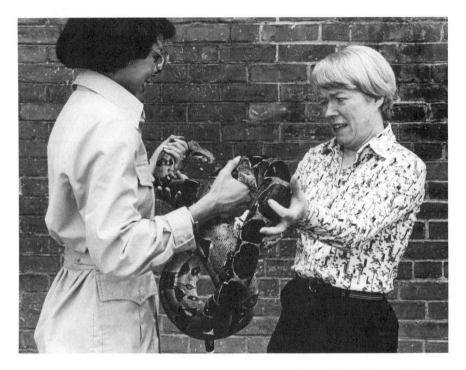

Guided Participation: *Bandura emphasizes the role of modeling and guided participation in behavior change. Here, a woman who is afraid of snakes is being helped to overcome her fear by a woman who models the desired behavior.*

in progressively more threatening interactions with a large king snake; subjects were also trained to relax while watching the film; (3) *systematic desensitization;* (4) control—no treatment. The results were that the control subjects remained unchanged in their avoidance behavior, the symbolic modeling and systematic desensitization subjects showed substantial reductions in phobic behavior, and the live modeling combined with guided participation subjects showed the greatest improvement. Live modeling with guided participation proved to be a superior and unusually powerful treatment that eliminated the snake phobia in virtually all subjects. As an illustration, all the subjects in this group progressed to the point where they were able to sit in a chair with a snake in their laps for 30 seconds.

A study of nursery school children who were afraid of dogs found that observation of another child playing with a dog helped to remove much of the fear and avoidance behavior (Bandura, Grusec, & Menlove, 1967). Significantly, these gains were maintained at a follow-up test one month later. In another study, Bandura and Menlove (1968) demonstrated that watching films of models playing with dogs could be helpful in reducing children's avoidance behavior. A particularly interesting finding was the possibility that the real-life models themselves were afraid of dogs. Whereas only one parent in a group of bold children reported any fear of dogs, in the group of avoidant children many of the parents were found to have such a fear.

One can see here many potential applications of modeling and guided participation with children and adults. For example, a beginning swimmer may be assisted in losing his or her fear of water by watching peers overcome their fears. The student may be helped to develop better study skills by observing more capable students and participating with them in study sessions. Thus, modeling and guided participation can be useful in eliminating unnecessary fears, as well as in acquiring new skills and competencies.

In these studies, fear and avoidance behavior are reduced through the observation of models. What is the process that underlies such changes? Bandura suggests that psychological procedures, whatever their form, alter the level and strength of *self-efficacy* or the perceived ability to cope with specific situations (Bandura, 1982). Cognitive processes are part of psychopathology in that these processes involve dysfunctional expectancies and perceptions of self-inefficacy. Therefore, it makes sense that an effective therapeutic procedure would alter such expectancies and self-perceptions. Modeling and guided participation facilitate such changes and thereby reduce anticipatory fears and avoidance behaviors. At the root of such procedures, as well as other therapeutic procedures, is a cognitive process involving changed expectations of personal efficacy.

Is there evidence to support this theory of psychological change? In a number of studies, individuals with phobias received treatment while their efficacy expectations and behaviors were measured (Bandura & Adams, 1977; Bandura, Adams, & Beyer, 1977; Bandura, Reese, & Adams, 1982; Williams, 1992). As predicted, subjects' statements of self-efficacy consistently predicted performance on tasks of varying levels of difficulty or threat. In other words, as therapeutic procedures led to improvement in perceived self-efficacy, individuals were increasingly able to confront previously feared objects.

For example, in one such study, subjects who suffered from chronic snake phobia were assigned to one of three conditions: *participant modeling* (the therapist models the threatening activities and subjects gradually perform the tasks, with therapist assistance, until they can be performed alone); *modeling* (subjects observe the therapist perform the tasks but do not engage in them); and *control condition* (Bandura, Adams, & Beyer, 1977). Both before and after these conditions, the subjects were tested on a Behavioral Avoidance Test (BAT), consisting of 29 performance tasks requiring increasingly threatening interactions with a red-tailed boa constrictor. The final task involved letting the snake crawl in their laps while holding their hands at their sides. To determine the generality of change, subjects were also tested after treatment with a dis-

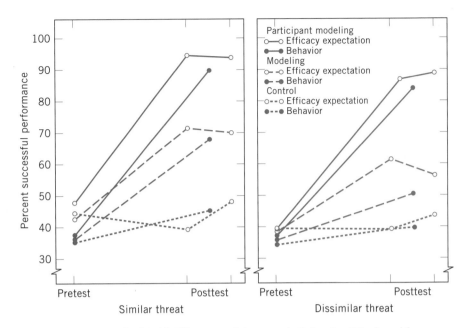

Figure 13.2 Level of Self-Efficacy and Approach Behavior Displayed by Subjects Toward Different Threats After Receiving Vicarious (Modeling) or Performance-based Participant Modeling Treatments or No Treatment. *(In the posttest phase, level of self-efficacy was measured prior to and after the behavioral avoidance tests with the two subjects.) Bandura, Adams, & Beyer, 1977. Copyright © 1977 American Psychological Association. Reprinted by permission.*

similar threat—a corn snake. In addition, efficacy expectations were obtained before treatment, after treatment but before the second administration of the BAT, following the second administration of the BAT, and again one month following the completion of treatment. The results indicated that participant modeling and modeling produced significant increases in approach behavior toward both the similar threat and the dissimilar threat, as well as significant increases in self-efficacy judgments (Figure 13.2). These gains clearly surpassed those made by subjects in the control condition. In addition, self-efficacy judgments (before the second BAT) were uniformly accurate predictors of performance; that is, strong self-efficacy judgments were associated with higher probabilities of successful task performance. These efficacy expectations in fact had superior predictive power over past performance! Follow-up data indicated that the subjects not only maintained their gains in self-efficacy and approach behavior but achieved further improvements. In sum, the data supported the utility of guided participation and the social cognitive view that treatments improve performance because they raise expectations of personal efficacy.

CURRENT APPLICATIONS

GIVING UP ADDICTIONS AND AVOIDING RELAPSE

Millions of people suffer from compulsive behavior patterns that have an addictive quality—smoking, overeating, gambling, drinking, drug abuse. Often they give up the troublesome behavior for a period of time, only to find that it returns. What accounts for the relapse, and how can its risks be minimized?

Although many people claim a physiological basis for addictive behavior, two points are noteworthy: (1) In some of these compulsive patterns, no true physiological addiction exists. Yet a psychological craving remains. Generally, periods of intense craving are associated with feelings of threat and inability to cope with events. (2) Many people are able to go through an extended period of absti-

nence, only to experience a relapse—overeating after weight loss, habitual smoking after abstinence, and so on. Researchers in this area have identified a common element in the relapse process. Those who are able to maintain abstinence perceive themselves as more able to cope with and affect events than those who relapse. They have better self-efficacy judgments. Many people show occasional lapses from total abstinence. Those who relapse, however, treat the event as a statement about themselves and their efficacy. Thus, they make statements such as "I'm a failure" or "I just can't do it" or "I have no willpower." Already feeling vulnerable in relation to the task at hand, they treat occasional lapses in a way that only serves to damage further their beliefs in themselves.

In treating addictions and compulsive patterns of behavior, getting people to abstain is only part of the job. In many cases, this turns out to be easier than helping them to remain abstinent. Evidently, changing the way they interpret occasional lapses and enhancing their feeling of self-efficacy concerning abstinence are an important part of the work that needs to be done.

SOURCE: Marlatt, Baer, & Quigley, 1995; Marlatt & Gordon, 1980; *The New York Times*, February 23, 1983, C1.

Self-efficacy: *Bandura suggests that feelings of self-efficacy are key in the responses of alcoholics and drug addicts to relapse.*

The preceding discussion has focused on the treatment of phobias and other fears. However, as indicated in the discussion of self-efficacy and health, the social cognitive approach has been used in the treatment of a wide variety of difficulties. For example, studies have demonstrated the utility of developing coping skills and increased self-efficacy in handling test anxiety (Smith, 1989) and of vulnerability to assault in women (Ozer & Bandura, 1990). In the latter case, women who participated in a modeling program in which they mastered the physical skills needed to defend themselves against unarmed sexual assailants gained increased freedom of action and decreased avoidant behavior. Fundamental to all of these studies is the experience of mastery that leads to a therapeutic increase in perceived self-efficacy (Figure 13.3).

Of particular significance for any therapeutic approach is the degree to which the positive effects endure and generalize to other aspects of the person's functioning. Skeptics of modeling and guided mastery approaches might expect there to be little evidence of enduring change or of generalization beyond, for example, the specific phobia treated. However, research suggests that the effects often are enduring and transfer to self-efficacy beliefs in other areas as well (Cervone & Scott, 1995; Williams, 1992). Bandura describes such effects as follows:

> Psychological treatments have traditionally attempted to change human behavior by talk. In the sociocognitive view, human functioning can be enhanced more dependably and fundamentally by mastery experiences than by conversation. In translating this notion to therapeutic practice for phobic disorders, my students and I evolved a powerful guided mastery treatment. It eradicates phobic behavior and biochemical stress reactions, eliminates phobic ruminations and recurrent nightmares, and creates positive attitudes toward formerly dreaded threats. These striking changes are achieved by everyone in a brief period. The changes endure...In follow-up assessments we discovered that the participants not only maintained their therapeutic gains, but made notable improvements in domains of functioning quite unrelated to the treated dysfunction. Thus, for example, after mastering an animal phobia, participants had reduced their social timidity, expanded their competencies in different spheres, and boosted their venturesomeness in a variety of ways. Success in overcoming, within a few hours of treatment, a phobic dread that had constricted and tormented their lives for twenty or thirty years produced a profound change in participants' beliefs in their personal efficacy to exercise better control over their lives. They were putting themselves to the test and enjoying their successes much to their surprise.
>
> SOURCE: Bandura, as quoted in Pervin, 1996, p. 82

GENERAL VIEW

Psychological procedures, whatever their format, serve as ways of creating and strengthening expectations of personal effectiveness. Social cognitive therapy emphasizes the acquisition of cognitive and behavioral competencies through modeling and guided participation.

ATTRIBUTES OF GOOD MODELS: RELEVANCE AND CREDIBILITY

Models who compel attention, who instill trust, who appear to be realistic figures for self-comparison, and whose standards seem reasonable to the learner will be good sources for therapeutic modeling effects. These attributes may be summarized in terms of the positive functions of relevance and credibility.

SOME ILLUSTRATIVE RULES FOR INDUCING AND MAINTAINING DESIRED CHANGES

1. Structure the tasks to be learned in an orderly, stepwise sequence.
2. Explain and demonstrate general rules or principles. Check client's understanding and provide opportunities for clarification.
3. Provide guided simulated practice with feedback concerning success and error.
4. Once the desired behavior is established, increase opportunities for self-directed accomplishment.
5. Test newly acquired skills in the natural environment under conditions likely to produce favorable results.
6. Test skills in increasingly more demanding situations until a satisfactory level of competence and self-efficacy has been obtained.
7. Provide opportunity for therapist consultation and feedback during periods of increased independent mastery.

THERAPEUTIC EFFECTS OF MODELING

1. *Development of New Skills.* Through observing models and through guided participation people acquire new patterns of behavior and new coping strategies. For example, submissive clients learn to model assertive behavior.
2. *Changes in Inhibitions About Self-expression.* As a result of modeling, responses already available to the person may be weakened or strengthened. For example, inhibitory effects can occur as a result of observing models receive negative consequences for certain behaviors. Disinhibitory effects, which are more common in therapy, result from observing models perform behaviors without adverse consequences or with positive consequences. Fears may be overcome in this way.
3. *Facilitation of Preexisting Patterns of Behavior.* Behaviors already available to the person and that are not associated with anxiety may occur more often as a result of modeling influences. For example, learners may be aided to become more skillful conversationalists.
4. *Adoption of More Realistic Standards for Judging One's Own Performance.* Observing models reward themselves for varying levels of performance can affect the learner's self-standards. For example, rigid self-demands characteristic of depressed people can be relaxed as a result of modeling.

CONCLUSION "A burgeoning literature confirms the value of modeling treatments for redressing deficits in social and cognitive skills, and for helping to remove defensive avoidance behavior."

Figure 13.3 *Summary of Social Cognitive Therapy. (Rosenthal and Bandura, 1978, p. 622)*

A Case Example: The Bombardier

It is interesting and perhaps significant that few, if any, in-depth individual cases have been reported by proponents of social cognitive theory.

Mischel (1968, 1976) has taken a case previously reported in the literature and interpreted it from a social cognitive standpoint. Originally reported by two psychiatrists–psychoanalysts in a book on the psychological trauma experienced by servicemen during World War II (Grinker & Spiegel, 1945), the case involved a bombardier who, during one of his missions, experienced psychological and physical trauma. His plane was damaged by flak, and although it began to dive, it pulled out of the dive just before crashing. However, the bombardier was hurled against the bombsight. Upon return to flight duty, he found that he became faint whenever the plane reached an altitude of about 10,000 feet. This, of course, interfered with his continuation on active duty.

Mischel notes that the analysts concluded that the bombardier's fainting was related to deep underlying anxieties rooted in his childhood experiences. Instead of such a dynamic explanation, Mischel suggests a social behavior analysis in which the emotional trauma probably was conditioned to the altitude the plane reached at about the time of the mishap. When the bombardier went on a flight and reached that altitude, he reexperienced the cues connected with the accident and became emotionally helpless. Therefore, the causes of the problem lay in the current conditions rather than in early childhood antecedents. Rather than needing insight therapy Mischel suggests that "the treatment implications seem clear for social behavior theory: render the traumatic cues neutral by desensitizing him to them through slow, graded exposure under conditions that prevent arousal and, instead, insure incompatible responses such as relaxation" (1968, p. 267). Mischel is critical of the approach that emphasizes events in childhood, defenses against feelings, dynamic explanations, and the value of insight. Instead, he argues for an emphasis on the conditions precipitating the difficulty, the situational factors maintaining the problem, and the kinds of structured tasks or situations that facilitate new kinds of learning.

THE CASE OF JIM

Social Cognitive Theory: Goals, Reinforcers, and Self-efficacy Beliefs

Twenty years ago Jim was assessed from various theoretical points of view—psychoanalytic, phenomenological, personal construct, and trait. At the time, social cognitive theory was just beginning to evolve, and thus he was not considered from this standpoint. Later, however, it was possible to gather at least some data from this theoretical standpoint as well. Although comparisons with earlier data may be problematic because of the time lapse, we can gain at least some insight into his personality from this theoretical point of view.

Goals

Jim was asked about his goals for the immediate future and for the long-range future. He felt that his immediate and long-term goals were pretty much the same: (1) getting to know his son and being a good parent; (2) becoming more accepting and less critical of his wife and others; and (3) feeling good about his professional work as a consultant. Generally he feels that there is a good chance of achieving these goals but he is guarded in that estimate, with some uncertainty about just how much he will be able to "get out of myself" and thereby be more able to give to his wife and child.

Subjective Values: Reinforcers

Jim was asked about positive and aversive reinforcers—things he found rewarding and things he found unpleasant—that were important to him. Concerning positive reinforcers, he reported that money was "a biggie." In addition he emphasized time with loved ones, the glamor of going to an opening night, and generally going to the theater or movies. He had a difficult time thinking of negative reinforcers. He described writing as a struggle and then noted, "I'm having trouble with this." When his concerns about rejection were mentioned, Jim responded: "Oh, to be sure. I agree. Somehow I'm blanking. I think there's more there, but I don't know."

Competencies and Self-efficacy Beliefs

Jim was asked about his competencies or skills, both intellectual and social. In the intellectual area he reported that he considered himself to be very bright and functioning at a very high intellectual level. He felt that he had no real intellectual deficiencies, though he distinguished between tight, logical thinking and loose, creative thinking, and felt that he was somewhat weak in the latter. Similarly, he felt that he writes well from the standpoint of a clear, organized presentation, but he had not written anything that is innovative or creative.

In the social area, Jim felt that he was very skilled: "I do it naturally, easily, well. I can pull off anything and have a lot of confidence in myself socially. If I was meeting with President Reagan tomorrow I could do it easily. I am at ease with both men and women, in both professional and social contexts." The one social concern noted was his constant struggle with "how egocentric I should be, how personally to take things." He felt that sometimes he takes things too personally. For example, he often feels hurt, offended, and disappointed if someone doesn't call him, wondering why they don't care about him and whether he's done something to offend them. He related this to the time he lived in a commune when he would nightly go over a checklist of people in the commune and wonder how he was doing with each of them: "My security is based on how I'm doing with others. I put a lot of energy into friendships, and when I'm relating well I feel good."

In terms of self-efficacy beliefs, it is clear that Jim has many positive views of himself. He believes that he does most things well; he is a good athlete, a competent consultant, bright, and socially skilled. Does he have areas of low self-efficacy? Jim mentioned three such areas. First, he feels that he does not genuinely accept his wife. He tends to be critical of others generally and of his wife in particular. Related to this is the second area mentioned, a difficulty in "getting out of myself so that I can be genuinely devoted to others." He is particularly concerned about this in relation to whether he will be able to maintain the parental interest and commitment that he would like. This is a high priority for him, but he is concerned that he will not want to be inconvenienced or put out by the new addition to the household. Finally, the third area of low self-efficacy concerned creativity: "I know I'm not good at being creative, so I don't try it."

Whereas Bandura emphasizes the situation-specific aspects of self-efficacy beliefs, Jim felt that these represented fairly broad, consistent areas of high and low self-efficacy and could not pick out more specific situations expressive of his beliefs in this area.

Comment

In many ways the social cognitive data on Jim are more limited than those associated with the previous theories of personality. We learn about important aspects of Jim's life, but clearly there also are major gaps. There are two reasons for this. First, only a limited amount of time was available for assessment. Second, and perhaps more important, social cognitive theorists have not developed comprehensive personality assessment tests. In part this is because of their greater concern with systematic research and the testing of hypotheses as opposed to the in-depth study of individuals. This also is because of the social cognitive criticism of traditional approaches to assessment that emphasize broad personality consistencies across many domains. In this regard, it is interesting that Jim had difficulty spelling out differences in his functioning in various areas. In this sense, he functions much more like a traditional personality theorist than like a social cognitive theorist, although with further questioning he probably would have been able to specify ways in which his goals, reinforcers, competencies, and self-efficacy beliefs varied from context to context.

It may be of interest at this point to consider social cognitive theory in relation to the theories previously discussed in the text. In part we will be helped in this endeavor by Bandura himself, since he begins his 1986 book with a critique of psychoanalytic theory, trait theory, and radical behaviorism. Our analysis may be simplified by keeping in mind four points emphasized by social cognitive theory: (1) Cognitive processes are important in motivation, emotion, and action. (2) People discriminate among situations, and behavior tends to be specific to contexts or domains. (3) There is an interactive, reciprocal relationship between persons and situations, as well as among thought, feeling, and behavior (i.e., people influence situations as well as are influenced by them, and thoughts, feelings, and overt behavior can influence one another). (4) Experimental research is important in defining concepts and providing support for the effectiveness of therapeutic methods.

COMPARATIVE ANALYSIS

SOCIAL COGNITIVE THEORY AND PSYCHOANALYSIS

Bandura is critical of psychoanalysis for its reliance on concepts that cannot be studied experimentally and on therapeutic procedures that have not demonstrated their effectiveness in changing actual psychosocial functioning. In particular, Bandura suggests that laboratory investigations have "failed to unearth an unconscious agency of the type assumed by psychodynamic theory" (1986, p. 3) and that "insight into dubious unconscious psychodynamics has little effect on behavior" (p. 5). In terms of anxiety, there is an emphasis on perceived inefficacy in coping with potentially aversive events rather than on intrapsychic conflict or the threat of unconscious impulses. In terms of therapy, it is suggested that people benefit more from changing their conscious cognitive functioning than from uncovering an unconscious.

Bandura's emphasis on experimental laboratory data contrasts strongly with the roots of psychoanalytic theory in the clinical therapeutic setting. Beyond this, however, there is a very different view of the functioning of the organism. Social cognitive theorists are critical of the psychoanalytic emphasis on broad personality dispositions (character types) and the relative fixity of behavior established during the early years. Instead, social cognitive theory suggests that behavior is situation or context specific and is governed by what is occurring in the present. Rather than broad stages of development, development in particular areas is emphasized; rather than generalized dynamics and defenses, specific expectancies and self-evaluations are emphasized; rather than early traumatic experiences, observational learning and vicarious conditioning are emphasized; rather than insight into unconscious dynamics, changes in conscious cognitive functioning are emphasized.

SOCIAL COGNITIVE THEORY AND PHENOMENOLOGY

Social cognitive theory shares with Rogers and proponents of the human potential movement an emphasis on the vast potential of humans, as well as an emphasis on the concept of self. However, such points of agreement are overshadowed by more important fundamental differences. According to social cognitive theory, people have self-conceptualizations and self-evaluations, but they do not have selves or generalized self-concepts: "A global self-conception does not do justice to the complexity of self-efficacy percepts, which vary across different activities, different levels of the same activity, and different circumstances" (Bandura, 1986, p. 410).

There are other differences between the two theoretical approaches. First, although Rogers emphasized the importance of research, he also valued clinical observations. Other members of the human potential movement have tended to ignore research, in particular laboratory research. Clearly this is not the case for Bandura and followers of social cognitive theory. Second, whereas Rogers was interested in the therapeutic climate as the primary ingredient of change, social cognitive theory emphasizes the importance of experiences in changing self-efficacy percepts. Finally, although both Rogerian theory and social cognitive theory emphasize emotions and cognitions, the primary emphasis for Rogers was on feelings (positive regard, empathic understanding, congruence), whereas for Bandura it is on cognitions.

SOCIAL COGNITIVE THEORY AND PERSONAL CONSTRUCT THEORY

Social cognitive theory and personal construct theory share an emphasis on cognitive processes in human behavior. They also share an emphasis on the utility of behavioral experiences in changing constructs or cognitions. Despite this, and despite Kelly's acknowledged influence on Mischel, followers of the two approaches tend to go their own ways and Bandura virtually ignores the work of Kelly.

Why should this be the case? It reflects in part the differing roots of the two approaches and in part their different groundings. Whereas Kelly set his views apart from traditional psychology, social cognitive theory was based on learning theory and continues to be rooted in developments in traditional psychology. Whereas personal construct theorists have tended to limit themselves to the study of constructs—and to the use of the Rep test as a measuring device—the social cognitive theory and approach to research have been much broader. In addition, to a certain extent personal construct theorists have been interested in what people think, whereas social cognitive theorists have been interested in the relation of what people think to what they feel and do. Whereas Kelly could dismiss the concept of motivation and "carrot and stick" theories of motivation, social cognitive theory emphasizes the importance of rewards in influencing outcome expectancies and performance.

SOCIAL COGNITIVE THEORY AND TRAIT THEORY

Social cognitive theorists are critical of trait theorists for their emphasis on broad dispositions as opposed to the study of processes that account for how behavior is acquired, maintained, and changed. As noted in Chapter 8, the differing views were crystallized and polarized in terms of the person–situation debate.

Although trait and social cognitive theorists share an emphasis on research, their basic assumptions and focus of investigation are different. Whereas trait theorists suggest that behavior is largely the product of dispositions, and is fairly consistent across situations and over time, social cognitive theorists emphasize the role of people's cognitive competencies in discriminating among situations, in terms of both their self-efficacy percepts and outcome expectancies. At this point, both trait and social cognitive theorists would agree that there is evidence of both consistency and variability in behavior. However, they disagree about how much of each there is, how to account for behavior, and what should be studied. Social cognitive theorists emphasize what a person *can do*, particularly in specific contexts, whereas trait theorists emphasize what a person *has* in terms of context-free traits; social cognitive theorists emphasize learned cognitive expectancies and competencies, whereas trait theorists emphasize broad dispositions that tend to be genetically based; social cognitive theorists emphasize adaptation to changing circumstances, whereas trait theorists emphasize stable factor structures; and, although both accept the value of self-report, social cognitive theorists emphasize the assessment of ongoing thoughts and feelings in relation to specific situations rather than global self-assessments of general functioning (Mischel, 1990; Mischel & Shoda, 1995).

SOCIAL COGNITIVE THEORY AND LEARNING THEORY

Social cognitive theory has its roots in learning theory. As noted, originally it was called *social learning theory*. It shares with Hullian and Skinnerian learning theories an emphasis on research, on the importance of learned behavior in relation to specific situations or contexts, and on the importance of rewards in influencing behavior. In addition, both theories reject the medical symptom–disease model and emphasize therapy as the learning of new patterns of thinking and behaving rather than as a cure for some underlying problem. However, in their emphasis on cognitive processes, social cognitive theorists argue that behavior is regulated not just by external consequences but by internal expectancies and self-regulatory processes.

Another important difference involves the use of verbal self-report data. Whereas learning theorists typically avoid the use of such data, and Skinnerians specifically argue against their use to infer internal events, Bandura takes a much different view. According to him, cognitive processes are not publicly observable, but self-report data can be useful in learning about such processes. As a minimum, the value of self-reports is seen as an open, empirical question. Beyond this, however, it is suggested that such data can be useful when reports are made specific and just prior to action.

CRITICAL EVALUATION

STRENGTHS OF THE THEORY

Social cognitive theory is perhaps the current favorite among academic personality psychologists, and many clinicians would also label themselves social cognitive psychologists. How can we account for this growth in popularity and influence? Probably the major factors have been the attention given to experimentation and a parallel consideration of important human phenomena. Beyond this, there is an impressive openness to change, as well as a continuing concern with other points of view. These strengths will be considered in greater detail.

Concern with Experimentation and Evidence

Developments in social cognitive theory have been grounded in careful experimental research. Bandura and Mischel have been concerned with defining concepts in ways that leave them open to empirical verification and have always conducted active research programs. The variety of phenomena investigated and the research methods used are impressive. For example, the research on modeling indicates that the observation of models can lead to the acquisition of new responses and to changes in the frequency of occurrence of behaviors already learned. The range of behaviors investigated includes aggression, moral judgments, setting of standards, vicarious conditioning of fears, delay of gratification, and helping behavior. Children and adults have been found to be influenced by a wide range of models—live humans, filmed humans, verbally presented models of behavior, and cartoons. The process of modeling has been studied in terms of the influences of model characteristics, observer characteristics, and observed consequences to the model of the demonstrated behavior. The concept of self-efficacy has been studied in terms of its determinants, implications for a wide range of behaviors, and potential for change—an impressive record of research.

Importance of Phenomena Considered

Most social cognitive research has been conducted with the social behaviors of humans. Thus, in considering the evidence, we are not asked to make large extrapolations from animal research to humans and from simple behaviors to complex human processes. Social cognitive theory investigates and attempts to account for the very phenomena that are of interest to most people—aggression, the effects of parents and mass media on children, the change of dysfunctional behaviors, the development of self-regulatory capacities, and the increase of control over one's life.

A Theory Open to Change

Social cognitive theory has changed and evolved over the years. A comparison of *Social Learning and Personality Development* (1963) by Bandura and Walters with Bandura's *Social Foundations of Thought and Action* (1986) gives ample testimony to the changes that have come about. The theory's emphasis on behavior, observational learning, and the importance of reinforcers in maintaining behavior has continued. However, with time there has been an increased emphasis on cognitive processes and self-regulation. Not only external events but internal ones as well are emphasized. In the process of reciprocal determinism we not only have environmental contingencies shaping people but also people shaping environmental contingencies. There is an emphasis not only on behavior but on cognition and emotion as well. Furthermore, there is an emphasis on the relationships among thought, feeling, and overt behavior. Social cognitive theorists have tried to remain informed about developments in other areas of psychology and to adjust their position so that it remains consistent with these developments. Beyond this, social cognitive theory itself has influenced and contributed to other parts of psychology. Although social cognitive theory draws on advances in fields such as cognition and development, it also contributes to these advances. As noted by one reviewer: "Bandura's contributions to a theoretical understanding of human development have been of major significance for the field...Social cognitive theory has evolved over the years in a way that is responsive to new data" (Grusec, 1992, p.784).

Focus on Important Issues

Social cognitive theorists have played a valuable role in criticizing other theoretical positions (psychoanalytic, trait, Skinnerian) and in bringing critical issues to the forefront, among them the role of reinforcement in the acquisition and performance of behavior. Mischel, in particular, has been influential in drawing attention to the problems associated with views that overemphasize trait factors. The person–situation controversy has led in some wasteful directions, such as examining whether persons or situations are more important in determining behavior. Generally, however, it has led to a more realistic assessment of the complex, interacting causes of behavior.

View of the Person and Social Concern

Social cognitive theory offers a view of the person that is more reasonable than a robot or telephone switchboard and suggests possible solutions to problems of genuine social concern. Social cognitive approaches are used to help people with common problems of life. Yet they are also considered in relation to larger problems of social change. Bandura (1977a) considers the soundness of a legal system of deterrence, the potential for creating environments conducive to learning and intellectual development, and the interplay between personal freedom and limits on conduct that must exist in every society. Interestingly enough, he concludes his book: "As a science concerned with the social consequences of its applications, psychology must promote public understanding of psychological issues that bear on social policies to ensure that its findings are used in the service of human betterment" (p. 213).

LIMITATIONS OF THE THEORY

Given these significant strengths, what are the limitations of social cognitive theory? Some of these are associated with new developments and the fact that many of the approaches are recent. Social cognitive theory has shown a constructive openness to change but has not followed a path that has led to a carefully integrated network of theoretical assumptions. Many of the concepts, findings, and therapeutic procedures have been challenged by proponents of alternative points of view. Finally, social cognitive theory still appears to ignore important phenomena that are recognized by other approaches. Again, these points will be considered in greater detail.

Not Yet a Systematic, Unified Theory

Social cognitive theory is not yet a systematic, unified theory—in the sense of a network of assumptions tied together in a systematic way leading to specific predictions. Bandura's (1986) recent effort in this direction are important. One reviewer suggests, for example, that the outline of a "grand theory" of human behavior is there, and "what more can we ask from a single colleague and scholar" (Baron, 1987, p. 415). At the same time, it is important to recognize that social cognitive theory represents a blend of contributions and concepts, some unique to the theory and others taken from other theories, rather than a unified theory. Occasionally diverse concepts are merely lumped together, and sometimes opposing findings appear to fit equally well into the theory. In attempting to go beyond a simplistic emphasis on internal (person) or external (environment) determinants and a simplistic emphasis on cognition, affect, or overt behavior as all important, social cognitive theory represents an important contribution. However, what it presents is a general view or orientation rather than a fully worked out statement of relationships.

New Problems with New Developments

Perhaps not unexpectedly, each new development in social cognitive theory creates new criticisms and new difficulties. The theory's emphasis on learning complex acts in the absence of reinforcement has been attacked consistently by Skinnerians, who suggest that observational learning may, in fact, illustrate a generalized imitative response that is sometimes—but not always—reinforced (Gewirtz, 1971). Skinnerians suggest that although an individual may learn a response performed by a model without being reinforced, this does not mean that reinforcement was not a necessary part of the overall learning process; one cannot determine this without knowing the reinforcement history of the individual. Other psychologists, working within a strict behaviorist framework, are critical of the recent emphasis on internal variables and verbal self-report. Developments here have occurred with an eye toward past pitfalls of research on the self and the use of verbal reports. It is strange, perhaps welcome, to see social cognitive psychologists emphasizing what people have to report about themselves. However, it remains to be seen whether detailed verbal report procedures and supportive reporting conditions can take care of the fact that people often are unaware of processes in themselves. Years of research on the concept of self have left us with a host of major unresolved problems (Wylie, 1974). Can social cognitive theory find a way to overcome them?

Most recently the concept of self-efficacy has come under attack. Three aspects of this criticism can be considered. First, there is the suggestion that self-efficacy beliefs are tied to outcome expectancies and that outcome expectancies govern behavior. Ordinarily, if people believe they can perform the tasks relevant to a situation, wouldn't they expect a positive outcome? Also, if they feel that they cannot perform the necessary tasks, wouldn't they expect a negative outcome? Thus, to the extent that one believes performance to be related to outcome, one's self-efficacy beliefs would be expected to relate fairly closely to one's outcome expectancies.

Bandura suggests, however, that self-efficacy beliefs do not always match outcome expectancies, particularly in situations where outcomes are partially or totally beyond the control of the person. Further, research suggests that self-efficacy beliefs predict behavior better than outcome expectancies. Thus, Bandura argues that self-efficacy beliefs are fundamentally different from outcome expectancies; what one believes one can do is different from what one believes will be the outcome of behavior. What remains to be worked out in this controversy are the factors that determine when self-efficacy beliefs and outcome expectancies match one another and when they diverge, as well as the contributions of each to behavior.

A second aspect of the criticism of the concept of self-efficacy is that although Bandura has broadly articulated the factors contributing to the development of self-efficacy beliefs, we do not understand such events as the sudden erosion of a self-efficacy belief or the rapid fluctuation between strong beliefs in efficacy and those in inefficacy. Thus, for example, people may first feel very confident in a situation and then rapidly lose all confidence or fluctuate rapidly in the sense of self-efficacy. It remains to be determined why some self-efficacy beliefs are stable and others unstable, some resistant to change and others open to change.

The third question concerns the relationship of self-efficacy beliefs to broad aspects of behavior. Self-efficacy is measured according to Bandura's microanalytic strategy—at specific moments in time and in relation to specific tasks. This allows considerable precision in measurement but does not provide broad explanatory power (Seligman, 1992). If self-efficacy percepts are so specific to tasks and contexts, of what value are they in relation to broader aspects of a person's life or new situations? Also, how are we to account for situations where self-efficacy beliefs appear to be unrelated to behavior—such as where persons indicate that they believe they have the ability to do something and it makes sense to do it, yet they still find themselves unable to act?

In sum, self-efficacy appears to be a valuable concept, but one in need of further examination and elaboration.

Relative Neglect of Important Areas

It is impossible for a theory of personality to be truly all-encompassing at this time. Accepting such qualifications, it would still appear that social cognitive theorists ignore or give minimal attention to significant aspects of human functioning. Without accepting all of the viewpoint of stage theorists, maturational factors would appear to be important in the feelings people experience and in the way they process information. Sexual feelings do become increasingly important at particular times in the life cycle, and the thinking of a child is fundamentally different from that of an adult in a variety of ways.

Beyond this, although social cognitive theory recognizes the importance of motivational factors and conflict, only recently has it begun to give serious attention to these processes. The concepts of standards and goals represent an important development in the social cognitive view of motivation. At the same time, this is an area in need of further development. In particular, there is need for study of the kinds of goals people have and the basis for their acquisition. Bandura seems to equate goals with standards, as if the only thing that motivates people is standards. But don't people pursue other goals? Similarly, Bandura suggests that people are motivated by the discrepancy between performance and a standard, but are not people also motivated by the desire to achieve the goal itself rather than to close a discrepancy between performance and a standard?

Turning to the concept of conflict, Bandura recognizes that most behavior is determined by multiple goals, yet he strangely ignores the concept of conflict. Most people can readily think of situations where

they felt in conflict between goals. For some people conflict is a fundamental part of their lives. Not only is the concept of conflict central to
psychoanalytic theory, but it was emphasized by the learning theorists
Dollard and Miller. Thus, it seems strange that such a seemingly important concept would be so neglected.

Preliminary Nature of Findings

Throughout its history, psychology generally and the field of psychotherapy in particular have been beset with fads. Therefore one must be cautious in distinguishing between actual progress and overzealous commitment to a new idea. Whereas theories that emphasized cognitive
processes were once viewed with skepticism, later they were adopted
readily: "1976 could well be designated the year of cognition for both theoretician and practitioner. Like the activities of Superman and the
Scarlet Pimpernel, cognition is in the air, it is here, there, and everywhere" (Franks & Wilson, 1978, p. vii). Without minimizing their importance in human behavior, we should be careful about prematurely
accepting cognitive processes as our basic explanatory concepts.

   Although the results of guided participation and modeling are significant, these therapeutic processes remain to be tested by other therapists,
with different patients and with different problems. Bandura has
answered critics who suggest that his results are of limited generaliz-
ability. However, the history of psychotherapy is filled with methods that
were introduced as solving the problems of those in psychological distress. Most recently, evaluation of efforts in the areas of behavior modification and behavior therapy should make us aware of the complexities
of the problem and of the work that remains to be done.

   In sum, there are good grounds both for enthusiasm about social cognitive theory and for caution, even skepticism. Social cognitive theory
represents a major development. It is still evolving, and its further efforts
are worthy of careful attention (Table 13.1).

Table 13.1 Summary of Strengths and Limitations of Social Cognitive Theory

Strengths	Limitations
1. Has impressive research record.	1. Is not a systematic, unified theory.
2. Considers important phenomena.	2. Contains potential problems associated with the utilization of verbal self report.
3. Shows consistent development and elaboration as a theory.	3. Requires more exploration and development in certain areas (e.g., motivation, affect, system properties of personality organization).
4. Focuses attention on important theoretical issues.	4. Provides findings concerning therapy that are tentative rather than conclusive.

SOCIAL COGNITIVE THEORY AT A GLANCE

Theorist or Theory	Structure	Process
Social Cognitive Theory	Expectancies; standards; goals; self-efficacy beliefs	Observational learning; vicarious conditioning; symbolic processes, self-evaluative and self-regulatory processes (standards)

MAJOR CONCEPTS

Dysfunctional expectancies. In social cognitive theory, maladaptive expectations concerning the consequences of specific behaviors.

Dysfunctional self-evaluations. In social cognitive theory, maladaptive standards for self-reward that have important implications for psychopathology.

Modeling. Bandura's concept for the process of reproducing behaviors learned through the observation of others.

Guided participation. A treatment approach emphasized in social cognitive theory in which a person is assisted in performing modeled behaviors.

REVIEW

1. Social cognitive theory rejects the medical–symptom disease model of psychopathology, emphasizing instead the dysfunctional learning of behaviors, expectancies, standards for self-reward, and, most significantly, self-efficacy beliefs.

2. Dysfunctional learning can occur through the observation of models, in particular through vicarious conditioning, or through direct experience.

3. People with low perceived self-efficacy in relation to potential threats experience high levels of anxiety.

4. Perceived inefficacy in relation to rewarding outcomes leads to depression. Another component of depression is excessively stringent standards, where the person is self-critical in relation to the failure to achieve them.

5. There is evidence that perceived self-efficacy can promote health by increasing the likelihood of health-related behaviors and by enhancing the immune system.

6. Social cognitive therapy emphasizes increases in self-efficacy so that previously avoided situations may be confronted and new expectancies

Growth and Development	Pathology	Change	Illustrative Case
Social learning through observation and direct experience; development of self-efficacy judgments and standards for self-regulation	Learned response patterns; excessive self-standards; problems in self-efficacy	Modeling; guided participation; increased self-efficacy	Reinterpretation of bombardier case

learned. The common denominator of all therapeutic change is seen to result from increases in the level and strength of self-efficacy beliefs.

7. Modeling and guided participation are procedures used to acquire cognitive and behavioral competencies. In modeling, models demonstrate the skills and subskills necessary in specific situations. In guided participation, the person is assisted in performing these modeled behaviors. Research supports the utility of these procedures in raising the perception of self-efficacy.

8. In relation to the theories considered previously, (a) social cognitive theory emphasizes conscious cognitive processes and experimental data as opposed to the psychoanalytic emphasis on unconscious processes and clinical data; (b) social cognitive theory emphasizes the specificity of self-efficacy beliefs as opposed to the global self-conceptions emphasized by Rogers; (c) social cognitive theory emphasizes the situational specificity and variability of behavior as opposed to the broad dispositions emphasized by trait theorists.

9. Social cognitive theory's strengths include its emphasis on research, its history of development and elaboration as a theory, and its focus on important theoretical issues. At the same time, it is not yet a systematic theory, requires further study of areas such as motivation and personality organization, and has yet to demonstrate its utility with a wide range of psychological difficulties.

14

A COGNITIVE, INFORMATION-PROCESSING APPROACH TO PERSONALITY

Chapter Focus

You walk out of an interview after having been offered the summer job of your dreams. Wow! You have to sit down on a street bench and think about what just happened. What runs through your mind? You may find yourself wondering how you managed to get this great job. Perhaps you pat yourself on the back for your diligent efforts in preparing for the interview, or you congratulate yourself for your effective interviewing skills. Alternatively, you may wonder whether it was just luck; a wave of doubtful thoughts washes over you as you begin to question whether you will be able to handle the job.

These kinds of thoughts, attributions, and expectations are the topic of cognitive theories of personality. Our complex and changing world is filled with information. Cognitive personality psychologists are interested in the various ways we process (that is, attend to and make sense of) this information in order to lead reasonably stable and productive lives. Their approach, the cognitive-information processing approach to personality, is based on a computer model of human functioning and is the focus of this chapter.

QUESTIONS TO BE ADDRESSED IN THIS CHAPTER

1. To what extent can humans be viewed as functioning like computers? Can we speak of computer personalities?

2. How do we organize and utilize information concerning the world around us and our own experience?

3. Does a computer have a self? If not, how might a model based on the computer interpret the self?

4. To what extent are psychological difficulties caused by problematic, irrational thoughts and cognitive processes? Can psychological functioning be improved through procedures aimed at correcting irrational thoughts and improving ways of processing information? Can we be "reprogrammed" to think in healthier ways?

Theories of personality tend to be associated with models of human nature. To take two illustrations already noted: in psychoanalytic theory, there is the model of the person as a hydraulic energy system; in personal construct theory, there is the model of the person as a scientist. Since the 1960s, we have witnessed in psychology a revolution—the cognitive revolution (Robins, Craik, & Gosling, 1995). This revolution in psychology has matched the technological revolution in industry. The technological revolution is dominated by the computer and information

Computers and Personality: *Cognitive psychologists use the computer as a model for personality and try to model human behavior on computers. (© Robert Schochet)*

processing. The cognitive revolution's model of the person is that of a complex, sophisticated—though error-prone—processor of information.

Like all such models, this one cannot be taken literally. No psychologist would suggest that people are the same as computers or that computers can now perform all the thinking operations of humans. However, such models are viewed as useful in conceptualizing how people think and in defining which issues are important to investigate. Thus, many psychologists have begun to probe the ways in which people do function like computers. Computers are information-processing devices in which information is received or encoded, stored or remembered, and retrieved when needed. The key terms here are *encoding, memory*, and *retrieval*, and cognitive personality psychologists are interested in how people go about encoding, storing, and retrieving information.

From the standpoint of a computer model of personality, what are the relevant structural units? That is, what are the cognitive units of personality? How do we organize and utilize information to make sense out of the world? What categories do we form to classify objects and people? How do we develop causal explanations for events? How do some of these categories and causal explanations sometimes help us to function effectively and at other times lead us into trouble?

COGNITIVE STRUCTURES

CATEGORIES

As we go about our daily lives we are exposed to an enormous amount of information, including information from outside stimuli and information from internal thoughts and feelings. How are we to function effectively while being exposed to such an enormous amount of information? We must find ways to simplify the world to function effectively and there are two ways to do this. First, we can be selective in what we attend to. In concentrating on a task we focus on information relevant to that task and screen out other things that may be going on. When unable to screen out such extraneous information, we find that our concentration and performance are impaired—an event familiar to most students. A second method of simplification is to form categories for treating many pieces of information as similar, if not identical. In this way we need not treat each piece of information as completely novel and have to decide on what to do with it. By treating a piece of information as a member of a category we can respond immediately in ways established for other members of the category. We do not treat each tree as unique but rather identify it as a member of a category and can respond accordingly. Similarly, for better or for worse, we meet people and treat them as members of a category rather than as totally unique individuals. The categories used may be gender, religion, race, nationality, or club membership. Or, perhaps in meeting a new person we use categories developed for our own purposes and unique to us. Whether common or unique, however, it is categories that we use much of the time.

In cognitive theories such categories often are called **schemas**. A *schema* is a cognitive structure that organizes information and thereby influences how we perceive and respond to further information such as physical objects, people, and events.

Categories for Physical Objects

Let us begin our consideration of categories or schemas by considering physical objects. What kinds of physical object categories can be formed? If I use the term *four-wheeled transportation vehicle*, do you know what I am referring to? You probably have a general idea, but you need more information to know exactly. So you know about a category, one that clearly is different from other categories such as people or plants, but then there are subcategories such as cars and trucks. How many such subcategories are there? Do people generally agree about these subcategories, about which objects are to be placed in them, and the characteristics that determine membership in one or another category?

Consider the hierarchical category structure represented in Figure 14.1. Do these seem to be reasonable subcategories of the larger category *vehicle*, and would most people agree about the characteristics of a sports car as opposed to a four-door sedan? Research on questions such as these suggests the following conclusions concerning people's categorizations of physical objects:

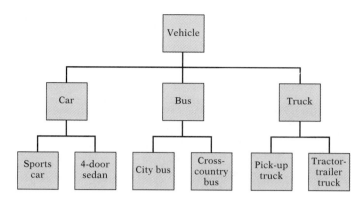

Figure 14.1 Illustrative Hierarchical Category Structure. *(Adapted from Rosch et al., 1976)*

1. Good agreement can be found concerning a taxonomy or hierarchical arrangement of categories.

2. Subjects can reach high levels of agreement concerning characteristics associated with specific categories. For example, subjects agree about characteristics defining a car.

3. No one characteristic may be critical or sufficient to define membership in that category. Thus, for example, no one characteristic may be necessary or sufficient to describe a car as a sports car. Rather, membership is defined by a pattern of characteristics. Sports cars can vary considerably in terms of specific details but share a general pattern of characteristics.

4. Although categories possess different patterns of characteristics, there may be some overlap between them. Thus, for example, sedans and sport cars have different patterns of characteristics, though they also have certain characteristics in common.

5. While no member of a category is likely to have all the characteristics descriptive of membership in that category, some members best exemplify the category. For example, a Porsche might best exemplify a sports car. Such an object is called a **prototype**.

6. At the other extreme, because of overlapping characteristics between categories, some objects are difficult to classify. There is a fuzziness or ambiguity at the boundaries. For example, is a hatchback a sedan or a sports car? We designate some such cases as *hybrids*, or crosses between categories (Figure 14.2).

7. The earliest categories used by children are middle-level categories (e.g., car). Higher-level categories (e.g., vehicle) are more abstract. Although distinctive (e.g., vehicle vs. human vs. plant), they are not very specific. Lower-level categories (e.g., sports car)

Figure 14.2   The sport utility vehicle. *A hybrid or cross between the categories of sports car and utility vehicle.*

are very specific but not economical to use. Thus, each level has its own value, but middle-level categories are particularly useful in combining richness of detail and economy.

Categories for Situations

If these are some of the principles established in relation to the categorization of physical objects, what about other categories—for example, situations? If behavior is influenced by the perceived environment, then we must be interested in how people organize information concerning situations and how they go about classifying them. Do the principles established for physical objects also hold for situations? In some relevant research, subjects were asked to sort situations into categories, describe the characteristics associated with each category, and then organize the categories into a hierarchy (Cantor, Mischel, & Schwartz, 1982). An illustrative situation hierarchy that resulted from this task is presented in Figure 14.3.

The conclusions drawn from this research are similar to those with which we are familiar: (1) People can readily form and agree on a hierarchical taxonomy of situations; (2) people can readily describe and agree on characteristics associated with situations; (3) situation prototypes generally include physical characteristics of the situation, personality and feeling characteristics of the participants, and expected behaviors; (4) middle-level situation categories (e.g., Being at a Party) are particularly rich in detail and well differentiated from characteristics associated with other categories.

Situation Scripts   In sum, there is evidence of the utility of people's using a categorical approach and forming behavioral expectations on the basis of these categories. Apparently in entering into a situation, we attend to and encode certain information that leads us to say "this is X kind of sit-

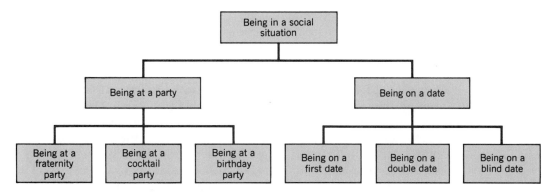

Figure 14.3   Illustrative Situation Taxonomy. *(Cantor, Mischel, & Schwartz, 1982)*

uation." On the basis of this categorization, we generate a range of additional feelings and behavioral expectations—both for ourselves and for those with whom we will be interacting.

The concept of **script** has been used by some proponents of a computer model to define a series or pattern of behaviors considered to be appropriate for a situation (Schank & Abelson, 1977). For example, behavior in a restaurant generally is highly scripted. Not only are specific behaviors well defined, but the order or sequence of behaviors is clearly set forth. Generally we act out roles in such situations, and our behavior is regulated by norms or sanctions for behaving in an inappropriate way. Violating the script in a restaurant may sometimes be funny, but more often it leads to errors in the meal being served or in being asked to leave, particularly if the restaurant is formal in atmosphere. Functioning in such cases requires us to recognize that we are in a scripted situation and to call forth images of the required scripts. A breakdown in either cognitive skill or skill in performing the requisite behaviors leads to difficulties. On the

Scripts: *Some situations, such as eating in a restaurant, require following a clearly defined series of behaviors.*

other hand, other situations are less structured or scripted. For example, an informal meeting among friends generally has fewer prescriptions and fewer well-defined scripts. Under such circumstances, people often feel less inhibited or more able to be themselves.

Analysis of an Individual's Situation Categories and Associated Feelings and Behaviors   Aside from abstract situation categories, how might one classify situations in one's own life? And, beyond the rules for behaving in specific situations, which feelings and behaviors are associated with these situation categories? Consider the following task presented to subjects. First, they are asked to form a list of situations in their current life or recent past. The subjects review their daily lives and list representative situations in terms of who is there, what is going on, where it takes place, and when it occurs. For example, a subject might list the situation of presenting an idea before a class, being on a date, or being alone with a good friend. The subjects then describe each situation, as well as their feelings and behaviors in the situation. This generates a list of situation characteristics, feelings, and behaviors. The subjects then rate the relevance of each situation characteristic, feeling, and behavior to each of the original situations listed. In this way it is possible to study each subject's categorizations of situations and perceptions of feelings and behaviors associated with these categories.

The data for each subject are factor-analyzed to determine which situation characteristics, feelings, and behaviors go together. The results for one subject are presented in Table 14.1. In this table, Jennifer groups some situations into a category titled "home—volatile." These situations are emotional; in them she feels angry and insecure and behaves in a caring, concerned fashion—at least in terms of her perceptions. She also perceives a group of situations with friends that, though again emotional, are now associated with caring and concerned feelings. Interestingly, she associates some of the same behaviors with these situations that she does with the home—volatile situations, where the feelings are quite different. According to her reports, Jennifer is almost always sensitive, vulnerable, and insightful. She also is friendly, warm, and accepting most of the time, except when she is in some volatile home situations, when she is uniquely irritable, angry, upset, depressed, uncontrolled, and rebellious. She also tends to be involved and caring, except when she is detached, preoccupied, introverted, controlled, and cool.

In terms of this analysis, to what extent does it make sense to consider Jennifer's personality as defined by the way in which she categorizes situations, the feelings and behaviors she associates with these situation categories, and the ways in which she sees herself as stable or variable across the situations?

Categories for People

When asked to describe people we know, which terms do we use? In thinking about friends, we find that we use particular terms to describe

Table 14.1 Illustrative Situation Categories—Jennifer

Situation Categories	Illustrative Situations	Situation Traits	Feelings	Behaviors
Home—Volatile	Mother blows up at me. Honest with parents about leaving. Mother refuses gift. Someone else comes home upset.	Emotional, angry, volatile, excitable	Angry, pressured, involved, insecure, unhappy	Sensitive, concerned, caring, suppressed, confused, not compulsive
School, Work—Pressure to Perform	Have to participate in class. Have to perform at work. Do the job wrong at work in a strange place.	Demanding, threatening, pressuring, awkward, challenging, embarrassing, unconcerned	Self-conscious, challenged, vulnerable, awkward, pressured, anxious	Self-conscious, controlled, ambitious, determined, compulsive, cool, responsive, diligent, nonrebellious
Friends, Alone	With friend—no problem. With friend—problem. Alone.	Emotional, gentle, friendly, generous	Caring, concerned, comfortable, melancholy, sad	Concerned, caring, emotional, involved, insightful, responsive
Uncertain	Come home from Philadelphia. In a crowd. Taking the bus to class. Want to leave to go to Philadelphia. In a strange place.	Ambiguous, nondefined, uncertain, unconcerned, ignoring	Bottled-up, melancholy, sad, lonely, frustrated, confused	Preoccupied, detached, quiet, self-conscious, controlled, cool, introverted

SOURCE: Pervin, 1976. Copyright © 1976 by the American Psychological Association. Reprinted by permission.

them and that sometimes we group people into types; we say that a friend has these characteristics or is this type of person. In meeting new people, we also find that we tend to be sensitive to particular characteristics and to perceive them in particular terms. In some cases, these perceived characteristics are more or less neutral; in other cases, they are heavily value laden. Thus, for example, one may describe someone in physical terms (e.g., tall, ruddy, angular) that may not express value preferences or in trait terms (e.g., honest, kind, hostile) that are generally associated with considerable emotion.

People differ in the terms they use to describe people and in the ways they organize these terms, but everyone seeks to organize the information they have about others. Given the diversity of people we encounter and their varying behavior in situations, such organization is necessary for us to make sense out of and provide stability to the world we encounter. In the chapter on the Five Factor Model of personality traits (Chapter 8), we considered what might be common categories of people—introverts and extraverts (*Extraversion*), neurotics and emotionally stable people (*Neuroticism*), responsible and irresponsible people (*Conscientiousness*), and so on. And, in the representation of the hierarchical organization of personality traits (Chapter 7), we considered how each of these categories could have subcategories of traits and then more specific responses. These represent the common denominator of trait descriptions across large numbers of subjects but individuals vary in the categories they use, in the content of these categories, and in the complexity of organization of their people categories. In many ways, this was what Kelly (Chapter 10) was trying to achieve with his personal construct view of personality. In other words, whereas the trait model gets at common categories used for people, and the characteristics used to define these categories, personal construct theory tries to get at individualistic ways of categorizing people.

The Self and Self-schema   Previous chapters in this text have emphasized the importance of the concept of the self for personality. At the same time, it also has been recognized that not all theories give prominence to the concept and that there have been times where the concept of the self fell into disfavor. During the early part of the cognitive revolution the concept was not given a great deal of attention. How could a computer model make sense out of such a concept? Then, Markus (1977) took a step that gave impetus for work in this area. She suggested that the self is a concept or category like any other concept or category, and that people form cognitive structures about the self just as they do about other phenomena. Such cognitive structures are called **self-schemas**. For example, one person might have an independence–dependence self-schema which another person does not, or a guilty–innocent self-schema that is not present in others. As noted in Chapter 5, some individuals may see parts of the self as malleable that others see as fixed (Dweck, Chiu, & Hong,

1995). For some people perhaps there is no self-schema relevant to malleable–fixed. That is, they are aschematic for this concept.

According to the cognitive view of the self, self-schemas are cognitive generalizations about the self, derived from past experience, that organize and guide the processing of self-related information. The concepts or dimensions we use to define ourselves (e.g., intelligent–unintelligent, sociable–introverted, assertive–unassertive, brave–cowardly) are all self-schemas. As is true of other schemas or concepts, self-schemas influence whether information is attended to, how it is structured, and how easily it can be remembered. For example, individuals with a self-schema for independence function differently than those with a self-schema of dependence, and both function differently than individuals without a self-schema related to either independence or dependence. Markus indeed demonstrated that people with a particular self-schema, such as independence or dependence, *process* relevant information with ease, *retrieve* relevant behavioral evidence, and *resist* evidence contrary to their self-schemas. In other words, once we have developed ways of thinking about ourselves (our self-schemas), there is a strong tendency for them to be maintained by a bias in what we attend to, a bias in what we remember, and a bias in what we are prepared to accept as true about ourselves. There is, in other words, a self-schema influence and, beyond this, a self-confirming bias.

A recent study illustrates how self-schemas are not only related to the processing of information but to action as well, in this case to sexual behavior and romantic involvement. The researchers in this study investigated the hypothesis that women with differing sexual self-schemas would process interpersonal information differently and function differently in their sexual and romantic relationships (Andersen & Cyranowski, 1994). Women were asked to rate themselves on a list of 50 adjectives, 26 of which were used to form a *Sexual Self-Schema Scale* (e.g., uninhibited, loving, romantic, passionate, direct). Since the relevant items were embedded in the longer list, subjects did not know of the existence of the specific scale, believing instead that they were making general self-ratings. The women were also asked to respond to sexuality measures selected to sample sexual experiences and romantic involvement. Clear evidence was found that women with high scores on the *Sexual Self-Schema Scale*, particularly those with positive sexual self-schemas, were more sexually active, experienced greater sexual arousal and sexual pleasure, and were more able to be involved in romantic love relationships relative to women with low scores on the scale. The authors concluded that sexual schemas, defined as cognitive generalizations about sexual aspects of the self, are significantly related to sexually relevant emotions and behaviors.

In this emphasis on the self, it should be clear that we are considering many self-schemas rather than a single self-schema, and the potential for many self categories rather than a single self category. In other words, there can be what has been called a *"family of selves"* rather than a single

SOURCES OF SELF-ESTEEM FOR MEN AND WOMEN: HOW DO SELF-SCHEMAS OPERATE?

Do men and women differ in their self-schemas? Josephs, Markus, and Tafarodi (1992) think so. Their work sheds light on the nature of gender differences in the self-concept and also illustrates how self-schemas operate—how they organize and guide the processing of self-related information.

The basic idea for this research is that culture provides us with norms about gender-appropriate behavior (i.e., behavior considered correct for each sex), and both men and women learn and represent these norms in their self-schemas for gender-appropriate behavior. What is the content of these schemas? An extensive literature review suggested that one important content domain is the degree to which men and women see themselves as separate from, or connected with, others. Men are more likely to have "individualist," "independent," and "autonomous" schemas for the self, and other individuals are represented not as part of the self but as separate and distinct from it. Women, in contrast, are more likely to have "collectivist," "ensembled," and "connected" schemas for the self, and relations with others are thought to be basic elements of the self.

Josephs et al. then hypothesized that how we feel about ourselves should depend on how successfully we measure up to our gender-appropriate self-schemas. Thus, for men thinking of self as *independent* and *unique* should be associated with self-esteem; for women,

in contrast, thinking of self as *connected* should be associated with self-esteem. To test this idea, Josephs et al. conducted three studies. In Study 1, subjects were asked to indicate the percentage of other people who are as good as they are with respect to various skills or abilities. As predicted, men with high self-esteem, in contrast to men with low self-esteem and women in general, construed themselves as having uniquely superior abilities in comparison to others.

Study 2 was based on the idea that the better one's *memory* for particular kinds of information, the more important is this information for the self-schema. Subjects learned to "encode," or associate, words either with themselves or with other people important to them. As predicted, high self-esteem women—in contrast with low self-esteem women and men in general—had better memory for words they had encoded with respect to others. These findings fit the hypothesis: supposedly, the high self-esteem women had better memory for words related to others because relationships with others are important or *self-relevant* to them.

Finally, Study 3 examined *reactions to threatening information* about the self. Subjects completed a bogus personality test and then received manipulated feedback regarding their (a) individual attainment and (b) interpersonal attainment. As predicted, when high self-esteem men received negative feedback about their *individual* attainment, they compensated for this threat to their self-worth by predicting they would improve on a future test. Similarly, when high self-esteem women received negative feedback on *interpersonal* attainment, they compensated for this threat to their self-worth by predicting improvement. These findings show both men and women feel threatened in their self-worth when they fail to confirm their self-schemas; however, they differ in the content of these schemas, with independence and individual attainment more central for men and connection and interdependence more central for women.

Together, the results of these three studies demonstrate that gender norms influence how we establish self-esteem. The studies also illustrate how self-schemas influence the way we process information: how we compare ourselves to others (Study 1), what information we remember (Study 2), and how we compensate for threatening information (Study 3). These are all important cognitive processes in which our self-schemas play a crucial role.

SOURCE: Josephs, Markus, and Tafarodi, 1992.

self (Cantor & Kihlstrom, 1987). According to this view, you are many things, in many places, with many people. Thus, you have many contextualized selves, each with a set of features. The features of these contextualized selves, this family of selves, will overlap in some ways and be distinctive in others. Returning to Jennifer in Table 14.1, we can see that there is a Home Self, a School–Work Self, a Friends Self, and an Uncertain Self. Associated with each contextual self is a group of situations, feelings, and behaviors. Her various selves contain some overlapping features, as well as some that are distinctive. Perhaps at a higher level of organization there is a Good Self and a Bad Self, the former characterized by situations in which she is caring with friends and the latter by situations in which she is cool and detached. Each of us, then, has a family of selves, the contents and organization of which are unique. Within this family of selves there may be a prototypic self, a self-concept in relation to which we say, "This is what I am *really* like." And within this family of selves there may be fuzzy selves, or parts of us that we are not sure how they fit in relation to the other selves.

In sum, the information-processing approach suggests that the self be treated and subjected to empirical study, just like any other category, with recognition being given to its special potential importance in the functioning of the person. In this sense it is similar to Kelly's suggestion that the self be treated as a construct that is part of a person's construct system. However, in treating the self as a schema within the context of an information-processing approach, cognitive personality psychologists are able to relate their research to other studies being done in the area of cognitive psychology. This was, and continues to be, an important contribution (Banaji & Prentice, 1994).

CAUSAL EXPLANATIONS AND ATTRIBUTIONS

In the preceding sections we discussed how people organize information relevant to people and situations. In this section we are concerned with how people organize information relevant to events, in particular with how they go about attributing causes to events. We see someone hit or yell at another person and we infer some reason for the action. Is the person generally hostile? Was something malicious done to him? We see someone act in a strange way. Was she not feeling well? Was our previous picture of these people inaccurate, and must we now view them in a new way? These are the kinds of inferences and attributions we are constantly making in our daily lives.

Causal Explanations

We are already familiar with the fact that individuals may maintain beliefs about their ability to influence or control events in their lives (e.g., learned helplessness and locus of control; see Chapter 2). A related area of research concerns people's explanations for success or failure. Weiner (1990,1996) suggests that there are three dimensions relevant to causal explanations. The first dimension, related to the work of Rotter on locus of control, concerns whether causes are perceived as coming from within (internal) or from outside (external) the person. This dimension has been named **locus of causality**. A second dimension of causality, **stability**, concerns whether the cause is stable and relatively fixed as opposed to being unstable or variable. The implications for causal attributions from combining these two dimensions can be seen in Table 14.2. Accordingly, we can attribute success or failure to *ability* ("I am bright."), *effort* ("I tried hard."), *task difficulty* ("The test was easy."), or *chance* or *luck* ("I was lucky in guessing right."). The third dimension, **controllability**, has to do with whether events are subject to control or influence through additional effort. For example, social rejection because of physical unattractiveness might be attributed to internal, stable, and uncontrollable causes, whereas social rejection because of obnoxious behavior might be attributed to internal, stable, and controllable causes. In each case it is the beliefs and causal ascriptions of the person that are important. Thus, for example, one person might see her physical appearance as uncontrollable, whereas another might see it as controllable. One person might see her intellectual performance as due to fixed intelligence,

Table 14.2   Possible Causal Attributions for Success and Failure

Cause	*Internal*	*External*
Stable	Ability	Task difficulty
Variable	Effort	Chance or luck

SOURCE: Weiner, 1979

whereas another might see it as due to effort and acquired knowledge (Dweck, 1991; Dweck, Chiu, & Hong, 1995).

Consequences of Causal Attributions

The practical implications of differing attributions for performance are illustrated in a study of college freshmen (Wilson & Linville, 1985). In this study, freshmen whose grades were below the median and who indicated that they were worried about their academic performance were put into one of two groups. Those in one group were given information suggesting that the causes of their poor performance were unstable. This information consisted of statistics indicating that grades typically improve after the first year and videotaped interviews of upper-class students who reported improved performance following poor grades during their freshman year. Students in the second group were given general information that did not relate to grade improvement and saw videotaped interviews in which there was no mention of grades. The hypothesis tested was that the attribution of poor grades to unstable causes would reduce anxiety about academic performance and increase expectations about future grades, leading to improvement in actual performance. Indeed, it was found that students in the first (unstable attribution) group improved in their subsequent grade performance significantly more than did subjects in the second (control) group. In addition, a smaller proportion of the students in the first group left college the following semester. Thus, the authors of the study concluded that showing college freshmen that the causes of low grades are temporary can greatly benefit academic performance.

Additional dimensions have been suggested, but the point here is that people make causal attributions, and that such attributions have important psychological implications. For example, such attributions have important implications for motivation. A person is more likely to persist at a task if it is viewed as one involving effort than if success or failure is viewed as being due to chance. Similarly, persons will behave differently if they believe health or illness is due to internal or external causes ("I am a sickly person" versus "The flu bug got me") and if they believe in the efficacy of self-care ("Basic health principles prevent illness" versus "One can do little to prevent illness") (Lau, 1982).

Causal attributions also are important aspects of stereotypes. For example, success in males and failure in females tend to be attributed to ability, whereas failure in men and success in women tend to be attributed to effort or luck (Deaux, 1976). Differences in causal attribution also have important implications for emotion. As noted in relation to learned helplessness, depression is seen as resulting from an internal, stable, global attribution. Other illustrations of emotional consequences of causal attributions are pride following success and a causal attribution to ability, and guilt following failure and a causal attribution to effort

(Weiner, 1990). Finally, causal attributions have important implications for moral judgments. For example, to the extent that we see failure as due to lack of effort we see punishment as appropriate, whereas this is not the case if failure is perceived to be due to lack of ability. And, to the extent that we see someone's "illness" as due to circumstances beyond their control we view it as a *sickness* and respond with sympathy, whereas if we view it as due to controllable influences we view it as a *sin* and respond with moral condemnation and anger (Weiner, 1993, 1996). Illustrative here would be differing views concerning the causes of alcoholism, drug abuse, and AIDS. In sum, it is suggested that attributions cause many of our emotions, motivations, and behaviors.

IMPLICIT PERSONALITY THEORY

How we organize information about the personality functioning of others and ourselves is known as **implicit personality theory**. The term implicit personality theory suggests that each of us has a theory of personality, defined in terms of the categories we use to describe people, the content and organization of these categories, and our explanations for why people behave as they do, including causal explanations and attributions. Such theories are considered implicit in that most people cannot make them explicit or organize them as part of a formal theory of personality.

Although difficult to make explicit, you can begin to examine your own implicit theory of personality in terms of the categories you use to perceive others, the characteristics that define membership in each category, and the explanations you typically give for events. Can the categories you use be arranged in a hierarchy—and if so, what are the fundamental distinctions (categories) you make among people? Are there prototypic people for each category? For example, if you use the category extravert, do you have an image of someone who best combines the characteristics of extraverted people? On the other hand, are there people who are hard to classify because they fall into the fuzzy area between categories? To what extent do you categorize people on the basis of some characteristic and then assume that they have all the other category characteristics (i.e., pigeonhole someone), as opposed to thinking of them in terms of their unique combination of attributes? Or, having categorized someone, to what extent are you prepared to observe behavior in a particular situation that is inconsistent with such a categorization? To what extent do you use middle-level categories, such as traits, as opposed to more abstract categories such as types or more situation-specific categories such as responses in your characterizations of people? Do your causal explanations vary depending on the people and circumstances involved or do you have a fairly standard set of explanations for events? From an information processing standpoint, these are some of the questions that would be relevant to understanding your personality.

Until now we have considered the structure and content of personality cognition. But what of the process aspects? Where does motivation enter into our cognitive functioning? In a certain sense, we are interested here in the operation of the software that directs the operation of the various units of information, or that which directs the encoding, storage, retrieval, and production of information. We can consider here two categories of cognitive processes—nonmotivational and motivational. **COGNITIVE PROCESSES**

NONMOTIVATED COGNITIVE PROCESSES

Initially cognitive personality psychologists focused their attention on nonmotivational cognitive processes, following almost literally the model of a computer devoid of emotion or motivation. There was consideration of how categories are formed and how already formed schemas influence the further processing of information. For example, we already have come across such an analysis in terms of how self-schemas can influence what is perceived to be relevant to our self-representation, how incoming information is stored in relation to other information, and how information is retrieved. Already established schemas, in other words, influence what is perceived and how information is stored and retrieved. As noted, there is a self-confirming bias in the way information is treated and this in part accounts for why our self-schemas are so difficult to change once they are established. In addition, apparently we operate in ways that will make others perceive us in the ways we perceive ourselves, regardless of whether our self-views are positive or negative (McNulty & Swann, 1994). Thus, once more there is a self-confirming bias to our functioning. This is what schemas are about. They are organizing units of information. In this sense there is nothing special about self-schema and at this point there are no motivational principles involved.

Although we tend to think of cognitive processes as operating on a rational basis, evidence suggests that this is not always the case. In other words, sometimes we make errors in our processing of information, errors that are common to virtually all of us and are not due to motivational causes (Kahneman & Tversky, 1984; Nisbett & Ross, 1980). For example, our bias in terms of preexisting beliefs leads us to see in others what we expect and to discount the significance of events that do not confirm our beliefs. We may view events that follow one another in time as causally related when they are unrelated or both are caused by something else. Such thinking often is seen in superstitious beliefs. We may believe that big events must have big causes. Many of our everyday beliefs about illness have some of these qualities. For example, we tend to believe that our illness is clearly due to an event just preceding it (e.g., "I caught a cold because I went out in the cold yesterday.") and that a serious illness must be due to a more major event than a less serious illness (e.g., cancer must have a more major cause than a cold; a torn Achilles tendon can't be due to just stepping off the sidewalk) (Taylor, 1982). If we are asked whether the flip of a coin would result in heads or tails after a string of heads, most of us probably would strongly feel that a tail must be coming up, despite our knowing that there is an equal probability of a head and tail on each flip of the coin. And, as noted in Chapter 3, we may be strongly inclined to believe that our chances of picking a red jelly bean out of a jar are greater if there are more in the jar, even if the percentage is less.

Of course, many of these beliefs may have some truth to them over the course of many events, but many of them do not and others are in any case incorrect in specific cases. In sum, according to this view, in our daily lives often we make serious errors in our processing of information—we look at the wrong data, weigh the data improperly, and make incorrect inferences. The suggestion is that, being the naive scientists we are, these errors are due to cognitive failings rather than to motivational factors.

MOTIVATED COGNITIVE PROCESSES

In contrast to the above analysis of cognitive processes, we turn here to cognitive processes influenced by motivational factors. We will consider both motivational influences on how information is processed and how certain categories or schemas can have motivational properties associated with them. More specifically, we will consider how self-schemas motivate a person to process information in particular ways and how self-schemas can represent motives or goals for action. As noted, this emphasis on motivational properties of schemas is a more recent component of the information-processing model (Banaji & Prentice, 1994; Kunda, 1990).

Self-verification and Self-enhancement

Two motives in relation to the self have been emphasized by cognitive personality psychologists—the motive for self-confirmation or self-verification and the motive for self-enhancement. Earlier we noted that self-schemas operate in terms of a self-confirming bias. It also was suggested that this was the nature of schema operation. Could there also be motivated reasons for such a phenomenon? Swann (1991, 1992) suggests that this indeed is the case. According to him, people actively solicit self-confirming evidence from others and present themselves in ways that will elicit such evidence. The reason for this, according to Swann, is that people have a need for consistency and predictability. Self-confirmation affords a degree of predictability and control that is not possible when events, such as feedback from others, violate our self-schemas. This may seem obvious, but the non-obvious part of Swann's view is the suggestion that people even seek self-confirmation when they have negative schemas. That is, a person with a negative self-schema will seek out information and social feedback that confirms the negative self-schema, becoming in a sense his or her own worst enemy. In accord with this view, Swann presents evidence to the effect that people gravitate toward relationships with people who see them as they see themselves. Thus, not only are persons with positive self-concepts more committed to spouses who think highly of them than to spouses who think poorly of them, but persons with negative self-concepts are more committed to spouses who think poorly of them than to spouses who think well of them (Swann, De La Ronde, & Hixon, 1992). In the words of the comedian Groucho Marx: "I'd never join a club that would have me as a member."

There also is evidence, however, of a bias toward seeing ourselves in a positive light, a self-enhancement or self-esteem motive (Tesser et al., 1989). In other words, according to the self-enhancement motive, we seek to establish and maintain positive self-images. We prefer positive feedback to negative feedback. Without necessarily being narcissists (Chapter 4), we overestimate our positive attributes and underestimate the negative attributes. Further, we compare ourselves favorably with those below us and try to associate ourselves with those perceived to have desirable features (Wood, 1989).

What happens, then, when the two motives conflict? If push comes to shove, do we prefer accurate feedback or positive feedback, the disagreeable truth or what fits our fancy, to be known for who we are or to be adored for who we would like to be (Strube, 1990; Swann, 1991)? In other words, what happens when our cognitive need for consistency or self-verification conflicts with our affective need for self-enhancement, what Swann has called the *cognitive–affective crossfire* (Swann et al., 1987, 1989)? A complete answer to this question is not at hand. The evidence to date suggests, however, that generally we prefer positive feedback but prefer negative feedback in relation to negative self-views. In line with this, there is evidence that life events inconsistent with the self-concept can lead to physical illness, even if these events are positive (Brown & McGill, 1989). In other words, positive life events can be bad for one's health if they conflict with a negative self-concept and disrupt one's negative identity. At the same time, there are individual differences in this regard and we may be more oriented toward self-enhancement in some relationships and self-verification in other relationships. For example, there is evidence that self-enhancement is more important during the early stages of a relationship but self-verification becomes increasingly important as the relationship becomes more intimate (Swann, De La Ronde, & Hixon, 1994).

Possible Selves and Self Guides

The information-processing view of the self is leading to investigation of many selves, including those that have emotional and motivational qualities. In other words, some self-schemas can have motivational properties. This is perhaps best captured by Markus's concept of **possible selves** (Markus & Nurius, 1986). Possible selves represent what people think they might become, what they would like to become, and what they are afraid of becoming. In this sense, possible selves not only serve to organize information but also have a powerful motivational influence, directing us toward becoming certain things and away from becoming other things (Markus & Ruvolo, 1989).

In relation to this, possible selves help us understand why people experience difficulties in self-control or willpower. According to Markus, we are able to carry out our intentions when the desired end state is experienced as self-relevant or a definite possible self. On the other hand, we are blocked in carrying out our intentions when the end state is not experienced as a possible self. Thus, for example, in attempting to diet, there must be an overlap between the "diet concept" and the self-concept, a sense of "*me* feeling lighter" and "*me* giving away clothes that are too big": "If the anticipation of satisfaction from wearing clothes two sizes smaller results in more, or more intense, cognitive, affective, or somatic self-representations than the anticipation of the delicious tastes and immediate gratification, the mandate to restrain oneself from eating for another hour can be more easily formulated" (Cross & Markus, 1990, p. 729).

Another illustrative concept is Higgins's (1987, 1989) concept of **self-guides**. Self-guides represent standards for individuals to meet. They result from early social learning experiences that are associated with emotional consequences for meeting or failing to meet standards. Like other self-schemas, self-guides organize information. In addition, however, self-guides play a major role in emotion and motivation. As we noted in Chapter 6, self-guides are of particular importance in the categories of ideal self and ought self. The *ideal self* represents the attributes that ideally we would like to possess, the *ought self* the attributes we feel we should possess. According to Higgins's self-discrepancy theory, we are motivated to reduce discrepancies between how we actually see ourselves and how ideally we would like to be, and motivated to reduce discrepancies between how we actually see ourselves and how we ought to be. Failure to meet each of these kinds of self-guides has different emotional implications. Failure to reduce the actual–ideal discrepancy is associated with sadness and disappointment, whereas failure to reduce the actual–ought discrepancy is associated with guilt and anxiety. The existence of such discrepancies apparently also decreases the effectiveness of the functioning of our immunological system in fighting disease (Strauman, Lemieux, & Coe, 1993).

SUMMARY

In sum, from an information-processing point of view, we can consider how information is processed as well as the content of the information.

And, we can now incorporate motivational as well as nonmotivational concepts in relation to explaining why information is processed in the way it is. In other words, we have a dynamic view as well as a structural view. For instance, from a cognitive perspective the self is viewed as an important cognitive structure that influences the encoding, organization, and memory of a great deal of information. Treatment of the self as a cognitive category allows one to study it in the same way as other cognitive categories and to understand its functioning in terms of cognitive processes followed by all cognitive categories. The self is an important conceptual category, but it is not some internal homunculus or controlling agent. Beyond this, what is distinctive about the self is that self-related schemas tend to be central to the organization of the person's cognitive system and of considerable emotional and motivational importance. Self-schemas may represent goals to achieve and may motivate us in the direction of self-verification and self-enhancement. Although similar to other concepts of the self noted in this book, perhaps most of all to Kelly's emphasis on constructs related to the self, the information-processing model of the self has distinctive features. What is most distinctive is the influence of self-schemas on the encoding, retrieval (memory) and enactment of events and their context-dependent nature.

The clinical, applied implications of the cognitive, information-processing model have been very significant, influencing vast parts of the health professions. Within a relatively short period of time, perhaps a decade or so, it has become one of the dominant themes among psychologists interested in understanding and treating stress-related disorders and serious psychological difficulties such as depression. Although there is no one theory or mode of therapy, the different approaches involved share some common assumptions: **CLINICAL APPLICATIONS**

1. Cognitions (attributions, beliefs, expectancies, memories concerning the self and others) are viewed as critical in determining feelings and behaviors. Thus, there is an interest in what people think and say to themselves.

2. The cognitions of interest tend to be specific to situations or categories of situations, though the importance of some generalized expectancies and beliefs is recognized.

3. Psychopathology is viewed as arising from distorted, incorrect, maladaptive cognitions concerning the self, others, and events in the world. Different forms of pathology are viewed as resulting from different cognitions or ways of processing information.

4. Faulty, maladaptive cognitions lead to problematic feelings and behaviors, and these in turn lead to further problematic cogni-

tions. Thus, a self-fulfilling cycle may set in whereby persons act so as to confirm and maintain their distorted beliefs.

5. Cognitive therapy involves a collaborative effort between therapist and patient to determine which distorted, maladaptive cognitions are creating the difficulty and then to replace them with other more realistic, adaptive cognitions. The therapeutic approach tends to be active, structured, and focused on the present.

6. In contrast with other approaches, cognitive approaches do not see the unconscious as important, except insofar as patients may not be aware of their routine, habitual ways of thinking about themselves and life. Further, there is an emphasis on changes in specific problematic cognitions rather than on global personality change.

STRESS AND COPING

The work of cognitively oriented psychologists has been very important in the area of stress and health. Lazarus, whose work has been very influential in this area, suggests that psychological stress depends on cognitions relating to the person and the environment (Lazarus, 1990).

Stress

According to the cognitive theory of psychological stress and coping, **stress** is viewed as occurring when the person views circumstances as taxing or exceeding his or her resources and endangering well-being. Involved in this are two stages of cognitive appraisal. In *primary appraisal*, the person evaluates whether there is anything at stake in the encounter, whether there is a threat or danger. For example, is there potential harm or benefit to self-esteem? Is one's personal health or that of a loved one at risk? In *secondary appraisal*, the person evaluates what, if anything, can be done to overcome harm, prevent harm, or improve the prospects for benefit. In other words, secondary appraisal involves an evaluation of the person's resources to cope with the potential harm or benefit evaluated in the stage of primary appraisal.

Ways of Coping with Stress

In a stressful situation, various means of *coping* are viewed as possible to manage, master, or tolerate the circumstances appraised as taxing or exceeding the person's resources. In particular a distinction is made between problem-focused forms of coping (e.g., efforts to alter the situation) and emotion-focused forms of coping (e.g., emotional distancing, escape–avoidance, seeking social support). Recent research on this model has focused on the development of a questionnaire to assess coping, the *Ways of Coping Scale*, and the health implications of differing

Escape–avoidance Coping: *People sometimes use activities such as shopping as a means of escaping from or avoiding stressful situations.*

coping strategies. This research suggests the following conclusions (Folkman, Lazarus, Gruen, & DeLongis, 1986; Lazarus, 1993):

1. There is evidence of both stability and variability in the methods individuals use to cope with stressful situations. Although the use of some coping methods appears to be influenced by personality factors, the use of many coping methods appears to be strongly influenced by the situational context.

2. In general, the greater the reported level of stress and efforts to cope, the poorer is the physical health and the greater is the likelihood of psychological symptoms. In contrast, the greater the sense of mastery, the better is the physical and psychological health.

3. Although the value of a particular form of coping depends on the context in which it is used, in general planful problem solving ("I made a plan of action and followed it" or "Just concentrated on the next step") is a more adaptive form of coping than escape–avoidance ("I hoped a miracle would happen" or "I tried to reduce tension by eating, drinking, or using drugs") or confrontative coping ("I let my feelings out somehow" or "I expressed anger to those who caused the problem").

Stress Inoculation Training

Although Lazarus did not develop procedures to reduce stress, Don Meichenbaum (1995) has developed what is called a **stress inoculation training** procedure based on a cognitive view of stress. In accord with Lazarus's view, Meichenbaum suggests that stress be viewed in cognitive terms; that is, stress involves cognitive appraisals, and individuals under stress often have a variety of self-defeating and interfering thoughts. In addition, such self-defeating cognitions and related behaviors have a built-in self-confirmatory component (e.g., people get others to treat them in an overprotective way). Finally, events are perceived and recalled in ways that are consistent with a negative bias. Meichenbaum's stress inoculation procedure is designed to help individuals cope better with stress and is seen as analogous to medical inoculation against biological disease.

Stress inoculation training involves teaching clients the cognitive nature of stress, followed by instruction in procedures to cope with stress and change faulty cognitions and, finally, training in the application of these procedures in actual situations. In terms of the cognitive nature of stress, the effort is to have the client become aware of such negative, stress-engendering, automatic thoughts as "It is such an effort to do anything" and "There is nothing I can do to control these thoughts or change the situation." The important point here is that the person may not be aware of having these automatic thoughts, and thus must be taught to be aware of them and their negative effects. In terms of coping procedures and correction of faulty cognitions, clients are taught relaxation as an active coping skill and taught cognitive strategies such as how to restructure problems so that they appear more manageable. In addition, clients are taught problem-solving strategies, such as how to define problems,

Don Meichenbaum

Imagery: *Cognitive therapists encourage patients to imagine scenes to determine the nature of their fears and develop positive courses of action.*

generate possible alternative courses of action, evaluate the pros and cons of each proposed solution, and implement the most practicable and desirable one. Clients also are taught to use coping self-statements such as "I can do it," "One step at time," "Focus on the present; what is it I have to do?" "I can be pleased with the progress I'm making," and "Keep trying; don't expect perfection or immediate success." Finally, through imagery rehearsal and practice in real-world situations clients are taught to feel comfortable with the utilization of these procedures. In imagery rehearsal the client imagines various stressful situations and the use of the coping skills and strategies. Practice involves role playing and modeling involving the therapist as well as practice in real-world situations.

The stress inoculation training procedure is active, focused, structured, and brief. It has been used with medical patients about to undergo surgery, with athletes to help them deal with the stress of competition, with rape victims to help them deal with the trauma of such assaults, and in the work environment to teach workers more efficient coping strategies and to help worker–management teams consider organizational change.

PATHOLOGY AND CHANGE

The cognitive, information-processing view holds that psychopathology results from unrealistic, maladaptive cognitions. Therapy, then, involves efforts to change such cognitive distortions and replace them with more realistic, adaptive cognitions.

Ellis's Rational-Emotive Therapy

Albert Ellis was a former psychoanalyst who developed a therapeutic system of personality change known as **rational–emotive therapy (RET)**. According to his theory, the causes of psychological difficulties are irrational beliefs or irrational statements we make to ourselves—that we *must* do something, that we *have* to feel some way, that we *should* be a certain kind of person, that we *cannot do* anything about our feelings or situation in life.

What kinds of maladaptive cognitions do people have? About as many different kinds as there are cognitive processes. Consider the following possibilities:

Irrational beliefs "If good things happen, bad things must be on the way." "If I express my needs, others will reject me."

Faulty reasoning "I failed on this effort, so I must be incompetent." "They didn't respond the way I wanted them to, so they must not think much of me."

Dysfunctional expectancies "If something can go wrong for me, it will." "Catastrophe is just around the corner."

Negative self-views "I always tend to feel that others are better than me." "Nothing I do ever turns out right."

Maladaptive attributions "I'm a poor test taker because I am a nervous person." "When I win, it's luck; when I lose, it's me."

Memory distortions "Life is horrible now and always has been this way." "I've never succeeded in anything."

Maladaptive attention "All I can think about is how horrible it will be if I fail." "It's better not to think about things; there's nothing you can do anyway."

Self-defeating strategies "I'll put myself down before others do." "I'll reject others before they reject me and see if people still like me."

Obviously there is overlap among the above maladaptive cognitions. Often important maladaptive cognitions have more than one flawed aspect. However, they illustrate the kinds of cognitions that create problematic feelings and situations for people. Through the use of logic, argument, persuasion, ridicule, or humor, an effort is made to change the irrational beliefs causing the difficulties. Although Ellis's views were long neglected by behavior therapists, with their emphasis on overt motor behavior, they have received greater interest with the development of cognitive therapy (Dobson & Shaw, 1995; Meichenbaum, 1995).

Beck's Cognitive Therapy for Depression

Like Albert Ellis, Aaron Beck is a former psychoanalyst who became disenchanted with psychoanalytic techniques and gradually developed a

Aaron T. Beck

cognitive approach to therapy. His therapy is best known for its relevance to the treatment of depression, but it has relevance to a wider variety of psychological disorders. According to Beck (1987), psychological difficulties are due to automatic thoughts, dysfunctional assumptions, and negative self-statements.

The Cognitive Triad of Depression   Beck's cognitive model of depression emphasizes that a depressed person systematically misevaluates ongoing and past experiences, leading to a view of the self as a loser, the view of the world as frustrating, and the view of the future as bleak. These three negative views are known as the **cognitive triad** and include negative views of the self such as "I am inadequate, undesirable, worthless," negative views of the world such as "The world makes too many demands on me and life represents constant defeat," and negative views of the future such as "Life will always involve the suffering and deprivation it has for me now." In addition, a depressed person is prone to faulty information processing, such as in magnifying everyday difficulties into disasters and overgeneralizing from a single instance of rejection to the belief that "Nobody likes me." It is these thinking problems, these negative schemas and cognitive errors, that cause depression.

Research on Faulty Cognitions   Considerable research has attempted to determine the role of faulty cognitions in depression and other psychological difficulties. Generally there is support for the presence of Beck's cognitive triad, as well as other faulty cognitions (Segal & Dobson, 1992). In particular, compared to nondepressed individuals, those who are depressed appear to focus more on themselves (Wood, Saltzberg, & Goldsamt, 1990), to have more accessible negative self-constructs (Bargh

& Tota, 1988; Strauman, 1990), and to have a bias toward pessimism rather than optimism, particularly in relation to the self (Epstein, 1992; Taylor & Brown, 1988). What is not clear from this research, however, is whether such cognitions *cause* depression, as opposed to being part of depression. And, even if they play a causal role, the question of how such faulty cognitions develop remains to be determined.

Cognitive Therapy   Cognitive therapy of depression is designed to identify and correct distorted conceptualizations and dysfunctional beliefs (Beck, 1993; Brewin, 1996). Therapy generally consists of 15 to 25 sessions at weekly intervals. The approach is described as involving highly specific learning experiences designed to teach the patient to monitor negative, automatic thoughts, to recognize how these thoughts lead to problematic feelings and behaviors, to examine the evidence for and against these thoughts, and to substitute more reality-oriented interpretations for these biased cognitions. The therapist helps the patient to see that interpretations of events lead to depressed feelings. For example, the following exchange between therapist (T) and patient (P) might occur:

P: I get depressed when things go wrong. Like when I fail a test.

T: How can failing a test make you depressed?

P: Well, if I fail I'll never get into law school.

T: So failing the test means a lot to you. But if failing a test could drive people into clinical depression, wouldn't you expect everyone who failed the test to have a depression?…Did everyone who failed get depressed enough to require treatment?

P: No, but it depends on how important the test was to the person.

T: Right, and who decides the importance?

P: I do.

SOURCE: Beck, Rush, and Shaw, 1979, p. 146

In addition to the examination of beliefs for their logic, validity, and adaptiveness, behavioral assignments are used to help the patient test certain maladaptive cognitions and assumptions. This may involve the assignment of activities designed to result in success and pleasure. In general, the therapy focuses on specific target cognitions that are seen as contributing to the depression. Beck contrasts cognitive therapy with traditional analytic therapy in terms of the therapist's being continuously active in structuring the therapy, in the focus on the here and now, and in the emphasis on conscious factors.

Beck's cognitive therapy has been expanded to include the treatment of other psychological difficulties, including anxiety, personality disorders, drug abuse, and marital difficulties (Beck, 1988; Beck & Freeman, 1990; Beck, Wright, Newman, & Liese, 1993; Clark, Beck, & Brown, 1989; Epstein & Baucom, 1988; Young, 1990). The basic view is that each difficulty is associated with a distinctive pattern of beliefs. For example, whereas in depression these concern failure and self-worth, in anxiety they concern danger. There is evidence for the effectiveness of cognitive therapy (Craighead, Craighead, & Ilardi, 1995; Hollon, Shelton, & Davis, 1993; Robins & Hayes, 1993). However, the distinctive therapeutic features of cognitive therapy and whether changes in beliefs and ways of processing information are the key therapeutic ingredients remains to be determined (Dobson & Shaw, 1995; Hollon, DeRubeis, & Evans, 1987).

Information-Processing Theory: Cognitions and Coping Strategies

THE CASE OF JIM

As noted in the discussion of social cognitive theory, at the time of the original assessment of Jim, the information-processing approach to personality had not yet emerged. Thus, at the time, it was impossible to assess him in relation to this theoretical approach. And, as noted in relation to social cognitive theory, information-processing approaches to personality have been more concerned with the testing of specific hypotheses than with the development of broader personality assessment instruments.

However, the results of other assessment devices would probably interest information-processing theorists. For example, the results of the Rep test concerning Jim's constructs, in particular those relating to the self (or self-schema), would be of great interest. In addition, there would be interest in his goals and self-efficacy beliefs, assessed in relation to social cognitive theory. Finally, we were able to obtain from Jim some estimate of his cognitions, attributions, dysfunctional thoughts, and coping strategies.

General Cognitions, Attributions, and Dysfunctional Thoughts

Jim was asked about specific or general beliefs he held. He noted that he believes in hard work, earning things, and being responsible for what one does. He believes that some people are natural winners and others are losers, the former making life easy for themselves and the latter making life difficult for themselves. Generally he feels that he likes life the easy way and enjoys being a winner. Other beliefs about himself are that he is intelligent, hardworking, personable, humorous, in need of approval, and possessing a depressive streak. Ideally he would like to be more selfless and generous, take setbacks more easily, and relax more. In terms of generalized expectancies, the *Life Orientation Test* (Scheier & Carver, 1985) was given to Jim as a measure of generalized optimism–pessimism. His responses indicated a strongly pessimistic orientation that fits with his depressive streak. For example, he strongly disagreed with the statements "I'm a believer in the idea that 'every cloud has a silver lining' " and "I'm always optimistic about my future." In contrast to these statements, he strongly disagreed with the statement "I hardly ever expect things to go my way," which probably reflects his clear belief that control is possible and desirable. Thus, he had an extremely high score on the *Desirability of Control Scale* (Burger & Cooper, 1979).

Jim gave the following as categories he used to view the world: successful–not successful, wealthy–not wealthy, attractive–not attractive, bright–not bright, interesting–not interesting, kind and loving–unloving, patient–impatient, generous–not generous, and deep–shallow. In terms of attributions, he again emphasized his belief in control and responsibility as opposed to belief in luck, chance, or fate. Jim filled out the *Attributional Style Questionnaire*; his responses reflected a general tendency toward internal, stable, and global attributions. Such an attributional style would fit with his tendency toward depressive streaks and belief in the desirability of control. However, an analysis of the subsections of this questionnaire reveals that this pattern holds more for positive events than for negative ones. In particular, his internal and stable attributions tend to be much more true for positive events than for negative ones. Thus, his belief that positive events can be controlled by his own efforts and can remain stable, reflected in the generalized expectancy that things can work out the way he wants, probably helps him to be less depressed than might otherwise be the case. In addition, his responses indicate a greater internal attribution for interpersonal events than for events having to do with professional achievement.

Finally, let us consider the area of irrational beliefs, dysfunctional thoughts, and cognitive distortions. One important point here is what Jim describes as his tendency to overpersonalize: "This is a problem of mine. If someone doesn't call, I attribute it to a feeling state in relation to me. I can feel terribly injured at times." Although he could not come up with any irrational beliefs or dysfunctional thoughts in the interview, his responses to the *Automatic Thoughts Questionnaire* (Hollon & Kendall, 1980) shed some light on this area of his functioning. He reported having the following thoughts frequently: "I've let people down," "I wish I were a better person," "I'm disappointed in myself," and "I can't stand this." These frequent thoughts have to do with his not being as loving or generous as he would like, his being very demanding of himself professionally and in athletics, his obsession about things that might go wrong, and his intolerance of things not going his way. For example, he cannot stand to be in traffic and will say: "I can't stand this. This is intolerable." Although Jim does not think much of Ellis's work and in the interview suggested that he didn't have many irrational beliefs, on the questionnaire he checked four out of nine items as frequent thoughts of his: "I must have love or approval," "When people act badly, I blame them," "I tend to view it as a catastrophe when I get seriously frustrated or feel rejected," and "I tend to get preoccupied with things that seem fearsome." He also described his tendency to catastrophize if he is going to be late for a movie: "It's a calamity if I'm going to be one minute late. It becomes a life and death emergency. I go through red lights, honk the horn, and pound on the wheel." This is in contrast to his own tendency to be at least a few minutes late for virtually all appointments, though rarely by more than a few minutes.

Coping Methods

When asked about his coping methods, Jim responded: "Heavy-duty compulsivity. It's part of my character, in everything—clean ashtrays in the car, the bed made in the morning, everything in the apartment in place. Order is very important. It's pervasive. Also intellectualization and humor." Jim also filled out the *Ways of Coping Scale* (Folkman, Lazarus, DeLongis, & Gruen, 1986). His responses to this scale indicate that his primary modes of coping with stressful events are to accept responsibility ("Criticize or lecture myself," "Realize I brought the problem on myself") and to engage in problem solving ("Just concentrated on what I had to do next," "Draw on my past experiences; I was in a similar position before"). In general, he tends to remain self-controlled and to think about the problem rather than use escape–avoidance methods, engage in risky solutions, or seek social support and sympathy from others. The latter reflects his not being forgiving of himself for getting into difficulty. Although there appear to be some positive aspects to his coping, other responses indicate that he feels he does not change or grow as a person as a result of these coping methods.

Summary

Combining the information from the social cognitive approach with that from the information-processing approach, what can be said about Jim as he approaches midlife? We see that in general Jim has a strong sense of self-efficacy in relation to intellectual and social skills, though he feels less efficacious in relation to creative thought and the ability to be loving, generous, and giving to people who are dear to him. He values money and financial success but has settled more on family intimacy and the quality of his work as a consultant as goals for the future. He has a strong sense of individual responsibility and belief in personal control over events. His attributions tend to be internal, stable, and global, and there is a streak of pessimism and depression to him. He is bothered by concerns about the approval of others, by his perfectionism and impatience, and by a tendency to worry about things. He tends to be self-controlled in coping with stress rather than avoiding problems or escaping from them. Generally he sees himself as a competent person and is guardedly optimistic about his chances of achieving his goals in the future.

RECENT DEVELOPMENTS

The view presented in this chapter started with the computer as a model for thinking about people and personality, but clearly work in the field is progressing beyond a narrow utilization of the model. In particular, three developments are noteworthy. First, there has been increased attention to the areas of emotion and motivation. Second, there has been increased attention to how thoughts, feelings, and motives are translated into action—that is, how people are not just left in thought but are directed toward doing things. Third, particularly in relation to the self, there is an interest in non-Western ways of thinking about the world.

FROM COGNITIONS TO FEELINGS AND MOTIVATION

Earlier editions of this text criticized the information-processing point of view for its neglect of affect (emotion) and motivation. According to this criticism, people may think like computers, or computers may be made to think like humans, but people also feel and are motivated. Our feelings and motives influence what we think, and our thoughts influence what we feel and do. Recent work within this approach has become strongly focused on such relationships, as illustrated by work on the self. Concepts such as *possible selves* and *self-guides* speak to the motivational properties of self-schemas; that is, we are motivated to become like some self-schemas and avoid being like other self-schemas, and we are motivated to behave in accord with ideal and ought self-standards. In addition, there is evidence that we are motivated toward a positive self-image but also toward self-verification, even if such verification involves a negative statement. Thus, cognitions such as self-schemas are always affecting our feelings and motives, but they in turn are always being affected by them.

FROM THINKING TO ACTION

The cognitive revolution threatened to leave the person in thought. If we are just sophisticated computers, why aren't we satisfied with processing information (Pervin, 1983)? As noted, current personality theorists following the information-processing view have become interested in questions of motivation. In contrast with an exclusively cognitive emphasis on thoughts, there is an added emphasis on action. In contrast with the trait emphasis on what people have, there is an emphasis on what people are trying to do (Cantor, 1990).

Once more, a variety of concepts have been used to express this motivational emphasis, concepts such as *goals, personal projects, personal strivings,* and *life tasks* (Cantor & Zirkel, 1990). Common to these concepts is an emphasis on the motivation to reach desired ends, as suggested by concepts such as *possible selves* and *self guides*. From a cognitive perspective, there is an interest in how people frame their goals and develop plans or strategies for reaching them (Cantor & Harlow, 1994). What is important here is that rather than leaving the person mired in thought, the theory focuses on how the person translates thought into action, that is, how the person sets a goal and maps out strategies for solving life's tasks.

FROM THE WESTERN SELF TO THE CROSS-CULTURAL SELF

Much of psychology is Western psychology. This is as true for the field of personality as it is for other parts of psychology. Yet, as suggested in Chapter 1, culture plays a role in defining one's personality. Therefore, one might expect the study of cross-cultural differences to play a major role in the field. Unfortunately, for the most part, it has not. In the absence of such comparative studies, it is often hard to tell whether the way we frame our questions, and the answers we come up with, make sense within the limits of our own cultural context or have wider relevance.

But, you may ask, aren't the personality structures and processes present in one culture also present in another culture? Just as people in all cultures have the same bodily parts and processes, don't they have the same personality structures and processes?

This is a very complicated question, one often debated, and we will not arrive at a conclusion here. However, let us consider the question of the self. We all know what the self is. Despite periods in the field where the concept came under attack, we might wonder how a theory of personality could do without such a concept. Doesn't everyone have a self? Well, some cultures have no word for self, and in other cultures the self is very different from that known in Western society (Roland, 1988; Shweder, 1991). A distinction gaining particular attention is that between the *individual self* and the *group self* or *collective self* (Cousins, 1989; Markus & Cross, 1990; Markus & Kitayama, 1991; Triandis, 1989; Triandis, McCusker, & Hui, 1990). In societies emphasizing the individual self, one's identity is based on unique qualities associated with the individual. When asked "Who are you?" most Americans respond with their name

The Self: *Cultural differences exist concerning how the self is defined and experienced.*

and what they do. In societies emphasizing the group, one's identity is based on ties to other members of the group. When asked "Who are you?" persons from such a society might answer in terms of the town they come from and the family they are part of. In individualistic societies, one's identity is based on what one owns and what one accomplishes. Value is placed on being independent and self-reliant. In collectivist societies, one's identity is based on membership in a group—the collective self—and value is placed on conformity. In the former, the private self is emphasized; in the latter, the public self.

Suggested here is that the very nature of the self—the information that is emphasized and the implications of that information for social behavior—can vary enormously from culture to culture. Indeed, one can even ask about the boundaries of the self. Most Americans, if asked about their "true self," would locate it somewhere within the body; but in India, the true self is the spiritual self that lies outside the body. It is not that members of the two societies have different views of where the parts of the body are and where they end, but rather that they have different views as to what constitutes the self and what forms its boundaries. What is self-relevant for one is not self-relevant for the other. In addition, there is the suggestion that attributional thinking is not a significant part of the thinking of members of all cultures, and that while attributions for physical events may be similar across cultures, those for social events vary considerably from culture to culture (Morris & Peng, 1994).

The issues raised here are profound. They have serious implications for the field of personality, ultimately questioning the limits of universal principles that can be established. To return to the computer metaphor, a computer consists of both hardware and software. The hardware (the machine itself) may be fairly standard and fixed. The software (the program), however, can vary enormously and change rapidly. The question then becomes, to what extent are people's personalities like computer hardware and to what extent are they like computer software? To what extent can we talk about structures and processes that hold for all people as opposed to those (i.e., programs) that are idiosyncratic to cultures and individuals? Proponents of the information-processing point of view are researching questions with implications for this issue. Regardless of the answers found, exploration of the issue will be of tremendous benefit to the field.

Now that we have considered the cognitive, information-processing approach to personality, what can be said about it relative to approaches previously considered? Clearly, certain concepts sound familiar. This is most clearly seen in the similarities with social cognitive theory. The cognitive emphasis in these chapters also reminds one of the work of George Kelly. In addition, one may be reminded of the work of Carl Rogers in the cognitive emphasis on the concept of self and in the emphasis on how people give meaning to the world about them.

THE RELATION OF INFORMATION-PROCESSING THEORY TO TRADITIONAL PERSONALITY THEORY

While noting these similarities, one can at the same time observe critical differences. For example, the works of Rogers and Kelly emanated from clinical experience, whereas the work in information processing derives from the experimental laboratory. Rogers and Kelly were attempting to develop a theory of personality, whereas the work presented here might better be construed as an *approach to* personality rather than a *theory of* personality. Both Rogers and Kelly were interested in the study of individuals, whereas cognitive personality psychologists have yet to demonstrate the utility of their approach for understanding an individual or the utility of studying the individual for learning about people generally. Even though Rogers emphasized process and change, he also emphasized the importance of structure and the continuity of personality. Cognitive personality psychologists tend to give greater emphasis to process and variability in personality functioning. This may be seen most clearly in the emphasis on the contextualized self and the family of selves, in contrast with Rogers's emphasis on the self as a more unitary concept.

Differences between cognitive personality theory and traditional personality theory (psychoanalytic and trait theory) are even more apparent

Table 14.3   Prototypic Characteristics of Two Personality Theories

Traditional Personality Theory	Cognitive, Information-Processing Theory
1. Stability and consistency of personality	1. Discriminativeness and flexibility of behavior
2. Generalized predictions of person's behavior	2. Predictions specific to situations
3. Emphasis on structure-stability	3. Emphasis on process-fluidity
4. Dispositions, traits, needs	4. Category stuctures, belief systems, inferential strategies, cognitive competencies
5. Motivation and dynamics	5. Cognitive economics and everyday cognitive processes
6. Self as unitary concept	6. Self as composed of multiple schema

and noteworthy (Table 14.3). At the heart of this difference lies the emphasis of traditional personality theory on structure and consistency in personality functioning. In contrast with this is the cognitive personality psychologist's emphasis on processes and flexibility, in the person's ability to discriminate among situations and manage behavior accordingly. In addition, traditional personality theory places much greater emphasis on human motivation than is true for cognitive personality approaches. As noted previously, the latter see people as *information seeking* rather than *pleasure seeking*. Finally, cognitive personality psychologists emphasize experimental observations of behavior and relate concepts of internal processes—such as cognitions—to behaviors that can be measured. In contrast, traditional personality theorists put greater faith in clinical observation (psychoanalytic theory) and in responses to questionnaires (trait theory). According to cognitive personality psychologists, we should be studying people's category structures and inference processes rather than their needs and dispositions; we should be studying behavior and cognitive representations of behavior rather than responses to questionnaires or projective techniques; and we should ally ourselves with other parts of psychology, such as cognitive and social psychology, rather than pursuing an entirely independent course of action.

CRITICAL EVALUATION

Earlier, we questioned whether the cognitive, information-processing approach has any distinctive contribution to make to personality. Having considered some of the relevant theory and research, what answers can be suggested?

STRENGTHS OF THE APPROACH

Ties to Cognitive Psychology

This approach appears to have three main contributions and strengths (Table 14.4). First, it is tied to an experimental foundation in cognitive psychology and continues to uphold that tradition while investigating issues in personality. Many personality theories have suffered from the problem of vague concepts and difficulty in suggesting relevant experimental efforts. To a certain extent, this has been true of psychoanalysis; to a greater extent, it has been true of humanistic and human growth potential theories. Also, most theories of personality have arisen independently of other ongoing efforts in psychology. Thus, when one considers the various theories covered in this book, one often finds it hard to say what has been learned from other areas of psychology. This is particularly true for the more clinical theories presented earlier in the text and somewhat less true for the theories of learning presented later. The cognitive, information-processing approach, however, marks a radical departure from this tradition. In going social and cognitive, personality psychologists following this approach have attempted to take from social psychology and cognitive psychology concepts and experimental procedures that might be useful in exploring personality.

Consideration of Important Aspects of Personality

The second strength of the cognitive, information-processing approach to personality lies in the phenomena investigated. Although it emphasizes an experimental tradition, important aspects of human personality functioning have not altogether been neglected. Consider here the issues covered—how individuals organize their representations of people, situations, events, and themselves. These indeed are topics that should be of concern to personality psychologists. Thus, when parallels are noted between issues explored by cognitive personality psychologists and earlier theories of personality, this may be taken as a strength. The approach does not neglect longstanding issues that remain of concern to us. Whereas for some time experimental psychologists ignored questions of the self and consciousness, these psychologists are prepared to tackle them. Though they remain committed to the laboratory, they also generally remain aware of and concerned about phenomena observed in daily living.

Contributions to Health Management and Therapy

Finally, one can note the importance of the clinical applications associated with this approach. The defining characteristic of cognitive therapy is an interest in what people think and say to themselves. Beyond this, there is an interest in how people process information, in the cognitive distortions that lead to psychological difficulties, and in the procedures that can be used to change these distortions. In the emphasis on an active, structured approach, this is a radical departure from psycho-analysis and Rogerian therapy. At the same time, in the emphasis on what goes on inside the person, it is a radical departure from behaviorism, and, in this regard, it continues to come under attack from conservative behaviorists. Still, the legions of those who consider themselves cognitive therapists are growing, and the application of the approach to a broad spectrum of difficulties is increasing.

LIMITATIONS OF THE APPROACH

Problems with the Computer as a Model

But what of the limitations of the approach? Here we may again consider three relevant points. First, we can examine the underlying model critically. How useful is the computer, information-processing model that underlies this approach to personality? We must recall that a model need not be an accurate reflection of human behavior to be useful in the study of that behavior. Thus, the basic question is not whether humans function like computers but whether studying people *as if* they function like computers assists us in understanding their behavior.

To a certain extent, the jury is still out on this question. We do know that in many ways people do not think like computers, let alone behave like them. George Miller, one of the early leaders in the development of computer models of human thinking, suggests that "how computers work seems to have no real relevance to how the mind works any more than a wheel shows how people walk" (1982, p. C1). Computers are becoming faster and capable of handling growing amounts of information. We are becoming increasingly sophisticated in writing programs to make computers think like humans. However, many people believe that human thinking is fundamentally different from machine thinking. Not only does a machine inevitably require a person to select the information to be stored and write the program for organizing information, two critical processes in information processing, but machines do not make the many economies and irrational connections that are part of human thought. In addition, people make judgments such as attributing intent to the action of others. Although it is possible to make a computer think in an analogous way, there remains a considerable gap between the two. Furthermore, it is possible that thinking about social phenomena in a social context is fundamentally different from the isolated processing of neutral information.

Neglect of Affect and Motivation

This last point brings us to the second criticism of this approach. This is that in going cognitive, psychology has neglected such important human phenomena as affect and motivation (Berscheid, 1992; Hastorf & Cole, 1992). In following in the footsteps of cognitive psychology, personality psychology may be in danger of committing the same errors without breaking new ground. In gaining our head, we may be in danger of losing our soul.

Some time ago the distinction was made between "cold cognition" and "hot cognition." Psychologists, including both cognitive and cognitive personality psychologists, tend to study cold cognition. Although they study important phenomena, they tend to study the more emotionally neutral aspects of these phenomena in the relatively cool setting of the laboratory. But true social cognition in important life situations may be fundamentally different from the cool, detached processes that have typically been the focus of investigation. In reviewing the results of research following the information-processing model, a leading cognitive psychologist suggested that "there is more to human intelligence than the pure cognitive system, and that a science of Cognition cannot afford to ignore these other aspects" (Norman, 1980, p. 4). Prominent among these other aspects were emotion and motivation.

Since 1980, the situation has changed and there are encouraging signs of an interest in hot cognition—emotion and motivation. The work on goals and possible selves represents one move in this direction, work on stress and cognitive coping strategies represents another, and work on the effects of emotions such as depression on cognitive processes represents a third. However, such efforts are in the early stages of development. How far they will take us in understanding such areas remains to be seen.

Table 14.4 Summary of Strengths and Limitations of a Cognitive, Information-Processing Approach to Personality

Strengths	Limitations
1. Ties its approach to work in experimental cognitive psychology. Defines concepts clearly and makes them accessible to experimental investigation.	1. Has yet to achieve an integrated theory of personality.
2. Considers some important aspects of human personality functioning (e.g., how people represent other people, situations, events, and themselves).	2. Neglects affect and motivation as important correlates and determinants of cognition.
3. Important contributions to health management and psychotherapy.	3. Questions concerning the conceptual status and clinical efficacy of cognitive therapies.

Status of Therapies Yet to Be Defined

Finally, let us consider some questions regarding cognitive therapy or, more accurately, cognitively based therapies. First, although many of these approaches share a common cognitive emphasis, there is no one theoretical model. Further, often there may be little direct tie to work in cognitive psychology itself (Brewin, 1989). Second, as noted, although these approaches suggest that cognitive distortions are causes of disturbances in emotion such as anxiety and depression, it is not yet clear that they determine negative affects rather than being associated with negative affect or a result of negative affect (Brewin, 1996; Segal & Dobson, 1992). Third, it is not clear whether cognitive therapy emphasizes rational, realistic cognitions or adaptive cognitions. Both are mentioned, often being used interchangeably. Yet, there is evidence that depressives, for example, suffer *less* cognitive distortion than do normals (Power & Champion, 1986). Is the goal of therapy, then, to help people learn how to distort better so as to feel better? If so, what kinds of scientists are we training them to be? Finally, although there is *some* evidence of the efficacy of *some* forms of cognitive therapy with *some* patients, the jury is still out in regard to the boundaries of therapeutic efficacy. Thus questions can be raised concerning the conceptual status and clinical efficacy of cognitive therapies.

In sum, cognitive approaches to personality and therapy represent promising leads. At this time we can recognize their contributions while remaining guarded in our optimism concerning the future.

MAJOR CONCEPTS

Schema. A cognitive structure that organizes information and thereby influences how we perceive and respond to further information.

Prototype. The pattern of characteristics that best illustrates or exemplifies membership in a category. The prototype represents an ideal type, with members of the category not necessarily possessing all the characteristics of the prototype.

Script. A series or pattern of behaviors considered to be appropriate for a situation.

Self-schemas. Cognitive generalizations about the self, derived from past experience, that organize and guide the processing of self-related information.

Locus of causality. In Weiner's scheme of causal attributions, a dimension that relates to whether the person perceives causes of events as coming from within (internal) or from outside (external). The two other causal dimensions are *stability* (stable–unstable causes) and *controllability* (events as controllable or uncontrollable).

Implicit personality theory. The layperson's beliefs concerning the characteristics or traits of people that go together, implicit in that they are not made explicit and are not part of a formal theory of personality.

Possible selves. Individuals' ideas of what they might become, would like to become, and are afraid of becoming.

Self-guides. Standards concerning the self that the individual feels should be met. They result from early learning experiences and have important emotional consequences.

Stress. The person's perception that circumstances exceed his or her resources and endanger well-being. In Lazarus's view this involves two stages of cognitive appraisal—primary and secondary.

Stress inoculation training. Meichenbaum's procedure for training individuals to cope with stress.

Cognitive therapy. An approach to therapy in which changes in unrealistic and maladaptive thinking are emphasized.

Rational–emotive therapy (RET). A therapeutic approach, developed by Albert Ellis, that emphasizes change in irrational beliefs that have destructive emotional and behavioral consequences.

Cognitive triad. Beck's description of the cognitive factors that lead to depression, involving a view of the self as a loser, a view of the world as frustrating, and a view of the future as bleak.

---

1. Using the computer as a model, cognitive personality psychologists are interested in how people process (encode, store, retrieve) information. **REVIEW**

2. Interest in how people represent the world (physical objects, situations, people) focuses on the categories people develop and the hierarchical organization of these categories. Categories are defined by a pattern of characteristics. A prototype represents an ideal type that best exemplifies the contents of a category.

3. People define scripts that are relevant to particular situations or categories of situations. A script represents a series or pattern of behaviors considered to be appropriate for the situation.

4. People develop self-schemas or cognitive generalizations about the self that organize and guide self-related information. Such schemas influence what information we see as self-relevant, and how that information is organized and remembered. Once developed, self-schemas may be difficult to change because of a bias toward self-consistent information, and because of a tendency to elicit self-confirming evidence from others.

5. Rather than a single self, we have a family of selves made up of the way we are in various situations and our various possible selves or what we think we might become, would like to become, and are afraid to become.

COGNITIVE INFORMATION-PROCESSING THEORY AT A GLANCE

Structure	Process	Growth and Development
Cognitive categories and schemas; attributions; generalized expectancies	Information-processing strategies; attributions	Development of cognitive competencies, self-schemas, expectancies, attributions

6. A key ingredient of the processing of information relevant to events is their causal explanations. According to Weiner, there are three dimensions of people's causal explanations: locus of causality (internal–external), stability (stable–unstable), and controllability. For example, events may be perceived to be due to ability, effort, task difficulty, or luck. Causal explanations (attributions) influence a broad range of psychological processes, including motivation and emotion.

7. In organizing information relevant to people, individuals develop an implicit personality theory or view that certain traits are associated with other traits.

8. The relation of information processing to affect and motivation is illustrated by the concepts of possible selves, self-guides (standards for the person to meet), as well as research on the self-verification and self-enhancement motives.

9. According to Lazarus, stress occurs when persons view events as exceeding their resources. This follows primary appraisal of the threat and secondary appraisal of one's resources to cope with the threat. People may use problem-focused or emotion-focused forms of coping, the method used being influenced both by the personality of the individual and by the context of the situation. Meichenbaum's stress inoculation training is a procedure developed to help individuals cope better with stress.

10. Cognitive approaches to psychopathology and change assume that cognitions determine feelings and behaviors, that maladaptive cognitions lead to problematic feelings and behaviors, and that therapy involves the replacement of problematic cognitions with more realistic, adaptive cognitions.

11. According to Ellis, the causes of psychological difficulties are irra-

Pathology	Change	Illustrative Case
Unrealistic or maladaptive beliefs; errors in information processing	Cognitive therapy—changes in irrational beliefs, dysfunctional thoughts, and maladaptive attributions	Jim

tional beliefs. In rational–emotive therapy (RET), various procedures are used to challenge and change these irrational beliefs.

12. In Beck's cognitive model of depression, depression is due to the cognitive triad of a negative view of the self, a negative view of the world, and a negative view of the future. Although research supports the presence of such cognitions in depression, it is not clear that they cause depression as opposed to being part of depression. Beck's cognitive therapy involves teaching the patient to become aware of negative automatic thoughts, to examine and challenge these thoughts, and to substitute more reality-oriented, adaptive cognitions for them.

13. Recent work in the area has focused on three topics: (a) the relation of information processing to affect and motivation; (b) how people move from thoughts to action, including an emphasis on goals and action strategies; and (c) cross-cultural differences in information processing, as in the study of the difference between the Western individualistic self and the collective self of other cultures.

14. Cognitive personality psychologists emphasize category structures and inference processes rather than needs or dispositions, and emphasize specific problematic cognitions in need of change as opposed to change in overall personality organization or isolated pieces of behavior.

15. The cognitive, information-processing approach to personality has valuable ties to cognitive psychology, considers important aspects of personality, and has made valuable contributions to the management of health difficulties and psychological problems. At the same time, questions can be raised concerning the computer as a model for human personality, the neglect of affect and motivation until recently, and the conceptual status and clinical efficacy of cognitive therapies.

15

AN OVERVIEW OF PERSONALITY THEORY, ASSESSMENT, AND RESEARCH

Chapter Focus

You might think of the many theories presented in this book as pieces in the complicated puzzle we call personality. Let's take a step back and consider how all these pieces might fit together. Ultimately, there may be several different ways of putting the puzzle together. In this final chapter, then, our goal is a deeper understanding of the issues in personality research. Through the process of contrast and comparison, we aim for a greater appreciation of the theories covered in this book. First, we return to some of the issues that divide personality theorists. Second, we provide an overview of the concepts that each theory uses to explain the what, how, and why of human behavior. Finally, we again consider relations among theory, assessment, and research. Throughout, we emphasize the distinctive contributions each theory can make toward a more complete understanding of human personality.

QUESTIONS TO BE ADDRESSED IN THIS CHAPTER

1. How can we understand the existence of the many different theories of personality covered in the text?

2. What can we conclude about the major issues on which the theories covered in the text disagree?

3. How can we make sense of the various pictures of Jim derived from the different theories and their preferred assessment instruments?

What theorists believe people to be influences which determinants and mechanisms of human functioning they explore most thoroughly and which they leave unexamined. The view of human nature embodied by psychological theories is more than just a philosophical issue.

SOURCE: Bandura, 1986, p. 1

This book has tried to achieve a greater understanding of why people behave as they do and of how we can better understand their behavior. The major focus has been on how different theories of personality conceptualize human behavior. We have also discussed alternative approaches to assessment and research. Finally, we have considered how different types of theories, assessment techniques, and research styles are related; we found that different theories of personality focus on different aspects of personality functioning and use different means for gathering and analyzing data. In this final chapter, let us take stock of some of the ground that has been covered and consider some of the issues that remain open.

498

STAGES OF SCIENTIFIC DEVELOPMENT

In Chapter 1, we discussed ways to evaluate theories and highlighted the importance of evaluating a theory in relation to its stage of development. A look at the history of developments in most fields of science will help us understand some of the relevant issues. According to Kuhn (1970), there are three distinct stages of scientific development: an early developmental stage, a stage of normal science, and a period of scientific revolution.

Developmental Stage

The early developmental stage of scientific activity is characterized by continual competition among a number of distinct schools or views of nature. Each school believes it functions according to the dictates of scientific method and observation. Indeed, what differentiates these competing views is not the degree of commitment to scientific method, but rather their differing ways of viewing the world and of practicing science within it. Since at this stage of development there is no common body of data and belief, each school builds the field anew from its own foundation and chooses its own supporting observations and experiments. Fact gathering during this time has a random quality; one rarely observes a systematic accumulation of knowledge. Essentially, during the early development stage, the field is without a commonly accepted model, or **paradigm**, that defines the field of observations and the methods to be used in research.

Normal Science: Paradigms

The stage of normal science begins with the acceptance of such a paradigm or model and is based on clear scientific achievement. During this stage there is acceptance of and commitment to a model that defines which problems are legitimate areas of inquiry and points out the appropriate methods of research. A more rigid definition of the field occurs, research is more focused, observations are more restricted, and knowledge is more cumulative. Each new bit of knowledge serves as a building block for the next. The scientists during this period are somewhat tradition-bound and are committed to the accepted model. Instead of many competing schools in the field, there tend to be relatively few, and frequently only one.

Scientific Revolutions

Since no paradigm or theory can ever explain all facts, ultimately there are some observations during the period of normal science that do not fit the accepted models. These observations or *anomalies* create a crisis in which tradition is shattered and, after a period of turmoil, a new paradigm is accepted. Copernicus, Newton, and Einstein were each associated with a stage of scientific revolution. In each case, a time-honored theory was rejected in favor of a new theory. In each case, also, the new the-

THE RISE AND FALL OF SCHOOLS IN PSYCHOLOGY: WHICH SCHOOL HAS BEEN MOST PROMINENT?

Since the birth of scientific psychology more than a century ago, many schools of thought have risen and fallen from prominence. One popular contention is that the cognitive perspective now dominates scientific psychology, having prevailed over psychoanalysis and behaviorism. In contrast, others argue that no such cognitive revolution has occurred: "The repeated declaration of a revolution may be more a reflection of the enthusiasm many cognitive psychologists have for their subdiscipline than of actual events" (Friman, Allen, Kerwin, & Larzelere, 1993, p. 662).

Despite the passionate claims and heated arguments, there have been few attempts to document these trends empirically. A recent study by Robins, Craik, and Gosling (1995) moves beyond mere speculation on this issue, measuring historical trends in the prominence of psychoanalysis, behaviorism, and cognitive psychology. (Note that this analysis studied the whole field of psychology, rather than personality psychology in particular; therefore, the trait approach was not included as a separate school.)

Prominence implies that a school's scientific achievements are capturing the attention of the rest of the field. Thus, Robins et al. argued, prominence in *mainstream scientific psychology* can be measured by what is cited and published in the most influential general psychology publications. These "flagship" publications (e.g., *Psychological Review* and the *American Psychologist*) serve dual roles in the field:

They reflect current trends and they define the agenda for the future. Thus, a school of thought's prominence in the flagship journals should be reflected in the *number of articles published on topics relevant to that school*. For example, if cognitive psychology has been increasing in scientific prominence, we would expect to find an increase in articles on cognitive topics appearing in the flagship publications.

To determine the number of relevant articles, Robins et al. used keywords to represent topics of central concern to each school, and then determined the frequency with which these keywords appeared in articles published since 1967. For each school, they calculated the percentage of articles published in the flagship publications that included at least one of the keywords selected to represent that school.

Figure 15.1 shows the publication trends from 1967 to 1994. Articles relevant to cognitive psychology have appeared with increasing frequency in the flagship publications, while the number of articles relevant to behavioral psychology has been decreasing. Note that Figure 15.1 also shows that psychoanalytic articles were almost nonexistent throughout the period examined. Over the past three decades, the percentage of flagship articles devoted to cognitive psychology has more than doubled from 1967 to the present (from less than 7% to more than 16%), whereas the percentage of articles devoted to behavioral psychology declined over this period to less than a third of its 1967 value (from about 9%

to about 2.5%). In contrast, psychoanalysis did not show any substantial changes.

These data suggest three major conclusions. (1) Cognitive psychology has overtaken behaviorism as the most prominent of the three major schools in scientific psychology. (2) Despite claims to the contrary, behavioral psychology seems to be on the decline. (3) Mainstream scientific psychology has paid little attention to psychoanalytic research and articles pertaining to the psychoanalytic school have been virtually nonexistent in the flagship publications over the past three decades. Although psychoanalytic ideas continue to influence research in psychology, contemporary psychoanalytic writing is not assimilated directly into scientific psychology.

How do these trends fit into the broader context of psychology as a science? Interpreted within a Kuhnian perspec-tive, Robins et al.'s findings might be taken to suggest that the cognitive school is the most recent in a succession of dominant paradigms. But that conclusion may be premature because additional evidence is required before a Kuhnian *revolution* can be declared. For example, Kuhn's emphasis on the socialization process within science would require that all textbooks of scientific psychology adopt the cognitive orientation, and that most young scientists work on cognitive topics. Certainly, this is not (yet) the case, as the present textbook amply demonstrates. Whether cognitive psychology will evolve into *the* dominant paradigm or remain a competing perspective, which both informs other perspectives and is informed by them, remains to be seen.

SOURCES: Robins, Craik, & Gosling, 1995; Friman, Allen, Kerwin, & Larzelere, 1993.

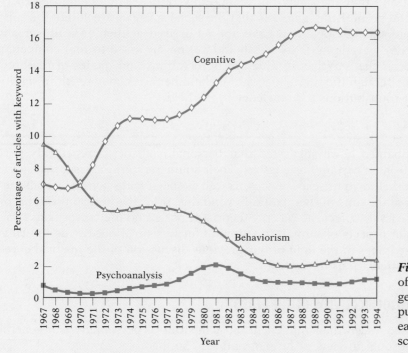

Figure 15.1 Percentage of articles published in general psychology publications relevant to each of three major schools of psychology.

ory was incompatible with the old one and offered explanations of critical observations that could not be explained within the earlier paradigm. Typically, however, acceptance of the new paradigm occurs after a period of intense struggle among competing views and a period of wide-open research. This period thus shares some characteristics with the early developmental phase—competition among alternative views, wide-open research, debate over fundamental issues, and additions to knowledge that are noncumulative. What differentiates this state from the early development stage is that it follows a period of articulation of a paradigm and is a response to specific observations that have presented problems for that paradigm. Although the new paradigm may be limited in scope, it is accepted because it offers solution to critical issues in the field. Rather than representing a competing paradigm or point of view, it replaces an old one and involves a reevaluation of prior facts. Once accepted, the new paradigm is associated with a new period of normal science until new observations arise and the stage is set for a further scientific revolution. The successive transition from one paradigm to another via revolution is the usual developmental pattern of a mature science.

Summary

The field of personality is filled with issues that divide scientists along sharply defined lines and lead to alternative, competing schools of thought. It is important to recognize that such theoretical differences exist and that they may not be speedily resolved by debate or experimental proof. Kuhn suggests that the social sciences are still in the early developmental stage and have not yet arrived at their first universally received paradigm. If so, we should not be surprised to find competing theories that emphasize different observations and modes of research. And although they compete with one another, each may result in significant contributions to knowledge in the field.

SOME ISSUES THAT DIVIDE PERSONALITY THEORISTS

In Chapter 1, we suggested that personality theorists repeatedly have confronted certain basic issues. Their solutions to these issues reflect in part their own life experiences, as well as social and scientific trends current at the time of their work. Beyond this, prior theoretical positions on these issues affect the way the theorist chooses and then investigates particular aspects of human functioning for investigation. Let us return to these issues in the light of our previous discussion of the major theoretical orientations in the text.

PHILOSOPHICAL VIEW OF THE PERSON

We have seen that implicit in most theories of personality is a general, philosophical view of human nature. The theorists covered in this text present a diversity of views: Freud's view of the person as an energy system; Rogers's view of the person as a self-actualizing organism; Kelly's view of the person as a scientist; the Skinnerian view of the person as responding to environmental reinforcement contingencies; the social cognitive view of the person as a problem-solving organism; the computer model of the person as a complex information processor. Of course, other views are possible—and within any single orientation, such as trait theory, different views can emerge. Furthermore, such capsule descriptions fail to do justice to the complexity inherent in each view. At the same time, these capsule descriptions capture a distinctive element in each theoretical perspective and help to make us aware of the differing views that do exist. Of particular interest here is the emphasis on cognition found in so many recent theoretical developments (psychoanalytic ego psychology, social cognitive theory, and cognitive information-processing personality theory).

Each view of the organism opens up certain avenues of thought, research, and analysis. Each also potentially closes off other important lines of emphasis and investigation. The early S–R view of the person inhibited recognition of the importance of cognitive functions. The current cognitive emphasis may correct this imbalance, but it may also lead us to ignore other important areas of experience such as motivation and emotion. The point here is not that one view is right or wrong but that such views exist and that it is important to be aware of them in understanding each theory, as well as in assessing its strengths and limitations.

INTERNAL AND EXTERNAL CAUSES OF BEHAVIOR

A second, related issue is whether the causes of behavior are inside the person or in the environment. In Chapter 1, Freud and Skinner were contrasted as representing extreme positions on this issue. We have also discussed how the questions asked by researchers have changed over the years. First, researchers asked *whether* behavior is caused by the person or by the situation, then *to what extent* behavior is caused by person and situation factors, and finally how person and situation factors *interact* with one another to determine behavior.

In the theories covered, this issue emerged most clearly in relation to trait theory and social cognitive theory. At one extreme, trait theory has been characterized as suggesting that people are stable and consistent in their behavior over time and across situations. Psychoanalytic theory, with its similar emphasis on personality structure, has been seen as emphasizing internal causes of behavior and general stability in personality functioning. At the other extreme, learning theory has been characterized as emphasizing environmental determinants of behavior and the variability or situational specificity of behavior. Such characterizations are useful in highlighting important theoretical differences. At the same time, it should be clear that none of these theories emphasizes only one set of causes. To a certain extent, they are all interactionist in their emphasis; they all emphasize the interaction between individual and environment, or person and situation, in determining behavior. Trait theory, for example, does recognize the importance of situational factors in affecting which traits are activated as well as affecting the moods of the individual. It is inconceivable that a trait theorist or a psychoanalytic theorist would expect a person to behave the same way in all situations. On the other hand, social cognitive theory recognizes the importance of person factors in terms of concepts such as goals, cognitive and behavioral competencies, self-efficacy, and self-regulation. Indeed, the concept of reciprocal determinism or the mutually causal relationship between person and situation is a cornerstone of social cognitive theory.

As with other issues in the field, emphasis often shifts in one direction or another—in this case in terms of relative emphasis on internal, person factors or on external, environmental factors. At one point considerable evidence was presented to suggest that human behavior is quite variable. Such evidence was used to challenge traditional trait and psychodynamic views of personality structure and personality dispositions (Mischel, 1968). More recently, evidence has been presented to suggest that human behavior is more consistent than had been suggested previously (Epstein, 1983; Pervin, 1985). Such consistency does not seem to be explained by unchanged environmental circumstances. Indeed, we often are impressed with how resistant some behavior is to change despite dramatic changes in environmental circumstances. Thus, whereas at one point situational determinants were emphasized, many psychologists are again emphasizing dispositions or reaction tendencies within individuals.

Although important differences remain in the relative emphasis on internal (person) and external (situation) causes, all theories of personality recognize that both are important in understanding behavior. Perhaps we can now expect to find theorists who increasingly will address questions in terms of both sets of causes rather than with an almost exclusive emphasis on one or another set of causes. All personality theorists recognize that there is both consistency and variability to individual behavior. The task, then, is to account for the pattern of stability and change that characterizes people.

CONSISTENCY ACROSS SITUATIONS AND OVER TIME

As we have seen, a major point of difference among theories of personality involves the issue of how consistent personality is across situations. Known as the *person–situation controversy*, this issue brings together such different views as psychoanalytic theory and trait theory, both arguing in favor of relative consistency across situations, as opposed to social-cognitive and information-processing approaches that emphasize context-specificity. Of course, psychoanalytic and trait theories differ in their explanations for the consistency of behavior, the former emphasizing the early development of a basic personality structure and the latter emphasizing the role of genetic determinants. However, both suggest a high degree of consistency to personality, particularly if one looks beyond what are seen as being superficial differences in appearance (phenotypes) as opposed to more basic structures (genotypes). In contrast to this, the more cognitive, information-processing approaches to personality emphasize the extent to which learning is context-specific and the extent to which people regulate their behavior according to the demands of particular situations.

There is greater agreement among the theories concerning longitudinal stability. All of the theories of personality accept some significant degree of stability of personality over time, particularly once adulthood has been reached. The theories vary, however, in the reasons they give for this stability and in their views about the individual's potential for change. Whereas trait theorists emphasize the role of genetic influences, psychoanalytic theorists emphasize the continuity of personality structures formed early in life, and cognitive theories emphasize the role of the person in selecting situations that maintain consistency over time and the role of others who confirm the person's self-concept. Thus, in the latter case cognitive motives, such as needs for self- verification and self-consistency, are emphasized. Perhaps not surprisingly, more cognitive theorists also suggest a greater potential for change than do psychoanalytic and trait theorists. Rogers was closer to the cognitive approaches in this regard. However, Rogers's optimistic view of the potential for change appears to have been more expressive of a philosophical view of the person than an emphasis on cognitive processes or the context-specificity of behavior.

Where do we go from here? We know that some people are more consistent than others, and that most people are consistent in some ways and variable in others. Similarly, we know that some people hardly change at all over time whereas others change a great deal, and that over time each of us changes a little in some ways and a great deal in other ways. Thus, the task ahead remains to account for both consistency and variability in functioning, and for both stability and change in personality over time. Ultimately a unified theory of personality will have to spell out the reasons for both consistency and variability, as well as the reasons for both stability and change. These reasons will involve factors both inside the person and in the environment that promote consistency or variability and that encourage or resist change.

THE UNITY OF BEHAVIOR AND THE CONCEPT OF THE SELF

There is movement in human organisms, as living systems, toward integrated functioning and the reduction of conflict. Personality theories differ in the extent to which they emphasize the patterned, unified system aspects of human functioning. An emphasis on the unity of behavior is greatest in the clinical theories of Freud, Rogers, and Kelly. With the exception of Allport, it is much less prominent in trait theories and learning theories. Why should this be? Undoubtedly the reasons are complex and varied, but a number of points can be considered. First, clinical theories are based on observations of many behaviors of a single individual. The theories of Freud, Rogers, and Kelly evolved out of these clinical observations. Their efforts were directed toward understanding relationships among thoughts, behaviors, and feelings. Almost of necessity, they were struck with the issues of conflict and threats to the coherence of the system, as reported to them by their patients. Although clinical approaches based on learning theory exist and are important, they evolved out of theories rather than initially serving as the basis for them.

A second point to be considered is the emphasis in trait theories and learning theories on exploring particular variables. The belief here is that human behavior can be understood through the systematic study of particular variables or processes. The strategy is to study phenomena systematically and to build from the simple to the complex. Pattern and organization become important when one has a clear enough grasp of the parts that constitute the pattern or organization.

The concept of self traditionally has been used to express the patterned, organized aspects of personality functioning. In psychoanalytic theory, the concept of ego expresses the "executive" or integrative aspects of system functioning. Although sometimes portrayed as a person or homunculus inside the individual ("The ego seeks to reduce conflict"), it actually describes processes going on within the person. For both Rogers and Kelly the concept of self plays an important integrative function. For Rogers, the person seeks self-actualization and to make the self and experience congruent with one another. For Kelly, the constructs associated with the self and how they are organized play a central role in the person's functioning. The emphasis on the concept of self as an organizing entity is perhaps most clearly expressed in the view of Allport. The concept of self, or *proprium*, as he called it, gave testimony to the complex, organized aspects of the mature human system.

In their efforts to avoid the vague, romantic, and fanciful, many theorists have avoided the concept of self. In particular, the self as a homunculus within the person that determines action has been criticized. Still, as we have witnessed, recent developments in social cognitive theory place heavy emphasis on the concept of self. This is a somewhat different concept of self, however, involving standards for self-praise and self-criticism as well as other self-regulatory functions. Nevertheless, it is a self-concept. The concept of efficacy, or ability to perform the behavior necessary for certain outcomes, an increasingly important part of Bandura's theory, involves cognitions or beliefs about the self. It is seen as a broadly integrative concept that can account for diverse findings. Thus, at this point, social cognitive theory also has come to emphasize both the organized aspects of the human personality and the importance of the self-concept in such organization. Finally, the organizing and directing functions of self-schemas are clearly articulated in the cognitive information-processing view. Just as any complex system may have higher-order control units, so the self may be viewed as consisting of schemas or constructs that organize and integrate the functioning of other parts of the system. It is noteworthy, however, to reemphasize the view of a multiplicity or family of selves rather than a single, all-encompassing self-concept.

Although the utility and necessity of the concept of self continue to be debated, theories of personality are drawn to it continuously. In one form or another, the concept of self enters into most theories and attests to the important ways in which we experience ourselves, to the myriad ways in which we understand ourselves, and to the organized aspects of our functioning.

VARYING STATES OF AWARENESS AND THE CONCEPT OF THE UNCONSCIOUS

Interest in varying states of awareness has been increasing in psychology. As noted at the outset, many theorists are uncomfortable with the concept of the unconscious as formulated by Freud. The notion of things buried in the unconscious or of unconscious forces striving for expression is too metaphorical for most systematic thinkers. Yet, if we accept the view that we are not always aware of factors affecting our behavior, how are we to conceptualize such phenomena? Is it merely that we do not attend to them and that focusing our attention brings them into awareness? Is it the case, as some cognitive theorists suggest, that what others view as unconscious processes actually consist of rehearsed behaviors that flow automatically, that they consist of overlearned responses? In other words, is there no need to consider special processes and label them as unconscious?

As we have seen, both Rogers and Kelly avoided the concept of the unconscious. Instead, they emphasized concepts that involve aspects of functioning that are not available to awareness. Rogers stated that experiences incongruent with the self-concept may be distorted and/or denied. Threatening feelings may be unavailable to awareness but experienced through the process of subception. Kelly suggested that one or both poles of a construct may be submerged and unavailable to awareness. Each of these theories describes a defensive process resulting in important aspects of personality functioning being unavailable to awareness. Though some learning theorists, such as Dollard and Miller, accepted such processes and attempted to interpret them within the framework of Hullian theory, others rejected such concepts as vague and unnecessary. Although initially expressing little interest in unconscious processes, cognitive theorists have recently been concerned with them—albeit not necessarily in the terms suggested by psychoanalytic theorists.

The problem of evaluating the importance of such phenomena and conceptualizing them remains. If much of our behavior is governed by reinforcements, both from within ourselves and from others, are we always aware of what these reinforcers are? If not, why not? Is it because some of them were learned in infancy, prior to the development of verbal labels? Is it because some are so much a part of our daily lives that we no longer attend to them? Or is it because often we choose not to be aware of things that make us anxious and uncomfortable? How much attention is paid to these phenomena and how they are interpreted continue to be important issues on which theories of personality differ.

RELATIONS AMONG COGNITION, AFFECT, AND OVERT BEHAVIOR

As we have seen, personality theories differ in the attention given to cognitive, affective, and behavioral processes. Understanding the intricate relations among them remains a significant task. Although Freud emphasized cognitive and drive processes, he assigned a central role to affects in his conceptualization of human behavior. This is seen most clearly in relation to the affect of anxiety, but he and his followers also were concerned with other affects such as anger, depression, guilt, shame, and jealousy. There is interest in overt behavior, but only as an expression of the workings of drive processes. Rogers and Kelly both emphasized the person as an active construer of events, but for Rogers the "felt experience" was central, whereas for Kelly emotions followed from cognitive interpretations. The latter emphasis also is found in current attribution and other cognitive theories. In these theories cognitive properties are central and primary to feelings and overt behavior. Radical behaviorism, of course, focused exclusively on overt behavior. However, behavior therapists increasingly have become concerned with cognitive processes and, even more recently, with the influences of affective processes.

Historically, many issues in psychology initially are framed in either–or terms. Is it heredity or environment? Person or situation? Then there is debate about which is more important. Finally, there is recognition that the issues are more complex than "either–or" and "more important than" solutions. There is recognition that multiple factors enter into complex functioning, each of them contributing to a greater or lesser extent at different times and in different situations. The critical question then becomes one of understanding relationships among variables, rather than choosing among them. Thus, the question becomes how heredity and environment interact, and how person and situation variables mutually affect one another. Similarly, we are coming to understand that people are always thinking, feeling, and behaving, and that what remains to be understood is how these processes interact in the ongoing stream of human functioning.

INFLUENCES OF THE PAST, PRESENT, AND FUTURE ON BEHAVIOR

When we think of Freud, we almost automatically think of behavior being governed by the past. When we think of Kelly, we think of a person as striving to anticipate the future. Prediction becomes the key to understanding behavior. Skinner's emphasis on past reinforcement contingencies can be contrasted with social cognitive theory's emphasis on expectancies. Is behavior regulated by the past or by our expectations of the future?

This is yet another issue that divides personality theorists. Often the differences among theorists are subtle but important in their implications. For example, Bandura's suggestion that past reinforcements are important for what has been *learned* but that expectancies about future reinforcement are important for what is *performed* is a subtle but important distinction. It involves not only the important distinction between the acquisition and the performance of behavior but also an important emphasis on cognitive functioning. In fact, there appears to be a close relationship between an emphasis on the future and an emphasis on cognitive processes. This is not surprising, since the development of higher mental processes and the capacity for language are necessary for an organism to be able to construct a future world.

In reality, of course, past events and our anticipation of future events affect one another, as well as our experiences in the present. How we anticipate the future is inevitably linked to our past. However, it is probably also the case that how we view the future influences our construction of the past. For example, if we are depressed about the future we may feel bound by our past, whereas if we are optimistic about the future we may perceive the past as having been liberating. Our views of the past, present, and future are all parts of our experience. An understanding of the relationships among these views, then, becomes the task of each theory of personality.

In Chapter 1 it was stated that a theory of personality should answer the questions of *what, how,* and *why*. In later chapters, the concepts and principles used by various theorists to account for human personality were considered. Some of the major concepts relevant to each theory are given in Table 15.1. At this point, let us review some of these concepts, consider the similarities among the theories, and raise some remaining questions.

PERSONALITY THEORY AS AN ANSWER TO THE QUESTIONS OF WHAT, HOW, AND WHY

PERSONALITY STRUCTURE

Each theory that has been studied here suggests concepts relevant to the structure of personality. The theories differ not only in the content of these units but also in their level of abstraction and in the complexity of the structural organization. Freud's structural units are at a very high level of abstraction. One cannot observe an id, ego, or superego, or a conscious, preconscious, or unconscious. Somewhat less abstract are the

Table 15.1 Summary of Major Theoretical Concepts

Theorist, Theory, or Approach	Structure	Process	Growth and Development	Pathology	Change	Illustrative Case
Freud	Id, ego, superego; unconscious, preconscious, conscious	Sexual and aggressive instincts; anxiety and the mechanisms of defense	Erogenous zones; oral, anal, phallic stages of development; Oedipus complex	Infantile sexuality; fixation and regression; conflict; symptoms	Transference; conflict resolution; "Where id was, ego shall be"	Little Hans
Rogers	Self; ideal self	Self-actualization; congruence of self and experience; incongruence and defensive distortion and denial	Congruence and self-actualization vs. incongruence and defensiveness	Defensive maintenance of self; incongruence	Therapeutic atmosphere: congruence, unconditional positive regard, empathic understanding	Mrs. Oak
Trait Approaches	Traits	Dynamic traits; motives associated with traits	Contributions of heredity and environment to traits	Extreme scores on trait dimensions (e.g., neuroticism)	(No formal model)	69-year-old man
Learning Approaches	Response	Classical conditioning; instrumental conditioning; operant conditioning	Imitation; schedules of reinforcement and successive approximations	Maladaptive learned response patterns	Extinction; discrimination learning; counterconditioning; positive reinforcement; imitation; systematic desensitization; behavior modification	Peter; Reinterpretation of Little Hans

510

Kelly	Constructs	Processes channelized by anticipation of events	Increased complexity and definition to construct system	Disordered functioning of construct system	Psychological reconstruction of life; invitational mood; fixed-role therapy	Reinterpretation of bombardier case	Ronald Barrett
Social Cognitive Theory	Expectancies; standards; goals; self-efficacy beliefs	Observational learning; vicarious conditioning; self-evaluative and self-regulatory processes	Social learning through observation and direct experience; development of self-efficacy judgments and standards for self-regulation	Learned response patterns; excessive self-standards; problems in self-efficacy	Modeling; guided participation; increased self-efficacy		
Cognitive Information-Processing Theory	Cognitive categories and schemas; attributions; generalized expectancies	Information-processing strategies; attributions; possible selves and self-guides	Development of cognitive competencies, self-schemas, expectancies, attributions	Unrealistic or maladaptive beliefs; errors in information-processing	Cognitive therapy—changes in irrational beliefs, dysfunctional thoughts, and maladaptive attributions		Jim

structural units used by Rogers and Kelly. Many problems remain in current definitions of the self, but the definitions offered by Rogers do suggest some methods of systematic investigation. Similarly, although the defining properties of constructs need to be clarified further, a technique for assessing the construct system of an individual is available.

The structural units of Cattell vary in their level of abstraction, with source traits being more abstract than surface traits. At the lowest level of abstraction is the major structural unit used by learning theorists to describe behavior—the response. Whether it refers to a simple reflex or a complex behavior, the response is always external and observable. It is defined by the behavior. In this case, one does not go from the specific act to an abstract structural unit. The act itself is the structural unit. Instead of being internal to the organism and only indirectly observable, the response is part of the observable behavior of the organism.

Social cognitive theory started with a similar emphasis on the overt, behavioral response. The units of the person were concrete, clearly defined, and objectively measured. Variations in response were tied to equally clearly defined and objectively measured variations in the environment. With the development of an emphasis on cognitive activities and self-regulatory behavior, however, there was a shift toward emphasis on more abstract structural units. Concepts such as standards, self-efficacy judgments, and goals tend to be more abstract than the concept of a response. Furthermore, they require different tools of measurement, and this has resulted in a defense of the use of verbal reports by social cognitive theorists. At the same time, it should be clear that this increasing emphasis on different kinds of units has not lessened the concern for rigor, objectivity, and measurement. Social cognitive theorists continue to emphasize concepts that are clear in their meaning and specific in the appropriate method of measurement. This is equally true for psychologists emphasizing cognitive, information-processing approaches. These psychologists, often associated with social cognitive theorists, emphasize concepts such as attributions and schemas that are measured in systematic ways.

In addition to differences in their level of abstraction, theories differ in the complexity of structural organization. This complexity may be considered in terms of the number of units involved and whether they are formed in some kind of *hierarchical arrangement* in relation to one another. For example, consider the fairly simple structure described by most learning theorists. There are few categories of responses; no suggestion that behavior generally involves the expression of many units at the same time; and a bias against the concept of personality types, which implies a stable organization of many different responses. Contrast this with the psychoanalytic framework, which includes many structural units and almost unlimited possibilities for interrelationships among the units. Or consider Kelly's system, which allows for a complex system involving many constructs, some superordinate and others subordinate.

These differences in complexity of structural organization can be related to differences in the general importance attached to structure in behavior. The concept of structure generally is used to account for the more stable aspects of personality and for the consistency of individual behavior over time and over situations. To consider two extremes: psychoanalytic theory places great emphasis on the stability of behavior over time, whereas learning theory does not; psychoanalytic theory places great emphasis on the consistency of behavior across situations, whereas learning theory does not. At one extreme, psychoanalytic theory involves abstract units and a complex structural organization. At the other extreme, learning theory involves concrete units and little emphasis on their organization. In other words, there appears to be a relationship between the importance attributed to structure by a theory and the theory's emphasis on stability and consistency in human behavior.

PROCESS

In our review of theories of personality, the major conceptions in psychology concerning the why of behavior have been identified. As indicated in Chapter 1, many theories of motivation emphasize the efforts of the individual to *reduce tension*. The push toward tension reduction is clearly indicated in psychoanalytic theory and in Hull's approach to learning theory. For Freud, the individual's efforts are directed toward expressing the sexual and aggressive instincts and, thereby, toward the reduction of the tension associated with these instincts. For Hull, and for Dollard and Miller, reinforcement is associated with the satisfaction of primary or secondary drives and, thereby, with the reduction of drive-induced tension.

Rogers's theory expresses the motivational model suggesting that individuals often *seek tension*. Rogers suggests that individuals seek self-actualization, that they want to grow and to realize their inner potentials even at the cost of increased tension. However, Rogers also places emphasis on a third motivational force—*consistency*. The particular kind of consistency emphasized by Rogers is a congruence between self and experience. For Kelly, who also emphasizes consistency, the relevant variables are different. According to Kelly, it is important that the individual's constructs be consistent with one another, so that the predictions from one do not cancel out the predictions from another. It is also important that predictions be consistent with experiences—in other words, that events confirm and validate the construct system.

Although operant learning theory and social cognitive theory both emphasize the importance of reinforcement, they do not do so in terms of drive reduction, as happens in Hullian S–R theory. For Skinner, reinforcements affect the probability of a response, but there is no use for an internal concept of drive or tension. In social cognitive theory the emphasis is on cognitive processes and the development of expectancies.

Reinforcers are critical for performance but not for the acquisition of behavior. Expectancies concerning reinforcement and evaluative standards guide and direct behavior. In this way they provide motivation. Finally, information-processing theorists suggest that many aspects of human performance attributed to motivational factors may, in fact, be better understood as the consequence of using particular cognitive strategies or heuristics.

Notice that these motivational models conflict with one another only if we assume that all behavior must follow the same motivational principles. In relation to structure, we need not assume that an individual only has drives, that one only has a concept of the self, or that one only has personal constructs. In the same way, we need not assume that an individual is always reducing tension, or always striving toward actualization, or always seeking consistency. It may be that all three models of motivation are relevant to human behavior. An individual may at some points be functioning to reduce tension, at other times to actualize his or her self, and at other times to achieve cognitive consistency. Another possibility is that, at one time, two kinds of motivation are operating, but they are in conflict with one another. For example, an individual may seek to relieve aggressive urges by hitting someone, but he or she may also like the person involved and view this behavior as out of character. A third possibility is that two kinds of motivation may combine to support one another. Thus, to make love to someone can represent the reduction of tension from sexual urges, an actualizing expression of the self, and an act consistent with the self-concept and with predictions from one's construct system. If room is left for more than one process model, it becomes the task of psychologists to define the conditions under which each type of motivation will occur and the ways in which the different types of motivation can combine to determine behavior.

GROWTH AND DEVELOPMENT

In Chapter 1 we considered the causes of personality—cultural, social class, familial, peers, and genetic. None of the theories studied gives adequate attention to the variety of factors that determine growth and development. Trait theorists have done important work on the influences of heredity and environment, and on age trends in personality development. Psychoanalytic theory gives attention to the role of biological and environmental factors in personality development, but in most cases this remains speculative. It is disappointing that Rogers and Kelly have so little to say in this area. Finally, although the learning theorists have done a great deal to interpret the processes through which cultural, social class, and familial influences are transmitted, they have seriously neglected biological factors. Also, until recently learning theorists tended to ignore the important area of cognitive growth and development. Important contributions are, however, now being made by cognitive theorists. For example, Bandura has been doing research on observational learning, and Mischel has been studying how children develop methods for tolerating increased delays in reinforcement. As personality psychologists increasingly emphasize cognitive variables, they become able to incorporate into their work the considerable body of research and theory devoted to cognitive development.

In considering the theorists covered in this text, differences concerning two questions about development become apparent. The first concerns the utility of the concept of stages of development, and the second concerns the importance of early experiences for later personality development. Psychoanalytic theory attaches great importance to the early years and to the concept of stages of development. In relation to the early years, they emphasize particularly experiences within the family. Such a view can be contrasted with the trait emphasis on heredity and the importance of the nonshared environment, including experiences outside the home. The psychoanalytic emphasis can be contrasted as well with the social cognitive criticism of the concept of stages of development and of suggestions that personality is relatively fixed by developments during the early years. Social cognitive theorists emphasize, instead, the potential for different parts of personality to develop in different ways and much greater potential for change as a result of later experience.

PSYCHOPATHOLOGY

The forces producing psychopathology are interpreted differently by the theorists. However, the concept of conflict is essential to a number of them. This is most clearly the case in psychoanalytic theory. According to Freud, psychopathology occurs when the instinctive urges of the id come into conflict with the functioning of the ego. Although Rogers does not emphasize the importance of conflict, one can interpret the problem of incongruence in terms of a conflict between experience and the self-concept. Learning theory offers a number of explanations for psychopathology, and at least one of these explanations emphasizes the importance of approach–avoidance conflicts. And, although cognitive theorists do not emphasize the importance of conflict, one can think of the implications of goal conflicts and conflicting beliefs or expectancies. In addition, as cognitive theorists consider motivational questions, they come to recognize the potential for conflict between the motives for self-verification and self-enhancement.

Many complex questions concerning psychopathology remain unanswered. For example, we know that cultures vary in the incidence of various forms of psychopathology. Depression is rare in Africa but is common in the United States. Why? Conversion symptoms, such as hysterical paralysis of the arm or leg, were quite common in Freud's time but are observed much less frequently today. Why? Are there important differences in the problems that people in different cultures face? Or do they face the same problems but cope with them differently? Or is it just that some problems are more likely to be reported than others and that this pattern varies with the culture? If people today are more concerned with problems of identity than with problems of guilt, if they are more concerned with the problem of finding meaning than of relieving sexual urges, what are the implications for psychoanalysis and the other theories of personality?

Psychopathology is a major concern for clinical theories of personality. In Kelly's terms, this is a major focus of convenience for these theories. However, we have seen that interpretations of the nature of psychopathology vary considerably among them. And, although other theories of personality are derived from observations outside the therapeutic setting, they have nonetheless recognized the importance of explaining psychopathology. The issue here is not whether personality theory should offer some understanding of psychopathology, but rather how central this topic is for the theory and the variables that are emphasized. It is fascinating to observe how each theory of personality, with its own set of structural units and process concepts, can come up with such varying interpretations of the same phenomena.

CHANGE

The following questions concerning change are given varying amounts of attention by each theorist: What is changed? What are the conditions for change? What is the process in change? Psychoanalytic theory, in its emphasis on changes in the relationship between the unconscious and the conscious and between the ego and the id, is particularly concerned with structural change. Kelly, in his analysis of psychotherapy as the psychological reconstruction of life, also deals with structural change. In contrast, Rogers is most concerned with the conditions that make change possible. Although his research has attended to structural change (e.g., changes in self–ideal self discrepancy), this has been for the purpose of having a criterion against which he could measure the effectiveness of different variables (e.g., congruence, unconditional positive regard, empathic understanding). Kelly pointed out the importance of an atmosphere of experimentation and invitational mood, but there is little research to suggest the variables critical in establishing this atmosphere or mood.

The process of change is a particular focus of convenience for learning theory. The following learning processes are used to account for a wide range of changes related to a variety of forms of psychotherapy: extinction, discrimination learning, counterconditioning, positive reinforcement, and imitation. Whereas initially learning concepts were used to explain treatment effects associated with other theories, more recently these concepts have been used to develop learning-based treatment methods. A clear illustration of therapeutic technique as an outgrowth of theory is Bandura's work on modeling and guided participation. It is also interesting to note here that although therapy or psychological change has not been a major aspect of social cognitive theory, it is becoming an increasingly important part of it. In fact, Bandura suggests that developments in this area may well serve as a test of the theory generally.

There are, of course, basic and important differences in the theories concerning the potential for change. At one extreme is psychoanalytic theory, which suggests that fundamental personality change is quite difficult. This view is related to the psychoanalytic emphasis on structure and the importance of early experiences. If structure is important and is developed early in life, it follows that basic change later in life is difficult. Many of the early learning theorists (e.g., Hull, Dollard, and Miller), particularly those who attempted to relate learning theory to psychoanalytic theory, were similarly pessimistic about the potential for change. However, more recent developments in operant conditioning, social cognitive theory, and cognitive therapy have led to much greater optimism about change. These theorists place little emphasis on structure and great emphasis on the potential to change behavior. With faith in their ability to shape behavior by manipulating external rewards or by changing cognitive beliefs and attributions, these psychologists are at the other extreme from psychoanalysts.

In considering the question of how people change, we again recognize the extent to which theories of personality emphasize different processes of change, different conditions for change, and change in different aspects of personality functioning. Some of these differences may well represent competing and conflicting points of view, and others merely various terms for similar processes. Finally, some differences may result from attending to different aspects of the person. Sorting these out is a task for both students and professionals in the field.

At various times in this book, theory, assessment, and research have been considered separately. However, an attempt has been made to keep in mind the intimate relationships among them. Indeed, this has been a major theme throughout the book.

In Chapter 1, theory as an attempt to fit together and explain a wide variety of facts with a few assumptions was considered. In Chapter 2 the tools that personality psychologists use to observe and measure behavior in a systematic way were discussed. It is clear that research involves the use of assessment techniques to develop and test theory. What of the relationships among theory, assessment, and research? Here we can note a relationship between the assumptions basic to theories and the techniques of assessment generally associated with these theories. For example, a psychodynamic theory such as psychoanalysis is associated with

RELATIONSHIPS AMONG THEORY, ASSESSMENT, AND RESEARCH

the Rorschach test, phenomenological theory such as that of Rogers with the interview and measures of the self-concept, factor-analytic theory with psychometric tests, a learning theory approach with objective tests, and cognitive theories with ways in which people process information and organize their worlds.

Are the observations obtained similar when assessment techniques associated with the different theories are applied to the same individual? Recall here the story of the wise blind men and the elephant. Each wise man examined a part of the elephant and assumed that he knew what it was. None knew that it was an elephant, and each came to a different conclusion on the basis of his observations. One felt the tail and thought it was a snake, another a leg and thought it was a tree, another a trunk and thought it was a hose, and another a body and thought it was a wall. Do the theories refer to different parts of the same individual, each representing an interesting though incomplete picture of the whole and describing the same qualities but in different terms? Or do the theories picture very different individuals?

THE CASE OF JIM

The case of Jim has given us the opportunity to follow an individual over the course of 20 years and to compare the observations gained from different theoretical perspectives. Let us compare the observations from the different tests, as well as those obtained at different times. Finally, we can consider Jim's impressions of the personality tests.

Comparison of the Assessment Data on Different Theories

A number of themes emerge consistently across the various tests administered to Jim when he was a college student. First, all of the tests show evidence of tension, insecurity, and anxiety. Second, they present evidence of difficulties in relating to women. Third, they show evidence of difficulties in interpersonal relationships, particularly in experiencing and expressing warmth. Finally, the tests present consistent evidence of rigidity, inhibition, compulsivity, and difficulty in being creative.

At the same time, the pictures that emerge from the different approaches are qualitatively different from one another—different and distinct, although not necessarily in conflict. For example, the vampires and "Count Dracula sucking blood" images on the Rorschach are qualitatively different from Jim's self-reports of problems in interpersonal relationships, and the evidence of sadism on the projectives is qualitatively different from the self-reports of difficulties in this area.

Finally, it is important to note that each assessment device seems able to pick up aspects of Jim's personality not necessarily detected by the other tests, or to highlight an aspect of his personality left vague on the other tests. For example, the projectives highlighted some of his conflicts and defenses; the 16 P.F. his somatic complaints and mood swings; and the interview and autobiography his perception of himself as deep, sensitive, kind, and basically good.

Stability and Change Over Time

We have been able to follow Jim over the course of 20 years, from a struggling college student undecided about his career to an established professional, husband, and father. During this period we have also been able to administer new personality tests as they have evolved in association with new theoretical developments in the field. The picture that emerges gives considerable evidence of stability in Jim's personality. Twenty years later, evidence remains of tension-neuroticism; difficulties in being as warm and tender as he would like to be, particularly in relation to his wife; and evidence of compulsive characteristics leading him to be less creative than he would like to be.

At the same time, important developments have occurred, developments that are spelled out in the interview and in responses to other tests. Twenty years later, Jim is a happier person, with a greater sense of self-efficacy in intellectual and social areas and a greatly reduced concern about his sexual adequacy. He is more able to get out of himself, though this still remains somewhat of a struggle. As he approaches midlife, Jim feels that he is moving in the right direction and is committed to the goals of being a good husband and father, as well as further development of his professional skills.

The picture that emerges is one of both stability and change, of continuity with the past although not a complete duplication of it. In all likelihood, it would have been difficult to predict the developments that have occurred; on the other hand, one can look back and see why his life has unfolded as it has.

Jim's Reflections on the Data

How did Jim view the various tests and personality sketches? Jim felt that the projective data did a good job of pointing up his conflicts and defenses, but that they overemphasized the insecurities present at the time. He believed that the phenomenological data (semantic differential, Rep test) gave an accurate picture of him at the time, although he has now become more aware of similarities to his mother. In addition, he felt that he now has a less constricted view of people and of the world, and can express more warmth. As with the other approaches, Jim felt that the trait approach captured a part of him that was present at the time, and in relation to which there have been changes. He is less insecure now, though he still has concerns about being liked and still has mood swings.

What of the cognitive approach considered at this time? As a psychologist Jim was somewhat aware of this general orientation, but he was not very familiar with it. Thus, in a sense, this was a professional learning experience for him. At the same time, it should be noted that he came to the material with a mixed psychodynamic and humanist slant. Thus, he said of the cognitive, information-processing approach: "It picked up some interesting things but we're not cut from the same cloth. There's something valuable in it but I don't see it as a whole approach. It captures a part of the truth, a part of me, but somehow it seems like a denuded frame of reference. It misses some of the power and drama of life."

What was his overall view of the alternative approaches? In general Jim felt that the various approaches captured different aspects of him, highlighting different aspects of his personality while picking up some consistent themes. In addition, he commented that he felt that different approaches to therapy could be useful with different people or as different ways of gaining access to people.

Overview

The emphasis here has not been on whether one or another approach to theory, assessment, and research is right or wrong. Rather we have focused on relations among the three approaches and on the strengths and limitations of each. It would appear that different aspects of personality are studied with greater or lesser ease in different settings and with greater or lesser accuracy with different assessment devices. Each research approach and assessment device appears to have its own special contribution to make, as well as its own potential for sources of error or bias. Thus, if we limit ourselves to one approach to research or assessment, we may restrict our observations to phenomena directly relevant to a specific theoretical position. Alternatively, we can appreciate the contributions that different theories, research procedures, and assessment devices can make to our understanding of human behavior. Like Jim, we can consider the possibility that each approach captures a glimpse of the person, highlighting different aspects of personality while picking up common themes.

In a certain sense, every person is a psychologist. Every person develops **A FINAL** a view of human nature and a strategy for predicting events. The theory **SUMMING UP** and research presented in this book represent the efforts of psychologists to systematize what is known about human personality and to suggest areas for future exploration. We have tried to highlight similarities in what different psychologists have been trying to do as well as differences in what they view as the best mode of conducting research. Although psychologists as a group are more explicit about their view of the person than is the average layperson, and although they are more systematic in their efforts to understand and predict human behavior, there are individual differences among them. In this book we have considered the theories of a number of psychologists in detail. They represent the major theories in the field although they are not the only ones, and they are representative of the diversity of approaches that can be considered reasonable and useful.

An effort has been made in this text to demonstrate that theory, assessment, and research are related to one another. In most cases some consistency can be found in the nature of theory proposed, the types of tests used to obtain data, and the problems selected for investigation. At the same time, it can be suggested that the theories of personality covered need not be considered mutually exclusive. In a very real sense, each represents a glimpse of the total picture. Human behavior is like a very complex jigsaw puzzle. The theories of personality considered have offered us many possible pieces for solution of the puzzle. Although some pieces may have to be discarded as not fitting the puzzle at all, and many remain outstanding, undoubtedly many of the pieces offered will be there when the final picture is put together.

1. The history of scientific progress suggests three distinct stages of sci- **REVIEW** entific development: (a) an early developmental stage; (b) a stage of normal science in which a paradigm or model is commonly accepted; and (c) a stage of scientific revolution.

2. Personality theories have repeatedly confronted basic problems, the solutions to these problems going far to define the basic nature of the theory. These issues are the philosophical view of the person; the relation between internal and external causes of behavior; consistency across situations and over time; the unity of behavior and the concept of the self; the concept of the unconscious; relations among cognition, affect, and overt behavior; and the relative importance of the past, present, and future.

3. All theories of personality seek to organize what is known and to advance our knowledge of what is not yet known. In doing so, the theories utilize concepts in relation to the following areas: structure,

process, growth and development, psychopathology, and personality change. The theories covered can be compared in terms of the concepts emphasized in each of these areas (Table 15.1).

4. It is again emphasized that theory, assessment, and research are generally closely linked with one another, with different observations leading to different theories that in turn suggest different approaches to assessment and research.

5. It is suggested that each of the theories covered in the text presents a glimpse of the complex totality that is personality.

ABA (own-control) research. A Skinnerian variant of the experimental method consisting of exposing one subject to three experimental phases: (A) a baseline period, (B) introduction of reinforcers to change the frequency of specific behaviors, and (A) withdrawal of reinforcement and observation of whether the behaviors return to their earlier frequency (baseline period).

ABC assessment. In behavioral assessment, an emphasis on the identification of antecedent (A) events and the consequences (C) of behavior (B); a functional analysis of behavior involving identification of the environmental conditions that regulate specific behaviors.

Ability, temperament, and dynamic traits. In Cattell's trait theory, the categories of traits that capture the major aspects of personality.

Acquiescence. A response style or bias in which there is a tendency to agree with test items regardless of their content.

Acquisition. The learning of new behaviors, viewed by Bandura as independent of reward and contrasted with performance—which is seen as dependent on reward.

Aggression. In Kelly's personal construct theory, the active expansion of the person's construct system.

Aggressive instincts. Freud's concept for those drives directed toward harm, injury, or destruction.

Anal personality. Freud's concept for a personality type that expresses a fixation at the anal stage of development and relates to the world in terms of the wish for control or power.

Anal stage. Freud's concept for that period of life during which the major center of bodily excitation or tension is the anus.

Anxiety. An emotion expressing a sense of impending threat or danger. In Kelly's personal construct theory, anxiety occurs when the person recognizes that his or her construct system does not apply to the events being perceived.

Approach–avoidance conflict. In S–R theory, the simultaneous presence of opposing drives to move toward an object and away from it.

Attachment Behavioral System (ABS). Bowlby's concept emphasizing the early formation of a bond between infant and caregiver, generally the mother.

Attributional Style Questionnaire (ASQ). A questionnaire designed to measure attributions concerning learned helplessness along three dimensions: internal (personal)–external (universal), specific–global, and stable–unstable.

Bandwidth. The area to which a theory or technique of assessment is applicable.

Behavior deficit. In the Skinnerian view of psychopathology, the failure to learn an adaptive response.

Behavior modification. The approach to therapeutic treatment (behavior change) based on Skinner's operant conditioning theory.

Behavior therapy. An approach to therapeutic treatment (behavior change) based on learning theory and focusing on specific behavioral difficulties.

Behavioral assessment. The emphasis in assessment on specific behaviors that are tied to defined situational characteristics (e.g., ABC approach).

Behavioral competencies. Ability to behave in particular ways, particularly emphasized in social cognitive theory in relation to performance, as in delay of gratification.

Behavioral signatures. Mischel's concept for individually distinctive profiles of situation-behavior relationships.

Behaviorism. An approach within psychology, developed by Watson, that restricts investigation to overt, observable behavior.

The big five. In trait factor theory, the five major trait categories (see Five-factor model).

Bivariate method. Cattell's description of the method of personality study that follows the classical experimental design of manipulating an independent variable and observing the effects on a dependent variable.

Cardinal trait.   Allport's concept for a disposition that is so pervasive and outstanding in a person's life that virtually every act is traceable to its influence.

Castration anxiety.   Freud's concept of the boy's fear, experienced during the phallic stage, that the father will cut off the son's penis because of their sexual rivalry for the mother.

Catharsis.   The release and freeing of emotion through talking about one's problems.

Causal attribution.   In the revised theory of learned helplessness and depression, attributions made on three dimensions: internal (personal)–external (universal), specific–global, and stable–unstable.

Central trait.   Allport's concept for a disposition to behave in a particular way in a range of situations.

Classical conditioning.   A process, emphasized by Pavlov, in which a previously neutral stimulus becomes capable of eliciting a response because of its association with a stimulus that automatically produces the same or a similar response.

Client-centered therapy.   Rogers's term for his earlier approach to therapy in which the counselor's attitude is one of interest in the ways in which the client experiences the self and the world.

Clinical method.   Cattell's description of the method of personality study in which there is an interest in complex patterns of behavior as they occur in life, but variables are not assessed in a systematic way.

Clinical research.   An approach to research involving the intensive study of individuals in terms of observation of naturally occurring behavior or verbal reports of what occurred in the natural setting.

Cognition.   The person's thought processes, including perception, memory, and language. The term is used to refer to the ways in which the organism processes information concerning the environment and the self.

Cognitive competencies.   Ability to think in a variety of ways, particularly emphasized in social

cognitive theory in relation to the ability to delay gratification.

Cognitive complexity–simplicity.   An aspect of a person's cognitive functioning that is defined at one end by the use of many constructs with many relationships to one another (complexity) and at the other end by the use of few constructs with limited relationships to one another (simplicity).

Cognitive therapy.   An approach to therapy in which changes in unrealistic and maladaptive thinking are emphasized.

Cognitive triad.   Beck's description of the cognitive factors that lead to depression, involving a view of the self as a loser, a view of the world as frustrating, and a view of the future as bleak.

Competencies.   A structural unit in social cognitive theory reflecting an individual's ability to solve problems or perform tasks necessary to achieve specific goals.

Conditioned emotional reaction.   Watson and Rayner's term for the development of an emotional reaction to a previously neutral stimulus, as in Little Albert's fear of rats.

Congruence.   Rogers's concept expressing an absence of conflict between the perceived self and experience. Also one of three conditions suggested as essential for growth and therapeutic progress. (*See* **empathic understanding** and **unconditional positive regard**)

Conscious.   Those thoughts, experiences, and feelings of which we are aware.

Constriction.   In Kelly's personal construct theory, the narrowing of the construct system so as to minimize incompatibilities.

Construct.   In Kelly's theory, a way of perceiving, construing, or interpreting events.

Construct system.   In Kelly's theory, the hierarchical arrangement of constructs.

Constructive alternativism.   Kelly's view that there is no objective reality or absolute truth but only alternative ways of construing events.

Contrast pole.   In Kelly's personal construct theory, the contrast pole of a construct is defined by the way in which a third element is perceived as different from two other elements that are used to form a similarity pole.

Controllability.   In Weiner's scheme of causal

attributions, a dimension that relates to whether events are perceived to be subject to control or influence through additional effort.

Core construct. In Kelly's personal construct theory, a construct that is basic to the person's construct system and cannot be altered without serious consequences for the rest of the system.

Correlational research. An approach to research, described by Cronbach, in which existing individual indifferences are measured and related to one another, in contrast with the experimental approach to research.

Death instinct. Freud's concept for drives or sources of energy directed toward death or a return to an inorganic state.

Defense mechanisms. Freud's concept for those devices used by the person to reduce anxiety. They result in the exclusion from awareness of some thought, wish, or feeling.

Delay of gratification. The postponement of pleasure until the optimum or proper time, a concept particularly emphasized in social cognitive theory in relation to self-regulation.

Demand characteristics. Cues that are implicit (hidden) in the experimental setting and influence the subject's behavior.

Denial. The defense mechanism in which a painful internal or external reality is denied.

Dilation. In Kelly's personal construct theory, the broadening of a construct system so that it will be more comprehensive.

Direct external consequences. In social cognitive theory, the external events that follow behavior and influence future performance, contrasted with vicarious consequences and self-produced consequences.

Discrimination. In conditioning, the differential response to stimuli depending on whether they have been associated with pleasure, pain, or neutral events.

Distortion. According to Rogers, a defensive process in which experience is changed so as to be brought into awareness in a form that is consistent with the self.

Drive, primary. In Hull's theory, an innate internal stimulus that activates behavior (e.g., hunger drive).

Drive, secondary. In Hull's theory, a learned internal stimulus, acquired through association with the satisfaction of primary drives, that activates behavior (e.g., anxiety).

Dysfunctional expectancies. In social cognitive theory, maladaptive expectations concerning the consequences of specific behaviors.

Dysfunctional self-evaluations. In social cognitive theory, maladaptive standards for self-reward that have important implications for psychopathology.

Ego. Freud's structural concept for the part of personality that attempts to satisfy drives (instincts) in accordance with reality and the person's moral values.

Empathic understanding. Rogers's term for the ability to perceive experiences and feelings and their meanings from the standpoint of another person. One of three therapist conditions essential for therapeutic progress. (*See also* **congruence** and **unconditional positive regard**)

Energy system. Freud's view of personality as involving the interplay among various forces (e.g., drives, instincts) or sources of energy.

Entity theory. Dweck's concept for the beliefs of some individuals that a particular characteristic is fixed or not malleable.

Erg. Cattell's concept for innate biological drives that provide the basic motivating power for behavior.

Erogenous zones. According to Freud, those parts of the body that are the sources of tension or excitation.

Existentialism. An approach to understanding people and conducting therapy, associated with the human potential movement, that emphasizes phenomenology and concerns inherent in existing as a person. Derived from a more general movement in philosophy.

Expectancies. In social cognitive theory, what the individual anticipates or predicts will occur as the result of specific behaviors in specific situations (anticipated consequences).

Experimental research. An approach to research in which the experimenter manipulates the variable and is interested in general laws, in contrast with the correlational approach to research.

Experimenter expectancy effects. Unintended experimenter effects involving behaviors that lead subjects to respond in accordance with the experimenter's hypothesis.

Extinction. In conditioning, the progressive weakening of the association between a stimulus and a response; in classical conditioning because the conditioned stimulus is no longer followed by the unconditioned stimulus; and in operant conditioning because the response is no longer followed by reinforcement.

Extraversion. In Eysenck's theory, one end of the introversion–extraversion dimension of personality characterized by a disposition to be sociable, friendly, impulsive, and risk taking.

Facet. In the five-factor model and on the NEO-PI, facets represent sub-components or sub-scales of the five factors.

Factor analysis. A statistical method for determining those variables or test responses that increase and decrease together. Used in the development of personality tests and of some trait theories (e.g., Cattell, Eysenck).

Fear (Kelly). In Kelly's personal construct theory, fear occurs when a new construct is about to enter the person's construct system.

Fidelity. The area to which a theory or technique of assessment is particularly applicable.

Five-factor model. An emerging consensus among trait theorists suggesting five basic factors to human personality: neuroticism, extraversion, openness, agreeableness, and conscientiousness.

Fixation. Freud's concept expressing a developmental arrest or stoppage at some point in the person's psychosexual development.

Fixed-role therapy. Kelly's therapeutic technique that makes use of scripts or roles for people to try out, thereby encouraging people to behave in new ways and to perceive themselves in new ways.

Focus of convenience. In Kelly's personal construct theory, those events or phenomena that are best covered by a construct or by the construct system.

Free association. In psychoanalysis, the patient's reporting to the analyst of every thought that comes to mind.

Functional analysis. In behavioral approaches, particularly Skinnerian, the identification of the environmental stimuli that control behavior.

Functional autonomy. Allport's concept that a motive may become independent of its origins; in particular, motives in adults may become independent of their earlier basis in tension reduction.

Fundamental lexical hypothesis. The hypothesis that over time the most important individual differences in human interaction have been encoded as single terms into language.

Generalization. In conditioning, the association of a response with stimuli similar to the stimulus to which the response was originally conditioned or attached.

Generalized reinforcer. In Skinner's operant conditioning theory, a reinforcer that provides access to many other reinforcers (e.g., money).

Genital stage. In psychoanalytic theory, the stage of development associated with the onset of puberty.

Goals. In social cognitive theory, desired future events that motivate the person over extended periods of time and enable the person to go beyond momentary influences.

Guided participation. A treatment approach emphasized in social cognitive theory in which a person is assisted in performing modeled behaviors.

Habit. In Hull's theory, an association between a stimulus and a response.

Hostility (Kelly). In Kelly's personal construct theory, making others behave in an expected way to validate one's own construct system.

Human potential movement. A group of psychologists, represented by Rogers and Maslow, who emphasize the actualization or fulfillment of individual potential, including an openness to experience.

Id. Freud's structural concept for the source of the instincts or all of the drive energy in people.

Ideal self. The self-concept the individual would most like to possess. A key concept in Rogers's theory.

Identification. The acquisition, as characteristics of the self, of personality characteristics perceived to be part of others (e.g., parents).

Idiographic approach. An approach emphasized by Allport in which particular attention is given to the intensive study of individuals and the organization of personality variables in each person.

Imitation. Behavior that is acquired through the observation of others. In S–R theory, the result of the process called *matched-dependent* behavior in which, for example, children match their behavior to that of their parents and are then rewarded.

Impermeable construct. In Kelly's personal construct theory, a construct that does not allow new elements into it.

Implicit personality theory. The layperson's beliefs concerning the characteristics or traits of people that go together, implicit in that they are not made explicit and are not part of a formal theory of personality.

Incongruence. Rogers's concept of the existence of a discrepancy of conflict between the perceived self and experience.

Incremental theory. Dweck's concept for the beliefs of some individuals that a particular characteristic is malleable or can be changed.

Instrumental learning. In S–R theory, the learning of responses that are instrumental in bringing about a desirable situation.

Internal–External (I–E) Scale. The personality scale developed by Rotter to measure the extent to which the person has developed a belief that he or she can control life's events (i.e., internal locus of control) as opposed to the belief that life's events are the result of external factors such as chance, luck, or fate (i.e., external locus of control).

Internal standards. A concept in social cognitive theory emphasizing how behavior may be regulated and maintained by learned standards for reinforcement (e.g., pride, shame) that are now part of the individual.

Internal working model. Bowlby's concept for the mental representations (images), associated with emotion, of the self and others that develop during the early years of development.

Introversion. In Eysenck's theory, one end of the introversion–extraversion dimension of personality characterized by a disposition to be quiet, reserved, reflective, and risk avoiding.

Isolation. The defense mechanism in which emotion is isolated from the content of a painful impulse or memory.

Latency stage. In psychoanalytic theory, the stage following the phallic stage in which there is a decrease in sexual urges and interest.

L-data. In Cattell's theory, life-record data relating to behavior in everyday life situations or to ratings of such behavior.

Learned helplessness. Seligman's concept for inappropriate passivity and diminished effort resulting from repeated experiences with uncontrollable events.

Libido. The psychoanalytic term for the energy associated first with the life instincts and later with the sexual instincts.

Life instinct. Freud's concept for drives or sources of energy (libido) directed toward the preservation of life and sexual gratification.

Locus of causality. In Weiner's scheme of causal attributions, a dimension that relates to whether the person perceives causes of events as coming from within (internal) or from outside (external).

Locus of control. Rotter's concept expressing a generalized expectancy or belief concerning the determinants of rewards and punishments. (*See* **Internal–External Scale**)

Loosening. In Kelly's personal construct theory, the use of the same construct to make varied predictions.

Maladaptive response. In the Skinnerian view of psychopathology, the learning of a response that is maladaptive or not considered acceptable by people in the environment.

Mechanisms of defense. (*See* **defense mechanisms**)

Microanalytic research. Bandura's suggested research strategy concerning the concept of self-efficacy in which specific rather than global self-efficacy judgments are recorded.

Modeling. Bandura's concept for the process of reproducing behaviors learned through the observation of others.

Multivariate method. Cattell's description of the method of personality study, favored by him, in which there is study of the interrelationships among many variables at once.

Need for positive regard.   (*See* **positive regard, need for**)

Neuroticism.   In Eysenck's theory, a dimension of personality defined by stability and low anxiety at one end and by instability and high anxiety at the other end.

Observational learning.   Bandura's concept for the process through which people learn merely by observing the behavior of others, called *models*.

Ocean.   The acronym for the five basic traits: openness, conscientiousness, extraversion, agreeableness, and neuroticism.

O-data.   Observer data (i.e., specific observations or ratings by knowledgeable observers such as parents, friends, or teachers based on observations.

Oedipus complex.   Freud's concept expressing the boy's sexual attraction to the mother and fear of castration by the father who is seen as a rival.

Operant conditioning.   Skinner's term for the process through which the characteristics of a response are determined by its consequences.

Operants.   In Skinner's theory, behaviors that appear (are emitted) without being specifically associated with any prior (eliciting) stimuli and are studied in relation to the reinforcing events that follow them.

Oral personality.   Freud's concept of a personality type that expresses a fixation at the oral stage of development and who relates to the world in terms of the wish to be fed or to swallow.

Oral stage.   Freud's concept for that period of life during which the major center of bodily excitation or tension is the mouth.

OT-data.   In Cattell's theory, objective test data or information about personality obtained from observing behavior in miniature situations.

Own-control design.   A Skinnerian variant of the experimental method in which one subject is used and serves as his or her own control while experimental conditions are varied. (*See* **ABA design**)

Paradigm.   Kuhn's concept for a model that is commonly accepted by scientists in a field and that defines the field of observations and the methods to be used in research.

Penis envy.   In psychoanalytic theory, the female's envy of the male's possession of a penis.

Perception without awareness.   Unconscious perception or perception of a stimulus without conscious awareness of such perception.

Perceptual defense.   The process by which an individual defends (unconsciously) against awareness of a threatening stimulus.

Performance.   The production of learned behaviors, viewed by Bandura as dependent on rewards, in contrast with the acquisition of new behaviors, which is seen as independent of reward.

Peripheral construct.   In Kelly's personal construct theory, a construct that is not basic to the construct system and can be altered without serious consequences for the rest of the system.

Permeable construct.   In Kelly's personal construct system, a construct that allows new elements into it.

Person–situation controversy.   A controversy between psychologists who emphasize the importance of personal (internal) variables in determining behavior and those who emphasize the importance of situational (external) influences.

Personality.   Those characteristics of the person that account for consistent patterns of behavior.

Phallic character.   Freud's concept of a personality type that expresses a fixation at the phallic stage of development and strives for success in competition with others.

Phallic stage.   Freud's concept for that period of life during which excitation or tension begins to be centered in the genitals and during which there is an attraction to the parent of the opposite sex.

Phenomenal field.   Rogers's concept for the individual's conscious and unconscious perceptions of the self and the world.

Phenomenology.   An approach within psychology that focuses on how the person perceives and experiences the self and the world.

Pleasure principle.   According to Freud, psychological functioning based on the pursuit of pleasure and the avoidance of pain.

Possible selves.   Individuals' ideas of what they might become, would like to become, and are afraid of becoming.

Positive regard, need for. Rogers's concept expressing the need for warmth, liking, respect, and acceptance from others.

Preconscious. Freud's concept for those thoughts, experiences, and feelings of which we are momentarily unaware but can readily bring into awareness.

Preverbal construct. In Kelly's personal construct theory, a construct that is used but cannot be expressed in words.

Primary process. In psychoanalytic theory a form of thinking which is not governed by logic or reality testing and which is seen in dreams and other expressions of the unconscious.

Process. In personality theory, the concept that refers to the motivational aspects of personality.

Projection. The defense mechanism in which one attributes to (projects onto) others one's own unacceptable instincts or wishes.

Projective test. A test that generally involves vague, ambiguous stimuli and allows subjects to reveal their personalities in terms of their distinctive responses (e.g., Rorschach, TAT).

Prototype. The pattern of characteristics that best illustrates or exemplifies membership in a category. The prototype represents an ideal type, with members of the category not necessarily possessing all the characteristics of the prototype.

Psychoticism. In Eysenck's theory, a dimension of personality defined by a tendency to be solitary and insensitive at one end and to accept social custom and care about others at the other end.

Q-data. In Cattell's theory, personality data obtained from questionnaires.

Q-sort. An assessment device in which the subject sorts statements into categories following a normal distribution. Used by Rogers as a measure of statements regarding the self and ideal self.

Range of convenience. In Kelly's personal construct theory, those events or phenomena that are covered by a construct or by the construct system.

Rational–emotive therapy (RET). A therapeutic approach, developed by Albert Ellis, that emphasizes change in irrational beliefs that have destructive emotional and behavioral consequences.

Rationalization. The mechanism of defense in which an acceptable reason is given for an unacceptable motive or act.

Reaction formation. The defense mechanism in which the opposite of an unacceptable impulse is expressed.

Reality principle. According to Freud, psychological functioning based on reality in which pleasure is delayed until an optimum time.

Reciprocal determinism. The mutual effects of variables on one another (e.g., Bandura's emphasis on person and environmental factors continuously affecting one another).

Regression. Freud's concept expressing a person's return to ways of relating to the world and the self that were part of an earlier stage of development.

Reinforcer. An event (stimulus) that follows a response and increases the probability of its occurrence.

Reliability. The extent to which observations are stable, dependable, and can be replicated.

Repression. The primary defense mechanism in which a thought, idea, or wish is dismissed from consciousness.

Response style. The tendency of some subjects to respond to test items in a consistent, patterned way that has to do with the form of the questions and/or answers rather than with their content.

Role. Behavior considered to be appropriate for a person's place or status in society. Emphasized by Cattell as one of a number of variables that limit the influence of personality variables on behavior relative to situational variables.

Role Construct Repertory Test (Rep test). Kelly's test to determine the constructs used by a person, the relationships among constructs, and how the constructs are applied to specific people.

Sample approach. Mischel's description of assessment approaches in which there is an interest in the behavior itself and its relation to environmental conditions, in contrast to sign approaches that infer personality from test behavior.

Schedule of reinforcement. In Skinner's operant conditioning theory, the rate and interval of reinforcement of responses (e.g., response ratio schedule and time intervals).

Schema. A cognitive structure that organizes information and thereby influences how we perceive and respond to further information.

Script. A series or pattern of behaviors considered to be appropriate for a situation.

S-data. Self-report data or information provided by the subject.

Second signal system. Pavlov's concept emphasizing the importance of speech and thought in human classical conditioning.

Secondary disposition. Allport's concept for a disposition to behave in a particular way that is relevant to few situations.

Secondary process. In psychoanalytic theory, a form of thinking that is governed by reality and associated with the development of the ego.

Self. A concept many psychologists use to express pattern, organization, and consistency in personality functioning; in social cognitive theory, cognitive processes (schemata) associated by the person with the I or Me.

Self-actualization. The fundamental tendency of the organism to actualize, maintain, and enhance itself. A concept emphasized by Rogers and other members of the human potential movement.

Self-concept. The perceptions and meaning associated with the self, Me, or I.

Self-conceptions. In social cognitive theory, cognitive evaluations of the self. Dysfunctional self-evaluations, for example, are viewed as being important in psychopathology.

Self-consistency. Rogers's concept expressing an absence of conflict among perceptions of the self.

Self-efficacy. In social cognitive theory, the perceived ability to cope with specific situations.

Self-efficacy judgments. In social cognitive theory, the person's expectations concerning his or her ability to perform specific behaviors in a situation.

Self-esteem. The person's evaluative regard for the self or personal judgment of worthiness.

Self-experience discrepancy. Rogers's emphasis on the potential for conflict between the concept of self and experience—the basis for psychopathology.

Self-guides. Standards concerning the self that the individual feels should be met. They result from early learning experiences and have important emotional consequences.

Self-produced consequences. In social cognitive theory, the consequences to behavior that are produced personally (internally) by the individual and that play a vital role in self-regulation and self-control.

Self-regulation. Bandura's concept for the process through which persons regulate their own behavior.

Self-reinforcement. In social cognitive theory, the process by which individuals reward themselves through self-evaluative responses such as praise and guilt. Such self-reinforcement processes are particularly important in the self-regulation of behavior over extended periods of time.

Self-schema. Cognitive generalizations about the self, derived from past experience, that organize and guide the processing of self-related information.

Semantic conditioning. The classical conditioning of responses to the meaning of words. Associated with Pavlov's emphasis on the second signal system.

Sentiment. Cattell's concept for environmentally determined patterns of behavior that are expressed in attitudes (i.e., readiness to act in a certain direction) and are linked to underlying ergs (i.e., innate biological drives).

Sexual instincts. Freud's concept for those drives directed toward sexual gratification or pleasure.

Sign approach. Mischel's description of assessment approaches that infer personality from test behavior, in contrast with sample approaches to assessment.

Similarity pole. In Kelly's personal construct theory, the similarity pole of a construct is defined by the way in which two elements are perceived to be similar.

Situational specificity. The emphasis on behavior as varying according to the situation, as opposed to the emphasis by trait theorists on consistency in behavior across situations.

Social desirability. The perceived social value of a response to a test item that may lead to a subject responding in terms of the perceived acceptability (desirability) of a response rather than in terms of its actual relevance to the self.

Source trait.   In Cattell's theory, behaviors that vary together to form an independent dimension of personality, which is discovered through the use of factor analysis.

Stability.   In Weiner's scheme of causal attributions, a dimension that relates to whether the person perceives the causes of events as stable and relatively fixed as opposed to being unstable or variable.

State.   Emotional and mood changes (e.g., anxiety, depression, fatigue) that Cattell suggested may influence the behavior of a person at a given time. The assessment of both traits and states is suggested to predict behavior.

Stress.   The person's perception that circumstances exceed his or her resources and endanger well-being. In Lazarus' view this involves two stages of cognitive appraisal—primary and secondary.

Stress inoculation training.   Meichenbaum's procedure for training individuals to cope with stress, involving the phases of Conceptualization, Skill Acquisition and Rehearsal, and Application–Follow-through.

Structure.   In personality theory, the concept that refers to the more enduring and stable aspects of personality.

Subception.   A process emphasized by Rogers in which a stimulus is experienced without being brought into awareness.

Sublimation.   The mechanism of defense in which the original expression of the instinct is replaced by a higher cultural goal.

Subliminal psychodynamic activation.   The research procedure associationed with psychoanalytic theory in which stimuli are presented below the perceptual threshold (subliminally) to stimulate unconscious wishes and fears.

Submerged construct.   In Kelly's personal construct theory, a construct that once could be expressed in words, but now either one or both poles of the construct cannot be verbalized.

Subordinate construct.   In Kelly's personal construct theory, a construct that is lower in the construct system and is thereby included in the context of another (superordinate) construct.

Successive approximation.   In Skinner's operant conditioning theory, the development of complex behaviors through the reinforcement of behaviors that increasingly resemble the final form of behavior to be produced.

Superego.   Freud's structural concept for the part of personality that expresses our ideals and moral values.

Superfactor.   A higher-order or secondary factor, representing a higher level organization of traits than the initial, primary factors derived from factor analysis.

Superordinate construct.   In Kelly's personal construct theory, a construct that is higher in the construct system and thereby includes other constructs within its context.

Surface trait.   In Cattell's theory, behaviors that appear to be linked to one another but do not in fact increase and decrease together.

Symptom.   In psychopathology, the expression of psychological conflict or disordered psychological functioning. For Freud, a disguised expression of a repressed impulse.

Systematic desensitization.   A technique in behavior therapy in which a competing response (relaxation) is conditioned to stimuli that previously aroused anxiety.

Target behaviors (target responses).   In behavioral assessment, the identification of specific behaviors to be observed and measured in relation to changes in environmental events.

T-data.   Test data or information obtained from experimental procedures or standardized tests.

Tension-reduction model.   A view of motivation that suggests that behavior is directed toward the reduction of tensions associated with drives or needs.

Threat (Kelly).   In Kelly's personal construct theory, threat occurs when the person is aware of an imminent, comprehensive change in his or her construct system.

Tightening.   In Kelly's personal construct theory, the use of constructs to make the same predictions regardless of circumstances.

Token economy. Following Skinner's operant conditioning theory, an environment in which individuals are rewarded with tokens for desirable behaviors.

Trait. A disposition to behave in a particular way, as expressed in a person's behavior over a range of situations.

Transference. In psychoanalysis, the patient's development toward the analyst of attitudes and feelings rooted in past experiences with parental figures.

Type. The classification of people into a few groups, each of which has its own defining characteristics (e.g., introverts and extraverts).

Unconditional positive regard. Rogers's term for the acceptance of a person in a total, unconditional way. One of three therapist conditions suggested as essential for growth and therapeutic progress. (*See* **congruence** and **empathic understanding**)

Unconscious. Those thoughts, experiences, and feelings of which we are unaware. According to Freud, this unawareness is the result of repression.

Undoing. The defense mechanism in which one magically undoes an act or wish associated with anxiety.

Validity. The extent to which our observations reflect the phenomena or variables of interest to us.

Verbal construct. In Kelly's personal construct theory, a construct that can be expressed in words.

Vicarious conditioning. Bandura's concept for the process through which emotional responses are learned through the observation of emotional responses in others.

Vicarious experiencing of consequences. In social cognitive theory, the observed consequences to the behavior of others that influence future performance.

ABRAMSON, L. Y., GARBER, J., & SELIGMAN, M. E. P. (1980). Learned helplessness in humans: An attributional analysis. In J. Garber & M. E. P. Seligman (Eds.), *Human helplessness* (pp. 3–37). New York: Academic Press.

ABRAMSON, L. Y., SELIGMAN, M. E. P., & TEASDALE, J. D. (1978). Learned helplessness in humans: Critique and reformulation. *Journal of Abnormal Psychology, 87*, 49–74.

ADAMS-WEBBER, J. R. (1979). *Personal construct theory: Concepts and applications.* New York: Wiley.

ADAMS-WEBBER, J. R. (1982). Assimilation and contrast in personal judgment: The dichotomy corollary. In J. C. Mancuso & J. R. Adams-Webber (Eds.), *The construing person* (pp. 96–112). New York: Praeger.

ADER, R., & COHEN, N. (1993). Psychoneuroimmunology: Conditioning and stress. *Annual Review of Psychology, 44*, 53–85.

AHADI, S., & DIENER, E. (1989). Multiple determinants and effect size. *Journal of Personality and Social Psychology, 56*, 398–406.

AINSWORTH, M. D. S., & BOWLBY, J. (1991). An ethological approach to personality development. *American Psychologist, 46*, 333–341.

ALEXANDER, F., & FRENCH, T. M. (1946). *Psychoanalytic therapy.* New York: Ronald.

ALLPORT, F. H., & ALLPORT, G. W. (1921). Personality traits: Their classification and measurement. *Journal of Abnormal and Social Psychology, 16*, 1–40.

ALLPORT, G. W. (1937). *Personality: A psychological interpretation.* New York: Holt, Rinehart & Winston.

ALLPORT, G. W. (1958). What units shall we employ? In G. Lindzey (Ed.), *Assessment of human motives* (pp. 239–260). New York: Holt, Rinehart & Winston.

ALLPORT, G. W. (1967). Autobiography. In E. G. Boring & G. Lindzey (Eds.), *A history of psychology in autobiography* (pp. 1–26). New York: Appleton-Century-Crofts.

ALLPORT, G. W., & ODBERT, H. S. (1936). Traitnames: A psycho-lexical study. *Psychological Monographs*, 47 (Whole No. 211).

AMERICAN PSYCHOLOGICAL SOCIETY OBSERVER, The accuracy of recovered memories. July 1992, p. 6.

ANDERSEN, B. L., & CYRANOWSKI, J. M. (1994). Women's sexual self-schema. *Journal of Personality and Social Psychology, 67*, 1079–1100.

ANDERSEN, S. M., & BAUM, A. (1994). Transference in interpersonal relations: Inferences and affect based on significant-other representations. *Journal of Personality, 62*, 459–498.

ANGELOU, M. (1993). *Wouldn't take nothing for my journey now.* Toronto, Canada: Random House.

APA ETHICAL PRINCIPLES OF PSYCHOLOGISTS. (1981). *American Psychologist, 36*, 633–638.

APA MONITOR. (1982). The spreading case of fraud, *13*, 1.

APA MONITOR. (1990). The risk of emotion suppression, July 14.

ARONSON, E., & METTEE, D. R. (1968). Dishonest behavior as a function of differential levels of induced self-esteem. *Journal of Personality and Social Psychology, 9*, 121–127.

AYLLON, T., & AZRIN, H. H. (1965). The measurement and reinforcement of behavior of psychotics. *Journal of the Experimental Analysis of Behavior, 8*, 357–383.

BALAY, J., & SHEVRIN, H. (1988). The subliminal psychodynamic activation method. *American Psychologist, 43*, 161–174.

BALAY, J., & SHEVRIN, H. (1989). SPA is subliminal, but is it psychodynamically activating? *American Psychologist, 44*, 1423–1426.

BALDWIN, A., CRITELLI, J. W., STEVENS, L. C., & RUSSELL, S. (1986). Androgyny and sex role measurement: A personal construct approach. *Journal of Personality and Social Psychology, 51*, 1081–1088.

BALDWIN, A. L. (1949). The effect of home environment on nursery school behavior. *Child Development, 20*, 49–61.

BANAJI, M., & PRENTICE, D. A. (1994). The self in social contexts. *Annual Review of Psychology, 45,* 297–332.

BANDURA, A. (1965). Influence of models' reinforcement contingencies on the acquisition of imitative responses. *Journal of Personality and Social Psychology, 1,* 589–595.

BANDURA, A. (1971). Psychotherapy based upon modeling principles. In A. E. Bergin & S. Garfield (Eds.), *Handbook of psychotherapy and behavior change* (pp. 653–708). New York: Wiley.

BANDURA, A. (1972). *The process and practice of participant modeling treatment.* Paper presented at the Conference on the Behavioral Basis of Mental Health, Ireland.

BANDURA, A. (1982). Self-efficacy mechanism in human agency. *American Psychologist, 37,* 122–147.

BANDURA, A. (1986). *Social foundations of thought and action: A social cognitive theory.* Englewood Cliffs, N. J. : Prentice Hall.

BANDURA, A. (1988). Self-efficacy conception of anxiety. *Anxiety Research, 1,* 77–98.

BANDURA, A. (1989a). Social cognitive theory. *Annals of Child Development, 6,* 1–60.

BANDURA, A. (1989b). Self-regulation of motivation and action through internal standards and goal systems. In L. A. Pervin (Ed.), *Goal concepts in personality and social psychology* (pp. 19–85). Hillsdale, N. J. : Erlbaum.

BANDURA, A. (1989c). Human agency in social cognitive theory. *American Psychologist, 44,* 1175–1184.

BANDURA, A. (1990). Self-regulation of motivation through anticipatory and self-reactive mechanisms. *Nebraska Symposium on Motivation, 38,* 69–164.

BANDURA, A. (1992). Self-efficacy mechanism in psychobiologic functioning. In R. Schwarzer (Ed.), *Self-efficacy: Thought control of action,* (pp. 335–394). Washington, D.C.: Hemisphere.

BANDURA, A. (1995). Exercise of personal and collective efficacy in changing societies. In A. Bandura (Ed.), *Self-efficacy in changing societies* (pp. 1–45). New York: Cambridge.

BANDURA, A., & ADAMS, N. E. (1977). Analysis of self-efficacy theory of behavioral change. *Cognitive Therapy and Research, 1,* 287–310.

BANDURA, A., ADAMS, N. E., & BEYER, J. (1977). Cognitive processes mediating behavioral change. *Journal of Personality and Social Psychology, 35,* 125–139.

BANDURA, A., & BARAB, P. G. (1971). Conditions governing nonreinforced imitation. *Developmental Psychology, 5,* 244–255.

BANDURA, A., BLANCHARD, E. B., & RITTER, B. J. (1967). *The relative efficacy of modeling therapeutic approaches for producing behavioral, attitudinal and affective changes.* Unpublished manuscript, Stanford University.

BANDURA, A., & CERVONE, D. (1983). Self-evaluative and self-efficacy mechanisms governing the motivational effect of goal systems. *Journal of Personality and Social Psychology, 45,* 1017–1028.

BANDURA, A., GRUSEC, J. E., & MENLOVE, F. L. (1967). Some social determinants of self-monitoring reinforcement systems. *Journal of Personality and Social Psychology, 5,* 449–455.

BANDURA, A., & KUPERS, C. J. (1964). Transmission of patterns of self-reinforcement through modeling. *Journal of Abnormal and Social Psychology, 69,* 1–9.

BANDURA, A., & MENLOVE, F. L. (1968). Factors determining vicarious extinction of avoidance behavior through symbolic modeling. *Journal of Personality and Social Psychology, 8,* 99–108.

BANDURA, A., & MISCHEL, W. (1965). Modification of self-imposed delay of reward through exposure to live and symbolic models. *Journal of Personality and Social Psychology, 2,* 698–705.

BANDURA, A., REESE, L., & ADAMS, N. E. (1982). Microanalysis of action and fear arousal as a function of differential levels of perceived self-efficacy. *Journal of Personality and Social Psychology, 43,* 5–21.

BANDURA, A., & ROSENTHAL, T. L. (1966). Vicarious classical conditioning as a function of arousal level. *Journal of Personality and Social Psychology, 3,* 54–62.

BANDURA, A., ROSS, D., & ROSS, S. (1963). Imitation of film-mediated aggressive models. *Journal of Abnormal and Social Psychology, 66,* 3–11.

BANDURA, A., & SCHUNK, D. H. (1981). Cultivating competence, self-efficacy, and intrinsic interest. *Journal of Personality and Social Psychology, 41,* 586–598.

BANNISTER, D. (1962). The nature and measurement of schizophrenic thought disorder. *Journal of Mental Science, 108,* 825–842.

BARGH, J. A., & TOTA, M. E. (1988). Context-dependent automatic processing in depression: Accessibility of negative constructs with regard to self but not others. *Journal of Personality and Social Psychology, 54,* 925–939.

BARLOW, D. H. (1991). Disorders of emotion. *Psychological Inquiry, 2,* 58–71.

BARON, R. A. (1987). Outlines of a grand theory. *Contemporary Psychology, 32,* 413–415.

BARRICK, M. R., & MOUNT, M. K. (1991). The Big Five personality dimensions and job performance: A meta-analysis. *Personnel Psychology, 44,* 1–26.

BARRON, F. (1953). An ego-strength scale which predicts response to psychotherapy. *Journal of Consulting Psychology, 17,* 327–333.

BARTHOLOMEW, K., & HOROWITZ, L. K. (1991). Attachment styles among young adults: A test of a four-category model. *Journal of Personality and Social Psychology, 61,* 226–244.

BASEN-ENGQUIST, K. (1994). Evaluation of theory-based HIV prevention intervention in college students. *AIDS Education and Prevention, 6,* 412–424.

BAUMEISTER, R. F. (1982). A self-presentational view of social phenomena. *Psychological Bulletin, 91,* 3–26.

BAUMEISTER, R. F. (Ed.) (1991). *Escaping the self.* New York: Basic Books.

BECK, A. T. (1987). Cognitive models of depression. *Journal of Cognitive Psychotherapy, 1,* 2–27.

BECK, A. T. (1988). *Love is never enough.* New York: Harper & Row.

BECK, A. T. (1991). Cognitive therapy: A 30–year retrospective. *American Psychologist, 46,* 368–375.

BECK, A. T. (1993). Cognitive therapy: Past, present, and future. *Journal of Consulting and Clinical Psychology, 61,* 194–198.

BECK, A. T., FREEMAN, A., & ASSOCIATES. (1990). *Cognitive therapy of personality disorders.* New York: Guilford Press.

BECK, A. T., WRIGHT, F. D., NEWMAN, C. D., & LIESE, B. S. (1993). *Cognitive therapy of drug abuse.* New York: Guilford Press.

BENET, V., & WALLER, N. G. (1995). The Big Seven factor model of personality description: Evidence for its cross-cultural generality in a Spanish sample. *Journal of Personality and Social Psychology, 69,* 701–718.

BENJAMIN, J., LIN, L., PATTERSON, C., GREENBERG, B. D., MURPHY, D. L., & HAMER, D. H. (1996). Population and familial association between the D4 dopamine receptor gene and measures of novelty seeking. *Nature Genetics, 12,* 81–84.

BERKOWITZ, L., & DONNERSTEIN, E. (1982). External validity is more than skin deep. *American Psychologist, 37,* 245–257.

BERSCHEID, E. (1992). A very personal view of person perception. *Psychological Inquiry, 1992, 2,* in press.

BIERI, J. (1953). Changes in interpersonal perceptions following social interaction. *Journal of Abnormal and Social Psychology, 48,* 61–66.

BIERI, J. (1986). Beyond the grid principle. *Contemporary Psychology, 31,* 672–673.

BIERI, J., ATKINS, A., BRIAR, S., LEAMAN, R. L., MILLER, H., & TRIPOLDI, T. (1966). *Clinical and social judgment.* New York: Wiley.

BLOCK, J. (1977). Advancing the psychology of personality: Paradigmatic shift or improving the quality of research? In D. Magnusson & N. Endler (Eds.), *Personality at the crossroads* (pp. 37–64). Hillsdale, N. J. : Erlbaum.

BLOCK, J. (1993). Studying personality the long way. In D. C. Funder, R. D. Parke, C. Tomlinson-Keasey, & K. Widaman (Eds.), *Studying lives through time,* (pp. 9–41). Washington, D.C.: American Psychological Association.

BLOCK, J. (1995). A contrarian view of the five-factor approach to personality description. *Psychological Bulletin, 117,* 187–215.

BLOCK, J. H., & BLOCK, J. (1980). The role of ego control and ego resiliency in the organization of behavior. In W. A. Collins (Ed.), *Development of cognitive, affect, and social relations: The Minnesota symposium in child psychology* (pp. 39–101). Hillsdale, N. J. : Erlbaum.

BLOCK, J. & ROBINS, R. W. (1993). A longitudinal

study of consistency and change in self-esteem from early adolescence to early adulthood. *Child Development, 64,* 909–923.

BONARIUS, H., HOLLAND, R., & ROSENBERG, S. (Eds.) (1981). *Personal construct psychology. Recent advances in theory and practice.* London: Macmillan.

BOND, M. H. (1994). Trait theory and cross-cultural studies of person perception. *Psychological Inquiry, 5,* 114–117.

BORGATTA, E. F. (1968). Traits and persons. In E. F. Borgatta & W. F. Lambert (Eds.), *Handbook of personality: Theory and research* (pp. 510–528). Chicago: Rand McNally.

BOUCHARD, T. J., JR., LYKKEN, D. T., MCGUE, M., SEGAL, N. L., & TELLEGEN, A. (1990). Sources of human psychological differences: The Minnesota study of twins reared apart. *Science, 250,* 223–250.

BOUTON, M. E. (1994). Context, ambiguity, and classical conditioning. *Current Directions in Psychological Science, 3,* 49–53.

BRAMEL, D., & FRIEND, R. (1981). Hawthorne, the myth of the docile worker, and the class bias in psychology. *American Psychologist, 36,* 867–878.

BRETHERTON, I. (1992). The origins of attachment theory: John Bowlby and Mary Ainsworth. *Developmental Psychology, 28,* 759–775.

BREWIN, C. R. (1989). Cognitive change processes in psychotherapy. *Psychological Review, 96,* 379–394.

BREWIN, C. R. (1996). Theoretical foundations of cognitive-behavior therapy for anxiety and depression. *Annual Review of Psychology, 47,* 33–57.

BRIGGS, S. R. (1989). The optimal level of measurement for personality constructs. In D. M. Buss & N. Cantor (Eds.), *Personality psychology: Recent trends and emerging directions* (pp. 246–260). New York: Springer-Verlag.

BRODY, N. (1988). *Personality: In search of individuality.* New York: Academic Press.

BROWN, I. B., JR., & INOUYE, D. K. (1978). Learned helplessness through modeling: The role of perceived similarity in competence. *Journal of Personality and Social Psychology, 36,* 900–908.

BROWN, J. D., & MCGILL, K. L. (1989). The cost of good fortune: When positive life events produce negative health consequences. *Journal of Personality and Social Psychology, 57,* 1103–1110.

BROWN, N. O. (1959). *Life against death.* New York: Random House.

BRUNER, J. S. (1956). You are your constructs. *Contemporary Psychology, 1,* 355–356.

BURGER, J. M., & COOPER, H. M. (1979). The desirability of control. *Motivation and Emotion, 3,* 381–387.

BUSS, A. H. (1988). *Personality: Evolutionary heritage and human distinctiveness.* Hillsdale, N. J. : Erlbaum.

BUSS, A. H. (1989). Personality as traits. *American Psychologist, 44,* 1378–1388.

BUSS, D. M. (1991). Evolutionary personality psychology. *Annual Review of Psychology, 42,* 459–492.

BUSS, D. M. (1995). Evolutionary psychology: A new paradigm for psychological science. *Psychological Inquiry, 6,* 1–30.

BUSS, D. M., & CRAIK, K. H. (1983). The act frequency approach to personality. *Psychological Review, 90,* 105–126.

CAMPBELL, J. B., & HAWLEY, C. W. (1982). Study habits and Eysenck's theory of extroversion–introversion. *Journal of Research in Personality, 16,* 139–146.

CAMPBELL, J. D., & LAVALLEE, L. F. (1993). Who am I? The role of self-concept confusion in understanding the behavior of people with low self-esteem. In R. F. Baumeister (Ed.), *Self-esteem: The puzzle of low self-regard* (pp. 3–20). New York: Plenum.

CANTOR, N. (1990). From thought to behavior: "Having" and "doing" in the study of personality and cognition. *American Psychologist, 45,* 735–750.

CANTOR, N. & HARLOW, R. E. (1994). Personality, strategic behavior, and daily-life problem solving. *Current Directions in Psychological Science, 3,* 169–172.

CANTOR, N. & KIHLSTROM, J. F. (1987). *Personality and social intelligence.* Englewood Cliffs, N. J. : Prentice Hall.

CANTOR, N., MISCHEL, W., & SCHWARTZ, J. C. (1982). A prototype analysis of psychological situations. *Cognitive Psychology, 14,* 45–77.

CANTOR, N., & ZIRKEL, S. (1990). Personality, cognition, and purposive behavior. In L. A. Pervin (Ed.), *Handbook of personality: Theory and research* (pp. 135–164). New York: Guilford Press.

CARLSON, R. (1971). Where is the person in personality research? *Psychological Bulletin, 75,* 203–219.

CARNELLEY, K. B., PIETROMONACO, P. R., & JAFFE, K. (1994). Depression, working models of others, and relationships functioning. *Journal of Personality and Social Psychology, 66,* 127–140.

CARTWRIGHT, D. S. (1956). Self-consistency as a factor affecting immediate recall. *Journal of Abnormal and Social Psychology, 52,* 212–218.

CASPI, A., & BEM, D. J. (1990). Personality continuity and change across the life course. In L. A. Pervin (Ed.), *Handbook of personality: Theory and research* (pp. 549–575). New York: Guilford Press.

CATTELL, R. B. (1959). Foundations of personality measurement theory in multivariate expressions. In B. M. Bass & I. A. Berg (Eds.), *Objective approaches to personality assessment* (pp. 42–65). Princeton, N. J. : Van Nostrand.

CATTELL, R. B. (1963a). Personality, role, mood, and situation perception: A unifying theory of modulators. *Psychological Review, 70,* 1–18.

CATTELL, R. B. (1963b). The nature and measurement of anxiety. *Scientific American, 208,* 96–104.

CATTELL, R. B. (1965). *The scientific analysis of personality.* Baltimore: Penguin.

CATTELL, R. B. (1979). *Personality and learning theory.* New York: Springer.

CATTELL, R. B. (1983). *Structured personality learning theory.* New York: Praeger.

CATTELL, R. B. (1985). *Human motivation and the dynamic calculus.* New York: Praeger.

CATTELL, R. B. (1990). Advances in Cattellian personality theory. In L. A. Pervin (Ed.), *Handbook of personality: Theory and research* (pp. 101–110). New York: Guilford Press.

CERVONE, D., & SCOTT, W. D. (1995). Self-efficacy theory of behavioral change: Foundations, conceptual issues, and therapeutic implications. In W. O'Donohue & L. Krasner (Eds.), *Theories in behavior therapy.* Washington, D.C.: American Psychological Association.

CERVONE, D., & WILLIAMS, S. L. (1992). Social cognitive theory and personality. In G. Caprara & G. L. Van Heck (Eds.), *Modern personality psychology* (pp. 200–252). New York: Harvester Wheatsheaf.

CHAPLIN, W. F., JOHN, O. P. & GOLDBERG, L. R. (1988). Conceptions of states and traits: Dimensional attributes with ideals as prototypes. *Journal of Personality and Social Psychology, 54,* 541–557.

CHODORKOFF, B. (1954). Self perception, perceptual defense, and adjustment. *Journal of Abnormal and Social Psychology, 49,* 508–512.

CHURCH, A. T., KATIGBAK, M. S., & REYES, J. A. (1995). Toward a taxonomy of trait adjectives in Filipino: Comparing personality lexicons across cultures. *European Journal of Personality,* in press.

CLARK, D. A., BECK, A. T., & BROWN, G. (1989). Cognitive mediation in general psychiatric outpatients: A test of the content-specificity hypothesis. *Journal of Personality and Social Psychology, 56,* 958–964.

COLVIN, C. R. (1993). "Judgable" people: Personality, behavior, and competing explanations. *Journal of Personality and Social Psychology, 64,* 861–873.

COLVIN, C. R., & BLOCK, J. (1994). Do positive illusions foster mental health? An examination of the Taylor and Brown formulation. *Psychological Bulletin, 116,* 3–20.

CONLEY, J. J.(1985). Longitudinal stability of personality traits: A multitrait-multimethod-multioccasion analysis. *Journal of Personality and Social Psychology, 49,* 1266–1282.

CONTRADA, R. J., LEVENTHAL, H., & O'LEARY, A. (1990). Personality and health. In L. A. Pervin (Ed.), *Handbook of Personality: Theory and research* (pp. 638–669). New York: Guilford Press.

COOPERSMITH, S. (1967). *The antecedents of self-esteem.* San Francisco: Freeman.

COSTA, P. T., JR. (1991). Clinical use of the five-factor model. *Journal of Personality Assessment, 57,* 393–398.

COSTA, P. T., JR., & McCRAE, R. R. (1985). *The NEO Personality Inventory manual.* Odessa, Fla.: Psychological Assessment Resources.

COSTA, P. T., JR., & McCRAE, R. R. (1992). NEO-PI-R: Professional Manual. Odessa, Fla.: Psychological Assessment Resources.

COSTA, P. T., JR., & McCRAE, R. R. (1994a). "Set like plaster?" Evidence for the stability of adult personality. In T. Heatherton & J. Weinberger (Eds.), *Can personality change?* (pp. 21–40). Washington, D.C.: American Psychological Association.

COSTA, P. T., JR., & McCRAE, R. R. (1994b). Stability and change in personality from adolescence through adulthood. In C. F. Halverson, Jr., G. A. Kohnstamm, & Roy P. Martin (Eds.), *The developing structure of temperament and personality from infancy to adulthood* (pp. 139–155). Hillsdale, N.J.: Erlbaum.

COSTA, P. T., JR., & McCRAE, R. R. (1995). Primary traits of Eysenck's P-E-N system: Three- and five-factor solutions. *Journal of Personality and Social Psychology, 69,* 308–317.

COSTA, P. T., JR., & WIDIGER, T. A. (Eds.) (1994). *Personality disorders and the five-factor model of personality.* Washington, D.C.: American Psychological Association.

COUSINS, S. D. (1989). Culture and self-perception in Japan and the United States. *Journal of Personality and Social Psychology, 56,* 124–131.

COX, T., & MACKAY, C. (1982). Psychosocial factors and psychophysiological mechanisms in the etiology and development of cancer. *Social Science and Medicine, 16,* 381–396.

COYNE, J. C.(1994). Self-reported distress: Analog or ersatz depression? *Psychological Bulletin, 116,* 29–45.

COZZARELLI, C. (1993). Personality and self-efficacy as predictors of coping with abortion. *Journal of Personality and Social Psychology, 65,* 1224–1236.

CRAIGHEAD, W. E., CRAIGHEAD, L. W., & ILARDI, S. S. (1995). Behavior therapies in historical perspective. In B. Bongar & L. E. Bentler (Eds.), *Comprehensive textbook of psychotherapy* (pp. 64–83). New York: Oxford University Press.

CREWS, F. (1993). The unknown Freud. *The New York Review of Books,* November 18, 55–66.

CROCKETT, W. H. (1965). Cognitive complexity and impression formation. In B. A. Maher (Ed.), *Progress in experimental personality research* (pp. 47–90). New York: Academic Press.

CROCKETT, W. H. (1982). The organization of construct systems: The organization corollary. In J. C. Mancuso & J. R. Adams-Webber (Eds.), *The construing person* (pp. 62–95). New York: Praeger.

CROSS, H. J. (1966). The relationship of parental training conditions to conceptual level in adolescent boys. *Journal of Personality, 34,* 348–365.

CROSS, S. E., & MARKUS, H. R. (1990). The willful self. *Personality and Social Psychology Bulletin, 16,* 726–742.

CURTIS, R. C., & MILLER, K. (1986). Believing another likes or dislikes you: Behaviors making the beliefs come true. *Journal of Personality and Social Psychology, 51,* 284–290.

DARLEY, J. M., & FAZIO, R. (1980). Expectancy confirmation processes arising in the social interaction sequence. *American Psychologist, 35,* 867–881.

DAVIS, P. J., & SCHWARTZ, G. E. (1987). Repression and the inaccessibility of affective memories. *Journal of Personality and Social Psychology, 52,* 155–162.

DECI, E. L., & RYAN, R. M. (1985). *Intrinsic motivation and self determination in human behavior.* New York: Plenum.

DECI, E. L., & RYAN, R. M. (1991). A motivational approach to self: Integration in personality. *Nebraska Symposium on Motivation, 38,* 237–288.

DEAUX, K. (1976). *The behavior of women and men.* Monterey, Calif. : Brooks/Cole.

DENES-RAJ, V. & EPSTEIN, S. (1994). Conflict between intuitive and rational processing: When people behave against their better judgment. *Journal of Personality and Social Psychology, 66,* 819–829.

DEPUE, R. A., LUCIANA, M., ARBISI, P., COLLINS, P., & LEON, A. (1994). Dopamine and the structure of personality: Relation of agonist-induced dopamine activity to positive emotionality. *Journal of Personality and Social Psychology, 67,* 485–498.

DERUBEIS, R. J., & HOLLON, S. D. (1995). Explanatory style in the treatment of depression.

In G. M. Buchanan & M. E. P. Seligman (Eds.), *Explanatory style* (pp. 99–112). Hillsdale, N.J.: Erlbaum.

DEVELLIS, R. F., DEVELLIS, B. M., & MCCAULEY, C. (1978). Vicarious acquisition of learned helplessness. *Journal of Personality and Social Psychology, 36,* 894–899.

DIGMAN, J. M. (1990). Personality structure: Emergence of the five-factor model. *Annual Review of Psychology, 41,* 417–440.

DOBSON, K. S., & SHAW, B. F. (1995). Cognitive therapies in practice. In B. Bongar & L. E. Bentler (Eds.), *Comprehensive textbook of psychotherapy* (pp. 159–172). New York: Oxford University Press.

DOLLARD, J., DOOB, L. W., MILLER, N. E., MOWRER, O. H., & SEARS, R. R. (1939). *Frustration and aggression.* New Haven, Conn.: Yale University Press.

DOLLARD, J., & MILLER, N. E. (1950). *Personality and psychotherapy.* New York: McGraw-Hill.

DONAHUE, E. M. (1994). Do children use the big Five, too? Content and structual form in personality descriptions. *Journal of Personality, 62,* 45–66.

DONAHUE, E. M., ROBINS, R. W., ROBERTS, B., & JOHN, O. P. (1993). The divided self: Concurrent and longitudinal effects of psychological adjustment and self-concept differentiation. *Journal of Personality and Social Psychology, 64,* 834–846.

DUCK, S. (1982). Two individuals in search of agreement: The commonality corollary. In J. C. Mancuso & J. R. Adams-Webber (Eds.), *The construing person* (pp. 222–234). New York: Praeger.

DUDYCHA, G. J. (1936). An objective study of punctuality in relation to personality and achievement. *Archives of Psychology, 29,* 1–53.

DUNN, J., & PLOMIN, R. (1990). *Separate lives: Why siblings are so different.* New York: Basic Books.

DWECK, C. S. (1991). Self-theories and goals: Their role in motivation, personality, and development. In R. D. Dienstbier (Ed.), *Nebraska Symposium on Motivation* (pp. 199–235). Lincoln: University of Nebraska Press.

DWECK, C. S., CHIU, C., & HONG, Y. (1995). Implicit theories and their role in judgments and reactions: A world from two perspectives. *Psychological Inquiry, 6,* in press.

EAGLE, M., WOLITZKY, D. L., & KLEIN, G. S. (1966). Imagery: Effect of a concealed figure in a stimulus. *Science, 18,* 837–839.

EBSTEIN, R. P. NOVICK, O. UMANSKY, R., PRIEL, B., OSHER, Y., BLAINE, D., BENNETT, E., NEWMANOV, L., KATZ, M., & BELMAKER, R. (1996). Dopamine D4 receptor (D4DR) exon III polymorphism associated with the human personality trait of Novelty Seeking. *Nature Genetics, 12,* 78–80.

EDELSON, M. (1984). *Hypothesis and evidence in psychoanalysis.* Chicago: University of Chicago Press.

EKMAN, P. (1992). An argument for basic emotions. *Cognition and Emotion, 6,* 169–200.

EKMAN, P. (1993). Facial expression and emotion. *American Psychologist, 48,* 384–392.

ELLIS, A., & HARPER, R. A. (1975). *A new guide to rational living.* North Hollywood, Calif. : Wilshire.

EMMONS, R. A. (1987). Narcissism: Theory and measurement. *Journal of Personality and Social Psychology, 52,* 11–17.

ENDLER, N. S., & MAGNUSSON, D. (Eds.) (1976). *Interactional psychology and personality.* Washington, D. C. : Hemisphere (Halsted-Wiley).

EPSTEIN, N., & BAUCOM, N. (1988). *Cognitive-behavioral marital therapy.* New York: Springer.

EPSTEIN, S. (1983). A research paradigm for the study of personality and emotions. In M. M. Page (Ed.), *Personality: Current theory and research* (pp. 91–154). Lincoln: University of Nebraska Press.

EPSTEIN, S. (1992). The cognitive self, the psychoanalytic self, and the forgotten selves. *Psychological Inquiry, 3,* 34–37.

EPSTEIN, S. (1994). Integration of the cognitive and the psychodynamic unconscious. *American Psychologist, 49,* 709–724.

ERDELYI, M. (1984). *Psychoanalysis: Freud's cognitive psychology.* New York: Freeman.

ERICSSON, K. A., & SIMON, H. A. (1993). *Protocol analysis: Verbal reports as data.* Cambridge, MA: MIT Press.

ERIKSON, E. (1950). *Childhood and society.* New York: Norton.

ERIKSON, E. H. (1982). *The life cycle completed: A review.* New York: Norton.

ESTERSON, A. (1993). *Seductive mirage: An exploration of the the work of Sigmund Freud*. New York: Open Court.

EVANS, R. I. (1976). *The making of psychology*. New York: Knopf.

EWART, C. K. (1992). The role of physical self-efficacy in recovery from heart attack. In R. Schwarzer (Ed.), *Self-efficacy: Thought control of action* (pp. 287–304). Washington, D.C.: Hemisphere.

EYSENCK, H. J. (1953). *Uses and abuses of psychology*. London: Penguin.

EYSENCK, H. J. (1975). *The inequality of man*. San Diego, Calif. : Edits Publishers.

EYSENCK, H. J. (1979). The conditioning model of neurosis. *Behavioral and Brain Sciences, 2*, 155–199.

EYSENCK, H. J. (1982). *Personality genetics and behavior*. New York: Praeger.

EYSENCK, H. J. (1990). Biological dimensions of personality. In L. A. Pervin (Ed.), *Handbook of personality: Theory and research* (pp. 244–276). New York: Guilford Press.

EYSENCK, H. J. (1991). Personality, stress, and disease: An interactionist perspective. *Psychological Inquiry, 2*, 221–232.

EYSENCK, H. J. (1993). Comment on Goldberg. *American Psychologist, 48*, 1299–1300.

EYSENCK, H. J., & BEECH, H. R. (1971). Counter conditioning and related methods. In A. E. Bergin & S. Garfield (Eds.), *Handbook of psychotherapy and behavior change* (pp. 543–611). New York: Wiley.

EYSENCK, S. B. G., & LONG, F. Y. (1986). A cross-cultural comparison of personality in adults and children: Singapore and England. *Journal of Personality and Social Psychology, 50*, 124–130.

FEENEY, J. A., & NOLLER, P. (1990). Attachment style as a predictor of adult romantic relationships. *Journal of Personality and Social Psychology, 58*, 281–291.

FISHER, S., & FISHER, R. L. (1981). *Pretend the world is funny and forever: A psychological analysis of comedians, clowns, and actors*. Hillsdale, N. J.: Erlbaum.

FOLKMAN, S., LAZARUS, R. S., GRUEN, R. J., &

DELONGIS, A. (1986). Appraisal, coping, health status, and psychological symptoms. *Journal of Personality and Social Psychology, 50*, 571–579.

FRANKL, V. E. (1955). *The doctor and the soul*. New York: Knopf.

FRANKL, V. E. (1958). On logotherapy and existential analysis. *American Journal of Psychoanalysis, 18*, 28–37.

FRANKS, C. M., & WILSON, G. T. (Eds.) (1978). *Annual review of behavior therapy: Theory and practice*. New York: Brunner/Mazel.

FRANKS, C. M., WILSON, G. T., KENDALL, P. C., & BROWNELL, K. D. (1982). *Annual review of behavior therapy: Theory and practice*. New York: Guilford Press.

FREUD, A. (1936). *The ego and the mechanisms of defense*. New York: International Universities Press.

FREUD, S. (1953). The interpretation of dreams. In *Standard edition*, Vols. 4 & 5. London: Hogarth Press. (First German edition, 1900.)

FREUD, S. (1953). *Three essays on sexuality*. London: Hogarth Press. (Original edition, 1905.)

FREUD, S. (1959). Analysis of a phobia in a five-year-old boy. In *Standard edition*, Vol. 10. London: Hogarth Press. (First German edition, 1909.)

FREUD, S. (1953). *A general introduction to psychoanalysis*. New York: Permabooks. (Boni & Liveright edition, 1924.)

FREUD, S. (1949). *Civilization and its discontents*. London: Hogarth Press. (Original edition, 1930.)

FREUD, S. (1933). *New introductory lectures on psychoanalysis*. New York: Norton.

FRIEDMAN, H. S., TUCHKER, J. S., SCHWARTZ, J. E., TOMLINSON-KEASY, C., MARTIN, L. R., WINGARD, D. L., & CRIQUI, M. H. (1995a). Psychosocial and behavioral predictors of longevity: The aging and death of the "Termites." *American Psychologist, 50*, 69–78.

FRIEDMAN, H. S., TUCKER, J. S., SCHWARTZ, J. E., MARTIN, L. R., TOMLINSON-KEASY, C., WINGARD, D. L., & CRIQUI, M. H. (1995b). Childhood conscientiousness and longevity: Health behaviors and cause of death. *Journal of Personality and Social Psychology, 68*, 696–703.

FRIMAN, P. C., ALLEN, K. D., KERWIN, M. L. E., &

LARZELERE, R. (1993). Changes in modern psychology: A citation analysis of the Kuhnian displacement thesis. *American Psychologist, 48,* 658–664.

FROMM, E. (1959). *Sigmund Freud's mission.* New York: Harper.

FUNDER, D. C. (1989). Accuracy in personality judgment and the dancing bear. In D. M. Buss & N. Cantor (Eds.), *Personality psychology: Recent trends and emerging directions* (pp. 210–223). New York: Springer-Verlag.

FUNDER, D. C. (1993). Judgments of personality and personality itself. In K. H. Craik, R. Hogan, & R. N. Wolfe (Eds.), *Fifty years of personality psychology* (pp. 207–214). New York: Plenum.

FUNDER, D. C. (1995). On the accuracy of personality judgment: A realistic approach. *Psychological Review, 102,* 652–670.

FUNDER, D. C., & BLOCK, J. (1989). The role of ego-control, ego-resiliency, and IQ in delay of gratification in adolescence. *Journal of Personality and Social Psychology, 57,* 1041–1050.

GAENSBAUER, T. J. (1982). The differentiation of discrete affects. *Psychoanalytic Study of the Child, 37,* 29–66.

GEEN, R. G. (1984). Preferred stimulation levels in introverts and extroverts: Effects on arousal and performance. *Journal of Personality and Social Psychology, 46,* 1303–1312.

GEISLER, C. (1986). The use of subliminal psychodynamic activation in the study of repression. *Journal of Personality and Social Psychology, 51,* 844–851.

GERARD, H. B., KUPPER, D. A., & NGUYEN, L. (1993). The causal link between depression and bulimia. In J. M. Masling & R. F. Bornstein (Eds.), *Psychoanalytic perspectives in psychopathology* (pp. 225–252). Washington, D.C.: American Psychological Association.

GERGEN, K. J. (1971). *The concept of self.* New York: Holt.

GEWIRTZ, J. L. (1971). Conditional responding as a paradigm for observational, imitative learning and vicarious imitative learning and vicarious reinforcement. In H. W. Reese (Ed.), *Advances in child development and behavior* (pp. 274–304). New York: Academic Press.

GOFFMAN, E. (1959). *The presentation of self in everyday life.* Garden City, N. Y. : Doubleday.

GOLDBERG, L. R. (1981). Language and individual differences: The search for universals in personality lexicons. In L. Wheeler (Ed.), *Review of personality and social psychology* (pp. 141–165). Beverly Hills, Calif. : Sage.

GOLDBERG, L. R. (1990). An alternative "description of personality": The big-five factor structure. *Journal of Personality and Social Psychology, 59,* 1216–1229.

GOLDBERG, L. (1992). The development of markers for the Big-Five factor structure. *Psychological Assessment, 4,* 26–42.

GOLDBERG, L. R. (1993). The structure of phenotypic personality traits. *American Psychologist, 48,* 26–34.

GOLDBERG, L. R., & SAUCIER, G. (1995). So what do you propose we use instead? A reply to Block. *Psychological Bulletin, 117,* 221–225.

GOLDSTEIN, K. (1939). *The organism.* New York: American Book.

GOTTESMAN, I. I. (1963). Heritability of personality: A demonstration. *Psychological Monographs, 77* (9, Whole No. 572).

GRAY, J. A. (1990). A critique of Eysenck's theory of personality. In H. J. Eysenck (Ed.), *A model for personality,* 2nd ed. Berlin: Springer-Verlag.

GREENBERG, J. R., & MITCHELL, S. A. (1983). *Object relations in psychoanalytic theory.* Cambridge, Mass. : Harvard University Press.

GREENSPOON, J. (1962). Verbal conditioning and clinical psychology. In A. J. Bachrach (Ed.), *Experimental foundations of clinical psychology.* New York: Basic Books.

GREENSPOON, J., & LAMAL, P. A. (1978). Cognitive behavior modification—Who needs it? *Psychological Record, 28,* 323–335.

GREENWALD, A. G., SPANGENBERG, E. R., PRATKANIS, A. R., & ESKENAZI, J. (1991). Double blind tests of subliminal self-help audiotapes. *Psychological Science, 2,* 119–122.

GRIFFIN, D., & BARTHOLOMEW, K. (1994). Models of the self and other: Fundamental dimensions underlying measures of adult attachment. *Journal of Personality and Social Psychology, 67,* 430–445.

GRINKER, R. R., & SPIEGEL, J. P. (1945). *Men under stress*. Philadelphia: Blakiston.

GRODDECK, G. (1961). *The book of the it*. New York: Vintage. (Original edition 1923.)

GRUNBAUM, A. (1984). *Foundations of psychoanalysis: A philosophical critique*. Berkeley: University of California Press.

GRUNBAUM, A. (1993). *Validation in the clinical theory of psychoanalysis: A study in the philosophy of psychoanalysis*. Madison, CT: International Universities Press.

GRUSEC, J. E. (1992). Social learning theory and developmental psychology: The legacies of Robert Sears and Albert Bandura. *Developmental Psychology, 28*, 776–786.

HALKIDES, G. (1958). *An experimental study of four conditions necessary for therapeutic change*. Unpublished Ph.D. dissertation, University of Chicago.

HALL, C. S. (1954). *A primer of Freudian psychology*. New York: Mentor.

HALL, C. S., & LINDZEY, G. (1957). *Theories of personality*. New York: Wiley.

HALPERN, J. (1977). Projection: A test of the psychoanalytic hypothesis. *Journal of Abnormal Psychology, 86*, 536–542.

HALVERSON, C. F., KOHNSTAMM, G. A., & MARTIN, R P. (Eds.) (1994). *The developing structure of temperament and personality from infancy to adulthood*. Hillsdale, N.J.: Erlbaum.

HARARY, K., & DONOHUE, E. (1994). *Who do you think you are?* San Francisco: Harper.

HARRINGTON, D. M., BLOCK, J. H., & BLOCK, J. (1987). Testing aspects of Carl Rogers's theory of creative environments: Child-rearing antecedents of creative potential in young adolescents. *Journal of Personality and Social Psychology, 52*, 851–856.

HARRIS, B. (1979). Whatever happened to Little Albert? *American Psychologist, 34*, 151–160.

HARRIS, J. R. (1995). Where is the child's environment? A group socialization theory of development. *Psychological Review, 102*, 458–489.

HASTORF, A., & COLE, S. W. (1992). On getting the whole person into interpersonal perception. *Psychological Inquiry, 2*, in press.

HAVENER, P. H., & IZARD, C. E. (1962). Unrealistic self-enhancement in paranoid schizophrenics. *Journal of Consulting Psychology, 26*, 65–68.

HAWKINS, R. P., PETERSON, R. F., SCHWEID, E., & BIJOU, S. W. (1966). Behavior therapy in the home: Amelioration of problem parent–child relations with the parent in a therapeutic role. *Journal of Experimental Child Psychology, 4*, 99–107.

HAYDEN, B. C. (1982). Experience—A case for possible change: The modulation corollary. In J. C. Mancuso & J. R. Adams-Webber (Eds.), *The construing person* (pp. 170–197). New York: Praeger.

HAZAN, C., & SHAVER, P. (1987). Romantic love conceptualized as an attachment process. *Journal of Personality and Social Psychology, 52*, 511–524.

HAZAN, C., & SHAVER, P. (1990). Love and work: An attachment-theoretical perspective. *Journal of Personality and Social Psychology, 59*, 270–280.

HEINE, R. W. (1950). *An investigation of the relationship between change in personality from psychotherapy as reported by patients and the factors seen by patients as producing change*. Unpublished Ph. D. dissertation, University of Chicago.

HELSON, R. (1993). Comparing longitudinal studies of adult development: Toward a paradigm of tension between stability and change. In D. Funder, R. D. Parke, C. Tomlinson-Keasey, & K. Widaman (Eds.), *Studying lives through time* (pp. 93–120). Washington, D.C.: American Psychological Association.

HELSON, R., & WINK, P. (1992). Personality change in women from college to midlife. *Psychology and Aging, 7*, 46–55.

HESSE, H. (1951). *Siddhartha*. New York: New Directions.

HESSE, H. (1965). *Demian*. New York: Harper. (Originally published in 1925.)

HIGGINS, E. T. (1987). Self-discrepancy: A theory relating self and affect. *Psychological Review, 94*, 319–340.

HIGGINS, E. T. (1989). Continuities and discontinuities in self-regulatory self-evaluative processes: A developmental theory relating self and affect. *Journal of Personality, 57*, 407–444.

HIGGINS, E. T., BOND, R. N., KLEIN, R., & STRAUMAN, T. (1986). Self-discrepancies and emotional vulnerability: How magnitude, accessibility, and type of discrepancy influence affect.

Journal of Personality and Social Psychology, 51, 5–15.

HIROTO, D. S. (1974). Locus of control and learned helplessness. *Journal of Experimental Psychology, 102,* 187–193.

HIROTO, D. S., & SELIGMAN, M. E. P. (1975). Generality of learned helplessness in man. *Journal of Personality and Social Psychology, 31,* 311–327.

HOFFMAN, L. W. (1991). The influence of the family environment on personality: Accounting for sibling differences. *Psychological Bulletin, 110,* 187–203.

HOFSTEE, W. K. B. (1994). Who should own the definition of personality? *European Journal of Personality, 8,* 149–162.

HOLENDER, D. (1986). Semantic activation without conscious identification in dichotic listening, paraforeal vision, and visual masking: A survey and appraisal. *Behavioral and Brain Sciences, 9,* 1–66.

HOLLAND, J. L. (1985). *Making vocational choices: A theory of vocational personality and work environments.* Englewood Cliffs, N.J.: Prentice-Hall.

HOLLON, S. D., DERUBEIS, R. J., & EVANS, M. D. (1987). Causal mediation of change in treatment for depression: Discriminating between nonspecificity and noncausality. *Psychological Bulletin, 102,* 139–149.

HOLLON, S. D., & KENDALL, P. C. (1980). Cognitive self-statements in depression: Development of an Automatic Thoughts Questionnaire. *Cognitive Therapy and Research, 4,* 383–395.

HOLLON, S. D., SHELTON, R. C., & DAVIS, D. D. (1993). Cognitive therapy for depression: Conceptual issues and clinical efficacy. *Journal of Consulting and Clinical Psychology, 61,* 270–275.

HOLMES, D. S. (1990). The evidence for repression: An examination of sixty years of research. In J. L. Singer (Ed.), *Regression and dissociation: Implications for personality theory, psychopathology and health* (pp. 85–102). Chicago: University of Chicago Press.

HOLT, R. R. (1978). *Methods in clinical psychology.* New York: Plenum.

HORNEY, K. (1937). *The neurotic personality of our time.* New York: Norton.

HORNEY, K. (1945). *Our inner conflicts.* New York: Norton.

HORNEY, K. (1973). *Feminine psychology.* New York: Norton.

HULL, C. L. (1940). *Mathematico-deductive theory of rote learning.* New Haven, Conn.: Yale University Press.

HULL, C. L. (1943). *Principles of behavior.* New York: Appleton.

HULL, J. G., YOUNG, R. D., & JOURILES, E. (1986). Applications of the self-awareness model of alcohol consumption: Predicting patterns of use and abuse. *Journal of Personality and Social Psychology, 51,* 790–796.

ICHHEISER, G. (1943). Misinterpretation of personality in everyday life and the psychologist's frame of reference. *Character and Personality, 12,* 145–152.

IZARD, C. E. (1991). *The psychology of emotion.* New York: Plenum.

JACOBY, L. L., LINDSAY, D. S., & TOTH, J. P. (1992). Unconscious influences revealed. *American Psychologist, 47,* 802–809.

JANKOWICZ, A. D. (1987). Whatever became of George Kelly? *American Psychologist, 42,* 481–487.

JENSEN, M. R. (1987). Psychobiological factors predicting the course of breast cancer. *Journal of Personality, 55,* 317–342.

JOHN, O. P. (1990). The "Big Five" factor taxomony: Dimensions of personality in the natural language and in questionnaires. In L. A. Pervin (Ed.), *Handbook of personality: Theory and research* (pp. 66–100). New York: Guilford Press.

JOHN, O. P., ANGLEITNER, A., & OSTENDORF, F. (1988). The lexical approach to personality: A historical review of trait taxonomic research. *European Journal of Personality, 2,* 171–203.

JOHN, O. P., CASPI, A., ROBINS, R. W., MOFFITT, T. E., & STOUTHAMER-LOEBER, M. (1994). The "Little Five": Exploring the nomological network of the five-Factor Model of personality in adolescent boys. *Child Development, 65,* 160–178.

JOHN, O. P., & ROBINS, R. W. (1993). Gordon Allport: Father and critic of the Five-Factor model. In K. H. Craik, R. T. Hogan, & R. N. Wolfe

(Eds.), *Fifty years of personality psychology* (pp. 215–236). New York: Plenum.

JOHN, O. P., & ROBINS, R. W. (1994a). Accuracy and bias in self-perception: Individual differences in self-enhancement and the role of narcissism. *Journal of Personality and Social Psychology, 66,* 206–219.

JOHN, O. P., & ROBINS, R. W. (1994b). Traits and types, dynamics and development : No doors should be closed in the study of personality. *Psychological Inquiry, 5,* 137–142.

JONES, A., & CRANDALL, R. (1986). Validation of a short index of self-actualization. *Personality and Social Psychology Bulletin, 12,* 63–73.

JONES, E. *The life and work of Sigmund Freud,* Vol. 1. New York: Basic Books, 1953; Vol. 2, 1955; Vol. 3, 1957.

JONES, M. C. (1924). A laboratory study of fear. The case of Peter. *Pedagogical Seminar, 31,* 308–315.

JOSEPHS, R. A., MARKUS, H., & TAFARODI, R. W. (1992). Gender and self-esteem. *Journal of Personality and Social Psychology, 63,* 391–402.

JOURARD, S. M., & REMY, R. M. (1955). Perceived parental attitudes, the self, and security. *Journal of Consulting Psychology, 19,* 364–366.

JUNG, C. G. (1939). *The integration of the personality.* New York: Farrar & Rinehart.

KAGAN, J. (1994). *Galen's prophecy: Temperament in human nature.* New York: Basic Books.

KAHNEMAN, D., & TVERSKY, A. (1984). Choices, values and frames. *American Psychologist, 39,* 341–350.

KANFER, F. H., & SASLOW, G. (1965). Behavioral analysis: An alternative to diagnostic classification. *Archives of General Psychiatry, 12,* 519–538.

KASSER, T., & RYAN, R. M. (1996). Further examining the American dream: Differential correlates of intrinsic and extrinsic goals. *Personality and Social Psychology Bulletin, 22,* 280–287.

KAVANAGH, D. (1992). Self-efficacy as a resource factor in stress appraisal processes. In R. Schwarzer (Ed.), *Self-efficacy: Thought control of action* (pp. 177–194). Washington, D.C.: Hemisphere.

KAZDIN, A. E. (1977). *The token economy: A review and evaluation.* New York: Plenum.

KAZDIN, A. E., & BOOTZIN, R. R. (1972). The token economy: An evaluative review. *Journal of Applied Behavior Analysis, 5,* 343–372.

KAZDIN, A. E., & WILSON, G. T. (1978). *Evaluation of behavior theory: Issues, evidence, and research strategies.* Cambridge, Mass. : Ballinger.

KELLY, G. A. (1955). *The psychology of personal constructs.* New York: Norton.

KELLY, G. A. (1958). Man's construction of his alternatives. In G. Lindzey (Ed.), *Assessment of human motives* (pp. 33–64). New York: Holt, Rinehart & Winston.

KELLY, G. A. (1961). Suicide: The personal construct point of view. In N. L. Faberow & E. S. Schneidman (Eds.), *The cry for help* (pp. 255–280). New York: McGraw-Hill.

KELLY, G. A. (1964). The language of hypothesis: Man's psychological instrument. *Journal of Individual Psychology, 20,* 137–152.

KELLY, G. A. (1969). *Clinical psychology and personality: The selected papers of George Kelly.* New York: Wiley.

KENNY, D. A., ALBRIGHT, L., MALLOY, T. E., & KASHY, D. A. (1994). Consensus in interpersonal perception: Acquaintance and the Big Five. *Psychological Bulletin, 116,* 245–258.

KENRICK, D. T., & FUNDER, D. C. (1988). Profiting from controversy: Lessons from the person–situation debate. *American Psychologist, 43,* 23–34.

KENRICK, D. T., SADALLA, E. K., GROTH, G., & TROST, M. R. (1990). Evolution, traits, and the stages of human courtship: Qualifying the parental investment model. *Journal of Personality, 58,* 97–116.

KIHLSTROM, J. F. (1990). The psychological unconscious. In L. A. Pervin (Ed.), *Handbook of personality: Theory and research* (pp. 445–464). New York: Guilford Press.

KIHLSTROM, J. F., BARNHARDT, T. M., & TATARYN, D. J. (1992). The cognitive perspective. In R. F. Bornstein & T. S. Pittman (Eds.), *Perception without awareness,* (pp. 17–54). New York: Guilford Press.

KIRKPATRICK, L. A., & DAVIS, K. E. (1994). Attachment style, gender, and relationship stability: A longitudinal analysis. *Journal of Personality and Social Psychology, 66,* 502–512.

Kirschenbaum, H. (1979). *On becoming Carl Rogers*. New York: Delacorte.

Kitiyama, S., & Markus, H. (Eds.) (1994). *Emotion and culture*. Washington, D.C.: American Psychological Association.

Kleinmuntz, B. (1967). *Personality measurement*. Homewood, Ill. : Dorsey.

Koestner, R., & McClelland, D. C. (1990). Perspectives on competence motivation. In L. A. Pervin (Ed.), *Handbook of personality: Theory and research* (pp. 527–548). New York: Guilford Press.

Kohut, H. (1977). *The restoration of the self*. New York: International Universities Press.

Kohut, H. (1984). *How does analysis cure?* Chicago: University of Chicago Press.

Krasner, L. (1971). The operant approach in behavior therapy. In A. E. Bergin & S. L. Garfield (Eds.), *Handbook of psychotherapy and behavior change* (pp. 612–652). New York: Wiley.

Kris, E. (1944). Danger and morale. *American Journal of Orthopsychiatry, 14*, 147–155.

Krosnick, J. A., Betz, A. L., Jussim, L. J., & Lynn, A. R. (1992). Subliminal conditioning of attitudes. *Journal of Personality and Social Psychology, 18*, 152–162.

Kuhn, T. S. (1970). *The structure of scientific revolutions*, 2nd ed. Chicago: University of Chicago Press.

Kunda, Z. (1990). The case for motivated reasoning. *Psychological Bulletin, 108*, 480–498.

Landfield, A. W. (1971). *Personal construct systems in psychotherapy*. Chicago: Rand McNally.

Landfield, A. W. (1982). A construction of fragmentation and unity. In J. C. Mancuso & J. R. Adams-Webber (Eds.), *The construing person* (pp. 198–221). New York: Praeger.

Lau, R. R. (1982). Origins of health locus of control beliefs. *Journal of Personality and Social Psychology, 42*, 322–324.

Lazarus, A. A. (1965). Behavior therapy, incomplete treatment and symptom substitution. *Journal of Nervous and Mental Disease, 140*, 80–86.

Lazarus, R. S. (1990). Theory-based stress measurement. *Psychological Inquiry, 1*, 3–13.

Lazarus, R. S. (1993). From psychological stress to the emotions: A history of changing outlooks. *Annual Review of Psychology, 44*, 1–21.

Lecky, P. (1945). *Self-consistency: A theory of personality*. New York: Island.

Lehman, D. R., & Taylor, S. E. (1987). Date with an earthquake: Coping with a probable, unpredictable disaster. *Personality and Social Psychology Bulletin, 13*, 546–555.

Lepper, M. R., Greene, D., & Nisbett, R. E. (1973). Undermining children's intrinsic interest with extrinsic rewards: A test of the "overjustification" hypothesis. *Journal of Personality and Social Psychology, 28*, 129–137.

Lester, D., Hvezda, J., Sullivan, S., & Plourde, R. (1983). Maslow's hierarchy of needs and psychological health. *Journal of General Psychology, 109*, 83–85.

Levinson, D. J., Darrow, C. N., Klein, E. B., Levinson, M. L., & McKee, B. (1978). *The seasons of a man's life*. New York: Knopf.

Levis, D. J., & Malloy, P. F. (1982). Research in infrahuman and human conditioning. In G. T. Wilson & C. M. Franks (Eds.), *Contemporary behavior therapy: Conceptual and empirical foundations* (pp. 65–118). New York: Guilford Press.

Levy, S. M. (1984). The expression of affect and its biological correlates: Mediating mechanisms of behavior and disease. In C. Van Dyke, L. Temoshok, & L. S. Zegans (Eds.), *Emotions in health and illness*. New York: Grune & Stratton.

Levy, S. (1991). Personality as a host risk factor: Enthusiasm, evidence and their interaction. *Psychological Inquiry, 2*, 254–257.

Lewis, M. (1995). *Unavoidable accidents and chance encounters*. New York: Guilford Press.

Lewis, M., & Brooks-Gunn, J. (1979). *Social cognition and the acquisition of self*. New York: Plenum.

Lewis, M., Feiring, C., McGuffog, C., & Jaskir, J. (1984). Predicting psychopathology in six year olds from early social relations. *Child Development, 55*, 123–136.

Liddell, H. S. (1944). Conditioned reflex method and experimental neurosis. In J. McV. Hunt (Ed.), *Personality and the behavior disorders* (pp. 389–412). New York: Ronald Press.

LOEHLIN, J. C. (1982). Rhapsody in G. *Contemporary Psychology, 27,* 623.

LOEHLIN, J. C. (1992). *Genes and environment in personality development.* Newbury Park, CA: Sage.

LOEVINGER, J. (1976). *Ego development: Conceptions and theories.* San Francisco: Jossey-Bass.

LOEVINGER, J. (1985). Revision of the Sentence Completion Test for ego development. *Journal of Personality and Social Psychology, 48,* 420–427.

LOEVINGER, J. (1993). Measurement in personality: True or false. *Psychological Inquiry, 4,* 1–16.

LOEVINGER, J., & KNOLL, E. (1983). Personality: Stages, traits, and the self. *Annual Review of Psychology, 34,* 195–222.

LOEVINGER, J., & WESSLER, R. (1970). *Measuring ego development: Vol. 1 Construction and use of a sentence completion test.* San Francisco: Jossey-Bass.

LOFTUS, E. F. (1993). The reality of repressed memories. *American Psychologist, 48,* 518–537.

LONDON, P. (1972). The end of ideology in behavior modification. *American Psychologist, 27,* 913–920.

LYKKEN, D. T. (1971). Multiple factor analysis and personality research. *Journal of Experimental Research in Personality, 5,* 161–170.

MACKENZIE, K. R. (1994). Using personality measurements in clinical practice. In P. T. Costa, Jr. & T. A. Widiger (Eds.), *Personality disorders and the five-factor model of personality* (pp. 237–250). Washington, D.C.: American Psychological Association.

MACLEOD, R. B. (1964). Phenomenology: A challenge to experimental psychology. In T. W. Wann (Ed.), *Behaviorism and phenomenology* (pp. 47–73). Chicago: University of Chicago Press.

MADISON, P. (1961). *Freud's concept of repression and defence: Its theoretical and observational language.* Minneapolis: University of Minnesota Press.

MAGNUSSON, D., & ENDLER, N. S. (Eds.) (1977). *Personality at the crossroads: Current issues in interactional psychology.* Hillsdale, N.J.: Erlbaum.

MANCUSO, J. C., & ADAMS-WEBBER, J. R. (Eds.) (1982). *The construing person.* New York: Praeger.

MARCIA, J. (1994). Ego identity and object relations. In J. M. Masling & R. F. Bornstein (Eds.), *Empirical perspectives on object relations theory,* (pp. 59–104). Washington, D.C.: American Psychological Association.

MARKUS, H. (1977). Self-schemata and processing information about the self. *Journal of Personality and Social Psychology, 35,* 63–78.

MARKUS, H. (1983). Self-knowledge: An expanded view. *Journal of Personality, 51,* 543–565.

MARKUS, H., & CROSS, S. (1990). The interpersonal self. In L. A. Pervin (Ed.), *Handbook of personality: Theory and research* (pp. 576–608). New York: Guilford Press.

MARKUS, H., & KITAYAMA, S. (1991). Culture and the self: Implications for cognition, emotion, and motivation. *Psychological Review, 98,* 224–253.

MARKUS, H., & NURIUS, P., (1986). Possible selves. *American Psychologist, 41,* 954–969.

MARKUS, H., & RUVOLO, A. (1989). Possible selves: Personalized representations of goals. In L. A. Pervin (Ed.), *Goal concepts in personality and social psychology* (pp. 211–241). Hillsdale, N. J. : Erlbaum.

MARLATT, G. A., BAER, J. S., & QUIGLEY, L. A. (1995). Self-efficacy and addictive behavior. In A. Bandura (Ed.), *Self-efficacy in changing societies* (pp. 289–315). New York: Cambridge.

MARLATT, G. A., & GORDON, J. R. (1980). Determinants of relapse: Implications for the maintenance of behavior change. In P. O. Davidson & S. M. Davidson (Eds.), *Behavioral medicine: Changing health lifestyles.* New York: Brunner/Mazel.

MASLOW, A. H. (1954). *Motivation and personality.* New York: Harper.

MASLOW, A. H. (1968). *Toward a psychology of being.* Princeton, N. J. : Van Nostrand.

MASLOW, A. H. (1971). *The farther reaches of human nature.* New York: Viking.

MAY, R. (1950). *The meaning of anxiety.* New York: Ronald Press.

MAYO, C. W., & CROCKETT, W. H. (1964). Cognitive complexity and primacy; recency effects in impression formation. *Journal of Abnormal and Social Psychology, 68,* 335–338.

McAdams, D. P. (1992). The five-factor model in personality: A critical appraisal. *Journal of Personality, 60,* 329–361.

McCoy, M. M. (1981). Positive and negative emotion: A personal construct theory interpretation. In H. Bonarius, R. Holland, & S. Rosenberg (Eds.), *Personal construct psychology: Recent advances in theory and practice* (pp. 96–104). London: Macmillan.

McCrae, R. R. (1994). New goals for trait psychology. *Psychological Inquiry, 5,* 148–153.

McCrae, R. R., & Costa, P. T. (1987). Validation of the five-factor model of personality across instruments and observers. *Journal of Personality and Social Psychology, 52,* 81–90.

McCrae, R. R., & Costa, P. T., Jr. (1990). *Personality in adulthood.* New York: Guilford Press.

McCrae, R. R., & Costa, P. T., Jr. (1994). The stability of personality: Observations and evaluations. *Current Directions in Psychological Science, 3,* 173–175.

McCrae, R. R., & John, O. P. (1992). An introduction to the five-factor model and its applications. *Journal of Personality, 60,* 175–215.

McGinnies, E. (1949). Emotionality and perceptual defense. *Psychological Review, 56,* 244–251.

McGuire, W. J. (1967). Some impending reorientations in social psychology: Some thoughts provoked by Kenneth Ring. *Journal of Experimental Social Psychology, 3,* 124–139.

McNulty, S. E., & Swann, W. B. Jr. (1994). Identity negotiation in roommate relationships: The self as architect and consequence of social reality. *Journal of Personality and Social Psychology, 67,* 1012–1023.

McPherson, D. A. (1990). *Order out of chaos: The autobiographical works of Maya Angelou.* New York: Peter Lang Publishing.

Medinnus, G. R., & Curtis, F. J. (1963). The relation between maternal self-acceptance and child acceptance. *Journal of Consulting Psychology, 27,* 542–544.

Meichenbaum, D. (1985). *Stress inoculation training.* New York: Pergamon.

Meichenbaum, D. (1995). Cognitive-behavioral therapy in historical perspective. In B. Bongar & L. E. Bentler (Eds.), *Comprehensive textbook of psychotherapy* (pp. 140–158). New York: Oxford University Press.

Mikulciner, M., Florain, V., & Weller, A. (1993). Attachment styles, coping strategies, and posttraumatic psychological distress: The impact of the Gulf War in Israel. *Journal of Personality and Social Psychology, 64,* 817–826.

Milgram, S. (1965). Some conditions of obedience and disobedience to authority. *Human Relations, 18,* 57–76.

Miller, G. Quoted in *The New York Times,* November 12, 1982, page C1.

Miller, N. E. (1951). Comments on theoretical models: Illustrated by the development of a theory of conflict behavior. *Journal of Personality, 20,* 82–100.

Miller, N. E. (1978). Biofeedback and visceral learning. *Annual Review of Psychology, 29,* 373–404.

Miller, N. E. (1983). Behavioral medicine: Symbiosis between laboratory and clinic. *Annual Review of Psychology, 34,* 1–31.

Miller, N. E., & Dollard, J. (1941). *Social learning and imitation.* New Haven, Conn.: Yale University Press.

Miller, S. M., & Mangan, C. E. (1983). Interacting effects of information and coping style in adapting to gynecologic stress: Should the doctor tell all? *Journal of Personality and Social Psychology, 45,* 223–236.

Miller, S. M., Shoda, Y., & Hurley, K. (1996). Applying cognitive-social theory to health-protective behavior: Breast self-examination in cancer screening. *Psychological Bulletin, 119,* 70–94.

Miller, T. R. (1991). Personality: A clinician's experience. *Journal of Personality Assessment, 57,* 415–433.

Mineka, S., Davidson, M., Cook, M., & Kleir, R. (1984). Observational conditioning of snake fear in rhesus monkeys. *Journal of Abnormal Psychology, 93,* 355–372.

Mischel, W. (1968). *Personality and assessment.* New York: Wiley.

Mischel, W. (1971). *Introduction to personality.* New York: Holt, Rinehart & Winston.

MISCHEL, W. (1973). Toward a cognitive social learning reconceptualization of personality. *Psychological Review, 80,* 252–283.

MISCHEL, W. (1976). *Introduction to personality.* New York: Holt, Rinehart & Winston.

MISCHEL, W. (1990). Personality dispositions revisited and revised: A view after three decades. In L. A. Pervin (Ed.), *Handbook of personality: Theory and research* (pp. 111–134). New York: Guilford Press.

MISCHEL, W. (1996). From good intentions to willpower. In P. M. Gollwitzer & J. A. Bargh (Eds.), *The psychology of action* (pp. 197–218). New York: Guilford Press.

MISCHEL, W., & LIEBERT, R. M. (1966). Effects of discrepancies between observed and imposed reward criteria on their acquisition and transmission. *Journal of Personality and Social Psychology, 3,* 45–53.

MISCHEL, W., & PEAKE, P. K. (1982). Beyond déjà vu in the search for cross-situational consistency. *Psychological Review, 89,* 730–755.

MISCHEL, W., & PEAKE, P. K. (1983). Analyzing the construction of consistency in personality. In M. M. Page (Ed.), *Personality: Current theory and research* (pp. 233–262). Lincoln: University of Nebraska Press.

MISCHEL, W., & SHODA, Y. (1995). A cognitive-affective system theory of personality: Reconceptualizing the invariances in personality and the role of situations. *Psychological Review, 102,* 246–286.

MONSON, T. C., HESLEY, J. W., & CHERNICK, L. (1982). Specifying when personality traits can and cannot predict behavior: An alternative to abandoning the attempt to predict single-act criteria. *Journal of Personality and Social Psychology, 43,* 385–399.

MOORE, M. K., & NEIMEYER, R. A. (1991). A confirmatory factor analysis of the threat index. *Journal of Personality and Social Psychology, 60,* 122–129.

MORGAN, M. (1985). Self-monitoring of attained subgoals in private study. *Journal of Educational Psychology, 77,* 623–630.

MOROKOFF, P. J. (1985). Effects of sex, guilt, repression, sexual "arousability," and sexual experience on female sexual arousal during erotica and fantasy. *Journal of Personality and Social Psychology, 49,* 177–187.

MORRIS, M. W., & PENG, K. (1994). Culture and cause: American and Chinese attributions for social and physical events. *Journal of Personality and Social Psychology, 67,* 949–971.

MORRISON, J. K., & COMETA, M. C. (1982). Variations in developing construct systems: The experience corollary. In J. C. Mancusco & J. R. Adams-Webber (Eds.), *The construing person* (pp. 152–169). New York: Praeger.

MOSS, P. D., & MCEVEDY, C. P. (1966). An epidemic of over-breathing among school-girls. *British Medical Journal,* 1295–1300.

MOWRER, O. H., & MOWRER, W. A. (1928). Enuresis: A method for its study and treatment. *American Journal of Orthopsychiatry, 8,* 436–447.

MURRAY, H. A. (1938). *Explorations in personality.* New York: Oxford University Press.

NATHAN, P. E. (1985). Aversion therapy in the treatment of alcoholism: Success and failure. *Annals of the New York Academy of Sciences, 443,* 357–364.

NEIMEYER, G. J. (1992). Back to the future with the psychology of personal constructs. *Contemporary Psychology, 37,* 994–997.

NEIMEYER, R. A. (1994). *Death anxiety handbook: Research, instrumentation, and application.* Washington, D. C. : Taylor & Francis.

NEIMEYER, R. A., & NEIMEYER, G. J. (Eds.) (1992). *Advances in personal construct psychology* (Vol. 2). Greenwich, Conn.: JAI Press.

NESSELROADE, J. R., & DELHEES, K. H. (1966). Methods and findings in experimentally based personality theory. In R. B. Cattell (Ed.), *Handbook of multivariate experimental psychology.* (pp. 563–610). Chicago: Rand McNally.

NISBETT, R., & ROSS, L. (1980). *Human inference: Strategies and shortcomings of social judgment.* Englewood Cliffs, N. J. : Prentice Hall.

NISBETT, R. E., & WILSON, T. D. (1977). Telling more than we know: Verbal reports on mental processes. *Psychological Review, 84,* 231–279.

NORMAN, D. A. (1980). Twelve issues for cognitive science. *Cognitive Science, 4,* 1–32.

NORMAN, W. T. (1963). Toward an adequate taxonomy of personality attributes. *Journal of Abnormal and Social Psychology, 66*, 574–583.

OGILVIE, D. M. (1987). The undesired self: A neglected variable in personality research. *Journal of Personality and Social Psychology, 52*, 379–385.

OHMAN, A., & SOARES, J. F. (1993). On the automaticity of phobic fear: Conditional skin conductance responses to masked phobic stimuli. *Journal of Abnormal Psychology, 102*, 121–132.

O'LEARY, A. (1990). Stress, emotion, and human immune function. *Psychological Bulletin, 108*, 363–382.

O'LEARY, A. (1992). Self-efficacy and health: Behavioral and stress-physiological mediation. *Cognitive Therapy and Research, 16*, 229–245.

O'LEARY, A., SHOOR, S., LORIG, K., & HOLMAN, H. R. (1988). A cognitive-behavioral treatment of rheumatoid arthritis. *Health Psychology, 7*, 527–544.

O'LEARY, K. D. (1972). The assessment of psychopathology in children. In H. C. Quay & J. S. Werry (Eds.), *Psychopathological disorders of childhood* (pp. 234–272). New York: Wiley.

ORNE, M. T. (1962). On the social psychology of the psychological experiment: With particular reference to demand characteristics and their implications. *American Psychologist, 17*, 776–783.

OSGOOD, C. E., & LURIA, Z. (1954). A blind analysis of a case of multiple personality using the semantic differential. *Journal of Abnormal and Social Psychology, 49*, 579–591.

OSGOOD, C. E., SUCI, G. J., & TANNENBAUM, P. H. (1957). *The measurement of meaning*. Urbana, Ill.: University of Illinois Press.

OZER, E., & BANDURA, A. (1990). Mechanisms governing empowerment effects: A self-efficacy analysis. *Journal of Personality and Social Psychology, 58*, 472–486.

PATTON, C. J. (1992). Fear of abandonment and binge eating. *Journal of Nervous and Mental Disease, 180*, 484–490.

PAULHUS, D. L. (1990). Measurement and control of response bias. In J. P. Robinson, P. R. Shaver, & L. Wrightsman (Eds.), *Measures of personality and social-psychological attitudes* (pp. 17–59). San Diego: Academic Press.

PAVLOV, I. P. (1927). *Conditioned reflexes*. London: Oxford University Press.

PENNEBAKER, J. W. (1985). Traumatic experience and psychosomatic disease: Exploring the roles of behavioral inhibition, obsession, and confiding. *Canadian Psychology, 26*, 82–95.

PENNEBAKER, J. W. (1990). *Opening up: The healing powers of confiding in others*. New York: Morrow.

PERVIN, L. A. (1960a). Rigidity in neurosis and general personality functioning. *Journal of Abnormal and Social Psychology, 61*, 389–395.

PERVIN, L. A. (1960b). Existentialism, psychotherapy, and psychology. *American Psychologist, 15*, 305–309.

PERVIN, L. A. (1964). Predictive strategies and the need to confirm them: Some notes on pathological types of decisions. *Psychological Reports, 15*, 99–105.

PERVIN, L. A. (1967a). A twenty-college study of Student/College interaction using TAPE (Transactional Analysis of Personality and Environment): Rationale, reliability, and validity. *Journal of Educational Psychology, 58*, 290–302.

PERVIN, L. A. (1967b). Satisfaction and perceived self-environment similarity: A semantic differential study of student–college interaction. *Journal of Personality, 35*, 623–634.

PERVIN, L. A. (1976). A free-response description approach to the analysis of person–situation interaction. *Journal of Personality and Social Psychology, 34*, 465–474.

PERVIN, L. A. (1978). *Current controversies and issues in personality*. New York: Wiley. (Second edition, 1984.)

PERVIN, L. A. (1983). Idiographic approaches to personality. In J. McV. Hunt & N. Endler (Eds.), *Personality and the behavior disorders* (pp. 261–282). New York: Wiley.

PERVIN, L. A. (1985). Personality: Current controversies, issues, and directions. *Annual Review of Psychology, 36*, 83–114.

PERVIN, L. A. (1988). Affect and addiction. *International Journal of Addictive Behaviors, 13*, 83–86.

PERVIN, L. A. (1990). A brief history of modern personality theory. In L. A. Pervin (Ed.), *Handbook of personality: Theory and research* (pp. 3–18). New York: Guilford Press.

PERVIN, L. A. (1994a). A critical analysis of current trait theory. *Psychological Inquiry, 5,* 103–113.

PERVIN, L. A. (1994b). Personality stability, personality change, and the question of process. In T. Heatherton & J. Weinberger (Eds.), *Can personality change?* (pp. 315–330). Washington, D.C.: American Psychological Association.

PERVIN, L. A. (1996). *The science of personality.* New York: Wiley.

PERVIN, L. A., & LEWIS, M. (Eds.) (1978). *Perspectives in interactional psychology.* New York: Plenum.

PETERSON, C. (1991). The meaning and measurement of explanatory style. *Psychological Inquiry, 2,* 1–10.

PETERSON, C. (1995). Explanatory style and health. In G. M. Buchanan & M. E. P. Seligman (Eds.), *Explanatory style* (pp. 233–246). Hillsdale, N.J.: Erlbaum.

PETERSON, C., MAIER, S. F., & SELIGMAN, M. E. P. (1993). *Learned helplessness: A theory for the age of personal control.* New York: Oxford University Press.

PETERSON, C., SCHWARTZ, S. M., & SELIGMAN, M. E. P. (1981). Self-blame and depressive symptoms. *Journal of Personality and Social Psychology, 41,* 253–259.

PETERSON, C., & SELIGMAN, M. E. P. (1984). Causal explanations as a risk factor for depression: Theory and evidence. *Psychological Review, 91,* 347–374.

PETERSON, C., SEMMEL, A., VON BAEYER, C., ABRAMSON, L. Y., METALSKY, G. I., & SELIGMAN, M. E. P. (1982). The Attributional Style Questionnaire. *Cognitive Therapy and Research, 6,* 287–300.

PFUNGST, O. (1911). Clever Hans: *A contribution to experimental, animal, and human psychology.* New York: Holt, Rinehart & Winston.

PLOMIN, R. (1994). *Genetics and experience: The interplay between nature and nurture.* Newbury Park, Calif.: Sage.

PLOMIN, R., & BERGEMAN, C. S. (1991). The nature of nurture: Genetic influence on "environmental" measures. *Behavioral and Brain Sciences, 14,* 373–385.

PLOMIN, R., CHIPUER, H. M., & LOEHLIN, J. C. (1990). Behavioral genetics and personality. In L. A. Pervin (Ed.), *Handbook of personality: Theory and research* (pp. 225–243). New York: Guilford Press.

PLOMIN, R., CHIPUER, H. M., & NEIDERHISER, J. M. (1994). Behavioral genetic evidence for the importance of nonshared environment. In E. M. Hetherington, D. Reiss, & R. Plomin (Eds.), *Separate social worlds of siblings: The impact of nonshared environment on development* (pp. 1–31). Hillsdale, N.J.: Erlbaum.

PLOMIN, R., & DANIELS, D. (1987). Why are children in the same family so different from each other? *Behavioral and Brain Sciences, 10,* 1–16.

POCH, S. M. (1952). *A study of changes in personal constructs as related to interpersonal prediction and its outcomes.* Unpublished Ph.D. dissertation, Ohio State University.

POWELL, R. A., & BOER, D. P. (1994). Did Freud mislead patients to confabulate memories of abuse? *Psychological Reports, 74,* 1283–1298.

POWER, M. J., & CHAMPION, L. A. (1986). Cognitive approaches to depression: A theoretical critique. *British Journal of Clinical Psychology, 25,* 201–212.

PSYCHOLOGICAL INQUIRY. (1991). Commentaries. *2,* 11–49.

RASKIN, R., & HALL, C. S. (1979). A narcissistic personality inventory. *Psychological Reports, 45,* 590.

RASKIN, R., & HALL, C. S. (1981). The Narcissistic Personality Inventory: Alternate form reliability and further evidence of construct validity. *Journal of Personality Assessment, 45,* 159–162.

RASKIN, R., & SHAW, R. (1987). *Narcissism and the use of personal pronouns.* Unpublished manuscript.

RASKIN, R., & TERRY, H. (1987). *A factor-analytic study of the Narcissistic Personality Inventory and further evidence of its construct validity.* Unpublished manuscript.

RAZRAN, G. (1939). A quantitative study of meaning by a conditioned salivary technique. *Science, 90,* 89–91.

RETTEW, D., & REIVICH, K. (1995). Sports and explanatory style. In G. M. Buchanan & M. E. P. Seligman (Eds.), *Explanatory style* (pp. 173–186). Hillsdale, N.J.: Erlbaum.

REYNOLDS, G. S. (1968). *A primer of operant conditioning*. Glenview, Ill. : Scott, Foresman.

RHODEWALT, F., & MORF, C. C. (1995). Self and interpersonal correlates of the Narcissistic Personality Inventory: A review and new findings. *Journal of Research in Personality, 29*, 1–23.

ROBERTS, J. A., GOTLIB, I. H., & KASSEL, I. D. (1996). Adult attachment security and symptoms of depression: The mediating roles of dysfunctional attitudes and low self-esteem. *Journal of Personality and Social Psychology, 70*, 310–320.

ROBINS, C. J., & HAYES, A. M. (1993). An appraisal of cognitive therapy. *Journal of Consulting and Clinical Psychology, 61*, 205–214.

ROBINS, C. J., & HAYES, A. M. (1995). The role of causal attributions in the prediction of depression. In G. M. Buchanan & M. E. P. Seligman (Eds.), *Explanatory style* (pp. 71–97). Hillsdale, N.J.: Erlbaum.

ROBINS, R. W., CRAIK, K. H., & GOSLING, S. D. (1995). The rise and fall of contemporary schools in psychology: Moving beyond speculation. Manuscript submitted for publication.

ROBINS, R. W., & JOHN, O. P. (1995). Self-perception, visual perspective, and narcissism: Is seeing believing? Manuscript submitted for publication.

ROBINS, R. W., & JOHN, O. P. (1996). The quest for self-insight: Theory and research on the accuracy of self-perception. In R. Hogan, J. Johnson, & S. Briggs (Eds.), *Handbook of personality psychology*. New York: Academic Press.

ROBINS, R. W., JOHN, O. P. & CASPI, A. (1994). Major dimensions of personality in early adolescence: The Big Five and beyond. In C. F. Halverson, G. A. Kohnstamm, & R. P. Martin (Eds.), *The developing structure of temperament and personality from infancy to adulthood* (pp. 267–291). Hillsdale, N.J.: Erlbaum.

ROBINS, R. W., JOHN, O. P., CASPI, A., MOFFITT, T. E., & STOUTHAMER-LOEBER, M. (1996). Resilient, overcontrolled, and undercontrolled boys: Three replicable personality types. *Journal of Personality and Social Psychology*, in press.

ROGERS, C. R. (1942). *Counseling and psychotherapy*. Boston: Houghton Mifflin.

ROGERS, C. R. (1946). Significant aspects of client-centered therapy. In H. M. Ruitenbeck (Ed.), *Varieties of personality theory* (pp. 168–183). New York: Dutton. (Originally published in 1946.)

ROGERS, C. R. (1947). Some observations on the organization of personality. *American Psychologist, 2*, 358–368.

ROGERS, C. R. (1951). *Client-centered therapy*. Boston: Houghton Mifflin.

ROGERS, C. R. (1954). The case of Mrs. Oak: A research analysis. In C. R. Rogers & R. F. Dymond (Eds.), *Psychotherapy and personality change* (pp. 259–348). Chicago: University of Chicago Press.

ROGERS, C. R. (1956). Some issues concerning the control of human behavior. *Science, 124*, 1057–1066.

ROGERS, C. R. (1959). A theory of therapy, personality, and interpersonal relationships as developed in the client-centered framework. In S. Koch (Ed.), *Psychology: A study of science* (pp. 184–256). New York: McGraw-Hill.

ROGERS, C. R. (1961). *On becoming a person*. Boston: Houghton Mifflin.

ROGERS, C. R. (1963). The actualizing tendency in relation to "motives" and to consciousness. In M. R. Jones (Ed.), *Nebraska symposium on motivation* (pp. 1–24). Lincoln: University of Nebraska Press.

ROGERS, C. R. (1964). Toward a science of the person. In T. W. Wann (Ed.), *Behaviorism and phenomenology* (pp. 109–133). Chicago: University of Chicago Press.

ROGERS, C. R. (1966). Client-centered therapy. In S. Arieti (Ed.), *American handbook of psychiatry* (pp. 183–200). New York: Basic Books.

ROGERS, C. R. (Ed.) (1967). *The therapeutic relationship and its impact: A study of psychotherapy with schizophrenics*. Madison: University of Wisconsin Press.

ROGERS, C. R. (1970). *On encounter groups*. New York: Harper.

ROGERS, C. R. (1972). *Becoming partners: Marriage and its alternatives*. New York: Delacorte Press.

ROGERS, C. R. (1977). *Carl Rogers on personal power*. New York: Delacorte Press.

ROGERS, C. R. (1980). *A way of being*. Boston: Houghton Mifflin.

ROLAND, A. (1988). *In search of self in India and Japan*. Princeton, N. J. : Princeton University Press.

ROSCH, E., MERVIS, C., GRAY, W., JOHNSON, D., & BOYES-BRAEM, P. (1976). Basic objects in natural categories. *Cognitive Psychology, 8*, 382–439.

ROSENBERG, S. (1980). A theory in search of its zeitgeist. *Contemporary Psychology, 25*, 898–900.

ROSENTHAL, R. (1994). Interpersonal expectancy effects: A 30–year perspective. *Current Directions in Psychological Science, 3*, 176–179.

ROSENTHAL, R., & RUBIN, D. (1978). Interpersonal expectancy effects: The first 345 studies. *Behavioral and Brain Sciences, 3*, 377–415.

ROSENTHAL, T., & BANDURA, A. (1978). Psychological modeling: Theory and practice. In S. L. Garfield & A. E. Bergin (Eds.), *Handbook of psychotherapy and behavior change* (pp. 621–658). New York: Wiley.

ROSENZWEIG, S. (1941). Need-persistive and ego-defensive reactions to frustration as demonstrated by an experiment on repression. *Psychological Review, 48*, 347–349.

ROTHBARD, J. C. & SHAVER, P. R. (1994). Continuity of attachment across the life-span. In M. B, Sperling & W. H. Berman (Eds.), *Attachment in adults: Clinical and developmental perspectives* (pp. 31–71). New York: Guilford Press.

ROTTER, J. B. (1966). Generalized expectancies for internal versus external control of reinforcement. *Psychological Monographs, 80* (Whole No. 609).

ROTTER, J. B. (1982). *The development and application of social learning theory*. New York: Praeger.

ROWE, D. C. (1987). Resolving the person–situation debate. *American Psychologist, 42*, 218–227.

ROWE, D. C. (1994). *The limits of family influence*. New York: Guilford Press.

ROZIN, P., & ZELLNER, D. (1985). The role of Pavlovian conditioning in the acquisition of food likes and dislikes. *Annals of the New York Academy of Sciences, 443*, 189–202.

RUSHTON, J. P., & ERDLE, S. (1987). Evidence for aggressive (and delinquent) personality. *British Journal of Social Psychology, 26*, 87–89.

SANDERSON, C., & CLARKIN, J. F. (1994). Use of the NEO-PI personality dimensions in differential treatment planning. In P. T. Costa, Jr. & T. A. Widiger (Eds.), *Personality disorders and the five-factor model of personality* (pp. 219–236). Washington, D.C.: American Psychological Association.

SCARR, S. (1992). Developmental theories for the 1990s: Development and individual differences. *Child Development, 63*, 1–19.

SCHACHTER, S., & SINGER, J. (1962). Cognitive, social, and physiological determinants of emotional state. *Psychological Review, 69*, 379–399.

SCHAFER, R. (1954). *Psychoanalytic interpretation in Rorschach testing*. New York: Grune & Stratton.

SCHAFER, R. (1984). The pursuit of failure and the idealization of unhappiness. *American Psychologist, 39*, 398–405.

SCHANK, R., & ABELSON, R. (1977). *Scripts, plans, goals, and understanding*. Hillsdale, N.J.: Erlbaum.

SCHEIER, M. F., & CARVER, C. S. (1985). Optimism, coping, and health: Assessment and implications of generalized outcome expectancies. *Health Psychology, 4*, 219–247.

SCHEIER, M. F., & CARVER, C. S. (1987). Dispositional optimism and physical well-being: The influence of generalized outcome expectancies on health. *Journal of Personality, 55*, 169–210.

SCHNEIDER, D. J. (1982). Personal construct psychology: An international menu. *Contemporary Psychology, 27*, 712–713.

SCHNEIDER, J. A., O'LEARY, A., & AGRAS, W. S. The role of perceived self-efficacy in recovery from bulimia: A preliminary examination. *Behavior Research and Therapy*, in press.

SCHULMAN, P. (1995). Explanatory style and achievement in school and work. In G. M. Buchanan & M. E. P. Seligman (Eds.), *Explanatory style* (pp. 159–172). Hillsdale, N. J. : Erlbaum.

SCHUNK, D. H., & COX, P. D. (1986). Strategy training and attributional feedback with learning disabled students. *Journal of Educational Psychology, 1986, 78*, 201–209.

SCHWARZER, R. (Ed.) (1992). *Self-efficacy: Thought control of action*. Washington, D. C. : Hemisphere.

SEARS, R. R., RAU, L., & ALPERT, R. (1965). *Identification and child-rearing*. Stanford, Calif. : Stanford University Press.

SECHREST, L. (1963). The psychology of personal constructs. In J. M. Wepman & R. W. Heine (Eds.), *Concepts of personality* (pp. 206–233). Chicago: Aldine.

SECHREST, L., & JACKSON, D. N. (1961). Social intelligence and accuracy of interpersonal predictions. *Journal of Personality, 29*, 167–182.

SEGAL, Z. V., & DOBSON, K. S. (1992). Cognitive models of depression: Report from a consensus development conference. *Psychological Inquiry, 3*, in press.

SELIGMAN, M. E. P. (1975). *Helplessness*. San Francisco: Freeman.

SELIGMAN, M. E. P. (1991). *Learned optimism*. New York: Knopf.

SELIGMAN, M. E. P. (1992). Power and powerlessness: Comments on "cognates of personal control." *Applied and Preventive Psychology, 1*, 119–120.

SHEDLER, J., MAYMAN, M., & MANIS, M. (1993). The illusion of mental health. *American Psychologist, 48*, 1117–1131.

SHODA, Y., MISCHEL, W., & WRIGHT, J. C. (1994). Intra-individual stability in the organization and patterning of behavior: Incorporating psychological situations into the idiographic analysis of personality. *Journal of Personality and Social Psychology, 67*, 674–687.

SHWEDER, R. A. (1991). *Thinking through cultures: Expeditions in cultural psychology*. Cambridge, Mass.: Harvard University Press.

SIEGEL, S. (1984). Pavlovian conditioning and heroin overdose: Reports by overdose victims. *Bulletin of the Psychonomic Society, 22*, 428–430.

SIEGEL, S., HINSON, R. E., KRANK, M. D., & Mc CULY, J. (1982). Heroin "overdose" death: Contribution of drug-associated environmental cues. *Science, 216*, 436–437.

SIGEL, I. E. (1981). Social experience in the development of representational thought: Distancing theory. In I. E. Sigel, D. Brodzinsky, & R. Golinkoff (Eds.), *New directions in Piagetian theory and practice* (pp. 203–217). Hillsdale, N.J.: Erlbaum.

SILVERMAN, L. H. (1976). Psychoanalytic theory: The reports of its death are greatly exaggerated. *American Psychologist, 31*, 621–637.

SILVERMAN, L. H. (1982). A comment on two subliminal psychodynamic activation studies. *Journal of Abnormal Psychology, 91*, 126–130.

SILVERMAN, L. H., ROSS, D. L., ADLER, J. M., & LUSTIG, D. A. (1978). Simple research paradigm for demonstrating subliminal psychodynamic activation: Effects of oedipal stimuli on dart-throwing accuracy in college men. *Journal of Abnormal Psychology, 87*, 341–357.

SKINNER, B. F. (1948). *Walden two*. New York: Macmillan.

SKINNER, B. F. (1953). *Science and human behavior*. New York: Macmillan.

SKINNER, B. F. (1956). A case history in the scientific method. *American Psychologist, 11*, 221–233.

SKINNER, B. F. (1959). *Cumulative record*. New York: Appleton-Century-Crofts.

SKINNER, B. F. (1967). Autobiography. In E. G. Boring & G. Lindzey (Eds.), *A history of psychology in autobiography* (pp. 385–414).

SKINNER, B. F. (1971). *Beyond freedom and dignity*. New York: Knopf.

SKINNER, B. F. (1990). Can psychology be a science of mind? *American Psychologist, 45*, 1206–1210.

SMITH, R. E. (1989). Effects of coping skills training on generalized self-efficacy and locus of control. *Journal of Personality and Social Psychology, 56*, 228–233.

SPERLING, M. B., & BERMAN, W. H. (Eds.) (1994). *Attachment in adults: Clinical and developmental perspectives*. New York: Guilford Press.

SROUFE, L. A., CARLSON, E., & SHULMAN, S. (1993). Individuals in relationships: Development from infancy. In D. C. Funder, R. D. Parke, C. Tomlinson-Keasey, & K. Widaman (Eds.), *Studying lives through time*, (pp. 315–342). Washington, D.C.: American Psychological Association.

STAATS, A. Q., & BURNS, G. L. (1982). Emotional personality repertoire as cause of behavior: Specification of personality and interaction principles. *Journal of Personality and Social Psychology*, 1982, *43*, 873–886.

STEINER. J. F. (1966). *Treblinka*. New York: Simon & Schuster.

STEPHENSON, W. (1953). *The study of behavior*. Chicago: University of Chicago Press.

STEWART, V., & STEWART, A. (1982). *Business applications of repertory grid*. London: McGraw-Hill.

STRAUMAN, T. J. (1990). Self-guides and emotionally significant childhood memories: A study of retrieval efficiency and incidental negative emotional content. *Journal of Personality and Social Psychology, 59*, 869–880.

STRAUMAN, T. J., LEMIEUX, A. M., & COE, C. L. (1993). Self-discrepancy and natural killer cell activity: Immunological consequences of negative self-evaluation. *Journal of Personality and Social Psychology, 64*, 1042–1052.

STRUBE, M. J. (1990). In search of self: Balancing the good and the true. *Personality and Social Psychology Bulletin, 16*, 699–704.

SUEDFELD, P., & TETLOCK, P. E. (Eds.) (1991). *Psychology and social policy*. New York: Hemisphere.

SUINN, R. M., OSBORNE, D., & WINFREE, P. (1962). The self concept and accuracy of recall of inconsistent self-related information. *Journal of Clinical Psychology, 18*, 473–474.

SULLIVAN, H. S. (1953). *The interpersonal theory of psychiatry*. New York: Norton.

SULLOWAY, F. J. (1979). *Freud: Biologist of the mind*. New York: Basic Books.

SULLOWAY, F. J. (1991). Reassessing Freud's case histories. *ISIS, 82*, 245–275.

SWANN, W. B., JR. (1991). To be adored or to be known? The interplay of self-enhancement and self-verification. In E. T. Higgins & R. M. Sorrentino (Eds.), *Handbook of motivation and cognition* (pp. 408–450). New York: Guilford Press.

SWANN, W. B., JR. (1992). Seeking "truth," finding despair: Some unhappy consequences of a negative self-concept. *Current Directions in Psychological Science, 1*, 15–18.

SWANN, W. B. JR., DE LA RONDE, C., & HIXON, J. G. (1994). Authenticity and positivity strivings in marriage and courtship. *Journal of Personality and Social Psychology, 66*, 857–869.

SWANN, W. B., JR., GRIFFIN, J. J., JR., PREDMORE, S. C., & GAINES, B. (1987). The cognitive–affective crossfire: When self-consistency confronts self-enhancement. *Journal of Personality and Social Psychology, 52*, 881–889.

SWANN, W. B., JR., PELHAM, B. W., & KRULL, D. S. (1989). Agreeable fancy or disagreeable truth? Reconciling self-enhancement and self-verification. *Journal of Personality and Social Psychology, 57*, 782–791.

TAYLOR, S. E. (1982). Social cognition and health. *Personality and Social Psychology Bulletin, 8*, 549–562.

TAYLOR, S. E. (1989). *Positive illusions: Creative self-deception and the healthy mind*. New York: Basic Books.

TAYLOR, S. E., & BROWN, J. D. (1988). Illusion and well-being: Where two roads meet. *Psychological Bulletin, 103*, 193–210.

TAYLOR, S. E., & BROWN, J. D. (1994). Positive illusions and well-being revisited: Separating fact from fiction. *Psychological Bulletin, 116*, 21–27.

TELLEGEN, A. (1993). Folk concepts and psychological concepts of personality and personality disorder. *Psychology and Inquiry, 4*, 122–130.

TELLEGEN, A., LYKKEN, D. T., BOUCHARD, T. J., JR., WILCOX, K. J., SEGAL, N. L., & RICH, S. (1988). Personality similarity in twins reared apart and together. *Journal of Personality and Social Psychology, 54*, 1031–1039.

TEMOSHOK, L. (1985). The relationship of psychosocial factors to prognostic indicators in cutaneous malignant melanoma. *Journal of Psychosomatic Research, 29*, 139–153.

TEMOSHOK, L. (1987). Personality, coping style, emotion and cancer: Towards an integrative model. *Cancer Surveys, 6*, 545–567.

TEMOSHOK, L. (1991). Assessing the assessment of psychosocial factors. *Psychological Inquiry, 2*, 276–280.

TESSER, A., PILKINGTON, C. J., & MCINTOSH, W. D. (1989). Self-evaluation maintenance and the mediational role of emotion: The perception of friends and strangers. *Journal of Personality and Social Psychology, 57*, 442–456.

TETLOCK, P. E., PETERSON, R. S., & BERRY, J. M.

(1993). Flattering and unflattering personality portraits of integratively simple and complex managers. *Journal of Personality and Social Psychology, 64*, 500–511.

TOBACYK, J. J., & DOWNS, A. (1986). Personal construct threat and irrational beliefs as cognitive predictors of increases in musical performance anxiety. *Journal of Personality and Social Psychology, 51*, 779–782.

TOMKINS, S. S. (1962). Commentary. The ideology of research strategies. In S. Messick & J. Ross (Eds.), *Measurement in personality and cognition* (pp. 285–294). New York: Wiley.

TOOBY, J., & COSMIDES, L. (1990). On the universality of human nature and the uniqueness of the individual: The role of genetics and adaptation. *Journal of Personality, 58*, 17–68.

TRIANDIS, H. C. (1989). The self and social behavior in differing cultural contexts. *Psychological Review, 96*, 506–520.

TRIANDIS, H. C., McCUSKER, C., & HUI, C. H. (1990). Multimethod probes of individualism and collectivism. *Journal of Personality and Social Psychology, 59*, 1006–1020.

TVERSKY, A., & KAHNEMAN, D. (1974). Judgment under uncertainty: Heuristics and biases. *Science, 185*, 1124–1131.

VAN KAAM, A. (1966). *Existential foundations of psychology*. Pittsburgh: Duquesne University Press.

VAN LIESHOUT, C. F., & HASELAGER, G. J. (1994). The Big Five personality factors in Q-sort descriptions of children and adolescents. In C. F. Halverson, G. A. Kohnstamm, & R. P. Martin (Eds.), *The developing structure of temperament and personality from infancy to childhood.* (pp. 293–318). Hillsdale, N.J.: Erlbaum.

VERNON, P. E. (1963). *Personality assessment*. New York: Wiley.

WACHTEL, P. L. (1973). Psychodynamics, behavior therapy, and the implacable experimenter: An inquiry into the consistency of personality. *Journal of Abnormal Psychology, 82*, 324–334.

WALLER, N. G., & SHAVER, P. R. (1994). The importance of nongenetic influences on romantic love styles. *Psychological Science, 5*, 268–274.

WALTERS, R. H., & PARKE, R. D. (1964). Influence of the response consequences to a social model on resistance to deviation. *Journal of Experimental Child Psychology, 1*, 269–280.

WARE, A. P., & JOHN, O. P. (1995). Punctuality revisited: Personality, situations, and consistency. Poster presented at the 103rd Annual Meetings of the American Psychological Association, New York, August 11–15, 1995.

WATSON, D., & CLARK, L. A. (1992). On traits and temperament: General and specific factors of emotional experience and their relation to the five-factor model. *Journal of Personality, 60*, 441–476.

WATSON, J. B. (1919). *Psychology from the standpoint of a behaviorist*. Philadelphia: Lippincott.

WATSON, J. B. (1924). *Behaviorism*. New York: People's Institute Publishing.

WATSON, J. B. (1936). Autobiography. In C. Murchison (Ed.), *A history of psychology in autobiography* (pp. 271–282). Worcester, Mass. : Clark University Press.

WATSON, J. B., & RAYNER, R. (1920). Conditioned emotional reactions. *Journal of Experimental Psychology, 3*, 1–14.

WATSON, J. D. (1968). *The double helix*. New York: Atheneum.

WATSON, M. W., & GETZ, K. (1990). The relationship between Oedipal behaviors and children's family role concepts. *Merrill-Palmer Quarterly, 36*, 487–506.

WEBER, S. J., & COOK, T. D. (1972). Subject effects in laboratory research: An examination of subject roles, demand characteristics, and valid inference. *Psychological Bulletin, 77*, 273–295.

WEGNER, D. M. (1992). You can't always think what you want: Problems in the suppression of unwanted thoughts. *Advances in Experimental Social Psychology, 25*, 193–225.

WEGNER, D. M. (1994). Ironic processes of mental control. *Psychological Review, 101*, 34–52.

WEGNER, D. M., SHORTT, G. W., BLAKE, A. W., & PAGE, M. S. (1990). The suppression of exciting thoughts. *Journal of Personality and Social Psychology, 58*, 409–418.

WEINBERG, R. S., GOULD, D., & JACKSON, A. (1979). Expectations and performance: An empirical test of Bandura's self-efficacy theory. *Journal of Sport Psychology, 1*, 320–331.

WEINBERGER, D. A. (1990). The construct reality of the repressive coping style. In J. L. Singer (Ed.), *Repression and dissociation: Implications for personality, psychopathology, and health*, (pp. 337–386). Chicago: University of Chicago Press.

WEINBERGER, D. A., & DAVIDSON, M. N. (1994). Styles of inhibiting emotional expression: Distinguishing repressive coping from impression management. *Journal of Personality, 62*, 587–595.

WEINBERGER, J. (1992). Validating and demystifying subliminal psychodynamic activation. In R. F. Bornstein & T. S. Pittman (Eds.), *Perception without awareness* (pp. 170–188). New York: Guilford Press.

WEINER, B. (1979). A theory of motivation for some classroom experiences. *Journal of Educational Psychology, 71*, 3–25.

WEINER, B. (1990). Attribution in personality psychology. In L. A. Pervin (Ed.), *Handbook of personality: Theory and research* (pp. 465–485). New York: Guilford Press.

WEINER, B. (1993). On sin versus sickness: A theory of perceived responsibility and social motivation. *American Psychologist, 48*, 957–965.

WEINER, B. (1996). Searching for order in social motivation. *Psychological Inquiry, 7*, 1–24.

WHITE, P. (1980). Limitations of verbal reports of internal events: A refutation of Nisbett and Wilson and of Bem. *Psychological Review, 87*, 105–112.

WHITE, R. W. (1959). Motivation reconsidered: The concept of competence. *Psychological Review, 66*, 297–333.

WIDIGER, T. A. (1993). The DSM-III-R categorical personality disorder diagnoses: A critique and an alternative. *Psychological Inquiry, 4*, 75–90.

WIDIGER, T. A., & TRULL, T. J. (1992). Personality and psychopathology: An application of the five-factor model. *Journal of Personality, 60*, 363–395.

WIEDENFELD, S. A., BANDURA, A., LEVINE, S., O'LEARY, A., BROWN, S., & RASKA, K. (1990). Impact of perceived self-efficacy in coping with stressors in components of the immune system. *Journal of Personality and Social Psychology, 59*, 1082–1094.

WIERSON, M. & FOREHAND, R. (1994). Parent behavioral training for child noncompliance: Rationale, concepts and effectiveness. *Current Directions in Psychological Science, 3*, 146–150.

WIGGINS, J. S. (1973). *Personality and prediction: Principles of personality assessment*. New York: Addison-Wesley.

WIGGINS, J. S. (1984). Cattell's system from the perspective of mainstream personality theory. *Multivariate Behavioral Research, 19*, 176–190.

WIGGINS, J. S., PHILLIPS, N., & TRAPNELL, P. (1989). Circular reasoning about interpersonal behavior: Evidence concerning some untested assumptions underlying diagnostic classification. *Journal of Personality and Social Psychology, 56*, 296–305.

WIGGINS, J. S., & PINCUS, A. L. (1994). Personality structure and the structure of personality disorders. In P. T. Costa, Jr., & T. A. Widiger (Eds.), *Personality disorders and the five-factor model of personality* (pp. 73–94). Washington, D.C.: American Psychological Association.

WILLIAMS, L. (1994). Recall of childhood trauma: A prospective study of women's memories of child sexual abuse. *Journal of Consulting and Clinical Psychology, 62*, 1167–1176.

WILLIAMS, S. L. (1992). Perceived self-efficacy and phobic disability. In R. Schwarzer (Ed.), *Self-efficacy: Thought control of action* (pp. 149–176). Washington, D. C. : Hemisphere.

WILSON, T. D. (1994). The proper protocol: Validity and completeness of verbal reports. *Psychological Science, 5*, 249–252.

WILSON, T. D., HULL, J. G., & JOHNSON, J. (1981). Awareness and self-perception: Verbal reports on internal states. *Journal of Personality and Social Psychology, 40*, 53–71.

WILSON, T. D., & LINVILLE, P. W. (1985). Improving the performance of college freshmen with attributional techniques. *Journal of Personality and Social Psychology, 49*, 287–293.

WINTER, D. G. (1992). Content analysis of archival productions, personal documents, and everyday verbal productions. In C. P. Smith (Ed.), *Motivation and personality: Handbook of thematic content analysis* (pp. 110–125). Cambridge, England: Cambridge University Press.

WOLF, S. (1977). "Irrationality" in a psychoanalytic psychology of the self. In T. Mischel (Ed.), *The self: Psychological and philosophical issues* (pp. 203–223). Totowa, N. J. : Rowman & Littlefield.

WOLPE, J. (1961). The systematic desensitization treatment of neuroses. *Journal of Nervous and Mental Disorders, 132,* 189–203.

WOLPE, J., & RACHMAN, S. (1960). Psychoanalytic "evidence." A critique based on Freud's case of Little Hans. *Journal of Nervous and Mental Disease, 130,* 135–148.

WOOD, J. V. (1989). Theory and research concerning social comparison of personal attributes. *Psychological Bulletin, 106,* 231–248.

WOOD, J. V., SALTZBERG, J. A., & GOLDSAMT, L. A. (1990). Does affect induce self-focused attention? *Journal of Personality and Social Psychology, 58,* 899–908.

WYLIE, R. C. (1974). *The self-concept,* rev. ed. Lincoln: University of Nebraska Press.

YANG, K., & BOND, M. H. (1990). Exploring implic-it personality theories with indigenous or important constructs: The Chinese case. *Journal of Personality and Social Psychology, 58,* 1087–1095.

YORK, K. L., & JOHN, O. P. (1992). The four faces of five: A typological analysis of women's personality at midlife. *Journal of Personality and Social Psychology, 51,* 993–1000.

ZIMBARDO, P. G. (1973). On the ethics of intervention in human psychological research: With special reference to the Stanford prison experiment. *Cognition, 2,* 243–256.

ZUCKERMAN, M. (1990). The psychophysiology of sensation seeking. *Journal of Personality, 58,* 313–345.

ZUCKERMAN, M. (1995). Good and bad humors: Biochemical bases of personality and its disorders. *Psychological Science, 6,* 325–332.

ZUROFF, D. C. (1986). Was Gordon Allport a trait theorist? *Journal of Personality and Social Psychology, 51,* 993–1000.

PHOTO CREDITS

CHAPTER 1

Page 8: Lori Adamski Peek/Tony Stone Images/ New York, Inc. Page 10: W. del Toro/Newsday, Inc. Page 11: Michael Weisbrot /Stock, Boston. Page 18: Elizabeth Crews/The Image Works. Page 19: Rosanne Olson/Tony Stone Images/ New York, Inc.

CHAPTER 2

Page 36: Bruce Ayers/Tony Stone Images/ New York, Inc. Page 38: Corbis-Bettmann. Page 39: Elizabeth Crews/Stock, Boston. Page 42: Gale Zucker/Stock, Boston. Page 43: Dratch/The Image Works. Page 50: Robert Kalman/The Image Works.

CHAPTER 3

Page 66: Max Halberstadt. Page 78: Martin Benjamin/The Image Works. Page 89 (left): ©New York Times Co., July 30, 1983. Page 89 (right): ©New York Times Co., April 4, 1987. Page 90: Kit Hedman/Jeroboam. Page 95: Charles Harbutt/Actuality. Page 101: Sara Krulwich/©New York Times Co. Page 102: Jon Erikson. Page 104: Gale Zucker/Stock, Boston.

CHAPTER 4

Page 114: Courtesy Dr. Henri Ellenberger. Pages 116 and 117: Reprinted by permission of Hans Huber, Publishers. Page 118: Reprinted by permission of the publishers from Henry A. Murray, Thematic Apperception Test, Cambridge, MA, Harvard University Press; ©1953 by the President & Fellows of Harvard University. Page 120: UPI/Corbis-Bettmann. Page 129: Edwin Engleman. Page 141: Courtesy Alfred Adler Consultation Center. Page 142: Courtesy NASA. Page 143: Yusef Karsh/Woodfin Camp & Associates. Page 146: Courtesy Karen Horney Clinic, Inc., NYC. Page 147 (top left): Dale Durfee/Tony Stone Images/ New York,

Inc. Page 147 (top right): Brent Petersen/The Stock Market. Page 147 (bottom): Tony Latham/Tony Stone Images/ New York, Inc. Page 148: Courtesy William Alanson, White Psychiatric Foundation. Page 149: Penny Tweedie/Tony Stone Images/ New York, Inc.

CHAPTER 5

Page 168: Antony di Gesu. Page 172: Bruce Ayres/Tony Stone Images/ New York, Inc. Page 178: Dean Abramson/Stock, Boston. Page 184: Jerome Tisne/Tony Stone Images/ New York, Inc. Page 190: Elizabeth Crews/The Image Works.

CHAPTER 6

Page 201: Dean Abramson/Stock, Boston. Page 210: Courtesy Kurt Goldstein. Page 211: Courtesy Brandeis University. Page 212: Dave Allocca/Retna.

CHAPTER 7

Page 228: Courtesy Harvard University News Office. Page 231: Arthur Tilley/Tony Stone Images/ New York, Inc. Page 233: Courtesy Hans Eysenck. Page 236: Penny Tweedie/Tony Stone Images/ New York, Inc. Page 242: Courtesy University of Illinois. Page 248: UPI/Corbis-Bettmann. Page 250: Comstock, Inc.

CHAPTER 8

Page 258: Courtesy L.R. Goldberg. Page 262: Courtesy Paul T. Costa, Jr., Ph.D. Page 263: William H. Newhall/Courtesy Robert R. McCrae. Page 268: Elizabeth Crews/Stock, Boston. Page 270: Joel Gordon.

CHAPTER 9

Pages 300 and 302: Corbis-Bettmann. Page 307: Courtesy Psychology Today. Page 316: Kathy Bendo. Page 317: Courtesy B.F. Skinner, 1956. Page 322: Dion Ogust/The Image Works. Page 329: Courtesy Clark Hull. Page 330: Courtesy Yale University. Page 331: Courtesy Rockefeller University. Page 335: Shirley Zeiberg/Photo Researchers.

CHAPTER 10

Page 349: Courtesy Ralph Norman. Page 355: Marianne Gontarz/Jeroboam. Page 357: Bruce Ayres/Tony Stone Images/ New York, Inc. Page 364: Peace Corps photo by Bill Strassberger. Page 368: Martha Stewart/The Picture Cube.

CHAPTER 11

Page 379: Drawing by Lippman; ©1972 *The New Yorker*.

CHAPTER 12

Page 400: Courtesy Stanford University.   Page 401: Charlyce Jones.   Page 420: Cary Wolinsky/Stock, Boston.

CHAPTER 13

Page 429: Robert E. Daemmrich/Tony Stone Images/ New York, Inc.   Page 432: Susan Rosenberg/Photo Researchers.   Page 435: Michael Siluk/The Image Works.

CHAPTER 14

Page 455: ©Robert Schochet.   Page 458: Courtesy Ford Motor Co.   Page 459: Comstock, Inc.   Page 475: Chris Craymer/Tony Stone Images/ New York, Inc. Page 476: Courtesy Dr. Donald T. Meichenbaum.   Page 477: Drawing by Gil Eiser; ©New York Times Co. Page 479: Courtesy Dr. Aaron T. Beck.   Page 486: Peter Menzel/Stock, Boston.

NAME INDEX

SUBJECT INDEX

569